NE능률 영어교과서

대한민국 고등학생 **10명** 중 **4.7명**이 보는 교과서

영어 고등 교과서 점유율 1위
(7차, 2007 개정, 2009 개정, 2015 개정)

리딩튜터

그동안 판매된
리딩튜터 1,900만 부
차곡차곡 쌓으면 19만 미터

에베레스트 21배 높이

190,000m

에베레스트 8,848m

능률보카

그동안 판매된
능률VOCA 1,100만 부

대한민국 박스오피스
천만명을 넘은 영화 단 28개

그래머존

그동안 판매된 450만 부의 그래머존을 바닥에 쭉 ~ 깔면
1000km 서울-부산 왕복가능

서울

부산

능률
EBS 수능특강

• • •

변형 문제
영어독해
연습(하)

733제

지은이	NE능률 영어교육연구소
선임 연구원	김지현
외주연구원	콘텐츠 인앤아웃
영문 교열	Angela Lan
맥편집	㈜하이테크컴
디자인	민유화, 김연주
영업	한기영, 이경구, 박인규, 정철교, 하진수, 김남준, 이우현
마케팅	박혜선, 남경진, 이지원, 김여진

능률
EBS 수능특강

변형 문제

영어독해
연습 (하)

733제

Structure & Features

1

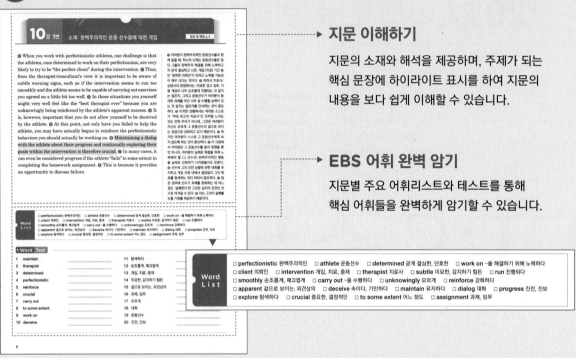

지문 이해하기

지문의 소재와 해석을 제공하며, 주제가 되는
핵심 문장에 하이라이트 표시를 하여 지문의
내용을 보다 쉽게 이해할 수 있습니다.

EBS 어휘 완벽 암기

지문별 주요 어휘리스트와 테스트를 통해
핵심 어휘들을 완벽하게 암기할 수 있습니다.

Word List

□ perfectionistic 완벽주의적인　□ athlete 운동선수　□ determined 굳게 결심한, 단호한　□ work on ~을 해결하기 위해 노력하다
□ client 의뢰인　□ intervention 개입, 치료, 중재　□ therapist 치료사　□ subtle 미묘한, 감지하기 힘든　□ run 진행되다
□ smoothly 순조롭게, 매끄럽게　□ carry out ~을 수행하다　□ unknowingly 모르게　□ reinforce 강화하다
□ apparent 겉으로 보이는, 외견상의　□ deceive 속이다, 기만하다　□ maintain 유지하다　□ dialog 대화　□ progress 진전, 진보
□ explore 탐색하다　□ crucial 중요한, 결정적인　□ to some extent 어느 정도　□ assignment 과제, 임무

2

내신 빈출 유형 집중 훈련하기

올바른 어법 및 어휘 고르기, 동사를 알맞은 형태로 고
쳐 쓰기, 우리말에 맞게 영작하기 등 학교 시험에 자주
출제되는 3가지 유형을 집중 훈련할 수 있습니다.

3

전 지문 변형 문제 풀기

한 지문당 3~4문제의 변형 문제로 지문을
완전히 숙지하고 다양한 유형의 변형 문제에
대비할 수 있습니다.

12강 3번

A large repertoire and proficient song performance
can only be acquired by an individual bird that
grew up in a secure nest, was subsequently
unencumbered by dis
in possession of sharp
foraging ability, and
engaged in hundreds c
practice. Whatever i
growth of a bird's s
whatever keeps the l
practicing song is late
size and perfection of
This makes a large r
direct causal reflectio
passage through a der
course. The more der
be acquired, the more
of an individual's per
lies implicit in the
performance. An indiv
its audience, in a wa
that the singer come
background." Potenti
do well to take a sing
virtuosity seriously.

*unencumbered 방해가 없는 **

고난도

03 **12강 3번**

다음 글의 밑줄 친 부분 중, 문맥상 낱말의 쓰임이
것은?

A large repertoire and proficient song
can only be acquired by an individu
grew up in a secure nest, was s
unencumbered by disease and paras
in possession of sharp faculties, mem
foraging ability, and predator watc
engaged in hundreds of hours of succe
practice. Whatever ① assists the p
growth of a bird's system of song
whatever keeps the bird from attending to and
practicing song is later evident as deficits in the size
and perfection of its mature song repertoire. This
makes a large repertoire of complex song a direct
causal reflection of an individual's ② successful
passage through a demanding and varied obstacle
course. The more demanding the performance
to be acquired, the ③ more comprehensive a
measure of an individual's personal history and
qualities lies implicit in the perfected, mature song
performance. An individual's song proficiency tells
its audience, in a way ④ impossible to counterfeit,
that the singer comes from, as it were, "a good

---

17 **12강 3번**

다음 글에서 전체 흐름과 관계 없는 문장은?

A large repertoire and proficient song performance
can only be acquired by an individual bird that
grew up in a secure nest, was subsequently
unencumbered by disease and parasites, and —
in possession of sharp faculties, memory capacity,
foraging ability, and predator watchfulness —
engaged in hundreds of hours of successful singing
practice. ① Whatever impairs the post-hatching

---

27 윗글의 밑줄 친 a good background가 문맥상 의미
하는 바를 찾아 우리말로 쓰시오. (40자 이내)

_____

_____

고난도

28 윗글의 내용을 한 문장으로 요약하려고 한다. 보기 의
단어를 순서대로 배열하여 문장을 완성하시오.

보기
developmental / provides / represents /
the entire / process / proof

A bird's song proficiency _____ _____
_____ _____ _____ of the singer, and
_____ _____ of all-around individual quality
and competence.

고난도 문항으로 수능·내신 완벽 대비

엄선된 고난도 문항을 통해 3점짜리
킬러 문항에 완벽하게 대비할 수 있습니다.

4

• 내신 만점 서술형

11강 1번

The ocean is ① important as a surface, as a
channel for travel. As anyone who has jumped
into the ocean knows, seawater is buoyant — it
supports your weight much better than the air
around you. This greatly ② reduces the amount
of fuel required to move goods from place to place.
20피트의 컨테이너를 상하이에서 프랑크푸르트로 배로 이동시키는
것은 비용의 고작을 비행기로 옮기는 것 만큼의 1/3만에 비용이 옳지
않는다. It is no surprise, therefore, that four-fifths
of international trade in goods depends on sea
freight. The ③ emergency of enormous container
ships has meant that fewer and fewer people now
work in shipping, but it remains very big business
— the biggest ocean industry of all in terms of total
income. Every day, ④ huge quantities of goods
pass through major bottlenecks like the Panama
and Suez Canals. The world was given a stark
reminder of the importance of these bottlenecks
in March 2021, when one of the world's largest
container ships, the Ever Given, blocked the Suez
Canal for six days, ⑤ prompting widespread
concern about the consequences for world trade.

*buoyant 부력이 있는, 뜨게 하는 **freight 화물 운송 ***stark 냉혹한

23 윗글의 밑줄 친 부분 중, 문맥상 어색한 것을 1개 찾아 그
번호를 쓰고 고쳐 쓰시오.

_____

24 윗글의 밑줄 친 (A)의 의미가 되도록 보기 의 단어를 배
열하여 문장을 완성하시오.

보기
shifting / by plane / costs / a / much /
as / it / third / mere / as

Moving a 20-foot container from Shanghai to
Frankfurt by ship _____

11강 2번

When the new coronavirus arrived in the United
States in January 2020, it hit an economy, society,
and constitutional democracy fundamentally
unprepared. As the scale of the challenge became
clear, the country simply could not deliver what
was needed to confront it. There was a solution, one
identified by scholars and policy experts as early
as the middle of March and publicly disseminated
by the middle of April. That solution was a large-
scale program of rapid testing of patients, tracing
and testing their contacts, and tracing and testing
their contacts again in turn. Such testing also
needed _____ from a culture of sticking
to universal precautions such as mask-wearing,
hand and bathroom hygiene, and robust practices
of infection control. The massive, rapid buildup
of such a public health campaign, as well as the
necessary systems and services to support it,
would have interrupted transmission of the virus
sufficiently to eliminate it even while keeping the
economy open. But the country did not have the
relevant infrastructure ready to go and was not
able to deliver this mobilization.

*disseminate 전파하다 **hygiene 위생 ***robust 강력한

25 윗글의 빈칸에 들어갈 단어를 영영 뜻풀이를 참고하여 쓰
시오. (단, 주어진 철자로 시작할 것)

the action of making an idea, belief, or feeling
stronger

r_____

26 윗글의 밑줄 친 this mobilization이 가리키는 바를 본
문에서 찾아 우리말로 쓰시오. (40글자 내외)

_____

_____

내신 만점 서술형

시험에 자주 등장하는 서술형 문제를 통해
까다로운 내신 유형에 대비할 수 있습니다.

Contents

◆ ◆ ◆

❶ When you work with perfectionistic athletes, one challenge is that the athletes, once determined to work on their perfectionism, are very likely to try to be "the perfect client" during the intervention. ❷ Thus, from the therapist/consultant's view it is important to be aware of subtle warning signs, such as if the intervention seems to run too smoothly and the athlete seems to be capable of carrying out exercises you agreed on a little bit too well. ❸ In these situations you yourself might very well feel like the "best therapist ever" because you are unknowingly being reinforced by the athlete's apparent success. ❹ It is, however, important that you do not allow yourself to be deceived by the athlete. ❺ At this point, not only have you failed to help the athlete, you may have actually begun to reinforce the perfectionistic behaviors you should actually be working on. ❻ Maintaining a dialog with the athlete about their progress and continually exploring their goals within the intervention is therefore crucial. ❼ In many cases, it can even be considered progress if the athlete "fails" to some extent in completing the homework assignment. ❽ This is because it provides an opportunity to discuss failure.

❶ 여러분이 완벽주의적인 운동선수들과 함께 일할 때, 하나의 난제는 운동선수들은 일단 그들의 완벽주의 해결을 위해 노력하고자 굳게 결심하고 나면, 개입 [치료] 기간 동안 '완벽한 의뢰인'이 되려고 노력할 가능성이 매우 크다는 것이다. ❷ 따라서 치료사/상담사의 관점에서는, 미묘한 경고 징후, 가령 개입이 너무 순조롭게 진행되는 것 같지는 않은지, 그리고 운동선수가 여러분이 동의한 과제를 약간 너무 잘 수행할 능력이 있는 것 같지는 않은지를 인식하는 것이 중요하다. ❸ 이러한 상황에서는 여러분 스스로가 '역대 최고의 치료사'인 것처럼 느끼는 것도 전혀 무리가 아닌데, 그것은 여러분이 자신도 모르게 그 운동선수의 겉으로 보이는 성공으로 강화되고 있기 때문이다. ❹ 하지만 여러분이 스스로 그 운동선수에게 속지 않도록 하는 것이 중요하다. ❺ 이 시점에서 여러분은 그 운동선수를 돕지 못했을 뿐만 아니라, 여러분이 실제로 해결을 위해 노력해야 할 (그 선수의) 완벽주의적인 행동을 실제로 강화하기 시작했을지도 모른다. ❻ 선수와 그의 진전 상황에 관한 대화를 유지하고 개입 과정 내에서 끊임없이 그의 목표를 탐색하는 것이 따라서 중요하다. ❼ 많은 경우에 선수가 과제를 완료하는 데 어느 정도 '실패한다'면 그것은 심지어 진전인 것으로 여겨질 수 있다. ❽ 이는 그것이 실패를 논할 기회를 제공하기 때문이다.

Word List

□ perfectionistic 완벽주의적인　□ athlete 운동선수　□ determined 굳게 결심한, 단호한　□ work on ~을 해결하기 위해 노력하다
□ client 의뢰인　□ intervention 개입, 치료, 중재　□ therapist 치료사　□ subtle 미묘한, 감지하기 힘든　□ run 진행되다
□ smoothly 순조롭게, 매끄럽게　□ carry out ~을 수행하다　□ unknowingly 모르게　□ reinforce 강화하다
□ apparent 겉으로 보이는, 외견상의　□ deceive 속이다, 기만하다　□ maintain 유지하다　□ dialog 대화　□ progress 진전, 진보
□ explore 탐색하다　□ crucial 중요한, 결정적인　□ to some extent 어느 정도　□ assignment 과제, 임무

• Word Test

1	maintain		11	탐색하다
2	therapist		12	순조롭게, 매끄럽게
3	determined		13	개입, 치료, 중재
4	perfectionistic		14	미묘한, 감지하기 힘든
5	reinforce		15	겉으로 보이는, 외견상의
6	crucial		16	과제, 임무
7	carry out		17	모르게
8	to some extent		18	대화
9	work on		19	운동선수
10	deceive		20	진전, 진보

When you work with perfectionistic athletes, one challenge is that the athletes, once determined to work on their perfectionism, are very likely to try to be "the perfect client" during the intervention. Thus, from the therapist/consultant's view it is important to be aware of ❶ subtle / obvious warning signs, such as if the intervention seems to run too ❷ smooth / smoothly and the athlete seems to be capable of carrying out exercises you agreed on a little bit too well. In these situations you yourself might very well feel like the "best therapist ever" because you are unknowingly being reinforced by the athlete's apparent success. It is, ❸ however / moreover , important that you do not allow yourself to be deceived by the athlete. At this point, not only ❹ you have / have you failed to help the athlete, you may have actually begun to reinforce the perfectionistic behaviors you should actually be working on. Maintaining a dialog with the athlete about their ❺ progress / regression and continually exploring their goals within the intervention is therefore crucial. In many cases, it can even be considered progress if the athlete "fails" to some extent in completing the homework assignment. This is because it provides an opportunity to discuss failure.

When you work with perfectionistic athletes, one challenge is that the athletes, once determined to work on their perfectionism, ❶ _____ (be) very likely to try to be "the perfect client" during the intervention. Thus, from the therapist/consultant's view it is important to be aware of subtle warning signs, such as if the intervention seems to run too smoothly and the athlete seems to be capable of carrying out exercises you ❷ _____ (agree) on a little bit too well. In these situations you yourself might very well feel like the "best therapist ever" because you are unknowingly ❸ _____ (reinforce) by the athlete's apparent success. It is, however, important that you do not allow yourself to ❹ _____ (deceive) by the athlete. At this point, not only have you failed to help the athlete, you may have actually begun to reinforce the perfectionistic behaviors you should actually be working on. Maintaining a dialog with the athlete about their progress and continually exploring their goals within the intervention is therefore crucial. In many cases, it can even ❺ _____ (consider) progress if the athlete "fails" to some extent in completing the homework assignment. This is because it provides an opportunity ❻ _____ (discuss) failure.

When you work with perfectionistic athletes, one challenge is that the athletes, ❶ _____ _____ _____ _____ _____ (일단 ~의 해결을 위해 노력하고자 굳게 결심하고 나면) their perfectionism, are very likely to try to be "the perfect client" during the intervention. Thus, from the therapist/consultant's view it is ❷ _____ _____ _____ _____ _____ (~을 인식하는 것이 중요한) subtle warning signs, such as if the intervention seems to run too smoothly and the athlete seems to be capable of carrying out exercises you agreed on a little bit too well. In these situations you yourself ❸ _____ _____ _____ _____ _____ (~처럼 느끼는 것도 전혀 무리가 아니다) the "best therapist ever" because you are unknowingly being reinforced by the athlete's apparent success. It is, however, important that you do not allow yourself to be deceived by the athlete. At this point, not only have you failed to help the athlete, you may have actually begun to reinforce the perfectionistic behaviors you should actually be working on. Maintaining a dialog with the athlete about their progress and ❹ _____ _____ _____ _____ (끊임없이 그들의 목표들을 탐색하는 것) within the intervention is therefore crucial. In many cases, it can even be considered progress if the athlete "fails" to some extent in completing the homework assignment. This is because it provides an opportunity to discuss failure.

❶ One of the ideas many scientists take as an ethical principle is that scientists should remain, like journalists, "objective" and not take sides on policy controversies. ❷ Indeed, historically, scientists such as the late astronomer Carl Sagan who appear to have become "too" public have risked losing the respect of other scientists. ❸ Under normal circumstances, some scientists might reasonably choose to avoid (as scientists) championing specific policy solutions, even on something like climate, lest they be mistaken for self-appointed (or media-appointed) authorities over what society should do. ❹ But scientists are also citizens, who may also reasonably choose to speak out, as citizens, on policy issues. ❺ To avoid involvement altogether can itself be seen as irresponsible. ❻ Scientists have the same rights and duties as other citizens, including the right and the duty to give thought to public issues and, on appropriate occasions, to take positions on them. ❼ For a climate scientist not to support appropriate action on climate might be likened to a medical doctor's not supporting routine cancer screening or prenatal nutrition initiatives.

*champion 옹호하다 **prenatal 태아기의

❶ 많은 과학자가 윤리적 원칙으로 받아들이는 생각 중 하나는, 과학자들은 기자들처럼 계속 '객관적'이어야 하면서 정책 논쟁에 있어 편을 들지 말아야 한다는 것이다. ❷ 실제로 역사를 살펴보면, 고인이 된 천문학자 Carl Sagan과 같이 '너무' 대중적으로 된 것처럼 보이는 과학자들은 다른 과학자들의 존중을 잃을 위험을 무릅써 왔다. ❸ 보통의 상황에서 일부 과학자들은 사회가 무엇을 해야 하는지에 대해 자기 혼자 정한 (혹은 언론에서 정한) 권위자로 오인되지 않도록 심지어 기후와 같은 것에서도 특정한 정책 해결책을 옹호하는 것을 (과학자로서) 피하고자 하는 것이 당연할 수도 있다. ❹ 하지만 과학자들도 시민이며, 그들은 또한 시민으로서 정책 문제에 대해 목소리를 내고자 하는 것이 당연할 수도 있다. ❺ 관여를 완전히 피하는 것 자체는 무책임한 것으로 보일 수 있다. ❻ 과학자들은 다른 시민들과 같은 권리와 의무를 지니고 있는데, 공공 문제에 대해 생각해 보고 그리고 적절한 경우에 그것에 대해 입장을 취할 수 있는 권리와 의무도 (여기에) 포함된다. ❼ 기후 과학자가 기후에 관한 적절한 조치를 지지하지 않는 것은 의사가 정기적인 암 검사 또는 태아기 영양 계획을 지지하지 않는 것에 비유될 수 있다.

Word List

□ ethical 윤리적인 □ principle 원칙, 원리 □ objective 객관적인; 목적 □ take sides 편을 들다 □ controversy 논쟁, 논란
□ late 고인이 된 □ astronomer 천문학자 □ respect 존중, 존경 □ circumstance 상황 □ reasonably 당연히, 합리적으로
□ specific 특정한 □ mistaken 오인된, 오해받는 □ self-appointed 자기 혼자 정한 □ authority 권위자, 권한
□ speak out 목소리를 내다, 공개적으로 말하다 □ give thought to ~에 대해 생각해 보다 □ appropriate 적절한
□ occasion 경우, 기회 □ liken ~ to ... ~을 …에 비유하다 □ routine 정기적인, 일상적인 □ screening 검사, 상영
□ initiative (목적 달성을 위한) 계획

• Word Test

1	authority		11	고인이 된	
2	give thought to		12	편을 들다	
3	circumstance		13	존중, 존경	
4	controversy		14	정기적인, 일상적인	
5	astronomer		15	원칙, 원리	
6	objective		16	(목적 달성을 위한) 계획	
7	specific		17	당연히, 합리적으로	
8	ethical		18	목소리를 내다, 공개적으로 말하다	
9	screening		19	오인된, 오해받는	
10	occasion		20	적절한	

One of the ideas many scientists take as an ethical principle is that scientists should remain, like journalists, "❶ objective / subjective " and not take sides on policy controversies. Indeed, historically, scientists such as the late astronomer Carl Sagan who appear to have become "too" ❷ public / private have risked losing the respect of other scientists. Under normal circumstances, some scientists might reasonably choose to avoid (as scientists) championing specific policy solutions, even on something like climate, lest they be mistaken for self-appointed (or media-appointed) authorities over ❸ that / what society should do. But scientists are also citizens, who may also reasonably choose to speak out, as citizens, on policy issues. To avoid involvement altogether can itself be seen as ❹ responsible / irresponsible . Scientists have the same rights and duties ❺ as / to other citizens, including the right and the duty to give thought to public issues and, on appropriate occasions, to take positions on them. For a climate scientist not to support appropriate action on climate might be likened to a medical doctor's not supporting routine cancer screening or prenatal nutrition initiatives.

*champion 옹호하다 **prenatal 태아기의

One of the ideas many scientists take as an ethical principle ❶ _____ (be) that scientists should remain, like journalists, "objective" and not take sides on policy controversies. Indeed, historically, scientists such as the late astronomer Carl Sagan who ❷ _____ (appear) to have become "too" public have risked losing the respect of other scientists. Under normal circumstances, some scientists might reasonably choose ❸ _____ (avoid) (as scientists) championing specific policy solutions, even on something like climate, lest they be mistaken for self-appointed (or media-appointed) authorities over what society should do. But scientists are also citizens, who may also reasonably choose to speak out, as citizens, on policy issues. To avoid involvement altogether can itself ❹ _____ (see) as irresponsible. Scientists have the same rights and duties as other citizens, including the right and the duty to give thought to public issues and, on appropriate occasions, to take positions on them. For a climate scientist not to support appropriate action on climate might be likened to a medical doctor's not ❺ _____ (support) routine cancer screening or prenatal nutrition initiatives.

*champion 옹호하다 **prenatal 태아기의

One of the ideas many scientists take as an ethical principle is that scientists should remain, like journalists, "objective" and not ❶ _____ _____ _____ _____ _____ (정책 논쟁들에 있어 편들을 들다). Indeed, historically, scientists such as the late astronomer Carl Sagan who appear to have become "too" public ❷ _____ _____ _____ _____ _____ (존중을 잃을 위험을 무릅써 왔다) of other scientists. Under normal circumstances, some scientists might reasonably choose to avoid (as scientists) championing specific policy solutions, even on something like climate, ❸ _____ _____ _____ _____ _____ (그들이 ~로 오인되지 않도록) self-appointed (or media-appointed) authorities over what society should do. But scientists are also citizens, who may also reasonably choose to speak out, as citizens, on policy issues. To avoid involvement altogether can itself be seen as irresponsible. Scientists have the same rights and duties as other citizens, including the right and the duty to give thought to public issues and, on appropriate occasions, to take positions on them. For a climate scientist not to support ❹ _____ _____ _____ _____ (기후에 관한 적절한 조치) might be likened to a medical doctor's not supporting routine cancer screening or prenatal nutrition initiatives.

*champion 옹호하다 **prenatal 태아기의

❶ In a study conducted by Griskevicius and his colleagues on behavioural cues, university students read a short story about a successful university graduate who obtained a high-status first job and was, relative to others, promoted quickly. ❷ Students in the control group read a neutral story of similar length. ❸ In subsequent experimental tasks, students could choose between different green and non-green hypothetical consumer products (car, household cleaner, dishwasher). ❹ Each time the products were equal in price, but the non-green product was more luxurious and had better performance than the green product, which was pro-environmental. ❺ The study showed that, in the treatment group, in which an activation of status motives occurred, 55 per cent chose the green car; in the control group, 37 per cent chose the green car. ❻ The corresponding figures for the household cleaner and dishwasher were 42 per cent versus 26 per cent, and 49 per cent versus 35 per cent, respectively.

*subsequent 뒤이은, 차후의

❶ Griskevicius와 그의 동료들이 행동 단서에 관해 수행한 연구에서, 대학생들은 높은 (사회적) 지위의 첫 직장을 얻어 다른 사람들에 비해 빠르게 승진한 한 성공한 대학 졸업자에 관한 짧은 이야기를 읽었다. ❷ 통제 집단의 학생들은 비슷한 길이의 평범한 이야기를 읽었다. ❸ 뒤이은 실험 과제에서 학생들은 다양한 가상의 친환경 및 비친환경 소비자 제품(자동차, 가정용 세제, 식기 세척기) 사이에서 선택할 수 있었다. ❹ 매번 제품 가격은 같았지만, 비친환경 제품이 환경친화적인 친환경 제품보다 더 고급스럽고 성능도 더 우수했다. ❺ 이 연구는 지위 동기의 활성화가 발생한 처치 집단에서는 55퍼센트가 친환경 자동차를 선택하고 통제 집단에서는 37퍼센트가 친환경 자동차를 선택한다는 것을 보여 주었다. ❻ 가정용 세제와 식기 세척기의 해당 수치는 각각 42퍼센트 대 26퍼센트, 그리고 49퍼센트 대 35퍼센트였다.

Word List

□ conduct 수행하다, 처리하다　□ colleague 동료　□ behavioural 행동의　□ cue 단서, 신호　□ obtain 얻다, 획득하다
□ high-status 높은 지위의　□ relative to ~에 비해　□ promote 승진시키다　□ control group (실험의) 통제 집단
□ neutral 평범한, 중립적인　□ green 친환경의　□ hypothetical 가상의　□ household cleaner 가정용 세제
□ luxurious 고급스러운, 호화로운　□ performance 성능, 수행　□ treatment group (실험의) 처치 집단(실험 효과를 측정하기 위해 인위적인 처치를 한 집단)　□ activation 활성화　□ corresponding 해당하는, 상응하는　□ figure 수치, 숫자　□ respectively 각각, 제각기

• Word Test

1	activation		10	단서, 신호
2	figure		11	높은 지위의
3	luxurious		12	가상의
4	behavioural		13	성능, 수행
5	obtain		14	승진시키다
6	green		15	각각, 제각기
7	relative to		16	해당하는, 상응하는
8	neutral		17	가정용 세제
9	conduct		18	동료

In a study conducted by Griskevicius and his colleagues on behavioural cues, university students read a short story about a successful university graduate ❶ who / which obtained a high-status first job and was, relative to others, promoted quickly. Students in the control group read a ❷ neutral / mutual story of similar length. In subsequent experimental tasks, students could choose between different green and non-green hypothetical consumer products (car, household cleaner, dishwasher). Each time the products were equal in price, but the non-green product was more luxurious and had better performance than the green product, ❸ who / which was pro-environmental. The study showed that, in the treatment group, ❹ which / in which an activation of status motives occurred, 55 per cent chose the green car; in the control group, 37 per cent chose the green car. The corresponding figures for the household cleaner and dishwasher were 42 per cent versus 26 per cent, and 49 per cent versus 35 per cent, ❺ respectively / simultaneously .

*subsequent 뒤이은, 차후의

In a study conducted by Griskevicius and his colleagues on behavioural cues, university students read a short story about a successful university graduate who obtained a high-status first job and ❶ _____ (be), relative to others, promoted quickly. Students in the control group read a neutral story of similar length. In subsequent experimental tasks, students could choose between different green and non-green hypothetical consumer products (car, household cleaner, dishwasher). Each time the products were equal in price, but the non-green product was more luxurious and ❷ _____ (have) better performance than the green product, which ❸ _____ (be) pro-environmental. The study showed that, in the treatment group, in which an activation of status motives ❹ _____ (occur), 55 per cent chose the green car; in the control group, 37 per cent chose the green car. The corresponding figures for the household cleaner and dishwasher ❺ _____ (be) 42 per cent versus 26 per cent, and 49 per cent versus 35 per cent, respectively.

*subsequent 뒤이은, 차후의

In a study conducted by Griskevicius and his colleagues on behavioural cues, university students read a short story about a successful university graduate who obtained a high-status first job and was, ❶ _____ _____ _____ (다른 사람들에 비해), promoted quickly. Students in the control group read a neutral story of similar length. In subsequent experimental tasks, students could choose between different green and non-green ❷ _____ _____ _____ (가상의 소비자 제품들) (car, household cleaner, dishwasher). Each time the products were ❸ _____ _____ _____ (가격이 같은), but the non-green product was more luxurious and had better performance than the green product, which was pro-environmental. The study showed that, in the treatment group, in which a(n) ❹ _____ _____ _____ _____ (지위 동기들의 활성화) occurred, 55 per cent chose the green car; in the control group, 37 per cent chose the green car. The corresponding figures for the household cleaner and dishwasher were 42 per cent versus 26 per cent, and 49 per cent versus 35 per cent, respectively.

*subsequent 뒤이은, 차후의

❶ Perhaps the variable found in research to distinguish entrepreneurs from others is self-efficacy — individuals' belief that they can successfully accomplish whatever they set out to accomplish. ❷ This is one reason why, despite the odds being highly stacked against them, many start new ventures: they believe that they can effectively complete the tasks needed to make these companies a success. ❸ Thus, self-efficacy is one characteristic that helps entrepreneurs get started and also persist in their efforts to succeed. ❹ Self-efficacy, however, has a downside. ❺ It may lead individuals to undertake tasks for which, in reality, they lack the required resources, leading to what can be disastrous results. ❻ In a sense, they have chosen to play in a game they cannot win, with negative results virtually guaranteed. ❼ These negative effects can be magnified by a high level of optimism — a general, and often unjustified belief that ultimately all will turn out well. ❽ In combination, high levels of optimism and high levels of self-efficacy can prove deadly for entrepreneurs with limited resources.

❶ 아마도 연구에서 발견된 사업가와 그 외 다른 사람들을 구분하는 변인은 자기 효능감, 즉 성취하려고 나선 것이 어떤 것이든 그것을 성공적으로 성취할 수 있다는 개인의 믿음일 것이다. ❷ 이것이 바로 자신이 성공할 가능성이 크지 않음에도 불구하고, 많은 사람이 새로운 벤처 사업을 시작하는 한 가지 이유인데, 그들은 자신들이 이 회사들을 성공한 것으로 만드는 데 필요한 과업을 효과적으로 완수할 수 있다고 믿는다. ❸ 따라서, 자기 효능감은 사업가가 시작하고 또한 성공하기 위한 노력을 지속할 수 있도록 돕는 하나의 특징이다. ❹ 그러나 자기 효능감에는 부정적인 면이 있다. ❺ 그것은 개인이 사실상 필요한 자원이 부족한 과업에 착수하도록 만들어, 비참한 결과가 될 수 있는 것을 초래할 수도 있다. ❻ 그들은 어떤 의미에서는 부정적인 결과가 거의 확실한 상황에서 자신들이 이길 수 없는 게임에 출전하기로 선택한 것이다. ❼ 이러한 부정적인 영향은 결국 모든 것이 잘될 것이라는 막연하고, 그리고 흔히 근거가 없는 믿음인 높은 수준의 낙관에 의해 확대될 수 있다. ❽ 서로 결합되면 높은 수준의 낙관과 높은 수준의 자기 효능감은 제한된 자원을 가진 사업가들에게 치명적인 것으로 판명될 수 있다.

Word List

□ **variable** 변인, 변수; 변하기 쉬운   □ **entrepreneur** 사업가, 기업가   □ **self-efficacy** 자기 효능감   □ **accomplish** 성취하다, 달성하다
□ **set out to** *do* ~하려고 나서다   □ **the odds are stacked against** ~이 성공할 가능성이 크지 않다   □ **venture** 벤처 사업, (사업상의) 모험
□ **characteristic** 특징   □ **persist** 지속하다, 계속하다   □ **downside** 부정적인 면   □ **undertake** 착수하다, 맡다
□ **disastrous** 비참한, 형편없는   □ **virtually** 거의, 사실상   □ **guaranteed** 확실한, 보장된   □ **magnify** 확대하다
□ **optimism** 낙관(주의)   □ **unjustified** 근거가 없는, 정당하지 않은   □ **ultimately** 결국, 궁극적으로

• Word Test

1	virtually	9	~하려고 나서다
2	venture	10	비참한, 형편없는
3	accomplish	11	특징
4	undertake	12	사업가, 기업가
5	unjustified	13	낙관(주의)
6	persist	14	확실한, 보장된
7	magnify	15	부정적인 면
8	variable	16	결국, 궁극적으로

Perhaps the variable found in research to ❶ distinguish/extinguish entrepreneurs from others is self-efficacy — individuals' belief that they can successfully accomplish whatever they set out to accomplish. This is one reason why, ❷ while/despite the odds being highly stacked against them, many start new ventures: they believe that they can effectively complete the tasks needed to make these companies a success. Thus, self-efficacy is one characteristic that helps entrepreneurs get started and also persist in their efforts to succeed. Self-efficacy, however, has a(n) ❸ upside/downside . It may lead individuals to undertake tasks for which, in reality, they lack the required resources, leading to what can be disastrous results. In a sense, they have chosen to play in a game they cannot win, with negative results virtually guaranteed. These negative effects can be magnified by a high level of optimism — a general, and often unjustified belief ❹ that/which ultimately all will turn out well. In combination, high levels of optimism and high levels of self-efficacy can prove ❺ deadly/beneficial for entrepreneurs with limited resources.

Perhaps the variable ❶ _____ (find) in research to distinguish entrepreneurs from others ❷ _____ (be) self-efficacy — individuals' belief that they can successfully accomplish whatever they set out to accomplish. This is one reason why, despite the odds being highly stacked against them, many start new ventures: they believe that they can effectively complete the tasks ❸ _____ (need) to make these companies a success. Thus, self-efficacy is one characteristic that helps entrepreneurs get started and also persist in their efforts to succeed. Self-efficacy, however, has a downside. It may lead individuals to undertake tasks for which, in reality, they lack the required resources, ❹ _____ (lead) to what can be disastrous results. In a sense, they have chosen to play in a game they cannot win, with negative results virtually ❺ _____ (guarantee). These negative effects can ❻ _____ (magnify) by a high level of optimism — a general, and often unjustified belief that ultimately all will turn out well. In combination, high levels of optimism and high levels of self-efficacy can prove deadly for entrepreneurs with limited resources.

Perhaps the variable found in research to distinguish entrepreneurs from others is self-efficacy — individuals' belief that they can successfully accomplish ❶ _____ _____ _____ _____ _____ _____ (그들이 성취하려고 나선 것이 어떤 것이든). This is one reason why, despite ❷ _____ _____ _____ _____ _____ _____ _____ (~이 성공할 가능성이 크지 않음) them, many start new ventures: they believe that they can effectively complete the tasks needed to make these companies a success. Thus, self-efficacy is one characteristic that helps entrepreneurs get started and also ❸ _____ _____ _____ _____ _____ _____ (성공하기 위한 그들의 노력을 지속하다). Self-efficacy, however, has a downside. It may lead individuals to undertake tasks for which, in reality, they lack the required resources, leading to ❹ _____ _____ _____ _____ _____ (비참한 결과들이 될 수 있는 것). In a sense, they have chosen to play in a game they cannot win, with negative results virtually guaranteed. These negative effects can be magnified by a(n) ❺ _____ _____ _____ _____ (높은 수준의 낙관) — a general, and often unjustified belief that ultimately all will turn out well. In combination, high levels of optimism and high levels of self-efficacy can prove deadly for entrepreneurs with limited resources.

❶ During her last year of community college, Krista worked as a full-time nanny to take care of Delia's four kids. ❷ Krista was the first person in her family to go to college and felt pressure all around, especially as her long days became consumed by her job as well as writing assignments for her classes. ❸ These, along with some other things to take care of, were a real struggle for Krista.

❹ Delia, Krista's boss at the time, had her own struggles. ❺ Just before Krista began working for her family, Delia's career in law enforcement was cut short when she'd broken her hip at work. ❻ Krista marveled at her attitude. ❼ She had endured surgery to replace her hip and was left with metal in her leg — rods that would remain in her bones forever. ❽ But nothing stopped her. ❾ She remained positive, day in and day out. ❿ One day when Delia saw Krista struggling with school and writing and general life pressures, she explained how she coped. ⓫ She told her that the only thing Krista could do was to take "one day at a time."

⓬ Delia's attitude made little sense to Krista. ⓭ She wanted to deal with everything all at once, but that just made her stress even worse. ⓮ Delia's one-day-at-a-time motto seemed nice in theory but impossible in reality. ⓯ As the days and weeks of the year melted by, Delia listened to Krista as Krista shared about life and how she was working through it. ⓰ After a year with Delia's family, Krista transferred to Ridge University and her job ended. ⓱ Krista and Delia stayed in touch, but Krista lived a few hours away on campus so they didn't see each other very often.

⓲ One day, after a tense situation with one of the girls who lived in her dorm, Krista found herself overcome with major anxiety, ⓳ She took a deep breath, looked at herself in the mirror, and said, "It's okay, Krista. Just get through today." ⓴ Krista shocked herself, because it was the first time she truly believed that she could survive *one day at a time.* ㉑ That is a gift Krista has carried with her over all the years since then. ㉒ She's so thankful for Delia's words.

*nanny 아이 돌보미

❶ 지역 전문대학의 마지막 해 동안에 Krista는 Delia의 네 아이를 돌보는 전일제 아이 돌보미로서 일했다. ❷ Krista는 자기 가족 중에서 대학에 간 첫 번째 사람이었는데, 특히 그녀의 긴 [힘든] 하루가 수업을 위한 쓰기 과제뿐만 아니라 그녀의 일로 소모되었으므로, 모든 면에서 압박을 느꼈다. ❸ 이것들은 처리할 몇 가지 다른 일들과 더불어 Krista에게 정말 힘든 일이었다.

❹ 당시에 Krista의 고용주였던 Delia도 그녀 자신의 힘든 일이 있었다. ❺ Krista가 그녀의 가족을 위해 일하기 바로 전에 직장에서 자신의 고관절 [엉덩이뼈]이 부러진 후 법률 집행 분야에서 Delia의 경력은 갑자기 끝났다. ❻ Krista는 그녀의 태도에 경탄했다. ❼ 그녀는 자신의 고관절을 교체하는 수술을 견디어 냈는데, 그녀의 다리에는 금속이, 즉 영원히 자기 뼛속에 있을 막대가 남아 있게 되었다. ❽ 하지만 아무것도 그녀를 멈추게 하지 못했다. ❾ 그녀는 매일매일 긍정적인 상태를 유지했다. ❿ Krista가 수업과 글쓰기와 일반적인 생활의 압박으로 힘들어하는 것을 본 어느 날, Delia는 자신이 어떻게 대처하는지를 설명했다. ⓫ 그녀는 그녀에게 Krista가 할 수 있는 유일한 것은 '한 번에 하루씩' 처리하는 것이라고 말했다.

⓬ Delia의 태도는 Krista에게 거의 이해가 되지 않았다. ⓭ 그녀는 모든 것을 동시에 처리하고 싶었지만, 그것은 그녀의 스트레스를 훨씬 더 악화시켰을 뿐이었다. ⓮ Delia의 한 번에 하루 좌우명은 이론상 근사하지만 실제로는 불가능해 보였다. ⓯ 그 해의 여러 날과 여러 주가 지나감에 따라, Delia는 Krista가 삶과 삶을 다루는 방식에 관해 이야기할 때 Krista의 말에 귀를 기울였다. ⓰ Delia의 가족과 함께한 일 년 후에, Krista는 Ridge University로 편입하였고 그녀의 일은 끝이 났다. ⓱ Krista와 Delia는 계속 연락은 했지만, Krista는 몇 시간 거리로 떨어져 대학 내에서 살았고 그래서 그들은 서로 그다지 자주 만나지 못했다.

⓲ 어느 날 그녀의 기숙사에 사는 친구들 중 한 명과 긴장 상황이 있고 나서, Krista는 자신이 큰 걱정으로 압도된 것을 알게 되었다. ⓳ 그녀는 심호흡을 하고 거울 속 자신을 바라보고는 "괜찮아, Krista. 오늘을 헤쳐 나가기만 하자."라고 말했다. ⓴ Krista는 깜짝 놀랐는데, 처음으로 그녀가 자신이 '한 번에 하루씩' 넘길 수 있다고 진정으로 믿었기 때문이었다. ㉑ 그것은 그때 이후로 여러 해에 걸쳐 Krista가 그녀의 몸에 지니고 다녔던 선물이다. ㉒ 그녀는 Delia의 말에 매우 고마워한다.

□ community 지역 사회   □ pressure 압박   □ consume 소모하다, 소비하다   □ assignment 과제
□ struggle 힘든 일: 힘들어하다, 고투하다   □ enforcement 집행, 시행   □ cut short ~을 갑자기 끝내다   □ hip 고관절, 엉덩이뼈, 엉덩이
□ marvel 놀라다   □ endure 견디어 내다, 오래가다   □ rod 막대   □ day in and day out 매일매일, 날이면 날마다
□ one day at a time (미래를 걱정하지 않고 당면한 문제에 집중하여 처리하는 방식으로) 한 번에 하루씩   □ all at once 동시에, 갑자기
□ motto 좌우명, 처세훈   □ theory 이론   □ melt by (서서히) 지나가다, (녹듯이) 사라지다   □ share (생각·경험·감정을) 말하다, 함께 나누다
□ work through (까다로운 것을) 다루다, 처리하다   □ transfer 편입하다, 전학하다   □ tense 긴장된   □ dorm 기숙사(dormitory)
□ overcome with ~로 압도된, ~ 때문에 꼼짝 못하는

• Word Test

1	rod	
2	melt by	
3	marvel	
4	consume	
5	motto	
6	struggle	
7	dorm	
8	cut short	
9	transfer	
10	share	

11	과제	
12	이론	
13	고관절, 엉덩이뼈, 엉덩이	
14	집행, 시행	
15	동시에, 갑자기	
16	압박	
17	견디어 내다, 오래가다	
18	긴장된	
19	~로 압도된, ~ 때문에 꼼짝 못하는	
20	지역 사회	

• 유형 1 네모 안에서 옳은 어법·어휘를 고르시오.

During her last year of community college, Krista worked as a full-time nanny to take care of Delia's four kids. Krista was the first person in her family to go to college and felt pressure all around, especially as her long days became ❶ [dynamic/consumed] by her job as well as writing assignments for her classes. These, along with some other things to take care of, were a real ❷ [reward/struggle] for Krista.

Delia, Krista's boss at the time, had her own struggles. Just before Krista began working for her family, Delia's career in law enforcement was cut short when she'd broken her hip at work. Krista marveled at her attitude. She had endured surgery to replace her hip and was left with metal in her leg — rods that would remain in her bones forever. But nothing stopped her. She remained ❸ [positive/negative], day in and day out. One day when Delia saw Krista struggling with school and writing and general life pressures, she explained how she ❹ [coped/boasted]. She told her that the only thing Krista could do was to take "one day at a time."

Delia's attitude made little sense to Krista. She wanted to deal with everything all at once, but that just made her stress even worse. Delia's one-day-at-a-time motto seemed nice in theory but impossible in reality. As the days and weeks of the year melted by, Delia listened to Krista as Krista shared about life and how she was working ❺ [over/through] it. After a year with Delia's family, Krista transferred to Ridge University and her job ended. Krista and Delia stayed in touch, but Krista lived a few hours away on campus ❻ [so/as] they didn't see each other very often.

One day, after a tense situation with one of the girls who lived in her dorm, Krista found ❼ [her / herself] overcome with major anxiety, She took a deep breath, looked at herself in the mirror, and said, "It's okay, Krista. Just get through today." Krista shocked herself, because it was the first time she truly believed that she could survive *one day at a time*. That is a gift Krista has carried with her over all the years since then. She's so thankful for Delia's words.

*nanny 아이 돌보미

During her last year of community college, Krista worked as a full-time nanny to take care of Delia's four kids. Krista was the first person in her family to go to college and felt pressure all around, especially as her long days became consumed by her job as well as writing assignments for her classes. These, along with some other things to take care of, ❶ _____ (be) a real struggle for Krista.

Delia, Krista's boss at the time, had her own struggles. Just before Krista began working for her family, Delia's career in law enforcement was cut short when she'd broken her hip at work. Krista marveled at her attitude. She ❷ _____ (endure) surgery to replace her hip and ❸ _____ (leave) with metal in her leg — rods that would remain in her bones forever. But nothing stopped her. She remained positive, day in and day out. One day when Delia saw Krista struggling with school and writing and general life pressures, she explained how she coped. She told her that the only thing Krista could do was to take "one day at a time."

Delia's attitude made little sense to Krista. She wanted to deal with everything all at once, but that just made her stress even worse. Delia's one-day-at-a-time motto seemed nice in theory but impossible in reality. As the days and weeks of the year ❹ _____ (melt) by, Delia listened to Krista as Krista shared about life and how she was working through it. After a year with Delia's family, Krista transferred to Ridge University and her job ended. Krista and Delia stayed in touch, but Krista lived a few hours away on campus so they didn't see each other very often.

One day, after a tense situation with one of the girls who lived in her dorm, Krista ❺ _____ (find) herself overcome with major anxiety, She took a deep breath, looked at herself in the mirror, and said, "It's okay, Krista. Just get through today." Krista shocked herself, because it was the first time she truly believed that she could survive *one day at a time*. That is a gift Krista ❻ _____ (carry) with her over all the years since then. She's so thankful for Delia's words.

*nanny 아이 돌보미

During her last year of community college, Krista worked as a full-time nanny to take care of Delia's four kids. Krista was the first person in her family to go to college and ❶ _____ _____ _____ _____ (모든 면에서 압박을 느꼈다), especially as her long days became consumed by her job as well as writing assignments for her classes. These, along with some other things to take care of, were a real struggle for Krista.

Delia, Krista's boss at the time, had her own struggles. Just before Krista began working for her family, Delia's career in law enforcement ❷ _____ _____ _____ (갑자기 끝났다) when she'd broken her hip at work. Krista marveled at her attitude. She had endured surgery to replace her hip and was left with metal in her leg — rods that would remain in her bones forever. But nothing stopped her. She remained positive, ❸ _____ _____ _____ _____ _____ (매일매일). One day when Delia saw Krista struggling with school and writing and general life pressures, she explained how she coped. She told her that the only thing Krista could do was to take "one day at a time."

Delia's attitude ❹ _____ _____ _____ _____ (~에게 거의 이해가 되지 않았다) Krista. She wanted to deal with everything all at once, but that just made her stress even worse. Delia's one-day-at-a-time motto seemed nice in theory but impossible in reality. As the days and weeks of the year melted by, Delia listened to Krista as Krista shared about life and how she was working through it. After a year with Delia's family, Krista transferred to Ridge University and her job ended. Krista and Delia ❺ _____ _____ _____ (계속 연락했다), but Krista lived a few hours away on campus so they didn't see each other very often.

One day, after a tense situation with one of the girls who lived in her dorm, Krista found herself ❻ _____ _____ _____ _____ (큰 걱정으로 압도된), She took a deep breath, looked at herself in the mirror, and said, "It's okay, Krista. Just get through today." Krista shocked herself, because it was the first time she truly believed that she could survive *one day at a time*. That is a gift Krista has carried with her over all the years since then. She's so thankful for Delia's words.

*nanny 아이 돌보미

❶ Do bacteria speak? ❷ Do they use sound to communicate with one another just as they use chemicals to send information from one cell to another? ❸ Given that communication among cells is one of the fundamental activities of bacteria, sound would at first seem a likely means of communication. ❹ Bacteria are social beings. ❺ They live in films and clusters that are so tightly woven that they are often invulnerable to chemical and physical attacks that easily kill solitary cells. ❻ Bacterial success depends on networked teamwork and, at the genetic and biochemical levels, bacteria are constantly exchanging molecules. ❼ But to date, there are no documented examples of sonic signaling among bacteria, although their increased growth rates when exposed to the sounds of their own kind may be a form of eavesdropping. ❽ Sonic communication may be ill-suited to bacterial societies. ❾ They live at a scale so tiny that molecules can zip from one cell to another in a fraction of a second. ❿ Bacteria use tens of thousands of molecules within their cells, an extensive, complex, and ready-made language. ⓫ For them, chemical communication may be cheaper, faster, and more nuanced than sound waves.

*eavesdropping 엿듣기 **zip 빠르게 이동하다 ***nuanced 미묘한 차이가 있는

❶ 박테리아가 말을 하는가? ❷ 한 세포에서 다른 세포로 정보를 보내기 위해 화학 물질을 사용하는 것처럼 서로 교신하기 위해 그것들은 소리를 사용할까? ❸ 세포 간의 교신이 박테리아의 필수적인 활동 중 하나라는 것을 고려할 때, 소리가 처음에는 교신의 그럴싸한 수단인 것처럼 보일 것이다. ❹ 박테리아는 무리를 이루어 사는 존재이다. ❺ 그것들은 매우 촘촘하게 짜여서, 고립된 세포를 쉽게 죽이는 화학적, 물리적 공격을 많은 경우 안전하게 막아 주는 얇은 막과 무리 속에서 산다. ❻ 박테리아의 성공은 네트워크로 연결된 협력에 달려 있으며, 유전적, 생화학적 수준에서 박테리아는 끊임없이 분자를 교환하고 있다. ❼ 그러나 지금까지는, 비록 박테리아가 자기 자신의 종의 소리를 접할 때 증가되는 생장률이 엿듣기의 한 형태일 수도 있지만, 박테리아들 사이의 음파 신호 전달에 대한 기록된 예가 없다. ❽ 음파 교신은 박테리아 사회에 적합하지 않을 수도 있다. ❾ 그것들은 아주 작은 규모로 살아서 분자들이 한 세포에서 다른 세포로 순식간에 빠르게 이동할 수 있다. ❿ 박테리아는 그것들의 세포 내에서 수만 개의 분자를 사용하는데, 이는 광범위하고 복잡하며 이미 만들어진 언어이다. ⓫ 그것들에게, 화학적 교신이 음파보다 더 저렴하고, 더 빠르고, 더 미묘한 차이가 있을 수 있다.

Word List

□ chemical 화학 물질 □ cell 세포 □ fundamental 필수적인, 중요한 □ means 수단, 방법 □ film 막 □ cluster 무리
□ woven 짜인 □ invulnerable to ~을 안전하게 막아 주는, ~에 손상되지 않는 □ solitary 고립된, 무리를 짓지 않는 □ genetic 유전의
□ biochemical 생화학의 □ molecule 분자 □ sonic 음파의 □ expose 노출시키다 □ in a fraction of a second 순식간에
□ extensive 광범위한

• Word Test

1	genetic	8	고립된, 무리를 짓지 않는
2	molecule	9	음파의
3	film	10	무리
4	fundamental	11	세포
5	invulnerable to	12	수단, 방법
6	expose	13	순식간에
7	chemical	14	생화학의

Do bacteria speak? Do they use sound to communicate with one another just as they use chemicals to send information from one cell to another? ❶ | Given / Giving | that communication among cells is one of the fundamental activities of bacteria, sound would at first seem a likely means of communication. Bacteria are social beings. They live in films and clusters that are so ❷ | tight / tightly | woven that they are often ❸ | vulnerable / invulnerable | to chemical and physical attacks that easily kill solitary cells. Bacterial success depends on networked teamwork and, at the genetic and biochemical levels, bacteria are constantly exchanging molecules. But to date, there are no documented examples of sonic signaling among bacteria, even although their increased growth rates when exposed to the sounds of their own kind may be a form of eavesdropping. Sonic communication may be ❹ | ill-suited / well-suited | to bacterial societies. They live at a scale so tiny that molecules can zip from one cell to ❺ | another / others | in a fraction of a second. Bacteria use tens of thousands of molecules within their cells, an extensive, complex, and ready-made language. For them, chemical communication may be cheaper, faster, and more nuanced than sound waves.

*eavesdropping 엿듣기　**zip 빠르게 이동하다　***nuanced 미묘한 차이가 있는

Do bacteria speak? Do they use sound to communicate with one another just as they use chemicals to send information from one cell to another? Given that communication among cells ❶ _____ (be) one of the fundamental activities of bacteria, sound would at first seem a likely means of communication. Bacteria ❷ _____ (be) social beings. They live in films and clusters that are so tightly woven that they are often invulnerable to chemical and physical attacks that easily kill solitary cells. Bacterial success ❸ _____ (depend) on networked teamwork and, at the genetic and biochemical levels, bacteria are constantly ❹ _____ (exchange) molecules. But to date, there are no documented examples of sonic signaling among bacteria, although their increased growth rates when ❺ _____ (expose) to the sounds of their own kind may be a form of eavesdropping. Sonic communication may be ill-suited to bacterial societies. They live at a scale so tiny that molecules can zip from one cell to another in a fraction of a second. Bacteria use tens of thousands of molecules within their cells, an extensive, complex, and ready-made language. For them, chemical communication may be cheaper, faster, and more nuanced than sound waves.

*eavesdropping 엿듣기　**zip 빠르게 이동하다　***nuanced 미묘한 차이가 있는

Do bacteria speak? Do they use sound to ❶ _____ _____ _____ _____ (서로 교신하다) just as they use chemicals to send information from one cell to another? Given that communication among cells is one of the fundamental activities of bacteria, sound would at first seem ❷ _____ _____ _____ _____ _____ (교신의 그럴싸한 수단). Bacteria are social beings. They live in films and clusters that are so tightly woven that they are often invulnerable to chemical and physical attacks that easily kill solitary cells. Bacterial success depends on networked teamwork and, at the genetic and biochemical levels, bacteria are constantly exchanging molecules. ❸ _____ _____ _____ (그러나 지금까지는), there are no documented examples of sonic signaling among bacteria, although their increased growth rates when exposed to the sounds of their own kind may be a form of eavesdropping. Sonic communication may be ill-suited to bacterial societies. They live at a scale so tiny that molecules can zip from one cell to another ❹ _____ _____ _____ _____ _____ (순식간에). Bacteria use tens of thousands of molecules within their cells, an extensive, complex, and ready-made language. For them, chemical communication may be cheaper, faster, and more nuanced than sound waves.

*eavesdropping 엿듣기　**zip 빠르게 이동하다　***nuanced 미묘한 차이가 있는

❶ Different listeners will have different interpretations. ❷ On hearing Brahms's Fourth Symphony, Elisabeth von Herzogenberg (among his closest friends, whose opinion he valued) wrote to say: ❸ "It is a walk through exquisite scenery at sunset, when the colours deepen and the crimson glows to purple." ❹ Her response is even more interesting juxtaposed with that of Richard Strauss, who "received an unforgettable impression of the new Brahms Symphony, the Andante of which 'reminded him of a funeral procession moving in silence across moonlit heights.'" ❺ It doesn't matter that the same movement evoked "moonlight" for Strauss and "sunset" for Herzogenberg. ❻ Moonlight and sunset may not be the same, but they have aspects in common, both invoking heavenly bodies, both striving for expression beyond words, and it is the similarities that tell us more about the music than the differences. ❼ The music could never, for instance, characterize a chase or a battle or a cartoon. ❽ If someone were to offer such an interpretation he would be subject to suspicion himself.

*exquisite 더없이 아름다운 **crimson 진홍색 ***juxtapose 나란히 놓다, 병치하다

❶ 듣는 사람이 다르면 해석도 달라질 것이다. ❷ 브람스의 교향곡 4번을 듣자 마자, (브람스가 의견을 존중하는 그의 가장 가까운 친구 가운데 한 사람인) Elisabeth von Herzogenberg는 다음과 같이 썼다. ❸ "그것은 해질 녘에 더없이 아름다운 경치 속으로 들어가는 산책인데, 그 시간에는 색이 짙어지고 진홍빛이 타올라 자줏빛이 된다." ❹ 그녀의 반응은 Richard Strauss의 반응과 나란히 놓일 때 훨씬 더 흥미로운데, 그는 "그 새로운 브람스 교향곡에 대한 잊을 수 없는 인상을 받았는데, 그것의 안단테 악장은 '그에게 달빛이 비치는 고원을 가로질러 고요히 이동하는 장례 행렬을 생각나게 했다." ❺ 같은 악장이 Strauss에게는 '달빛'을, Herzogenberg에게는 '일몰'을 불러일으켰다는 것은 중요하지 않다. ❻ 달빛과 일몰이 똑같지 않을지는 모르나, 둘 다 천체를 상기시키고 둘 다 말로 나타낼 수 없는 표현을 추구하면서 공통적인 면을 가지고 있는데, 우리에게 그 차이점보다 음악에 대해 더 많은 것을 말해 주는 것은 바로 그 유사점이다. ❼ 예를 들어, 그 음악은 결코 추격이나, 전투나, 만화의 특징을 나타낼 수는 없을 것이다. ❽ 만약 누군가 그런 해석을 내놓는다면 그 자신이 의심을 면하기 힘들 것이다.

Word List

□ interpretation 해석 □ value 중요하게 여기다 □ glow 타오르다 □ funeral 장례, 장례식 □ procession 행렬 □ heights 고원
□ evoke 불러일으키다 □ aspect 양상, 측면 □ invoke 상기시키다 □ heavenly bodies 천체
□ strive for ~을 추구하다, ~을 얻고자 하다 □ similarity 유사점 □ characterize ~의 특징을 나타내다 □ chase 추격
□ subject to ~을 면하기 힘든 □ suspicion 의심

• Word Test

1	procession	9	추격
2	invoke	10	천체
3	characterize	11	양상, 측면
4	evoke	12	의심
5	strive for	13	장례, 장례식
6	glow	14	유사점
7	subject to	15	중요하게 여기다
8	interpretation	16	고원

Different listeners will have different interpretations. On hearing Brahms's Fourth Symphony, Elisabeth von Herzogenberg (among his closest friends, ❶ |whom / whose| opinion he valued) wrote to say: "It is a walk through exquisite scenery at sunset, when the colours deepen and the crimson glows to purple." Her response is even more interesting juxtaposed with ❷ |that / those| of Richard Strauss, who "received an unforgettable impression of the new Brahms Symphony, the Andante ❸ |by / of| which 'reminded him of a funeral procession moving in silence across moonlit heights.'" It doesn't matter that the same movement evoked "moonlight" for Strauss and "sunset" for Herzogenberg. Moonlight and sunset may not be the same, but they have aspects in common, both invoking heavenly bodies, both striving for expression beyond words, and it is the ❹ |similarities/dissimilarities| that tell us more about the music than the differences. The music could never, for instance, characterize a chase or a battle or a cartoon. If someone ❺ |is / were| to offer such an interpretation he would be subject to suspicion himself.

*exquisite 더없이 아름다운 **crimson 진홍색 ***juxtapose 나란히 놓다, 병치하다

Different listeners will have different interpretations. On hearing Brahms's Fourth Symphony, Elisabeth von Herzogenberg (among his closest friends, whose opinion he valued) wrote ❶ _____ (say) to say: "It is a walk through exquisite scenery at sunset, when the colours deepen and the crimson ❷ _____ (glow) to purple." Her response is even more interesting juxtaposed with that of Richard Strauss, who "received an unforgettable impression of the new Brahms Symphony, the Andante of which 'reminded him of a funeral procession ❸ _____ (move) in silence across moonlit heights.'" It doesn't matter that the same movement evoked "moonlight" for Strauss and "sunset" for Herzogenberg. Moonlight and sunset may not be the same, but they have aspects in common, both ❹ _____ (invoke) heavenly bodies, both ❺ _____ (strive) for expression beyond words, and it is the similarities that tell us more about the music than the differences. The music could never, for instance, characterize a chase or a battle or a cartoon. If someone were to offer such an interpretation he would be subject to suspicion himself.

*exquisite 더없이 아름다운 **crimson 진홍색 ***juxtapose 나란히 놓다, 병치하다

Different listeners will have different interpretations. On hearing Brahms's Fourth Symphony, Elisabeth von Herzogenberg (❶ _____ _____ _____ _____ (그의 가장 가까운 친구들 가운데), whose opinion he valued) wrote to say: "It is a walk through exquisite scenery at sunset, when the colours deepen and the crimson glows to purple." Her response is even more interesting juxtaposed with that of Richard Strauss, who "received an unforgettable impression of the new Brahms Symphony, the Andante of which 'reminded him of a funeral procession moving in silence ❷ _____ _____ _____ (달빛이 비치는 고원들을 가로질러).'" It doesn't matter that the same movement evoked "moonlight" for Strauss and "sunset" for Herzogenberg. Moonlight and sunset may not be the same, but they have ❸ _____ _____ _____ (공통적인 면들), both invoking heavenly bodies, both striving for expression beyond words, and it is the similarities that tell us more about the music than the differences. The music could never, for instance, characterize a chase or a battle or a cartoon. If someone were to offer such an interpretation he ❹ _____ _____ _____ _____ _____ _____ (그 자신이 의심을 면하기 힘들 것이다).

*exquisite 더없이 아름다운 **crimson 진홍색 ***juxtapose 나란히 놓다, 병치하다

❶ In general, two approaches to learning have been distinguished — a surface approach and a deep approach to learning. ❷ A student with a surface approach to learning sees the work or task as an unwelcome external imposition, a hurdle they want to clear with as little time and effort as possible. ❸ One of the most common strategies for the surface approach is rote learning content without understanding, in order to subsequently reproduce the material. ❹ Students with a deep approach to learning, on the other hand, have the intention of comprehending the material, and activating conceptual analysis. ❺ Learning strategies that characterize a deep approach to learning can vary in terms of the characteristics and requirements of the task. ❻ Possible strategies are reflecting, discussing, using various information sources, relating ideas to previous knowledge, looking for patterns, checking evidence, and critically examining arguments.

*imposition 부담 **rote learn 무턱대고 암기하다

❶ 일반적으로 학습에 대한 두 가지 접근법, 즉 학습에 대한 표면 접근법과 심층 접근법이 구분되어 왔다. ❷ 학습에 표면 접근법을 취하는 학생은 공부나 과제를 달갑지 않은 외적인 부담, 즉 가능한 한 적은 시간과 노력으로 치워 버리고 싶은 장애물로 본다. ❸ 표면 접근법에 대한 가장 일반적인 전략 중 하나는 이후에 자료를 상기하기 위해, 이해하지 않고 내용을 무턱대고 암기하는 것이다. ❹ 반면 학습에 대한 심층 접근법을 취하는 학생은 자료를 이해하고 개념 분석을 활성화하려는 의도를 가지고 있다. ❺ 학습에 대한 심층 접근법의 특징이 되는 학습 전략은 과제의 특성과 요구 사항의 측면에서 차이가 있을 수 있다. ❻ 가능한 전략으로는 곰곰이 생각해 보기, 토론하기, 다양한 정보 출처 사용하기, 아이디어를 이전 지식과 연관시키기, 패턴 찾아보기, 증거 확인하기, 주장을 비판적으로 검토하기가 있다.

Word List

□ in general 일반적으로   □ approach 접근법   □ distinguish 구분하다   □ external 외적인   □ hurdle 장애물   □ content 내용
□ subsequently 이후에   □ reproduce 상기하다, 재현하다   □ comprehend 이해하다   □ activate 활성화하다
□ conceptual 개념의   □ analysis 분석   □ reflect 곰곰이 생각하다   □ critically 비판적으로   □ argument 주장

• Word Test

1 external _____
2 critically _____
3 activate _____
4 content _____
5 analysis _____
6 reproduce _____
7 approach _____

8 이해하다 _____
9 개념의 _____
10 이후에 _____
11 주장 _____
12 장애물 _____
13 곰곰이 생각하다 _____
14 구분하다 _____

In general, two approaches to learning have been distinguished — a surface approach and a deep approach to learning. A student with a surface approach to learning sees the work or task as an unwelcome ❶ external / internal imposition, a hurdle they want to ❷ miss / clear with as little time and effort as possible. One of the most common strategies for the surface approach is rote learning content without understanding, in order to subsequently reproduce the material. Students with a deep approach to learning, ❸ in other words / on the other hand , have the intention of comprehending the material, and activating conceptual analysis. Learning strategies ❹ what / that characterize a deep approach to learning can vary in terms of the characteristics and requirements of the task. Possible strategies are reflecting, discussing, using various information sources, relating ideas to ❺ previous / potential knowledge, looking for patterns, checking evidence, and critically examining arguments.

*imposition 부담 **rote learn 무턱대고 암기하다

In general, two approaches to learning have ❶ _____ (distinguish) — a surface approach and a deep approach to learning. A student with a surface approach to learning ❷ _____ (see) the work or task as an unwelcome external imposition, a hurdle they want to clear with as little time and effort as possible. One of the most common strategies for the surface approach ❸ _____ (be) rote learning content without understanding, in order to subsequently reproduce the material. Students with a deep approach to learning, on the other hand, ❹ _____ (have) the intention of comprehending the material, and ❺ _____ (activate) conceptual analysis. Learning strategies that characterize a deep approach to learning can vary in terms of the characteristics and requirements of the task. Possible strategies are reflecting, discussing, using various information sources, relating ideas to previous knowledge, looking for patterns, checking evidence, and critically examining arguments.

*imposition 부담 **rote learn 무턱대고 암기하다

In general, two approaches to learning have been distinguished — a surface approach and a deep approach to learning. A student with a surface approach to learning sees the work or task as an unwelcome external imposition, a hurdle they want to clear with ❶ _____ _____ _____ _____ _____ _____ _____ (가능한 한 적은 시간과 노력). One of the most common strategies for the surface approach is rote learning content without understanding, in order to ❷ _____ _____ _____ _____ (이후에 자료를 상기하다). Students with a deep approach to learning, on the other hand, have the intention of comprehending the material, and activating conceptual analysis. Learning strategies that characterize a deep approach to learning ❸ _____ _____ _____ _____ _____ (~의 측면에서 차이가 있을 수 있다) the characteristics and requirements of the task. Possible strategies are reflecting, discussing, using various information sources, relating ideas to previous knowledge, looking for patterns, checking evidence, and ❹ _____ _____ _____ (주장들을 비판적으로 검토하기).

*imposition 부담 **rote learn 무턱대고 암기하다

❶ So many of our feelings can be made so much easier to manage, and perhaps more fun to experience, just by saying them aloud and letting them build a bridge between us and another person. ❷ Exposing our fears makes them much less frightening; affirming our triumphs makes them much more real; revealing our grief relieves us of carrying the burden completely alone. ❸ A compassionate and empathetic friend, much like a therapist, can give us and our emotions a foundation to cling to. ❹ It's the reason that merely having someone listen can be such a powerful experience, even if that person was secretly paying more attention to the cheerleaders at the halftime show. ❺ All jokes about therapists' fees aside, it is no shame that part of their ability to help lies in just being there, in the moment and attuned — those nods can be meaningful. ❻ A quality friend understands this and runs with it, knowing just how to validate their buddy's emotional state — whether that state stems from a hard-won personal triumph or just a particularly arduous commute home.

*attuned 이해를 해 주는 **arduous 힘든

❶ 우리의 감정 가운데 아주 많은 것이 그저 그것을 (남이 들을 수 있게) 소리 내어 말해 우리와 다른 사람 사이에 다리를 놓게 함으로써, 관리하기 훨씬 더 쉽고, 아마도 겪기가 더 재미있어질 수도 있을 것이다. ❷ 우리의 두려움을 드러내는 것은 그것을 훨씬 덜 두렵게 만들고, 우리의 승리를 긍정하는 것은 그것을 훨씬 더 현실적으로 만들고, 우리의 슬픔을 드러내는 것은 그 짐을 완전히 혼자 짊어지고 가는 것에서 우리를 해방한다. ❸ 인정이 많고 이해심이 있는 친구는 치료 전문가와 마찬가지로, 매달릴 수 있는 토대를 우리와 우리의 감정에 줄 수 있다. ❹ 그렇기 때문에 단지 어떤 사람에게 이야기를 들려주는 것만으로도 매우 강력한 경험이 될 수 있는데, 그가 하프타임 쇼에서 몰래 치어리더들에게 더 많은 관심을 기울이고 있다 하더라도 그렇다. ❺ 치료 전문가의 치료비에 관한 모든 농담은 차치하고라도, 도움을 줄 수 있는 그들의 능력 일부가 그 순간에 이해를 해 주며 그저 그 자리에 존재한다는 데 있다는 것은 유감스러운 일이 아니며, 그런 고개 끄덕임이 유의미할 수 있다. ❻ 좋은 친구는 이것을 이해하고 받아들이며, 자기 벗의 감정 상태가 어렵게 얻은 개인적 승리에서 비롯되는 것이든, 그저 특히 힘든 귀갓길에서 비롯되는 것이든, 그것을 그저 인정하는 법을 안다.

Word List

□ expose 드러내다, 보여 주다   □ frightening 두려운   □ affirm 긍정하다   □ triumph 승리   □ reveal 드러내다   □ grief 슬픔
□ relieve - of... ~을 …에서 해방시키다   □ burden 짐, 부담   □ compassionate 인정이 많은   □ empathetic 이해심 있는, 공감하는
□ therapist 치료 전문가   □ foundation 토대   □ cling 매달리다   □ nod 고개 끄덕임   □ quality 좋은   □ run with ~을 받아들이다,
~을 이용하기 시작하다   □ validate 인정하다, 확인하다   □ stem from ~에서 비롯되다   □ commute 통근

• Word Test

1	foundation	9	치료 전문가
2	validate	10	승리
3	reveal	11	인정이 많은
4	empathetic	12	두려운
5	burden	13	매달리다
6	affirm	14	좋은
7	nod	15	슬픔
8	expose	16	통근

So many of our feelings can be made so much easier to manage, and perhaps more fun to experience, just by ❶ |saying/laughing| them aloud and letting them build a bridge between us and another person. Exposing our fears makes them much ❷ |more/less| frightening; affirming our triumphs makes them much more real; revealing our grief relieves us of carrying the burden completely alone. A compassionate and ❸ |pathetic/empathetic| friend, much like a therapist, can give us and our emotions a foundation to cling to. It's the reason that merely having someone listen can be such a powerful experience, ❹ |despite/even if| that person was secretly paying more attention to the cheerleaders at the halftime show. All jokes about therapists' fees aside, it is no shame that part of their ability to help lies in just being there, in the moment and attuned — those nods can be meaningful. A quality friend understands this and runs with it, knowing just how to ❺ |validate/invalidate| their buddy's emotional state — whether that state stems from a hard-won personal triumph or just a particularly arduous commute home.

*attuned 이해를 해 주는 **arduous 힘든

So many of our feelings can be made so much easier to manage, and perhaps more fun ❶ _____ (experience), just by saying them aloud and letting them ❷ _____ (build) a bridge between us and another person. Exposing our fears makes them much less frightening; affirming our triumphs makes them much more real; revealing our grief ❸ _____ (relieve) us of carrying the burden completely alone. A compassionate and empathetic friend, much like a therapist, can give us and our emotions a foundation to cling to. It's the reason that merely having someone listen can be such a powerful experience, even if that person was secretly paying more attention to the cheerleaders at the halftime show. All jokes about therapists' fees aside, it is no shame that part of their ability to help ❹ _____ (lie) in just being there, in the moment and attuned — those nods can be meaningful. A quality friend understands this and runs with it, ❺ _____ (know) just how to validate their buddy's emotional state — whether that state stems from a hard-won personal triumph or just a particularly arduous commute home.

*attuned 이해를 해 주는 **arduous 힘든

So many of our feelings can be made so much easier to manage, and perhaps more fun to experience, just by saying them aloud and letting them build a bridge between us and another person. Exposing our fears makes them much less frightening; affirming our triumphs makes them much more real; revealing our grief relieves us of ❶ _____ _____ _____ _____ _____ (그 짐을 완전히 혼자 짊어지고 가는 것). A compassionate and empathetic friend, much like a therapist, can give us and our emotions a(n) ❷ _____ _____ _____ _____ (매달릴 수 있는 토대). It's the reason that merely having someone listen can be such a powerful experience, even if that person was secretly paying more attention to the cheerleaders at the halftime show. All jokes about therapists' fees aside, it is no shame that part of their ability to help lies in ❸ _____ _____ _____ (그저 그 자리에 존재하는 것), in the moment and attuned — those nods can be meaningful. A quality friend understands this and ❹ _____ _____ _____ (그것을 받아들인다), knowing just how to validate their buddy's emotional state — whether that state stems from a hard-won personal triumph or just a particularly arduous commute home.

*attuned 이해를 해 주는 **arduous 힘든

❶ To understand connection regrets, let me tell you the story of two women. ❷ In the late 1980s, Cheryl attended Drake University in Des Moines, where she became fast friends with Jen. ❸ Cheryl and Jen belonged to the same sorority and lived in a house with about forty other women. ❹ Among the group, these two stood out for their seriousness and ambition. ❺ Cheryl became president of the sorority; Jen was elected president of the entire student body. ❻ They supported each other's enthusiasms and aspirations.

❼ Shortly after graduation in 1990, Jen married — Cheryl was a bridesmaid — and moved to Virginia. ❽ And shortly after that, Jen invited Cheryl to visit her at her new home. ❾ Jen said that she wanted Cheryl to meet a friend of Jen's husband, who she thought might be a good romantic match. ❿ Cheryl was taken aback. ⓫ She'd been dating another Drake student for two years. ⓬ "I thought he was the one." ⓭ Jen knew the guy, but Cheryl said, she "clearly did not think he was the one." ⓮ Cheryl politely declined the invitation to visit.

⓯ Over the next few years, Cheryl and Jen, living in different parts of the country at a time before widespread email, exchanged letters and cards. ⓰ Cheryl eventually ditched the boyfriend, whom she refers to today only as "Mr. Wrong," and says, "Now that I've matured into the person I am, I can see what Jen saw." ⓱ Within a couple of years, the letters dwindled. ⓲ Then they stopped. ⓳ Cheryl hasn't talked to Jen for twenty-five years. ⓴ "We didn't have a falling-out of any kind. ㉑ I just let it kind of drift away, " she told me. ㉒ "I regret not having that relationship in my life. ㉓ I've missed having another person in my life who could share with me the kind of growth I've experienced over the years."

㉔ The absence disquiets Cheryl. ㉕ I asked Cheryl, "If you're going to die in a month, are there things you would want tied up?" ㉖ Cheryl said, "I would like her to know that the friendship feels significant to me even twenty-five years later." ㉗ During a conversation one spring afternoon, I asked Cheryl if she'd consider trying to revive the friendship — or at least to call, email, or write Jen. ㉘ "I think the door's open," she replied. ㉙ "If I were not a coward, I would reach out."

*sorority (미국 대학의) 여학생 사교 클럽 **ditch (교제하던 사람을) 차 버리다 ***dwindle 줄어들다

❶ 관계에 대한 후회를 이해하기 위해, 두 여성의 이야기를 해 보겠다. ❷ 1980년대 후반에 Cheryl은 Des Moines에 있는 Drake University에 다녔고 그곳에서 그녀는 Jen과 절친한 친구 사이가 되었다. ❸ Cheryl과 Jen은 같은 여학생 사교 클럽에 속해 있었고 약 40명의 다른 여자들과 한 건물에 살았다. ❹ 그 집단에서 이 두 사람은 진지함과 야망이 두드러졌다. ❺ Cheryl은 여학생 클럽의 회장이 되었고 Jen은 전체 학생회 회장으로 선출되었다. ❻ 그들은 서로의 열정과 열망을 응원했다.

❼ 1990년에 졸업한 후 얼마 안 되어 Jen은 결혼했고-Cheryl이 신부 들러리였다-Virginia로 이사했다. ❽ 그리고 그 후 얼마 지나지 않아 Jen은 Cheryl을 자신의 새집에 방문하도록 초대했다. ❾ Jen은 Cheryl이 자기 남편의 친구를 만나길 원한다고 말했는데 그녀는 남편의 친구가 훌륭한 연애 상대가 될 수도 있을 것이라고 생각했다. ❿ Cheryl은 깜짝 놀랐다. ⓫ 그녀는 2년 동안 다른 Drake 학생과 데이트를 해 왔다. ⓬ "저는 그가 운명적인 제 짝이라고 생각했어요." ⓭ Jen은 그 남자를 알고 있었지만, Cheryl의 말로는, 그녀는 "분명 그가 운명적인 제 짝이라고 생각하지 않았어요." ⓮ Cheryl은 방문 초대를 정중하게 거절했다.

⓯ 그 후 몇 년 동안 Cheryl과 Jen은, 이메일이 널리 퍼지기 전의 시기에 나라의 다른 지역에 살았으므로, 편지와 카드를 주고받았다. ⓰ Cheryl은 자신이 오늘날 단지 "Mr. Wrong"이라고 언급하는 그 남자 친구를 결국 차 버렸고, "이제 제가 성숙하여 현재의 제가 되고 보니, Jen이 본 것이 저에게도 보입니다."라고 말한다. ⓱ 몇 년 안에 편지가 줄어들었다. ⓲ 그러더니 편지는 중단되었다. ⓳ Cheryl은 25년 동안 Jen과 이야기하지 않았다. ⓴ "우리는 어떤 형태로도 사이가 틀어진 것은 없었습니다. ㉑ 저는 그냥 상황이 약간 흘러가도록 내버려 두었습니다."라고 그녀는 내게 말했다. ㉒ "저는 제 인생에서 그런 관계를 갖지 못한 것을 후회합니다. ㉓ 오랜 세월 동안 겪어 온 그런 종류의 성장을 저와 나눌 수 있는 다른 사람을 제 인생에서 가지지 못했습니다."

㉔ 그 부재가 Cheryl을 불안하게 한다. ㉕ 나는 Cheryl에게 물었다. "만약 당신이 한 달 후에 죽는다면, 연결되도록 하고 싶은 것이 있습니까?" ㉖ Cheryl은 "25년이 지난 후에도 우정이 나에게 중요하게 느껴진다는 것을 그녀가 알았으면 좋겠어요,"라고 말했다. ㉗ 어느 봄날 오후 대화하는 동안 나는 Cheryl에게 그 우정을 되살리려고 애써 보는 것, 즉 적어도 Jen에게 전화를 걸거나, 이메일을 보내거나, 편지를 쓰려고 애써 보는 것을 고려할 것인지를 물었다. ㉘ "문은 열려 있다고 생각해요."라고 그녀가 대답했다. ㉙ "제가 겁쟁이가 아니라면 연락을 취하려 할 텐데요."

• Word Test

1	drift away	9	불안하게 하다
2	take aback	10	열정
3	significant	11	성숙하다
4	connection	12	거절하다
5	eventually	13	속하다
6	coward	14	신부 들러리
7	aspiration	15	연락을 취하려고 하다
8	ambition	16	되살리다, 재개시키다

• 유형 1 네모 안에서 옳은 어법·어휘를 고르시오.

To understand connection regrets, let me tell you the story of two women. In the late 1980s, Cheryl attended Drake University in Des Moines, ❶ which / where she became fast friends with Jen. Cheryl and Jen belonged to the same sorority and lived in a house with about forty other women. Among the group, these two stood out for their seriousness and ambition. Cheryl became president of the sorority; Jen was elected president of the entire student body. They supported each other's enthusiasms and aspirations.

Shortly after graduation in 1990, Jen married — Cheryl was a bridesmaid — and moved to Virginia. And shortly after that, Jen invited Cheryl to visit her at her new home. Jen said that she wanted Cheryl to meet a friend of Jen's husband, who she thought might be a good romantic match. Cheryl was taken aback. She'd been dating another Drake student for two years. "I thought he was the one." Jen knew the guy, but Cheryl said, she "clearly did not think he was the one." Cheryl politely ❷ declined / inclined the invitation to visit.

Over the next few years, Cheryl and Jen, living in different parts of the country at a time before widespread email, exchanged letters and cards. Cheryl eventually ditched the boyfriend, ❸ whom / which she refers to today only as "Mr. Wrong,", and says, "Now that I've matured into the person I am, I can see what Jen saw." Within a couple of years, the letters dwindled. Then they stopped. Cheryl hasn't talked to Jen ❹ for / since twenty-five years. "We didn't have a falling-out of any kind. I just let it kind of drift away, " she told me. "I regret not having that relationship in my life. I've missed ❺ to have / having another person in my life who could share with me the kind of growth I've experienced over the years."

The absence disquiets Cheryl. I asked Cheryl, "If you're going to die in a month, are there things you would want tied up?" Cheryl said, "I would like her to know that the friendship feels significant to me even twenty-five years later." During a conversation one spring afternoon, I asked Cheryl if she'd consider trying to ❻ remove / revive the friendship — or at least to call, email, or write Jen. "I think the door's open," she replied. "If I were not a coward, I would reach out."

*sorority (미국 대학의) 여학생 사교 클럽 **ditch (교제하던 사람을) 차 버리다 ***dwindle 줄어들다

To understand connection regrets, let me tell you the story of two women. In the late 1980s, Cheryl attended Drake University in Des Moines, where she became fast friends with Jen. Cheryl and Jen belonged to the same sorority and lived in a house with about forty other women. Among the group, these two stood out for their seriousness and ambition. Cheryl became president of the sorority; Jen ❶ _____ (elect) president of the entire student body. They supported each other's enthusiasms and aspirations.

Shortly after graduation in 1990, Jen married — Cheryl was a bridesmaid — and moved to Virginia. And shortly after that, Jen invited Cheryl ❷ _____ (visit) her at her new home. Jen said that she wanted Cheryl to meet a friend of Jen's husband, who she thought might be a good romantic match. Cheryl was taken aback. She'd been dating another Drake student for two years. "I thought he was the one." Jen knew the guy, but Cheryl said, she "clearly did not think he was the one." Cheryl politely declined the invitation to visit.

Over the next few years, Cheryl and Jen, ❸ _____ (live) in different parts of the country at a time before widespread email, exchanged letters and cards. Cheryl eventually ditched the boyfriend, whom she refers to today only as "Mr. Wrong,", and says, "Now that I've matured into the person I am, I can see what Jen ❹ _____ (see)." Within a couple of years, the letters dwindled. Then they stopped. Cheryl hasn't talked to Jen for twenty-five years. "We didn't have a falling-out of any kind. I just let it kind of drift away, " she told me. "I regret not ❺ _____ (have) that relationship in my life. I've missed having another person in my life who could share with me the kind of growth I've experienced over the years."

The absence disquiets Cheryl. I asked Cheryl, "If you're going to die in a month, are there things you would want ❻ _____ (tie) up?" Cheryl said, "I would like her to know that the friendship feels significant to me even twenty-five years later." During a conversation one spring afternoon, I asked Cheryl if she'd consider ❼ _____ (try) to revive the friendship — or at least to call, email, or write Jen. "I think the door's open," she replied. "If I were not a coward, I would reach out."

*sorority (미국 대학의) 여학생 사교 클럽   **ditch (교제하던 사람을) 차 버리다   ***dwindle 줄어들다

To understand connection regrets, let me tell you the story of two women. In the late 1980s, Cheryl attended Drake University in Des Moines, where she became fast friends with Jen. Cheryl and Jen belonged to the same sorority and lived in a house with about forty other women. Among the group, these two ❶ _____ _____ _____ _____ _____ _____ _____ (그들의 진지함과 야망이 두드러졌다). Cheryl became president of the sorority; Jen was elected president of the entire student body. They supported each other's enthusiasms and aspirations.

Shortly after graduation in 1990, Jen married — Cheryl was a bridesmaid — and moved to Virginia. And shortly after that, Jen invited Cheryl to visit her at her new home. Jen said that she wanted Cheryl to meet a friend of Jen's husband, who she thought might be a good romantic match. Cheryl ❷ _____ _____ _____ (깜짝 놀랐다). She'd been dating another Drake student for two years. "I thought he was the one." Jen knew the guy, but Cheryl said, she "clearly did not think he was the one." Cheryl politely declined the invitation to visit.

Over the next few years, Cheryl and Jen, living in different parts of the country ❸ _____ _____ _____ _____ _____ _____ (이메일이 널리 퍼지기 전의 시기에), exchanged letters and cards. Cheryl eventually ditched the boyfriend, whom she refers to today only as "Mr. Wrong,", and says, "Now that I've matured into the person I am, I can see what Jen saw." Within a couple of years, the letters dwindled. Then they stopped. Cheryl hasn't talked to Jen for twenty-five years. "We didn't have a falling-out of any kind. I just ❹ _____ _____ _____ _____ _____ _____ (상황이 약간 흘러가도록 내버려 두었다), " she told me. "I regret not having that relationship in my life. I've missed having another person in my life who could share with me the kind of growth I've experienced over the years."

The absence disquiets Cheryl. I asked Cheryl, "If you're going to die in a month, are there things you would want tied up?" Cheryl said, "I would like her to know that the friendship feels significant to me even twenty-five years later." During a conversation one spring afternoon, I asked Cheryl if she'd consider trying to revive the friendship — or at least to call, email, or write Jen. "I think the door's open," she replied. "❺ _____ _____ _____ _____ _____ (내가 겁쟁이가 아니라면), I would reach out."

*sorority (미국 대학의) 여학생 사교 클럽   **ditch (교제하던 사람을) 차 버리다   ***dwindle 줄어들다

01 10강 1번

다음 빈칸에 들어갈 말로 가장 적절한 것은?

When you work with perfectionistic athletes, one challenge is that the athletes, once determined to work on their perfectionism, are very likely to try to be "the perfect client" during the intervention. Thus, from the therapist/consultant's view it is important to be aware of subtle warning signs, such as if the intervention seems to run too smoothly and the athlete seems to be capable of carrying out exercises you agreed on a little bit too well. In these situations you yourself might very well feel like the "best therapist ever" because you are unknowingly being reinforced by the athlete's apparent success. It is, however, important that you do not allow yourself to _____ . At this point, not only have you failed to help the athlete, you may have actually begun to reinforce the perfectionistic behaviors you should actually be working on. Maintaining a dialog with the athlete about their progress and continually exploring their goals within the intervention is therefore crucial. In many cases, it can even be considered progress if the athlete "fails" to some extent in completing the homework assignment. This is because it provides an opportunity to discuss failure.

① reveal your client's secrets
② be disappointed by the results
③ be deceived by the athlete
④ slow down your counseling pace
⑤ doubt about your client's response

02 10강 2번

밑줄 친 To avoid involvement altogether can itself be seen as irresponsible.이 다음 글에서 의미하는 바로 가장 적절한 것은?

One of the ideas many scientists take as an ethical principle is that scientists should remain, like journalists, "objective" and not take sides on policy controversies. Indeed, historically, scientists such as the late astronomer Carl Sagan who appear to have become "too" public have risked losing the respect of other scientists. Under normal circumstances, some scientists might reasonably choose to avoid (as scientists) championing specific policy solutions, even on something like climate, lest they be mistaken for self-appointed (or media-appointed) authorities over what society should do. But scientists are also citizens, who may also reasonably choose to speak out, as citizens, on policy issues. To avoid involvement altogether can itself be seen as irresponsible. Scientists have the same rights and duties as other citizens, including the right and the duty to give thought to public issues and, on appropriate occasions, to take positions on them. For a climate scientist not to support appropriate action on climate might be likened to a medical doctor's not supporting routine cancer screening or prenatal nutrition initiatives.

*champion 옹호하다 **prenatal 태아기의

① Scientists should remain objective no matter what the situation is.
② Scientists' political involvement has little to do with their rights and duties as scientists.
③ Scientists should express their thoughts on policy issues, when it is needed, for the greater good.
④ Scientists might lose the respect of other scientists if they are involved in political championing.
⑤ Scientists cannot easily avoid speaking out on policy issues but they should be careful not to be involved.

다음 글의 제목으로 가장 적절한 것은?

In a study conducted by Griskevicius and his colleagues on behavioural cues, university students read a short story about a successful university graduate who obtained a high-status first job and was, relative to others, promoted quickly. Students in the control group read a neutral story of similar length. In subsequent experimental tasks, students could choose between different green and non-green hypothetical consumer products (car, household cleaner, dishwasher). Each time the products were equal in price, but the non-green product was more luxurious and had better performance than the green product, which was pro-environmental. The study showed that, in the treatment group, in which an activation of status motives occurred, 55 per cent chose the green car; in the control group, 37 per cent chose the green car. The corresponding figures for the household cleaner and dishwasher were 42 per cent versus 26 per cent, and 49 per cent versus 35 per cent, respectively.

*subsequent 뒤이은, 차후의

① Eco-friendly Products: Helpful or Harmful?
② Why the Non-Green Products Perform Better
③ The Triggering of Status Motives: A Variable in Eco-Friendly Choice
④ Pro-Environmental Attitude: A Product of Education
⑤ What Is the Difference Between Green Products and Non-Green Ones?

다음 글의 주제로 가장 적절한 것은?

Perhaps the variable found in research to distinguish entrepreneurs from others is self-efficacy — individuals' belief that they can successfully accomplish whatever they set out to accomplish. This is one reason why, despite the odds being highly stacked against them, many start new ventures: they believe that they can effectively complete the tasks needed to make these companies a success. Thus, self-efficacy is one characteristic that helps entrepreneurs get started and also persist in their efforts to succeed. Self-efficacy, however, has a downside. It may lead individuals to undertake tasks for which, in reality, they lack the required resources, leading to what can be disastrous results. In a sense, they have chosen to play in a game they cannot win, with negative results virtually guaranteed. These negative effects can be magnified by a high level of optimism — a general, and often unjustified belief that ultimately all will turn out well. In combination, high levels of optimism and high levels of self-efficacy can prove deadly for entrepreneurs with limited resources.

① pros and cons of starting new ventures
② optimal levels of self-efficacy and optimism
③ the impact self-efficacy can have on entrepreneurs
④ the importance of self-efficacy to becoming an entrepreneur
⑤ how to solve problems out of a lack of the required resources

[5~6] 다음 글을 읽고, 물음에 답하시오.

During her last year of community college, Krista worked as a full-time nanny to take care of Delia's four kids. Krista was the first person in her family to go to college and felt pressure all around, especially as her long days became consumed by her job as well as writing assignments for her classes. These, along with some other things to take care of, were a real (a) struggle for Krista.

Delia, Krista's boss at the time, had her own struggles. Just before Krista began working for her family, Delia's career in law enforcement was cut short when she'd broken her hip at work. Krista marveled at her attitude. She had endured surgery to replace her hip and was left with metal in her leg — rods that would remain in her bones forever. But nothing stopped her. She remained (b) positive, day in and day out. One day when Delia saw Krista struggling with school and writing and general life pressures, she explained how she coped. She told her that the only thing Krista could do was to take "one day at a time."

Delia's attitude made (c) little sense to Krista. She wanted to deal with everything all at once, but that just made her stress even worse. Delia's one-day-at-a-time motto seemed nice in theory but impossible in reality. As the days and weeks of the year melted by, Delia listened to Krista as Krista shared about life and how she was working through it. After a year with Delia's family, Krista transferred to Ridge University and her job ended. Krista and Delia stayed in touch, but Krista lived a few hours away on campus so they didn't see each other very often.

One day, after a tense situation with one of the girls who lived in her dorm, Krista found herself overcnme with major (d) anxiety, She took a deep breath, looked at herself in the mirror, and said, "It's okay, Krista. Just get through today." Krista shocked herself, because it was the first time she truly believed that she could (e) give up *one day at a time*. That is a gift Krista has carried with her over all the years since then. She's so thankful for Delia's words.

*nanny 아이 돌보미

05

윗글의 제목으로 가장 적절한 것은?

① How to Defeat Powerlessness
② A Gift from Delia: One Day at a Time
③ Positivity: Ever in Dreams, Never in Reality
④ What's the Right Attitude for Your Success?
⑤ What Happened to the Woman after the Surgery?

06

밑줄 친 (a)~(e) 중, 문맥상 낱말의 쓰임이 적절하지 <u>않은</u> 것은?

① (a)　　② (b)　　③ (c)　　④ (d)　　⑤ (e)

07 10강 8번

다음 글의 내용을 한 문장으로 요약하고자 한다. 빈칸 (A), (B)에 들어갈 말로 가장 적절한 것은?

Do bacteria speak? Do they use sound to communicate with one another just as they use chemicals to send information from one cell to another? Given that communication among cells is one of the fundamental activities of bacteria, sound would at first seem a likely means of communication. Bacteria are social beings. They live in films and clusters that are so tightly woven that they are often invulnerable to chemical and physical attacks that easily kill solitary cells. Bacterial success depends on networked teamwork and, at the genetic and biochemical levels, bacteria are constantly exchanging molecules. But to date, there are no documented examples of sonic signaling among bacteria, although their increased growth rates when exposed to the sounds of their own kind may be a form of eavesdropping. Sonic communication may be ill-suited to bacterial societies. They live at a scale so tiny that molecules can zip from one cell to another in a fraction of a second. Bacteria use tens of thousands of molecules within their cells, an extensive, complex, and ready-made language. For them, chemical communication may be cheaper, faster, and more nuanced than sound waves.

*eavesdropping 엿듣기 **zip 빠르게 이동하다
***nuanced 미묘한 차이가 있는

↓

Although bacteria are   (A)   beings, constantly networking with one another,   (B)   do not seem to be an appropriate means to communicate for bacterial societies.

	(A)		(B)
①	reserved	......	sounds
②	reserved	......	chemicals
③	social	......	chemicals
④	communicative	......	sounds
⑤	communicative	......	motions

08 10강 9번

주어진 글 다음에 이어질 글의 순서로 가장 적절한 것은?

Different listeners will have different interpretations. On hearing Brahms's Fourth Symphony, Elisabeth von Herzogenberg (among his closest friends, whose opinion he valued) wrote to say: "It is a walk through exquisite scenery at sunset, when the colours deepen and the crimson glows to purple."

(A) It doesn't matter that the same movement evoked "moonlight" for Strauss and "sunset" for Herzogenberg. Moonlight and sunset may not be the same, but they have aspects in common, both invoking heavenly bodies, both striving for expression beyond words, and it is the similarities that tell us more about the music than the differences.

(B) Her response is even more interesting juxtaposed with that of Richard Strauss, who "received an unforgettable impression of the new Brahms Symphony, the Andante of which 'reminded him of a funeral procession moving in silence across moonlit heights.'"

(C) The music could never, for instance, characterize a chase or a battle or a cartoon. If someone were to offer such an interpretation he would be subject to suspicion himself.

*exquisite 더없이 아름다운 **crimson 진홍색
***juxtapose 나란히 놓다, 병치하다

① (A) – (C) – (B)
② (B) – (A) – (C)
③ (B) – (C) – (A)
④ (C) – (A) – (B)
⑤ (C) – (B) – (A)

다음 빈칸에 들어갈 말로 가장 적절한 것은?

In general, two approaches to learning have been distinguished — a surface approach and a deep approach to learning. A student with a surface approach to learning sees the work or task as an unwelcome external imposition, a hurdle they want to clear with as little time and effort as possible. One of the most common strategies for the surface approach is rote learning content without _____, in order to subsequently reproduce the material. Students with a deep approach to learning, on the other hand, have the intention of comprehending the material, and activating conceptual analysis. Learning strategies that characterize a deep approach to learning can vary in terms of the characteristics and requirements of the task. Possible strategies are reflecting, discussing, using various information sources, relating ideas to previous knowledge, looking for patterns, checking evidence, and critically examining arguments.

*imposition 부담 **rote learn 무턱대고 암기하다

① creating
② replacing
③ distorting
④ presenting
⑤ understanding

다음 글의 요지로 가장 적절한 것은?

So many of our feelings can be made so much easier to manage, and perhaps more fun to experience, just by saying them aloud and letting them build a bridge between us and another person. Exposing our fears makes them much less frightening; affirming our triumphs makes them much more real; revealing our grief relieves us of carrying the burden completely alone. A compassionate and empathetic friend, much like a therapist, can give us and our emotions a foundation to cling to. It's the reason that merely having someone listen can be such a powerful experience, even if that person was secretly paying more attention to the cheerleaders at the halftime show. All jokes about therapists' fees aside, it is no shame that part of their ability to help lies in just being there, in the moment and attuned — those nods can be meaningful. A quality friend understands this and runs with it, knowing just how to validate their buddy's emotional state — whether that state stems from a hard-won personal triumph or just a particularly arduous commute home.

*attuned 이해를 해 주는 **arduous 힘든

① 감정을 치유하기 위해서는 전문 치료사의 도움이 필요하다.
② 친밀한 친구 관계를 만드는 데 있어 중요한 것은 감정의 공유이다.
③ 자신의 감정을 터놓기 전에 상대방의 감정에 먼저 귀 기울여야 한다.
④ 감정을 있는 그대로 드러내는 것만으로도 감정 관리에 큰 도움이 된다.
⑤ 자신의 감정을 충분히 이해하기 위해서 장기적이고 체계적으로 접근해야 한다.

[11~12] 다음을 읽고 물음에 답하시오.

To understand connection regrets, let me tell you the story of two women. In the late 1980s, Cheryl attended Drake University in Des Moines, where she became fast friends with Jen. Cheryl and Jen belonged to the same sorority and lived in a house with about forty other women. Among the group, these two stood out for their seriousness and ambition. Cheryl became president of the sorority; Jen was elected president of the entire student body. They supported each other's enthusiasms and aspirations.

Shortly after graduation in 1990, Jen married — Cheryl was a bridesmaid — and moved to Virginia. And shortly after that, Jen invited Cheryl to visit her at her new home. Jen said that she wanted Cheryl to meet a friend of Jen's husband, who she thought might be a good romantic match. Cheryl was taken (a) aback. She'd been dating another Drake student for two years. "I thought he was the one." Jen knew the guy, but Cheryl said, she "clearly did not think he was the one." Cheryl politely declined the invitation to visit.

Over the next few years, Cheryl and Jen, living in different parts of the country at a time before widespread email, exchanged letters and cards. Cheryl eventually (b) ditched the boyfriend, whom she refers to today only as "Mr. Wrong," and says, "Now that I've matured into the person I am, I can see what Jen saw." Within a couple of years, the letters dwindled. Then they (c) stopped. Cheryl hasn't talked to Jen for twenty-five years. "We didn't have a falling-out of any kind. I just let it kind of drift away," she told me. "I regret not having that relationship in my life. I've missed having another person in my life who could share with me the kind of growth I've experienced over the years."

The (d) connection disquiets Cheryl. I asked Cheryl, "If you're going to die in a month, are there things you would want tied up?" Cheryl said, "I would like her to know that the friendship feels significant to me even twenty-five years later." During a conversation one spring afternoon, I asked Cheryl if she'd consider trying to (e) revive the friendship — or at least to call, email, or write Jen. "I think the door's open," she replied. "If I were not a coward, I would reach out."

*sorority (미국 대학의) 여학생 사교 클럽   **ditch (교제하던 사람을) 차 버리다
***dwindle 줄어들다

11
윗글의 제목으로 가장 적절한 것은?

① Reunion: Easier Said Than Done
② How to Reconnect with an Old Friend
③ What's the Right Attitude to a Friendship?
④ Connections: Worth Cherishing and Keeping
⑤ The Ties of Friendship Aren't Easily Broken

12
밑줄 친 (a)~(e) 중, 문맥상 낱말의 쓰임이 적절하지 않은 것은?

① (a)　　② (b)　　③ (c)　　④ (d)　　⑤ (e)

13 10강 1번

글의 흐름으로 보아, 주어진 문장이 들어가기에 가장 적절한 곳은?

> It is, however, important that you do not allow yourself to be deceived by the athlete.

When you work with perfectionistic athletes, one challenge is that the athletes, once determined to work on their perfectionism, are very likely to try to be "the perfect client" during the intervention. Thus, from the therapist/consultant's view it is important to be aware of subtle warning signs, such as if the intervention seems to run too smoothly and the athlete seems to be capable of carrying out exercises you agreed on a little bit too well. (①) In these situations you yourself might very well feel like the "best therapist ever" because you are unknowingly being reinforced by the athlete's apparent success. (②) At this point, not only have you failed to help the athlete, you may have actually begun to reinforce the perfectionistic behaviors you should actually be working on. (③) Maintaining a dialog with the athlete about their progress and continually exploring their goals within the intervention is therefore crucial. (④) In many cases, it can even be considered progress if the athlete "fails" to some extent in completing the homework assignment. (⑤) This is because it provides an opportunity to discuss failure.

14 10강 2번

다음 글에서 필자가 주장하는 바로 가장 적절한 것은?

One of the ideas many scientists take as an ethical principle is that scientists should remain, like journalists, "objective" and not take sides on policy controversies. Indeed, historically, scientists such as the late astronomer Carl Sagan who appear to have become "too" public have risked losing the respect of other scientists. Under normal circumstances, some scientists might reasonably choose to avoid (as scientists) championing specific policy solutions, even on something like climate, lest they be mistaken for self-appointed (or media-appointed) authorities over what society should do. But scientists are also citizens, who may also reasonably choose to speak out, as citizens, on policy issues. To avoid involvement altogether can itself be seen as irresponsible. Scientists have the same rights and duties as other citizens, including the right and the duty to give thought to public issues and, on appropriate occasions, to take positions on them. For a climate scientist not to support appropriate action on climate might be likened to a medical doctor's not supporting routine cancer screening or prenatal nutrition initiatives.

*champion 옹호하다 **prenatal 태아기의

① 과학자들의 윤리적 기준은 시대가 바뀌어도 변하지 말아야 한다.
② 과학자들이 정책 논쟁에 참여하는 것은 시민들에게 혼란을 줄 수 있다.
③ 과학자들은 필요에 따라서 정책에 관한 입장을 표명할 수 있어야 한다.
④ 과학자들은 대중적 인기와 무관하게 객관적 진리 탐구를 추구해야 한다.
⑤ 과학자들은 자신과 관련된 정책 사안이라도 정치적으로 개입해서는 안 된다.

15 10강 3번

다음 빈칸에 들어갈 말로 가장 적절한 것은?

In a study conducted by Griskevicius and his colleagues on behavioural cues, university students read a short story about a successful university graduate who obtained a high-status first job and was, relative to others, promoted quickly. Students in the control group read a neutral story of similar length. In subsequent experimental tasks, students could choose between different green and non-green hypothetical consumer products (car, household cleaner, dishwasher). Each time the products were equal in price, but the non-green product was more luxurious and had better performance than the green product, which was pro-environmental. The study showed that, in the treatment group, in which an activation of status motives occurred, 55 per cent chose the green car; in the control group, 37 per cent chose the green car. The corresponding figures for the household cleaner and dishwasher were 42 per cent versus 26 per cent, and 49 per cent versus 35 per cent, respectively. In brief, ＿＿＿＿＿＿＿＿ led to a higher proportion of students selecting eco-friendly products.

*subsequent 뒤이은, 차후의

① the stimulation of status motives
② the desire for the higher education
③ using various kinds of products
④ experience with the green product
⑤ participation in the pro-environmental experiment

16 10강 4번

글의 흐름으로 보아, 주어진 문장이 들어가기에 가장 적절한 곳은?

> Self-efficacy, however, has a downside.

Perhaps the variable found in research to distinguish entrepreneurs from others is self-efficacy — individuals' belief that they can successfully accomplish whatever they set out to accomplish. This is one reason why, despite the odds being highly stacked against them, many start new ventures: they believe that they can effectively complete the tasks needed to make these companies a success. (①) Thus, self-efficacy is one characteristic that helps entrepreneurs get started and also persist in their efforts to succeed. (②) It may lead individuals to undertake tasks for which, in reality, they lack the required resources, leading to what can be disastrous results. (③) In a sense, they have chosen to play in a game they cannot win, with negative results virtually guaranteed. (④) These negative effects can be magnified by a high level of optimism — a general, and often unjustified belief that ultimately all will turn out well. (⑤) In combination, high levels of optimism and high levels of self-efficacy can prove deadly for entrepreneurs with limited resources.

17 10강 8번

다음 글에서 전체 흐름과 관계 <u>없는</u> 문장은?

Do bacteria speak? Do they use sound to communicate with one another just as they use chemicals to send information from one cell to another? Given that communication among cells is one of the fundamental activities of bacteria, sound would at first seem a likely means of communication. Bacteria are social beings. They live in films and clusters that are so tightly woven that they are often invulnerable to chemical and physical attacks that easily kill solitary cells. Bacterial success depends on networked teamwork and, at the genetic and biochemical levels, bacteria are constantly exchanging molecules. But to date, there are no documented examples of sonic signaling among bacteria, although their increased growth rates when exposed to the sounds of their own kind may be a form of eavesdropping. ① Some bacteria are harmful, but most serve a useful purpose; they support many forms of life, both plant and animal, and they are used in industrial and medicinal processes. ② Sonic communication may be ill-suited to bacterial societies. ③ They live at a scale so tiny that molecules can zip from one cell to another in a fraction of a second. ④ Bacteria use tens of thousands of molecules within their cells, an extensive, complex, and ready-made language. ⑤ For them, chemical communication may be cheaper, faster, and more nuanced than sound waves.

*eavesdropping 엿듣기　**zip 빠르게 이동하다
***nuanced 미묘한 차이가 있는

18 10강 9번

다음 글의 밑줄 친 부분 중, 어법상 <u>틀린</u> 것은?

Different listeners will have different interpretations. On ① <u>hearing</u> Brahms's Fourth Symphony, Elisabeth von Herzogenberg (among his closest friends, whose opinion he valued) wrote to say: "It is a walk through exquisite scenery at sunset, when the colours deepen and the crimson glows to purple." Her response is even more interesting juxtaposed with ② <u>that</u> of Richard Strauss, who "received an unforgettable impression of the new Brahms Symphony, the Andante of which 'reminded him of a funeral procession moving in silence across moonlit heights.'" It doesn't matter that the same movement ③ <u>evoking</u> "moonlight" for Strauss and "sunset" for Herzogenberg. Moonlight and sunset may not be the same, but they have aspects in common, both invoking heavenly bodies, both striving for expression beyond words, and it is the similarities that ④ <u>tell</u> us more about the music than the differences. The music could never, for instance, characterize a chase or a battle or a cartoon. If someone ⑤ <u>were</u> to offer such an interpretation, he would be subject to suspicion himself.

*exquisite 더없이 아름다운　**crimson 진홍색
***juxtapose 나란히 놓다, 병치하다

19 10강 10번

글의 흐름으로 보아, 주어진 문장이 들어가기에 가장 적절한 곳은?

> Students with a deep approach to learning, on the other hand, have the intention of comprehending the material, and activating conceptual analysis.

In general, two approaches to learning have been distinguished — a surface approach and a deep approach to learning. (①) A student with a surface approach to learning sees the work or task as an unwelcome external imposition, a hurdle they want to clear with as little time and effort as possible. (②) One of the most common strategies for the surface approach is rote learning content without understanding, in order to subsequently reproduce the material. (③) Learning strategies that characterize a deep approach to learning can vary in terms of the characteristics and requirements of the task. (④) Possible strategies are reflecting, discussing, using various information sources, relating ideas to previous knowledge, looking for patterns, checking evidence, and critically examining arguments. (⑤) In short, students adopting a surface approach to learning see learning tasks as enforced work, while students with a deep approach to learning seek comprehension by using various learning strategies.

*imposition 부담 **rote learn 무턱대고 암기하다

20 10강 11번

다음 글에서 전체 흐름과 관계 없는 문장은?

So many of our feelings can be made so much easier to manage, and perhaps more fun to experience, just by saying them aloud and letting them build a bridge between us and another person. Exposing our fears makes them much less frightening; affirming our triumphs makes them much more real; revealing our grief relieves us of carrying the burden completely alone. ① A compassionate and empathetic friend, much like a therapist, can give us and our emotions a foundation to cling to. ② To completely understand what a therapist does, it's important to understand various therapeutic approaches, licensure, and titles. ③ It's the reason that merely having someone listen can be such a powerful experience, even if that person was secretly paying more attention to the cheerleaders at the halftime show. ④ All jokes about therapists' fees aside, it is no shame that part of their ability to help lies in just being there, in the moment and attuned — those nods can be meaningful. ⑤ A quality friend understands this and runs with it, knowing just how to validate their buddy's emotional state — whether that state stems from a hard-won personal triumph or just a particularly arduous commute home.

*attuned 이해를 해 주는 **arduous 힘든

_____

_____

• **내신 만점** 서술형

10강 1번

When you work with perfectionistic athletes, one challenge is that the athletes, once determined to work on their perfectionism, are very likely to try to be "the perfect client" during the intervention. Thus, from the therapist/consultant's view it is important to be aware of subtle warning signs, such as if the intervention seems to run too smoothly and the athlete seems to be capable of carrying out exercises you agreed on a little bit too well. In these situations you yourself might very well feel like the "best therapist ever" because you are unknowingly being reinforced by the athlete's apparent success. It is, however, important that you do not allow yourself to be deceived by the athlete. At this point, 여러분은 그 운동 선수를 돕지 못했을 뿐만 아니라, 여러분이 실제로 해결을 위해 노력해야 할 (그 선수의) 완벽주의적인 행동을 실제로 강화하기 시작했을지도 모른다. Maintaining a dialog with the athlete about their progress and continually exploring their goals within the intervention is therefore crucial. In many cases, it can even be considered progress if the athlete "fails" to some extent in completing the homework assignment. This is because it provides an opportunity to discuss failure.

21 윗글의 밑줄 친 우리말의 의미와 일치하도록 [보기]의 단어를 배열하여 [조건]에 맞게 문장을 완성하시오.

[보기] help / to / failed / only / you / have / the / athlete

[조건] • 도치 구문으로 할 것

Not _____ _____ _____ _____

_____ _____ _____ _____ , you may have actually begun to reinforce the perfectionistic behaviors you should actually be working on.

One of the ideas many scientists take as an ethical principle is that scientists should remain, like journalists, "objective" and not take sides on policy controversies. Indeed, historically, scientists such as the late astronomer Carl Sagan who appear to have become "too" public have risked losing the respect of other scientists. Under normal circumstances, some scientists might reasonably choose to avoid (as scientists) championing specific policy solutions, even on something like climate, 그들은 사회가 무엇을 해야 하는지에 대해 자기 혼자 정한 권위자로 오인되지 않도록. But scientists are also citizens, who may also reasonably choose to speak out, as citizens, on policy issues. To avoid involvement altogether can itself <u>be seen as irresponsible</u>. Scientists have the same rights and duties as other citizens, including the right and the duty to give thought to public issues and, on appropriate occasions, to take positions on them. For a climate scientist not to support appropriate action on climate might be likened to a medical doctor's not supporting routine cancer screening or prenatal nutrition initiatives.

*champion 옹호하다 **prenatal 태아기의

고난도

23 윗글의 밑줄 친 우리말의 의미에 맞게 [보기]의 단어를 배열하여 영작하시오.

> [보기] authorities / over / society / they / be / should / mistaken / lest / for / what / self-appointed / do

_____

_____

24 윗글에서 다음 질문에 대한 답을 찾아 우리말로 쓰시오.

Q: What are two examples of the underlined part in the passage?

A: (1) _____

(2) _____

In a study (A) <u>conducting</u> by Griskevicius and his colleagues on behavioural cues, university students read a short story about a successful university graduate who obtained a high-status first job and was, relative to others, promoted quickly. Students in the control group read a neutral story of similar length. In subsequent experimental tasks, students could choose between different green and non-green hypothetical consumer products (car, household cleaner, dishwasher). Each time the products were equal in price, but the non-green product was more luxurious and had better performance than the green product, (B) <u>in which</u> was pro-environmental. The study showed that, in the treatment group, in which an _____ of status motives occurred, 55 per cent chose the green car; in the control group, 37 per cent chose the green car. The corresponding figures for the household cleaner and dishwasher (C) <u>was</u> 42 per cent versus 26 per cent, and 49 per cent versus 35 per cent, respectively.

*subsequent 뒤이은, 차후의

25 윗글의 밑줄 친 부분을 어법상 알맞은 형태로 고쳐 쓰시오.

(A) conducting → _____

(B) in which   → _____

(C) was   → _____

26 윗글의 빈칸에 들어갈 단어를 영영 뜻풀이를 참고하여 쓰시오. 쓰시오. (단, 주어진 글자로 시작할 것)

> the state in which the equipment or process is working

a_____

고난도

28 윗글의 밑줄 친 우리말 의미와 일치하도록 보기 의 단어들을 배열하여 문장을 완성하시오.

> 보기 get started / entrepreneurs / helps /
> and also / persist / one / characteristic /
> that / in / succeed / their efforts / to

Thus, self-efficacy is _____

_____ .

10강 4번

Perhaps the variable found in research to distinguish entrepreneurs from others is self-efficacy — individuals belief that they can ① successfully accomplish whatever they set out to accomplish. This is one reason why, despite the odds being highly stacked against them, many start new ventures: they ② believe that they can effectively complete the tasks needed to make these companies a success. 따라서 자기 효능감은 사업가가 시작하고 또한 성공하기 위한 노력을 지속할 수 있도록 돕는 하나의 특징이다. Self-efficacy, however, has a downside. It may lead individuals to undertake tasks for which, in reality, they lack the required resources, leading to what can be ③ fortunate results. In a sense, they have chosen to play in a game they cannot win, with negative results virtually ④ guaranteed. These negative effects can be magnified by a high level of optimism — a general, and often ⑤ unjustified belief that ultimately all will turn out well. In combination, high levels of optimism and high levels of self-efficacy can prove deadly for entrepreneurs with limited resources.

27 윗글의 밑줄 친 부분 중, 문맥상 어색한 것을 1개 찾아 그 번호를 쓰고 고쳐 쓰시오.

_____ → _____

① While her last year of community college, Krista worked as a full-time nanny to take care of Delia's four kids. Krista was the first person in her family to go to college and felt pressure all around, especially as her long days became consumed by her job as well as writing assignments for her classes. These, along with some other things to take care of, ② were a real struggle for Krista.

Delia, Krista's boss at the time, had her own struggles. Just before Krista began working for her family, Delia's career in law enforcement was cut short when she'd broken her hip at work. Krista marveled at her attitude. She had endured surgery to replace her hip and was left with metal in her leg — rods that would remain in her bones forever. But nothing stopped her. She remained positive, day in and day out. One day when Delia saw Krista ③ struggled with school and writing and general life pressures, she explained how she coped. She told her that the only thing Krista could do was to take "one day at a time."

Delia's attitude made little sense to Krista. She wanted to deal with everything all at once, but that just made her stress even worse. Delia's one-day-at-a-time motto seemed nice in theory but ④ impossible in reality. As the days and weeks of the year melted by, Delia listened to Krista as Krista shared about life and how she was working through it. After a year with Delia's family, Krista transferred to Ridge University and her job ended. Krista and Delia stayed in touch, but Krista lived a few hours away on campus so they didn't see each other very often.

One day, after a tense situation with one of the girls who lived in her dorm, Krista found ⑤ herself overcome with major anxiety, She took a deep breath, looked at herself in the mirror, and ⑥ saying, "It's okay, Krista. Just get through today." Krista shocked herself, because it was the first time she truly believed that she could survive *one day at a time*. That is a gift Krista has carried with her over all the years since then. She's so thankful for Delia's words.

*nanny 아이 돌보미

29 윗글의 밑줄 친 부분 중, 어법상 틀린 것을 3개 찾아 그 번호를 쓰고 고쳐 쓰시오.

(1) ＿＿＿＿＿ → ＿＿＿＿＿

(2) ＿＿＿＿＿ → ＿＿＿＿＿

(3) ＿＿＿＿＿ → ＿＿＿＿＿

30 윗글에서 다음 질문에 대한 답을 본문에서 찾아 쓰시오. (단, 5단어로 쓸 것)

Q: What does the underlined "a giftt" refer to specifically in the passage?

A: ＿＿＿＿＿＿＿＿＿＿＿＿＿＿＿＿＿

Do bacteria speak? Do they use sound to communicate with one another just as they use chemicals to send information from one cell to another? Given that communication among cells is one of the fundamental activities of bacteria, sound would at first seem a likely means of communication. Bacteria are ① social beings. They live in films and clusters that are so tightly woven that they are often ② vulnerable to chemical and physical attacks that easily kill solitary cells. Bacterial success depends on networked teamwork and, at the genetic and biochemical levels, bacteria are constantly ③ exchanging molecules. But to date, there are no documented examples of sonic signaling among bacteria, although their increased growth rates when exposed to the sounds of their own kind may be a form of eavesdropping. Sonic communication may be ④ ill-suited to bacterial societies. They live at a scale so ⑤ tiny that molecules can zip from one cell to another in a fraction of a second. Bacteria use tens of thousands of molecules within their cells, an extensive, complex, and ready-made language. For them, ＿＿(A)＿＿ communication may be cheaper, faster, and more nuanced than ＿＿(B)＿＿ waves.

*eavesdropping 엿듣기 **zip 빠르게 이동하다
***nuanced 미묘한 차이가 있는

31 윗글의 밑줄 친 부분 중, 문맥상 어색한 것을 1개 찾아 바르게 고쳐 쓰시오.

_____ → _____

32 윗글의 빈칸 (A)와 (B)에 들어갈 알맞은 말을 본문에서 찾아 쓰시오.

(A) _____ (B) _____

10강 9번

Different listeners will have different interpretations. ① On hearing Brahms's Fourth Symphony, Elisabeth von Herzogenberg (among his closest friends, whose opinion he valued) wrote to say: "It is a walk through exquisite scenery at sunset, when the colours deepen and the crimson glows to purple." Her response is even more interesting juxtaposed with ② Richard Strauss, who "received an unforgettable impression of the new Brahms Symphony, the Andante of which reminded him of a funeral procession ③ moving in silence across moonlit heights.'" It doesn't matter ④ that the same movement evoked "moonlight" for Strauss and "sunset" for Herzogenberg. Moonlight and sunset may not be the same, but they have aspects in common, both invoking heavenly bodies, both striving for expression beyond words, and it is the _____ that tell us more about the music than the differences. The music could never, for instance, characterize a chase or a battle or a cartoon. If someone were to offer such an interpretation he ⑤ would be subject to suspicion himself.

*exquisite 더없이 아름다운 **crimson 진홍색
***juxtapose 나란히 놓다, 병치하다

고난도

33 윗글의 밑줄 친 부분 중, 어법상 틀린 것 1개를 찾아 그 번호를 쓰고 고쳐 쓰시오.

_____ → _____

34 윗글의 빈칸에 들어갈 단어를 영영 뜻풀이를 참고하여 쓰시오. (단, 필요시 어형을 바꿔 쓸 것)

> the degree to which one thing is similar to another thing, or the fact that they are similar

_____

10강 10번

In general, two approaches to learning have ① distinguished — a surface approach and a deep approach to learning. A student with a surface approach to learning sees the work or task as an unwelcome external imposition, a hurdle they want to clear with as little time and effort ② as possible. One of the most common strategies for the surface approach is rote learning content without ③ understanding, in order to subsequently reproduce the material. Students with a deep approach to learning, on the other hand, have the intention of comprehending the material, and ④ activating conceptual analysis. Learning strategies that characterize a deep approach to learning can vary in terms of the characteristics and requirements of the task. Possible strategies are reflecting, discussing, using various information sources, relating ideas to previous knowledge, looking for patterns, checking evidence, and critically ⑤ examining arguments.

*imposition 부담 **rote learn 무턱대고 암기하다

35 윗글의 밑줄 친 부분 중, 어법상 틀린 것을 1개 찾아 그 번호를 쓰고 고쳐 쓰시오.

_____ → _____

고난도

36 윗글에서 다음 질문에 대한 답을 찾아 우리말로 쓰시오. (단, 두 가지 전략을 각각 나누어 쓸 것)

Q: What are the described strategies of a surface and a deep approach to learning?

A: (1) _____

(2) _____

_____

So many of our feelings can be made so much easier to manage, and perhaps more fun to experience, just by saying them aloud and letting them build a bridge between us and another person. Exposing our fears makes them much less frightening; affirming our triumphs makes them much more real; revealing our grief relieves us of carrying the burden completely alone. A compassionate and empathetic friend, much like a therapist, can give us and our emotions a foundation to cling to. 단지 어떤 사람에게 이야기를 들려주는 것만으로도 매우 강력한 경험이 될 수 있다는 것이 그 이유이다, even if that person was secretly paying more attention to the cheerleaders at the halftime show. All jokes about therapists' fees aside, it is no shame that part of their ability to help lies in just being there, in the moment and attuned — those nods can be meaningful. A quality friend understands this and runs with it, knowing just how to validate their buddy's emotional state — whether that state stems from a hard-won personal triumph or just a particularly arduous commute home.

*attuned 이해를 해주는 **arduous 힘든

37 윗글의 밑줄 친 우리말 의미와 일치하도록 보기 의 단어를 활용하여 조건 에 맞게 문장을 완성하시오.

> 보기 listen / such / merely / have / someone / the reason / experience / powerful / an

> 조건 · 가주어-진주어 구문을 활용할 것
> · 필요시 어형을 바꿔 쓸 것
> · 총 13단어로 쓸 것

It's _____

_____ .

38 윗글의 내용을 한 문장으로 요약하려고 한다. 빈칸 (A)와 (B)에 들어갈 알맞은 말을 본문에서 찾아 쓰시오.

> Exposing our feelings can make them easier to ___(A)___ and more fun to experience, so it is important to have someone who understands this and validates our ___(B)___ state.

(A) _____ (B) _____

To understand connection regrets, let me tell you the story of two women. In the late 1980s, Cheryl attended Drake University in Des Moines, ① where she became fast friends with Jen. Cheryl and Jen belonged to the same sorority and lived in a house with about forty other women. Among the group, these two stood out for their seriousness and ambition. Cheryl became president of the sorority; Jen was elected president of the entire student body. They supported each other's enthusiasms and aspirations.

Shortly after graduation in 1990, Jen married — Cheryl was a bridesmaid — and moved to Virginia. And shortly after that, Jen invited Cheryl to visit her at her new home. Jen said that she wanted Cheryl to meet a friend of Jen's husband, who ② she thought might be a good romantic match. Cheryl was taken aback. She'd been dating another Drake student for two years. "I thought he was the one." Jen knew the guy, but Cheryl said, she "clearly did not think he was the one." Cheryl politely declined the invitation to visit.

Over the next few years, Cheryl and Jen, living in different parts of the country at a time before widespread email, ③ exchanging letters and cards. Cheryl eventually ditched the boyfriend, whom she refers to today only as "Mr. Wrong, and says, "④ Now that I've matured into the person I am, I can see what Jen saw." Within a couple of years, the letters dwindled. Then they stopped. Cheryl hasn't talked to Jen for twenty-five years. "We didn't have a falling-out of any kind. I just let it kind of drift away," she told me. "I ___(A)___ not having that relationship in my life. I've missed having another person in my life who could ___(B)___ with me the kind of growth I've experienced over the years."

The absence disquiets Cheryl. I asked Cheryl, "If you're going to die in a month, are there things you would want tied up?" Cheryl said, "I would like her to know that the friendship feels significant to me even twenty-five years later." During a conversation one spring afternoon, I asked Cheryl if she'd consider trying to revive the friendship — or at least to call, email, or write Jen. "I think the door's open," she replied. "If I ⑤ were not a coward, I would reach out."

*sorority (미국 대학의) 여학생 사교 클럽   **ditch (교제하던 사람을) 차 버리다
***dwindle 줄어들다

39 윗글의 밑줄 친 부분 중, 어법상 틀린 것을 1개 찾아 그 번호를 쓰고 고쳐 쓰시오.

_____ → _____

40 윗글의 빈칸 (A)와 (B)에 들어갈 단어를 영영 뜻풀이를 참고하여 쓰시오. (단, 주어진 글자로 시작할 것)

> (A) to feel sorry or sad about something that you have said or done
> (B) to use or to have something at the same time as someone else

(A) r_____   (B) s_____

❶ The ocean is important as a surface, as a channel for travel. ❷ As anyone who has jumped into the ocean knows, seawater is buoyant — it supports your weight much better than the air around you. ❸ This greatly reduces the amount of fuel required to move goods from place to place. ❹ Moving a 20-foot container from Shanghai to Frankfurt by ship costs a mere third as much as shifting it by plane. ❺ It is no surprise, therefore, that four-fifths of international trade in goods depends on sea freight. ❻ The emergence of enormous container ships has meant that fewer and fewer people now work in shipping, but it remains very big business — the biggest ocean industry of all in terms of total income. ❼ Every day, huge quantities of goods pass through major bottlenecks like the Panama and Suez Canals. ❽ The world was given a stark reminder of the importance of these bottlenecks in March 2021, when one of the world's largest container ships, the *Ever Given*, blocked the Suez Canal for six days, prompting widespread concern about the consequences for world trade.

*buoyant 부력이 있는, 뜨게 하는 **freight 화물 운송 ***stark 냉혹한

❶ 대양은 수면으로서, 이동의 경로로서 중요하다. ❷ 대양에 뛰어들어 본 사람은 누구나 알듯이, 바닷물은 부력이 있어서 여러분의 체중을 주변의 공기보다 훨씬 더 잘 떠받친다. ❸ 이것은 이리저리 상품을 이동시키기 위해 필요한 연료의 양을 크게 줄여준다. ❹ 20피트의 컨테이너를 상하이에서 프랑크푸르트로 배로 이동시키는 것은 비용이 그것을 비행기로 옮기는 것의 겨우 1/3밖에 들지 않는다. ❺ 그러므로 국제 상품 무역의 4/5가 해상 화물 운송에 의존하는 것은 놀라운 일이 아니다. ❻ 거대한 컨테이너선들이 출현하는 것은 이제는 점점 더 적은 사람들이 해상 운송에서 작업하는 것을 의미하게 됐지만, 그것은 여전히 매우 큰 사업으로 총수입의 측면에서 모든 것 중에서 가장 큰 해양 산업이다. ❼ 매일 엄청난 양의 상품이 파나마 운하와 수에즈 운하 같은 주요 병목 지역을 통과한다. ❽ 세계는 2021년 3월에 이 병목 지역들의 중요성을 냉혹하게 상기하게 되었는데, 그때 세계의 가장 큰 컨테이너선들 중 하나인 *Ever Given*호가 6일 동안 수에즈 운하를 막아서, 세계 무역에 미치는 결과에 관하여 광범위한 우려를 유발했다.

Word List

□ **surface** 수면, 지면, 표면   □ **weight** 체중, 무게   □ **goods** 물품, 상품   □ **mere** 겨우 ~의, ~에 불과한   □ **shift** 이동하다
□ **emergence** 출현   □ **enormous** 거대한, 막대한   □ **shipping** 해상 운송, 해운, 선적   □ **in terms of** ~의 측면[관점]에서
□ **quantity** 양   □ **bottleneck** 병목 지역, 좁은 통로   □ **canal** 운하   □ **prompt** 유발하다, 불러일으키다, 고무하다
□ **widespread** 광범위한, 널리 퍼진   □ **consequence** 결과

• Word Test

1	quantity	_____	8	결과
2	enormous	_____	9	해상 운송, 해운, 선적
3	widespread	_____	10	유발하다, 불러일으키다, 고무하다
4	shift	_____	11	겨우 ~의, ~에 불과한
5	goods	_____	12	병목 지역, 좁은 통로
6	canal	_____	13	체중, 무게
7	surface	_____	14	출현

네모 안에서 옳은 어법·어휘를 고르시오.

The ocean is important as a surface, as a channel for travel. As anyone ❶ who / whom has jumped into the ocean knows, seawater is buoyant — it supports your weight much better than the air around you. This ❷ great / greatly reduces the amount of fuel required to move goods from place to place. Moving a 20-foot container from Shanghai to Frankfurt by ship costs a mere third as much as shifting it by plane. It is no surprise, ❸ however / therefore , that four-fifths of international trade in goods depends on sea freight. The emergence of enormous container ships has meant that ❹ more and more / fewer and fewer people now work in shipping, but it remains very big business — the biggest ocean industry of all in terms of total income. Every day, huge ❺ qualities / quantities of goods pass through major bottlenecks like the Panama and Suez Canals. The world was given a stark reminder of the importance of these bottlenecks in March 2021, when one of the world's largest container ships, the *Ever Given*, blocked the Suez Canal for six days, prompting widespread concern about the consequences for world trade. 　　　　　*buoyant 부력이 있는, 뜨게 하는　**freight 화물 운송　***stark 냉혹한

• 유형 2 괄호 안의 동사를 알맞은 형태로 쓰시오.

The ocean is important as a surface, as a channel for travel. As anyone who has jumped into the ocean ❶ _____ (know), seawater is buoyant — it supports your weight much better than the air around you. This greatly reduces the amount of fuel ❷ _____ (require) to move goods from place to place. Moving a 20-foot container from Shanghai to Frankfurt by ship ❸ _____ (cost) a mere third as much as shifting it by plane. It is no surprise, therefore, that four-fifths of international trade in goods depends on sea freight. The emergence of enormous container ships ❹ _____ (mean) that fewer and fewer people now work in shipping, but it remains very big business — the biggest ocean industry of all in terms of total income. Every day, huge quantities of goods pass through major bottlenecks like the Panama and Suez Canals. The world ❺ _____ (give) a stark reminder of the importance of these bottlenecks in March 2021, when one of the world's largest container ships, the *Ever Given*, blocked the Suez Canal for six days, prompting widespread concern about the consequences for world trade. 　　　　　*buoyant 부력이 있는, 뜨게 하는　**freight 화물 운송　***stark 냉혹한

• 유형 3 우리말에 맞게 빈칸에 알맞은 말을 쓰시오.

The ocean is important as a surface, as a channel for travel. As anyone who has jumped into the ocean knows, seawater is buoyant — it supports your weight much better than the air around you. This greatly reduces the amount of fuel required to move goods from place to place. Moving a 20-foot container from Shanghai to Frankfurt by ship costs a(n) ❶ _____ _____ _____ _____ _____ (~의 겨우 3 분의 1 만큼) shifting it by plane. It is no surprise, therefore, that ❷ _____ _____ _____ _____ (국제 무역의 5 분에 4) in goods depends on sea freight. The emergence of enormous container ships has meant that fewer and fewer people now work in shipping, but it remains very big business — the biggest ocean industry of all ❸ _____ _____ _____ _____ (총수입의 측면에서). Every day, huge quantities of goods pass through major bottlenecks like the Panama and Suez Canals. The world was given a stark reminder of the importance of these bottlenecks in March 2021, when one of the world's largest container ships, the *Ever Given*, blocked the Suez Canal for six days, ❹ _____ _____ _____ (광범위한 우려를 유발한) about the consequences for world trade. 　　　　　*buoyant 부력이 있는, 뜨게 하는　**freight 화물 운송　***stark 냉혹한

❶ When the new coronavirus arrived in the United States in January 2020, it hit an economy, society, and constitutional democracy fundamentally unprepared. ❷ As the scale of the challenge became clear, the country simply could not deliver what was needed to confront it. ❸ There was a solution, one identified by scholars and policy experts as early as the middle of March and publicly disseminated by the middle of April. ❹ That solution was a large-scale program of rapid testing of patients, tracing and testing their contacts, and tracing and testing their contacts again in turn. ❺ Such testing also needed reinforcement from a culture of sticking to universal precautions such as mask-wearing, hand and bathroom hygiene, and robust practices of infection control. ❻ The massive, rapid buildup of such a public health campaign, as well as the necessary systems and services to support it, would have interrupted transmission of the virus sufficiently to eliminate it even while keeping the economy open. ❼ But the country did not have the relevant infrastructure ready to go and was not able to deliver this mobilization.

*disseminate 전파하다   **hygiene 위생   ***robust 강력한

❶ 새로운 코로나바이러스가 2020년 1월 미국에 도착했을 때, 그것은 기본적으로 준비되지 않은 경제, 사회, 그리고 입헌 민주 국가를 타격했다. ❷ 그 문제의 규모가 명백해졌을 때, 국가는 그것에 맞서기 위해 필요한 것(정책이나 조치 등)을 전혀 내놓을 수가 없었다. ❸ 한 해결책이 있었는데, 벌써 3월 중순에 학자들과 정책 전문가들이 확인하고 4월 중순까지는 공공연하게 전파된 것이었다. ❹ 그 해결책은 환자를 신속히 검사하고, 그들의 접촉자를 추적하고 검사하며, 다시 차례차례 그들의 접촉자를 추적하고 검사하는 대규모 계획이었다. ❺ 그런 검사는 또한 마스크 착용, 손위생과 화장실 위생, 그리고 강력한 감염 관리 실행과 같은 보편적 예방책을 충실히 지키는 문화에서 오는 보강이 필요했다. ❻ 그런 공중위생 캠페인을, 그것을 지원하는 필수적 시스템 및 서비스와 함께, 대규모로 신속하게 강화했다면, 경제를 개방된 상태로 유지하면서도 바이러스를 제거할 만큼 충분히 바이러스의 전염을 차단했을 것이다. ❼ 그러나 국가는 관련된 사회 기반 시설을 작동하도록 준비하지 못했고 이 동원을 해낼 수 없었다.

Word List

□ constitutional 입헌의, 헌법에 따르는   □ democracy 민주 국가, 민주주의   □ fundamentally 근본적으로   □ scale 규모
□ deliver 내놓다, 산출하다, 해내다   □ confront 맞서다, 대항하다   □ identify 확인하다   □ scholar 학자   □ policy 정책
□ expert 전문가   □ patient 환자   □ trace 추적하다   □ reinforcement 보강, 강화   □ stick to ~을 충실히 지키다
□ precaution 예방책, 예방조치   □ infection 감염, 감염병   □ buildup 강화, 증가   □ interrupt 차단하다, 가로막다
□ transmission 전염, 전달   □ eliminate 제거하다   □ mobilization 동원

• Word Test

1	reinforcement		11 학자	
2	infection		12 맞서다, 대항하다	
3	deliver		13 예방책, 예방조치	
4	policy		14 동원	
5	patient		15 민주 국가, 민주주의	
6	identify		16 전염, 전달	
7	fundamentally		17 추적하다	
8	interrupt		18 강화, 증가	
9	eliminate		19 규모	
10	constitutional		20 전문가	

When the new coronavirus arrived in the United States in January 2020, it hit an economy, society, and constitutional democracy fundamentally ❶ prepared/unprepared . As the scale of the challenge became clear, the country simply could not deliver what was needed to confront it. There was a solution, one identified by scholars and policy experts as early as the middle of March and publicly disseminated by the middle of April. That solution was a large-scale program of ❷ rapid/gradual testing of patients, tracing and testing their contacts, and tracing and testing their contacts again in turn. Such testing also needed reinforcement from a culture of sticking to universal precautions such as mask-wearing, hand and bathroom hygiene, and robust practices of infection control. The massive, rapid buildup of such a public health campaign, as well as the necessary systems and services to support ❸ it / them , would have interrupted transmission of the virus sufficiently to eliminate it even while keeping the economy open. But the country did not have the relevant ❹ enterprise/infrastructure ready to go and was not able to deliver this mobilization.

*disseminate 전파하다 **hygiene 위생 ***robust 강력한

When the new coronavirus arrived in the United States in January 2020, it ❶ _____ (hit) an economy, society, and constitutional democracy fundamentally unprepared. As the scale of the challenge ❷ _____ (become) clear, the country simply could not deliver what was needed to confront it. There was a solution, one ❸ _____ (identify) by scholars and policy experts as early as the middle of March and publicly disseminated by the middle of April. That solution was a large-scale program of rapid testing of patients, tracing and testing their contacts, and tracing and testing their contacts again in turn. Such testing also ❹ _____ (need) reinforcement from a culture of sticking to universal precautions such as mask-wearing, hand and bathroom hygiene, and robust practices of infection control. The massive, rapid buildup of such a public health campaign, as well as the necessary systems and services to support it, would have interrupted transmission of the virus sufficiently ❺ _____ (eliminate) it even while keeping the economy open. But the country did not have the relevant infrastructure ready to go and was not able to deliver this mobilization.

*disseminate 전파하다 **hygiene 위생 ***robust 강력한

When the new coronavirus arrived in the United States in January 2020, it hit an economy, society, and constitutional democracy ❶ _____ _____ (기본적으로 준비되지 않은). As the scale of the challenge became clear, the country simply could not deliver ❷ _____ _____ _____ _____ _____ _____ (그것에 맞서기 위해 필요한 것). There was a solution, one identified by scholars and policy experts as early as the middle of March and publicly disseminated by the middle of April. That solution was a large-scale program of rapid testing of patients, tracing and testing their contacts, and tracing and testing their contacts again in turn. Such testing also needed reinforcement from a culture of ❸ _____ _____ _____ _____ (보편적 예방책들을 충실히 지키는) such as mask-wearing, hand and bathroom hygiene, and robust practices of infection control. The massive, rapid buildup of such a public health campaign, as well as the necessary systems and services to support it, would have interrupted transmission of the virus sufficiently to eliminate it even ❹ _____ _____ _____ _____ _____ (경제를 개방된 상태로 유지하는 동안). But the country did not have the relevant infrastructure ready to go and was not able to deliver this mobilization.

*disseminate 전파하다 **hygiene 위생 ***robust 강력한

52

❶ The only way to produce crystal-clear writing is to know how a reader will respond to the choices you make in composing text and graphics. ❷ You need to know which sentence structures are most easily understood, which organization of material into sections is most easily followed, and so on. ❸ It's certainly possible to offer some general rules along these lines: for example, "use the active voice," "divide the paper into Introduction, Methods, Results, and Discussion sections," and "use a figure instead of a table when quantities are to be compared." ❹ In principle, you could tape a long list of such rules above your computer and treat it as the voice of authority on how to reach readers. ❺ But long lists of rules are boring. ❻ Besides, using them makes writing mechanical, and good writing sometimes entails knowing when to bend the rules instead of following them. ❼ Furthermore, using a list of rules is oddly indirect: instead of relying on rules you've been told will produce clear text, surely it would be more effective to understand how readers think, and write to that understanding.

❶ 아주 명료한 글쓰기를 하는 유일한 방법은 글과 그래픽을 작성할 때 여러분이 하는 선택에 독자가 어떻게 반응할지를 아는 것이다. ❷ 여러분은 어떤 문장 구조가 가장 쉽게 이해되는지, 자료를 섹션으로 어떻게 조직해야 (독자가) 가장 쉽게 따라올 수 있는지 등을 알아야 한다. ❸ 다음과 같은 몇몇 일반적인 규칙을 제공하는 것이 확실히 가능한데, 예를 들면 '능동태를 사용하기', '논문을 '서론', '연구 방법', '연구 결과' 및 '토의' 섹션으로 나누기', 그리고 '양이 비교되어야 할 때는 표 대신에 도표를 사용하기'이다. ❹ 원칙적으로 여러분은 그런 규칙의 긴 목록을 여러분의 컴퓨터 위에 테이프로 붙여 놓고 그것을 독자들에게 닿는 방법에 관한 권위 있는 목소리로 취급할 수도 있을 것이다. ❺ 그러나 긴 규칙 목록은 지루하다. ❻ 게다가 그것을 사용하는 것은 글쓰기를 기계적으로 만드는데, 좋은 글쓰기는 때로 언제 그 규칙을 따르는 대신에 그것들을 유연하게 적용할지를 아는 것을 수반한다. ❼ 더욱이, 규칙 목록을 사용하는 것은 이상하게도 간접적인데, 여러분이 명료한 텍스트를 만들어 낼 것이라고 들었던 규칙에 의존하는 것 대신에, 독자가 사고하는 방식을 이해하고 그 이해에 부합하게 글을 쓰는 것이 분명히 더 효과적일 것이다.

Word List

□ **crystal-clear** 아주 명료한   □ **compose** 작성하다, 작곡하다   □ **graphic** 그래픽(사진, 그림, 도형, 그래프 등 다양한 시각적 형상)   □ **section** 부분   □ **active voice** 능동태   □ **figure** 도표, 도형   □ **quantity** 양   □ **in principle** 원칙적으로   □ **authority** 권위   □ **entail** 수반하다   □ **bend** (사정에 따라) 유연하게 적용하다, 수정하다   □ **oddly** 이상하게, 기이하게   □ **indirect** 간접적인   □ **effective** 효과적인

• Word Test

1 figure		7 양	
2 entail		8 이상하게, 기이하게	
3 section		9 작성하다, 작곡하다	
4 in principle		10 효과적인	
5 indirect		11 권위	
6 crystal-clear		12 능동태	

The only way to produce crystal-clear writing is to know how a reader will respond to the choices you make in composing text and graphics. You need to know ❶ how / which sentence structures are most easily understood, which organization of material into sections is most easily followed, and so on. It's certainly possible to offer some general rules along these lines: ❷ for example / in addition , "use the active voice," "divide the paper into Introduction, Methods, Results, and Discussion sections," and "use a figure instead of a table when quantities are to be compared." In principle, you could tape a long list of such rules above your computer and treat it as the voice of authority on how to reach readers. But long lists of rules are boring. ❸ Besides / Nevertheless , using them makes writing mechanical, and good writing sometimes entails knowing when to bend the rules instead of following ❹ it / them . Furthermore, using a list of rules is oddly ❺ direct / indirect : instead of relying on rules you've been told will produce clear text, surely it would be more effective to understand how readers think, and write to that understanding.

The only way to produce crystal-clear writing is to know how a reader will respond to the choices you make in composing text and graphics. You need to know which sentence structures are most easily understood, which organization of material into sections ❶ _____ (be) most easily followed, and so on. It's certainly possible to offer some general rules along these lines: for example, "use the active voice," "divide the paper into Introduction, Methods, Results, and Discussion sections," and "use a figure instead of a table when quantities are to ❷ _____ (compare)." In principle, you could tape a long list of such rules above your computer and treat it as the voice of authority on how to reach readers. But long lists of rules are boring. Besides, using them ❸ _____ (make) writing mechanical, and good writing sometimes entails knowing when to bend the rules instead of following them. Furthermore, using a list of rules ❹ _____ (be) oddly indirect: instead of relying on rules you've been told will produce clear text, surely it would be more effective ❺ _____ (understand) how readers think, and write to that understanding.

The only way to produce crystal-clear writing is to know how a reader will respond to the choices you make in composing text and graphics. You need to know which sentence structures ❶ _____ _____ _____ _____ (가장 쉽게 이해된다), which organization of material into sections is most easily followed, and so on. It's certainly possible to offer some general rules ❷ _____ _____ _____ (다음과 같은): for example, "use the active voice," "divide the paper into Introduction, Methods, Results, and Discussion sections," and "use a figure instead of a table when quantities are to be compared." ❸ _____ _____ (원칙적으로), you could tape a long list of such rules above your computer and treat it ❹ _____ _____ _____ _____ _____ (권위 있는 목소리로) on how to reach readers. But long lists of rules are boring. Besides, using them makes writing mechanical, and good writing sometimes entails knowing ❺ _____ _____ _____ _____ _____ (언제 규칙들을 유연하게 적용할지를) instead of following them. Furthermore, using a list of rules is oddly indirect: instead of relying on rules you've been told will produce clear text, surely it would be more effective to understand how readers think, and write to that understanding.

❶ Masting is the synchronized production of large crops of acorns across a broad geographic range of a species, alternating with one or more years of little or no acorn production. ❷ This is an adaption to increase acorn survival and dispersibility. ❸ Populations of some specialist seed consumers crash following non-mast years so that more acorns survive following the mast years. ❹ This works pretty well, but when crops of acorns fluctuate dramatically across years, it can send shock waves through the animal community. ❺ Acorn mast is an important resource in the community for a wide variety of animals far beyond those that serve as agents of acorn dispersal. ❻ Deer, bear, woodpeckers, turkeys, mice, and many other animals direct their attention to the acorn mast during mast years. ❼ People are also sometimes affected by masting. ❽ When mouse populations increase in mast years, so do the populations of ticks and the incidence of Lyme disease.

*mast (도토리 등이 일정한 주기로) 대량으로 결실하다; 열매
**dispersibility (열매 등의) 분산 가능성　***tick (동물) 진드기

❶ 대량 결실이란 종의 광범위한 지리적 범위에 걸쳐서 대규모 수확량의 도토리가 동시에 생산 되는 것인데, 일 년 이상 동안 도토리 생산이 거의 또는 전혀 없는 해와 번갈아 발생한다. ❷ 이것은 도토리의 생존과 분산 가능성을 증가시킬 수 있는 적응이다. ❸ 대량 결실이 없는 해 다음에는 일부 전문적으로 씨앗을 먹는 동물들의 개체 수가 급감하여 대량 결실이 있는 해 다음에 더 많은 도토리가 살아남는다. ❹ 이것은 매우 잘 작용하지만, 여러 해에 걸쳐 도토리 수확량이 극적으로 변동할 때, 동물 군집 전체에 걸쳐 충격파를 보낼 수 있다. ❺ 도토리 열매는 도토리 분산의 행위자 역할을 하는 동물들을 훨씬 넘어서 매우 다양한 동물들에게 군집 내의 중요한 자원이다. ❻ 사슴, 곰, 딱따구리, 칠면조, 생쥐, 그리고 다른 많은 동물은 대량 결실이 있는 해 동안에는 도토리 열매로 관심을 돌린다. ❼ 사람들 또한 때때로 대량 결실로 영향을 받는다. ❽ 대량 결실이 있는 해에 생쥐 개체 수가 증가할 때, 진드기 개체 수와 라임병 발생률도 그렇게 된다.

Word List

□ synchronize 동시에 발생하다, 시간대를 맞추다　□ crop (한 철에 거둔) 수확량, 농작물　□ acorn 도토리　□ geographic 지리적
□ range 범위　□ species (생물의) 종　□ alternate 번갈아 일어나다　□ adaption 적응(adaptation)　□ population 개체 수, 개체군
□ specialist 전문적인; 전문가　□ seed 씨, 씨앗　□ crash 급감하다, 붕괴하다, 추락하다　□ fluctuate 변동하다, 오르내리다
□ shock wave 충격파　□ agent 행위자　□ woodpecker 딱따구리　□ turkey 칠면조　□ mouse 생쥐(*pl.* mice)
□ direct 향하다, 돌리다　□ incidence 발생률, 발생

• Word Test

1	species		9	씨, 씨앗
2	adaption		10	발생률, 발생
3	direct		11	번갈아 일어나다
4	synchronize		12	범위
5	crash		13	개체 수, 개체군
6	specialist		14	행위자
7	shock wave		15	변동하다, 오르내리다
8	geographic		16	(한 철에 거둔) 수확량, 농작물

Masting is the synchronized production of large crops of acorns across a broad geographic range of a species, alternating with one or more years of little or no acorn production. This is an ❶ adoption / adaption to increase acorn survival and dispersibility. Populations of some specialist seed consumers crash following non-mast years so that more acorns ❷ destroy / survive following the mast years. This works pretty well, but when crops of acorns fluctuate dramatically across years, it can send shock waves ❸ along / through the animal community. Acorn mast is an important resource in the community for a wide variety of animals far beyond those ❹ who / that serve as agents of acorn dispersal. Deer, bear, woodpeckers, turkeys, mice, and many other animals direct their attention to the acorn mast during mast years. People are also sometimes affected by masting. When mouse populations increase in mast years, ❺ so / and do the populations of ticks and the incidence of Lyme disease.

*mast (도토리 등이 일정한 주기로) 대량으로 결실하다; 열매 **dispersibility (열매 등의) 분산 가능성 ***tick (동물) 진드기

Masting is the synchronized production of large crops of acorns across a broad geographic range of a species, ❶ _____ (alternate) with one or more years of little or no acorn production. This is an adaption to increase acorn survival and dispersibility. Populations of some specialist seed consumers crash following non-mast years so that more acorns survive following the mast years. This ❷ _____ (work) pretty well, but when crops of acorns fluctuate dramatically across years, it can send shock waves through the animal community. Acorn mast is an important resource in the community for a wide variety of animals far beyond those that ❸ _____ (serve) as agents of acorn dispersal. Deer, bear, woodpeckers, turkeys, mice, and many other animals direct their attention to the acorn mast during mast years. People are also sometimes ❹ _____ (affect) by masting. When mouse populations increase in mast years, so ❺ _____ (do) the populations of ticks and the incidence of Lyme disease.

*mast (도토리 등이 일정한 주기로) 대량으로 결실하다; 열매 **dispersibility (열매 등의) 분산 가능성 ***tick (동물) 진드기

Masting is the synchronized production of large crops of acorns ❶ _____ _____ _____ _____ _____ (광범위한 지리적 범위에 걸쳐서) of a species, alternating with one or more years of little or no acorn production. This is an adaption to increase acorn survival and dispersibility. Populations of some specialist seed consumers crash following non-mast years so that more acorns survive following the mast years. This works pretty well, but when crops of acorns ❷ _____ _____ _____ _____ (여러 해에 걸쳐 극적으로 변동하다), it can send shock waves through the animal community. Acorn mast is an important resource in the community for ❸ _____ _____ _____ _____ (매우 다양한) animals far beyond those that serve as agents of acorn dispersal. Deer, bear, woodpeckers, turkeys, mice, and many other animals ❹ _____ _____ _____ _____ (~로 그들의 관심을 돌리다) the acorn mast during mast years. People are also sometimes affected by masting. When mouse populations increase in mast years, so do the populations of ticks and the incidence of Lyme disease.

*mast (도토리 등이 일정한 주기로) 대량으로 결실하다; 열매 **dispersibility (열매 등의) 분산 가능성 ***tick (동물) 진드기

❶ Early one morning the doorbell rang. ❷ "How can I help you?" Vera asked the child who was standing there. ❸ "My mother is ill. She needs some medicine," he said. ❹ "Who's your mom?" Vera asked. ❺ "Charity," he answered. ❻ Charity was the woman who cleaned their house each week. ❽ Vera's mom came to talk to Washington, Charity's son, ❾ "I will take you home and we can take some medicine to her." ❿ "But Mom," Vera objected, "you promised to take me to the mall today!" ⓫ "I know," her mom replied. ⓬ "But Charity seems to be seriously ill. ⓭ We can go shopping later on."

⓮ Vera frowned. ⓯ Newtown was far from where they lived. ⓰ *There won't be time to go to the mall after this*, she realized. ⓱ "Come with me!" her mom invited. ⓲ After a while they turned off onto a dirt road. ⓳ Children in old clothes and no shoes were playing in the dust. ⓴ Washington asked Vera's mom to stop outside a run-down house. ㉑ The house was neat and clean. ㉒ Faded red linoleum covered the floor and pictures cut from magazines were pasted against the walls. ㉓ A small stove stood in the front room, and in front of it was a table and three old chairs. ㉔ Charity was in the bedroom. ㉕ She coughed when she greeted them. ㉖ Vera's mom gave her some medicine and put a carrier bag filled with groceries onto the table. ㉗ Vera went outside and looked over the top of the run-down houses in the squatter camp to the blue mountains in the distance. ㉘ "Lord, forgive me for being so ungrateful," she said.

㉙ Back home she took out a suitcase and packed it full of clothes and other things that she didn't need any more. ㉚ She put her favorite blue T-shirt on top of everything. ㉛ *That's for Washington*, she thought. ㉜ She felt a lot of respect for the young boy who had walked for more than two hours without complaining to get some medicine for his mother.

*run-down 낡고 허름한　**linoleum 리놀륨(마루의 깔개)　***squatter camp 빈민가

❶ 어느 이른 아침 초인종이 울렸다. ❷ "무슨 일이니?" 거기 서 있는 아이에게 Vera가 물었다. ❸ "엄마가 아파. 약이 필요해." 그가 말했다. ❹ "너네 엄마가 누구야?" Vera가 물었다. ❺ "Charity야." 그가 대답했다. ❻ Charity는 매주 그들의 집을 청소하는 여자였다. ❽ Vera의 엄마가 Charity의 아들 Washington에게 다가와서 말했다. ❾ "내가 너를 집에 데려다주고 우리가 그녀에게 약을 좀 가져다줄 수 있어." ❿ "하지만 엄마, 오늘 쇼핑몰에 데려가겠다고 제게 약속하셨잖아요!"라고 Vera가 반대했다. ⓫ "알아." 그녀의 엄마가 대답했다. ⓬ "하지만 Charity가 심하게 아픈 것 같아. ⓭ 우리는 나중에 쇼핑하러 갈 수 있어."

⓮ Vera는 뚱한 표정을 지었다. ⓯ Newtown은 그들이 사는 곳에서 멀리 떨어져 있었다. ⓰ '이 일이 끝나면 쇼핑몰에 갈 시간이 없을 거야.' 그녀는 깨달았다. ⓱ "함께 가자!"라고 그녀의 엄마가 권했다. ⓲ 잠시 후 그들은 비포장 도로로 들어갔다. ⓳ 낡은 옷을 입고 신발을 신지 않은 아이들이 먼지 속에서 놀고 있었다. ⓴ Washington은 Vera의 엄마에게 한 낡고 허름한 집 밖에서 세워 달라고 부탁했다. ㉑ 그 집은 깔끔하고 깨끗했다. ㉒ 색이 바랜 붉은 리놀륨이 바닥을 덮고 잡지에서 오려낸 그림들이 벽에 붙여져 있었다. ㉓ 앞방에는 작은 스토브가 서 있었고, 그 앞에는 테이블과 낡은 의자 세 개가 놓여 있었다. ㉔ Charity는 침실에 있었다. ㉕ 그들에게 인사할 때 그녀는 기침을 했다. ㉖ Vera의 엄마는 그녀에게 약을 좀 주고 식료품으로 가득 찬 캐리어 가방을 테이블 위에 놓았다. ㉗ Vera는 밖으로 나가서 빈민가에 있는 황폐한 집들의 꼭대기 너머 멀리 있는 푸른 산들을 바라보았다. ㉘ "하느님, 제가 너무 감사할 줄 모르는 것을 용서해 주세요."라고 그녀는 말했다.

㉙ 집으로 돌아온 그녀는 여행 가방을 꺼내 더 이상 필요 없는 옷과 다른 물건들로 가득 채웠다. ㉚ 그녀는 자신이 가장 좋아하는 파란색 티셔츠를 모든 것 위에 올렸다. ㉛ '그건 Washington을 위한 거야'라고 그녀는 생각했다. ㉜ 그녀는 어머니에게 드릴 약을 얻기 위해 불평하지 않고 두 시간 이상 걸어온 그 어린 소년에게 많은 존경심을 느꼈다.

Word List

□ doorbell 초인종　□ medicine 약　□ object 반대하다　□ frown 뚱한 표정을 짓다　□ invite 권하다　□ dirt road 비포장 도로, 흙길　□ neat 깔끔한　□ faded 빛이 바랜　□ paste (풀로) 붙이다　□ cough 기침하다　□ greet 인사하다　□ ungrateful 감사할 줄 모르는　□ suitcase 여행 가방　□ pack 채우다　□ respect 존경심

1	suitcase		8	빛이 바랜
2	neat		9	채우다
3	medicine		10	기침하다
4	frown		11	감사할 줄 모르는
5	paste		12	존경심
6	greet		13	권하다
7	doorbell		14	반대하다

• 유형 1 네모 안에서 옳은 어법·어휘를 고르시오.

Early one morning the doorbell rang. "How can I help you?" Vera asked the child who was standing there. "My mother is ill. She needs some medicine," he said. "Who's your mom?" Vera asked. "Charity," he answered. Charity was the woman who cleaned their house each ❶ week / weeks . Vera's mom came to talk to Washington, Charity's son, "I will take you home and we can take some medicine to her." "But Mom," Vera ❷ approved / objected , "you promised to take me to the mall today!" "I know," her mom replied. "But Charity seems to be seriously ill. We can go shopping later on."

Vera ❸ frowned / grinned . Newtown was far from where they lived. *There won't be time to go to the mall after this*, she realized. "Come with me!" her mom invited. After a while they turned ❹ off / down onto a dirt road. Children in old clothes and no shoes were playing in the dust. Washington asked Vera's mom to stop outside a run-down house.

The house was neat and clean. ❺ Faded / Glowing red linoleum covered the floor and pictures cut from magazines were pasted against the walls. A small stove stood in the front room, and in front of it was a table and three old chairs. Charity was in the bedroom. She coughed when she greeted them. Vera's mom gave her some medicine and put a carrier bag filled with groceries onto the table. Vera went outside and looked over the top of the run-down houses in the squatter camp to the blue mountains in the distance. "Lord, forgive me for being so ungrateful," she said.

Back home she took out a suitcase and ❻ picked / packed it full of clothes and other things that she didn't need any more. She put her favorite blue T-shirt on top of everything. *That's for Washington*, she thought. She felt a lot of ❼ regret / respect for the young boy who had walked for more than two hours without complaining to get some medicine for his mother.

*run-down 낡고 허름한　**linoleum 리놀륨(마루의 깔개)　***squatter camp 빈민가

Early one morning the doorbell rang. "How can I help you?" Vera asked the child who was standing there. "My mother is ill. She needs some medicine," he said. "Who's your mom?" Vera asked. "Charity," he answered. Charity was the woman who cleaned their house each week. Vera's mom came to talk to Washington, Charity's son, "I will take you home and we can take some medicine to her." "But Mom," Vera objected, "you promised ❶ _____ (take) me to the mall today!" "I know," her mom replied. "But Charity seems to be seriously ill. We can go shopping later on."

Vera frowned. Newtown was far from where they lived. *There won't be time to go to the mall after this,* she realized. "Come with me!" her mom invited. After a while they turned off onto a dirt road. Children in old clothes and no shoes were playing in the dust. Washington asked Vera's mom ❷ _____ (stop) outside a run-down house.

The house was neat and clean. Faded red linoleum covered the floor and pictures ❸ _____ (cut) from magazines were pasted against the walls. A small stove stood in the front room, and in front of it was a table and three old chairs. Charity was in the bedroom. She coughed when she ❹ _____ (greet) them. Vera's mom gave her some medicine and put a carrier bag ❺ _____ (fill) with groceries onto the table. Vera went outside and looked over the top of the run-down houses in the squatter camp to the blue mountains in the distance. "Lord, forgive me for being so ungrateful," she said.

Back home she took out a suitcase and packed it full of clothes and other things that she didn't need any more. She put her favorite blue T-shirt on top of everything. *That's for Washington,* she thought. She felt a lot of respect for the young boy who ❻ _____ (walk) for more than two hours without complaining to get some medicine for his mother.

*run-down 낡고 허름한   **linoleum 리놀륨(마루의 깔개)   ***squatter camp 빈민가

Early one morning the doorbell rang. "How can I help you?" Vera asked the child who was standing there. "My mother is ill. She needs some medicine," he said. "Who's your mom?" Vera asked. "Charity," he answered. Charity was the woman who cleaned their house each week. Vera's mom came to talk to Washington, Charity's son, "I will take you home and we can take some medicine to her." "But Mom," Vera objected, "you promised to take me to the mall today!" "I know," her mom replied. "But Charity ❶ _____ _____ _____ _____ _____ (심하게 아픈 것 같다). We can go shopping later on."

Vera frowned. Newtown was ❷ _____ _____ _____ _____ _____ (그들이 사는 곳에서 멀리 떨어진). *There won't be time to go to the mall after this*, she realized. "Come with me!" her mom invited. After a while they turned off onto a dirt road. Children in old clothes and no shoes were playing in the dust. Washington asked Vera's mom to stop outside a run-down house.

The house was ❸ _____ _____ _____ (깔끔하고 깨끗한). Faded red linoleum covered the floor and pictures cut from magazines were pasted against the walls. A small stove stood in the front room, and in front of it was a table and three old chairs. Charity was in the bedroom. She coughed when she greeted them. Vera's mom gave her some medicine and put a carrier bag filled with groceries onto the table. Vera went outside and looked over the top of the run-down houses in the squatter camp to the blue mountains in the distance. "Lord, forgive me ❹ _____ _____ _____ _____ (너무 감사할 줄 모르는 것에 대해)," she said.

Back home she took out a suitcase and packed it full of clothes and other things that she didn't need any more. She put her favorite blue T-shirt on top of everything. *That's for Washington*, she thought. She felt a lot of respect for the young boy who had walked for more than two hours ❺ _____ _____ (불평하지 않고) to get some medicine for his mother.

*run-down 낡고 허름한 **linoleum 리놀륨(마루의 깔개) ***squatter camp 빈민가

❶ Recent advances in electronic media and computer networks have allowed the creation of large and distributed repositories of information. ❷ However, the immediate availability of extensive resources for use by broad classes of computer users gives rise to new challenges in everyday life. ❸ These challenges arise from the fact that users cannot exploit available resources effectively when the amount of information requires prohibitively long user time spent on acquaintance with and comprehension of the information content. ❹ Thus, the risk of information overload of users imposes new requirements on the software systems that handle the information. ❺ One of these requirements is the incorporation into the software systems of mechanisms that help their users when they face difficulties during human-computer interaction sessions or lack the knowledge to make decisions by themselves. ❻ Such mechanisms attempt to identify user information needs and to personalize human-computer interactions. ❼ (Personalized) Recommender Systems (RS) provide an example of software systems that attempt to address some of the problems caused by information overload.

*repository 저장소

❶ 최근 전자 미디어와 컴퓨터 네트워크의 발전으로 대규모의 분산된 정보 저장소를 만들 수 있게 되었다. ❷ 그러나 넓은 부류의 컴퓨터 이용자가 사용할 수 있는 광범위한 자원의 즉각적인 가용성은 일상생활에서 새로운 난제를 야기한다. ❸ 이러한 난제가 발생하는 것은, 정보의 양 때문에 그 정보 내용을 알고 이해하는 데 엄청나게 긴 이용자 시간이 요구될 때 이용자가 가용 자원을 효과적으로 활용하지 못한다는 사실 때문이다. ❹ 따라서 이용자의 정보 과부하에 대한 위험은 정보를 처리하는 소프트웨어 시스템에 새로운 요구 사항을 부과한다. ❺ 이러한 요구 사항 중 하나는, 이용자가 인간과 컴퓨터가 상호 작용을 하는 시간에 어려움에 직면하거나 스스로 의사 결정을 내릴 수 있는 지식이 없을 때 그들에게 도움이 되는 메커니즘을 소프트웨어 시스템에 통합하는 것이다. ❻ 이러한 메커니즘은 이용자의 정보 요구를 식별하고 인간과 컴퓨터의 상호 작용을 개인에게 맞추려고 시도한다. ❼ (개인화된) 추천 시스템(RS)은 정보 과부하로 인해 야기되는 문제들의 일부를 해결하려고 시도하는 소프트웨어 시스템의 예를 제공한다.

Word List

□ advance 발전, 진보　□ electronic 전자의　□ distributed 분산된　□ extensive 광범위한　□ give rise to ~을 야기하다
□ arise from ~에서 발생하다　□ exploit 활용하다　□ prohibitively 엄청나게　□ acquaintance 알고 있음　□ comprehension 이해
□ content 내용　□ risk 위험　□ overload 과부하　□ impose 부과하다, (부담을) 지우다　□ requirement 요구 사항
□ incorporation 통합　□ interaction 상호 작용　□ attempt 시도하다　□ identify 식별하다
□ personalize 개인에게 맞추다, 개인화하다　□ address a problem 문제를 해결하다

• Word Test

1 overload _____
2 content _____
3 interaction _____
4 give rise to _____
5 acquaintance _____
6 identify _____
7 distributed _____
8 requirement _____
9 advance _____
10 exploit _____

11 부과하다, (부담을) 지우다 _____
12 이해 _____
13 ~에서 발생하다 _____
14 전자의 _____
15 엄청나게 _____
16 위험 _____
17 개인에게 맞추다, 개인화하다 _____
18 광범위한 _____
19 시도하다 _____
20 통합 _____

Recent advances in electronic media and computer networks have allowed the creation of large and distributed repositories of information. ❶ However / Moreover , the immediate availability of extensive resources for use by broad classes of computer users gives rise to new challenges in everyday life. These challenges arise from the fact ❷ that / which users cannot exploit available resources effectively when the amount of information requires prohibitively long user time spent on acquaintance with and comprehension of the information content. Thus, the risk of information ❸ overload / shortage of users imposes new requirements on the software systems that handle the information. One of these requirements is the ❹ corporation / incorporation into the software systems of mechanisms that help their users when they face difficulties during human-computer interaction sessions or lack the knowledge to make decisions by themselves. Such mechanisms attempt to identify user information needs and to personalize human-computer interactions. (Personalized) Recommender Systems (RS) provide an example of software systems that attempt to ❺ analyze / address some of the problems caused by information overload.

*repository 저장소

Recent advances in electronic media and computer networks have allowed the creation of large and distributed repositories of information. However, the immediate availability of extensive resources for use by broad classes of computer users gives rise to new challenges in everyday life. These challenges arise from the fact that users cannot exploit available resources effectively when the amount of information requires prohibitively long user time ❶ _____ (spend) on acquaintance with and comprehension of the information content. Thus, the risk of information overload of users ❷ _____ (impose) new requirements on the software systems that handle the information. One of these requirements ❸ _____ (be) the incorporation into the software systems of mechanisms that help their users when they face difficulties during human-computer interaction sessions or lack the knowledge to make decisions by themselves. Such mechanisms attempt ❹ _____ (identify) user information needs and to personalize human-computer interactions. (Personalized) Recommender Systems (RS) provide an example of software systems that attempt to address some of the problems ❺ _____ (cause) by information overload.

*repository 저장소

Recent advances in electronic media and computer networks have allowed the creation of large and distributed repositories of information. However, the immediate availability of extensive resources for use by broad classes of computer users ❶ _____ _____ _____ _____ (새로운 난제들을 야기하다) in everyday life. These challenges ❷ _____ _____ (~에서 발생하다) the fact that users cannot exploit available resources effectively when the amount of information requires prohibitively long user time spent ❸ _____ _____ _____ _____ _____ _____ (~을 알고 이해하는 데) the information content. Thus, the risk of information overload of users imposes new requirements on the software systems that handle the information. One of these requirements is the incorporation into the software systems of mechanisms that help their users when they face difficulties during human-computer interaction sessions or lack the knowledge to ❹ _____ _____ _____ _____ (그들 스스로 의사 결정을 내린다). Such mechanisms attempt to identify user information needs and to personalize human-computer interactions. (Personalized) Recommender Systems (RS) provide an example of software systems that attempt to address some of the problems caused by information overload.

*repository 저장소

❶ Trade deregulation has brought down barriers to the movement of capital and jobs, but it has not freed up movement of people in pursuit of a better livelihood. ❷ The result is that work is allowed to circulate around the globe with impunity, but workers themselves are not — in fact, many are criminalized if they cross borders. ❸ The higher up the skills curve, the less strictly this rule applies, if only because it has not proven so easy to separate skills from employees. ❹ Nonetheless, corporate strategies loosely known as "knowledge transfer" have been devised to migrate brainpower from the heads of well-paid employees to a cheaper labor pool offshore. ❺ Increasingly sophisticated work-flow technologies can now slice up the contents of a job into work tasks, assign them to different parts of the globe, and reassemble the results into a meaningful whole. ❻ Most recently, trade liberalization, in India and China in particular, has enabled large amounts of skilled, professional work to be performed in discount offshore locations. ❼ As more and more countries strive to enter the upper reaches of industry and services, the competition to attract high-tech investment has intensified, and so these skill-intensive sectors are now seen as key to the game of catch-up.

*impunity 처벌되지 않음

❶ 무역 규제 완화는 자본과 일자리의 이동에 대한 장벽을 무너뜨렸지만, 그것은 더 나은 생계 수단을 추구하는 사람들의 이동을 자유롭게 해 주지 못했다. ❷ 그 결과 일은 전 세계로 퍼지는 것이 처벌되지 않고 허용되지만, 노동자 자체는 그렇지 않아서, 사실 많은 사람이 국경을 넘으면 법으로 처벌된다. ❸ 단지 기술을 직원과 분리하기가 그리 쉽지 않다는 것이 입증되었다는 이유 때문이라 해도, 기술 향상 곡선에서 위치가 더 높아질수록, 이 규칙은 덜 엄격하게 적용된다. ❹ 그럼에도 불구하고, 고임금 직원의 머리로부터 해외의 더 저렴한 노동력으로 지력을 이전하기 위해 '지식 이전'이라고 막연히 알려진 기업 전략이 고안되었다. ❺ 점점 더 정교한 작업 흐름 기술이 이제 일의 내용을 업무 과제로 분할하고, 그것들을 세계의 여러 지역으로 할당하고, 그 결과를 의미 있는 전체로 다시 모을 수 있다. ❻ 가장 최근에, 무역 자유화는, 특히 인도와 중국에서, 많은 양의 숙련된 전문적인 업무가 더 싼 해외 지역에서 이루어질 수 있게 해 주었다. ❼ 점점 더 많은 나라들이 산업과 서비스의 상층부에 진입하기 위해 노력함에 따라, 첨단 기술 투자를 유치하기 위한 경쟁이 심해졌고, 따라서 이러한 기술 집약적인 부문이 이제 격차 해소 게임의 비결로 간주되고 있다.

Word List

□ deregulation 규제 완화   □ barrier 장벽, 장애물   □ capital 자본   □ free up ~을 자유롭게 해주다   □ in pursuit of ~을 추구하여
□ livelihood 생계 수단   □ circulate 퍼지다, 순환하다   □ criminalize 법으로 처벌하다   □ border 국경   □ strictly 엄격하게
□ apply 적용되다   □ corporate 기업의   □ strategy 전략   □ transfer 이전, 이동   □ migrate 이전하다   □ labor pool 노동력
□ offshore 해외에서; 해외의   □ sophisticated 정교한   □ slice up ~ into... ~을 …으로 분할하다   □ content 내용
□ assign 할당하다   □ reassemble 다시 모으다   □ liberalization 자유화   □ discount (보통 가격보다) 더 싸게 제공되는
□ intensify 심해지다   □ skill-intensive 기술 집약적인   □ catch-up 격차 해소

• Word Test

1	transfer		12	적용되다
2	corporate		13	격차 해소
3	strictly		14	~을 추구하여
4	offshore		15	장벽, 장애물
5	reassemble		16	전략
6	criminalize		17	퍼지다, 순환하다
7	capital		18	자유화
8	content		19	정교한
9	livelihood		20	국경
10	intensify		21	이전하다
11	deregulation		22	할당하다

Trade deregulation has brought down barriers to the movement of capital and jobs, but it has not freed up movement of people in pursuit of a better livelihood. The result is ❶ which / that work is allowed to circulate around the globe with impunity, but workers themselves are not — in fact, many are criminalized if they cross borders. The higher up the skills curve, the ❷ more / less strictly this rule applies, if only because it has not proven so easy to separate skills from employees. Nonetheless, corporate strategies loosely known as "knowledge transfer" have been devised to ❸ migrate / immigrate brainpower from the heads of well-paid employees to a cheaper labor pool offshore. Increasingly sophisticated work-flow technologies can now slice up the contents of a job into work tasks, assign them to different parts of the globe, and reassemble the results into a meaningful whole. Most recently, trade liberalization, in India and China in particular, has ❹ assured / enabled large amounts of skilled, professional work to be performed in discount offshore locations. As more and more countries strive to enter the upper reaches of industry and services, the competition to attract high-tech investment has intensified, and so these skill-intensive sectors are now seen ❺ as / by key to the game of catch-up.

*impunity 처벌되지 않음

Trade deregulation has brought down barriers to the movement of capital and jobs, but it has not freed up movement of people in pursuit of a better livelihood. The result is that work ❶ _____ (allow) to circulate around the globe with impunity, but workers themselves are not — in fact, many ❷ _____ (criminalize) if they cross borders. The higher up the skills curve, the less strictly this rule applies, if only because it has not proven so easy to separate skills from employees. Nonetheless, corporate strategies loosely known as "knowledge transfer" have been devised to migrate brainpower from the heads of well-paid employees to a cheaper labor pool offshore. Increasingly sophisticated work-flow technologies can now slice up the contents of a job into work tasks, assign them to different parts of the globe, and ❸ _____ (reassemble) the results into a meaningful whole. Most recently, trade liberalization, in India and China in particular, has enabled large amounts of skilled, professional work to ❹ _____ (perform) in discount offshore locations. As more and more countries strive to enter the upper reaches of industry and services, the competition to attract high-tech investment ❺ _____ (intensify), and so these skill-intensive sectors are now seen as key to the game of catch-up.

*impunity 처벌되지 않음

Trade deregulation has brought down barriers to the movement of capital and jobs, but it has not freed up movement of people ❶ _____ _____ _____ _____ _____ _____ (더 나은 생계 수단을 추구하는). The result is that work is allowed to circulate around the globe with impunity, but workers themselves are not — in fact, many are criminalized if they cross borders. ❷ _____ _____ _____ _____ _____ _____ (기술 향상 곡선에서 위치가 더 높아질수록), the less strictly this rule applies, if only because it has not proven so easy to separate skills from employees. Nonetheless, corporate strategies loosely known as "knowledge transfer" have been devised to migrate brainpower from the heads of well-paid employees to a cheaper labor pool offshore. Increasingly sophisticated work-flow technologies can now slice up the contents of a job into work tasks, assign them to different parts of the globe, and reassemble the resulfs ❸ _____ _____ _____ _____ (의미 있는 전체로). Most recently, trade liberalization, in India and China in particular, has enabled large amounts of skilled, professional work to be performed ❹ _____ _____ _____ _____ (더 싼 해외 지역들에서). As more and more countries strive to enter the upper reaches of industry and services, the competition to attract high-tech investment has intensified, and so these skill-intensive sectors are now seen as key to the game of catch-up.

*impunity 처벌되지 않음

❶ From the time that dogs evolved from wolves, they have developed numerous behavioral traits that have supported and enhanced their interactions with humans. ❷ Science is now discovering that dogs seem to have more advanced cognitive skills than previously thought, skills that have helped them coexist with humans. ❸ For example, it was once believed that dogs were not capable of understanding verbal communication but rather relied on their advanced nonverbal abilities to help them understand human gestures and behavior. ❹ However, Andics and Miklosi reported in *Science* that research now suggests that some dogs may be capable of recognizing more than 1,000 words. ❺ This capability is definitely an asset in their interactions with humans. ❻ Furthermore, research by Udell and Vonholdt suggests that one of the biggest transformations of dogs in the process of domestication from the wolf may be due to two genes (GTF2I and GTF2IDI). ❼ These genes appear to have a direct impact on dogs' intense ability and desire for social contact. ❽ They are considered the "friendly genes" and help foster positive interactions with people.

❶ 늑대로부터 진화했을 때부터, 개는 인간과의 상호 작용을 지원하고 증진시킨 수많은 행동적 특성을 발달시켰다. ❷ 과학은 이제 개가 이전에 생각되었던 것보다 더 높은 수준의 인지 기술, 즉 그들이 인간과 공존하는 데 도움을 준 기술을 가지고 있는 것으로 보인다는 점을 발견하고 있다. ❸ 예를 들어, 한때는 개가 언어적 의사소통을 이해할 수 있는 능력이 있는 것이 아니라 인간의 몸짓과 행동을 이해하는 것을 돕는 그들의 발달된 비언어적 능력에 의존한다고 믿어졌다. ❹ 그러나 Andics와 Miklosi가 Science지에 보고한 바에 따르면, 연구는 이제 일부 개들이 1,000개가 넘는 단어를 인식할 수 있을지도 모른다는 것을 시사한다. ❺ 이 능력은 분명히 그들이 인간과 상호 작용을 할 때 유용한 것이다. ❻ 나아가, Udell과 Vonholdt의 연구는 늑대로부터 가축화되는 과정에서 개들의 가장 큰 변화 중 하나가 두 개의 유전자(GTF21와 GTF21DI) 때문일 수도 있다는 것을 시사한다. ❼ 이 유전자들은 개의 사회적 접촉에 대한 강한 능력과 열망에 직접적인 영향을 미치는 것으로 보인다. ❽ 그것은 '친절한 유전자'로 여겨지고 사람들과의 긍정적인 상호 작용을 촉진하는 데 도움을 준다.

Word List

□ evolve 진화하다 □ behavioral 행동의 □ trait 특성 □ enhance 강화하다 □ interaction 상호 작용
□ cognitive 인지의, 인지적인 □ coexist 공존하다 □ capable 할 수 있는 □ verbal 언어적인, 언어의 □ rely on ~에 의존하다
□ advanced 높은 수준의, 발달된 □ nonverbal 비언어적인 □ definitely 분명히 □ asset 유용한 것, 이점
□ transformation 변화, 변형 □ domestication 가축화 □ gene 유전자 □ impact 영향 □ intense 강한 □ contact 접촉
□ foster 촉진하다

• Word Test

1	nonverbal	11	분명히
2	trait	12	높은 수준의, 발달된
3	coexist	13	강한
4	contact	14	행동의
5	domestication	15	변화, 변형
6	evolve	16	유전자
7	impact	17	강화하다
8	interaction	18	촉진하다
9	asset	19	할 수 있는
10	verbal	20	인지의, 인지적인

From the time that dogs evolved from wolves, they have developed numerous behavioral traits ❶ that / what have supported and enhanced their interactions with humans. Science is now discovering that dogs seem to have more advanced ❷ rational / cognitive skills than previously thought, skills that have helped them coexist with humans. For example, it was once believed that dogs were not capable of understanding verbal communication but rather relied on their advanced ❸ verbal / nonverbal abilities to help them understand human gestures and behavior. However, Andies and Miklosi reported in *Science* that research now suggests that some dogs may be capable of recognizing more than 1,000 words. This capability is definitely an asset in their interactions with humans. ❹ Furthermore / Nonetheless , research by Udell and Vonholdt suggests that one of the biggest transformations of dogs in the process of ❺ civilization / domestication from the wolf may be due to two genes (GTF2I and GTF2IDI). These genes appear to have a direct impact on dogs' intense ability and desire for social contact. They are considered the "friendly genes" and help foster positive interactions with people.

From the time that dogs evolved from wolves, they ❶ _____ (develop) numerous behavioral traits that have supported and enhanced their interactions with humans. Science is now discovering that dogs seem to have more advanced cognitive skills than previously thought, skills that ❷ _____ (help) them coexist with humans. For example, it was once believed that dogs were not capable of understanding verbal communication but rather ❸ _____ (rely) on their advanced nonverbal abilities to help them understand human gestures and behavior. However, Andies and Miklosi reported in *Science* that research now suggests that some dogs may be capable of recognizing more than 1,000 words. This capability is definitely an asset in their interactions with humans. Furthermore, research by Udell and Vonholdt ❹ _____ (suggest) that one of the biggest transformations of dogs in the process of domestication from the wolf may be due to two genes (GTF2I and GTF2IDI). These genes appear ❺ _____ (have) a direct impact on dogs' intense ability and desire for social contact. They are considered the "friendly genes" and help foster positive interactions with people.

From the time that dogs evolved from wolves, they have developed numerous behavioral traits that have supported and enhanced their interactions with humans. Science is now discovering that dogs seem to have more advanced cognitive skills ❶ _____ _____ _____ (이전에 생각되었던 것보다), skills that have helped them coexist with humans. For example, it was once believed that dogs were ❷ _____ _____ _____ _____ _____ _____ (언어적 의사소통을 이해할 수 있는 능력이 없는) but rather relied on their advanced nonverbal abilities to help them understand human gestures and behavior. However, Andies and Miklosi reported in *Science* that research now suggests that some dogs may be capable of recognizing more than 1,000 words. This capability is definitely an asset ❸ _____ _____ _____ _____ _____ (그들의 인간들과의 상호 작용들에). Furthermore, research by Udell and Vonholdt suggests that one of the biggest transformations of dogs in the process of domestication from the wolf may be ❹ _____ _____ _____ _____ (두 개의 유전자 때문인) (GTF2I and GTF2IDI). These genes appear to have a direct impact on dogs' intense ability and desire for social contact. They are considered the "friendly genes" and help foster positive interactions with people.

❶ The way cultures differ regarding external societal constraints is captured by the tightnesslooseness dimension. ❷ South Asian and Confucian nations are among the tightest whereas Latin American and Eastern European nations are the least tight. ❸ Tightness is associated with strong norms and low tolerance of deviant behavior, which restricts the range of behavior deemed appropriate across everyday situations and settings. ❹ By contrast, looseness is associated with weak norms and high tolerance of deviant behavior, affording a wider range of permissible behavior across everyday situations. ❺ The strength (or weakness) of everyday recurring situations within nations simultaneously reflects and supports the degree of order and coordination in the larger cultural context. ❻ Compared to individuals in loose cultures, individuals in tight cultures are more concerned with conforming to normative rules and have psychological qualities that promote social order.

*Confucian 유교의 **deviant 일탈적인 ***deem 여기다

❶ 외부의 사회적 제약에 관하여 문화가 상이한 방식은 경직성과 유연성의 관점으로 포착된다. ❷ 남아시아와 유교 국가들은 가장 경직된 국가에 속하지만, 라틴 아메리카와 동유럽 국가들은 가장 덜 경직된 국가이다. ❸ 경직성은 강한 규범과 일탈 행동에 대한 낮은 관용과 관련이 있는데, 이는 일상적인 상황과 환경 전반에서 적절하다고 여겨지는 행동의 범위를 제한한다. ❹ 이와 대조적으로, 유연성은 약한 규범과 일탈 행동에 대한 높은 관용과 관련이 있고, 일상적인 상황 전반에서 허용되는 더 넓은 범위의 행동을 갖게 한다. ❺ 국가 내에서 매일 되풀이되는 상황의 강함(또는 약함)은 더 큰 문화적 상황에서 질서와 조직화의 정도를 반영하고 동시에 뒷받침한다. ❻ 유연한 문화의 개인에 비해, 경직된 문화의 개인은 규범적인 규칙을 따르는 것에 더 관심을 두며 사회 질서를 조성하는 심리적 특성을 가지고 있다.

Word List

□ external 외부의, 외적인   □ constraint 제약   □ capture 포착하다   □ dimension 관점, 차원   □ tight 경직된
□ associated with ~과 관련이 있는   □ norm 규범   □ tolerance 관용, 참음   □ restrict 제한하다   □ range 범위
□ permissible 허용되는   □ recur 되풀이되다   □ simultaneously 동시에   □ coordination 조직화, 조화
□ conform to ~을 따르다   □ normative 규범적인   □ order 질서

• Word Test

1	recur	9	~을 따르다
2	range	10	제약
3	tolerance	11	제한하다
4	tight	12	관점, 차원
5	normative	13	허용되는
6	coordination	14	질서
7	capture	15	규범
8	external	16	동시에

The way cultures differ regarding external societal constraints is captured by the tightnesslooseness dimension. South Asian and Confucian nations are among the tightest ❶ unless/whereas Latin American and Eastern European nations are the least tight. Tightness is associated with strong norms and low tolerance of deviant behavior, ❷ that/which restricts the range of behavior deemed appropriate across everyday situations and settings. By contrast, looseness is associated with weak norms and high tolerance of deviant behavior, affording a wider range of ❸ permissible/unacceptable behavior across everyday situations. The strength (or weakness) of everyday recurring situations within nations ❹ subsequently/simultaneously reflects and supports the degree of order and coordination in the larger cultural context. Compared to individuals in loose cultures, individuals in tight cultures are more concerned with conforming to normative rules and have psychological qualities ❺ that/who promote social order.

*Confucian 유교의 **deviant 일탈적인 ***deem 여기다

The way cultures differ regarding external societal constraints ❶ _____ (capture) by the tightnesslooseness dimension. South Asian and Confucian nations are among the tightest whereas Latin American and Eastern European nations are the least tight. Tightness ❷ _____ (associate) with strong norms and low tolerance of deviant behavior, which ❸ _____ (restrict) the range of behavior deemed appropriate across everyday situations and settings. By contrast, looseness is associated with weak norms and high tolerance of deviant behavior, ❹ _____ (afford) a wider range of permissible behavior across everyday situations. The strength (or weakness) of everyday recurring situations within nations simultaneously reflects and supports the degree of order and coordination in the larger cultural context. Compared to individuals in loose cultures, individuals in tight cultures are more concerned with ❺ _____ (conform) to normative rules and have psychological qualities that promote social order.

*Confucian 유교의 **deviant 일탈적인 ***deem 여기다

The way cultures differ ❶ _____ _____ _____ _____ (외부의 사회적 제약들에 관하여) is captured by the tightnesslooseness dimension. South Asian and Confucian nations are among the tightest whereas Latin American and Eastern European nations are the least tight. Tightness is associated with strong norms and low tolerance of deviant behavior, which restricts the range of ❷ _____ _____ _____ (적절하다고 여겨지는 행동) across everyday situations and settings. By contrast, looseness is associated with weak norms and high tolerance of deviant behavior, affording a wider range of permissible behavior across everyday situations. The strength (or weakness) of everyday recurring situations within nations simultaneously reflects and supports the ❸ _____ _____ _____ _____ (질서와 조직화의 정도) in the larger cultural context. Compared to individuals in loose cultures, individuals in tight cultures are more concerned with ❹ _____ _____ _____ (규범적인 규칙들을 따르는 것) and have psychological qualities that promote social order.

*Confucian 유교의 **deviant 일탈적인 ***deem 여기다

❶ My father was an Air Force master sergeant stationed in Ohio. ❷ The Cincinnati Reds offered tickets at a discounted price to military personnel, and my father decided to take me and a group of airmen to a baseball game between the hometown Reds and the Pittsburgh Pirates. ❸ I was thrilled at finally being able to see a big-league game. ❹ Although I was a New York Yankees fan, one of my favorite baseball players, Roy Face, was a star pitcher for the Pirates and I was hoping to get his autograph.

❺ My father even bought me a brand-new baseball just in case I ran into him. ❻ I could hardly contain myself on the drive to Cincinnati. ❼ We arrived at the stadium a few minutes before the players were due to take the field, and I lined up with other fans at the entrance to the Pirates locker room to see the players. ❽ As the players came out to enter the runway to the dugout, I looked anxiously for Roy Face. ❾ I finally saw him coming and in my best manners asked him for his autograph.

❿ He calmly ignored me and proceeded down the runway. ⓫ I was shocked! ⓬ One of my favorite heroes had brushed me off! ⓭ I stood there pondering what to do next when a large arm appeared around my shoulders and a hand took the ball from my grasp. ⓮ I looked up to see a broad smile beneath a Pirates hat and a large 21 on the uniform. ⓯ The man handed me the ball with a wink and headed onto the field. ⓰ I looked down at the ball and could not believe that it now proudly bore the name ROBERTO CLEMENTE in black ink. ⓱ Roy Face's spot on my hero list had just been filled by one of the greatest players in the game. ⓲ Clemente played an important part in the Pirates' win on that day and helped lead his team to a World Series victory over my Yankees that October. ⓳ Despite that, he remained one of my greatest heroes until his death in a 1972 airplane crash while flying relief supplies to earthquake victims in Nicaragua. ⓴ When I learned of Clemente's death, I could only marvel that the man who had helped find me a hero had been a true hero trying to help an entire nation.

*master sergeant (미 공군) 1등 중사   **dugout (야구장의) 선수 대기석   ***ponder 곰곰이 생각하다

❶ 아버지께서는 Ohio에 배치된 공군 1등 중사이셨다. ❷ Cincinnati Reds는 군인들에게 할인된 가격으로 (경기)입장권을 제공했고, 아버지는 나와 항공 대원 몇 명을 홈팀인 Reds와 Pittsburgh Pirates의 야구 경기에 데려가기로 결정하셨다. ❸ 나는 마침내 메이저 리그 경기를 볼 수 있게 되어서 정말 신이 났다. ❹ 비록 나는 New York Yankees의 팬이었지만, 내가 가장 좋아하는 야구 선수 중 한 명인 Roy Face는 Pirates의 스타 투수였고 나는 그의 사인을 받기를 바라고 있었다.

❺ 아버지께서는 혹시라도 내가 그와 우연히 마주칠 때를 대비해서 심지어 새 야구공까지 사 주셨다. ❻ 나는 Cincinnati로 가는 차 안에서 거의 감정을 자제할 수 없었다. ❼ 우리는 선수들이 경기장으로 나가기로 예정된 시간 몇 분전에 야구장에 도착했고, 나는 선수들을 보기 위해 다른 팬들과 함께 Pirates 탈의실 입구에 줄을 섰다. ❽ 선수들이 선수 대기석으로 가는 통로에 진입하기 위해 나올 때 나는 애타게 Roy Face를 찾았다. ❾ 나는 마침내 그가 오고 있는 것을 보았고, 가장 예의 바르게 그에게 사인을 요청했다.

❿ 그는 조용히 나를 무시하고 통로를 따라 내려갔다. ⓫ 나는 충격을 받았다! ⓬ 내가 가장 좋아하는 영웅 중 한 명이 나를 매정하게 무시해 버렸다! ⓭ 나는 거기에 서서 다음에 무엇을 해야 할지를 곰곰이 생각하고 있었는데, 그때 어깨 언저리에 커다란 팔이 나타나더니 손 하나가 꽉 쥔 내 손에서 공을 가져갔다. ⓮ 내가 고개를 들어보니 Pirates 모자 아래 함박웃음과 유니폼 위의 커다란 21이라는 숫자가 보였다. ⓯ 그 남자는 나에게 윙크를 하며 공을 건네주고 경기장으로 향했다. ⓰ 나는 그 공을 내려다 보았고 이제 그것에 ROBERTO CLEMENTE 라는 이름이 위풍당당하게 검정 잉크로 적혀져 있다는 것이 믿기지 않았다. ⓱ 내 영웅 목록에서 Roy Face의 자리는 바로 그 순간 그 게임[야구]에서 가장 위대한 선수 중 한 명에 의해 채워졌다. ⓲ Clemente는 그날 Pirates의 승리에 중요한 역할을 했고, 그의 소속팀이 그해 10월 나의 Yankees를 꺾고 월드 시리즈에서 우승하는 데 기여했다. ⓳ 그럼에도 불구하고, 그는 1972년에 니카라과의 지진 피해자들을 위한 구호물자를 공수하던 중 비행기 사고로 죽을 때까지 나의 위대한 영웅 중 한 명으로 남아 있었다. ⓴ Clemente의 죽음을 알게 되었을 때, 나는 내가 한 영웅을 찾도록 도와준 사람이 한 나라 전체를 도우려고 애썼던 진정한 영웅이었다는 것에 단지 경탄할 뿐이었다.

Word List

□ **Air Force** 공군   □ **station** (군인을) 배치하다[주둔시키다]   □ **military personnel** 군인   □ **airman** 항공 대원
□ **thrilled** 정말 신이 난, 아주 흥분한   □ **big-league** 메이저 리그의   □ **pitcher** 투수   □ **run into** ~과 우연히 마주치다
□ **anxiously** 애타게, 간절히   □ **autograph** (유명인의) 사인   □ **proceed** 나아가다, 이동하다   □ **runway** 통로, 활주로
□ **brush ~ off** ~을 매정하게 무시하다   □ **grasp** 꽉 쥐기[움켜잡기], 이해   □ **broad smile** 함박웃음
□ **bear** (기재된 서명, 날짜 등을) 지니고 있다, 가지고 있다   □ **fly** (비행기로) 공수하다[실어 나르다]   □ **relief supplies** 구호물자
□ **victim** 피해자   □ **marvel** 경탄하다, 놀라다

• Word Test

1	runway	_____	9	(유명인의) 사인	_____
2	grasp	_____	10	정말 신이 난, 아주 흥분한	_____
3	anxiously	_____	11	군인	_____
4	airman	_____	12	피해자	_____
5	bear	_____	13	~과 우연히 마주치다	_____
6	fly	_____	14	나아가다, 이동하다	_____
7	station	_____	15	구호물자	_____
8	pitcher	_____	16	경탄하다, 놀라다	_____

• 유형 1 네모 안에서 옳은 어법·어휘를 고르시오.

My father was an Air Force master sergeant stationed in Ohio. The Cincinnati Reds offered tickets at a discounted price to military personnel, and my father decided to take me and a group of airmen to a baseball game between the hometown Reds and the Pittsburgh Pirates. I was ❶ thrilled/frustrated at finally being able to see a big-league game. ❷ Since/Although I was a New York Yankees fan, one of my favorite baseball players, Roy Face, was a star pitcher for the Pirates and I was hoping to get his autograph.

My father even bought me a brand-new baseball just in case I ran into him. I could ❸ always/hardly contain myself on the drive to Cincinnati. We arrived at the stadium a few minutes before the players were due to take the field, and I lined up with other fans at the entrance to the Pirates locker room to see the players. As the players came out to enter the runway to the dugout, I looked ❹ anxious/anxiously for Roy Face. I finally saw him coming and in my best manners asked him for his autograph. He calmly ignored me and ❺ proceeded/progressed down the runway. I was shocked! One of my favorite heroes had brushed me off! I stood there pondering what to do next when a large arm appeared around my shoulders and a hand took the ball from my grasp. I looked up to see a broad smile beneath a Pirates hat and a large 21 on the uniform. The man handed me the ball with a wink and headed onto the field. I looked down at the ball and could not believe that it now proudly bore the name ROBERTO CLEMENTE in black ink.

Roy Face's spot on my hero list had just been filled by one of the greatest players in the game. Clemente played an important part in the Pirates' win on that day and helped lead his team to a World Series victory over my Yankees that October. ❻ Despite/Because of that, he remained one of my greatest heroes until his death in a 1972 airplane crash while flying relief supplies to earthquake victims in Nicaragua. When I learned of Clemente's death, I could only marvel that the man who had helped find me a hero ❼ has/had been a true hero trying to help an entire nation.

*master sergeant (미 공군) 1등 중사   **dugout (야구장의) 선수 대기석   ***ponder 곰곰이 생각하다

My father was an Air Force master sergeant ❶ _____ (station) in Ohio. The Cincinnati Reds offered tickets at a discounted price to military personnel, and my father decided to take me and a group of airmen to a baseball game between the hometown Reds and the Pittsburgh Pirates. I was thrilled at finally ❷ _____ (be) able to see a big-league game. Although I was a New York Yankees fan, one of my favorite baseball players, Roy Face, was a star pitcher for the Pirates and I was hoping to get his autograph.

My father even ❸ _____ (buy) me a brand-new baseball just in case I ran into him. I could hardly contain myself on the drive to Cincinnati. We arrived at the stadium a few minutes before the players were due to take the field, and I lined up with other fans at the entrance to the Pirates locker room to see the players. As the players came out to enter the runway to the dugout, I looked anxiously for Roy Face. I finally saw him ❹ _____ (come) and in my best manners asked him for his autograph.

He calmly ignored me and proceeded down the runway. I was shocked! One of my favorite heroes had brushed me off! I stood there pondering what to do next when a large arm appeared around my shoulders and a hand took the ball from my grasp. I looked up to see a broad smile beneath a Pirates hat and a large 21 on the uniform. The man handed me the ball with a wink and ❺ _____ (head) onto the field. I looked down at the ball and could not believe that it now proudly bore the name ROBERTO CLEMENTE in black ink.

Roy Face's spot on my hero list had just ❻ _____ (fill) by one of the greatest players in the game. Clemente played an important part in the Pirates' win on that day and helped lead his team to a World Series victory over my Yankees that October. Despite that, he remained one of my greatest heroes until his death in a 1972 airplane crash while ❼ _____ (fly) relief supplies to earthquake victims in Nicaragua. When I learned of Clemente's death, I could only marvel that the man who ❽ _____ (help) find me a hero had been a true hero trying to help an entire nation.

*master sergeant (미 공군) 1등 중사 **dugout (야구장의) 선수 대기석 ***ponder 곰곰이 생각하다

My father was an Air Force master sergeant stationed in Ohio. The Cincinnati Reds offered tickets
❶ _____ _____ _____ _____ (할인된 가격으로) to military personnel, and my father decided
to take me and a group of airmen to a baseball game between the hometown Reds and the Pittsburgh
Pirates. I was thrilled at finally being able to see a big-league game. Although I was a New York
Yankees fan, one of my favorite baseball players, Roy Face, was a star pitcher for the Pirates and I was
hoping to get his autograph.

My father even bought me a brand-new baseball ❷ _____ _____ _____ _____ _____
_____ _____ (혹시라도 내가 그와 우연히 마주칠 때를 대비해서). I could hardly contain myself on the drive
to Cincinnati. We arrived at the stadium a few minutes before the players were due to take the field,
and I lined up with other fans at the entrance to the Pirates locker room to see the players. As the
players came out to enter the runway to the dugout, I looked anxiously for Roy Face. I finally saw him
coming and ❸ _____ _____ _____ _____ (내 최고의 예의로) asked him for his autograph.
He calmly ignored me and proceeded down the runway. I was shocked! One of my favorite heroes
❹ _____ _____ _____ _____ (나를 매정하게 무시했다)! I stood there pondering what to do
next when a large arm appeared around my shoulders and a hand took the ball from my grasp. I looked
up to see a broad smile beneath a Pirates hat and a large 21 on the uniform. The man handed me the
ball with a wink and headed onto the field. I looked down at the ball and could not believe that it now
❺ _____ _____ _____ _____ (이름이 위풍당당하게 적혀있다) ROBERTO CLEMENTE in black
ink.

Roy Face's spot on my hero list had just been filled by one of the greatest players in the game. Clemente
❻ _____ _____ _____ _____ (중요한 역할을 했다) in the Pirates' win on that day and helped
lead his team to a World Series victory over my Yankees that October. Despite that, he remained one of
my greatest heroes until his death in a 1972 airplane crash while flying relief supplies to earthquake
victims in Nicaragua. When I learned of Clemente's death, I could only marvel that the man who had
helped find me a hero had been a true hero trying to help an entire nation.

*master sergeant (미 공군) 1등 중사   **dugout (야구장의) 선수 대기석   ***ponder 곰곰이 생각하다

01 11강 1번

다음 글에서 전체 흐름과 관계 없는 문장은?

The ocean is important as a surface, as a channel for travel. As anyone who has jumped into the ocean knows, seawater is buoyant — it supports your weight much better than the air around you. This greatly reduces the amount of fuel required to move goods from place to place. Moving a 20-foot container from Shanghai to Frankfurt by ship costs a mere third as much as shifting it by plane. ① It is no surprise, therefore, that four-fifths of international trade in goods depends on sea freight. ② The emergence of enormous container ships has meant that fewer and fewer people now work in shipping, but it remains very big business — the biggest ocean industry of all in terms of total income. ③ Despite this fact, the main disadvantage of sea freight transportation might be the time it takes to get cargo from one location to the next. ④ Every day, huge quantities of goods pass through major bottlenecks like the Panama and Suez Canals. ⑤ The world was given a stark reminder of the importance of these bottlenecks in March 2021, when one of the world's largest container ships, the *Ever Given*, blocked the Suez Canal for six days, prompting widespread concern about the consequences for world trade.

*buoyant 부력이 있는, 뜨게 하는 **freight 화물 운송 ***stark 냉혹한

02 11강 2번

다음 글의 밑줄 친 부분 중, 어법상 틀린 것은?

When the new coronavirus arrived in the United States in January 2020, it hit an economy, society, and constitutional democracy fundamentally ① unprepared. As the scale of the challenge became clear, the country simply could not deliver ② what was needed to confront it. There was a solution, one identified by scholars and policy experts as early as the middle of March and publicly disseminated by the middle of April. That solution was a large-scale program of rapid testing of patients, tracing and testing their contacts, and tracing and testing their contacts again in turn. Such testing also needed reinforcement from a culture of ③ sticking to universal precautions such as mask-wearing, hand and bathroom hygiene, and robust practices of infection control. The massive, rapid buildup of such a public health campaign, as well as the necessary systems and services to support ④ them, would have interrupted transmission of the virus sufficiently to eliminate it even while ⑤ keeping the economy open. But the country did not have the relevant infrastructure ready to go and was not able to deliver this mobilization.

*disseminate 전파하다 **hygiene 위생 ***robust 강력한

03 11강 3번

다음 글의 요지로 가장 적절한 것은?

The only way to produce crystal-clear writing is to know how a reader will respond to the choices you make in composing text and graphics. You need to know which sentence structures are most easily understood, which organization of material into sections is most easily followed, and so on. It's certainly possible to offer some general rules along these lines: for example, "use the active voice," "divide the paper into Introduction, Methods, Results, and Discussion sections," and "use a figure instead of a table when quantities are to be compared." In principle, you could tape a long list of such rules above your computer and treat it as the voice of authority on how to reach readers. But long lists of rules are boring. Besides, using them makes writing mechanical, and good writing sometimes entails knowing when to bend the rules instead of following them. Furthermore, using a list of rules is oddly indirect: instead of relying on rules you've been told will produce clear text, surely it would be more effective to understand how readers think, and write to that understanding.

① 독자의 반응 방식을 생각하여 글쓰기의 일반적인 규칙을 목록화한 후 활용해야 한다.
② 좋은 글을 쓰기 위해 일반적인 규칙 대신 자신만의 개성 있는 스타일을 적용해야 한다.
③ 명료한 글을 쓰기 위해서는 작가의 관점들을 목록화한 후 이를 빠짐없이 적용해야 한다.
④ 좋은 글쓰기를 위해 규칙을 융통성 있게 적용하며 독자의 사고방식에 맞추는 것이 좋다.
⑤ 지루하고 기계적인 글을 피하기 위해서는 독자와 직접 만나 글쓰기 규칙을 정해야 한다.

04 11강 4번

글의 흐름으로 보아, 주어진 문장이 들어가기에 가장 적절한 곳은?

This works pretty well, but when crops of acorns fluctuate dramatically across years, it can send shock waves through the animal community.

Masting is the synchronized production of large crops of acorns across a broad geographic range of a species, alternating with one or more years of little or no acorn production. (①) This is an adaption to increase acorn survival and dispersibility. (②) Populations of some specialist seed consumers crash following non-mast years so that more acorns survive following the mast years. (③) Acorn mast is an important resource in the community for a wide variety of animals far beyond those that serve as agents of acorn dispersal. (④) Deer, bear, woodpeckers, turkeys, mice, and many other animals direct their attention to the acorn mast during mast years. (⑤) People are also sometimes affected by masting. When mouse populations increase in mast years, so do the populations of ticks and the incidence of Lyme disease.

*mast (도토리 등이 일정한 주기로) 대량으로 결실하다; 열매
**dispersibility (열매 등의) 분산 가능성   ***tick (동물) 진드기

[5~7] 다음 글을 읽고, 물음에 답하시오.

(A)

Early one morning the doorbell rang. "How can I help you?" Vera asked the child who was standing there. "My mother is ill. She needs some medicine, he said. "Who's your mom?" Vera asked. "Charity," he answered. Charity was the woman who cleaned their house each week. Vera's mom came to talk to Washington, Charity's son, "(a) I will take you home and we can take some medicine to her."

(B)

Washington asked Vera's mom to stop outside a run-down house. The house was neat and clean. Faded red linoleum covered the floor and pictures cut from magazines were pasted against the walls. A small stove stood in the front room, and in front of it was a table and three old chairs. Charity was in the bedroom. She coughed when she greeted them. (b) Vera's mom gave her some medicine and put a carrier bag filled with groceries onto the table.

*run-down 낡고 허름한   **linoleum 리놀륨(마루의 깔개)

(C)

Vera went outside and looked over the top of the run-down houses in the squatter camp to the blue mountains in the distance. "Lord, forgive me for being so ungrateful," she said. Back home she took out a suitcase and packed it full of clothes and other things that (c) she didn't need any more. She put her favorite blue T-shirt on top of everything. *That's for Washington*, she thought. She felt a lot of respect for the young boy who had walked for more than two hours without complaining to get some medicine for his mother.

*squatter camp 빈민가

(D)

"But Mom," Vera objected, "(d) you promised to take me to the mall today!" "I know," her mom replied. "But she seems to be seriously ill. We can go shopping later on." Vera frowned. Newtown was far from where they lived. *There won't be time to go to the mall after this*, she realized. "Come with (e) me!" her mom invited. After a while they turned off onto a dirt road. Children in old clothes and no shoes were playing in the dust.

05

주어진 글 (A)에 이어질 내용을 순서에 맞게 배열한 것으로 가장 적절한 것은?

① (B) – (D) – (C)　　　② (C) – (B) – (D)
③ (C) – (D) – (B)　　　④ (D) – (B) – (C)
⑤ (D) – (C) – (B)

06

밑줄 친 (a)~(e) 중에서 가리키는 대상이 나머지 넷과 다른 것은?

① (a)　② (b)　③ (c)　④ (d)　⑤ (e)

07

윗글에 관한 내용으로 적절하지 않은 것은?

① Washington의 엄마는 매주 Vera의 집을 청소하는 일을 하는 사람이었다.
② Washington의 집의 외관은 낡고 허름했지만, 내부는 깔끔하고 깨끗했다.
③ Vera의 엄마는 몸이 아픈 Charity에게 약과 식료품을 전해 주었다.
④ Vera의 엄마는 집으로 돌아온 뒤, Washington에게 줄 옷가지를 챙겼다.
⑤ Vera는 원래 엄마와 함께 쇼핑몰에 가려던 참이었다.

08 11강 8번

주어진 글 다음에 이어질 글의 순서로 가장 적절한 것은?

Recent advances in electronic media and computer networks have allowed the creation of large and distributed repositories of information. However, the immediate availability of extensive resources for use by broad classes of computer users gives rise to new challenges in everyday life.

(A) Such mechanisms attempt to identify user information needs and to personalize human-computer interactions. (Personalized) Recommender Systems (RS) provide an example of software systems that attempt to address some of the problems caused by information overload.

(B) One of these requirements is the incorporation into the software systems of mechanisms that help their users when they face difficulties during human-computer interaction sessions or lack the knowledge to make decisions by themselves.

(C) These challenges arise from the fact that users cannot exploit available resources effectively when the amount of information requires prohibitively long user time spent on acquaintance with and comprehension of the information content. Thus, the risk of information overload of users imposes new requirements on the software systems that handle the information.

*repository 저장소

① (A) – (C) – (B) 　② (B) – (A) – (C)
③ (B) – (C) – (A) 　④ (C) – (A) – (B)
⑤ (C) – (B) – (A)

09 11강 9번

다음 글의 밑줄 친 부분 중, 문맥상 낱말의 쓰임이 적절하지 않은 것은?

Trade deregulation has brought down barriers to the movement of capital and jobs, but it has not freed up movement of people in pursuit of a better livelihood. The result is that work is allowed to circulate around the globe with impunity, but workers themselves are not — in fact, many are ① criminalized if they cross borders. The higher up the skills curve, the ② less strictly this rule applies, if only because it has not proven so easy to separate skills from employees. Nonetheless, corporate strategies loosely known as "knowledge transfer" have been devised to migrate brainpower from the heads of well-paid employees to a cheaper labor pool offshore. Increasingly sophisticated work-flow technologies can now slice up the contents of a job into work tasks, assign them to different parts of the globe, and ③ reassemble the results into a meaningful whole. Most recently, trade liberalization, in India and China in particular, has ④ enbled large amounts of skilled, professional work to be performed in discount offshore locations. As more and more countries strive to enter the upper reaches of industry and services, the competition to attract high-tech investment has ⑤ weakened, and so these skill-intensive sectors are now seen as key to the game of catch-up.

*impunity 처벌되지 않음

10 [11강 10번]

글의 흐름으로 보아, 주어진 문장이 들어가기에 가장 적절한 곳은?

> However, Andies and Miklosi reported in *Science* that research now suggests that some dogs may be capable of recognizing more than 1,000 words.

From the time that dogs evolved from wolves, they have developed numerous behavioral traits that have supported and enhanced their interactions with humans. (①) Science is now discovering that dogs seem to have more advanced cognitive skills than previously thought, skills that have helped them coexist with humans. (②) For example, it was once believed that dogs were not capable of understanding verbal communication but rather relied on their advanced nonverbal abilities to help them understand human gestures and behavior. (③) This capability is definitely an asset in their interactions with humans. Furthermore, research by Udell and Vonholdt suggests that one of the biggest transformations of dogs in the process of domestication from the wolf may be due to two genes (GTF2I and GTF2IDI). (④) These genes appear to have a direct impact on dogs' intense ability and desire for social contact. (⑤) They are considered the "friendly genes" and help foster positive interactions with people.

---

behavior deemed appropriate across everyday situations and settings. By contrast, looseness is associated with weak norms and high tolerance of deviant behavior, affording a wider range of permissible behavior across everyday situations. The strength (or weakness) of everyday recurring situations within nations simultaneously reflects and supports the degree of order and coordination in the larger cultural context. Compared to individuals in loose cultures, individuals in tight cultures are more concerned with conforming to normative rules and have psychological qualities that promote social order.

*Confucian 유교의 **deviant 일탈적인 ***deem 여기다

> The way cultures differ regarding external
> ___(A)___ constraints is captured by how
> ___(B)___ cultures are made.

(A)	(B)
① societal	...... tight
② economic	...... tight
③ societal	...... strong
④ economic	...... strong
⑤ religious	...... tolerant

고난도

11 [11강 11번]

다음 글의 내용을 한 문장으로 요약하고자 한다. 빈칸 (A), (B)에 들어갈 말로 가장 적절한 것은?

South Asian and Confucian nations are among the tightest whereas Latin American and Eastern European nations are the least tight. Tightness is associated with strong norms and low tolerance of deviant behavior, which restricts the range of

---

[11강 12~14번]

[12~14] 다음 글을 읽고, 물음에 답하시오.

(A)

My father was an Air Force master sergeant stationed in Ohio. The Cincinnati Reds offered tickets at a discounted price to military personnel, and my father decided to take me and a group of airmen to a baseball game between the hometown Reds and the Pittsburgh Pirates. I was thrilled at finally being able to see a big-league game. Although I was a New York Yankees fan, one of my favorite baseball players, Roy Face, was a star pitcher for the Pirates and I was hoping to get his autograph. My father even bought me a brand-new baseball just in case I ran into him. I could hardly contain myself on the drive to Cincinnati.

*master sergeant (미 공군) 1등 중사

(B)

I stood there pondering what to do next when a large arm appeared around my shoulders and a hand took the ball from my grasp. I looked up to see a broad smile beneath a Pirates hat and a large 21 on the uniform. (a)The man handed me the ball with a wink and headed onto the field. I looked down at the ball and could not believe that it now proudly bore the name ROBERTO CLEMENTE in black ink. Roy Face's spot on my hero list had just been filled by (b)one of the greatest players in the game.

*ponder 곰곰이 생각하다

(C)

We arrived at the stadium a few minutes before the players were due to take the field, and I lined up with other fans at the entrance to the Pirates locker room to see the players. As the players came out to enter the runway to the dugout, I looked anxiously for Roy Face. I finally saw him coming and in my best manners asked (c)him for his autograph. He calmly ignored me and proceeded down the runway. I was shocked! One of my favorite heroes had brushed me off!

*dugout (야구장의) 선수 대기석

(D)

Clemente played an important part in the Pirates' win on that day and helped lead (d)his team to a World Series victory over my Yankees

that October. Despite that, he remained one of my greatest heroes until (e)his death in a 1972 airplane crash while flying relief supplies to earthquake victims in Nicaragua. When I learned of Clemente's death, I could only marvel that the man who had helped find me a hero had been a true hero trying to help an entire nation.

12

주어진 글 (A)에 이어질 내용을 순서에 맞게 배열한 것으로 가장 적절한 것은?

① (B) – (D) – (C)　　② (C) – (B) – (D)
③ (C) – (D) – (B)　　④ (D) – (B) – (C)
⑤ (D) – (C) – (B)

13

밑줄 친 (a)~(e) 중에서 가리키는 대상이 나머지 넷과 다른 것은?

① (a)　② (b)　③ (c)　④ (d)　⑤ (e)

14

윗글에 관한 내용으로 적절하지 않은 것은?

① 'I'는 아버지와 함께 홈팀인 Reds와 Pittsburgh Pirates 의 야구 경기를 관람하러 갔다.
② 'I'는 Pittsburgh Pirates팀의 스타 투수에게 사인을 받고 싶은 마음에 들떠 있었다.
③ 'I'의 손에 있던 야구공을 가져가 자신의 이름을 적은 후 건네 준 선수는 21번이었다.
④ 'I'는 Pirates 탈의실 입구에서 Roy Face를 기다렸지만 결국 그의 사인을 받진 못했다.
⑤ Roy Face는 지진 피해자들을 위한 구호물자를 공수하던 중 비행기 사고로 사망했다.

15 [11강 1번]

다음 글의 주제로 가장 적절한 것은?

The ocean is important as a surface, as a channel for travel. As anyone who has jumped into the ocean knows, seawater is buoyant — it supports your weight much better than the air around you. This greatly reduces the amount of fuel required to move goods from place to place. Moving a 20-foot container from Shanghai to Frankfurt by ship costs a mere third as much as shifting it by plane. It is no surprise, therefore, that four-fifths of international trade in goods depends on sea freight. The emergence of enormous container ships has meant that fewer and fewer people now work in shipping, but it remains very big business — the biggest ocean industry of all in terms of total income. Every day, huge quantities of goods pass through major bottlenecks like the Panama and Suez Canals. The world was given a stark reminder of the importance of these bottlenecks in March 2021, when one of the world's largest container ships, the *Ever Given*, blocked the Suez Canal for six days, prompting widespread concern about the consequences for world trade.

*buoyant 부력이 있는, 뜨게 하는 **freight 화물 운송 ***stark 냉혹한

① reasons why global shipping is harmful to the planet
② the importance of maritime shipping in international trade
③ the role and importance of the Suez Canals in contemporary shipping
④ advantages and disadvantages of air transport for international trade
⑤ the differences and similarities between transport by sea, land and air

16 [11강 2번]

주어진 글 다음에 이어질 글의 순서로 가장 적절한 것은?

When the new coronavirus arrived in the United States in January 2020, it hit an economy, society, and constitutional democracy fundamentally unprepared.

(A) As the scale of the challenge became clear, the country simply could not deliver what was needed to confront it. There was a solution, one identified by scholars and policy experts as early as the middle of March and publicly disseminated by the middle of April. That solution was a large-scale program of rapid testing of patients, tracing and testing their contacts, and tracing and testing their contacts again in turn.

(B) The massive, rapid buildup of such a public health campaign, as well as the necessary systems and services to support it, would have interrupted transmission of the virus sufficiently to eliminate it even while keeping the economy open. But the country did not have the relevant infrastructure ready to go and was not able to deliver this mobilization.

(C) Such testing also needed reinforcement from a culture of sticking to universal precautions such as mask-wearing, hand and bathroom hygiene, and robust practices of infection control.

*disseminate 전파하다 **hygiene 위생 ***robust 강력한

① (A) – (C) – (B)　　　② (B) – (A) – (C)
③ (B) – (C) – (A)　　　④ (C) – (A) – (B)
⑤ (C) – (B) – (A)

17 11강 3번

다음 글의 밑줄 친 부분 중, 문맥상 낱말의 쓰임이 적절하지 <u>않은</u> 것은?

The only way to produce crystal-clear writing is to know how a reader will respond to the choices you make in ① <u>composing</u> text and graphics. You need to know which sentence structures are most easily understood, which organization of material into sections is most easily followed, and so on. It's certainly possible to offer some ② <u>general</u> rules along these lines: for example, "use the active voice," "divide the paper into Introduction, Methods, Results, and Discussion sections," and "use a figure instead of a table when quantities are to be compared." In principle, you could tape a long list of such rules above your computer and treat it as the voice of ③ <u>authority</u> on how to reach readers. But long lists of rules are boring. Besides, using them makes writing mechanical, and good writing sometimes entails knowing when to ④ <u>bend</u> the rules instead of following them. Furthermore, using a list of rules is oddly indirect: instead of relying on rules you've been told will produce clear text, surely it would be ⑤ <u>less</u> effective to understand how readers think, and write to that understanding.

18 11강 4번

다음 글에서 전체 흐름과 관계 <u>없는</u> 문장은?

Masting is the synchronized production of large crops of acorns across a broad geographic range of a species, alternating with one or more years of little or no acorn production. This is an adaption to increase acorn survival and dispersibility. Populations of some specialist seed consumers crash following non-mast years so that more acorns survive following the mast years. This works pretty well, but when crops of acorns fluctuate dramatically across years, it can send shock waves through the animal community. ① Acorn mast is an important resource in the community for a wide variety of animals far beyond those that serve as agents of acorn dispersal. ② Dispersal is especially critical for offspring, as they find new resources and mates following the dispersal event. ③ Deer, bear, woodpeckers, turkeys, mice, and many other animals direct their attention to the acorn mast during mast years. ④ People are also sometimes affected by masting. ⑤ When mouse populations increase in mast years, so do the populations of ticks and the incidence of Lyme disease.

*mast (도토리 등이 일정한 주기로) 대량으로 결실하다; 열매
**dispersibility (열매 등의) 분산 가능성   ***tick (동물) 진드기

19 11강 8번

다음 빈칸에 들어갈 말로 가장 적절한 것은?

Recent advances in electronic media and computer networks have allowed the creation of large and distributed repositories of information. However, the immediate availability of extensive resources for use by broad classes of computer users gives rise to new challenges in everyday life. These challenges arise from the fact that users cannot exploit available resources effectively when the amount of information requires prohibitively long user time spent on acquaintance with and comprehension of the information content. Thus, the risk of _____ imposes new requirements on the software systems that handle the information. One of these requirements is the incorporation into the software systems of mechanisms that help their users when they face difficulties during human-computer interaction sessions or lack the knowledge to make decisions by themselves. Such mechanisms attempt to identify user information needs and to personalize human-computer interactions. (Personalized) Recommender Systems (RS) provide an example of software systems that attempt to address some of the problems caused by information overload.

*repository 저장소

① identity theft
② more competitive pressure
③ information overload of users
④ mistakes in analyzing big data
⑤ scams and illegal or fraud deals

20 11강 9번

trade deregulation에 관한 다음 글의 내용과 일치하지 <u>않는</u> 것은?

Trade deregulation has brought down barriers to the movement of capital and jobs, but it has not freed up movement of people in pursuit of a better livelihood. The result is that work is allowed to circulate around the globe with impunity, but workers themselves are not — in fact, many are criminalized if they cross borders. The higher up the skills curve, the less strictly this rule applies, if only because it has not proven so easy to separate skills from employees. Nonetheless, corporate strategies loosely known as "knowledge transfer" have been devised to migrate brainpower from the heads of well-paid employees to a cheaper labor pool offshore. Increasingly sophisticated work-flow technologies can now slice up the contents of a job into work tasks, assign them to different parts of the globe, and reassemble the results into a meaningful whole. Most recently, trade liberalization, in India and China in particular, has enabled large amounts of skilled, professional work to be performed in discount offshore locations. As more and more countries strive to enter the upper reaches of industry and services, the competition to attract high-tech investment has intensified, and so these skill-intensive sectors are now seen as key to the game of catch-up.

*impunity 처벌되지 않음

① 무역 규제 완화는 더 나은 생계 수단을 추구하는 사람들의 이동을 자유롭게 하지는 못했다.
② 기업들은 고임금 직원의 지력을 해외의 더 저렴한 노동력으로 이전하는 전략을 고안했다.
③ 기업들은 세계로 할당된 작은 과제를 조합해 일 단위로 묶어 고임금 직원에게 주고 있다.
④ 무역 자유화는 숙련된 전문적인 업무가 더 싼 해외 지역에서 이루어질 수 있게 해 주었다.
⑤ 첨단 기술 투자 유치 경쟁 심화에 따라 기술 집약적인 부분이 격차 해소의 비결이 되었다.

21 11강 10번

다음 글의 밑줄 친 부분 중, 문맥상 낱말의 쓰임이 적절하지 <u>않은</u> 것은?

From the time that dogs evolved from wolves, they have developed numerous behavioral traits that have supported and enhanced their interactions with humans. Science is now discovering that dogs seem to have more advanced ① <u>cognitive</u> skills than previously thought, skills that have helped them coexist with humans. For example, it was once believed that dogs were not capable of understanding verbal communication but rather relied on their advanced ② <u>nonverbal</u> abilities to help them understand human gestures and behavior. However, Andies and Miklosi reported in *Science* that research now suggests that some dogs may be capable of recognizing more than 1,000 words. This capability is definitely an ③ <u>asset</u> in their interactions with humans. Furthermore, research by Udell and Vonholdt suggests that one of the biggest transformations of dogs in the process of ④ <u>domestication</u> from the wolf may be due to two genes (GTF2I and GTF2IDI). These genes appear to have a direct impact on dogs' intense ability and desire for social contact. They are considered the "⑤ <u>hostile</u> genes" and help foster positive interactions with people.

22 11강 11번

다음 글에서 전체 흐름과 관계 <u>없는</u> 문장은?

The way cultures differ regarding external societal constraints is captured by the tightness-looseness dimension. South Asian and Confucian nations are among the tightest whereas Latin American and Eastern European nations are the least tight. ① Tightness is associated with strong norms and low tolerance of deviant behavior, which restricts the range of behavior deemed appropriate across everyday situations and settings. ② Given their differing colonial histories, Latin American and Confucian Asian societies differ also in contemporary cultural diversity. ③ By contrast, looseness is associated with weak norms and high tolerance of deviant behavior, affording a wider range of permissible behavior across everyday situations. ④ The strength (or weakness) of everyday recurring situations within nations simultaneously reflects and supports the degree of order and coordination in the larger cultural context. ⑤ Compared to individuals in loose cultures, individuals in tight cultures are more concerned with conforming to normative rules and have psychological qualities that promote social order.

*Confucian 유교의 **deviant 일탈적인 ***deem 여기다

11강 1번

The ocean is ① underline(important) as a surface, as a channel for travel. As anyone who has jumped into the ocean knows, seawater is buoyant — it supports your weight much better than the air around you. This greatly ② underline(reduces) the amount of fuel required to move goods from place to place. 20피트의 컨테이너를 상하이에서 프랑크푸르트로 배로 이동시키는 것은 비용이 그것을 비행기로 옮기는 것 만큼의 1/3밖에 비용이 들지 않는다. It is no surprise, therefore, that four-fifths of international trade in goods depends on sea freight. The ③ underline(emergency) of enormous container ships has meant that fewer and fewer people now work in shipping, but it remains very big business — the biggest ocean industry of all in terms of total income. Every day, ④ underline(huge) quantities of goods pass through major bottlenecks like the Panama and Suez Canals. The world was given a stark reminder of the importance of these bottlenecks in March 2021, when one of the world's largest container ships, the *Ever Given*, blocked the Suez Canal for six days, ⑤ underline(prompting) widespread concern about the consequences for world trade.

*buoyant 부력이 있는, 뜨게 하는 **freight 화물 운송 ***stark 냉혹한

23 윗글의 밑줄 친 부분 중, 문맥상 어색한 것을 1개 찾아 그 번호를 쓰고 고쳐 쓰시오.

_____ → _____

24 윗글의 밑줄 친 (A)의 의미가 되도록 보기 의 단어를 배열하여 문장을 완성하시오.

> 보기 shifting / by plane / costs / a / much / as / it / third / mere / as

Moving a 20-foot container from Shanghai to Frankfurt by ship _____
_____.

11강 2번

When the new coronavirus arrived in the United States in January 2020, it hit an economy, society, and constitutional democracy fundamentally unprepared. As the scale of the challenge became clear, the country simply could not deliver what was needed to confront it. There was a solution, one identified by scholars and policy experts as early as the middle of March and publicly disseminated by the middle of April. That solution was a large-scale program of rapid testing of patients, tracing and testing their contacts, and tracing and testing their contacts again in turn. Such testing also needed _____ from a culture of sticking to universal precautions such as mask-wearing, hand and bathroom hygiene, and robust practices of infection control. The massive, rapid buildup of such a public health campaign, as well as the necessary systems and services to support it, would have interrupted transmission of the virus sufficiently to eliminate it even while keeping the economy open. But the country did not have the relevant infrastructure ready to go and was not able to deliver this mobilization.

*disseminate 전파하다 **hygiene 위생 ***robust 강력한

25 윗글의 빈칸에 들어갈 단어를 영영 뜻풀이를 참고하여 쓰시오. (단, 주어진 철자로 시작할 것)

> the action of making an idea, belief, or feeling stronger

r_____

26 윗글의 밑줄 친 **this mobilization**이 가리키는 바를 본문에서 찾아 우리말로 쓰시오. (40글자 내외)

_____
_____

The only way to produce crystal-clear writing is to know how a reader will respond to the choices you make in composing text and graphics. You need to know which sentence structures are most easily understood, which organization of material into sections is most easily followed, and so on. It's certainly possible to offer some general rules along these lines: for example, "use the active voice," "divide the paper into Introduction, Methods, Results, and Discussion sections," and "use a figure instead of a table when quantities are to be compared." In principle, you could tape a long list of such rules above your computer and treat it as the voice of authority on how to reach readers. But long lists of rules are boring. Besides, using them makes writing mechanical, and good writing sometimes entails knowing when to bend the rules instead of following them. Furthermore, using a list of rules is oddly indirect: 여러분이 명료한 텍스트를 만들어 낼 것이라고 들었던 규칙에 의존하는 것 대신에, surely it would be more effective to understand how readers think, and write to that understanding.

27 윗글의 밑줄 친 우리말의 의미에 맞게 [보기]의 단어를 모두 이용하여 [조건]에 맞게 문장을 완성하시오.

> [보기] rules / you've / instead of / that / text / will / rely on / be told / produce / clear

> [조건] · 필요시 어형을 바꿔 쓸 것

_____

_____

28 윗글을 읽고 다음 질문에 대한 답을 찾아 우리말로 쓰시오. (단, 두 가지를 각각 나누어 쓸 것)

Q: What are two things you can do in order to produce clear writing?

A: (1) _____

　　(2) _____

Masting is the synchronized production of large crops of acorns across a broad geographic range of a species, (A) alternate with one or more years of little or no acorn production. This is an adaption to increase acorn survival and dispersibility. Populations of some specialist seed consumers (B) to crash following non-mast years so that more acorns survive following the mast years. This works pretty well, but when crops of acorns fluctuate dramatically across years, it can send shock waves through the animal community. Acorn mast is an important resource in the community for a wide variety of animals far beyond those that serve as agents of acorn dispersal. Deer, bear, woodpeckers, turkeys, mice, and many other animals direct their attention to the acorn mast during mast years. People are also sometimes affected by masting. When mouse populations increase in mast years, so (C) are the populations of ticks and the incidence of Lyme disease.

*mast (도토리 등이 일정한 주기로) 대량으로 결실하다; 열매
**dispersibility (열매 등의) 분산 가능성　***tick (동물) 진드기

🚩 고난도

29 윗글의 밑줄 친 부분을 어법상 알맞은 형태로 고쳐 쓰시오.

(A) alternate → _____

(B) to crash　→ _____

(C) are　　　→ _____

30 윗글의 밑줄 친 This가 가리키는 것을 본문에서 찾아 우리말로 쓰시오.

_____

Early one morning the doorbell rang. "How can I help you?" Vera asked the child who was standing there. "My mother is ill. She needs some medicine, he said. "Who's your mom?" Vera asked. "Charity," he answered. Charity was the woman who cleaned their house each week. Vera's mom came to talk to Washington, Charity's son, "I will take you home and we can take some medicine to her." "But Mom," Vera objected, "you promised ① to take me to the mall today!" "I know," her mom replied. "But Charity seems to be seriously ill. We can go ② shopping later on."

Vera frowned. Newtown was far from ③ where they lived. *There won't be time to go to the mall after this*, she realized. "Come with me!" her mom invited. After a while they turned off onto a dirt road. Children in old clothes and no shoes were playing in the dust. Washington asked Vera's mom to stop outside a run-down house.

The house was neat and clean. Faded red linoleum covered the floor and pictures cut from magazines were pasted against the walls. A small stove stood in the front room, and in front of it was a table and three old chairs. Charity was in the bedroom. She coughed when she greeted them. Vera's mom gave her some medicine and put a carrier bag ④ filling with groceries onto the table. Vera went outside and looked over the top of the run-down houses in the squatter camp to the blue mountains in the distance. "Lord, forgive me for being so ungrateful," she said.

Back home she took out a suitcase and packed it full of clothes and other things ⑤ what she didn't need any more. She put her favorite blue T-shirt on top of everything. *That's for Washington*, she thought. 어머니에게 드릴 약을 얻기 위해 불평하지 않고 두 시간 이상 걸어온 그 소년에게 그녀는 많은 존경심을 느꼈다.

*run-down 낡고 허름한   **linoleum 리놀륨(마루의 깔개)
***squatter camp 빈민가

31 윗글의 밑줄 친 부분 중, 어법상 틀린 것을 2개 찾아 그 번호를 쓰고 고쳐 쓰시오.

(1) _____ → _____
(2) _____ → _____

32 윗글의 밑줄 친 우리말 의미에 맞도록 보기 의 단어를 순서대로 배열하여 문장을 완성하시오.

> 보기   two hours / who / had walked / complaining / without / more than / for

She felt a lot of respect for the young boy _____

_____

to get some medicine for his mother.

Recent advances in electronic media and computer networks have ① allowed the creation of large and distributed repositories of information. However, the immediate availability of ② limited resources for use by broad classes of computer users gives rise to new challenges in everyday life. These challenges arise from the fact that users cannot exploit ③ available resources effectively when the amount of information requires prohibitively long user time spent on acquaintance with and comprehension of the information content. Thus, the risk of information overload of users imposes new requirements on the software systems that handle the information. One of these requirements is the incorporation into the software systems of mechanisms that help their users when they face difficulties during human-computer interaction sessions or ④ lack the knowledge to make decisions by themselves. Such mechanisms attempt to identify user information needs and to personalize human-computer interactions. (Personalized) Recommender Systems (RS) provide an example of software systems that attempt to ⑤ address some of the problems caused by information overload.

*repository 저장소

33 윗글의 밑줄 친 부분 중, 문맥상 어색한 것을 1개 찾아 그 번호를 쓰고 고쳐 쓰시오.

_____ → _____

34 윗글의 주제를 다음과 같이 할 때, 빈칸에 들어갈 알맞은 말을 본문에서 찾아 쓰시오.

> a solution for some of the problems that computer users face due to information _____

Trade deregulation has brought down barriers to the movement of capital and jobs, but it has not freed up movement of people in pursuit of a better livelihood. The result is that work is allowed to circulate around the globe with impunity, but workers ① themselves are not — in fact, many are criminalized if they cross borders. The higher up the skills curve, the less strictly this rule applies, if only because it has not proven so easy ② to separate skills from employees. Nonetheless, corporate strategies loosely known as "knowledge transfer" ③ has been devised to migrate brainpower from the heads of well-paid employees to a cheaper labor pool offshore. Increasingly sophisticated work-flow technologies can now slice up the contents of a job into work tasks, ④ assigning them to different parts of the globe, and reassemble the results into a meaningful whole. Most recently, trade liberalization, in India and China in particular, (A) has enabled large amounts of skilled, professional work to be performed in discount offshore locations. As more and more countries strive to enter the upper reaches of industry and services, the competition to attract high-tech investment has intensified, and so these skill-intensive sectors are now seen as key ⑤ to the game of catch-up.

*impunity 처벌되지 않음

35 윗글의 밑줄 친 부분 중, 어법상 틀린 것을 2개 찾아 그 번호를 쓰고 고쳐 쓰시오.

(1) _____ → _____

(2) _____ → _____

36 윗글의 밑줄 친 (A)가 의미하는 바를 구체적인 2단어로 본문에서 찾아 쓰시오.

_____

From the time that dogs evolved from wolves, they have developed numerous behavioral traits that have supported and enhanced their interactions with humans. Science is now discovering that dogs seem to have more advanced   (A)   skills than previously thought, skills that have helped them coexist with humans. For example, it was once believed that dogs were not capable of understanding verbal communication but rather relied on their advanced nonverbal abilities to help them understand human gestures and behavior. However, Andies and Miklosi reported in *Science* that research now suggests that some dogs may be capable of recognizing more than 1,000 words. This capability is definitely an asset in their interactions with humans. Furthermore, research by Udell and Vonholdt suggests that one of the biggest transformations of dogs in the process of domestication from the wolf may be due to two genes (GTF2I and GTF2IDI). (B) These genes appear to have a direct impact on dogs' intense ability and desire for social contact. They are considered the "friendly genes" and help foster positive interactions with people.

37 윗글의 빈칸 (A)에 들어갈 단어를 영영 뜻풀이를 참고하여 쓰시오. (단, 주어진 글자로 시작할 것)

> of involving or relating conscious intellectual activity such as thinking, reasoning, or remembering

c _____

38 윗글의 밑줄 친 (B)를 It으로 시작하는 문장으로 다시 쓰시오.

It _____

_____ .

The way ① how cultures differ regarding external societal constraints is captured by the tightness-looseness dimension. South Asian and Confucian nations are among the tightest whereas Latin American and Eastern European nations are the least tight. Tightness is associated with strong norms and low tolerance of deviant behavior, which restricts the range of behavior ② deemed appropriate across everyday situations and settings. By contrast, looseness is associated with weak norms and high tolerance of deviant behavior, ③ affording a wider range of permissible behavior across everyday situations. The strength (or weakness) of everyday recurring situations within nations simultaneously reflects and supports the degree of order and coordination in the larger cultural context. ④ Comparing to individuals in loose cultures, individuals in tight cultures are more concerned with conforming to normative rules and have psychological qualities ⑤ that promote social order.

*Confucian 유교의   **deviant 일탈적인   ***deem 여기다

39 윗글의 밑줄 친 부분 중, 어법상 틀린 것을 2개 찾아 그 번호를 쓰고 고쳐 쓰시오.

(1) _____ → _____

(2) _____ → _____

🚩 고난도

40 윗글에서 다음 질문에 대한 답을 찾아 우리말로 쓰시오.

Q: What are the characteristics of tight cultures and loose cultures?

A:
<tight cultures>	<loose cultures>
(1)	(3)
(2)	(4)

My father was an Air Force master sergeant ① stationed in Ohio. The Cincinnati Reds offered tickets at a discounted price to military personnel, and my father decided to take me and a group of airmen to a baseball game between the hometown Reds and the Pittsburgh Pirates. I was thrilled at finally being able to see a big-league game. Although I was a New York Yankees fan, one of my favorite baseball players, Roy Face, was a star pitcher for the Pirates and I was hoping to get his autograph.

My father even bought me a brand-new baseball just in case I ran into him. I could hardly contain myself on the drive to Cincinnati. We arrived at the stadium a few minutes before the players were due to take the field, and I lined up with other fans at the entrance to the Pirates locker room to see the players. As the players came out to enter the runway to the dugout, I looked anxiously for Roy Face. I finally saw him ② coming and in my best manners asked him for his autograph.

He calmly ignored me and proceeded down the runway. I was shocked! One of my favorite heroes had brushed me off! I stood there ③ pondered what to do next when a large arm appeared around my shoulders and a hand took the ball from my grasp. I looked up to see a broad smile beneath a Pirates hat and a large 21 on the uniform. The man handed me the ball with a wink and headed onto the field. I looked down at the ball and could not believe that it now proudly bore the name ROBERTO CLEMENTE in black ink.

Roy Face's spot on my hero list had just been filled by one of the greatest players in the game. Clemente played an important part in the Pirates' win on that day and helped ④ lead his team to a World Series victory over my Yankees that October. Despite that, he remained one of my greatest heroes until his death in a 1972 airplane crash while ⑤ flew relief supplies to earthquake victims in Nicaragua. When I learned of Clemente's death, I could only marvel that the man who had helped find me (A) a hero had been (B) a true hero trying to help an entire nation.

*master sergeant (미 공군) 1등 중사   **dugout (야구장의) 선수 대기석
***ponder 곰곰이 생각하나

41 윗글의 밑줄 친 부분 중 어법상 틀린 것을 2개 찾아 그 번호를 쓰고 고쳐 쓰시오.

(1) _____ → _____
(2) _____ → _____

42 윗글의 밑줄 친 (A)와 (B)가 가리키는 대상이 구체적으로 누구인지 쓰시오.

(A) _____
(B) _____

❶ Perhaps one of the greatest challenges is to find the will, the courage, and the undefeatable attitude to persist. ❷ To challenge oneself to exceed the comfort zone and to push beyond one's self-perceived outer limits is to practice with firm faith and devotion. ❸ Reaching beyond anything done previously, always knocking on that door of a new record, a farther reach than ever reached before — what Daniel Coyle called "reachfulness" — is what "peaking" involves. ❹ *Reachfulness* is the constant pounding in one's head to stretch and stretch and stretch to that new limit, no matter how minuscule. ❺ It is a new high. ❻ The role of the teacher, coach, or mentor is to keep tipping the learner forward from passivity toward reachable action. ❼ It is a continuous cycle that maintains and sustains skillfulness, yet also scores a plus within the learner for the new mark that has been reached. ❽ This requires constant dissatisfaction with the current specs or data and a yearning to do one's personal best, each and every outing. ❾ It is exhausting on the one hand, and on the other it is thrilling and truly invigorated by the tiny, barely noticeable successes that keep the learner moving ever forward.

*minuscule 미미한   **invigorate 고무하다

❶ 아마도 가장 큰 도전 중 하나는 끝까지 해낼 의지와 용기, 그리고 난공불락의 태도를 찾는 것일 것이다. ❷ 안락한 지대를 넘어 자신이 인식하는 외적 한계를 벗어나도록 자신에게 도전한다는 것은 확고한 신념을 가지고 전념하여 실천하는 것이다. ❸ 무엇이든 이전에 수행한 것 너머에 도달하는 것, 항상 새로운 기록의 그 문을 두드리는 것, 이전에 도달한 적이 있는 것보다 더 멀리 도달하는 것 ― Daniel Coyle이 'reachfulness'라고 부른 것-은 '절정에 이르는 것'이 수반하는 것이다. ❹ Reachfulness는 아무리 미미하더라도 그 새로운 한계까지 뻗어 나가고, 뻗어 나가고, 또 뻗어 나가기 위해 머릿속에서 끊임없이 두드리는 것이다. ❺ 그것은 새로운 정점이다. ❻ 교사, 코치 또는 멘토의 역할은 학습자를 계속 살짝 건드려서 수동성에서 도달 가능한 행동을 향해 앞으로 나아가도록 하는 것이다. ❼ 그것은 숙련도를 유지하고 지속하면서도, 도달된 새로운 기록에 대하여 학습자의 마음 속에 플러스 점수를 매기는 끊임없는 순환이다. ❽ 이를 위해서는 현재의 (역량에 대한) 상세한 기록이나 자료에 대한 끊임없는 불만족과 모든 출전에서 자신의 개인 최고 기록을 내고자 하는 열망이 필요하다. ❾ 그것은 한편으로는 고단하지만, 다른 한편으로는 짜릿하며 학습자를 계속 끊임없이 앞으로 나아가게 하는 아주 작고, 거의 눈에 띄지 않는 성공에 의해 진정으로 고무된다.

Word List

□ **undefeatable** 난공불락의, 무적의   □ **persist** 끝까지 해내다, 고집스럽게 계속하다   □ **exceed** 넘어서다, 초과하다   □ **perceive** 인식하다
□ **peak** 절정[최고조]에 이르다   □ **involve** 수반하다   □ **pound** 두드리다   □ **stretch** 뻗어 나가다, 늘어나다, 미치다   □ **high** 정점, 최고 기록
□ **tip** (어떤 것이 어느 방향으로 가도록) 살짝 건드리다   □ **maintain** 유지하다   □ **sustain** 지속하다   □ **spec**(= specification) 상세한 기록[설명]
□ **yearning** 열망, 갈망   □ **outing** (스포츠 대회) 출전[출장]   □ **exhausting** 고단한, 심신을 피로[소모]하게 하는
□ **noticeable** 눈에 띄는, 이목을 끄는

• Word Test

1	maintain	9	눈에 띄는, 이목을 끄는
2	exceed	10	인식하다
3	high	11	지속하다
4	exhausting	12	(스포츠 대회) 출전[출장]
5	undefeatable	13	뻗어 나가다, 늘어나다, 미치다
6	yearning	14	살짝 건드리다
7	pound	15	수반하다
8	peak	16	끝까지 해내다, 고집스럽게 계속하다

Perhaps one of the greatest challenges is to find the will, the courage, and the ❶ defeatable / undefeatable attitude to persist. To challenge oneself to exceed the comfort zone and to push beyond one's self-perceived outer limits is to practice with firm faith and devotion. Reaching beyond anything done previously, always knocking on that door of a new record, a farther reach than ever reached before — what Daniel Coyle called "reachfulness" — is ❷ that / what "peaking" involves. *Reachfulness* is the constant pounding in one's head to stretch and stretch and stretch to that new limit, no matter how minuscule. It is a new high. The role of the teacher, coach, or mentor is to keep tipping the learner ❸ forward / backward from passivity toward reachable action. It is a continuous cycle that maintains and sustains skillfulness, yet also scores a plus within the learner for the new mark that has been reached. This requires constant dissatisfaction with the current specs or data and a ❹ despair / yearning to do one's personal best, each and every outing. It is exhausting on the one hand, and on ❺ another / the other it is thrilling and truly invigorated by the tiny, barely noticeable successes that keep the learner moving ever forward. 　　　　　　　　*minuscule 미미한　**invigorate 고무하다

Perhaps one of the greatest challenges is to find the will, the courage, and the undefeatable attitude to persist. To challenge oneself to exceed the comfort zone and to push beyond one's self-perceived outer limits ❶ _____ (be) to practice with firm faith and devotion. Reaching beyond anything done previously, always knocking on that door of a new record, a farther reach than ever reached before — what Daniel Coyle called "reachfulness" — is what "peaking" ❷ _____ (involve). *Reachfulness* is the constant pounding in one's head to stretch and stretch and stretch to that new limit, no matter how minuscule. It is a new high. The role of the teacher, coach, or mentor ❸ _____ (be) to keep tipping the learner forward from passivity toward reachable action. It is a continuous cycle that maintains and sustains skillfulness, yet also ❹ _____ (score) a plus within the learner for the new mark that has been reached. This requires constant dissatisfaction with the current specs or data and a yearning to do one's personal best, each and every outing. It is exhausting on the one hand, and on the other it is thrilling and truly invigorated by the tiny, barely noticeable successes that keep the learner ❺ _____ (move) ever forward. 　　　　　　　*minuscule 미미한　**invigorate 고무하다

Perhaps one of the greatest challenges is to find the will, the courage, and the undefeatable attitude to persist. To challenge oneself to exceed the comfort zone and to push beyond one's self-perceived outer limits is to practice with firm faith and devotion. Reaching beyond ❶ _____ _____ _____
(이전에 수행한 무엇이든), always knocking on that door of a new record, a farther reach than ever reached before — what Daniel Coyle called "reachfulness" — is what "peaking" involves. *Reachfulness* is the constant pounding in one's head to stretch and stretch and stretch to that new limit, ❷ _____ _____ _____ (아무리 ~하더라도) minuscule. It is a new high. The role of the teacher, coach, or mentor is to keep tipping the learner forward ❸ _____ _____ _____ _____ _____
(수동성에서 도달 가능한 행동을 향해). It is a continuous cycle that maintains and sustains skillfulness, yet also scores a plus within the learner for the new mark that has been reached. This requires constant dissatisfaction with the current specs or data and a yearning to do one's personal best, each and every outing. It is exhausting on the one hand, and on the other it is thrilling and truly invigorated by the tiny, barely noticeable successes that ❹ _____ _____ _____ _____ _____
(학습자를 계속 끊임없이 앞으로 나가게 한다). 　　　　　　　*minuscule 미미한　**invigorate 고무하다

❶ Every time that a cell multiplies, there is risk of an error at the time when the DNA is copied. ❷ Consequently, as multicellular animals increased in complexity and size and the lifespan got longer and longer, the risk of cancer was expected to grow in direct proportion; the larger and longer-lived the animal, the higher the number of mitosis occurring in its body, and therefore the higher the chance of DNA damage to occur. ❸ However, this turned out not to be the case as large dimensions and longer life do not necessarily mean increased risk of cancer: ❹ this is the 'Peto's paradox', which gets its name from a study published in 1995 by Richard Peto and his colleagues. ❺ In this experiment, a large group of mice of different ages were exposed to topical application of a carcinogen. ❻ The rate of appearance by epithelial tumours was related to the duration of exposure to the chemical but not to the mouse's age. ❼ That is, it was the time of exposure to the carcinogen agent that dictated the risk of developing cancer and not the age of the exposed mouse — and neither the span of survival after the exposure. ❽ This study demonstrated that, against the then current wisdom, increased lifespan in itself can be irrelevant as far as increase in cancer risk is concerned.

*mitosis 체세포 분열 **carcinogen 발암 물질 ***epithelial tumour 상피 종양

❶ 세포가 증식할 때마다 DNA가 복제되는 시점에서 오류가 발생할 위험이 있다. ❷ 결과적으로, 다세포 동물의 복잡성과 크기가 증가하고 수명이 점점 길어짐에 따라 암의 위험이 정비례하여 증가할 것으로 예상되었는데, 즉 동물이 더 크고 오래 살수록 몸에서 일어나는 체세포 분열의 수가 더 많아지고, 따라서 DNA 손상이 발생할 가능성이 더 높아진다는 것이었다. ❸ 그러나 이것은 사실이 아닌 것으로 밝혀졌는데, 큰 크기와 더 긴 수명이 반드시 암 위험 증가를 의미하는 것은 아니기 때문이다. ❹ 이것이 'Peto의 역설'인데, 이는 Richard Peto와 그의 동료들이 1995년에 발표한 연구에서 그 이름을 가져온다. ❺ 이 실험에서 나이가 다른 쥐들의 대규모 집단이 발암 물질의 국소적 도포에 노출되었다. ❻ 상피 종양의 발생 비율은 그 화학 물질에 노출된 기간과 관련이 있었지만, 쥐의 나이와는 관련이 없었다. ❼ 즉, 암 발병 위험을 결정한 것은 발암 물질에 노출된 시간이지 노출된 쥐의 나이가 아니었고, 노출 후 생존 기간도 아니었다. ❽ 이 연구는 당시의 지식에 반하여, 암 위험 증가에 관한 한, 증가한 수명 그 자체는 무관할 수 있다는 것을 보여 주었다.

Word List

□ multiply 증식하다, 번식하다 □ multicellular 다세포의 □ complexity 복잡성 □ lifespan 수명 □ in direct proportion 정비례하여
□ dimension 크기, 규모 □ paradox 역설 □ experiment 실험 □ topical 국소의, 국부의 □ application 도포, 바르기, 적용
□ rate 비율 □ duration (지속되는) 기간 □ exposure 노출 □ agent 물질, 동인 □ dictate 결정하다, 영향을 미치다
□ demonstrate 보여 주다, 증명하다 □ irrelevant 무관한, 상관없는

• Word Test

1	agent		9	역설	
2	duration		10	노출	
3	dimension		11	결정하다, 영향을 미치다	
4	application		12	국소의, 국부의	
5	complexity		13	수명	
6	demonstrate		14	다세포의	
7	experiment		15	무관한, 상관없는	
8	multiply		16	비율	

Every time that a cell multiplies, there is risk of an error at the time ❶ which / when the DNA is copied. Consequently, as multicellular animals increased in complexity and size and the lifespan got longer and longer, the risk of cancer was expected to grow in direct proportion; the larger and longer-lived the animal, the higher the number of mitosis occurring in its body, and therefore the higher the chance of DNA damage to occur. However, this turned out not to be the case as large dimensions and longer life do not necessarily mean ❷ decreased / increased risk of cancer: this is the 'Peto's paradox', which gets its name from a study published in 1995 by Richard Peto and his colleagues. In this experiment, a large group of mice of different ages were exposed to topical application of a carcinogen. The rate of appearance by epithelial tumours was related to the ❸ duration / accuracy of exposure to the chemical but not to the mouse's age. That is, it was the time of exposure to the carcinogen agent that dictated the risk of developing cancer and not the age of the exposed mouse — and ❹ yet / neither the span of survival after the exposure. This study demonstrated that, against the then current wisdom, increased lifespan in itself can be ❺ relevant / irrelevant as far as increase in cancer risk is concerned.

*mitosis 체세포 분열 **carcinogen 발암 물질 ***epithelial tumour 상피 종양

Every time that a cell multiplies, there is risk of an error at the time when the DNA ❶ _____ (copy). Consequently, as multicellular animals increased in complexity and size and the lifespan got longer and longer, the risk of cancer ❷ _____ (expect) to grow in direct proportion; the larger and longer-lived the animal, the higher the number of mitosis occurring in its body, and therefore the higher the chance of DNA damage ❸ _____ (occur). However, this turned out not to be the case as large dimensions and longer life do not necessarily mean increased risk of cancer: this is the 'Peto's paradox', which gets its name from a study ❹ _____ (publish) in 1995 by Richard Peto and his colleagues. In this experiment, a large group of mice of different ages ❺ _____ (expose) to topical application of a carcinogen. The rate of appearance by epithelial tumours was related to the duration of exposure to the chemical but not to the mouse's age. That is, it was the time of exposure to the carcinogen agent that dictated the risk of developing cancer and not the age of the exposed mouse — and neither the span of survival after the exposure. This study demonstrated that, against the then current wisdom, increased lifespan in itself can be irrelevant as far as increase in cancer risk is concerned.

*mitosis 체세포 분열 **carcinogen 발암 물질 ***epithelial tumour 상피 종양

Every time that a cell multiplies, there is risk of an error at the time when the DNA is copied. Consequently, as multicellular animals increased in complexity and size and the ❶ _____ _____ _____ _____ _____ (수명이 점점 길어졌다), the risk of cancer was expected to grow in direct proportion; the larger and longer-lived the animal, the higher the number of mitosis occurring in its body, and therefore the higher the chance of DNA damage to occur. However, ❷ _____ _____ _____ _____ _____ _____ _____ _____ (이것은 사실이 아닌 것으로 밝혀졌다) as large dimensions and longer life do not necessarily mean increased risk of cancer: this is the 'Peto's paradox', which gets its name from a study published in 1995 by Richard Peto and his colleagues. In this experiment, a large group of mice of different ages were exposed to topical application of a carcinogen. The rate of appearance by epithelial tumours was related to the duration of exposure to the chemical but not to the mouse's age. That is, it was the time of exposure to the carcinogen agent that dictated the risk of developing cancer and not the age of the exposed mouse — and neither the ❸ _____ _____ _____ _____ _____ _____ (노출 후 생존 기간). This study demonstrated that, against the then current wisdom, increased lifespan in itself can be irrelevant ❹ _____ _____ _____ (~에 관한 한) increase in cancer risk is concerned.

*mitosis 체세포 분열 **carcinogen 발암 물질 ***epithelial tumour 상피 종양

❶ A large repertoire and proficient song performance can only be acquired by an individual bird that grew up in a secure nest, was subsequently unencumbered by disease and parasites, and — in possession of sharp faculties, memory capacity, foraging ability, and predator watchfulness — engaged in hundreds of hours of successful singing practice. ❷ Whatever impairs the post-hatching growth of a bird's system of song nuclei, and whatever keeps the bird from attending to and practicing song is later evident as deficits in the size and perfection of its mature song repertoire. ❸ This makes a large repertoire of complex song a direct causal reflection of an individual's successful passage through a demanding and varied obstacle course. ❹ The more demanding the performance to be acquired, the more comprehensive a measure of an individual's personal history and qualities lies implicit in the perfected, mature song performance. ❺ An individual's song proficiency tells its audience, in a way impossible to counterfeit, that the singer comes from, as it were, "a good background." ❻ Potential mates and rivals thus do well to take a singer displaying mastery and virtuosity seriously.

*unencumbered 방해가 없는 **counterfeit 위조하다 ***virtuosity 기교

❶ 풍부한 레퍼토리와 능숙한 노래 솜씨는 안전한 둥지에서 자랐으며, 그 후에 질병과 기생충의 방해가 없었고, 기민한 기능, 기억력, 먹이 찾기 능력, 포식자 경계력을 가진 상태에서, 수백 시간의 성공적인 노래 연습을 한 새 개체에 의해서만 습득될 수 있다. ❷ 무엇이든 부화 후 새의 노래 핵 체계의 성장을 손상시키는 것은, 그리고 무엇이든 새가 노래에 주의를 기울이고 노래를 연습하는 것을 방해하는 것은, 나중에 새의 원숙한 노래 레퍼토리의 크기와 완벽성의 부족으로 명백해진다. ❸ 이 때문에 복잡한 노래의 풍부한 레퍼토리는 개체가 힘들고 다양한 장애물 코스를 성공적으로 통과한 것을 직접적이며 인과 관계적으로 반영한다. ❹ 습득되어야 할 솜씨가 더 노력을 요할수록, 개체의 개별적인 이력과 자질의 척도는, 완벽하고 원숙한 노래 솜씨에 내재된 채, 더 포괄적이게 된다. ❺ 한 개체의 숙달된 노래 솜씨는 듣는 개체들에게 노래하는 그 새가 이를테면 '좋은 배경' 출신이라는 것을 위조가 불가능한 방식으로 말해 준다. ❻ 따라서 잠재적인 짝과 경쟁자들은 숙달된 솜씨와 기교를 보여 주는 노래하는 새를 진지하게 받아들이는 것이 현명하다.

Word List

□ repertoire 레퍼토리, 연주 목록 □ proficient 능숙한 □ performance 공연, 연주 □ secure 안전한 □ subsequently 그 후에
□ parasite 기생충 □ faculty 기능, 능력 □ forage 먹이를 찾다 □ predator 포식자 □ impair 손상시키다
□ post-hatching 부화 후의 □ song nucleus 노래 핵 (앵무새 등의 전뇌에 있는 부분) □ evident 명백한, 분명한 □ deficit 부족, 결손
□ mature 원숙한 □ causal 인과 관계의 □ obstacle 장애물, 장애 □ comprehensive 포괄적인 □ measure 척도, 측정
□ implicit 내재된, 내포된 □ do well to *do* ~하는 것이 현명하다

• Word Test

1	predator		10 안전한	
2	faculty		11 부족, 결손	
3	measure		12 능숙한	
4	performance		13 손상시키다	
5	obstacle		14 먹이를 찾다	
6	subsequently		15 포괄적인	
7	evident		16 내재된, 내포된	
8	mature		17 인과 관계의	
9	repertoire		18 기생충	

A large repertoire and proficient song performance can only be acquired by an individual bird that grew up in a secure nest, was subsequently unencumbered by disease and parasites, and — in possession of sharp faculties, memory capacity, foraging ability, and predator watchfulness — engaged in hundreds of hours of successful singing practice. ❶ Whatever/Whenever impairs the post-hatching growth of a bird's system of song nuclei, and whatever keeps the bird from attending to and practicing song is later ❷ hidden/evident as deficits in the size and perfection of its mature song repertoire. This makes a large repertoire of complex song a direct causal reflection of an individual's successful passage through a demanding and ❸ varied/unvarying obstacle course. The more demanding the performance to be acquired, the ❹ more/less comprehensive a measure of an individual's personal history and qualities lies implicit in the perfected, mature song performance. An individual's song proficiency tells its audience, in a way impossible to counterfeit, ❺ that/which the singer comes from, as it were, "a good background." Potential mates and rivals thus do well to take a singer displaying mastery and virtuosity seriously.

*unencumbered 방해가 없는   **counterfeit 위조하다   ***virtuosity 기교

A large repertoire and proficient song performance can only ❶ _____ (acquire) by an individual bird that grew up in a secure nest, was subsequently unencumbered by disease and parasites, and — in possession of sharp faculties, memory capacity, foraging ability, and predator watchfulness — engaged in hundreds of hours of successful singing practice. Whatever impairs the post-hatching growth of a bird's system of song nuclei, and whatever keeps the bird from attending to and practicing song ❷ _____ (be) later evident as deficits in the size and perfection of its mature song repertoire. This makes a large repertoire of complex song a direct causal reflection of an individual's successful passage through a demanding and varied obstacle course. The more demanding the performance to be acquired, the more comprehensive a measure of an individual's personal history and qualities ❸ _____ (lie) implicit in the perfected, mature song performance. An individual's song proficiency ❹ _____ (tell) its audience, in a way impossible to counterfeit, that the singer comes from, as it were, "a good background." Potential mates and rivals thus do well to take a singer ❺ _____ (display) mastery and virtuosity seriously.

*unencumbered 방해가 없는   **counterfeit 위조하다   ***virtuosity 기교

A large repertoire and proficient song performance can only be acquired by an individual bird that grew up in a secure nest, was subsequently unencumbered by disease and parasites, and — ❶ _____ _____ _____ (~을 가진 상태에서) sharp faculties, memory capacity, foraging ability, and predator watchfulness — engaged in hundreds of hours of successful singing practice. Whatever impairs the post-hatching growth of a bird's system of song nuclei, and whatever ❷ _____ _____ _____ _____ _____ _____ (새가 ~에 주의를 기울이는 것을 방해한다) and practicing song is later evident as deficits in the size and perfection of its mature song repertoire. This makes a large repertoire of complex song a(n) ❸ _____ _____ _____ (직접적이며 인과 관계적인 반응) of an individual's successful passage through a demanding and varied obstacle course. The more demanding the performance to be acquired, the more comprehensive a measure of an individual's personal history and qualities lies implicit in the perfected, mature song performance. An individual's song proficiency tells its audience, ❹ _____ _____ _____ _____ _____ _____ (위조하기에 불가능한 방식으로), that the singer comes from, as it were, "a good background." Potential mates and rivals thus do well to take a singer displaying mastery and virtuosity seriously.

*unencumbered 방해가 없는 **counterfeit 위조하다 ***virtuosity 기교

❶ Are you Othello or Hamlet? ❷ Are you more likely to think — and act — too fast, or to get mired in analysis paralysis? ❸ While jumping to conclusions and actions is a widespread fault in individuals, analysis paralysis is frequent in large, bureaucratic organizations that pile up studies and reports before taking any action or no action at all. ❹ On the one hand, being fast or lazy in our thinking allows us to economize on scarce and expensive mental resources, but the resulting solutions are often poor and ineffective. ❺ On the other hand, slow thinking and thorough investigation are necessary to tackle complex business problems but the reflection process might create delays in decision-making and frustrate action. ❻ For organizations and institutions to be both effective and efficient, they need people who can overcome these challenges to solving complex business problems. ❼ These people must be as thorough as Hamlet and as action oriented as Othello, without jumping to conclusions like the latter or being stuck in a loop of endless questioning like the former.

*mired 수렁에 빠진

❶ 여러분은 Othello인가, 아니면 Hamlet 인가? ❷ 여러분은 너무 빨리 생각할, 그리고 행동할, 가능성이 더 높은가, 아니면 (정보 과다로 인한) 분석 불능의 수렁에 빠질 가능성이 더 높은가? ❸ 성급하게 결론을 내리고 행동을 취하는 것은 개인들에게서 널리 퍼진 잘못인 반면, (정보 과다로 인한) 분석 불능은 어떤 조치를 취하기 전에 혹은 전혀 조치를 취하지 않기 전에 연구와 보고서를 쌓아 두는 거대한 관료 조직들에서 흔하다. ❹ 한편으로는, 생각이 빠르거나 태만한 것은 우리가 부족하고 비용이 많이 드는 정신적 자원을 절약하게 해 주지만, 그 결과로 생기는 해결책은 흔히 부실하고 효과적이지 못하다. ❺ 다른 한편으로는 복잡한 비즈니스 문제를 다루려면 느린 사고와 철저한 조사가 필요하지만, 심사숙고의 과정은 의사 결정에서 지연을 초래하고 행동을 방해할 수도 있을 것이다. ❻ 조직과 기관이 효과적이고 효율적이기 위해서는 복잡한 비즈니스 문제를 해결하는 것에 대한 이러한 도전을 극복할 수 있는 사람들이 필요하다. ❼ 이 사람들은 Hamlet처럼 철저해야 하고 Othello처럼 행동 지향적이어야 하며, 후자처럼 성급하게 결론을 내리거나 전자처럼 끝없는 질문의 고리에 갇히지 않아야 한다.

Word List

□ analysis 분석　□ paralysis 불능, 마비　□ conclusion 결론　□ widespread 널리 퍼진, 광범위한　□ fault 잘못
□ frequent 빈번한, 잦은　□ bureaucratic 관료적인, 관료주의의　□ pile up ~을 쌓다, 축적하다　□ economize 절약하다, 아끼다
□ scarce 부족한　□ thorough 철저한, 빈틈없는　□ investigation 조사　□ tackle 다루다, 씨름하다　□ reflection 심사숙고
□ delay 지연, 지체　□ frustrate 방해하다, 좌절시키다　□ institution 기관, 단체　□ be stuck in ~에 갇히다　□ loop 고리

• Word Test

1	conclusion		10	부족한	
2	thorough		11	~을 쌓다, 축적하다	
3	delay		12	고리	
4	tackle		13	조사	
5	analysis		14	널리 퍼진, 광범위한	
6	economize		15	빈번한, 잦은	
7	institution		16	심사숙고	
8	fault		17	불능, 마비	
9	bureaucratic		18	방해하다, 좌절시키다	

Are you Othello or Hamlet? Are you more likely to think — and act — too fast, or to get mired in analysis paralysis? ❶ Since / While jumping to conclusions and actions is a widespread fault in individuals, analysis paralysis is frequent in large, bureaucratic organizations that pile up studies and reports before taking any action or no action at all. ❷ On the contrary / On the one hand , being fast or lazy in our thinking allows us to economize on scarce and expensive mental resources, but the resulting solutions are often poor and ineffective. On the other hand, slow thinking and ❸ thorough / inattentive investigation are necessary to tackle complex business problems but the reflection process might create delays in decision-making and frustrate action. ❹ For / On organizations and institutions to be both effective and efficient, they need people who can overcome these challenges to solving complex business problems. These people must be as thorough as Hamlet and as action oriented as Othello, without jumping to conclusions like the ❺ later / latter or being stuck in a loop of endless questioning like the former.

*mired 수렁에 빠진

Are you Othello or Hamlet? Are you more likely to think — and act — too fast, or to get mired in analysis paralysis? While jumping to conclusions and actions ❶ _____ (be) a widespread fault in individuals, analysis paralysis is frequent in large, bureaucratic organizations that pile up studies and reports before ❷ _____ (take) any action or no action at all. On the one hand, being fast or lazy in our thinking allows us ❸ _____ (economize) on scarce and expensive mental resources, but the resulting solutions are often poor and ineffective. On the other hand, slow thinking and thorough investigation ❹ _____ (be) necessary to tackle complex business problems but the reflection process might create delays in decision-making and frustrate action. For organizations and institutions to be both effective and efficient, they need people who can overcome these challenges to ❺ _____ (solve) complex business problems. These people must be as thorough as Hamlet and as action oriented as Othello, without jumping to conclusions like the latter or being stuck in a loop of endless questioning like the former.

*mired 수렁에 빠진

Are you Othello or Hamlet? Are you more likely to think — and act — too fast, or to get mired in ❶ _____ _____ (분석 불능)? While jumping to conclusions and actions is a(n) ❷ _____ _____ _____ _____ (개인들에게서 널리 퍼진 잘못), analysis paralysis is frequent in large, bureaucratic organizations that pile up studies and reports before taking any action or no action at all. On the one hand, being fast or lazy in our thinking allows us to economize on scarce and expensive mental resources, but the resulting solutions are often poor and ineffective. On the other hand, slow thinking and thorough investigation are necessary to tackle complex business problems but the reflection process might create delays in decision-making and frustrate action. For organizations and institutions to be both effective and efficient, they need people who can overcome these challenges to solving complex business problems. These people must be as thorough as Hamlet and ❸ _____ _____ _____ _____ (~처럼 행동 지향적인) Othello, without jumping to conclusions like the latter or being ❹ _____ _____ _____ _____ _____ _____ (끊임없는 질문의 고리에 갇힌) like the former.

*mired 수렁에 빠진

❶ One day in the spring of 2011, San Francisco resident Tina Case finally agreed to allow her daughter Danielle to acquire a dog of her own if she promised to take care of it, and saved up the money necessary in order to bring one home. ❷ After receiving her permission, Danielle got busy, knocking on neighbors' doors to offer her pet- and babysitting services. ❸ Once she had saved up enough money, off she went to pick out a suitable dog. ❹ She found Koa, a golden retriever, who quickly settled into her new home. ❺ Koa set her mind to becoming an integral part of the family, offering companionship to the Cases who in turn provided her with plenty of opportunity to pursue more doggy pursuits. ❻ Soon Koa's favorite activity became chasing lizards in the backyard, and to Danielle's relief, the dog always let the reptiles go after providing them with a little bit of exercise. ❼ One day, Koa was on her usual lizard hunt when she became obsessed with exploring a raised spot of dirt alongside the house. ❽ Danielle came to investigate what her beloved dog was so intent on investigating, and to her great surprise, she found a nest full of wild baby rabbits. ❾ She rushed them to a neighbor who was also a vet, who diligently checked them over. ❿ After a thorough examination and clean bill of health, the baby rabbits were returned to the Case family along with instructions on how to care for them. ⓫ Danielle and her mom were prepared to take care of the baby rabbits themselves, but then Koa stepped in to help care for and nurture her discoveries. ⓬ It was an unusual situation, because many breeds of dogs would rather chase rabbits than nuzzle them, but she was determined to protect them. ⓭ After some initial hesitation, Tina Case decided to allow the dog to exercise her maternal instincts. ⓮ "Koa has never been a mother, so she thinks these are her little puppies," she said. ⓯ "They hop all over her and always find their way to the crook of her leg and find warmth and shelter."

*nuzzle 코로 문지르다[비비다] **maternal 모성의 ***crook (팔꿈치나 무릎 등의) 안쪽

❶ 2011년 봄의 어느 날, 샌프란시스코 주민 Tina Case는 개를 돌보겠다고 약속하고 개를 집으로 데려오기 위해 필요한 돈을 모은다면 딸 Danielle이 개를 사는 것을 허락하는 데 마침내 동의했다. ❷ 그녀의 허락을 받은 후, Danielle은 자신에게 반려동물과 아기 돌보는 일자리를 제공해 달라고 이웃집 문을 두드리느라 바빠졌다. ❸ 일단 돈을 충분히 모은 다음, 그녀는 적당한 개를 고르러 갔다. ❹ 그녀는 골든 리트리버 Koa를 발견했는데, 그 개는 금세 그녀의 새집에 정착했다. ❺ Koa는 Case 가족에게 동료애를 보여 주면서 그 가족의 없어서는 안 될 일부가 되는 데 전념하였으며, 이에 그 가족도 개와 관련된 더 많은 놀거리를 쫓아다닐 수 있는 많은 기회를 그녀에게 제공했다. ❻ 곧 Koa가 가장 좋아하는 활동은 뒷마당에서 도마뱀을 쫓아다니는 것이 되었고, Danielle에게는 다행히도, 그 개는 그 파충류에게 약간의 운동을 제공한 후에 그들을 항상 놓아주었다. ❼ 어느 날, Koa가 늘 하던 도마뱀 사냥을 하다가 그녀는 집 옆에 흙이 솟아오른 곳을 탐험하는 데 사로잡히게 되었다. ❽ Danielle은 자신이 사랑하는 개가 무엇을 그렇게 열중해서 조사하려고 했는지 살피러 왔는데, 매우 놀랍게도 그녀는 야생 새끼 토끼가 가득한 보금자리를 발견했다. ❾ 그녀는 그것들을 수의사이기도 한 이웃에게 급히 데려갔고, 그 이웃은 토끼들을 공들여 검사했다. ❿ 철저한 검사와 건강 증명서를 받은 후, 그 새끼 토끼들은 그들을 돌보는 방법에 대한 지침과 함께 Case 가족에게 돌려보내졌다. ⓫ Danielle과 그녀의 엄마는 새끼 토끼들을 직접 돌볼 준비가 되어 있었지만, 그때 Koa가 자신이 발견한 것들을 돌보고 양육하는 것을 돕기 위해 개입했다. ⓬ 많은 품종의 개들이 토끼를 코로 문지르기보다는 뒤쫓으려 하기 때문에 그것은 특이한 상황이었지만, 그녀는 토끼를 보호하기로 결심했다. ⓭ 처음에 약간 망설인 후에, Tina Case는 그 개가 자신의 모성 본능을 발휘하도록 허락하기로 결정했다. ⓮ "Koa는 엄마가 되어 본 적이 없어서, 이것들이 자신의 작은 강아지라고 생각하죠."라고 그녀가 말했다. ⓯ "그들은 그녀의 온몸 위를 뛰어다니고 항상 그녀의 다리 안쪽을 찾아가서 온기와 보호를 얻는답니다."

Word List

□ **resident** 주민 □ **permission** 허락 □ **babysit** 아이를 돌봐 주다 □ **suitable** 적당한 □ **golden retriever** 골든 리트리버(누런 털을 가진 영국 원산의 순한 조류사냥개) □ **settle** 정착하다 □ **integral** 없어서는 안 될 □ **companionship** 동료애, 우정 □ **pursue** 쫓아다니다 □ **reptile** 파충류 □ **lizard** 도마뱀 □ **obsessed with** ~에 사로잡힌 □ **investigate** 조사하다, 살피다 □ **intent on** ~에 열중하고 있는 □ **vet** 수의사 □ **clean bill of health** 건강 증명서 □ **step in** 개입하다 □ **nurture** 양육하다 □ **hesitation** 망설임 □ **shelter** 보호

1	obsessed with	10	도마뱀
2	hesitation	11	조사하다, 살피다
3	settle	12	쫓아다니다
4	companionship	13	양육하다
5	step in	14	수의사
6	babysit	15	없어서는 안 될
7	reptile	16	허락
8	intent on	17	적당한
9	resident	18	보호

• 유형 **1** 네모 안에서 옳은 어법·어휘를 고르시오.

One day in the spring of 2011, San Francisco resident Tina Case finally agreed to allow her daughter Danielle to acquire a dog of her own if she promised to take care of it, and saved up the money necessary in order to bring one home. After receiving her ❶ application/permission , Danielle got busy, knocking on neighbors' doors to offer her pet- and babysitting services. Once she had saved up enough money, off she went to pick out a suitable dog. She found Koa, a golden retriever, who quickly settled into her new home. Koa set her mind to becoming an integral part of the family, offering companionship to the Cases ❷ who/which in turn provided her with plenty of opportunity to pursue more doggy pursuits. Soon Koa's favorite activity became chasing lizards in the backyard, and to Danielle's relief, the dog always let the reptiles go after providing them with a little bit of exercise. One day, Koa was on her usual lizard hunt when she became obsessed with exploring a raised spot of dirt alongside the house. Danielle came to ❸ investigate/demonstrate what her beloved dog was so intent on investigating, and to her great surprise, she found a nest full of wild baby rabbits, She rushed them to a neighbor who was also a vet, who diligently ❹ checked/controlled them over. After a thorough examination and clean bill of health, the baby rabbits were returned to the Case family along with instructions on how to care for them. Danielle and her mom were prepared to take care of the baby rabbits themselves, but then Koa stepped in to help care for and ❺ nurture/separate her discoveries. It was an unusual situation, because many breeds of dogs would rather chase rabbits than nuzzle them, but she was determined to protect them. After some initial ❻ enthusiasm/hesitation , Tina Case decided to allow the dog to exercise her maternal instincts. "Koa has never been a mother, so she thinks these are her little puppies," she said. "They hop all over her and always find their way to the crook of her leg and find warmth and shelter."

*nuzzle 코로 문지르다[비비다]　**maternal 모성의　***crook (팔꿈치나 무릎 등의) 안쪽

One day in the spring of 2011, San Francisco resident Tina Case finally agreed to allow her daughter Danielle ❶ _____ (acquire) a dog of her own if she promised to take care of it, and saved up the money necessary in order to bring one home. After receiving her permission, Danielle got busy, ❷ _____ (knock) on neighbors' doors to offer her pet- and babysitting services. Once she had saved up enough money, off she went to pick out a suitable dog. She found Koa, a golden retriever, who quickly settled into her new home. Koa set her mind to ❸ _____ (become) an integral part of the family, offering companionship to the Cases who in turn provided her with plenty of opportunity to pursue more doggy pursuits. Soon Koa's favorite activity became chasing lizards in the backyard, and to Danielle's relief, the dog always let the reptiles go after ❹ _____ (provide) them with a little bit of exercise. One day, Koa was on her usual lizard hunt when she became obsessed with exploring a raised spot of dirt alongside the house. Danielle came to investigate what her beloved dog was so intent on investigating, and to her great surprise, she found a nest full of wild baby rabbits, She rushed them to a neighbor who was also a vet, who diligently checked them over. After a thorough examination and clean bill of health, the baby rabbits ❺ _____ (return) to the Case family along with instructions on how to care for them. Danielle and her mom were prepared to take care of the baby rabbits themselves, but then Koa stepped in to help care for and nurture her discoveries. It was an unusual situation, because many breeds of dogs would rather chase rabbits than nuzzle them, but she was determined to protect them. After some initial hesitation, Tina Case decided to allow the dog ❻ _____ (excercise) her maternal instincts. "Koa has never been a mother, so she thinks these are her little puppies," she said. "They hop all over her and always find their way to the crook of her leg and find warmth and shelter."

*nuzzle 코로 문지르다[비비다] **maternal 모성의 ***crook (팔꿈치나 무릎 등의) 안쪽

One day in the spring of 2011, San Francisco resident Tina Case finally agreed to allow her daughter Danielle to acquire a dog of her own if she promised to take care of it, and saved up the money necessary in order to bring one home. After receiving her permission, Danielle got busy, knocking on neighbors' doors to offer her pet- and babysitting services. Once she had saved up enough money, off she ❶ _____ _____ _____ _____ (~을 고르러 갔다) a suitable dog. She found Koa, a golden retriever, who quickly settled into her new home. Koa set her mind to becoming an integral part of the family, offering companionship to the Cases who in turn provided her with ❷ _____ _____ _____ (많은 기회) to pursue more doggy pursuits. Soon Koa's favorite activity became chasing lizards in the backyard, and to Danielle's relief, the dog always let the reptiles go after providing them with a little bit of exercise. One day, Koa was on her usual lizard hunt when she ❸ _____ _____ _____ (~에 사로잡히게 되었다) exploring a raised spot of dirt alongside the house. Danielle came to investigate what her beloved dog was ❹ _____ _____ _____ _____ (그렇게 열중해서 조사하는), and to her great surprise, she found a nest full of wild baby rabbits, She rushed them to a neighbor who was also a vet, who diligently checked them over. After a thorough examination and clean bill of health, the baby rabbits were returned to the Case family along with instructions on how to care for them. Danielle and her mom were prepared to take care of the baby rabbits themselves, but then Koa ❺ _____ _____ _____ _____ (~을 돕기 위해 개입했다) care for and nurture her discoveries. It was an unusual situation, because many breeds of dogs would rather chase rabbits than nuzzle them, but she ❻ _____ _____ _____ _____ (~을 보호하기로 결심했다) them. After some initial hesitation, Tina Case decided to allow the dog to exercise her maternal instincts. "Koa has never been a mother, so she thinks these are her little puppies," she said. "They hop all over her and always find their way to the crook of her leg and find warmth and shelter."

*nuzzle 코로 문지르다[비비다]   **maternal 모성의   ***crook (팔꿈치나 무릎 등의) 안쪽

❶ With the rise of the Internet, particularly in the light of on-line auctions, it is easier for customers to establish the lowest price of any product. ❷ However, the destabilizing effect this has on prices affects commodities more than brands. ❸ Indeed, it is interesting to note that it is the major brand leading organizations who have embraced e-commerce, not just to reduce transaction costs, but also to create added values for customers. ❹ For example, the travel specialists at Thomas Cook have used the Internet to make it easier for customers to contact them using whatever medium suits them best. ❺ This is a far cry from the traditional approach of viewing the customer as a passive entity to absorb whatever the supplier decides to do to them. ❻ Indeed, in the electronic age, given that customers today have as much information about suppliers as they have about them, the most powerful brands will be customer-centric. ❼ Successful companies will know the customer and will be the customer's advocate.

*a far cry from ~과 전혀 다른

❶ 인터넷의 출현과 함께, 특히 온라인 경매의 관점에서, 고객들이 모든 제품에 대해 가장 낮은 가격을 확인하기가 더 쉽다. ❷ 그러나 이것이 가격을 불안정하게 만드는 효과는 브랜드보다 상품에 더 많은 영향을 미친다. ❸ 실제로 거래 비용을 절감하기 위해서뿐만 아니라 고객을 위한 부가 가치를 창출하기 위해 전자 상거래를 수용해 온 이들이 바로 주요 브랜드 선도 기관이라는 점에 주목하는 것은 흥미롭다. ❹ 예를 들어, Thomas Cook 그룹의 여행 전문가들은 고객이 어떤 매체이든지 자신에게 가장 적합한 매체를 사용하여 그들에게 더 쉽게 연락할 수 있도록 인터넷을 사용해 왔다. ❺ 이것은 공급 회사가 고객에게 어떻게 하기로 결정하든지 간에 그것을 받아들이는 수동적인 존재로 고객을 바라보는 전통적인 접근법과는 전혀 다르다. ❻ 실제로, 전자 시대에는 공급 회사가 고객에 대해 가지고 있는 정보만큼이나 오늘날에는 고객도 공급 회사에 대한 정보를 가지고 있다는 점을 고려할 때 가장 강력한 브랜드는 고객 중심의 브랜드일 것이다. ❼ 성공적인 기업은 고객을 이해하고 있을 것이고 고객의 옹호자가 될 것이다.

Word List

□ rise 출현   □ in the light of ~의 관점에서, ~에 비춰 보면   □ auction 경매   □ establish 확인[확증]하다, 입증하다
□ destabilizing 불안정하게 만드는   □ affect 영향을 미치다   □ commodity 상품   □ e-commerce 전자 상거래, 제품이나 서비스의 온라인 매매   □ transaction 거래, 매매   □ added value 부가 가치   □ specialist 전문가   □ contact 연락하다   □ medium 매체
□ suit 적합하다   □ approach 접근법   □ entity 존재, 실체   □ absorb 받아들이다, 흡수하다   □ supplier 공급 회사
□ given that ~을 고려할 때   □ advocate 옹호자, 지지자

• Word Test

1	approach		10	상품
2	medium		11	옹호자, 지지자
3	specialist		12	연락하다
4	affect		13	공급 회사
5	rise		14	부가 가치
6	transaction		15	적합하다
7	absorb		16	존재, 실체
8	given that		17	경매
9	establish		18	불안정하게 만드는

With the rise of the Internet, particularly in the light of on-line auctions, it is easier for customers to establish the lowest price of any product. However, the ❶ stabilizing/destabilizing effect this has on prices affects commodities more than brands. Indeed, it is interesting to note that it is the major brand leading organizations who have embraced e-commerce, not just to reduce transaction costs, but also to create added values for customers. For example, the travel specialists at Thomas Cook have used the Internet to make ❷ it/them easier for customers to contact them using whatever medium suits them best. This is a far cry from the traditional approach of viewing the customer ❸ as/if a passive entity to absorb whatever the supplier decides to do to them. Indeed, in the electronic age, given that customers today have as much information about suppliers as they have about them, the most powerful brands will be customer-centric. Successful companies will know the customer and will be the customer's ❹ advocate/adversary .

*a far cry from ~과 전혀 다른

With the rise of the Internet, particularly in the light of on-line auctions, it is easier for customers to establish the lowest price of any product. However, the destabilizing effect this has on prices ❶ _____ (affect) commodities more than brands. Indeed, it is interesting to note that it is the major brand leading organizations who ❷ _____ (embrace) e-commerce, not just to reduce transaction costs, but also to create added values for customers. For example, the travel specialists at Thomas Cook ❸ _____ (use) the Internet to make it easier for customers to contact them ❹ _____ (use) whatever medium suits them best. This is a far cry from the traditional approach of viewing the customer as a passive entity to absorb whatever the supplier ❺ _____ (decide) to do to them. Indeed, in the electronic age, given that customers today have as much information about suppliers as they have about them, the most powerful brands will be customer-centric. Successful companies will know the customer and will be the customer's advocate.

*a far cry from ~과 전혀 다른

With the rise of the Internet, particularly ❶ _____ _____ _____ _____ (~의 관점에서) on-line auctions, it is easier for customers to establish the lowest price of any product. However, the destabilizing effect this has on prices ❷ _____ _____ _____ _____ _____ (브랜드들보다 상품들에 더 많은 영향을 미친다). Indeed, it is interesting to note that it is the major brand leading organizations who have embraced e-commerce, not just to reduce transaction costs, but also to create added values for customers. For example, the travel specialists at Thomas Cook have used the Internet to make it easier for customers to contact them using whatever medium suits them best. This is a far cry from the traditional approach of viewing the customer ❸ _____ _____ _____ _____ _____ _____ (~을 받아들이는 수동적인 존재로) whatever the supplier decides to do to them. Indeed, in the electronic age, ❹ _____ _____ (~을 고려할 때) customers today have as much information about suppliers as they have about them, the most powerful brands will be customer-centric. Successful companies will know the customer and will be the customer's advocate.

*a far cry from ~과 전혀 다른

❶ In order to be meaningful, the claim concerning wholeness and coherence must have a cognitive function, which may be related to economy of time as well as to the communication itself. ❷ Irrelevant elements take up valuable time and disturb comprehension, as the reader assumes at the outset that they have a function and tries to interpret the whole in such a way that they fit in. ❸ It is a convention of non-fiction to contain only relevant elements, and traditional views of literature have transferred this convention to literary fiction. ❹ We crave logical coherence and relevance because we do not want to waste time on something that is unnecessary. ❺ However, fictional literature leaves room for other priorities, for we read not only to receive information but also for entertainment or to pass the time. ❻ Although entertainment and the passing of time are products of the cognitive content, the reader often regards reading primarily as a way of passing the time and not as cognition. ❼ Consequently, independent of coherence and relevance, he is ready to accept every aspect of the work that makes time pass in an agreeable or at least meaningful way.

*crave 갈망하다

❶ 통일성과 일관성에 관한 주장이 의미를 가지기 위해서는 인지적 기능을 가져야 하는데, 그 기능은 내용 전달 자체뿐만 아니라 시간의 절약과도 관련이 있을 수도 있다. ❷ 상관없는 요소들이 귀중한 시간을 잡아먹고 이해를 방해하는데 이는 독자가 처음에 그것들이 기능을 가지고 있다고 가정하고 전체를 그것들이 들어맞는 그런 방식으로 해석하려고 노력하기 때문이다. ❸ 관련 있는 요소만 담는 것이 논픽션의 관례인데, 문학에 대한 전통적인 견해는 이 관례를 문학적 허구에 이입했다. ❹ 우리는 불필요한 것에 시간을 낭비하고 싶지 않기 때문에 논리적 일관성과 관련성을 갈망한다. ❺ 하지만 허구의 문학은 다른 우선 사항들을 위한 여지를 남겨 두는데, 왜냐하면 우리가 정보를 얻기 위해서뿐 아니라 오락이나 시간을 보내기 위해서도 읽기 때문이다. ❻ 비록 오락이나 시간을 보내는 것이 인지적 내용의 산물이긴 하지만, 독자는 흔히 독서를 주로 시간을 보내는 방법으로 여기지 인지로 여기지는 않는다. ❼ 결과적으로 일관성 및 관련성과는 관계없이 그는 기분 좋은 혹은 적어도 의미 있는 방식으로 시간을 보내게 해 주는 작품의 모든 측면을 받아들일 준비가 되어 있다.

Word List
□ claim 주장 □ wholeness 통일성, 일체성 □ coherence 일관성 □ cognitive 인지적인 □ function 기능 □ irrelevant 상관없는 □ element 요소 □ disturb 방해하다 □ comprehension 이해 □ assume 가정하다 □ at the outset 처음에 □ interpret 해석하다 □ convention 관례, 관습 □ relevance 관련성 □ priority 우선 사항, 우선권 □ primarily 주로 □ independent of ~과는 관계없이 □ aspect 측면 □ agreeable 기분 좋은, 쾌활한

• Word Test

1	priority		10	관련성
2	convention		11	주로
3	coherence		12	해석하다
4	at the outset		13	기분 좋은, 쾌활한
5	comprehension		14	상관없는
6	aspect		15	가정하다
7	element		16	방해하다
8	claim		17	통일성, 일체성
9	function		18	인지적인

In order to be meaningful, the claim concerning wholeness and coherence must have a cognitive function, which may be related to economy of time as well as to the communication itself. Irrelevant elements take ❶ in / up valuable time and disturb comprehension, as the reader assumes at the outset that they have a function and tries to interpret the whole in such a way ❷ how / that they fit in. It is a convention of non-fiction to contain only relevant elements, and traditional views of literature have transferred this convention to literary fiction. We crave logical coherence and relevance because we do not want to waste time on something ❸ what / that is unnecessary. However, fictional literature leaves room for other priorities, for we read not only to receive information but also for entertainment or to pass the time. ❹ Unless / Although entertainment and the passing of time are products of the cognitive content, the reader often regards reading primarily as a way of passing the time and not as cognition. Consequently, independent of coherence and relevance, he is ready to accept every ❺ aspect / aspects of the work that makes time pass in an agreeable or at least meaningful way.   *crave 갈망하다

In order to be meaningful, the claim concerning wholeness and coherence must have a cognitive function, which may be related to economy of time as well as to the communication itself. Irrelevant elements take up valuable time and disturb comprehension, as the reader assumes at the outset that they have a function and tries to interpret the whole in such a way that they fit in. It is a convention of non-fiction ❶ _____ (contain) only relevant elements, and traditional views of literature ❷ _____ (transfer) this convention to literary fiction. We crave logical coherence and relevance because we do not want to waste time on something that is unnecessary. However, fictional literature leaves room for other priorities, for we read not only to receive information but also for entertainment or to pass the time. Although entertainment and the passing of time ❸ _____ (be) products of the cognitive content, the reader often ❹ _____ (regard) reading primarily as a way of passing the time and not as cognition. Consequently, independent of coherence and relevance, he is ready to accept every aspect of the work that ❺ _____ (make) time pass in an agreeable or at least meaningful way.   *crave 갈망하다

In order to be meaningful, the claim concerning wholeness and coherence must have a cognitive function, which may be ❶ _____ _____ _____ _____ _____ (시간의 절약과 관련된) as well as to the communication itself. Irrelevant elements take up valuable time and disturb comprehension, as the reader assumes ❷ _____ _____ _____ (처음에) that they have a function and tries to interpret the whole in such a way that they fit in. It is a convention of non-fiction to contain only relevant elements, and traditional views of literature have transferred this convention to literary fiction. We crave logical coherence and relevance because we do not want to waste time on something that is unnecessary. However, fictional literature ❸ _____ _____ _____ _____ _____ (다른 우선 사항들을 위한 여지를 남겨 두다), for we read not only to receive information but also for entertainment or to pass the time. Although entertainment and the passing of time are products of the cognitive content, the reader often regards reading primarily as a way of passing the time and not as cognition. Consequently, ❹ _____ _____ _____ _____ _____ (일관성 및 관련성과는 관계없이), he is ready to accept every aspect of the work that makes time pass in an agreeable or at least meaningful way.   *crave 갈망하다

❶ Ten years ago, when search engines were powered by data mining (rather than by machine learning), if a person searched for "gourmet restaurants," then for "clothing," his or her search for the latter would be independent of his or her search for the former. ❷ Both times, a search engine would collect as much information as possible, then provide the inquirer options — something like a digital phone book or catalog of a subject. ❸ But contemporary search engines are guided by models informed by observed human behavior. ❹ If a person searches for "gourmet restaurants," then searches for "clothing," he or she may be presented with designer clothing rather than more affordable alternatives. ❺ Designer clothing may be what the searcher is after. ❻ But there is a difference between choosing from a range of options and taking an action — in this case, making a purchase; in other cases, adopting a political or philosophical position or ideology — without ever knowing what the initial range of possibilities or implications was, entrusting a machine to preemptively shape the options.

*gourmet (음식이) 고급인   **entrust 위임하다   ***preemptively 우선적으로

❶ 10년 전에 검색 엔진이 (기계 학습에 의해서라기보다는) 데이터 마이닝에 의해 작동되었을 때 어떤 사람이 '고급 식당'을 검색한 다음 '옷'을 검색하면, 후자에 대한 그 사람의 검색은 전자에 대한 그 사람의 검색과는 무관한 것이었다. ❷ 두 번 모두, 검색 엔진은 가능한 한 많은 정보를 수집하고, 그런 다음 문의자에게 디지털 전화번호부 혹은 주제별 카탈로그와 같은 선택 사항을 제공하곤 했다. ❸ 하지만 요즘의 검색 엔진은 관찰된 사람의 행동에 의해 정보를 받은 모형에 의해 처리된다. ❹ 어떤 사람이 '고급 식당'을 검색한 다음 '옷'을 검색하면, 그 사람은 더 저렴한 가격의 대안보다는 오히려 유명 디자이너 의류를 제시받을 수도 있다. ❺ 유명 디자이너 의류가 검색자가 찾는 것일 수도 있다. ❻ 그러나 다양한 선택 사항 중에서 고르는 것과, 기계에게 우선적으로 선택 사항을 만들도록 위임하면서 초기 범위의 가능성이나 함의가 무엇인지 전혀 알지 못한 채로 행동을 취하는 것 — 이번 경우에는 구매하는 것이지만, 다른 경우에는 정치적 혹은 철학적 입장이나 이데올로기를 받아들이는 것일 수도 있는데 — 사이에는 차이가 있다.

Word List

□ data mining 데이터 마이닝(대규모 자료를 토대로 새로운 정보를 찾아내는 것)   □ the latter 후자   □ independent of ~과 무관한
□ the former 전자   □ inquirer 문의자   □ subject 주제   □ contemporary 요즘의   □ affordable (가격 등이) 저렴한, 알맞은
□ alternative 대안   □ designer clothing 유명 디자이너 의류   □ adopt 받아들이다, 채택하다   □ ideology 이데올로기
□ initial 초기의, 처음의   □ range 범위   □ implication 함의, 영향

• Word Test

1	ideology	8	함의, 영향
2	subject	9	~과 무관한
3	designer clothing	10	받아들이다, 채택하다
4	affordable	11	요즘의
5	range	12	초기의, 처음의
6	the latter	13	문의자
7	the former	14	대안

Ten years ago, when search engines were powered by data mining (rather than by machine learning), if a person searched for "gourmet restaurants," then for "clothing," his or her search for the latter would be ❶ dependent/independent of his or her search for the ❷ formal/former. Both times, a search engine would collect as much information as possible, then provide the inquirer options — something like a digital phone book or catalog of a subject. But ❸ temporary/contemporary search engines are guided by models informed by observed human behavior. If a person searches for "gourmet restaurants," then searches for "clothing," he or she may be presented with designer clothing rather than more affordable alternatives. Designer clothing may be ❹ what/that the searcher is after. But there is a difference between choosing from a range of options and taking an action — in this case, making a purchase; in other cases, ❺ adopting/admiring a political or philosophical position or ideology — without ever knowing what the initial range of possibilities or implications was, entrusting a machine to preemptively shape the options.

*gourmet (음식이) 고급인 **entrust 위임하다 ***preemptively 우선적으로

Ten years ago, when search engines ❶ _____ (power) by data mining (rather than by machine learning), if a person ❷ _____ (search) for "gourmet restaurants," then for "clothing," his or her search for the latter would be independent of his or her search for the former. Both times, a search engine would collect as much information as possible, then provide the inquirer options — something like a digital phone book or catalog of a subject. But contemporary search engines are guided by models ❸ _____ (inform) by observed human behavior. If a person searches for "gourmet restaurants," then searches for "clothing," he or she may ❹ _____ (present) with designer clothing rather than more affordable alternatives. Designer clothing may be what the searcher is after. But there is a difference between choosing from a range of options and ❺ _____ (take) an action — in this case, making a purchase; in other cases, adopting a political or philosophical position or ideology — without ever ❻ _____ (know) what the initial range of possibilities or implications was, entrusting a machine to preemptively shape the options.

*gourmet (음식이) 고급인 **entrust 위임하다 ***preemptively 우선적으로

Ten years ago, when search engines were powered by data mining (rather than by machine learning), if a person searched for "gourmet restaurants," then for "clothing," his or her search for the latter would be independent of his or her search for the former. Both times, a search engine would ❶ _____ _____ _____ _____ _____ (가능한 한 많은 정보를 수집하다), then provide the inquirer options — something like a digital phone book or catalog of a subject. But contemporary search engines are guided by models informed ❷ _____ _____ _____ _____ (관찰된 사람의 행동에 의해). If a person searches for "gourmet restaurants," then searches for "clothing," he or she may be presented with designer clothing rather than more affordable alternatives. Designer clothing may be what the searcher is after. But there is a difference between ❸ _____ _____ _____ _____ _____ (다양한 선택 사항들 중에서 고르기) and taking an action — in this case, making a purchase; in other cases, adopting a political or philosophical position or ideology — ❹ _____ _____ _____ (전혀 알지 못한 채) what the initial range of possibilities or implications was, entrusting a machine to preemptively shape the options.

*gourmet (음식이) 고급인 **entrust 위임하다 ***preemptively 우선적으로

❶ Throughout nature, the process of natural selection seldom favours organisms that lack the capacity to disperse to new areas. ❷ Even among sedentary plants, evolution has found ways for species to spread from one place to another, 'hitchhiking' on animals or using the wind to scatter their seeds and pollen. ❸ Almost all species have some mechanism for exploratory movement — and the longest of these movements are often vital for the longterm survival of populations, for a whole suite of reasons. ❹ In the absence of long-distance dispersal, populations will invariably become threatened by inbreeding, as local gene pools become more and more impoverished over time through the lack of mixing with individuals elsewhere. ❺ Dispersal can also be essential in allowing populations to persist when environmental conditions change, or when population densities within a local area grow to the point that competition for resources limits survival chances.

*disperse (새 지역으로) 분산하다, 흩어지다 **sedentary 정착하여 사는

❶ 자연계를 통틀어 자연 선택의 과정이 새 지역으로 분산하는 능력이 결여된 유기체에 유리한 경우는 드물다. ❷ 정착하여 사는 식물 사이에서까지도 진화를 통해 종들은 씨앗과 꽃가루를 퍼뜨리기 위해 동물에 '편승하면서' 혹은 바람을 이용하면서 한곳에서 다른 곳으로 퍼지는 방법을 알아냈다. ❸ 거의 모든 종은 탐사 이동을 위한 어떤 기제를 가지고 있는데, 보통 이 이동 중 가장 장거리인 것이 모든 일련의 이유로 개체군의 장기 생존에 매우 중요하다. ❹ 장거리 분산이 일어나지 않는 경우, 개체군은 예외 없이 동계 교배로 멸종의 위기에 처하게 될 것인데, 그 이유는 다른 곳에 사는 개체와의 교배의 결여 때문에 국지적인 유전자 풀이 시간이 지나면서 점점 더 빈약해지기 때문이다. ❺ 환경의 조건이 변할 때, 혹은 자원 경쟁이 생존 가능성을 제한할 정도로 국지적인 영역 안에서 개체군의 밀도가 증가할 때, 분산은 또한 개체군이 존속하도록 하는 데 필수적일 수도 있다.

Word List

□ **natural selection** 자연 선택, 자연 도태 □ **favour** (~에) 유리하다, 총애하다 □ **organism** 유기체 □ **lack** 없다, 결여되다
□ **hitchhike** 편승하다, 얻어 타고 이동하다 □ **scatter** 퍼뜨리다 □ **seed** 씨앗 □ **pollen** 꽃가루, 화분
□ **mechanism** (생물체 내에서 특정한 기능을 수행하는) 기제, 구조 □ **a suite of** 일련의, 한 벌의 □ **invariably** 예외 없이, 변함없이
□ **threatened** 멸종의 위기에 처한 □ **inbreeding** 동계 교배(계통이 같은 생물끼리의 교배), 근친 교배 □ **gene pool** 유전자 풀, 유전자 공급원
□ **impoverish** 빈약하게 하다, 저하시키다 □ **essential** 필수적인, 극히 중요한 □ **persist** 계속되다 □ **density** 밀도

• Word Test

1	seed		9	꽃가루, 화분	
2	invariably		10	밀도	
3	organism		11	멸종의 위기에 처한	
4	persist		12	퍼뜨리다	
5	mechanism		13	없다, 결여되다	
6	impoverish		14	일련의, 한 벌의	
7	natural selection		15	필수적인, 극히 중요한	
8	hitchhike		16	(~에) 유리하다, 총애하다	

Throughout nature, the process of natural selection ❶ `often / seldom` favours organisms that lack the capacity to disperse to new areas. Even among sedentary plants, evolution has found ways for species to spread from one place to another, 'hitchhiking' on animals or using the wind to scatter their seeds and pollen. Almost all species have some mechanism for ❷ `explanatory / exploratory` movement — and the longest of these movements are often vital for the longterm survival of populations, for a whole suite of reasons. In the absence of long-distance dispersal, populations will ❸ `abruptly / invariably` become threatened by inbreeding, as local gene pools become more and more ❹ `prosperous / impoverished` over time through the lack of mixing with individuals elsewhere. Dispersal can also be essential in allowing populations to persist when environmental conditions change, or when population densities within a local area grow to the point ❺ `that / which` competition for resources limits survival chances.

*disperse (새 지역으로) 분산하다, 흩어지다   **sedentary 정착하여 사는

Throughout nature, the process of natural selection seldom ❶ _____ (favour) organisms that lack the capacity to disperse to new areas. Even among sedentary plants, evolution ❷ _____ (find) ways for species to spread from one place to another, 'hitchhiking' on animals or using the wind ❸ _____ (scatter) their seeds and pollen. Almost all species have some mechanism for exploratory movement — and the longest of these movements are often vital for the longterm survival of populations, for a whole suite of reasons. In the absence of long-distance dispersal, populations will invariably become threatened by inbreeding, as local gene pools become more and more impoverished over time through the lack of mixing with individuals elsewhere. Dispersal can also be essential in allowing populations to persist when environmental conditions ❹ _____ (change), or when population densities within a local area grow to the point that competition for resources ❺ _____ (limit) survival chances.

*disperse (새 지역으로) 분산하다, 흩어지다   **sedentary 정착하여 사는

Throughout nature, the process of natural selection seldom favours organisms that ❶ _____ _____ _____ _____ (~하는 능력이 결여되다) disperse to new areas. Even among sedentary plants, evolution has found ways for species to ❷ _____ _____ _____ _____ _____ (한 곳에서 다른 곳으로 퍼지다), 'hitchhiking' on animals or using the wind to scatter their seeds and pollen. Almost all species have some mechanism for exploratory movement — and the longest of these movements are often vital for the longterm survival of populations, ❸ _____ _____ _____ _____ _____ _____ (모든 일련의 이유들로). In the absence of long-distance dispersal, populations will invariably become threatened by inbreeding, as local gene pools become more and more impoverished over time through the lack of mixing with individuals elsewhere. Dispersal can also be essential in allowing populations to persist when environmental conditions change, or when ❹ _____ _____ _____ _____ _____ (국지적인 영역 안에서 개체군의 밀도들) grow to the point that competition for resources limits survival chances.

*disperse (새 지역으로) 분산하다, 흩어지다   **sedentary 정착하여 사는

❶ It was three days before Christmas. ❷ My sister Sherry and I were so excited. ❸ Every time another commercial came on TV, we ran to our lengthy Christmas list and added another toy or game. ❹ Finally Mom had enough, and she sat us down and gave us "the speech." ❺ She asked us if we had considered anyone besides ourselves. ❻ "Did either of you buy a gift for your little brother, your grandmother or your father?" she asked. ❼ I felt ashamed. ❽ Sherry and I made a list of our family, pooled our meager allowance, and walked to the dollar store. ❾ At home we wrapped and labeled each gift, chatting and laughing together. ❿ Our French poodle, Jacques, was right up under us the whole time. ⓫ Finally Sherry and I looked down, really noticing him for the first time. ⓬ "The dog!" we exclaimed together. ⓭ We had forgotten to put the dog on our Christmas list. ⓮ "What do you think he would like?" I asked Sherry. ⓯ "What about a bone?" she whispered with her hand to her mouth so Jacques wouldn't hear. ⓰ Out we went again to the meat market to get a bone. ⓱ We wrapped this gift and placed the bone under the tree. ⓲ The next day as we piled into the car for church, we noticed our damp, drippy dog standing in the rain. ⓳ "Can't we let him into the warm house?" I begged. ⓴ "He has a doghouse," Mom reminded us, but we could tell she thought he was pitiful too. ㉑ "Pleeeeeaaaaase," we begged together. ㉒ "OK." Mom caved in. ㉓ Sherry hurried to undo his chain and lead him in the front door. ㉔ A few hours later, when we got home, we didn't expect the scene that greeted us. ㉕ I stood in the front doorway and gasped. ㉖ There was ripped gift paper scattered all over the living room floor. ㉗ Sherry and I rushed to the tree to count the presents. ㉘ It looked as if all of them were still there. ㉙ Mom looked for the dog. ㉚ "Come and see," she shouted. ㉛ Jacques was crouched under a bed busily chewing his bone. ㉜ We couldn't believe it. ㉝ He had opened only one present... *his present*. ㉞ How did he know which one to open? ㉟ "He must have read the gift tag and knew it was his!" I exclaimed. ㊱ Our dog could read! ㊲ Our dog was the smartest dog I'd ever heard of. ㊳ I started planning TV shows for him. ㊴ Maybe we could get him on *America's Funniest Home Videos* or *Good Morning America* because our dog could read! ㊵ Mom waited till after Christmas to break the news. ㊶ It was quite a blow when she told me, "You know, he probably just smelled the bone." ㊷ I felt as deflated as last year's birthday balloons. ㊸ I guess there will be no *America's Funniest Home Videos* prize in our future. ㊹ But still, I think there will never be a Christmas to beat that one. ㊺ I still smile when I think that for two whole days I was sure we owned the smartest dog on earth.

*meager 얼마 안 되는 **pile 우르르 가다 ***crouch (몸을) 웅크리다

❶ 크리스마스 3일 전이었다. ❷ 여동생 Sherry와 나는 매우 신이 났다. ❸ TV에 다른 광고가 나올 때마다 우리는 우리의 긴 크리스마스 선물 리스트로 달려가 다른 장난감이나 게임을 추가했다. ❹ 마침내 엄마는 참을 만큼 참으셨고, 우리를 앉히고 '연설'을 하셨다. ❺ 그녀는 우리가 우리 자신 외에 다른 사람을 고려했는지 물으셨다. ❻ "너희 둘 중 누구라도 남동생, 할머니, 혹은 아버지를 위한 선물을 샀니?" 그녀가 물으셨다. ❼ 나는 부끄러움을 느꼈다. ❽ Sherry와 나는 우리 가족의 리스트를 작성하고 우리의 얼마 안 되는 용돈을 모아 염가 판매점으로 걸어갔다. ❾ 집에서 우리는 함께 수다를 떨고 웃으며 각각의 선물을 포장하고 이름표를 붙였다. ❿ 우리의 프랑스 푸들 Jacques는 내내 우리 바로 밑에 있었다. ⓫ 마침내 Sherry와 나는 아래를 내려다보았고 처음으로 진정 그를 알아차렸다. ⓬ "개!" 우리는 함께 외쳤다. ⓭ 우리는 개를 우리의 크리스마스 선물 리스트에 넣는 것을 잊었던 것이었다. ⓮ "그가 무엇을 원할 것 같니?" 나는 Sherry에게 물었다. ⓯ "뼈는 어때?" 그녀는 Jacques가 듣지 않도록 손을 입에 대고 속삭였다. ⓰ 우리는 뼈를 사기 위해 다시 나가 정육점에 갔다. ⓱ 우리는 이 선물을 포장해서 그 뼈를 나무 아래에 놓았다. ⓲ 다음 날 우리가 교회로 가기 위해 우르르 차에 탔을 때, 우리는 우리의 개가 축축하게 젖어, 물방울을 떨어뜨리며, 빗속에 서 있는 것을 알아차렸다. ⓳ "그를 따뜻한 집 안에 들어오게 하면 안 돼요?" 나는 간청했다. ⓴ "그는 개집이 있어." 엄마가 우리에게 상기시키셨지만 우리는 그녀도 그가 불쌍하다고 생각한다는 것을 알 수 있었다. ㉑ "제...바...알...요." 우리는 함께 간청했다. ㉒ "알았어." 엄마가 항복하셨다. ㉓ Sherry는 서둘러 그의 사슬을 풀고 그를 현관문 안으로 이끌었다. ㉔ 몇 시간 후, 우리가 집에 도착했을 때 우리는 우리를 맞이한 장면을 예상하지 못했다. ㉕ 나는 현관 출입구에 서 있었고, 말을 제대로 하지 못했다. ㉖ 거실 바닥에는 찢어진 선물 포장지가 여기저기 사방으로 흩어져 있었다. ㉗ Sherry와 나는 선물을 세기 위해 나무로 달려갔다. ㉘ 그것들을 모두 여전히 거기 있는 것처럼 보였다. ㉙ 엄마는 개를 찾고 계셨다. ㉚ "이리 와서 봐."라고 그녀가 소리쳤다. ㉛ Jacques는 침대 밑에 웅크린 채 바쁘게 자신의 뼈를 씹고 있었다. ㉜ 우리는 그것을 믿을 수 없었다. ㉝ 그는 단 하나의 선물만, '자신의 선물'만 풀어 놓았던 것이었다. ㉞ 그는 어떤 것을 풀어야 하는지 어떻게 알았던 것일까? ㉟ 나는 "그는 틀림없이 선물 태그를 읽었을 것이고 그래서 그것이 자신의 것이라는 것을 알았어!"라고 외쳤다. ㊱ 우리 개는 글을 읽을 줄 알아! ㊲ 우리 개는 내가 여태껏 들어 본 개 중에서 가장 똑똑해. ㊳ 나는 그를 위해 TV 쇼를 계획하기 시작했다. ㊴ 우리 개는 글을 읽을 수 있으므로 어쩌면 America's Funniest Home Videos나 Good Morning America에 그를 데려갈 수도 있을 거야! ㊵ 엄마는 나쁜 소식을 전하기 위해 크리스마스가 끝날 때까지 기다리셨다. ㊶ 그녀가 나에게 "있잖아, 그는 아마도 단지 뼈 냄새를 맡았을 거야."라고 말씀하셨을 때 그것은 상당한 타격이었다. ㊷ 나는 작년의 생일 풍선처럼 바람이 빠진[위축된] 기분이 들었다. ㊸ 나는 우리의 미래에 America's Funniest Home Videos상이 없을 것이라고 생각한다. ㊹ 하지만 그럼에도 불구하고, 나는 그 크리스마스를 능가할 수 있는 크리스마스는 결코 없을 거라고 생각한다. ㊺ 나는 이틀 내내 우리가 지구상에서 가장 똑똑한 개를 가졌다고 확신했던 것을 생각할 때면 여전히 웃음이 나온다.

• Word Test

1	greet		9	축축한
2	drippy		10	사방으로 흐트러뜨리다
3	rip		11	말을 제대로 못 하다, 숨이 턱 막히다
4	commercial		12	포장하다, 싸다
5	whisper		13	풀다, 열다
6	label		14	바람이 빠진, 위축된, 기가 꺾인
7	blow		15	외치다
8	allowance		16	모으다

• 유형 1 네모 안에서 옳은 어법·어휘를 고르시오.

It was three days before Christmas. My sister Sherry and I were so excited. Every time another commercial came on TV, we ran to our lengthy Christmas list and added another toy or game. Finally Mom had enough, and she sat us down and gave us "the speech." She asked us if we had considered anyone ❶ besides / despite ourselves. "Did either of you buy a gift for your little brother, your grandmother or your father?" she asked. I felt ❷ humble / ashamed . Sherry and I made a list of our family, pooled our meager ❸ allowance / assignment , and walked to the dollar store. At home we wrapped and labeled each gift, chatting and laughing together. Our French poodle, Jacques, was right up under us the whole time. Finally Sherry and I looked down, really noticing him for the first time. "The dog!" we exclaimed together. We had forgotten to put the dog on our Christmas list. "What do you think he would like?" I asked Sherry. "What about a bone?" she whispered with her hand to her mouth so Jacques wouldn't hear. Out we went again to the meat market to get a bone. We wrapped this gift and placed the bone under the tree. The next day as we piled into the car for church, we noticed our damp, drippy dog standing in the rain. "Can't we let him into the warm house?" I begged. "He has a doghouse," Mom reminded us, but we could tell she thought he was pitiful too. "Pleeeeeaaaaase," we begged together. "OK." Mom caved in. Sherry hurried to ❹ redo / undo his chain and lead him in the front door. A few hours later, when we got home, we didn't expect the scene that greeted us. I stood in the front doorway and gasped. There was ripped gift paper scattered all over the living room floor. Sherry and I rushed to the tree to count the presents. It looked as if all of them were still there. Mom looked for the dog. "Come and see," she shouted. Jacques was ❺ crouched / shrugged under a bed busily chewing his bone. We couldn't believe it. He had opened only one present... *his present*. How did he know which one to open? "He must have read the gift tag and knew it was his!" I exclaimed. Our dog could read! Our dog was the smartest dog I'd ever heard of. I started planning TV shows for him. Maybe we could get him on *America's Funniest Home Videos* or *Good Morning America* because our dog could read! Mom waited ❻ till / over after Christmas to break the news. It was quite a blow when she told me, "You know, he probably just smelled the bone." I felt as ❼ deflated / inflated as last year's birthday balloons. I guess there will be no *America's Funniest Home Videos* prize in our future. But still, I think there will never be a Christmas to beat that one. I still smile when I think that for two whole days I was sure we owned the smartest dog on earth.

*meager 얼마 안 되는 **pile 우르르 가다 ***crouch (몸을) 웅크리다

It was three days before Christmas. My sister Sherry and I ❶ _____ (be) so excited. Every time another commercial came on TV, we ran to our lengthy Christmas list and added another toy or game. Finally Mom had enough, and she sat us down and gave us "the speech." She asked us if we ❷ _____ (consider) anyone besides ourselves. "Did either of you buy a gift for your little brother, your grandmother or your father?" she asked. I felt ashamed. Sherry and I made a list of our family, pooled our meager allowance, and walked to the dollar store. At home we wrapped and labeled each gift, chatting and laughing together. Our French poodle, Jacques, was right up under us the whole time. Finally Sherry and I looked down, really noticing him for the first time. "The dog!" we exclaimed together. We ❸ _____ (forget) to put the dog on our Christmas list. "What do you think he would like?" I asked Sherry. "What about a bone?" she whispered with her hand to her mouth so Jacques wouldn't hear. Out we went again to the meat market to get a bone. We wrapped this gift and placed the bone under the tree. The next day as we piled into the car for church, we noticed our damp, drippy dog ❹ _____ (stand) in the rain. "Can't we let him into the warm house?" I begged. "He has a doghouse," Mom reminded us, but we could tell she thought he was pitiful too. "Pleeeeeaaaaase," we begged together. "OK." Mom caved in. Sherry hurried to undo his chain and lead him in the front door. A few hours later, when we got home, we didn't expect the scene that greeted us. I stood in the front doorway and gasped. There was ripped gift paper ❺ _____ (scatter) all over the living room floor. Sherry and I rushed to the tree to count the presents. It looked as if all of them were still there. Mom looked for the dog. "Come and see," she shouted. Jacques was crouched under a bed busily ❻ _____ (chew) his bone. We couldn't believe it. He had opened only one present... *his present.* How did he know which one to open? "He must have read the gift tag and knew it was his!" I exclaimed. Our dog could read! Our dog was the smartest dog I'd ever heard of. I started planning TV shows for him. Maybe we could get him on *America's Funniest Home Videos* or *Good Morning America* because our dog could read! Mom waited till after Christmas to break the news. It was quite a blow when she told me, "You know, he probably just ❼ _____ (smell) the bone." I felt as deflated as last year's birthday balloons. I guess there will be no *America's Funniest Home Videos* prize in our future. But still, I think there will never be a Christmas to beat that one. I still smile when I think that for two whole days I was sure we owned the smartest dog on earth.

*meager 얼마 안 되는   **pile 우르르 가다   ***crouch (몸을) 웅크리다

114

It was three days before Christmas. My sister Sherry and I were so excited. Every time another commercial came on TV, we ran to our lengthy Christmas list and added another toy or game. Finally Mom had enough, and she sat us down and gave us "the speech." She asked us if we had considered anyone besides ourselves. "Did either of you buy a gift for your little brother, your grandmother or your father?" she asked. I felt ashamed. Sherry and I made a list of our family, pooled our meager allowance, and walked to the dollar store. At home we wrapped and labeled each gift, ❶ _____ _____ _____ _____ (함께 수다를 떨고 웃으며). Our French poodle, Jacques, was right up under us the whole time. Finally Sherry and I looked down, ❷ _____ _____ _____ _____ _____ _____ _____ (처음으로 진정 그를 알아차렸다). "The dog!" we exclaimed together. We had forgotten to put the dog on our Christmas list. "What do you think he would like?" I asked Sherry. "What about a bone?" she whispered with her hand to her mouth so Jacques wouldn't hear. Out we went again to the meat market to get a bone. We wrapped this gift and placed the bone under the tree. The next day as we piled into the car for church, we noticed our damp, drippy dog standing in the rain. "Can't we let him into the warm house?" I begged. "He has a doghouse," Mom reminded us, but we could tell she thought he was pitiful too. "Pleeeeeaaaaase," we begged together. "OK." Mom ❸ _____ _____ (항복했다). Sherry hurried to undo his chain and lead him in the front door. A few hours later, when we got home, we didn't expect the scene that greeted us. I stood in the front doorway and gasped. There was ripped gift paper scattered all over the living room floor. Sherry and I rushed to the tree to count the presents. It looked ❹ _____ _____ _____ _____ _____ _____ (그것들 모두 여전히 거기 있는 것처럼). Mom looked for the dog. "Come and see," she shouted. Jacques was crouched under a bed busily chewing his bone. We couldn't believe it. He had opened only one present... *his present*. How did he know which one to open? "He ❺ _____ _____ _____ _____ _____ _____ (선물 태그를 읽었음이 틀림없다) and knew it was his!" I exclaimed. Our dog could read! Our dog was the smartest dog I'd ever heard of. I started planning TV shows for him. Maybe we could get him on *America's Funniest Home Videos* or *Good Morning America* because our dog could read! Mom waited till after Christmas to ❻ _____ _____ _____ (나쁜 소식을 전하다). It was quite a blow when she told me, "You know, he probably just smelled the bone." I felt as deflated as last year's birthday balloons. I guess there will be no *America's Funniest Home Videos* prize in our future. But still, I think there will never be a Christmas to beat that one. I still smile when I think that for two whole days I was sure we owned the smartest dog on earth.

*meager 얼마 안 되는 **pile 우르르 가다 ***crouch (몸을) 웅크리다

01 12강 1번

다음 글의 제목으로 가장 적절한 것은?

Perhaps one of the greatest challenges is to find the will, the courage, and the undefeatable attitude to persist. To challenge oneself to exceed the comfort zone and to push beyond one's self-perceived outer limits is to practice with firm faith and devotion. Reaching beyond anything done previously, always knocking on that door of a new record, a farther reach than ever reached before — what Daniel Coyle called "reachfulness" — is what "peaking" involves. *Reachfulness* is the constant pounding in one's head to stretch and stretch and stretch to that new limit, no matter how minuscule. It is a new high. The role of the teacher, coach, or mentor is to keep tipping the learner forward from passivity toward reachable action. It is a continuous cycle that maintains and sustains skillfulness, yet also scores a plus within the learner for the new mark that has been reached. This requires constant dissatisfaction with the current specs or data and a yearning to do one's personal best, each and every outing. It is exhausting on the one hand, and on the other it is thrilling and truly invigorated by the tiny, barely noticeable successes that keep the learner moving ever forward.

*minuscule 미미한 **invigorate 고무하다

① Coaching: Seeking Extraordinary Excellence from Learners
② Practice Makes Perfect: Strive to Develop Expertise
③ Design Defining Moments That Inspire and Sustain Your Growth
④ Seek Challenges to Go Beyond Your Limit and Reach a New Peak
⑤ Success Breeds Success: The Importance of Providing Winning Experiences

02 12강 2번

밑줄 친 Peto's paradox가 다음 글에서 의미하는 바로 가장 적절한 것은?

Every time that a cell multiplies, there is risk of an error at the time when the DNA is copied. Consequently, as multicellular animals increased in complexity and size and the lifespan got longer and longer, the risk of cancer was expected to grow in direct proportion; the larger and longer-lived the animal, the higher the number of mitosis occurring in its body, and therefore the higher the chance of DNA damage to occur. However, this turned out not to be the case: this is the 'Peto's paradox', which gets its name from a study published in 1995 by Richard Peto and his colleagues. In this experiment, a large group of mice of different ages were exposed to topical application of a carcinogen. The rate of appearance by epithelial tumours was related to the duration of exposure to the chemical but not to the mouse's age. That is, it was the time of exposure to the carcinogen agent that dictated the risk of developing cancer and not the age of the exposed mouse — and neither the span of survival after the exposure. This study demonstrated that, against the then current wisdom, increased lifespan in itself can be irrelevant as far as increase in cancer risk is concerned.

*mitosis 체세포 분열 **carcinogen 발암 물질
***epithelial tumour 상피 종양

① harmful effects of environmental hormones on tumors
② cancer as a disease of old age due to accumulated mutations
③ the lack of correlation between body size or age and cancer risk
④ higher resistance to cancer in smaller and shorter-lived organisms
⑤ cancer risks associated with radiation from diagnostic imaging procedures

03 12강 3번

다음 글의 밑줄 친 부분 중, 문맥상 낱말의 쓰임이 적절하지 않은 것은?

A large repertoire and proficient song performance can only be acquired by an individual bird that grew up in a secure nest, was subsequently unencumbered by disease and parasites, and — in possession of sharp faculties, memory capacity, foraging ability, and predator watchfulness — engaged in hundreds of hours of successful singing practice. Whatever ① assists the post-hatching growth of a bird's system of song nuclei, and whatever keeps the bird from attending to and practicing song is later evident as deficits in the size and perfection of its mature song repertoire. This makes a large repertoire of complex song a direct causal reflection of an individual's ② successful passage through a demanding and varied obstacle course. The more demanding the performance to be acquired, the ③ more comprehensive a measure of an individual's personal history and qualities lies implicit in the perfected, mature song performance. An individual's song proficiency tells its audience, in a way ④ impossible to counterfeit, that the singer comes from, as it were, "a good background." Potential mates and rivals thus do well to take a singer displaying mastery and virtuosity ⑤ seriously.

*unencumbered 방해가 없는 **counterfeit 위조하다 ***virtuosity 기교

04 12강 4번

글의 흐름으로 보아, 주어진 문장이 들어가기에 가장 적절한 곳은?

On the other hand, slow thinking and thorough investigation are necessary to tackle complex business problems but the reflection process might create delays in decision-making and frustrate action.

Are you Othello or Hamlet? Are you more likely to think — and act — too fast, or to get mired in analysis paralysis? (①) While jumping to conclusions and actions is a widespread fault in individuals, analysis paralysis is frequent in large, bureaucratic organizations that pile up studies and reports before taking any action or no action at all. (②) On the one hand, being fast or lazy in our thinking allows us to economize on scarce and expensive mental resources, but the resulting solutions are often poor and ineffective. (③) For organizations and institutions to be both effective and efficient, they need people who can overcome these challenges to solving complex business problems. (④) These people must be as thorough as Hamlet and as action oriented as Othello, without jumping to conclusions like the latter or being stuck in a loop of endless questioning like the former. (⑤) Conventional wisdom suggests these people should be chosen for their intelligence, experience, and expertise, but these qualities might not be enough: a systematic problem-solving method is also necessary.

*mired 수렁에 빠진

[5~7] 다음 글을 읽고, 물음에 답하시오.

(A)

One day in the spring of 2011, San Francisco resident Tina Case finally agreed to allow her daughter Danielle to acquire a dog of her own if she promised to take care of it, and saved up the money necessary in order to bring one home. After receiving her permission, Danielle got busy, knocking on neighbors' doors to offer (a) her pet- and babysitting services.

(B)

Danielle came to investigate what (b) her beloved dog was so intent on investigating, and to her great surprise, she found a nest full of wild baby rabbits. (c) She rushed them to a neighbor who was also a vet, who diligently checked them over. After a thorough examination and clean bill of health, the baby rabbits were returned to the Case family along with instructions on how to care for them. Danielle and her mom were prepared to take care of the baby rabbits themselves, but then Koa stepped in to help care for and nurture her discoveries.

(C)

It was an unusual situation, because many breeds of dogs would rather chase rabbits than nuzzle them, but she was determined to protect them. After some initial hesitation, Tina Case decided to allow the dog to exercise her maternal instincts. "Koa has never been a mother, so she thinks these are her little puppies," (d) she said. "They hop all over her and always find their way to the crook of her leg and find warmth and shelter."

*nuzzle 코로 문지르다[비비다] **maternal 모성의
***crook (팔꿈치나 무릎 등의) 안쪽

(D)

Once (e) she had saved up enough money, off she went to pick out a suitable dog. She found Koa, a golden retriever, who quickly settled into her new home. Koa set her mind to becoming an integral part of the family, offering companionship to the Cases who in turn provided her with plenty of opportunity to pursue more doggy pursuits. Soon Koa's favorite activity became chasing lizards in the backyard, and to Danielle's relief, the dog always let the reptiles go after providing them with a little bit of exercise. One day, Koa was on her usual lizard hunt when she became obsessed with exploring a raised spot of dirt alongside the house.

05

주어진 글 (A)에 이어질 내용을 순서에 맞게 배열한 것으로 가장 적절한 것은?

① (B) – (D) – (C)
② (C) – (B) – (D)
③ (C) – (D) – (B)
④ (D) – (B) – (C)
⑤ (D) – (C) – (B)

06

밑줄 친 (a)~(e) 중에서 가리키는 대상이 나머지 넷과 다른 것은?

① (a)　② (b)　③ (c)　④ (d)　⑤ (e)

07

윗글에 관한 내용으로 적절하지 않은 것은?

① Danielle은 돈을 벌기 위해 이웃들에게 일자리 제공을 부탁했다.
② Danielle이 Koa보다 먼저 집 주변의 솟아오른 흙더미를 발견했다.
③ Case 가족들은 토끼들을 발견한 후, 수의사인 이웃에게 데려가 건강 검사를 받았다.
④ 다른 품종의 개들은 토끼를 뒤쫓지만, Koa는 토끼를 보호하며 돌봤다.
⑤ Koa는 도마뱀을 쫓아다니기는 했으나 항상 도마뱀을 놓아주었다.

08 12강 8번

다음 글의 밑줄 친 부분 중, 어법상 틀린 것은?

With the rise of the Internet, particularly in the light of on-line auctions, it is easier for customers to establish the lowest price of any product. However, the destabilizing effect this has on prices ① affects commodities more than brands. Indeed, it is interesting to note that it is the major brand leading organizations who have embraced e-commerce, not just to reduce transaction costs, but also ② to create added values for customers. For example, the travel specialists at Thomas Cook have used the Internet to ③ make easier for customers to contact them using whatever medium suits them best. This is a far cry from the traditional approach of viewing the customer as a passive entity to absorb ④ whatever the supplier decides to do to them. Indeed, in the electronic age, given that customers today have as much information about suppliers as they have about ⑤ them, the most powerful brands will be customer-centric. Successful companies will know the customer and will be the customer's advocate.

*a far cry from ~과 전혀 다른

09 12강 9번

주어진 글 다음에 이어질 글의 순서로 가장 적절한 것은?

In order to be meaningful, the claim concerning wholeness and coherence must have a cognitive function, which may be related to economy of time as well as to the communication itself.

(A) Although entertainment and the passing of time are products of the cognitive content, the reader often regards reading primarily as a way of passing the time and not as cognition. Consequently, independent of coherence and relevance, he is ready to accept every aspect of the work that makes time pass in an agreeable or at least meaningful way.

(B) We crave logical coherence and relevance because we do not want to waste time on something that is unnecessary. However, fictional literature leaves room for other priorities, for we read not only to receive information but also for entertainment or to pass the time.

(C) Irrelevant elements take up valuable time and disturb comprehension, as the reader assumes at the outset that they have a function and tries to interpret the whole in such a way that they fit in. It is a convention of non-fiction to contain only relevant elements, and traditional views of literature have transferred this convention to literary fiction.

*crave 갈망하다

① (A) – (C) – (B) ② (B) – (A) – (C)
③ (B) – (C) – (A) ④ (C) – (A) – (B)
⑤ (C) – (B) – (A)

10 〔12강 10번〕

다음 글에서 전체 흐름과 관계 <u>없는</u> 문장은?

Ten years ago, when search engines were powered by data mining (rather than by machine learning), if a person searched for "gourmet restaurants," then for "clothing," his or her search for the latter would be independent of his or her search for the former. ① Both times, a search engine would collect as much information as possible, then provide the inquirer options — something like a digital phone book or catalog of a subject. ② But contemporary search engines are guided by models informed by observed human behavior. ③ What search engines often do once they have collected information about a user's habits is to create a profile of them, which helps the search engine decide which ads to target that user with. ④ If a person searches for "gourmet restaurants," then searches for "clothing," he or she may be presented with designer clothing rather than more affordable alternatives. ⑤ Designer clothing may be what the searcher is after. But there is a difference between choosing from a range of options and taking an action — in this case, making a purchase; in other cases, adopting a political or philosophical position or ideology — without ever knowing what the initial range of possibilities or implications was, entrusting a machine to preemptively shape the options.

*gourmet (음식이) 고급인   **entrust 위임하다
***preemptively 우선적으로

11 〔12강 11번〕

다음 글의 주제로 가장 적절한 것은?

Throughout nature, the process of natural selection seldom favours organisms that lack the capacity to disperse to new areas. Even among sedentary plants, evolution has found ways for species to spread from one place to another, 'hitchhiking' on animals or using the wind to scatter their seeds and pollen. Almost all species have some mechanism for exploratory movement — and the longest of these movements are often vital for the longterm survival of populations, for a whole suite of reasons. In the absence of long-distance dispersal, populations will invariably become threatened by inbreeding, as local gene pools become more and more impoverished over time through the lack of mixing with individuals elsewhere. Dispersal can also be essential in allowing populations to persist when environmental conditions change, or when population densities within a local area grow to the point that competition for resources limits survival chances.

*disperse (새 지역으로) 분산하다, 흩어지다   **sedentary 정착하여 사는

① reasons why birds are critical to life on Earth
② roles of animals in varied seed dispersal
③ the importance of dispersal for the survival of plants and animals
④ the necessity of estimating dispersal for endangered bird management
⑤ the settlement of plants and animals following long-distance dispersal

〔12강 12~14번〕

[12~14] 다음 글을 읽고, 물음에 답하시오.

(A)

It was three days before Christmas. My sister Sherry and I were so excited. Every time another commercial came on TV, we ran to our lengthy Christmas list and added another toy or game. Finally Mom had enough, and (a) she sat us down and gave us "the speech." She asked us if we had considered anyone besides ourselves. "Did either of you buy a gift for your little brother, your grandmother or your father?" she asked.

(B)

"He must have read the gift tag and knew it was his!" I exclaimed. Our dog could read! Our dog was the smartest dog I'd ever heard of. I started planning TV shows for him. Maybe we could get him on *America's Funniest Home Videos* or *Good Morning America* because our dog could read! Mom waited till after Christmas to break the news. It was quite a blow when (b) <u>she</u> told me, "You know, he probably just smelled the bone." I felt as deflated as last year's birthday balloons. I guess there will be no *America's Funniest Home Videos* prize in our future. But still, I think there will never be a Christmas to beat that one. I still smile when I think that for two whole days I was sure we owned the smartest dog on earth.

(C)

I felt ashamed. Sherry and I made a list of our family, pooled our meager allowance, and walked to the dollar store. At home we wrapped and labeled each gift, chatting and laughing together. Our French poodle, Jacques, was right up under us the whole time. Finally Sherry and I looked down, really noticing him for the first time. "The dog!" we exclaimed together. We had forgotten to put the dog on our Christmas list. "What do you think he would like?" I asked Sherry. "What about a bone?" she whispered with (c) <u>her</u> hand to her mouth so Jacques wouldn't hear. Out we went again to the meat market to get a bone. We wrapped this gift and placed the bone under the tree. The next day as we piled into the car for church, we noticed our damp, drippy dog standing in the rain.

*meager 얼마 안 되는 **pile 우르르 가다

(D)

"Can't we let him into the warm house?" I begged. "He has a doghouse," Mom reminded us, but we could tell she thought he was pitiful too. "Pleeeeeeaaaaase," we begged together.

"OK." (d) <u>She</u> caved in. Sherry hurried to undo his chain and lead him in the front door. A few hours later, when we got home, we didn't expect the scene that greeted us. I stood in the front doorway and gasped. There was ripped gift paper scattered all over the living room floor. Sherry and I rushed to the tree to count the presents. It looked as if all of them were still there. Mom looked for the dog. "Come and see," (e) <u>she</u> shouted. Jacques was crouched under a bed busily chewing his bone. We couldn't believe it. He had opened only one present... *his present*. How did he know which one to open?

*crouch (몸을) 웅크리다

12

주어진 글 (A)에 이어질 내용을 순서에 맞게 배열한 것으로 가장 적절한 것은?

① (B) – (D) – (C) ② (C) – (B) – (D)
③ (C) – (D) – (B) ④ (D) – (B) – (C)
⑤ (D) – (C) – (B)

13

밑줄 친 (a)~(e) 중에서 가리키는 대상이 나머지 넷과 <u>다른</u> 것은?

① (a) ② (b) ③ (c) ④ (d) ⑤ (e)

14

윗글에 관한 내용으로 적절하지 <u>않은</u> 것은?

① 엄마는 크리스마스 선물을 받는 데에만 신경쓰는 Sherry와 'I'의 태도를 한동안 참아오셨다.
② 'I'는 Jacques가 글을 읽는 능력이 있다고 여겨 텔레비전 프로그램에 출연시킬 생각까지 했다.
③ Sherry와 'I'는 성탄 선물을 사기 위해 가족의 선물 리스트를 작성해 염가 판매점으로 갔다.
④ Sherry와 'I'는 정육점에 들러 Jacques의 선물을 따로 산 뒤 포장해 나무 아래에 두었다.
⑤ 'I'가 집으로 돌아왔을 때 선물들이 모두 제자리에 없고 선물 포장지들이 찢어진 채 나뒹굴었다.

15 12강 1번

다음 글의 밑줄 친 부분 중, 어법상 틀린 것은?

Perhaps one of the greatest challenges is to find the will, the courage, and the undefeatable attitude to persist. To challenge oneself to exceed the comfort zone and ① to push beyond one's self-perceived outer limits is to practice with firm faith and devotion. Reaching beyond anything done previously, always knocking on that door of a new record, a farther reach than ever reached before — what Daniel Coyle called "reachfulness" — is ② what "peaking" involves. *Reachfulness* is the constant pounding in one's head to stretch and stretch and stretch to that new limit, no matter ③ how minuscule. It is a new high. The role of the teacher, coach, or mentor is to keep tipping the learner forward from passivity toward reachable action. It is a continuous cycle that maintains and sustains skillfulness, yet also scores a plus within the learner for the new mark that has ④ reached. This requires constant dissatisfaction with the current specs or data and a yearning to do one's personal best, each and every outing. It is exhausting on the one hand, and on the other it is thrilling and truly invigorated by the tiny, barely noticeable successes ⑤ that keep the learner moving ever forward.

*minuscule 미미한   **invigorate 고무하다

16 12강 2번

다음 빈칸에 들어갈 말로 가장 적절한 것은?

Every time that a cell multiplies, there is risk of an error at the time when the DNA is copied. Consequently, as multicellular animals increased in complexity and size and the lifespan got longer and longer, the risk of cancer was expected to grow in direct proportion; the larger and longer-lived the animal, the higher the number of mitosis occurring in its body, and therefore the higher the chance of DNA damage to occur. However, this turned out not to be the case as large dimensions and longer life do not necessarily mean increased risk of cancer: this is the 'Peto's paradox', which gets its name from a study published in 1995 by Richard Peto and his colleagues. In this experiment, a large group of mice of different ages were exposed to topical application of a carcinogen. The rate of appearance by epithelial tumours was related to the duration of exposure to the chemical but not to the mouse's age. That is, it was the time of exposure to the carcinogen agent that dictated the risk of developing cancer and not the age of the exposed mouse — and neither the span of survival after the exposure. This study demonstrated that, against the then current wisdom, _____ as far as increase in cancer risk is concerned.

*mitosis 체세포 분열   **carcinogen 발암 물질
***epithelial tumour 상피 종양

① an organism's body size plays a key role
② the growth rate of each individual is critical
③ increased lifespan in itself can be irrelevant
④ the genetic makeup of each individual is negligible
⑤ the duration of exposure to the carcinogen could be insignificant

17 [12강] 3번

다음 글에서 전체 흐름과 관계 <u>없는</u> 문장은?

A large repertoire and proficient song performance can only be acquired by an individual bird that grew up in a secure nest, was subsequently unencumbered by disease and parasites, and — in possession of sharp faculties, memory capacity, foraging ability, and predator watchfulness — engaged in hundreds of hours of successful singing practice. ① Whatever impairs the post-hatching growth of a bird's system of song nuclei, and whatever keeps the bird from attending to and practicing song is later evident as deficits in the size and perfection of its mature song repertoire. ② This makes a large repertoire of complex song a direct causal reflection of an individual's successful passage through a demanding and varied obstacle course. ③ The more demanding the performance to be acquired, the more comprehensive a measure of an individual's personal history and qualities lies implicit in the perfected, mature song performance. ④ In fact, several species of urban-dwelling birds have modified their songs in response to human-generated noise. ⑤ An individual's song proficiency tells its audience, in a way impossible to counterfeit, that the singer comes from, as it were, "a good background." Potential mates and rivals thus do well to take a singer displaying mastery and virtuosity seriously.

*unencumbered 방해가 없는　**counterfeit 위조하다
***virtuosity 기교

18 [12강] 4번

다음 빈칸에 들어갈 말로 가장 적절한 것은?

Are you Othello or Hamlet? Are you more likely to think — and act — too fast, or to get mired in analysis paralysis? While jumping to conclusions and actions is a widespread fault in individuals, analysis paralysis is frequent in large, bureaucratic organizations that pile up studies and reports before taking any action or no action at all. On the one hand, being fast or lazy in our thinking allows us to economize on scarce and expensive mental resources, but the resulting solutions are often poor and ineffective. On the other hand, slow thinking and thorough investigation are necessary to tackle complex business problems but the reflection process might create delays in decision-making and frustrate action. For organizations and institutions to be both effective and efficient, they need people who can overcome these challenges to solving complex business problems. These people must be _____, without jumping to conclusions like the latter or being stuck in a loop of endless questioning like the former.

*mired 수렁에 빠진

① as careful as Othello and as quick as Hamlet
② as reckless as Hamlet and as hasty as Othello
③ as fast as Othello and as energetic as Hamlet
④ as thorough as Hamlet and as action oriented as Othello
⑤ as thorough as Hamlet and as thought oriented as Othello

19 12강 8번

다음 글의 내용과 일치하지 <u>않는</u> 것은?

With the rise of the Internet, particularly in the light of on-line auctions, it is easier for customers to establish the lowest price of any product. However, the destabilizing effect this has on prices affects commodities more than brands. Indeed, it is interesting to note that it is the major brand leading organizations who have embraced e-commerce, not just to reduce transaction costs, but also to create added values for customers. For example, the travel specialists at Thomas Cook have used the Internet to make it easier for customers to contact them using whatever medium suits them best. This is a far cry from the traditional approach of viewing the customer as a passive entity to absorb whatever the supplier decides to do to them. Indeed, in the electronic age, given that customers today have as much information about suppliers as they have about them, the most powerful brands will be customer-centric. Successful companies will know the customer and will be the customer's advocate.

*a far cry from ~과 전혀 다른

① 인터넷으로 인한 가격 불안정의 효과는 브랜드보다 상품에 더 많은 영향을 끼친다.
② 주요 브랜드는 비용 절감 및 고객을 위한 부가가치 창출을 위해 전자상거래를 수용해 왔다.
③ 전통적인 관점에서 고객은 공급 회사의 결정을 수용할 수밖에 없는 수동적인 존재였다.
④ 전자 시대가 도래했음에도 공급자의 고객 정보는 고객의 공급자 정보를 여전히 앞선다.
⑤ 강력하고 성공한 브랜드는 고객 중심으로 고객을 이해하며 고객의 옹호자가 될 것이다.

20 12강 9번

다음 글의 밑줄 친 부분 중, 문맥상 낱말의 쓰임이 적절하지 <u>않은</u> 것은?

In order to be meaningful, the claim concerning wholeness and coherence must have a cognitive function, which may be related to ① <u>economy</u> of time as well as to the communication itself. Irrelevant elements take up valuable time and ② <u>disturb</u> comprehension, as the reader assumes at the outset that they have a function and tries to interpret the whole in such a way that they fit in. It is a convention of ③ <u>fiction</u> to contain only relevant elements, and traditional views of literature have transferred this convention to literary fiction. We crave logical coherence and relevance because we do not want to waste time on something that is unnecessary. However, fictional literature ④ <u>leaves</u> room for other priorities, for we read not only to receive information but also for entertainment or to pass the time. Although entertainment and the passing of time are products of the cognitive content, the reader often regards reading primarily as a way of passing the time and not as cognition. Consequently, ⑤ <u>independent</u> of coherence and relevance, he is ready to accept every aspect of the work that makes time pass in an agreeable or at least meaningful way.

*crave 갈망하다

21 12강 10번

다음 빈칸에 들어갈 말로 가장 적절한 것은?

Ten years ago, when search engines were powered by data mining (rather than by machine learning), if a person searched for "gourmet restaurants," then for "clothing," his or her search for the latter would be independent of his or her search for the former. Both times, a search engine would collect as much information as possible, then provide the inquirer options — something like a digital phone book or catalog of a subject. But contemporary search engines are guided by models informed by _____. If a person searches for "gourmet restaurants," then searches for "clothing," he or she may be presented with designer clothing rather than more affordable alternatives. Designer clothing may be what the searcher is after. But there is a difference between choosing from a range of options and taking an action — in this case, making a purchase; in other cases, adopting a political or philosophical position or ideology — without ever knowing what the initial range of possibilities or implications was, entrusting a machine to preemptively shape the options.

*gourmet (음식이) 고급인   **entrust 위임하다
***preemptively 우선적으로

① personal shopping histories
② observed human behavior
③ location-dependent results
④ restaurant selection preference
⑤ big data from public authorities

22 12강 11번

다음 글에서 전체 흐름과 관계 없는 문장은?

Throughout nature, the process of natural selection seldom favours organisms that lack the capacity to disperse to new areas. ① Even among sedentary plants, evolution has found ways for species to spread from one place to another, 'hitchhiking' on animals or using the wind to scatter their seeds and pollen. ② Almost all species have some mechanism for exploratory movement — and the longest of these movements are often vital for the long-term survival of populations, for a whole suite of reasons. ③ In the absence of long-distance dispersal, populations will invariably become threatened by inbreeding, as local gene pools become more and more impoverished over time through the lack of mixing with individuals elsewhere. ④ However, an increase in distance in seed dispersal does not always translate into benefits for plant recruitment, and even when it does, the relationship can be quite complex. ⑤ Dispersal can also be essential in allowing populations to persist when environmental conditions change, or when population densities within a local area grow to the point that competition for resources limits survival chances.

*disperse (새 지역으로) 분산하다, 흩어지다   **sedentary 정착하여 사는

Perhaps one of the greatest challenges is to find the will, the courage, and the undefeatable attitude to persist. To challenge oneself to exceed the comfort zone and to push beyond one's self-perceived outer limits is to practice with firm faith and devotion. Reaching beyond anything done previously, always knocking on that door of a new record, a farther reach than ever reached before — what Daniel Coyle called "reachfulness" — (A) be what "peaking" involves. *Reachfulness* is the constant pounding in one's head to stretch and stretch and stretch to that new limit, no matter how minuscule. It is a new high. The role of the teacher, coach, or mentor is to keep tipping the learner forward from passivity toward reachable action. It is a continuous cycle that maintains and sustains skillfulness, yet also (B) scored a plus within the learner for the new mark that has been reached. This requires constant dissatisfaction with the current specs or data and a yearning to do one's personal best, each and every outing. It is exhausting on the one hand, and on the other it is thrilling and truly (C) invigorating by the tiny, barely noticeable successes that keep the learner moving ever forward.

*minuscule 미미한 **invigorate 고무하다

23 윗글의 밑줄 친 부분을 어법상 알맞은 형태로 고쳐 쓰시오.

(A) be　　　　　→ _____

(B) scored　　　→ _____

(C) invigorating → _____

24 윗글의 밑줄 친 This가 가리키는 것을 우리말로 쓰시오.
(65글자 내외)

_____

_____

Every time that a cell multiplies, there ① is risk of an error at the time when the DNA is copied. Consequently, as multicellular animals increased in complexity and size and the _____ got longer and longer, the risk of cancer was expected to grow in direct proportion; the larger and longer-lived the animal, the higher the number of mitosis occurring in its body, and therefore ② high the chance of DNA damage to occur. However, this turned out not to be the case as large dimensions and longer life do not ③ necessary mean increased risk of cancer: this is the 'Peto's paradox', which gets its name from a study published in 1995 by Richard Peto and his colleagues. In this experiment, a large group of mice of different ages were exposed to topical application of a carcinogen. The rate of appearance by epithelial tumours ④ was related to the duration of exposure to the chemical but not to the mouse's age. That is, it was the time of exposure to the carcinogen agent ⑤ that dictated the risk of developing cancer and not the age of the exposed mouse — and neither the span of survival after the exposure. This study demonstrated that, against the then current wisdom, increased _____ in itself can be irrelevant as far as increase in cancer risk is concerned.

*mitosis 체세포 분열 **carcinogen 발암 물질
***epithelial tumour 상피 종양

25 윗글의 밑줄 친 부분 중, 어법상 **틀린** 것을 2개 찾아 그 번호를 쓰고 고쳐 쓰시오.

(1) _____ → _____

(2) _____ → _____

26 윗글의 빈칸에 공통으로 들어갈 단어를 영영 뜻풀이를 참고하여 쓰시오. (단, 주어진 글자로 시작할 것)

the length of time that a person or animal lives or is expected to live

l_____

A large repertoire and proficient song performance can only be acquired by an individual bird that grew up in a secure nest, was subsequently unencumbered by disease and parasites, and — in possession of sharp faculties, memory capacity, foraging ability, and predator watchfulness — engaged in hundreds of hours of successful singing practice. Whatever impairs the post-hatching growth of a bird's system of song nuclei, and whatever keeps the bird from attending to and practicing song is later evident as deficits in the size and perfection of its mature song repertoire. This makes a large repertoire of complex song a direct causal reflection of an individua's successful passage through a demanding and varied obstacle course. The more demanding the performance to be acquired, the more comprehensive a measure of an individual's personal history and qualities lies implicit in the perfected, mature song performance. An individual's song proficiency tells its audience, in a way impossible to counterfeit, that the singer comes from, as it were, "a good background." Potential mates and rivals thus do well to take a singer displaying mastery and virtuosity seriously.

*unencumbered 방해가 없는 **counterfeit 위조하다 ***virtuosity 기교

27 윗글의 밑줄 친 a good background가 문맥상 의미하는 바를 찾아 우리말로 쓰시오. (40자 이내)

_____

_____

고난도

28 윗글의 내용을 한 문장으로 요약하려고 한다. 보기 의 단어를 순서대로 배열하여 문장을 완성하시오.

> 보기   developmental / provides / represents / the entire / process / proof

A bird's song proficiency _____ _____ _____ _____ _____ of the singer, and _____ _____ of all-around individual quality and competence.

Are you Othello or Hamlet? Are you more likely to think — and act — too fast, or to get mired in analysis paralysis? While jumping to conclusions and actions is a widespread fault in individuals, analysis paralysis is frequent in large, bureaucratic organizations that pile up studies and reports before taking any action or no action at all. On the one hand, being fast or lazy in our thinking allows us to economize on scarce and expensive mental resources, but the resulting solutions are often poor and ineffective. On the other hand, slow thinking and thorough investigation are necessary to tackle complex business problems but the reflection process might create delays in decision-making and frustrate action. For organizations and institutions to be both effective and efficient, they need people who can overcome these challenges to solving complex business problems. These people must be as thorough as Hamlet and as action oriented as Othello, without jumping to conclusions like (A) the latter or being stuck in a loop of endless questioning like (B) the former.

*mired 수렁에 빠진

29 윗글의 밑줄 친 (A)와 (B)가 가리키는 것을 영어로 쓰시오.

(A) _____

(B) _____

30 윗글에서 다음 질문에 대한 답을 찾아 우리말로 쓰시오. (60글자 내외)

Q: What type of people do we need to solve complex business problems according to the passage?

A: _____

_____

One day in the spring of 2011, San Francisco resident Tina Case finally agreed to allow her daughter Danielle (A) acquiring a dog of her own if she promised to take care of it, and saved up the money necessary in order to bring one home. After receiving her permission, Danielle got busy, knocking on neighbors' doors to offer her pet- and babysitting services. Once she had saved up enough money, off she went to pick out a suitable dog. She found Koa, a golden retriever, who quickly settled into her new home.

Koa set her mind to becoming an integral part of the family, offering companionship to the Cases who in turn provided her with plenty of opportunity to pursue more doggy pursuits. Soon Koa's favorite activity became chasing lizards in the backyard, and to Danielle's relief, the dog always let the reptiles go after providing them with a little bit of exercise.

One day, Koa was on her usual lizard hunt when she became obsessed with (B) exploration a raised spot of dirt alongside the house. Danielle came to investigate what her beloved dog was so intent on investigating, and to her great surprise, she found a nest full of wild baby rabbits, She rushed them to a neighbor who was also a vet, who diligently checked (C) over them. After a thorough examination and clean bill of health, the baby rabbits were returned to the Case family along with instructions on how to care for them.

Danielle and her mom were prepared to take care of the baby rabbits themselves, but then Koa stepped in to help care for and nurture her discoveries. It was an unusual situation, because many breeds of dogs would rather (D) to chase rabbits than nuzzle them, but she was determined to protect them. After some initial hesitation, Tina Case decided to allow the dog to exercise her maternal instincts. "Koa has never been a mother, so she thinks these are her little puppies," she said. "They hop all over her and always find their way to the crook of her leg and find warmth and shelter."

*nuzzle 코로 문지르다[비비다]   **maternal 모성의
***crook (팔꿈치나 무릎 등의) 안쪽

고난도

31 윗글의 밑줄 친 부분 (A)~(D)를 어법상 알맞은 형태로 고쳐 쓰시오.

(A) acquiring → _____

(B) exploration → _____

(C) over them → _____

(D) to chase → _____

32 윗글의 밑줄 친 to exercise her maternal instincts 가 드러난 구체적인 내용을 찾아 우리말로 쓰시오. (45글자 내외)

_____

_____

With the rise of the Internet, particularly in the light of on-line auctions, it is easier for customers to establish the lowest price of any product. However, (A) 이것이 가격에게 주는 불안정한 효과는 affects commodities more than brands. Indeed, it is interesting to note that it is the major brand leading organizations who have embraced e-commerce, not just to reduce transaction costs, but also to create added values for ① them. For example, the travel specialists at Thomas Cook have used the Internet (B) 고객들이 그들과 더 쉽게 연락할 수 있도록 using whatever medium suits ② them best. This is a far cry from the traditional approach of viewing the customer as a passive entity to absorb whatever the supplier decides to do to ③ them. Indeed, in the electronic age, given that customers today have as much information about suppliers as ④ they have about them, the most powerful brands will be customer-centric. Successful companies will know ⑤ them and will be the customers' advocate.

*a far cry from ~과 전혀 다른

33 윗글의 밑줄 친 (A), (B)의 우리말 의미와 일치하도록 보기 의 단어를 순서대로 배열하여 각각의 문장을 완성하시오.

보기
(A) effect / on / this / the destabilizing / has / prices
(B) easier / to make / for customers / to / it / contact / them

(A) _____
(B) _____

34 윗글의 밑줄 친 ①~⑤ 중 가리키는 것이 나머지 넷과 다른 것을 고르고, 그것이 가리키는 것을 찾아 쓰시오.

_____ → _____

In order to be meaningful, the claim concerning wholeness and coherence must have a ① cognitive function, which may be related to economy of time as well as to the communication itself. Irrelevant elements take up valuable time and ② disturb comprehension, as the reader assumes at the outset that they have a function and tries to interpret the whole in such a way that they fit in. It is a convention of ③ non-fiction to contain only relevant elements, and traditional views of literature have transferred this convention to literary fiction. We crave logical coherence and relevance because we do not want to waste time on something that is unnecessary. However, fictional literature leaves room for other _____, for we read not only to receive information but also for entertainment or to pass the time. Although entertainment and the passing of time are products of the cognitive content, the reader often regards reading primarily as ④ a way of passing the time and not as cognition. Consequently, ⑤ dependent of coherence and relevance, he is ready to accept every aspect of the work that makes time pass in an agreeable or at least meaningful way.

*crave 갈망하다

35 윗글의 밑줄 친 부분 중, 문맥상 어색한 것을 1개 찾아 그 번호를 쓰고 고쳐 쓰시오.

_____ → _____

36 윗글의 빈칸에 들어갈 단어를 영영 뜻풀이를 참고하여 쓰시오. (단, 주어진 글자로 시작하고 필요시 어형을 바꿔 쓸 것)

something important that must be done first or needs more attention than anything else

p_____

Ten years ago, when search engines were powered by data mining (rather than by machine learning), if a person searched for "gourmet restaurants," then for "clothing," his or her search for the latter would be independent of his or her search for the former. Both times, <u>a search engine would collect as much information as possible</u>, then provide the inquirer options — something like a digital phone book or catalog of a subject. But contemporary search engines are guided by models informed by observed human behavior. If a person searches for "gourmet restaurants," then searches for "clothing," he or she may be presented with designer clothing rather than more affordable alternatives. Designer clothing may be what the searcher is after. But there is a difference between choosing from a range of options and taking an action — in this case, making a purchase; in other cases, adopting a political or philosophical position or ideology — without ever knowing what the initial range of possibilities or implications was, entrusting a machine to preemptively shape the options.

*gourmet (음식이) 고급인   **entrust 위임하다
***preemptively 우선적으로

37 윗글의 밑줄 친 부분을 다음과 같이 다시 쓸 때, 빈칸에 들어갈 알맞은 말을 쓰시오.

= a search engine would collect as much information as _____ _____

38 윗글에서 다음 질문에 대한 답을 찾아 우리말로 쓰시오. (50글자 내외)

Q: What is the obvious difference between search engines 10 years ago and contemporary search engines, as mentioned in the passage?

A: _____

_____

Throughout nature, the process of natural selection seldom ① <u>favours</u> organisms that lack the capacity to disperse to new areas. Even among sedentary plants, evolution has found ways for species to spread from one place to another, 'hitchhiking' on animals or using the wind to ② <u>gather</u> their seeds and pollen. Almost all species have some mechanism for exploratory movement — and the longest of these movements are often vital for the longterm survival of populations, for a whole suite of reasons. In the ③ <u>presence</u> of long-distance dispersal, populations will invariably become threatened by inbreeding, as local gene pools become more and more ④ <u>impoverished</u> over time through the lack of mixing with individuals elsewhere. _____ can also be essential in allowing populations to persist when environmental conditions change, or when population densities within a local area grow to the point that competition for resources ⑤ <u>limits</u> survival chances.

*disperse (새 지역으로) 분산하다, 흩어지다   **sedentary 정착하여 사는

고난도

39 윗글의 밑줄 친 부분 중, 문맥상 어색한 것을 2개 찾아 그 번호를 쓰고 고쳐 쓰시오.

(1) _____ → _____
(2) _____ → _____

40 윗글의 빈칸에 들어갈 단어를 영영 뜻풀이를 참고하여 본문에서 찾아 쓰시오. (단, 대·소문자 구분할 것)

the process of spreading things or people in different directions over a wide area

_____

It was three days before Christmas. My sister Sherry and I were so excited. Every time another commercial came on TV, we ran to our lengthy Christmas list and added another toy or game. Finally Mom had enough, and she sat us down and gave us "the speech." She asked us if we ① had considered anyone besides ourselves. "Did either of you buy a gift for your little brother, your grandmother or your father?" she asked. I felt ashamed. Sherry and I made a list of our family, pooled our meager allowance, and walked to the dollar store. At home we wrapped and labeled each gift, chatting and laughing together. Our French poodle, Jacques, was right up under us the whole time.

Finally Sherry and I looked down, really noticing him for the first time. "The dog!" we exclaimed together. We had forgotten to put the dog on our Christmas list. "What do you think he would like?" I asked Sherry. "What about a bone?" she whispered with her hand to her mouth so Jacques wouldn't hear. Out we went again to the meat market to get a bone. We wrapped this gift and placed the bone under the tree. The next day as we piled into the car for church, we noticed our damp, drippy dog ② standing in the rain. "Can't we let him into the warm house?" I begged. "He has a doghouse," Mom reminded us, but we could tell she thought he was pitiful too. "Pleeeeeaaaaase," we begged together.

"OK." Mom caved in. Sherry hurried to undo his chain and lead him in the front door. A few hours later, when we got home, we didn't expect the scene that greeted us. I stood in the front doorway and gasped. There was ripped gift paper ③ scattering all over the living room floor. Sherry and I rushed to the tree to count the presents. It looked as if all of them were still there. Mom looked for the dog. "Come and see," she shouted. Jacques was crouched under a bed busily chewing his bone. We couldn't believe it. He had opened only one present... *his present.* How did he know which one

to open? "He ④ must read the gift tag and knew it was his!" I exclaimed.

Our dog could read! Our dog was the smartest dog I'd ever heard of. I started planning TV shows for him. Maybe we could get him on *America's Funniest Home Videos* or *Good Morning America* because our dog could read! Mom waited till after Christmas to break the news. It was quite a blow when she told me, "You know, he probably just smelled the bone." I felt as ⑤ deflating as last year's birthday balloons. I guess there will be no *America's Funniest Home Videos* prize in our future. But still, I think there will never be a Christmas to beat that one. I still smile when I think that for two whole days I was sure we owned the smartest dog on earth.

*meager 얼마 안 되는 *pile 우르르 가다 *crouch (몸을) 웅크리다

41 윗글의 밑줄 친 부분 중, 어법상 틀린 것을 3개 찾아 바르게 고쳐 쓰시오.

(1) _____ → _____

(2) _____ → _____

(3) _____ → _____

42 윗글을 읽고 다음 질문에 대한 답을 영어로 쓰시오. (12 단어 내외)

Q: How did the girl find out the way the dog found his gift without opening any other gifts?

A: _____

_____

❶ I am a graduate student majoring in political science. ❷ I am writing this letter to tell you about the inconvenience students experience on campus. ❸ An increasing number of students are riding their bicycles to school. ❹ However, since there are not enough bicycle racks on campus, students have trouble finding places to park their bicycles. ❺ Often we spend a lot of time looking for a place for our bicycles, which often leads us to be late for class. ❻ It gets even worse on rainy or snowy days. ❼ Last month, I heard that five bicycles parked on the roadside due to the lack of bicycle facilities on campus had been stolen. ❽ So I hope you take this matter very seriously and take necessary action to resolve it. ❾ More than anything, I ask you to create more bicycle racks.

❶ 저는 정치학을 전공하고 있는 대학원생입니다. ❷ 저는 학생들이 교정에서 겪고 있는 불편함에 대해 말씀드리려고 이 편지를 쓰고 있습니다. ❸ 점점 더 많은 수의 학생이 자전거를 타고 등교하고 있습니다. ❹ 하지만 교정에 자전거 보관대가 충분하지 않기 때문에, 학생들은 자신들의 자전거를 주차할 장소를 찾는 데 어려움을 겪고 있습니다. ❺ 자주 저희는 자전거를 둘 장소를 찾느라 많은 시간을 보내고 있고, 이는 자주 저희가 수업에 늦는 결과를 초래합니다. ❻ 비가 오거나 눈이 오는 날에는 상황이 훨씬 더 나쁩니다. ❼ 지난달 저는 교정에 자전거 관련 시설이 부족해서 길가에 주차해 둔 5대의 자전거가 도난당했다고 들었습니다. ❽ 그래서 저는 관계자 분께서 이 문제를 매우 심각하게 받아들이시고 그것을 해결하는 데 필요한 조치를 취해 주시기를 바랍니다. ❾ 무엇보다 저는 더 많은 자전거 보관대를 만들어 주시기를 요청드립니다.

Word List

□ graduate student 대학원생 □ major in ~을 전공하다 □ political science 정치학 □ inconvenience 불편
□ bicycle rack 자전거 보관대 □ park 주차하다 □ lead (결과적으로) ~에 이르다 □ roadside 길가 □ due to ~ 때문에 □ lack 부족
□ facility 시설 □ matter 문제, 사안 □ seriously 심각하게 □ resolve 해결하다

• Word Test

1	seriously	8	부족
2	political science	9	길가
3	due to	10	주차하다
4	graduate student	11	문제, 사안
5	facility	12	해결하다
6	lead	13	불편
7	bicycle rack	14	~을 전공하다

I am a graduate student majoring ❶ in / for political science. I am writing this letter to tell you about the inconvenience students experience on campus. An increasing number of students ❷ is / are riding their bicycles to school. ❸ However / Furthermore , since there are not enough bicycle racks on campus, students have trouble finding places to park their bicycles. Often we spend a lot of time looking for a place for our bicycles, ❹ what / which often leads us to be late for class. It gets even worse on rainy or snowy days. Last month, I heard that five bicycles parked on the roadside due to the lack of bicycle facilities on campus had been stolen. So I hope you take this matter very seriously and take necessary action to ❺ resolve / dissolve it. More than anything, I ask you to create more bicycle racks.

I am a graduate student ❶ _____ (major) in political science. I am writing this letter to tell you about the inconvenience students experience on campus. An increasing number of students are riding their bicycles to school. However, since there are not enough bicycle racks on campus, students have trouble finding places ❷ _____ (park) their bicycles. Often we spend a lot of time ❸ _____ (look) for a place for our bicycles, which often leads us to be late for class. It gets even worse on rainy or snowy days. Last month, I heard that five bicycles ❹ _____ (park) on the roadside due to the lack of bicycle facilities on campus had ❺ _____ (steal). So I hope you take this matter very seriously and take necessary action to resolve it. More than anything, I ask you to create more bicycle racks.

I am a graduate student majoring in political science. I am writing this letter to tell you about the inconvenience students experience on campus. A(n) ❶ _____ _____ _____ _____ (점점 더 많은 수의 학생들) are riding their bicycles to school. However, since there are not enough bicycle racks on campus, students ❷ _____ _____ _____ (~을 찾는 데 어려움을 겪는다) places to park their bicycles. Often we spend a lot of time looking for a place for our bicycles, which often ❸ _____ _____ _____ _____ _____ _____ (우리가 수업에 늦는 결과를 초래한다). It gets even worse on rainy or snowy days. Last month, I heard that five bicycles parked on the roadside due to the ❹ _____ _____ _____ _____ (자전거 관련 시설의 부족) on campus had been stolen. So I hope you take this matter very seriously and take necessary action to resolve it. More than anything, I ask you to create more bicycle racks.

❶ I was working through college selling children's books door to door in Florida. ❷ One particularly blistering day nothing was going right. ❸ I had knocked on every door without a single answer; ❹ I was hot, tired, and felt like a total failure. ❺ Then, I looked down the street at a small white house and was drawn toward it. ❻ I had barely knocked on the door when an older woman opened it and immediately asked me in. ❼ She gave me a drink and invited me to share a meal with her and her husband. ❽ It was obvious that they did not have much money. ❾ During the two hours I was there, the woman and her husband shared stories of the hardships and experiences in their lives and told me that it was very important to always love and care deeply about others — even strangers. ❿ As I left, the man gave me money and said he just wanted to help me out and that he had no need for my books. ⓫ As I walked back down the street I broke into tears and kept crying for blocks. ⓬ These people who at first seemed to have so little had given me more than I could ever have asked for.

*blistering 지독히 더운

❶ 나는 플로리다에서 집집마다 돌아다니며 아동 도서를 판매하면서 고학으로 대학을 다니고 있었다. ❷ 특히나 지독히 더웠던 어느 날에 어느 것도 제대로 되는 것이 없었다. ❸ 나는 모든 문을 노크했으나 아무 응답이 없었다. ❹ 나는 덥고, 피곤하고, 완전한 실패자처럼 느껴졌다. ❺ 그러다가 나는 길을 따라 있는 작은 하얀 집을 보았고 그 집에 이끌렸다. ❻ 내가 문을 노크하자마자 연로한 여성이 문을 열고 즉시 나에게 들어오라고 했다. ❼ 그녀는 내게 마실 것을 주고 자신과 자기 남편과 함께 식사를 하자고 내게 권했다. ❽ 그들은 돈이 많지 않은 것이 분명했다. ❾ 내가 그곳에 있었던 두 시간 동안 그 여자와 그녀의 남편은 자신들 삶에서 겪었던 고난과 경험의 이야기를 해 주었고 항상 다른 사람, 심지어 낯선 사람까지도 깊이 사랑하고 보살피는 것이 매우 중요하다고 내게 말했다. ❿ 내가 떠날 때 그 남자는 나에게 돈을 주었고 그는 단지 나를 돕고 싶을 뿐이며 내 책은 필요하지 않다고 말했다. ⓫ 다시 거리를 따라 걸으면서 나는 울음을 터뜨렸고 몇 블록을 가는 동안 계속 울었다. ⓬ 처음에는 가진 것이 거의 없는 것처럼 보였던 이 사람들이 내가 요청할 수도 있었던 것보다 더 많은 것을 내게 주었다.

Word List

□ work through college 고학으로 대학을 다니다   □ failure 실패자   □ immediately 즉시   □ obvious 분명한
□ hardship 고난, 어려움   □ deeply 깊이   □ break into tears 울음을 터뜨리다

• Word Test

1	break into tears	4	깊이
2	immediately	5	실패자
3	hardship	6	분명한

네모 안에서 옳은 어법·어휘를 고르시오.

I was working through college selling children's books door to door in Florida. One particularly blistering day nothing was going right. I had knocked on every door without a single answer; I was hot, tired, and felt like a total ❶ success / failure . Then, I looked down the street at a small white house and was drawn toward it. I had barely knocked on the door when an older woman opened it and immediately asked me in. She gave me a drink and invited me to share a meal with her and her husband. It was ❷ unclear / obvious that they did not have much money. During the two hours I was there, the woman and her husband shared stories of the ❸ hungers / hardships and experiences in their lives and told me that it was very important to always love and care deeply about others — even strangers. ❹ As / If I left, the man gave me money and said he just wanted to help me out and that he had no need for my books. As I walked back down the street I broke into tears and kept crying for blocks. These people who at first seemed to have so ❺ much / little had given me more than I could ever have asked for.

*blistering 지독히 더운

괄호 안의 동사를 알맞은 형태로 쓰시오.

I was working through college ❶ _____ (sell) children's books door to door in Florida. One particularly blistering day nothing was going right. I had knocked on every door without a single answer; I was hot, tired, and felt like a total failure. Then, I looked down the street at a small white house and ❷ _____ (draw) toward it. I had barely knocked on the door when an older woman ❸ _____ (open) it and immediately asked me in. She gave me a drink and invited me to share a meal with her and her husband. It was obvious that they did not have much money. During the two hours I was there, the woman and her husband shared stories of the hardships and experiences in their lives and told me that it was very important to always love and care deeply about others — even strangers. As I left, the man gave me money and said he just wanted to help me out and that he had no need for my books. As I walked back down the street I broke into tears and kept ❹ _____ (cry) for blocks. These people who at first ❺ _____ (seem) to have so little had given me more than I could ever have asked for.

*blistering 지독히 더운

우리말에 맞게 빈칸에 알맞은 말을 쓰시오.

I was working through college selling children's books ❶ _____ _____ _____ (집집마다 돌아다니며) in Florida. One particularly blistering day nothing was going right. I had knocked on every door without a single answer; I was hot, tired, and felt like a total failure. Then, I looked down the street at a small white house and was drawn toward it. ❷ _____ _____ _____ _____ _____ _____ _____ (내가 문을 노크하자마자) when an older woman opened it and immediately asked me in. She gave me a drink and invited me to share a meal with her and her husband. It was obvious that they did not have much money. During the two hours I was there, the woman and her husband shared stories of the hardships and experiences in their lives and told me that it was very important to always love and care deeply about others — even strangers. As I left, the man gave me money and said he just wanted to help me out and that he had no need for my books. As I walked back down the street I ❸ _____ _____ _____ (울음을 터뜨렸다) and kept crying for blocks. These people who at first seemed to have so little had given me ❹ _____ _____ _____ _____ _____ _____ _____ (내가 요청할 수도 있었던 것보다 더 많은 것).

*blistering 지독히 더운

❶ It's probably worth mentioning that Socrates was put to death for his beliefs — and for spreading those beliefs too widely to the youth of Athens. ❷ So it's safe to say that challenging established thinking doesn't always sit well with people. ❸ But I'd argue it's not only a good idea to harness constructive conflict, it's critical to the decision-making process. ❹ You can't effectively set a strategy or decide direction if you're unwilling to grapple with tough questions and have some disagreement over ideas. ❺ Thoughtful leaders thrive on disagreement because it gives them the information they need to improve their ideas before they reach the world. ❻ We all have our own personal threshold of comfort around conflict. ❼ Some people thrive on lively debate; others find it deeply stressful. ❽ But if the boss can't be challenged safely, then no one can. ❾ I believe it's your job as a leader to invite good criticism. ❿ By constructively harnessing disagreements within your team, you improve ideas and fuel productivity.

*harness 활용하다 **grapple with ~을 해결하려고 노력하다 ***threshold 한계점

❶ 소크라테스가 자신의 신념 때문에, 그리고 그 신념들을 아테네의 젊은이들에게 너무 널리 전파해서 죽임을 당했다는 것은 아마도 언급할 만한 가치가 있을 것이다. ❷ 따라서 기성의 사고에 도전하는 것이 항상 사람들에게 받아들여지는 것은 아니라고 말하는 것에 무리는 없다. ❸ 하지만 나는 건설적인 갈등을 활용하는 것이 좋은 생각일 뿐만 아니라 그것이 의사 결정 과정에 매우 중요하다고 주장하고자 한다. ❹ 만약 여러분이 어려운 문제를 해결하려고 노력하기를 꺼리거나 아이디어에 대해서 어떤 의견 차이를 수용하기를 꺼린다면 효과적으로 전략을 세우거나 방향을 정할 수 없다. ❺ 사려 깊은 리더들은 의견 차이를 즐기는데 이는 그것이 그들에게 자신들의 아이디어들이 세상에 나아가기 전에 그것들을 발전시키는 데 필요한 정보를 주기 때문이다. ❻ 우리 모두는 갈등에 대해서 편안함을 느끼는 개인적인 한계점을 가지고 있다. ❼ 어떤 사람들은 활기찬 토론을 즐기는 반면 다른 사람들은 그것이 매우 스트레스를 준다고 생각한다. ❽ 하지만 상사에게 안전하게 이의를 제기할 수 없다면 어느 누구에게도 할 수 없다. ❾ 나는 건전한 비판을 청하는 것이 리더로서 여러분이 할 일이라고 믿는다. ❿ 팀 내의 의견 차이를 건설적으로 활용함으로써 여러분은 아이디어를 발전시키고 생산성을 증가시킨다.

Word List

□ mention 언급하다 □ spread 퍼뜨리다 □ challenge 도전하다 □ established 기성의, 확립된
□ sit well with (사람, 사물에) 받아들여지다 □ conflict 갈등 □ critical 매우 중요한 □ effectively 효과적으로 □ strategy 전략
□ thrive on ~을 즐기다[잘하다] □ disagreement 의견 차이, 불일치 □ lively 활기찬 □ fuel 증가시키다

• **Word Test**

1	mention	7	증가시키다
2	lively	8	전략
3	challenge	9	의견 차이, 불일치
4	thrive on	10	매우 중요한
5	conflict	11	기성의, 확립된
6	effectively	12	퍼뜨리다

It's probably worth mentioning that Socrates was put to death for his beliefs — and for spreading those beliefs too ❶ [wide / widely] to the youth of Athens. So it's safe to say that challenging ❷ [abandoned / established] thinking doesn't always sit well with people. But I'd argue it's not only a good idea to harness constructive conflict, it's critical to the decision-making process. You can't effectively set a strategy or decide direction if you're ❸ [inclined / unwilling] to grapple with tough questions and have some disagreement over ideas. ❹ [Thoughtful / Inconsiderate] leaders thrive on disagreement because it gives them the information they need to improve their ideas before they reach the world. We all have our own personal threshold of comfort around conflict. Some people thrive on lively debate; others find it deeply ❺ [relaxing / stressful]. But if the boss can't be challenged safely, then no one can. I believe it's your job as a leader to invite good criticism. By constructively harnessing disagreements within your team, you improve ideas and fuel productivity.

*harness 활용하다   **grapple with ~을 해결하려고 노력하다   ***threshold 한계점

It's probably worth ❶ _____ (mention) that Socrates was put to death for his beliefs — and for ❷ _____ (spread) those beliefs too widely to the youth of Athens. So it's safe to say that challenging established thinking doesn't always sit well with people. But I'd argue it's not only a good idea to harness constructive conflict, it's critical to the decision-making process. You can't effectively set a strategy or decide direction if you're unwilling to grapple with tough questions and ❸ _____ (have) some disagreement over ideas. Thoughtful leaders thrive on disagreement because it gives them the information they need to improve their ideas before they reach the world. We all have our own personal threshold of comfort around conflict. Some people thrive on lively debate; others find it deeply stressful. But if the boss can't ❹ _____ (challenge) safely, then no one can. I believe it's your job as a leader to invite good criticism. By constructively harnessing disagreements within your team, you improve ideas and fuel productivity.

*harness 활용하다   **grapple with ~을 해결하려고 노력하다   ***threshold 한계점

It's probably worth mentioning that Socrates ❶ _____ _____ _____ _____ _____ (~ 때문에 죽임을 당했다) his beliefs — and for spreading those beliefs too widely to the youth of Athens. So it's safe to say that challenging established thinking doesn't always ❷ _____ _____ _____ _____ (사람들에게 받아들여진다). But I'd argue it's not only a good idea to harness constructive conflict, it's critical to the decision-making process. You can't effectively set a strategy or decide direction if you're unwilling to grapple with tough questions and have some disagreement over ideas. Thoughtful leaders ❸ _____ _____ _____ (의견 차이를 즐긴다) because it gives them the information they need to improve their ideas before they reach the world. We all have our own personal threshold of comfort around conflict. Some people thrive on lively debate; others find it deeply stressful. But if the boss can't be challenged safely, then no one can. I believe it's your job as a leader to ❹ _____ _____ _____ (건전한 비판을 청한다). By constructively harnessing disagreements within your team, you improve ideas and fuel productivity.

*harness 활용하다   **grapple with ~을 해결하려고 노력하다   ***threshold 한계점

❶ Antiracist educator and author Debby Irving uses an often-cited headwinds and tailwinds metaphor to explain the invisibility of the systemic, group-level differences that treat different groups of people differently. ❷ Headwinds are the challenges — some big, some small, some visible, some invisible — that make life harder for some people, but not for all people. ❸ When you run against a headwind, your speed slows down and you have to push harder. ❹ You can feel the headwind. ❺ When you have a tailwind pushing you, it is a force that propels you forward. ❻ It is consequential but easily unnoticed or forgotten. ❼ In fact, if you are like me when I jog with a tailwind, you may glow with pride at your great running time that day, as if it were your own athletic prowess. ❽ When you have the tailwind, you will not notice that some runners are running into headwinds. ❾ They may be running as hard as, or even harder than, you, but they will appear lazier and slower to you. ❿ When some of them grow tired and stop trying, they will appear self-destructive to you.

*prowess 기량, 훌륭한 솜씨

❶ 반인종주의 교육자이자 저술가인 Debby Irving은 자주 인용되는 역풍과 순풍의 비유를 사용하여, 서로 다른 집단의 사람들을 다르게 취급하는 조직적인 집단 수준의 눈에 보이지 않는 차이를 설명한다. ❷ 역풍은 크기도 하고 작기도 하며, 눈에 보이기도 하고 눈에 보이지 않기도 하는 힘든 문제로서 일부 사람들에게 삶을 더 힘들게 하지만, 모든 사람들에게 다 그렇지는 않다. ❸ 역풍을 맞으며 달리면 속도가 느려져서 더 세게 밀고 나아가야 한다. ❹ 여러분은 그 역풍을 느낄 수 있다. ❺ 순풍이 여러분을 밀고 있을 때, 그것은 여러분을 앞으로 나아가게 하는 힘이다. ❻ 그것은 중요하지만 쉽게 간과되거나 잊혀진다. ❼ 사실, 여러분이 순풍에 조깅을 할 때의 나와 같다면, 여러분은 마치 그것이 자신의 운동 기량인 양 그날의 뛰어난 달리기 시간에 자부심으로 가슴이 뿌듯할 수도 있다. ❽ 여러분은 순풍을 타고 있을 때, 일부 주자가 역풍을 맞고 있다는 사실을 눈치채지 못할 것이다. ❾ 그들은 여러분만큼, 혹은 여러분보다 더 열심히 달리고 있을 수도 있지만, 여러분에게는 더 게으르고 더 느리게 보일 것이다. ❿ 그들 중 일부가 지쳐서 시도를 중단하면, 그들은 여러분에게 자멸적으로 보일 것이다.

Word List

□ antiracist 반인종주의의 □ cite 인용하다 □ headwind 역풍 □ tailwind 순풍 □ metaphor 비유
□ invisibility 눈에 보이지 않음, 불가시성 □ systemic 체계의 □ slow down 느려지다 □ propel 나아가게 하다
□ consequential 중요한 □ unnoticed 간과되는 □ glow (강한 감정 따위로) 가슴이 뿌듯하다, 북받치다 □ athletic 운동의
□ self-destructive 자멸적인

• **Word Test**

1	headwind		7	운동의	
2	systemic		8	눈에 보이지 않, 불가시성	
3	unnoticed		9	인용하다	
4	antiracist		10	순풍	
5	propel		11	느려지다	
6	metaphor		12	중요한	

Antiracist educator and author Debby Irving uses an often-cited headwinds and tailwinds metaphor to explain the ❶ visibility / invisibility of the systemic, group-level differences that treat different groups of people differently. Headwinds are the challenges — some big, some small, some visible, some invisible — ❷ that / what make life harder for some people, but not for all people. When you run against a headwind, your speed ❸ keeps up / slows down and you have to push harder. You can feel the headwind. When you have a tailwind pushing you, it is a force that propels you forward. It is consequential but easily unnoticed or forgotten. In fact, if you are like me when I jog with a tailwind, you may glow with pride at your great running time that day, ❹ as / even if it were your own athletic prowess. When you have the tailwind, you will not notice that some runners are running into headwinds. They may be running as hard as, or even harder than, you, but they will ❺ appear / disappear lazier and slower to you. When some of them grow tired and stop trying, they will appear self-destructive to you.

*prowess 기량, 훌륭한 솜씨

Antiracist educator and author Debby Irving uses an often-cited headwinds and tailwinds metaphor ❶ _____ (explain) the invisibility of the systemic, group-level differences that ❷ _____ (treat) different groups of people differently. Headwinds are the challenges — some big, some small, some visible, some invisible — that ❸ _____ (make) life harder for some people, but not for all people. When you run against a headwind, your speed slows down and you have to push harder. You can feel the headwind. When you have a tailwind ❹ _____ (push) you, it is a force that propels you forward. It is consequential but easily unnoticed or forgotten. In fact, if you are like me when I jog with a tailwind, you may glow with pride at your great running time that day, as if it were your own athletic prowess. When you have the tailwind, you will not notice that some runners are running into headwinds. They may be running as hard as, or even harder than, you, but they will appear lazier and slower to you. When some of them grow tired and stop ❺ _____ (try), they will appear self-destructive to you.

*prowess 기량, 훌륭한 솜씨

Antiracist educator and author Debby Irving uses an often-cited headwinds and tailwinds metaphor to explain the invisibility of the systemic, group-level differences that treat different groups of people differently. Headwinds are the challenges — some big, some small, some visible, some invisible — that make life harder for some people, ❶ _____ _____ _____ _____ _____ (하지만 모든 사람들에게 다 그렇지는 않은). When you run against a headwind, your speed slows down and you have to push harder. You can feel the headwind. When you have a tailwind pushing you, it is a force that propels you forward. It is consequential but ❷ _____ _____ _____ _____ (쉽게 간과되거나 잊혀지는). In fact, if you are like me when I jog with a tailwind, you may ❸ _____ _____ _____ (자부심으로 가슴이 뿌듯하다) at your great running time that day, as if it were your own athletic prowess. When you have the tailwind, you will not notice that some runners are running into headwinds. They may be running as hard as, or even harder than, you, but they will appear lazier and slower to you. When some of them grow tired and stop trying, they will ❹ _____ _____ (자멸적으로 보인다) to you.

*prowess 기량, 훌륭한 솜씨

❶ Like in the early days of industrialization, workers today are no longer reaping the gains of progress. ❷ Worse, many have been left behind in the backwaters of progress. ❸ In the same way that opportunity dried up for middle-income artisans as a consequence of the industrialization process, the age of automation has meant diminishing opportunities for the American middle class. ❹ Like the victims of the early factories, many Americans have adjusted to the computerization of work by unwillingly shifting into lower-paying jobs or have failed to adjust and dropped out of the workforce completely. ❺ And similar to the victims of the factories, the losers to automation have primarily been men in the prime of life. ❻ Up until the 1980s, manufacturing jobs allowed ordinary working men to attain a middle-class lifestyle without going to college. ❼ As employment opportunities in manufacturing receded, a path of upward mobility was closed to many citizens.

*artisan 장인 **recede 줄다

❶ 산업화 초기처럼, 오늘날의 노동자들은 더 이상 진보의 이익을 거두지 못하고 있다. ❷ 더욱 심각한 것은, 많은 이들이 진보의 변두리에 남겨진 채로 있어 왔다는 것이다. ❸ 산업화 과정의 결과로 중간 소득 계층의 장인에게 기회가 고갈된 것과 같은 방식으로, 자동화의 시대는 미국 중산층에게 기회의 감소를 의미했다. ❹ 초기 공장의 희생자들처럼 많은 미국인들은 마지못해 저임금 직업으로 옮겨 노동의 컴퓨터화에 적응했거나 적응에 실패하여 노동 인구에서 완전히 탈락하였다. ❺ 그리고 공장의 희생자들과 비슷하게, 자동화의 패배자들은 주로 인생의 전성기에 있는 남성들이었다. ❻ 1980년대까지만 해도 제조업은 평범한 직장인들이 대학에 가지 않고도 중산층 생활을 이룰 수 있도록 했다. ❼ 제조업의 고용 기회가 줄어들면서, 많은 시민들에게 상향 이동의 길이 막혔다.

Word List

□ industrialization 산업화   □ reap (성과·이익 등을) 거두다   □ gains 이득   □ progress 진보, 발전
□ leave - behind 남겨 두다, 둔 채 잊고 가다   □ backwater 변두리, 벽지   □ dry up 고갈되다   □ as a consequence of ~의 결과로
□ diminish 감소하다, 줄어들다   □ victim 희생자   □ adjust to ~에 적응하다   □ computerization 컴퓨터화   □ unwillingly 마지못해
□ shift into ~로 옮기다, ~로 이동하다   □ drop out of ~에서 탈락하다, 낙오하다   □ primarily 주로   □ prime 전성기
□ manufacturing 제조업의   □ attain 이루다   □ mobility 이동, 유동성

• Word Test

1	unwillingly		10	~로 옮기다, ~로 이동하다
2	industrialization		11	(성과·이익 등을) 거두다
3	gains		12	이동, 유동성
4	prime		13	진보, 발전
5	attain		14	고갈되다
6	victim		15	~에 적응하다
7	drop out of		16	제조업의
8	as a consequence of		17	주로
9	backwater		18	감소하다, 줄어들다

Like in the early days of industrialization, workers today are no longer ❶ leaping / reaping the gains of progress. Worse, many have been left behind in the backwaters of progress. In the same way that opportunity dried up for middle-income artisans as a consequence of the industrialization process, the age of automation has meant ❷ diminishing / increasing opportunities for the American middle class. Like the victims of the early factories, many Americans have adjusted to the computerization of work by ❸ unwillingly / voluntarily shifting into lower-paying jobs or have failed to adjust and dropped out of the workforce completely. And similar to the victims of the factories, the losers to automation have ❹ primary / primarily been men in the prime of life. Up until the 1980s, manufacturing jobs allowed ordinary working men to attain a middle-class lifestyle without going to college. ❺ As / Since employment opportunities in manufacturing receded, a path of upward mobility was closed to many citizens.

*artisan 장인 **recede 줄다

Like in the early days of industrialization, workers today are no longer reaping the gains of progress. Worse, many have been left behind in the backwaters of progress. In the same way that opportunity ❶ _____ (dry) up for middle-income artisans as a consequence of the industrialization process, the age of automation ❷ _____ (mean) diminishing opportunities for the American middle class. Like the victims of the early factories, many Americans ❸ _____ (adjust) to the computerization of work by unwillingly ❹ _____ (shift) into lower-paying jobs or have failed to adjust and dropped out of the workforce completely. And similar to the victims of the factories, the losers to automation have primarily been men in the prime of life. Up until the 1980s, manufacturing jobs allowed ordinary working men to attain a middle-class lifestyle without going to college. As employment opportunities in manufacturing receded, a path of upward mobility ❺ _____ (close) to many citizens.

*artisan 장인 **recede 줄다

Like in the early days of industrialization, workers today are no longer reaping the gains of progress. Worse, ❶ _____ _____ _____ _____ _____ (많은 이들이 ~에 남겨진 채로 있어 왔다) in the backwaters of progress. In the same way that opportunity dried up for middle-income artisans as a consequence of the industrialization process, the age of automation has meant diminishing opportunities for the American middle class. Like the victims of the early factories, many Americans have adjusted to the computerization of work by unwillingly shifting into lower-paying jobs or have failed to adjust and ❷ _____ _____ _____ _____ _____ _____ (노동 인구에서 완전히 탈락하였다). And similar to the victims of the factories, the losers to automation have primarily been ❸ _____ _____ _____ _____ _____ (인생의 전성기에 있는 남성들). Up until the 1980s, manufacturing jobs allowed ordinary working men to attain a middle-class lifestyle without going to college. As employment opportunities in manufacturing receded, a(n) ❹ _____ _____ _____ _____ (상향 이동의 길) was closed to many citizens.

*artisan 장인 **recede 줄다

❶ We do not have an environmental problem so much as we have a *story* problem. ❷ Or so says David Korten, who argues that the grave environmental challenges we face today have been set in motion by the predominating cultural lens of what he calls the "sacred money and markets story." ❸ This has been a story with catastrophic outcomes, contends Korten. ❹ Is there a way to fix it? ❺ Korten thinks there is: intervene. ❻ *Change the Story, Change the Future*, Korten proclaims in his book on creating more sustainable and just earth economies. ❼ Intervening in the "sacred money and markets story" and supplanting it with the "sacred life and living earth story" as the prevailing story of our time, he argues, will result in changing the human cognition and behavior that got us into our current environmental mess. ❽ Change the story, and we will climb our way out of destruction and despair and begin the repair and recovery of life systems on the planet. ❾ Permit the dominant "sacred money and markets story" instead to proceed on its current trajectory uninterrupted, with *no* effective intervention, and we seal our own doom.

*catastrophic 파멸적인   **trajectory 궤도

❶ 우리는 환경 문제라기보다는 '이야기'문제를 가지고 있다. ❷ 혹은 David Korten이 그렇게 말하는데, 그는 오늘날 우리가 직면하고 있는 심각한 환경적 난제가 그가 '신성시되는 돈과 시장 이야기'라고 부르는 것인 지배적인 문화적 렌즈에 의해 시작되었다고 주장한다. ❸ 이것은 파멸적인 결과를 가져온 이야기였다고 Korten은 주장한다. ❹ 그것을 고칠 방법이 있는가? ❺ Korten은 있다고 생각하는데, 그것은 바로 개입하는 것이다. ❻ '이야기를 바꾸고, 미래를 바꾸라'고 Korten은 더 지속 가능하고 공정한 지구 경제를 만드는 것에 관한 자신의 저서에서 선언한다. ❼ '신성시되는 돈과 시장 이야기'에 개입하여 그것을, 우리 시대의 지배적인 이야기로서 '신성시되는 생명과 살아있는 지구 이야기'로 대체하는 것은 우리를 현재의 환경적 혼란에 빠지게 한 인간의 인식과 행동을 바꾸는 결과를 가져올 것이라고 그는 주장한다. ❽ 이야기를 바꾸면, 우리는 파괴와 절망에서 빠져나와 지구상의 생명 시스템의 복구와 회복을 시작할 것이다. ❾ 그렇게 하지 않고 지배적인 '신성시되는 돈과 시장 이야기'가 효과적인 개입 '없이', 아무런 방해도 받지 않고, 현재의 궤도로 진행되도록 허용한다면, 우리는 우리 자신의 파멸을 확정한다.

Word List

□ environmental 환경의   □ argue 주장하다   □ grave 심각한   □ set in motion 시동을 걸다   □ predominating 지배적인, 우세한
□ sacred 신성시되는, 성스러운   □ outcome 결과   □ contend 주장하다   □ intervene 개입하다, 중재하다   □ proclaim 선언하다
□ sustainable 지속 가능한   □ supplant 대체[대신]하다   □ prevailing 지배적인, 우세한   □ cognition 인식, 인지
□ mess 혼란, 엉망인 상황   □ dominant 지배적인, 우세한   □ proceed 진행되다, 진행하다   □ seal 확정하다, 결정하다
□ doom 파멸, 운명

• Word Test

1	contend	10	환경의
2	prevailing	11	진행되다, 진행하다
3	supplant	12	파멸, 운명
4	seal	13	결과
5	sacred	14	인식, 인지
6	dominant	15	지속 가능한
7	argue	16	개입하다, 중재하다
8	proclaim	17	심각한
9	predominating	18	혼란, 엉망인 상황

We do not have an environmental problem ❶ | more than / so much as | we have a *story* problem. Or so says David Korten, who argues that the grave environmental challenges we face today have been set in motion by the ❷ | demonstrating / predominating | cultural lens of what he calls the "sacred money and markets story." This has been a story with catastrophic outcomes, contends Korten. Is there a way to fix it? Korten thinks there is: intervene. *Change the Story, Change the Future*, Korten ❸ | proclaims / provokes | in his book on creating more sustainable and just earth economies. Intervening in the "sacred money and markets story" and supplanting ❹ | it / them | with the "sacred life and living earth story" as the prevailing story of our time, he argues, will result in changing the human cognition and behavior ❺ | that / what | got us into our current environmental mess. Change the story, and we will climb our way out of destruction and despair and begin the repair and recovery of life systems on the planet. Permit the dominant "sacred money and markets story" instead to proceed on its current trajectory uninterrupted, with *no* effective intervention, and we seal our own doom.

*catastrophic 파멸적인   **trajectory 궤도

We do not have an environmental problem so much as we have a *story* problem. Or so says David Korten, who ❶ _____ (argue) that the grave environmental challenges we face today have been set in motion by the predominating cultural lens of what he calls the "sacred money and markets story." This _____ ❷ (be) a story with catastrophic outcomes, contends Korten. Is there a way to fix it? Korten thinks there is: intervene. *Change the Story, Change the Future*, Korten proclaims in his book on creating more sustainable and just earth economies. ❸ _____ (Intervene) in the "sacred money and markets story" and ❹ _____ (supplant) it with the "sacred life and living earth story" as the prevailing story of our time, he argues, will result in changing the human cognition and behavior that ❺ _____ (get) us into our current environmental mess. Change the story, and we will climb our way out of destruction and despair and begin the repair and recovery of life systems on the planet. Permit the dominant "sacred money and markets story" instead to proceed on its current trajectory uninterrupted, with *no* effective intervention, and we seal our own doom.

*catastrophic 파멸적인   **trajectory 궤도

We do not have an environmental problem so much as we have a *story* problem. Or so says David Korten, who argues that the grave environmental challenges we face today ❶ _____ _____ _____ _____ _____ _____ (~에 의해 시동이 걸려졌다) the predominating cultural lens of what he calls the "sacred money and markets story." This has been a story with catastrophic outcomes, contends Korten. Is there a way to fix it? Korten thinks there is: intervene. *Change the Story, Change the Future*, Korten proclaims in his book on creating ❷ _____ _____ _____ _____ (더 지속 가능하고 공정한) earth economies. Intervening in the "sacred money and markets story" and supplanting it with the "sacred life and living earth story" as the ❸ _____ _____ _____ _____ _____ (우리 시대의 지배적인 이야기), he argues, will result in changing the human cognition and behavior that got us into our current environmental mess. Change the story, and we will climb our way ❹ _____ _____ _____ _____ _____ (파괴와 절망에서 빠져나와) and begin the repair and recovery of life systems on the planet. Permit the dominant "sacred money and markets story" instead to proceed on its current trajectory uninterrupted, with *no* effective intervention, and we seal our own doom.

*catastrophic 파멸적인　**trajectory 궤도

144

❶ Imagination often *seems* unbounded and without constraint. ❷ However, if this were the case then it would be *more* likely to generate falsehoods than truths. ❸ Imagination must be constrained in order to provide knowledge. ❹ On the other hand, if we want to generate any new knowledge, what we imagine cannot be entirely "up to us," as it must go beyond what we already know. ❺ The knowledge-generating capacity of the imagination can be explained by suggesting that some constraints on the imagination are fixed and within our control, allowing for exploratory activity within these constraints. ❻ For example, if one wants to know whether a sofa will fit through a door, one must constrain one's imagination to keep the relevant shapes and sizes and the laws of physics fixed, while allowing for exploration of various possible ways of manipulating the sofa.

❶ 상상력은 흔히 무한하고 제약이 없는 것처럼 '보인다'. ❷ 하지만, 만약 이것이 사실이라면, 그렇다면 그것은 진실보다 거짓말을 만들어 낼 가능성이 '더' 클 것이다. ❸ 지식을 제공하려면 상상력이 제한되어야 한다. ❹ 반면에, 만약 우리가 어떤 새로운 지식을 생성하고 싶다면, 우리가 상상하는 것은 그것이 우리가 이미 알고 있는 것을 넘어서야 하기 때문에 전적으로 '우리에게만 달려' 있을 수는 없다. ❺ 상상력의 지식 생성 능력은 상상력에 대한 몇 가지 제약이 고정되어 있고 우리가 통제할 수 있는 범위 내에 있으므로 이러한 제약 내에서 탐색적 활동을 허용한다고 말함으로써 설명될 수 있다. ❻ 예를 들어, 소파가 문을 통과할 수 있는지 알고 싶다면, 소파를 조작하는 여러 가지 가능한 방법의 탐색을 허용하면서도 관련된 모양과 크기 및 물리학 법칙을 고정시켜 두기 위하여 우리의 상상력을 제한해야 한다.

Word List

□ unbounded 무한한   □ constraint 제약   □ generate 만들어 내다   □ falsehood 거짓말, 기만   □ constrain 제한[제약]하다
□ go beyond ~을 넘어서다   □ capacity 능력   □ fixed 고정된   □ exploratory 탐색의, 탐구의   □ relevant 관련된, 적절한
□ physics 물리학   □ manipulate 조작하다, 다루다

• Word Test

1	capacity	_____	7	조작하다, 다루다	_____
2	physics	_____	8	관련된, 적절한	_____
3	unbounded	_____	9	고정된	_____
4	exploratory	_____	10	거짓말, 기만	_____
5	constrain	_____	11	~을 넘어서다	_____
6	generate	_____	12	제약	

Imagination often *seems* unbounded and without constraint. ❶ However / Moreover, if this were the case then it would be *more* likely to generate falsehoods than truths. Imagination must be constrained in order to provide knowledge. On the other hand, if we want to generate any new knowledge, ❷ what / which we imagine cannot be entirely "up to us," as it must go beyond what we already know. The knowledge-generating capacity of the imagination can be explained by suggesting ❸ that / which some constraints on the imagination are fixed and within our control, allowing for exploratory activity within these constraints. For example, if one wants to know ❹ though / whether a sofa will fit through a door, one must constrain one's imagination to keep the relevant shapes and sizes and the laws of physics fixed, while allowing for exploration of various possible ways of ❺ eliminating / manipulating the sofa.

Imagination often *seems* unbounded and without constraint. However, if this were the case then it would be *more* likely to generate falsehoods than truths. Imagination must ❶ _____ (constrain) in order to provide knowledge. On the other hand, if we want to generate any new knowledge, what we imagine cannot be entirely "up to us," as it must go beyond what we already know. The knowledge-generating capacity of the imagination can ❷ _____ (explain) by suggesting that some constraints on the imagination ❸ _____ (be) fixed and within our control, allowing for exploratory activity within these constraints. For example, if one ❹ _____ (want) to know whether a sofa will fit through a door, one must constrain one's imagination to keep the relevant shapes and sizes and the laws of physics fixed, while ❺ _____ (allow) for exploration of various possible ways of manipulating the sofa.

Imagination often *seems* unbounded and without constraint. However, if this were the case then it would be *more* likely to generate falsehoods than truths. Imagination must be constrained ❶ _____ _____ _____ _____ _____ (지식을 제공하려면). On the other hand, if we want to generate any new knowledge, what we imagine cannot be entirely "up to us," as it must ❷ _____ _____ _____ _____ _____ _____ (우리가 이미 알고 있는 것을 넘어선다). The knowledge-generating capacity of the imagination can be explained by suggesting that some constraints on the imagination are fixed and ❸ _____ _____ _____ (우리가 통제할 수 있는 범위 내에 있는), allowing for exploratory activity within these constraints. For example, if one wants to know whether a sofa will fit through a door, one must constrain one's imagination to keep the relevant shapes and sizes and the laws of physics fixed, while allowing for ❹ _____ _____ _____ _____ _____ (여러 가지 가능한 방법들의 탐색) of manipulating the sofa.

146

Average Rainfall and Total Water Consumption in Australia

Financial Year	Average Rainfall (mm)	Total Water Consumption (gigaliter)
2014-2015	416	14,877
2015-2016	453	13,669
2016-2017	580	14,303
2017-2018	433	15,386
2018-2019	347	13,288
2019-2020	347	11,231

❶ The table above shows the average rainfall and the total water consumption in Australia in six financial years. ❷ During these six financial years, the highest average rainfall was recorded in financial year 2016-2017, and total water consumption reached its peak in financial year 2017-2018, with more than 15,000 gigaliters used. ❸ From financial year 2014-2015 to 2015-2016, the average rainfall increased, but during the same period, the total amount of water used fell by more than 1,000 gigaliters. ❹ However, from financial year 2016-2017 to 2017-2018, the total water consumption showed an increase, whereas average rainfall dropped by 147 millimeters. ❺ From financial year 2017-2018 to 2019-2020, the total amount of water consumed in Australia steadily declined. ❻ The average rainfall in financial years 2018-2019 and 2019-2020 was just below 350 millimeters in both periods.

*gigaliter 기가리터(10억 리터)

❶ 위의 표는 호주의 여섯 회계 연도 동안의 평균 강수량과 총 물 소비량을 보여 준다. ❷ 이 여섯 회계 연도 동안 2016~2017 회계 연도에 가장 높은 평균 강수량이 기록되었고, 총 물 소비량은 2017~2018 회계 연도에 1만 5,000기가리터 넘게 사용되며 최대량을 기록했다. ❸ 2014~ 2015 회계 연도부터 2015~2016 회계 연도까지 평균 강수량은 증가했지만, 같은 기간에 총 물 사용량은 1,000기가리터 넘게 감소했다. ❹ 하지만 2016~2017 회계 연도부터 2017~2018 회계 연도까지는 총물 소비량이 증가를 보였고, 반면에 평균 강수량은 147밀리미터 정도 감소했다. ❺ 2017~2018 회계 연도부터 2019~2020 회계 연도까지 호주에서 소비된 총 물의 양은 꾸준히 감소했다. ❻ 2018~2019 회계 연도와 2019~2020 회계 연도의 평균 강수량은 두 기간 모두에서 350밀리미터를 약간 밑돌았다.

Word List

□ table 표 □ rainfall 강수 □ consumption 소비(량) □ financial year 회계 연도 □ record 기록하다 □ reach 도달하다
□ peak 최대량, 최고점 □ drop 감소하다, 떨어지다 □ steadily 꾸준히 □ decline 감소하다 □ period 기간

• Word Test

1 decline _____
2 consumption _____
3 table _____
4 drop _____
5 reach _____

6 기간 _____
7 꾸준히 _____
8 기록하다 _____
9 강수 _____
10 최대량, 최고점 _____

The table above shows the average rainfall and the total water consumption in Australia in six financial years. ❶ [Since / During] these six financial years, the highest average rainfall was recorded in financial year 2016-2017, and total water consumption reached its ❷ [peak / slope] in financial year 2017-2018, with more than 15,000 gigaliters used. From financial year 2014-2015 to 2015-2016, the average rainfall ❸ [increased / decreased], but during the same period, the total amount of water used fell by ❹ [more / less] than 1,000 gigaliters. However, from financial year 2016-2017 to 2017-2018, the total water consumption showed an increase, ❺ [even if / whereas] average rainfall dropped by 147 millimeters. From financial year 2017-2018 to 2019-2020, the total amount of water consumed in Australia steadily declined. The average rainfall in financial years 2018-2019 and 2019-2020 was just below 350 millimeters in both periods.

*gigaliter 기가리터(10억 리터)

The table above shows the average rainfall and the total water consumption in Australia in six financial years. During these six financial years, the highest average rainfall ❶ _____ (record) in financial year 2016-2017, and total water consumption reached its peak in financial year 2017-2018, with more than 15,000 gigaliters ❷ _____ (use). From financial year 2014-2015 to 2015-2016, the average rainfall increased, but during the same period, the total amount of water used fell by more than 1,000 gigaliters. However, from financial year 2016-2017 to 2017-2018, the total water consumption showed an increase, whereas average rainfall ❸ _____ (drop) by 147 millimeters. From financial year 2017-2018 to 2019-2020, the total amount of water ❹ _____ (consume) in Australia steadily declined. The average rainfall in financial years 2018-2019 and 2019-2020 ❺ _____ (be) just below 350 millimeters in both periods.

*gigaliter 기가리터(10억 리터)

The table above shows the average rainfall and the total water consumption in Australia in six financial years. During these six financial years, ❶ _____ _____ _____ _____ (가장 높은 평균 강수량) was recorded in financial year 2016-2017, and total water consumption reached its peak in financial year 2017-2018, with more than 15,000 gigaliters used. From financial year 2014-2015 to 2015-2016, the average rainfall increased, but ❷ _____ _____ _____ _____ (같은 기간에), the total amount of water used fell by more than 1,000 gigaliters. However, from financial year 2016-2017 to 2017-2018, the total water consumption showed an increase, whereas average rainfall dropped by 147 millimeters. From financial year 2017-2018 to 2019-2020, the total amount of water consumed in Australia ❸ _____ _____ (꾸준히 감소했다). The average rainfall in financial years 2018-2019 and 2019-2020 was just below 350 millimeters ❹ _____ _____ _____ (두 기간 모두에서).

*gigaliter 기가리터(10억 리터)

❶ Zhang Heng was born in Henan, China in 78 CE. ❷ In his youth, he traveled to Chang'an and Luoyang to receive his education. ❸ Zhang Heng showed an early aptitude for literary pursuits and achieved fame for his poetry in his 20s. ❹ His work *To Live in Seclusion* is considered a masterpiece of the late Han dynasty. ❺ While most educated young men in China at the time sought to obtain government posts, Zhang Heng spent many years learning mathematics and astronomy instead. ❻ His accomplishments in these fields are extremely noteworthy and rival his literary fame. ❼ He was able to create an accurate chart of the stars, which assisted in keeping the imperial calendar accurate. ❽ He also invented a flying machine, which was able to leave the ground, though only for a few moments. ❾ In 132, he invented the first seismograph, which traced the direction of earthquakes and their seismic waves. ❿ It was only later in his life that Zhang Heng held a series of important government positions in the capital and remote regions, beginning in 116 and continuing until his death.

*aptitude 소질, 재능   **seismograph 지진계

❶ Zhang Heng(장형)은 중국 Henan(허난)에서 서기 78년에 태어났다. ❷ 어린 시절에 그는 교육을 받기 위해 Chang'an(장안)과 Luoyang(낙양)으로 갔다. ❸ Zhang Heng은 문학 활동에 일찍이 소질을 보였고 20대에 시로 명성을 얻었다. ❹ 그의 작품 *To Live in Seclusion*(귀전부)은 한 왕조 후기의 걸작으로 여겨진다. ❺ 당시 중국에서 대부분의 교육받은 젊은이들이 관직을 얻기 위해 노력했지만, Zhang Heng은 대신 수학과 천문학을 배우며 여러 해를 보냈다. ❻ 이들 분야에서의 그의 업적은 매우 주목할 만하고 그의 문학적 명성에 필적한다. ❼ 그는 정확한 성도(星圖)를 만들 수 있었는데, 그것은 황실의 달력을 정확하게 유지하는 데 도움이 되었다. ❽ 그는 또한 비행 장치를 발명했는데, 그것은 비록 잠깐 동안이었지만 이륙할 수 있었다. ❾ 132년에 그는 최초의 지진계를 발명했는데, 그것은 지진의 방향과 지진파를 추적할 수 있었다. ❿ 말년이 되어서야 비로소 Zhang Heng은 116년부터 죽을 때까지 계속 수도와 외진 지역에서 일련의 중요한 관직을 맡았다.

Word List

□ literary 문학의   □ pursuit 활동, 취미, 추구   □ achieve 성취하다   □ fame 명성   □ masterpiece 걸작
□ Han dynasty (중국의) 한 왕조   □ obtain 얻다, 획득하다   □ government post 관직, 벼슬   □ astronomy 천문학
□ accomplishment 업적   □ noteworthy 주목할 만한   □ rival ~에 필적하다[버금가다]   □ chart 도(圖), 도표   □ assist 도움이 되다
□ imperial 황실의, 제국의   □ trace 추적하다; 흔적   □ seismic wave 지진파   □ remote 외진, 먼

• Word Test

1	literary	___	9	얻다, 획득하다	___
2	achieve	___	10	도(圖), 도표	___
3	assist	___	11	외진, 먼	___
4	accomplishment	___	12	황실의, 제국의	___
5	trace	___	13	주목할 만한	___
6	rival	___	14	활동, 취미, 추구	___
7	government post	___	15	명성	___
8	masterpiece	___	16	천문학	___

Zhang Heng was born in Henan, China in 78 CE. In his youth, he traveled to Chang'an and Luoyang to receive his education. Zhang Heng showed an early aptitude for literary ❶ leisures / pursuits and achieved fame for his poetry in his 20s. His work *To Live in Seclusion* is considered a masterpiece of the late Han dynasty. While most educated young men in China at the time sought to obtain government posts, Zhang Heng spent many years learning mathematics and ❷ astronomy / astrology instead. His accomplishments in these fields are extremely noteworthy and rival his literary fame. He was able to create an accurate chart of the stars, which assisted in keeping the imperial calendar ❸ accurate / inaccurate. He also invented a flying machine, ❹ which / what was able to leave the ground, though only for a few moments. In 132, he invented the first seismograph, which traced the direction of earthquakes and their seismic waves. It was only later in his life ❺ that / which Zhang Heng held a series of important government positions in the capital and remote regions, beginning in 116 and continuing until his death.

*aptitude 소질, 재능   **seismograph 지진계

Zhang Heng was born in Henan, China in 78 CE. In his youth, he traveled to Chang'an and Luoyang to receive his education. Zhang Heng showed an early aptitude for literary pursuits and achieved fame for his poetry in his 20s. His work *To Live in Seclusion* ❶ _____ (consider) a masterpiece of the late Han dynasty. While most educated young men in China at the time sought to obtain government posts, Zhang Heng spent many years ❷ _____ (learn) mathematics and astronomy instead. His accomplishments in these fields are extremely noteworthy and rival his literary fame. He was able to create an accurate chart of the stars, which assisted in ❸ _____ (keep) the imperial calendar accurate. He also invented a flying machine, which was able to leave the ground, though only for a few moments. In 132, he invented the first seismograph, which traced the direction of earthquakes and their seismic waves. It was only later in his life that Zhang Heng ❹ _____ (hold) a series of important government positions in the capital and remote regions, ❺ _____ (begin) in 116 and continuing until his death.

*aptitude 소질, 재능   **seismograph 지진계

Zhang Heng was born in Henan, China in 78 CE. In his youth, he traveled to Chang'an and Luoyang to receive his education. Zhang Heng showed an early aptitude for literary pursuits and ❶ _____ _____ _____ _____ _____ (그의 시로 명성을 얻었다) in his 20s. His work *To Live in Seclusion* is considered a masterpiece of the late Han dynasty. While most educated young men in China at the time ❷ _____ _____ _____ _____ _____ (관직들을 얻기 위해 노력했다), Zhang Heng spent many years learning mathematics and astronomy instead. His accomplishments in these fields are extremely noteworthy and ❸ _____ _____ _____ _____ (그의 문학적 명성에 필적하는). He was able to create an accurate chart of the stars, which assisted in keeping the imperial calendar accurate. He also invented a flying machine, which was able to leave the ground, ❹ _____ _____ _____ _____ _____ _____ (비록 잠깐 동안이었지만). In 132, he invented the first seismograph, which traced the direction of earthquakes and their seismic waves. It was only later in his life that Zhang Heng held a series of important government positions in the capital and remote regions, beginning in 116 and continuing until his death.

*aptitude 소질, 재능   **seismograph 지진계

❶ **2023 Westland Student Art Contest**

❷ Do you want to see your artwork displayed at an exhibition?

❸ If so, sign up for the 2023 Westland Student Art Contest

❹ Contest Theme: Our Growing Community

- ❺ All fine art media allowed (oils, acrylics, watercolours, pastels, pencils, collage, etc.)
- ❻ All submitted pieces must be A3 in size.
- ❼ Two age groups: 7-12 and 13-18 years old

❽ **Prizes for Each Age Group**

► ❾ First Place (1 person)

- ❿ A $200 gift card to use at Westland Shopping Center

► ⓫ Second Place (3 persons)

- ⓬ A $150 gift card to use at Westland Shopping Center

► ⓭ Third Place (5 persons)

- ⓮ A $100 gift card to use at Westland Shopping Center

※ ⓯ All entries will be displayed at our exhibition.

⓰ The contest will run from June 5th to July 7th.

⓱ Find terms and conditions on our website: www.westsac.org.

❶ 2023년 Westland 학생 미술 대회

❷ 여러분의 미술 작품이 전시회에 전시되는 것을 보고 싶나요?

❸ 그렇다면 2023년 Westland 학생 미술 대회에 신청하세요.

❹ 대회 주제: 성장하는 우리의 공동체

- ❺ 모든 순수 미술 표현 수단 허용(유화 물감, 아크릴 물감, 수채화 물감, 파스텔, 연필, 콜라주 등)
- ❻ 모든 제출 작품의 크기는 A3이어야 합니다.
- ❼ 두 연령대: 7~12세와 13~18세

❽ 각 연령 그룹별 상

► ❾ 일등상 (1명)

- ❿ Westland 쇼핑센터에서 사용할 수 있는 200달러 기프트 카드

► ⓫ 2등상 (3명)

— ⓬ Westland 쇼핑센터에서 사용할 수 있는 150달러 기프트 카드

► ⓭ 3등상 (5명)

- ⓮ Westland 쇼핑센터에서 사용할 수 있는 100달러 기프트 카드

※ ⓯ 모든 출품작은 우리 전시회에 전시될 것입니다.

⓰ 대회는 6월 5일부터 7월 7일까지 진행될 것입니다.

⓱ 저희 웹 사이트 www.westsac.org에서 계약 조건을 찾아보십시오.

Word List

□ artwork 미술 작품   □ display 전시하다   □ exhibition 전시회   □ community 지역사회   □ acrylics 아크릴 물감
□ watercolour 수채화   □ collage 콜라주(색종이나 사진 등의 조각들을 붙여 그림을 만드는 미술 기법, 또는 그렇게 만든 그림)
□ submit 제출하다   □ piece 작품   □ entry 출품작   □ terms and conditions 계약 조건

• Word Test

1	collage	6	제출하다
2	acrylics	7	전시하다
3	piece	8	출품작
4	artwork	9	수채화
5	exhibition	10	지역사회

2023 Westland Student Art Contest

Do you want to see your artwork displayed at an ❶ admission / exhibition ?

If so, sign up for the 2023 Westland Student Art Contest

Contest ❷ Theme / Region : Our Growing Community

- All ❸ fare / fine art media allowed (oils, acrylics, watercolours, pastels, pencils, collage, etc.)
- All submitted pieces must be A3 in size.
- Two age groups: 7-12 and 13-18 years old

Prizes for Each Age Group

► First Place (1 person)

- A $200 gift card to use at Westland Shopping Center

► Second Place (3 persons)

- A $150 gift card to use at Westland Shopping Center

► Third Place (5 persons)

- A $100 gift card to use at Westland Shopping Center

※ All ❹ hosts / entries will be displayed at our exhibition.

The contest will ❺ take / run from June 5th to July 7th.

Find terms and conditions on our website: www.westsac.org.

2023 Westland Student Art Contest

Do you want to see your artwork ❶ _____ (display) at an exhibition?

If so, sign up for the 2023 Westland Student Art Contest

Contest Theme: Our ❷ _____ (Grow) Community

- All fine art media allowed (oils, acrylics, watercolours, pastels, pencils, collage, etc.)
- All ❸ _____ (submit) pieces must be A3 in size.
- Two age groups: 7-12 and 13-18 years old

Prizes for Each Age Group

► First Place (1 person)

- A $200 gift card ❹ _____ (use) at Westland Shopping Center

► Second Place (3 persons)

-A $150 gift card to use at Westland Shopping Center

► Third Place (5 persons)

-A $100 gift card to use at Westland Shopping Center

※ All entries will ❺ _____ (display) at our exhibition.

The contest will run from June 5th to July 7th.

Find terms and conditions on our website: www.westsac.org.

2023 Westland Student Art Contest

Do you want to see your artwork displayed at an exhibition?

If so, ❶ _____ _____ _____ (~에 신청하다) the 2023 Westland Student Art Contest

Contest Theme: Our Growing Community

• All fine art media allowed (oils, acrylics, watercolours, pastels, pencils, collage, etc.)
• All submitted pieces must be A3 ❷ _____ _____ (크기는).
• Two age groups: 7-12 and 13-18 years old

❸ _____ _____ _____ _____ _____ (각 연령 그룹별 상들)

► First Place (1 person)
– A $200 gift card to use at Westland Shopping Center
► Second Place (3 persons)
– A $150 gift card to use at Westland Shopping Center
► Third Place (5 persons)
– A $100 gift card to use at Westland Shopping Center

※ All entries will be displayed at our exhibition.

The contest will run from June 5th to July 7th.

Find ❹ _____ _____ _____ (계약과 조건들) on our website: www.westsac.org.

❶ 2023 Happy Mall Dance Challenge with Your Dad

❷ In partnership with the trendy short-video platform ShortClip, we want to level up the "home date" fun this Father's Day. ❸ We invite kids and dads to show their dance moves and take on the dance challenge!

❹ The challenge has three super easy steps:

1. ❺ Together with your dad, record a ShortClip video dancing to your favorite song.

2. ❻ Your video should be 15-30 seconds long.

3. ❼ Post it only on ShortClip with the hashtags #FathersDay DanceChallenge and #happymall by June 12.

※ ❽ Make sure your account is set to public to validate your entry.

❾ The top 5 most viewed videos from June 12 to 18 will get a special prize from Happy Mall. ❿ So join now!

⓫ For more information, scan the QR code below.

❶ 아빠와 함께하는 2023 Happy Mall 댄스 챌린지

❷ 최신 유행인 짧은 비디오 플랫폼 Short Clip과 협력하여 저희는 이번 아버지의 날 '홈 데이트'의 재미를 끌어올리고자 합니다.

❸ 우리는 춤 동작을 보여 주어 댄스 챌린지에 응하도록 아이와 아빠들을 초대합니다!

❹ 도전에는 매우 쉬운 세 가지 단계가 있습니다.

1. ❺ 아빠와 함께, 여러분이 가장 좋아하는 노래에 맞춰 춤을 추는 짧은 ShortClip 동영상을 녹화하세요.

2. ❻ 동영상의 길이는 15~30초여야 합니다.

3. ❼ 6월 12일까지 #FathersDay DanceChallenge와 #happymall의 해시태그를 달아 ShortClip에만 게시하세요.

※ ❽ 참가를 인증하기 위해 반드시 여러분의 계정이 공개로 설정되도록 하세요.

❾ 6월 12일부터 18일까지 가장 많이 시청된 5개의 동영상은 Happy Mall에서 특별 상품이 주어집니다. ❿ 그러니 지금 참여하세요!

⓫ 더 많은 정보를 원하시면, 아래의 QR 코드를 스캔하세요.

Word List

☐ **in partnership with** ~과 협력하여   ☐ **trendy** 최신 유행의   ☐ **platform** 플랫폼(사용 기반이 되는 컴퓨터 시스템·소프트웨어)
☐ **move** 동작, 움직임   ☐ **take on** 응하다, 받아들이다   ☐ **super** 아주, 특히   ☐ **dance to** ~에 맞추어 춤추다   ☐ **post** 게시하다
☐ **hashtag** 해시태그   ☐ **make sure** 반드시 ~하도록 하다   ☐ **account** 계정   ☐ **validate** 인증하다, 확인하다   ☐ **entry** 참가
☐ **view** 보다

• Word Test

1	account		7	보다
2	super		8	~에 맞추어 춤추다
3	move		9	인증하다, 확인하다
4	entry		10	응하다, 받아들이다
5	in partnership with		11	반드시 ~하도록 하다
6	post		12	최신 유행의

2023 Happy Mall Dance Challenge with Your Dad

In partnership with the trendy short-video platform ShortClip, we want to level up the "home date" fun this Father's Day. We invite kids and dads to show their dance ❶ moves / changes and take on the dance challenge!

The challenge has three super easy steps:

1. Together with your dad, record a ShortClip video dancing to your favorite song.

2. Your video should be 15-30 seconds ❷ short / long.

3. ❸ Mail / Post it only on ShortClip with the hashtags #FathersDayDanceChallenge and #happymall by June 12.

※ Make sure your account is set to public to ❹ validate / invalidate your entry.

The top 5 most viewed videos from June 12 to 18 will get a special prize from Happy Mall. So join now!

For more information, ❺ scan / skim the QR code below.

2023 Happy Mall Dance Challenge with Your Dad

In partnership with the trendy short-video platform ShortClip, we want to level up the "home date" fun this Father's Day. We invite kids and dads ❶ _____ (show) their dance moves and take on the dance challenge!

The challenge ❷ _____ (have) three super easy steps:

1. Together with your dad, record a ShortClip video ❸ _____ (dance) to your favorite song.

2. Your video should be 15-30 seconds long.

3. Post it only on ShortClip with the hashtags #FathersDayDanceChallenge and #happymall by June 12.

※ Make sure your account ❹ _____ (set) to public to validate your entry.

The top 5 most ❺ _____ (view) videos from June 12 to 18 will get a special prize from Happy Mall. So join now!

For more information, scan the QR code below.

2023 Happy Mall Dance Challenge with Your Dad

❶ _____ _____ _____ (~와 협력하여) the trendy short-video platform ShortClip, we want to level up the "home date" fun this Father's Day. We invite kids and dads to show their dance moves and ❷ _____ _____ _____ _____ _____ (댄스 챌린지에 응하다)!

The challenge has three super easy steps:

1. Together with your dad, record a ShortClip video dancing to your favorite song.

2. Your video should be 15-30 seconds long.

3. Post it only on ShortClip with the hashtags #FathersDayDanceChallenge and #happymall by June 12.

※ Make sure your account is set to public to validate your entry.

The top 5 ❸ _____ _____ _____ (가장 많이 시청된 동영상들) from June 12 to 18 will get a special prize from Happy Mall. So join now!

❹ _____ _____ _____ (더 많은 정보를 원하면), scan the QR code below.

❶ When we are young, we see our parents as people who always know the answers. ❷ That's probably why as soon as we can think independently, around the ages of 4-5, we start asking a lot of questions. ❸ Parents try to answer these questions in a way that a young mind can comprehend. ❹ However, when it comes to learning lessons about money, our parents' answers to these questions get written into a money blueprint. ❺ Even worse, a passing comment about money in the kitchen or at the dinner table can have a lasting effect. ❻ For example, a common phrase used by parents in response to a child's request for something is "No, we can't afford that." ❼ Think for a moment about how a young mind might interpret that. ❽ The message could be interpreted as "we don't have enough money" or "there isn't enough money." ❾ These beliefs about money can lead to an entire life designed around making sure there is always enough money through an obsession around work. ❿ It could lead to someone feeling deprived and a propensity for overspending in adulthood to avoid the feeling of deprivation.

*obsession 집착 **propensity 경향

❶ 어릴 때, 우리는 부모를 항상 정답을 아는 사람으로 생각한다. ❷ 아마도 그것이 우리가 4~5세 무렵에 독립적으로 생각할 수 있게 되면 곧 많은 질문을 하기 시작하는 이유일 것이다. ❸ 부모는 이러한 질문에 대해 어린 아이가 이해할 수 있는 방식으로 답하려고 노력한다. ❹ 하지만 돈에 대한 교훈을 얻는 것에 관한 한, 이러한 질문에 대한 우리 부모의 대답은 돈의 청사진에 기록된다. ❺ 설상가상으로, 부엌이나 저녁 식탁에서 이루어지는 돈에 관한 지나가는 말이 지속적인 영향을 미칠 수 있다. ❻ 예를 들어, 무언가에 대한 아이의 요구에 대응하여 부모가 흔히 사용하는 구절은 "안 돼, 우리는 그럴 여유가 없다."이다. ❼ 어린아이가 그것을 어떻게 해석할지 잠시 생각해 보라. ❽ 그 메시지는 "우리는 돈이 충분치 않다." 또는 "충분한 돈이 없다."로 해석될 수 있다. ❾ 돈에 관한 이러한 믿음은 일에 대한 집착을 통해 반드시 돈이 항상 충분히 있게 하는 것을 중심으로 설계된 평생의 삶으로 이어질 수 있다. ❿ 그것은 누군가가 박탈감을 느끼고 그 박탈감을 피하기 위해 성인이 되었을 때 과소비를 하는 경향을 초래할 수 있다.

Word List

□ independently 독립적으로 □ comprehend 이해하다 □ when it comes to ~에 관한 한 □ learn a lesson 교훈을 얻다
□ write ~ into ... ~을 …에 기록하다[명시하다] □ blueprint 청사진, 설계도 □ passing 지나가는, 잠깐의 □ lasting 지속적인
□ effect 효과 □ phrase 구절, 어구 □ in response to ~에 대응하여 □ request 요구 □ afford (~할) 여유가 있다
□ interpret 해석하다 □ overspending 과소비, 돈의 탕진 □ deprivation 박탈, 궁핍, 가난

• Word Test

1	afford			
2	independently			
3	effect			
4	when it comes to			
5	in response to			
6	overspending			
7	passing			
8	이해하다			
9	박탈, 궁핍, 가난			
10	요구			
11	해석하다			
12	구절, 어구			
13	지속적인			
14	청사진, 설계도			

When we are young, we see our parents as people who always know the answers. That's probably why as soon as we can think ❶ dependently / independently , around the ages of 4-5, we start asking a lot of questions. Parents try to answer these questions in a way that a young mind can ❷ comprehend / misunderstand . However, when it comes to learning lessons about money, our parents' answers to these questions get written into a money blueprint. Even ❸ better / worse , a passing comment about money in the kitchen or at the dinner table can have a lasting effect. For example, a common phrase used by parents in response to a child's request for something is "No, we can't afford that." Think for a moment about how a young mind might interpret that. The message could be interpreted ❹ as / on "we don't have enough money" or "there isn't enough money." These beliefs about money can lead to an entire life designed around making sure there is always enough money through an obsession around work. It could lead to someone feeling deprived and a propensity for ❺ overeating / overspending in adulthood to avoid the feeling of deprivation.

*obsession 집착 **propensity 경향

When we are young, we see our parents as people who always know the answers. That's probably why as soon as we can think independently, around the ages of 4-5, we start asking a lot of questions. Parents try ❶ _____ (answer) these questions in a way that a young mind can comprehend. However, when it comes to ❷ _____ (learn) lessons about money, our parents' answers to these questions get written into a money blueprint. Even worse, a passing comment about money in the kitchen or at the dinner table can have a lasting effect. For example, a common phrase ❸ _____ (use) by parents in response to a child's request for something is "No, we can't afford that." Think for a moment about how a young mind might interpret that. The message could ❹ _____ (interpret) as "we don't have enough money" or "there isn't enough money." These beliefs about money can lead to an entire life ❺ _____ (design) around making sure there is always enough money through an obsession around work. It could lead to someone feeling deprived and a propensity for overspending in adulthood to avoid the feeling of deprivation.

*obsession 집착 **propensity 경향

When we are young, we see our parents as people who always know the answers. That's probably why as soon as we can think independently, around the ages of 4-5, we start asking a lot of questions. Parents try to answer these questions in a way that a young mind can comprehend. However, ❶ _____ _____ _____ _____ (~에 관한 한) learning lessons about money, our parents' answers to these questions ❷ _____ _____ _____ _____ _____ _____ (돈의 청사진에 기록되다). Even worse, a passing comment about money in the kitchen or at the dinner table can ❸ _____ _____ _____ _____ (지속적인 영향을 미치다). For example, a common phrase used by parents in response to a child's request for something is "No, we can't afford that." Think for a moment about how a young mind might interpret that. The message could be interpreted as "we don't have enough money" or "there isn't enough money." These beliefs about money can lead to an entire life designed around making sure there is always enough money through an obsession around work. It could lead to someone feeling deprived and a propensity for overspending in adulthood to ❹ _____ _____ _____ _____ _____ (박탈감을 피하다).

*obsession 집착 **propensity 경향

❶ The idea that zebra stripes work to confuse predators while the zebra is in motion is a relatively early theory. ❷ This is a plausible possibility; zebras have the high-contrast patterning generally thought to promote dazzle effects, and as herd animals they might benefit from an interaction between dazzle effects and confusion effects created when targeting individuals in groups. ❸ They also have visually oriented lions and hyenas as their main predators, and as large animals that live in the open, they might find camouflaging via other mechanisms difficult. ❹ The motion dazzle hypothesis has been studied in zebras by modelling the motion signals created by moving zebra stripes. ❺ This analysis shows that zebra stripes create strong motion signals in directions other than the true direction of movement, supporting the hypothesis that zebra stripes make movement processing difficult. ❻ While most recent work focuses on whether zebra stripes function as protection against biting insects rather than mammalian carnivores, this idea is not necessarily mutually exclusive with the dazzle hypothesis. ❼ Rather than (or in addition to) lions and hyenas, stripes may target the motion processing of much smaller but no less fitness-reducing flies instead.

*dazzle 현혹 **camouflage 위장하다 ***carnivore 육식 동물

❶ 얼룩말이 움직이는 동안 얼룩말 줄무늬가 작용하여 포식자를 혼란스럽게 한다는 생각은 비교적 초기 이론이다. ❷ 이것은 그럴듯한 가능성인데, 왜냐하면 얼룩말은 일반적으로 현혹 효과를 촉진하는 것으로 생각되는 고대비 무늬를 가지고 있으며, 무리 동물로서 그들은 집단 속의 개체를 표적으로 삼을 때 생성되는 현혹 효과와 혼란 효과의 상호 작용으로부터 이익을 얻을 수도 있기 때문이다. ❸ 그들은 또한 시각 위주의 사자와 하이에나를 자신들의 주요 포식자로 가지고 있는데, 야외에 사는 대형 동물로서 다른 방법을 통한 위장이 어렵다는 것을 알고 있을지도 모른다. ❹ 움직임 현혹 가설은 움직이는 얼룩말 줄무늬에 의해 생성되는 움직임 신호의 모형을 만들어 얼룩말에서 연구되었다. ❺ 이 분석은 얼룩말 줄무늬가 실제 이동 방향이 아닌 방향으로 강한 움직임 신호를 생성한다는 것을 보여 주고, 이는 얼룩말 줄무늬가 이동 정보 처리를 어렵게 만든다는 가설을 뒷받침한다. ❻ 아주 최근의 연구는 얼룩말 줄무늬가 포유류 육식 동물보다 무는 곤충에 대한 보호 기능을 하는지 여부에 초점을 맞추지만, 이 견해가 현혹 가설과 반드시 상호 배타적인 것은 아니다. ❼ 줄무늬는 사자와 하이에나보다는 (혹은 사자와 하이에나뿐만 아니라), 대신 훨씬 더 작지만 못지않게 적응도를 감소시키는 파리의 움직임 정보 처리를 겨냥할 수도 있다.

Word List

□ zebra 얼룩말 □ stripe 줄무늬 □ confuse 혼란스럽게 만들다 □ predator 포식자 □ in motion 움직이고 있는
□ relatively 상대적으로 □ plausible 그럴듯한 □ possibility 가능성 □ contrast 대조, 차이 □ patterning 무늬
□ promote 촉진하다 □ herd 무리, 떼 □ target 표적[목표]으로 삼다, 겨냥하다 □ via ~을 통하여 □ mechanism 방법, 메커니즘
□ hypothesis 가설 □ analysis 분석 □ bite 물다 □ mammalian 포유류의

• Word Test

1	plausible		10 방법, 메커니즘	
2	zebra		11 포식자	
3	hypothesis		12 무리, 떼	
4	confuse		13 무늬	
5	promote		14 상대적으로	
6	contrast		15 줄무늬	
7	via		16 포유류의	
8	bite		17 가능성	
9	in motion		18 분석	

The idea that zebra stripes work to confuse predators while the zebra is in motion is a relatively early theory. This is a ❶ plausible / improbable possibility; zebras have the high-contrast patterning generally thought to promote dazzle effects, and as herd animals they might benefit from an interaction between dazzle effects and confusion effects created when targeting individuals in groups. They also have visually oriented lions and hyenas as their main predators, and as large animals ❷ that / what live in the open, they might find camouflaging via other mechanisms difficult. The motion dazzle hypothesis has been studied in zebras by modelling the motion signals created by moving zebra stripes. This analysis shows that zebra stripes create strong motion signals in directions other than the true direction of movement, supporting the hypothesis that zebra stripes make movement processing ❸ difficult / effortless. While most recent work focuses on whether zebra stripes function as ❹ prevention / protection against biting insects rather than mammalian carnivores, this idea is not necessarily mutually exclusive with the dazzle hypothesis. Rather than (or in addition to) lions and hyenas, stripes may target the motion processing of much smaller but no ❺ more / less fitness-reducing flies instead.

*dazzle 현혹   **camouflage 위장하다   ***carnivore 육식 동물

The idea that zebra stripes work to confuse predators while the zebra is in motion is a relatively early theory. This is a plausible possibility; zebras have the high-contrast patterning generally ❶ _____ (think) to promote dazzle effects, and as herd animals they might benefit from an interaction between dazzle effects and confusion effects ❷ _____ (create) when targeting individuals in groups. They also have visually oriented lions and hyenas as their main predators, and as large animals that live in the open, they might find camouflaging via other mechanisms difficult. The motion dazzle hypothesis has ❸ _____ (study) in zebras by modelling the motion signals created by moving zebra stripes. This analysis shows that zebra stripes create strong motion signals in directions other than the true direction of movement, ❹ _____ (support) the hypothesis that zebra stripes make movement processing difficult. While most recent work focuses on whether zebra stripes function as protection against ❺ _____ (bite) insects rather than mammalian carnivores, this idea is not necessarily mutually exclusive with the dazzle hypothesis. Rather than (or in addition to) lions and hyenas, stripes may target the motion processing of much smaller but no less fitness-reducing flies instead.

*dazzle 현혹   **camouflage 위장하다   ***carnivore 육식 동물

The idea that zebra stripes work to confuse predators while the zebra is in motion is a relatively early theory. This is a plausible possibility; zebras have the high-contrast patterning generally thought to promote dazzle effects, and as herd animals they might ❶ _____ _____ _____ _____ (상호 작용으로부터 이익을 얻는다) between dazzle effects and confusion effects created when targeting individuals in groups. They also have visually oriented lions and hyenas as their main predators, and as large animals that ❷ _____ _____ _____ _____ (야외에 산다), they might find camouflaging via other mechanisms difficult. The motion dazzle hypothesis has been studied in zebras by modelling the motion signals created by moving zebra stripes. This analysis shows that zebra stripes create strong motion signals in directions other than the ❸ _____ _____ _____ _____ (실제 이동 방향), supporting the hypothesis that zebra stripes make movement processing difficult. While most recent work focuses on whether zebra stripes function as protection against biting insects rather than mammalian carnivores, this idea is ❹ _____ _____ _____ _____ (반드시 상호 배타적인 것은 아닌) with the dazzle hypothesis. Rather than (or in addition to) lions and hyenas, stripes may target the motion processing of much smaller but no less fitness-reducing flies instead.

*dazzle 현혹 **camouflage 위장하다 ***carnivore 육식 동물

❶ It is interesting to reflect on the possible connection between increasing individualism and rising mental ill-health. ❷ This is discussed at length in Oliver James's book *Affluenza*, in which he points out that the United States, the world's most individualist society, is also on the top of the league for mental disorders (as recorded by the World Health Organization's World Mental Health Survey). ❸ Several other countries that rate highly on individualism also figure highly in this league table. ❹ Comparing just 14 countries, including New Zealand (2nd), France (4th) and the Netherlands (7th), James defines 'affluenza' as 'the placing of a high value on money, possessions, appearances (physical and social) and fame', and he attributes this to what he calls 'selfish capitalism'. ❺ It could certainly be argued that the relative importance attached to materialistic factors related to self-esteem is particularly important in cultures where 'selfish capitalism' is strong.

❶ 증가하는 개인주의와 늘어나는 정신 질환 사이에 있을 수도 있는 연관성에 관해 생각해 보는 것은 흥미롭다. ❷ 이는 Oliver James의 저서 *Affluenza*에서 상세히 다루어지는데, 여기에서 그는 세계에서 가장 개인주의적인 사회인 미국이 (세계보건기구의 세계정신건강조사에 의해 기록된 바와 같이) 정신 질환의 범주에서도 최고라는 점을 지적한다. ❸ 개인주의가 높다고 평가되는 몇몇 다른 나라들 또한 이 비교 일람표에서 높게 나타난다. ❹ 뉴질랜드(2위), 프랑스(4위), 그리고 네덜란드(7위)를 포함하여 정확히 14개국을 비교해 본 뒤에, James는 '부자병'을 '돈, 소유물, (신체적·사회적) 외양과 평판에 높은 가치를 두는 것'으로 정의하며, 이것을 자신이 '이기적 자본주의'라고 부르는 것 때문으로 여긴다. ❺ '이기적 자본주의'가 강한 문화에서는 자존감과 관련된 물질적 요소에 부여되는 상대적 중요성이 특히 중요하다고 확실히 주장할 수 있을 것이다.

Word List

□ reflect on ~에 관해 (곰곰이) 생각하다 □ connection 연관성 □ individualism 개인주의 □ ill-health 질환, 병마
□ at length 상세히, 길게 □ point out ~을 지적하다 □ individualist 개인주의의 □ league 범주, 부류 □ mental disorder 정신 질환
□ record 기록하다 □ rate 평가되다, 여겨지다 □ figure (두각) 나타내다, 두드러지다 □ league table 비교 일람표
□ possession 소유물 □ appearance 외양, 외모 □ fame 평판, 명성 □ attribute - to ... ~을 …때문으로 여기다
□ capitalism 자본주의 □ relative 상대적인 □ attach 부여하다 □ factor 요소 □ self-esteem 자존감

• Word Test

1	rate		11	질환, 병마	
2	mental disorder		12	범주, 부류	
3	individualism		13	자본주의	
4	factor		14	외양, 외모	
5	at length		15	연관성	
6	possession		16	평판, 명성	
7	figure		17	자존감	
8	relative		18	~을 지적하다	
9	reflect on		19	기록하다	
10	individualist		20	부여하다	

● 유형 1 네모 안에서 옳은 어법·어휘를 고르시오.

It is interesting to reflect on the possible connection between increasing individualism and rising mental ill-health. This is discussed at length in Oliver James's book *Affluenza*, ❶ in / by which he points out that the United States, the world's most individualist society, is also on the top of the league for ❷ mental / physical disorders (as recorded by the World Health Organization's World Mental Health Survey). ❸ Severe / Several other countries that rate highly on individualism also figure highly in this league table. Comparing just 14 countries, including New Zealand (2nd), France (4th) and the Netherlands (7th), James ❹ defines / refines 'affluenza' as 'the placing of a high value on money, possessions, appearances (physical and social) and fame', and he attributes this to ❺ what / which he calls 'selfish capitalism'. It could certainly be argued that the relative importance attached to materialistic factors related to self-esteem is particularly important in cultures where 'selfish capitalism' is strong.

● 유형 2 괄호 안의 동사를 알맞은 형태로 쓰시오.

It is interesting to reflect on the possible connection between increasing individualism and rising mental ill-health. This is discussed at length in Oliver James's book *Affluenza*, in which he ❶ _____ (point) out that the United States, the world's most individualist society, is also on the top of the league for mental disorders (as recorded by the World Health Organization's World Mental Health Survey). Several other countries that ❷ _____ (rate) highly on individualism also figure highly in this league table. ❸ _____ (Compare) just 14 countries, including New Zealand (2nd), France (4th) and the Netherlands (7th), James defines 'affluenza' as 'the placing of a high value on money, possessions, appearances (physical and social) and fame', and he attributes this to what he calls 'selfish capitalism'. It could certainly ❹ _____ (argue) that the relative importance attached to materialistic factors related to self-esteem is particularly important in cultures where 'selfish capitalism' is strong.

● 유형 3 우리말에 맞게 빈칸에 알맞은 말을 쓰시오.

It is interesting to ❶ _____ _____ _____ _____ _____ (있을 수도 있는 연관성에 관해 생각해 보다) between increasing individualism and rising mental ill-health. This is discussed at length in Oliver James's book *Affluenza*, in which he points out that the United States, the world's most individualist society, is also on the top of the league for mental disorders (as recorded by the World Health Organization's World Mental Health Survey). Several other countries that ❷ _____ _____ _____ _____ (개인주의에 대해 높게 평가되다) also figure highly in this league table. Comparing just 14 countries, including New Zealand (2nd), France (4th) and the Netherlands (7th), James defines 'affluenza' as 'the placing of a high value on money, possessions, appearances (physical and social) and fame', and he ❸ _____ _____ _____ (이것을 ~ 때문으로 여긴다) what he calls 'selfish capitalism'. It could certainly be argued that the relative importance ❹ _____ _____ _____ _____ (물질적 요소들에 부여되는) related to self-esteem is particularly important in cultures where 'selfish capitalism' is strong.

❶ Sensors are opening vast new windows on the cosmos. ❷ Thanks to the constant advance of sensors and effectors in the form of adaptive optics, discovery of extrasolar planets moved from science fiction to commonplace with breathtaking speed. ❸ In the near future, sensor advances will allow us to analyze exoplanetary atmospheres and look for signatures of civilization. ❹ The same trends will open new horizons for amateur astronomers, who will soon enjoy affordable technical means to match the *Kepler* space telescope in planet-finding skills. ❺ Sensors are thus as much about democratizing amateur science as the creation of ever more powerful instruments. ❻ The *Kepler* satellite imaged a field of 115°, or a mere 0.25 percent of the sky. ❼ Planet-finding amateurs using digitally empowered backyard scopes could put a serious dent in the 99.75 percent of the sky yet to be examined.

*effector 이펙터(영상이나 음성 신호 등을 전기 신호로 바꿔 다양한 효과를 연출하는 장치)
**optics 광학   ***dent (초기 단계의) 진척, 영향

❶ 센서는 우주를 이해할 방대한 새로운 창을 열고 있다. ❷ 적응 제어 광학의 형태로 센서와 이펙터가 지속적으로 발전한 덕분에 태양계 밖에 있는 행성의 발견은 놀라운 속도로 공상 과학 소설에서 흔히 있는 일로 이동했다. ❸ 가까운 미래에 센서의 발전으로 우리는 태양계 밖에 있는 행성의 대기를 분석하고 문명의 표시를 찾을 수 있을 것이다. ❹ 동일한 추세가 아마추어 천문학자들에게 새로운 지평을 열어 줄 것인데, 이들은 곧 행성을 찾는 기량에서 '케플러' 우주 망원경에 필적할 만한 적당한 가격의 기술적 수단을 누리게 될 것이다. ❺ 따라서 센서는 더욱더 강력한 도구를 만드는 것만큼이나 아마추어 과학을 대중화하는 것과 관련이 있다. ❻ '케플러' 위성은 115°의 시계, 즉 단지 하늘의 0.25퍼센트의 이미지를 촬영했다. ❼ 디지털 방식으로 작동되는 뒷마당의 관찰용 기구[망원경]를 사용하여 행성을 찾는 아마추어들은 아직 조사되지 않은 하늘의 99.75퍼센트에서 큰 진척을 이루어 낼 수 있을 것이다.

Word List

□ **sensor** 센서, 원격측정기(다른 천체를 관측하는 장치)   □ **vast** 방대한   □ **cosmos** 우주   □ **constant** 지속적인, 부단한
□ **adaptive optics** 적응 (제어) 광학   □ **extrasolar** 태양계 밖의   □ **planet** 행성   □ **commonplace** 흔히 있는 일, 다반사
□ **breathtaking** 놀라운, 놀랄 만한   □ **analyze** 분석하다   □ **exoplanetary** 태양계 밖 행성의   □ **signature** 표시, 특징
□ **civilization** 문명   □ **trend** 추세, 동향   □ **horizon** 지평   □ **astronomer** 천문학자   □ **affordable** (가격이) 적당한
□ **telescope** 망원경   □ **instrument** 도구, 기구   □ **empower** 작동시키다, 권한을 주다   □ **scope** 관찰용 기구

• Word Test

1	trend		10	흔히 있는 일, 다반사
2	signature		11	지평
3	breathtaking		12	문명
4	telescope		13	태양계 밖의
5	vast		14	관찰용 기구
6	constant		15	분석하다
7	empower		16	우주
8	astronomer		17	도구, 기구
9	planet		18	(가격이) 적당한

네모 안에서 옳은 어법·어휘를 고르시오.

Sensors are opening vast new windows on the cosmos. ❶ Thanks to / In spite of the constant advance of sensors and effectors in the form of adaptive optics, discovery of extrasolar planets moved from science fiction to ❷ placement / commonplace with breathtaking speed. In the near future, sensor advances will allow us to analyze exoplanetary atmospheres and look for signatures of civilization. The same trends will open new horizons for amateur astronomers, ❸ who / what will soon enjoy ❹ affordable / confidential technical means to match the *Kepler* space telescope in planet-finding skills. Sensors are thus as much about democratizing amateur science as the creation of ever more powerful instruments. The *Kepler* satellite imaged a field of 115°, or a mere 0.25 percent of the sky. Planet-finding amateurs using digitally ❺ empowered / empowering backyard scopes could put a serious dent in the 99.75 percent of the sky yet to be examined.

*effector 이펙터(영상이나 음성 신호 등을 전기 신호로 바꿔 다양한 효과를 연출하는 장치)   **optics 광학   ***dent (초기 단계의) 진척, 영향

괄호 안의 동사를 알맞은 형태로 쓰시오.

Sensors are opening vast new windows on the cosmos. Thanks to the constant advance of sensors and effectors in the form of adaptive optics, discovery of extrasolar planets ❶ _____ (move) from science fiction to commonplace with breathtaking speed. In the near future, sensor advances will allow us ❷ _____ (analyze) exoplanetary atmospheres and look for signatures of civilization. The same trends will open new horizons for amateur astronomers, who will soon enjoy affordable technical means ❸ _____ (match) the *Kepler* space telescope in planet-finding skills. Sensors are thus as much about democratizing amateur science as the creation of ever more powerful instruments. The *Kepler* satellite ❹ _____ (image) a field of 115°, or a mere 0.25 percent of the sky. Planet-finding amateurs ❺ _____ (use) digitally empowered backyard scopes could put a serious dent in the 99.75 percent of the sky yet to be examined.

*effector 이펙터(영상이나 음성 신호 등을 전기 신호로 바꿔 다양한 효과를 연출하는 장치)   **optics 광학   ***dent (초기 단계의) 진척, 영향

우리말에 맞게 빈칸에 알맞은 말을 쓰시오.

Sensors are opening vast new windows on the cosmos. Thanks to the constant advance of sensors and effectors ❶ _____ _____ _____ _____ (~의 형태로) adaptive optics, discovery of extrasolar planets moved from science fiction to commonplace ❷ _____ _____ _____ (놀라운 속도로). In the near future, sensor advances will allow us to analyze exoplanetary atmospheres and look for signatures of civilization. The same trends will open new horizons for amateur astronomers, who will soon enjoy affordable technical means to match the *Kepler* space telescope in planet-finding skills. Sensors are thus as much about ❸ _____ _____ _____ (아마추어 과학을 대중화하는 것) as the creation of ever more powerful instruments. The *Kepler* satellite imaged a field of 115°, or a mere 0.25 percent of the sky. Planet-finding amateurs using digitally empowered backyard scopes could put a serious dent in the 99.75 percent of the sky ❹ _____ _____ _____ _____ (아직 조사되지 않은).

*effector 이펙터(영상이나 음성 신호 등을 전기 신호로 바꿔 다양한 효과를 연출하는 장치)   **optics 광학   ***dent (초기 단계의) 진척, 영향

❶ Basic manners fit into the category of fundamentally important social phenomena we tend to overlook. ❷ When I moved to Vancouver from California, one of the first things that struck me was that the natives, when exiting public buses through the back door, always shouted out a loud and cheerful *Thank you*! to the bus driver. ❸ It initially struck me as a bit excessive, but I've since come to see it not only as an expression of a fundamentally more pleasant populace but also as a ritual that probably helps to create more pleasant people. ❹ The bus driver, whether she realizes it or not, feels better having been thanked; she is now more inclined to drive courteously, or to remain at the stop that extra second to allow someone running late to hop on the bus. ❺ This behavior ripples out across my rainy city in subtle waves, inclining people toward virtue like wind blowing over the grass.

*populace 대중 **courteously 친절하게 ***ripple 파문처럼 퍼지다

❶ 기본 예절은 우리가 간과하는 경향이 있는 근본적으로 중요한 사회 현상의 범주에 꼭 들어맞는다. ❷ 내가 캘리포니아에서 밴쿠버로 이사했을 때 가장 먼저 나에게 특별한 인상을 준 것 중 하나는 그곳 주민들이 뒷문으로 공공 버스에서 내릴 때 버스 기사에게 항상 크고 쾌활하게 '감사합니다!'라고 외친 것이었다. ❸ 처음에는 다소 과하다는 느낌이 들었지만, 그 이후로 나는 그것을 근본적으로 더 유쾌한 주민들의 말투일 뿐만 아니라 아마도 더 즐거운 사람들을 만들어 내는 데 도움이 되는 의식으로도 보게 되었다. ❹ 버스 기사는, 그녀가 깨닫든 그렇지 않든, 감사를 받아 더 기분이 좋아서, 이제 친절하게 운전하거나 늦게 도착하는 사람이 버스에 탈 수 있도록 조금 더 정류장에 머무르고 싶어 하는 생각이 더 든다. ❺ 이 행동은 비가 많이 오는 우리 도시 전역에 미묘한 파장으로 파문처럼 퍼져서, 바람이 풀 위로 불어가는 것처럼 사람들의 마음을 선으로 기울게 한다.

Word List

□ manners 예절   □ fit into ~에 꼭 들어맞다   □ category 범주, 카테고리   □ fundamentally 근본적으로
□ phenomenon 현상 (*pl.* phenomena)   □ overlook 간과하다   □ strike 특별한 인상을 주다, 느낌이 들게 하다   □ native 현지인, 토착민
□ exiting 기존의   □ initially 처음에   □ excessive 과한   □ expression 말투, 표현법   □ ritual 의식   □ inclined ~하고 싶어 하는
□ hop (버스, 기차 등에) 타다   □ rainy 비가 많이 오는   □ subtle 미묘한   □ incline ~ toward ... ~의 마음을 …쪽으로 기울게 하다

• Word Test

1	native		9	범주, 카테고리
2	manners		10	현상
3	overlook		11	처음에
4	inclined		12	미묘한
5	expression		13	과한
6	rainy		14	의식
7	strike		15	기존의
8	fundamentally		16	(버스, 기차 등에) 타다

Basic manners fit into the category of ❶ comparatively / fundamentally important social phenomena we tend to overlook. When I moved to Vancouver from California, one of the first things that struck me was ❷ that / which the natives, when exiting public buses through the back door, always shouted out a loud and cheerful *Thank you!* to the bus driver. It initially struck me as a bit excessive, but I've since come to see it not only as an expression of a fundamentally more pleasant populace but also as a ❸ ritual / campaign that probably helps to create more pleasant people. The bus driver, ❹ whether / though she realizes it or not, feels better having been thanked; she is now more inclined to drive courteously, or to remain at the stop that extra second to allow someone running late to hop on the bus. This behavior ripples out across my rainy city in subtle waves, inclining people toward ❺ vanity / virtue like wind blowing over the grass.

*populace 대중 **courteously 친절하게 ***ripple 파문처럼 퍼지다

Basic manners fit into the category of fundamentally important social phenomena we tend to overlook. When I moved to Vancouver from California, one of the first things that ❶ _____ (strike) me was that the natives, when exiting public buses through the back door, always shouted out a loud and cheerful *Thank you!* to the bus driver. It initially struck me as a bit excessive, but I've since come to see it not only as an expression of a fundamentally more pleasant populace but also as a ritual that probably ❷ _____ (help) to create more pleasant people. The bus driver, whether she realizes it or not, ❸ _____ (feel) better having been thanked; she is now more inclined to drive courteously, or to remain at the stop that extra second to allow someone running late ❹ _____ (hop) on the bus. This behavior ripples out across my rainy city in subtle waves, inclining people toward virtue like wind ❺ _____ (blow) over the grass.

*populace 대중 **courteously 친절하게 ***ripple 파문처럼 퍼지다

Basic manners fit into the category of fundamentally important social phenomena ❶ _____ _____ _____ _____ (우리가 간과하는 경향이 있다). When I moved to Vancouver from California, one of the first things that struck me was that the natives, when exiting public buses through the back door, always shouted out a loud and cheerful *Thank you!* to the bus driver. It initially struck me ❷ _____ _____ _____ _____ (다소 과하다는), but I've since come to see it not only as an expression of a fundamentally more pleasant populace but also as a ritual that probably helps to create more pleasant people. The bus driver, whether she realizes it or not, ❸ _____ _____ _____ _____ _____ (감사를 받았기에 더 기분이 좋다); she is now more inclined to drive courteously, or to remain at the stop that extra second to allow someone running late to hop on the bus. This behavior ripples out across my rainy city ❹ _____ _____ _____ (미묘한 파장들로), inclining people toward virtue like wind blowing over the grass.

*populace 대중 **courteously 친절하게 ***ripple 파문처럼 퍼지다

❶ It matters to us how things are. ❷ But how things are not can be equally important. ❸ It matters when something you want is not there. ❹ In a variety of circumstances, it matters that a drink is sugar-free. ❺ A migraine sufferer might want any pudding as long as it is not chocolate. ❻ Anyone with an allergy or intolerance will have a similar type of negative preference. ❼ It could matter to someone that a particular train does not stop in Wakefield, if they were planning to get off there. ❽ Bereavement matters too. ❾ When a loved one is no longer around, the feeling of their absence is profound. ❿ Some fear their own non-existence more than anything else. ⓫ In other cases, things not being a certain way can be entirely mundane. ⓬ Someone might regret not being six-feet tall or not being a better chess player. ⓭ But some cases of what is not are of great, even cosmic importance. ⓮ It matters enormously that the planet Earth is not closer to the sun than it is. ⓯ It is likely that there would be no human life on the planet if it were.

*migraine 편두통 **bereavement 사별 ***mundane 평범한, 세속적인

❶ 상황이 어떠한지는 우리에게 중요하다. ❷ 하지만 상황이 어떠하지 않은지도 똑같이 중요할 수 있다. ❸ 여러분이 원하는 것이 거기에 있지 않을 때, 그것은 중요하다. ❹ 여러 상황에서 음료에 설탕이 들어 있지 않다는 것은 중요하다. ❺ 편두통 환자는 초콜릿이 아니기만 하면 아무 푸딩이라도 원할지 모른다. ❻ 알레르기나 과민증이 있는 사람은 비슷한 종류의 부정의 선호를 갖고 있을 것이다. ❼ 누군가에게는 특정한 기차가 Wakefield에서 서지 않는 것이, 그 사람이 거기서 내릴 계획을 하고 있다면, 중요할 수 있다. ❽ 사별 또한 중요하다. ❾ 사랑하는 사람이 더는 존재하지 않을 때, 그 사람의 부재에 대한 느낌은 엄청나다. ❿ 어떤 사람은 그 밖의 어떤 것보다 더 자기 자신이 존재하지 않는 것을 두려워한다. ⓫ 다른 경우에는, 상황이 특정한 방식이 아닌 것이 완전히 평범할 수 있다. ⓬ 누군가는 키가 육 피트가 안 되는 것이나 더 나은 체스 플레이어가 아닌 것을 유감으로 여길 수 있다. ⓭ 하지만 그렇지 않은 것의 몇몇 경우는 대단히, 심지어 어마어마하게 중요하다. ⓮ 지구 행성이 현재 (실제로) 그러한 것보다 태양에 더 가깝지 않은 것은 엄청나게 중요하다. ⓯ 만일 그렇다면[더 가깝다면], 지구에는 어떤 인간 생명체도 없게 될 것 같다.

• Word Test

1	enormously		8	똑같이, 동등하게	
2	matter		9	~이기만 하면, ~하는 동안은	
3	profound		10	어마어마한, 우주의	
4	intolerance		11	상황	
5	preference		12	존재하여, 있어, 근처에	
6	negative		13	다양한	
7	sufferer		14	행성, 지구	

It matters to us how things are. But how things are not can be ❶ equal / equally important. It matters when something you want is not there. In a variety of circumstances, it matters that a drink is sugar-free. A migraine sufferer might want any pudding as long as it is not chocolate. Anyone with an allergy or intolerance will have a similar type of negative preference. It could matter to someone ❷ that / who a particular train does not stop in Wakefield, if they were planning to get off there. Bereavement matters too. When a loved one is no longer around, the feeling of their absence is ❸ profound / superficial . Some fear their own non-existence more than anything else. In other cases, things not being a certain way can be entirely mundane. Someone might regret not being six-feet tall or not being a better chess player. But some cases of what is not are of great, even ❹ cosmic / universal importance. It matters enormously that the planet Earth is not closer to the sun than it is. It is likely that there would be no human life on the planet ❺ if / whether it were.

*migraine 편두통 **bereavement 사별 ***mundane 평범한, 세속적인

It matters to us how things are. But how things are not can be equally important. It matters when something you want ❶ _____ (be) not there. In a variety of circumstances, it matters that a drink is sugar-free. A migraine sufferer might want any pudding as long as it is not chocolate. Anyone with an allergy or intolerance will have a similar type of negative preference. It could matter to someone that a particular train does not stop in Wakefield, if they were ❷ _____ (plan) to get off there. Bereavement matters too. When a loved one is no longer around, the feeling of their absence is profound. Some ❸ _____ (fear) their own non-existence more than anything else. In other cases, things not being a certain way can be entirely mundane. Someone might regret not being six-feet tall or not being a better chess player. But some cases of what is not ❹ _____ (be) of great, even cosmic importance. It matters enormously that the planet Earth is not closer to the sun than it is. It is likely that there would be no human life on the planet if it ❺ _____ (be).

*migraine 편두통 **bereavement 사별 ***mundane 평범한, 세속적인

It matters to us how things are. But how things are not can be equally important. It matters when something you want is not there. ❶ _____ _____ _____ _____ _____ (여러 상황들에서), it matters that a drink is sugar-free. A migraine sufferer might want any pudding ❷ _____ _____ _____ (~이기만 하면) it is not chocolate. Anyone with an allergy or intolerance will have a similar type of negative preference. It could matter to someone that a particular train does not stop in Wakefield, if they were planning to get off there. Bereavement matters too. When a loved one is no longer around, the feeling of their absence is profound. Some fear their own non-existence more than anything else. In other cases, ❸ _____ _____ _____ _____ _____ _____ (상황이 특정한 방식이 아닌 것) can be entirely mundane. Someone might regret not being six-feet tall or not being a better chess player. But some cases of what is not are of great, ❹ _____ _____ _____ (심지어 어마어마하게 중요한). It matters enormously that the planet Earth is not closer to the sun than it is. It is likely that there would be no human life on the planet if it were.

*migraine 편두통 **bereavement 사별 ***mundane 평범한, 세속적인

168

❶ 'Mindreading' refers to the cognitive ability to attribute psychological states to other people. ❷ It is distinct from 'social cognition' which has the broader referent base of 'the cognitive structures that facilitate our ability to navigate the social world'. ❸ Social cognition is a broader category than mindreading because it is possible to successfully interact with other people without attributing psychological states to them. ❹ One might have a perfectly successful social interaction with another by responding to their behaviours, without giving any thought to the psychological states that caused them. ❺ Alternatively, one might anticipate the behaviours of another person based on social protocols about how one ought to behave in a particular situation, for example, at a pedestrian crossing or waiting in line to get on a bus. ❻ Such social protocols extend to how we expect people in different roles to behave, for example, the behaviours we expect of a bus driver and a fellow passenger. ❼ These are all instances of interacting with others which do not obviously involve reasoning about their psychological states.

*protocol 관습, (군대·궁전 등의) 의례

❶ '마음 읽기'는 심리 상태가 다른 사람에게 있다고 생각하는[다른 사람의 심리 상태를 파악하는] 인지 능력을 일컫는다. ❷ 그것은 '사회 인지'와는 뚜렷이 다른데, 사회 인지는 '우리가 사회적 세상을 항해하는 것을 용이하게 하는 인지 구조'라는 더 넓은 지시 대상 기반을 가지고 있다. ❸ 사회 인지는 마음 읽기보다 더 넓은 범주인데, 심리 상태가 다른 사람들에게 있다고 생각하지 않고 그들과 성공적으로 상호 작용하는 것이 가능하기 때문이다. ❹ 우리는 다른 사람의 행동을 일으킨 심리 상태를 전혀 생각하지 않고 그 사람의 행동에 반응함으로써 그 사람과 완전히 성공적인 사회적 상호 작용을 할 수도 있을 것이다. ❺ 그 대신에, 우리가 특정 상황에서, 예를 들어 횡단보도에서나 버스를 타기 위해 줄을 서서 기다릴 때, 어떻게 행동해야 하는지에 대한 사회적 관습을 토대로, 우리는 다른 사람의 행동을 예상할 수도 있을 것이다. ❻ 그러한 사회적 관습은 서로 다른 역할을 하는 사람들이 어떻게 행동하리라고 우리가 기대하느냐에까지, 예를 들어 버스 운전사와 동승객에게 우리가 기대하는 행동에까지 확장된다. ❼ 이것들은 모두, 명백히 다른 사람들의 심리적 상태에 대한 추론을 수반하지 않는, 다른 사람들과 상호 작용하는 사례들이다.

Word List

☐ refer to ~을 언급하다   ☐ cognitive 인지의   ☐ attribute ~ to ... ~이 …에 있다고[속한다고] 생각하다   ☐ psychological 심리적인
☐ state 상태   ☐ distinct 뚜렷이 다른, 구별되는   ☐ social 사회적인, 사교적인   ☐ cognition 인지, 인식   ☐ referent 지시 대상
☐ structure 구조   ☐ facilitate 용이하게[가능하게] 하다   ☐ navigate 항해하다, 돌아다니다   ☐ alternatively 그 대신에, 그렇지 않으면
☐ anticipate 예상하다   ☐ pedestrian crossing 횡단보도   ☐ extend 확장되다, 미치다   ☐ fellow passenger 동승객
☐ reason 추론하다; 이유

• Word Test

1	navigate		9	용이하게[가능하게] 하다
2	structure		10	추론하다; 이유
3	extend		11	그 대신에, 그렇지 않으면
4	anticipate		12	사회적인, 사교적인
5	cognition		13	지시 대상
6	psychological		14	횡단보도
7	refer to		15	상태
8	distinct		16	인지의

'Mindreading' refers to the cognitive ability to attribute psychological states to other people. It is ❶ distinct / indistinct from 'social cognition' which has the broader referent base of 'the cognitive structures that facilitate our ability to navigate the social world'. Social cognition is a ❷ broader / narrower category than mindreading because it is possible to successfully interact with other people without attributing psychological states to them. One might have a perfectly successful social interaction with ❸ another / the other by responding to their behaviours, without giving any thought to the psychological states that caused them. Alternatively, one might anticipate the behaviours of another person based on social protocols about how one ought to behave in a particular situation, for example, at a pedestrian crossing or waiting in line to get on a bus. Such social protocols ❹ intend / extend to how we expect people in different roles to behave, for example, the behaviours we expect of a bus driver and a fellow passenger. These are all instances of interacting with others which do not ❺ obvious / obviously involve reasoning about their psychological states.

*protocol 관습, (군대·궁전 등의) 의례

'Mindreading' refers to the cognitive ability to attribute psychological states to other people. It is distinct from 'social cognition' which has the broader referent base of 'the cognitive structures that facilitate our ability ❶ _____ (navigate) the social world'. Social cognition is a broader category than mindreading because it is possible to successfully ❷ _____ (interact) with other people without attributing psychological states to them. One might have a perfectly successful social interaction with another by responding to their behaviours, without giving any thought to the psychological states that ❸ _____ (cause) them. Alternatively, one might anticipate the behaviours of another person based on social protocols about how one ought to behave in a particular situation, for example, at a pedestrian crossing or ❹ _____ (wait) in line to get on a bus. Such social protocols extend to how we expect people in different roles to behave, for example, the behaviours we expect of a bus driver and a fellow passenger. These are all instances of interacting with others which do not obviously involve ❺ _____ (reason) about their psychological states.

*protocol 관습, (군대·궁전 등의) 의례

'Mindreading' ❶ _____ _____ (~을 일컫는다) the cognitive ability to attribute psychological states to other people. It is distinct from 'social cognition' which has the ❷ _____ _____ _____ (더 넓은 지시 대상 기반) of 'the cognitive structures that facilitate our ability to navigate the social world'. Social cognition is a broader category than mindreading because it is ❸ _____ _____ _____ _____ _____ (~와 성공적으로 상호 작용하는 것이 가능한) other people without attributing psychological states to them. One might have a perfectly successful social interaction with another by responding to their behaviours, without giving any thought to the psychological states that caused them. Alternatively, one might anticipate the behaviours of another person based on social protocols about how one ought to ❹ _____ _____ _____ _____ _____ (특정 상황에서 행동하다), for example, at a pedestrian crossing or waiting in line to get on a bus. Such social protocols extend to how we expect people in different roles to behave, for example, the behaviours we expect of a bus driver and a fellow passenger. These are all ❺ _____ _____ _____ _____ _____ (다른 사람들과 상호 작용하는 사례들) which do not obviously involve reasoning about their psychological states.

*protocol 관습, (군대·궁전 등의) 의례

❶ The problem of free will has real-world implications for our self-understanding, our interpersonal relationships, and our moral and legal practices. ❷ The assumption that we have free will lurks behind the justification of many of our everyday attitudes and judgments. ❸ For instance, when someone morally wrongs us, not only do we experience resentment and moral anger; we typically feel that we are *justified* in doing so, since we assume that, absent any excusing conditions, people are free and morally responsible for what they do and are therefore appropriate targets for such responses. ❹ We also typically assume that when individuals "act of their own free will," they *justly deserve* to be praised and blamed, punished and rewarded for their actions since they are morally responsible for what they do. ❺ Similar assumptions are made in the criminal law. ❻ The US Supreme Court, for instance, has asserted: "A 'universal and persistent' foundation stone in our system of law, and particularly in our approach to punishment, sentencing, and incarceration, is the 'belief in freedom of the human will and a consequent ability and duty of the normal individual to choose between good and evil.'"

*lurk 잠재하다 **incarceration 감금, 투옥

❶ 자유 의지의 문제는 우리의 자기 이해, 우리의 대인 관계, 그리고 도덕적, 법적 관행에 현실적인 영향을 미친다. ❷ 우리가 자유 의지를 갖고 있다고 상정하는 것은 우리의 많은 일상적 태도와 판단에 대한 정당화 뒤에 잠재해 있다. ❸ 예를 들어, 누군가 우리를 도덕적으로 부당하게 취급할 때, 우리는 분개와 도덕적 분노를 경험할 뿐만 아니라 우리가 그렇게 할 때 '정당화된다'고 보통 느끼는데, 왜냐하면 우리는 변명이 되는 어떤 여건도 없을 때, 사람들이 자유롭고 자신이 하는 일에 도덕적으로 책임이 있으며, 그러므로 그런 반응의 적절한 대상이라고 상정하기 때문이다. ❹ 우리는 또한 개인들이 '자기 자신의 자유 의지에 따라 행동할' 때, 자신이 하는 일에 대해 도덕적으로 책임이 있으므로, 자기 행동에 대해 칭찬과 비난, 처벌과 보상을 '마땅히 받을 만하다'고 보통 상정한다. ❺ 비슷한 상정이 형사법에서 이뤄진다. ❻ 예를 들어, 미국 연방 대법원은 "우리 법체계에서, 그리고 특히 형벌, 선고, 감금에 대한 우리의 접근에서, '보편적이고 지속적인' 토대는 '인간 의지의 자유가 있고 그에 따라 평범한 개인에게 선과 악 중에서 선택할 능력과 의무가 있다는 믿음'이다"라고 단언했다.

Word List

□ implication 영향, 함의   □ interpersonal 대인 관계의, 사람과 사람 사이의   □ moral 윤리적   □ practice 관행, 관습
□ assumption 상정, 추정   □ justification 정당화   □ wrong 부당하게 취급하다, 모욕하다   □ resentment 분개, 분함
□ typically 보통, 전형적으로   □ absent ~이 없을 때   □ excuse 변명이 되다, 용서하다   □ responsible for ~에 책임이 있는
□ appropriate 적절한   □ criminal law 형사법, 형법   □ Supreme Court (연방) 대법원   □ persistent 지속적인
□ foundation stone 초석, 주춧돌   □ sentence 선고하다   □ consequent 그에 따르는, 결과로서 일어나는

• Word Test

1	excuse		10	지속적인
2	moral		11	형사법, 형법
3	implication		12	~에 책임이 있는
4	typically		13	~이 없을 때
5	assumption		14	정당화
6	appropriate		15	관행, 관습
7	consequent		16	선고하다
8	interpersonal		17	초석, 주춧돌
9	wrong		18	분개, 분함

The problem of free will has real-world implications for our self-understanding, our interpersonal relationships, and our moral and legal practices. The assumption that we have free will lurks behind the justification of many of our everyday attitudes and judgments. ❶ For instance / On the contrary , when someone morally wrongs us, not only ❷ we / do we experience resentment and moral anger; we typically feel that we are *justified* in doing so, since we assume that, absent any excusing conditions, people are free and morally responsible for what they do and are therefore ❸ appropriate / inappropriate targets for such responses. We also typically assume that when individuals "act of their own free will," they *justly deserve* to be praised and blamed, punished and rewarded for their actions ❹ unless / since they are morally responsible for what they do. Similar assumptions are made in the criminal law. The US Supreme Court, for instance, has asserted: "A 'universal and persistent' foundation stone in our system of law, and particularly in our approach to punishment, sentencing, and incarceration, is the 'belief in freedom of the human will and a consequent ability and ❺ duty / liberty of the normal individual to choose between good and evil.'"

*lurk 잠재하다 **incarceration 감금, 투옥

The problem of free will has real-world implications for our self-understanding, our interpersonal relationships, and our moral and legal practices. The assumption that we have free will lurks behind the justification of many of our everyday attitudes and judgments. For instance, when someone morally ❶ _____ (wrong) us, not only do we experience resentment and moral anger; we typically feel that we are *justified* in doing so, since we assume that, absent any excusing conditions, people are free and morally responsible for what they do and are therefore appropriate targets for such responses. We also typically assume that when individuals "act of their own free will," they *justly deserve* to ❷ _____ (praise) and blamed, punished and rewarded for their actions since they are morally responsible for what they do. Similar assumptions ❸ _____ (make) in the criminal law. The US Supreme Court, for instance, ❹ _____ (assert): "A 'universal and persistent' foundation stone in our system of law, and particularly in our approach to punishment, sentencing, and incarceration, ❺ _____ (be) the 'belief in freedom of the human will and a consequent ability and duty of the normal individual to choose between good and evil.'"

*lurk 잠재하다 **incarceration 감금, 투옥

The problem of free will has real-world implications for our self-understanding, our interpersonal relationships, and our moral and legal practices. The assumption that we have free will lurks behind the justification of many of ❶ _____ (우리의 일상적 태도들과 판단들). For instance, when someone morally wrongs us, not only do we experience resentment and moral anger; we typically feel that we are *justified* in doing so, since we assume that, absent any excusing conditions, people are ❷ _____ (자유롭고 도덕적으로 책임이 있는) for what they do and are therefore appropriate targets for such responses. We also typically assume that when individuals "❸ _____ (그들 자신의 자유 의지에 따라 행동하다)," they *justly deserve* to be praised and blamed, punished and rewarded for their actions since they are morally responsible for what they do. Similar assumptions are made in the criminal law. The US Supreme Court, for instance, has asserted: "A 'universal and persistent' foundation stone in our system of law, and particularly in our approach to punishment, sentencing, and incarceration, is the 'belief in ❹ _____ (인간 의지의 자유) and a consequent ability and duty of the normal individual to choose between good and evil.'"

*lurk 잠재하다   **incarceration 감금, 투옥

❶ An aeronautical engineer who sets about the task of developing a new airplane will start by performing theoretical analyses involving thrust, lift, and drag. ❷ Next, she will build models and run experiments. ❸ And most important, as the plane is built, its components will be assembled, adjusted, and tested while the plane is safely on the ground. ❹ Evolution has no such luxury. ❺ As a species evolves it always has to be done "in flight." ❻ Every sequential modification has to be fully functional and competitive. ❼ The neuroscientist David Linden has described the human brain as the progressive accumulation of evolutionary kludges, or quick-and-dirty fixes. ❽ During brain evolution, new structures were placed on top of the older functional structures, leading to redundancy, waste of resources, unnecessary complexity, and sometimes competing solutions to the same problem. ❾ Furthermore, as new computational requirements emerged, they had to be implemented with the current hardware. ❿ There is no switching from analog to digital along the way.

*aeronautical 항공학의
**kludge 클루지(컴퓨터 속어) (호환성 없는 요소로 이루어진 장치 혹은 못쓰게 된 프로그램)
***redundancy 불필요한 중복

❶ 새로운 비행기를 개발하는 일을 시작하는 항공 엔지니어는 추진력, 양력, 항력을 포함한 이론적 분석을 수행함으로써 시작할 것이다. ❷ 다음으로, 그녀는 모형을 만들고 실험을 할 것이다. ❸ 그리고 가장 중요한 것으로서, 비행기가 만들어질 때 그것의 부품이 비행기가 안전하게 땅에 있는 동안 조립되고, 조정되고, 테스트될 것이다. ❹ 진화에는 그런 호사가 없다. ❺ 종이 진화할 때 그것은 항상 '비행 중에' 행해져야 한다. ❻ 모든 순차적인 변이는 충분히 기능적이고 경쟁력이 있어야 한다. ❼ 신경 과학자 David Linden은 인간의 뇌를 진화적 클루지, 즉 임시변통의 해결책이 점진적으로 축적된 것으로 묘사했다. ❽ 두뇌가 진화하는 동안 새로운 구조물이 더 오래된 기능적 구조물 위에 놓여 불필요한 중복, 자원의 낭비, 불필요한 복잡성, 그리고 때로는 같은 문제에 대한 대립되는 해결책을 가져왔다. ❾ 게다가 새로운 계산상의 필요가 생겼을 때 그것들은 현재의 하드웨어를 가지고 실행되어야 했다. ❿ 그 과정에서 아날로그에서 디지털로 바뀌는 것은 불가능하다.

Word List

□ **perform** 수행하다　□ **theoretical** 이론적인　□ **analysis** 분석(*pl.* analyses)　□ **thrust** 추진력
□ **lift** 양력(항공기가 비행할 때 밑에서 위로 작용하는 압력)　□ **drag** 항력(운동 방향과 반대로 물체에 미치는 유체의 저항력)
□ **component** 부품, 요소　□ **assemble** 조립하다　□ **adjust** 조정하다　□ **evolution** 진화　□ **luxury** 호사, 사치
□ **sequential** 순차적인　□ **modification** 변이, 수정　□ **functional** 기능적인　□ **competitive** 경쟁력 있는
□ **neuroscientist** 신경 과학자　□ **progressive** 점진적인　□ **accumulation** 축적　□ **quick-and-dirty** 임시변통의　□ **fix** 해결책
□ **computational** 계산상의, 컴퓨터와 관련된　□ **requirement** 필요한 것, 요구 사항　□ **emerge** 생기다, 나타나다
□ **implement** 실행하다, 시행하다

Word Test

1	quick-and-dirty		13	신경 과학자
2	competitive		14	이론적인
3	analysis		15	진화
4	progressive		16	해결책
5	component		17	실행하다, 시행하다
6	lift		18	기능적인
7	modification		19	추진력
8	computational		20	필요한 것, 요구 사항
9	perform		21	조립하다
10	luxury		22	항력
11	emerge		23	순차적인
12	adjust		24	축적

네모 안에서 옳은 어법·어휘를 고르시오.

An aeronautical engineer who sets about the task of developing a new airplane will start by performing ❶ practical / theoretical analyses involving thrust, lift, and drag. Next, she will build models and run experiments. And most important, as the plane is built, its components will be ❷ assembled / scattered, adjusted, and tested while the plane is safely on the ground. Evolution has no such luxury. ❸ Since / As a species evolves it always has to be done "in flight." Every sequential modification has to be fully functional and competitive. The neuroscientist David Linden has described the human brain as the progressive accumulation of evolutionary kludges, or quick-and-dirty fixes. During brain evolution, new structures were placed on top of the older functional structures, leading to redundancy, waste of resources, ❹ essential / unnecessary complexity, and sometimes competing solutions to the same problem. ❺ Otherwise / Furthermore, as new computational requirements emerged, they had to be implemented with the current hardware. There is no switching from analog to digital along the way.

*aeronautical 항공학의 **kludge 클루지(컴퓨터 속어)(호환성 없는 요소로 이루어진 장치 혹은 못쓰게 된 프로그램) ***redundancy 불필요한 중복

• 유형 2 괄호 안의 동사를 알맞은 형태로 쓰시오.

An aeronautical engineer who sets about the task of developing a new airplane will start by performing theoretical analyses involving thrust, lift, and drag. Next, she will build models and run experiments. And most important, as the plane ❶ _____ (build), its components will be assembled, adjusted, and tested while the plane is safely on the ground. Evolution has no such luxury. As a species ❷ _____ (evolve) it always has to be done "in flight." Every sequential modification has to be fully functional and competitive. The neuroscientist David Linden ❸ _____ (describe) the human brain as the progressive accumulation of evolutionary kludges, or quick-and-dirty fixes. During brain evolution, new structures ❹ _____ (place) on top of the older functional structures, leading to redundancy, waste of resources, unnecessary complexity, and sometimes competing solutions to the same problem. Furthermore, as new computational requirements emerged, they had to ❺ _____ (implement) with the current hardware. There is no switching from analog to digital along the way.

*aeronautical 항공학의 **kludge 클루지(컴퓨터 속어)(호환성 없는 요소로 이루어진 장치 혹은 못쓰게 된 프로그램) ***redundancy 불필요한 중복

• 유형 3 우리말에 맞게 빈칸에 알맞은 말을 쓰시오.

An aeronautical engineer who ❶ _____ _____ (~을 시작하다) the task of developing a new airplane will start by performing theoretical analyses involving thrust, lift, and drag. Next, she will build models and run experiments. And most important, as the plane is built, its components will be assembled, adjusted, and tested while the plane is safely on the ground. ❷ _____ _____ _____ _____ _____ (진화에는 그런 호사가 없다). As a species evolves it always has to be done "in flight." Every sequential modification has to be fully functional and competitive. The neuroscientist David Linden has described the human brain as the progressive accumulation of evolutionary kludges, or quick-and-dirty fixes. During brain evolution, new structures were placed on top of the ❸ _____ _____ _____ (더 오래된 기능적 구조물들), leading to redundancy, waste of resources, unnecessary complexity, and sometimes competing solutions to the same problem. Furthermore, as new computational requirements emerged, they had to be implemented with the current hardware. There is no switching from analog to digital ❹ _____ _____ _____ (그 과정에서).

*aeronautical 항공학의 **kludge 클루지(컴퓨터 속어)(호환성 없는 요소로 이루어진 장치 혹은 못쓰게 된 프로그램) ***redundancy 불필요한 중복

❶ Self-presentation and/or impression management have been long identified as motivators for SNS use. ❷ Specific to image sharing, Facebook users choose certain profile pictures to portray themselves as attractive or fun-loving, as popular, or to show their relationship status, which aim to create a particular image of the individual and to shape others' impressions of them. ❸ Instagram users also report posting images to express themselves or present a particular image to others. ❹ In line with this, Facebook users also report untagging themselves from images posted by others if those photos are unattractive or portray them doing something they don't want others to know about. ❺ However, this is not to say that Facebook identities are completely divorced from who the person is offline. ❻ Researchers compared self-ratings of individuals' actual personality and their idealized self with ratings made by observers of their Facebook profile. ❼ Observer ratings corresponded more closely with actual personality than idealized personality, suggesting that although people can use social media to influence others' perceptions of them, the images presented are not wildly different from their actual selves.

❶ 자기표현 그리고/또는 인상 관리는 SNS 사용의 동기를 부여하는 것으로 오랫동안 인정되어 왔다. ❷ 이미지 공유와 관련하여 Facebook 사용자는 자신을 매력적이거나 재미를 추구하는 사람으로, 혹은 인기 있는 사람으로 나타내거나 자신의 관계 상태를 보여 주기 위해 특정 프로필 사진을 선택하는데, 이는 개인의 특정 이미지를 만들고 자신에 대한 다른 사람들의 인상을 형성하는 것을 목표로 한다. ❸ Instagram 사용자도 자신을 표현하거나 특정 이미지를 다른 사람에게 보여 주기 위해 이미지를 게시한다고 말한다. ❹ 이와 비슷하게 Facebook 사용자는 또한 다른 사람들에 의해 게시된 사진들이 매력적이지 않거나 다른 사람들이 알기를 원하지 않는 것을 자신이 하고 있는 것을 나타내는 경우 그 이미지들로부터 자신의 태그를 해제한다고 말한다. ❺ 하지만 이것이 Facebook의 정체성이 오프라인에서 그 사람의 모습과 완전히 동떨어져 있다는 의미는 아니다. ❻ 연구자들은 개인의 실제 개성과 이상화된 자아에 대한 자체 평가를 그들의 Facebook 프로필의 관찰자들이 한 평가와 비교했다. ❼ 관찰자 평가는 이상화된 개성보다 실제 개성과 더 밀접하게 일치하였는데, 이는 사람들이 자신들에 대한 다른 사람들의 인식에 영향을 주기 위해 소셜 미디어를 사용할 수 있지만, 제시된 이미지가 실제 자신과 크게 다르지 않음을 시사한다.

Word List

□ self-presentation 자기표현, 자기 제시   □ impression management 인상 관리   □ identify 확인하다, 식별하다
□ motivator 동기를 부여하는 것   □ specific 특정한   □ portray 나타내다, 보여 주다   □ fun-loving 재미를 추구하는   □ status 상태
□ shape (중요한 영향을 미쳐서) 형성하다   □ present 보여 주다, 제시하다   □ in line with ~과 비슷하게   □ untag 태그를 해제하다
□ divorce 분리하다, 단절시키다   □ observer 관찰자, 보는 사람   □ correspond 일치하다   □ perception 인식

• Word Test

1	present	_____	8	형성하다	_____
2	status	_____	9	인식	_____
3	motivator	_____	10	재미를 추구하는	_____
4	correspond	_____	11	~과 비슷하게	_____
5	divorce	_____	12	특정한	_____
6	self-presentation	_____	13	확인하다, 식별하다	_____
7	portray	_____	14	관찰자, 보는 사람	_____

Self-presentation and/or impression management have been long identified as motivators for SNS use. Specific to image sharing, Facebook users choose certain profile pictures to portray themselves as attractive or fun-loving, as popular, or to show their relationship status, ❶ who / which aim to create a particular image of the individual and to ❷ view / shape others' impressions of them. Instagram users also report posting images to express themselves or present a particular image to others. In line with this, Facebook users also report untagging themselves from images posted by others if those photos are ❸ attractive / unattractive or portray them doing something they don't want others to know about. However, this is not to say that Facebook identities are completely ❹ divorced / connected from who the person is offline. Researchers compared self-ratings of individuals' actual personality and their idealized self with ratings made by observers of their Facebook profile. Observer ratings ❺ communicated / corresponded more closely with actual personality than idealized personality, suggesting that although people can use social media to influence others' perceptions of them, the images presented are not wildly different from their actual selves.

Self-presentation and/or impression management have been long identified as motivators for SNS use. Specific to image sharing, Facebook users choose certain profile pictures to portray themselves as attractive or fun-loving, as popular, or to show their relationship status, which ❶ _____ (aim) to create a particular image of the individual and to shape others' impressions of them. Instagram users also report posting images to express themselves or present a particular image to others. In line with this, Facebook users also report untagging themselves from images ❷ _____ (post) by others if those photos are unattractive or portray them doing something they don't want others ❸ _____ (know) about. However, this is not to say that Facebook identities are completely divorced from who the person is offline. Researchers compared self-ratings of individuals' actual personality and their idealized self with ratings made by observers of their Facebook profile. Observer ratings corresponded more closely with actual personality than idealized personality, ❹ _____ (suggest) that although people can use social media to influence others' perceptions of them, the images ❺ _____ (present) are not wildly different from their actual selves.

Self-presentation and/or impression management ❶ _____ _____ _____ _____ (오랫동안 인정되어 왔다) as motivators for SNS use. Specific to image sharing, Facebook users choose certain profile pictures to portray themselves as attractive or fun-loving, as popular, or to show their relationship status, which aim to create a particular image of the individual and to shape others' impressions of them. Instagram users also report posting images to express themselves or present a particular image to others. ❷ _____ _____ _____ _____ (이와 비슷하게), Facebook users also report untagging themselves from images posted by others if those photos are unattractive or portray them doing something they don't want others to know about. However, this is not to say that Facebook identities are completely divorced from who the person is offline. Researchers compared self-ratings of individuals' ❸ _____ _____ _____ _____ _____ _____ (실제 개성과 그들의 이상화된 자아) with ratings made by observers of their Facebook profile. Observer ratings corresponded more closely with actual personality than idealized personality, suggesting that although people can use social media to influence others' perceptions of them, the images presented are ❹ _____ _____ _____ _____ (~와 크게 다르지 않은) their actual selves.

❶ Researchers like Blau, Scott, and Evan acknowledge that the concept of organization set was developed by analogy from Robert K. Merton's concept of role set. ❷ Merton noted that a single position such as "mother" is associated with not one, but a cluster of different roles depending on the identity of the counterpositions. ❸ Thus, a mother has specific role obligations toward her children, others toward the father, still others toward the child's teachers, and so on. ❹ Similarly, a given organization participates in a variety of relations depending on the identity of its specific partners and competitors. ❺ For example, a small grocery store will relate in one manner with its suppliers, another with its customers, yet another with city officials, and so on. ❻ The fundamental idea is a simple one, but its implications are quite rich. ❼ One is led to ask questions regarding, for example, the relative size of the organization set, the extent to which one group of role partners is aware of the demands made by another, and the extent to which expectations held by partners coincide.

*organization set 조직 집합

❶ Blau, Scott, 그리고 Evan과 같은 연구자는 조직 집합이라는 개념이 Robert K. Merton의 역할 군이라는 개념에서 유추되어 개발되었다는 것을 인정한다. ❷ Merton은 '어머니'와 같은 단일 지위는 하나가 아니라, 상대 지위의 정체성에 따라 다양한 역할 군과 연관된다는 점에 주목했다. ❸ 따라서, 어머니에게는 자녀에 대한 구체적인 역할 의무가 있고, 아버지에 대해서는 다른 역할 의무가 있으며, 그리고 아이의 선생님에 대해서는 또 다른 역할 의무가 있다는 것 기타 등등이다. ❹ 마찬가지로, 특정 조직도 특정 파트너와 경쟁자의 정체성에 따라 다양한 관계에 참여한다. ❺ 예를 들어, 작은 식료품점은 공급자와 어느 한 방식으로, 고객들과는 다른 방식으로, 그리고 시 공무원과는 또 다른 방식으로 관계를 맺게 될 것이고, 기타 등등이다. ❻ 근본적인 개념은 간단한 것이지만. 그것이 미치는 영향은 상당히 다채롭다. ❼ 사람은 예를 들어 조직 집합의 상대적 규모, 한 역할 파트너 그룹이 다른 그룹의 요구를 인지하고 있는 정도, 그리고 파트너가 가지고 있는 기대치가 부합하는 정도에 관한 질문을 하게 된다.

Word List

□ acknowledge 인정하다　□ concept 개념　□ by analogy from ~에서 유추하여　□ note 주목하다
□ be associated with ~과 연관되다　□ cluster 군, 무리　□ counterposition 상대 지위　□ obligation 의무　□ given 특정한
□ participate in ~에 참여하다　□ identity 정체성　□ competitor 경쟁자　□ supplier 공급자　□ official 공무원
□ fundamental 근본적인　□ implication (보통 복수형으로) 영향, 결과　□ rich 다채로운, 많은　□ regarding ~에 관하여
□ coincide 부합하다

• Word Test

1	competitor	9	공급자
2	regarding	10	~과 연관되다
3	acknowledge	11	의무
4	note	12	부합하다
5	cluster	13	정체성
6	implication	14	개념
7	participate in	15	다채로운, 많은
8	official	16	근본적인

Researchers like Blau, Scott, and Evan acknowledge that the concept of organization set was developed by ❶ analogy / analysis from Robert K. Merton's concept of role set. Merton noted that a single position such as "mother" is associated with not one, but a cluster of different roles depending on the identity of the counterpositions. Thus, a mother has specific role obligations toward her children, others toward the father, still others toward the child's teachers, and so on. ❷ Similarly / Conversely , a given organization participates in a variety of relations depending on the identity of its specific partners and competitors. ❸ For example / In addition , a small grocery store will relate in one manner with its suppliers, another with its customers, yet ❹ others / another with city officials, and so on. The fundamental idea is a simple one, but its implications are quite rich. One is led to ask questions regarding, for example, the relative size of the organization set, the extent ❺ to / for which one group of role partners is aware of the demands made by another, and the extent to which expectations held by partners coincide.

*organization set 조직 집합

• 유형 2 괄호 안의 동사를 알맞은 형태로 쓰시오.

Researchers like Blau, Scott, and Evan acknowledge that the concept of organization set ❶ _____ (develop) by analogy from Robert K. Merton's concept of role set. Merton noted that a single position such as "mother" is associated with not one, but a cluster of different roles depending on the identity of the counterpositions. Thus, a mother has specific role obligations toward her children, others toward the father, still others toward the child's teachers, and so on. Similarly, a given organization participates in a variety of relations ❷ _____ (depend) on the identity of its specific partners and competitors. For example, a small grocery store will relate in one manner with its suppliers, another with its customers, yet another with city officials, and so on. The fundamental idea is a simple one, but its implications are quite rich. One ❸ _____ (lead) to ask questions regarding, for example, the relative size of the organization set, the extent to which one group of role partners ❹ _____ (be) aware of the demands made by another, and the extent to which expectations ❺ _____ (hold) by partners coincide.

*organization set 조직 집합

• 유형 3 우리말에 맞게 빈칸에 알맞은 말을 쓰시오.

Researchers like Blau, Scott, and Evan acknowledge that the concept of organization set was developed by analogy from Robert K. Merton's concept of role set. Merton noted that a single position such as "mother"is associated with not one, but a cluster of different roles ❶ _____ _____ _____ _____ (정체성에 따라) of the counterpositions. Thus, a mother has specific role obligations toward her children, others toward the father, still others toward the child's teachers, and so on. Similarly, a given organization participates in a variety of relations depending on the identity of its specific partners and competitors. For example, a small grocery store will ❷ _____ _____ _____ _____ (어느 한 방식으로 관계를 맺다) with its suppliers, another with its customers, yet another with city officials, and so on. The fundamental idea is a simple one, but ❸ _____ _____ _____ _____ _____ (그것의 영향들은 상당히 다채롭다). One is led to ask questions regarding, for example, the relative size of the organization set, the extent to which one group of role partners is aware of the demands made by another, and the extent to which expectations held by partners coincide.

*organization set 조직 집합

❶ There are arguments about why faith in 'more education' might be misplaced. ❷ The entrepreneur Peter Thiel offers the most provocative version of that case. ❸ He claims that higher education is a 'bubble', arguing that it is 'overpriced' because people do not get 'their money's worth' but go to college 'simply because that's what everybody's doing.' ❹ Thiel does not deny that those who are better educated tend to earn more on average. ❺ Instead, he is suspicious that we never get to see the counterfactual: how these students would have done without their education. ❻ His sense is that many of them would have earned just as much, and that universities are 'just good at identifying talented people rather than adding value'. ❼ Thiel now offers $100,000 grants to young students who choose to 'skip or stop out of college' to start companies instead. ❽ The Thiel Foundation, which manages the grants, points out that its recipients have started sixty companies worth a combined total of over $1.1 billion.

*provocative 도발적인

❶ 왜 '더 많은 교육'에 대한 믿음이 부적절할 수도 있을지에 대한 논쟁이 있다. ❷ 기업가 Peter Thiel은 그 사례의 가장 도발적인 견해를 제시한다. ❸ 그는 고등 교육은 '거품'이라고 주장하며, 사람들이 '자신들의 돈의 가치'를 얻지 못하면서도 '단순히 모두가 그렇게 하고 있기 때문에' 대학에 가는 것이므로 그것은 '너무 비싸다'는 논지를 편다. ❹ Thiel은 더 나은 교육을 받은 사람들이 평균적으로 더 많이 버는 경향이 있다는 것을 부인하지 않는다. ❺ 대신에, 그는 우리가 이 학생들이 교육이 없었다면 어떻게 했을지와 같은 사실과 반대되는 것을 보는 기회를 결코 갖지 못하는 것이 아닐까 하고 생각한다. ❻ 그의 판단은 그들 중 많은 이들이 그만큼의 돈을 벌었을 것이고, 대학은 '가치를 더하기보다는 인재를 가려내는 데 능숙할 뿐'이라는 것이다. ❼ Thiel은 이제 '대학을 건너뛰거나 중퇴하고' 대신에 회사를 설립하기로 선택한 어린 학생들에게 10만 달러의 보조금을 제공한다. ❽ 보조금을 관리하는 Thiel 재단은 수령자들이 모두 합해 총 11억 달러 이상의 가치가 있는 60개의 회사를 시작했음을 지적한다.

Word List

□ misplaced 부적절한   □ entrepreneur 기업가   □ version 견해, 생각   □ bubble 거품   □ overpriced 너무 비싼
□ on average 평균적으로   □ be suspicious that ~이 아닐까 하고 생각하다   □ counterfactual 반사실적 조건문   □ talented 재능 있는
□ grant 보조금   □ recipient 수령자

• Word Test

1	overpriced		6	수령자
2	be suspicious that		7	평균적으로
3	grant		8	기업가
4	misplaced		9	거품
5	version		10	재능 있는

There are arguments about why faith in 'more education' might be misplaced. The entrepreneur Peter Thiel offers the most provocative version of that case. He claims that higher education is a 'bubble', arguing that it is '❶ overpriced / underpriced ' because people do not get 'their money's worth' but go to college 'simply because that's ❷ why / what everybody's doing.' Thiel does not deny that those who are better educated tend to earn more on average. Instead, he is suspicious that we never get to see the counterfactual: how these students would have done ❸ with / without their education. His sense is that many of them would have earned just as much, and that universities are 'just good at identifying talented people rather than adding ❹ price / value '. Thiel now offers $100,000 grants to young students who choose to 'skip or stop out of college' to start companies instead. The Thiel Foundation, which manages the grants, points out ❺ that / what its recipients have started sixty companies worth a combined total of over $1.1 billion.

*provocative 도발적인

There are arguments about why faith in 'more education' might ❶ _____ (misplace). The entrepreneur Peter Thiel offers the most provocative version of that case. He claims that higher education is a 'bubble', ❷ _____ (argue) that it is 'overpriced' because people do not get 'their money's worth' but go to college 'simply because that's what everybody's doing.' Thiel does not deny that those who are better educated tend to earn more on average. Instead, he is suspicious that we never get to see the counterfactual: how these students would ❸ _____ (do) without their education. His sense is that many of them would have earned just as much, and that universities are 'just good at identifying talented people rather than ❹ _____ (add) value'. Thiel now offers $100,000 grants to young students who choose to 'skip or stop out of college' to start companies instead. The Thiel Foundation, which manages the grants, points out that its recipients ❺ _____ (start) sixty companies worth a combined total of over $1.1 billion.

*provocative 도발적인

There are arguments about why faith in 'more education' might be misplaced. The entrepreneur Peter Thiel offers the most provocative version of that case. He claims that higher education is a 'bubble', arguing that it is 'overpriced' because people do not get 'their money's worth' but go to college 'simply because that's what everybody's doing.' Thiel does not deny that those who are better educated ❶ _____ _____ _____ _____ _____ (평균적으로 더 많이 버는 경향이 있다). Instead, he is suspicious that we never get to see the counterfactual how these students would have done without their education. His sense is that many of them would have earned just as much, and that universities are 'just ❷ _____ _____ _____ _____ _____ (인재들을 가려내는 데 능숙한) rather than adding value'. Thiel now offers $100,000 grants to young students who choose to '❸ _____ _____ _____ _____ _____ (대학을 건너뛰거나 중퇴하다)' to start companies instead. The Thiel Foundation, which manages the grants, points out that its recipients have started sixty companies ❹ _____ _____ _____ _____ _____ _____ (모두 합해 ~ 이상의 가치가 있는) $1.1 billion.

*provocative 도발적인

❶ To illustrate the connection between thought and feeling, consider a soft drink dispenser in a self-service restaurant. ❷ Our particular model has a row of labeled buttons at the top and spouts underneath that dispense the desired beverage if the corresponding button is pushed. ❸ In our case, the buttons represent our interpretations — *Wrong, Unfortunate, Terrible, Right* and *Shameful* (or "*I am wrong*"). ❹ Should I, in any given situation, arrive at the interpretation that something is wrong and consequently push the soda fountain button for "*I am wrong,*" then the machine would ideally dispense the corresponding beverage, namely anger.

❺ As long as I have awareness of pushing a certain button, the buttons are labeled correctly and they are properly connected to the corresponding beverage container, the machine will function without a hitch. ❻ Unfortunately, most of us are unaware of the connections between interpretations on the mental level and our corresponding reactions on the emotional level, however. ❼ Because of this, we often behave like people who continuously push buttons on a soda machine and watch in desperation as the cup overflows. ❽ We do not notice that we are pushing the button since we are completely unaware of its existence. ❾ We are oblivious to the fact that a particular interpretation is made before anger, for example, arises in our system — namely, "*This is wrong.*" ❿ When we become aware of this interpretation, it is like suddenly watching our own thumb continuously push the soda button despite the fact that we have already filled up our cup or would actually prefer lemonade or water instead.

*dispenser 자판기, 디스펜서　**spout (주전자 등의) 주둥이　***hitch 문제, 장애

❶ 생각과 느낌 사이의 연관성을 설명하기 위해, 셀프서비스 식당의 청량 음료 자판기를 생각해 보자. ❷ 우리의 특정 모델은 꼭대기에 라벨이 부착된 일련의 버튼이 있고, 아래에는 해당 버튼을 누르면 원하는 음료를 내놓는 주둥이가 있다. ❸ 우리의 경우, 그 버튼이 '틀렸다, 불행하다, 끔찍하다, 옳다, 부끄럽다 (혹은 "내가 틀렸다")'와 같은 우리의 해석을 나타낸다. ❹ 만약 내가, 어떤 특정한 상황에서, 무언가가 잘못되었다는 해석에 도달해서 결과적으로 "내가 틀렸다"는 탄산음료가 나오는 버튼을 누르면, 그 기계는 그에 해당하는 음료, 즉 분노를 완벽하게 내놓을 것이다. ❺ 내가 특정 버튼을 누르는 것에 대한 의식이 있고, 버튼에 표시가 올바르게 붙어 있고, 그것들이 해당 음료수 통에 적절하게 연결되어 있기만 하면, 그 기계는 문제없이 작동할 것이다. ❻ 하지만 불행히도, 우리들 대부분은 정신적인 관점에서의 해석과 감정적인 관점에서의 그에 해당하는 반응 사이의 연관성에 대해 알지 못한다. ❼ 이것 때문에, 우리는 자주 탄산음료 기계의 버튼을 계속해서 누르고 컵이 넘쳐 날 때 절망적으로 지켜보는 사람처럼 행동한다. ❽ 우리는 버튼의 존재를 전혀 모르기 때문에 우리가 그것을 누르고 있다는 것을 알아차리지 못한다. ❾ 우리는 예를 들어 분노가 우리 시스템에서 발생하기 전에 특정한 해석, 즉 "이것은 잘못된 것이다."라는 사실을 알아차리지 못한다. ❿ 우리가 이 해석을 알게 되었을 때, 그것은 우리가 이미 잔을 채웠거나 실제로는 그 대신에 레모네이드나 물을 더 선호하리라는 사실에도 불구하고 갑자기 우리 엄지손가락이 계속해서 탄산음료 버튼을 누르는 것을 보는 것과 같다.

Word List

□ illustrate 설명하다　□ connection 연관성, 연결　□ labeled 라벨이 부착된　□ underneath 아래에　□ corresponding 해당하는
□ represent 나타내다　□ interpretation 해석　□ consequently 결과적으로　□ soda 탄산음료　□ fountain 식수대　□ namely 즉
□ awareness 인식, 지각　□ properly 제대로, 적절히　□ function 작동하다　□ mental 정신적인　□ in desperation 절망하여
□ oblivious 잘 잊는, 의식하지 못하는　□ arise 발생하다　□ prefer 선호하다

1	function	_____	10	정신적인	_____
2	labeled	_____	11	선호하다	_____
3	in desperation	_____	12	아래에	_____
4	interpretation	_____	13	속	_____
5	awareness	_____	14	제대로, 적절히	_____
6	illustrate	_____	15	잘 잊는, 의식하지 못하는	_____
7	arise	_____	16	결과적으로	_____
8	corresponding	_____	17	연관성, 연결	_____
9	fountain	_____	18	나타내다	_____

• 유형 1 네모 안에서 옳은 어법·어휘를 고르시오.

To illustrate the connection between thought and feeling, consider a soft drink dispenser in a self-service restaurant. Our particular model has a row of labeled buttons at the top and spouts underneath that dispense the desired beverage if the ❶ comparing / corresponding button is pushed. In our case, the buttons represent our interpretations — *Wrong, Unfortunate, Terrible, Right* and *Shameful* (or "*I am wrong*"). Should I, in any given situation, arrive at the interpretation ❷ that / which something is wrong and consequently push the soda fountain button for "*I am wrong*," then the machine would ideally dispense the corresponding beverage, namely anger.

As long as I have awareness of pushing a certain button, the buttons are labeled correctly and they are properly connected to the corresponding beverage container, the machine will function without a hitch. ❸ Fortunately / Unfortunately , most of us are unaware of the connections between interpretations on the mental level and our corresponding reactions on the emotional level, however. ❹ Because of / According to this, we often behave like people who continuously push buttons on a soda machine and watch in desperation as the cup overflows. We do not notice that we are pushing the button since we are completely unaware of its existence. We are ❺ obsolete / oblivious to the fact that a particular interpretation is made before anger, for example, arises in our system —namely, "*This is wrong*." When we become aware of this interpretation, it is like suddenly watching our own thumb continuously push the soda button ❻ due to / despite the fact that we have already filled up our cup or would actually prefer lemonade or water instead.

*dispenser 자판기, 디스펜서 **spout (주전자 등의) 주둥이 ***hitch 문제, 장애

To illustrate the connection between thought and feeling, consider a soft drink dispenser in a self-service restaurant. Our particular model has a row of labeled buttons at the top and spouts underneath that dispense the desired beverage if the corresponding button ❶ _____ (push). In our case, the buttons represent our interpretations — *Wrong, Unfortunate, Terrible, Right* and *Shameful* (or *"I am wrong"*). Should I, in any given situation, ❷ _____ (arrive) at the interpretation that something is wrong and consequently push the soda fountain button for *"I am wrong,"* then the machine would ideally dispense the corresponding beverage, namely anger.

As long as I have awareness of pushing a certain button, the buttons are labeled correctly and they are properly connected to the corresponding beverage container, the machine will function without a hitch. Unfortunately, most of us ❸ _____ (be) unaware of the connections between interpretations on the mental level and our corresponding reactions on the emotional level, however. Because of this, we often behave like people who continuously push buttons on a soda machine and watch in desperation as the cup ❹ _____ (overflow). We do not notice that we are pushing the button since we are completely unaware of its existence. We are oblivious to the fact that a particular interpretation is made before anger, for example, ❺ _____ (arise) in our system —namely, *"This is wrong."* When we become aware of this interpretation, it is like suddenly watching our own thumb continuously push the soda button despite the fact that we have already filled up our cup or would actually prefer lemonade or water instead.

*dispenser 자판기, 디스펜서 **spout (주전자 등의) 주둥이 ***hitch 문제, 장애

To illustrate the connection between thought and feeling, consider a soft drink dispenser in a self-service restaurant. Our particular model has ❶ _____ _____ _____ _____ _____ (라벨이 부착된 일련의 버튼들) at the top and spouts underneath that dispense the desired beverage if the corresponding button is pushed. In our case, the buttons represent our interpretations — *Wrong, Unfortunate, Terrible, Right* and *Shameful* (or *"I am wrong"*). Should I, ❷ _____ _____ _____ _____ (어떤 특정한 상황에서), arrive at the interpretation that something is wrong and consequently push the soda fountain button for *"I am wrong,"* then the machine would ideally dispense the corresponding beverage, namely anger.

As long as ❸ _____ _____ _____ _____ (내가 ~에 대한 의식이 있다) pushing a certain button, the buttons are labeled correctly and they are properly connected to the corresponding beverage container, the machine will function without a hitch. Unfortunately, most of us are unaware of the connections between interpretations on the mental level and our corresponding reactions on the emotional level, however. Because of this, we often behave like people who continuously push buttons on a soda machine and watch ❹ _____ _____ (절망하여) as the cup overflows. We do not notice that we are pushing the button since we are ❺ _____ _____ _____ _____ _____ (그것의 존재를 전혀 모르는). We are oblivious to the fact that a particular interpretation is made before anger, for example, arises in our system —namely, *"This is wrong."* When we become aware of this interpretation, it is like suddenly watching our own thumb continuously push the soda button despite the fact that we have already filled up our cup or would actually prefer lemonade or water instead.

*dispenser 자판기, 디스펜서 **spout (주전자 등의) 주둥이 ***hitch 문제, 장애

186

❶ I was once sitting in Ben Gurion Airport, waiting for my flight to be announced. ❷ Suddenly I heard a strange, almost animal-like noise. ❸ I looked around and realized that a woman sitting a few rows in front of me was weeping loudly. ❹ I was a little thrown and did not know what to do. ❺ Should I allow her privacy? ❻ Should I approach her? ❼ My heart went out to her crying alone in an airport.

❽ An older woman, who had also noticed her, went up to her and said something, but then moved away again and I guessed that she had refused an offer of help. ❾ She continued with her aching crying, and I continued to wonder if I should do something nonetheless. ❿ Eventually I took my courage and went over. ⓫ Rather than asking if everything was OK, which would probably have elicited a polite rebuttal as in the case of the other woman, I sat down next to her and said, "I don't want to bother you, but I couldn't help noticing that you are in distress."

⓬ I guess she saw the genuine empathy in my eyes, as she proceeded to pour out her story. ⓭ Her sister, who was relatively young, had just lost her husband, and this woman had spent the week being the rock upon which her sister could lean. ⓮ Only now that she was leaving did she allow the flood of grief for her sister to deluge her, to the point where she abandoned her inhibitions and cried her heart out in such a public place.

⓯ She spoke to me for just a few minutes, but I sensed that she parted from me a little comforted; for somebody else had just for a moment reached out to her and provided a shoulder for her to cry on, in a reversal of her usual role. ⓰ I am often afraid of rejection and assume that no one would want me specifically to comfort them. ⓱ But it's not true — where there is real emotion, there can never be enough warm hands to hold, empathetic eyes to reflect the pain, and shoulders to cry on.

*elicit (정보나 반응 등을 어렵게)끌어내다 **rebuttal 항변 *deluge 밀려들다

❶ 언젠가 나는 Ben Gurion 공항에 앉아서 내 비행편이 방송으로 공지되기를 기다리고 있었다. ❷ 갑자기 나는 이상한, 거의 동물과 같은 소리를 들었다. ❸ 주위를 둘러보았고 몇 줄 내 앞에 앉아 있던 여자가 큰 소리로 울고 있는 것을 알아차렸다. ❹ 나는 약간 충격을 받아서 어떻게 해야 할지 몰랐다. ❺ 그녀의 사생활을 인정해야 하나? ❻ 내가 그녀에게 다가가야 하나? ❼ 나의 마음은 공항에서 혼자 울고 있는 그녀에게로 향했다.

❽ 역시 그녀를 인지한, 한 나이 든 여자가 그녀에게 다가가서 무엇인가를 말했으나, 그러고 나서 물러났는데, 나는 그녀가 도와주겠다는 제의를 거절했다고 추측했다. ❾ 그녀는 마음 아픈 울음을 계속했고, 그럼에도 나는 내가 무엇인가를 해 주어야 하는 게 아닐까 계속 생각했다. ❿ 결국 나는 용기를 내어 다가갔다. ⓫ 모든 것이 괜찮은지 묻기보다는, 그랬으면 아마 그 다른 여성의 경우처럼 정중한 항변을 끌어냈을 것인데, 나는 그녀 옆에 앉아서 "당신을 성가시게 하고 싶지는 않지만, 저는 당신이 비탄에 빠져 있다는 것을 눈치챌 수밖에 없었어요."라고 말했다.

⓬ 그녀가 이어서 자신의 이야기를 쏟아 내기 시작했기에, 나는 그녀가 내 눈에서 진정한 공감을 보았다고 생각한다. ⓭ 비교적 어렸던 그녀의 여동생이 자신의 남편을 잃은 지 얼마 되지 않았고, 이 여자는 자신의 여동생이 기댈 수 있는 바위가 되어 주며 그 주를 보냈었다. ⓮ 그녀는 떠나는 지금에서야, 그런 공공장소에서 억제하지 못하고 가슴이 미어지게 소리 내어 울 정도로, 여동생에 대한 슬픔의 홍수가 밀려들도록 두었던 것이었다.

⓯ 그녀는 단지 몇 분 동안 나에게 말을 했지만, 나는 그녀가 조금 위안을 받고 나와 헤어진다고 느꼈는데, 왜냐하면 다른 누군가가 그녀에게 아주 잠깐이라도 관심을 보이고 그녀의 평소 역할과는 반대로 그녀가 기대어 울 수 있는 어깨를 제공했기 때문이었다. ⓰ 나는 자주 거절(받는 것)을 두려워하고 아무도 내가 그들을 특별히 위로하기를 원하지 않을 것이라고 추정한다. ⓱ 하지만 그것은 사실이 아닌데, 진실한 감정이 있는 곳에서, 잡을 수 있는 따뜻한 손, 고통을 비추는 공감하는 눈, 그리고 기대어 울 수 있는 어깨는 아무리 충분해도 지나치지 않은 것이다.

Word List

□ row 줄, 열 □ thrown 충격을 받은, 당황한 □ privacy 사생활 □ notice 알아차리다 □ aching 아픈, 쑤시는 □ distress 비탄, 고통
□ genuine 진정한 □ empathy 공감, 감정 이입 □ proceed (먼저 다른 일을 한 후에) 계속해서[이어서] ~을 하다 □ pour out 쏟아 내다
□ abandon 그만두다, 버리다 □ inhibition 억제 □ reversal 반대 □ rejection 거절 □ empathetic 공감하는
□ reflect 비추다, (감정을) 나타내다

1	proceed	9	쏟아 내다
2	privacy	10	공감, 감정 이입
3	genuine	11	비추다, (감정을) 나타내다
4	row	12	충격을 받은, 당황한
5	reversal	13	알아차리다
6	empathetic	14	비탄, 고통
7	abandon	15	억제
8	aching	16	거절

• 유형 1 네모 안에서 옳은 어법·어휘를 고르시오.

I was once sitting in Ben Gurion Airport, ❶ waited / waiting for my flight to be announced. Suddenly I heard a strange, almost animal-like noise. I looked around and realized that a woman sitting a few rows in front of me was weeping loudly. I was a little thrown and did not know what to do. Should I allow her privacy? Should I approach her? My heart went out to her crying alone in an airport.

An older woman, who had also noticed her, went up to her and said something, but then moved away again and I guessed that she had refused an offer of help. She continued with her aching crying, and I continued to wonder if I should do something ❷ nonetheless / furthermore . Eventually I took my courage and went over. Rather than asking if everything was OK, which would probably have elicited a polite rebuttal as in the case of the other woman, I sat down next to her and said, "I don't want to bother you, but I couldn't help noticing that you are in ❸ dispute / distress ."

I guess she saw the genuine empathy in my eyes, as she proceeded to pour out her story. Her sister, who was relatively young, had just lost her husband, and this woman had spent the week being the rock ❹ upon / among which her sister could lean. Only now that she was leaving did she allow the flood of grief for her sister to deluge her, to the point ❺ when / where she abandoned her inhibitions and cried her heart out in such a public place.

She spoke to me for just a few minutes, but I sensed that she parted from me a little comforted; for somebody else had just for a moment reached out to her and provided a shoulder for her to cry on, in a reversal of her usual role. I am often afraid of ❻ rejection / acceptance and assume that no one would want me specifically to comfort them. But it's not true — where there is real emotion, there can never be enough warm hands to hold, ❼ empathetic / indifferent eyes to reflect the pain, and shoulders to cry on.

*elicit (정보나 반응 등을 어렵게)끌어내다   **rebuttal 항변   *deluge 밀려들다

I was once sitting in Ben Gurion Airport, waiting for my flight to ❶ _____ (announce). Suddenly I heard a strange, almost animal-like noise. I looked around and realized that a woman sitting a few rows in front of me ❷ _____ (be) weeping loudly. I was a little thrown and did not know what to do. Should I allow her privacy? Should I approach her? My heart went out to her crying alone in an airport.

An older woman, who had also noticed her, went up to her and said something, but then moved away again and I guessed that she ❸ _____ (refuse) an offer of help. She continued with her aching crying, and I continued to wonder if I should do something nonetheless. Eventually I took my courage and went over. Rather than ❹ _____ (ask) if everything was OK, which would probably have elicited a polite rebuttal as in the case of the other woman, I sat down next to her and said, "I don't want to bother you, but I couldn't help noticing that you are in distress."

I guess she saw the genuine empathy in my eyes, as she ❺ _____ (proceed) to pour out her story. Her sister, who was relatively young, had just lost her husband, and this woman had spent the week ❻ _____ (be) the rock upon which her sister could lean. Only now that she was leaving did she allow the flood of grief for her sister to deluge her, to the point where she abandoned her inhibitions and cried her heart out in such a public place.

She spoke to me for just a few minutes, but I sensed that she parted from me a little comforted; for somebody else had just for a moment reached out to her and provided a shoulder for her to cry on, in a reversal of her usual role. I am often afraid of rejection and assume that no one would want me specifically to comfort them. But it's not true — where there is real emotion, there can never be enough warm hands ❼ _____ (hold), empathetic eyes to reflect the pain, and shoulders to cry on.

*elicit (정보나 반응 등을 어렵게)끌어내다   **rebuttal 항변   *deluge 밀려들다

I was once sitting in Ben Gurion Airport, waiting for my flight to be announced. Suddenly I heard a strange, almost animal-like noise. I looked around and realized that a woman sitting ❶ _____ _____ _____ _____ _____ _____ (몇 줄 내 앞에) was weeping loudly. I was a little thrown and did not know what to do. Should I allow her privacy? Should I approach her? My heart went out to her crying alone in an airport.

An older woman, who had also noticed her, went up to her and said something, but then moved away again and I guessed that she had refused an offer of help. She continued with her aching crying, and I continued to wonder if I should do something nonetheless. Eventually I ❷ _____ _____ _____ (용기를 냈다) and went over. Rather than asking if everything was OK, which would probably have elicited a polite rebuttal as in the case of the other woman, I sat down next to her and said, "I don't want to bother you, but I ❸ _____ _____ _____ (눈치챌 수밖에 없었다) that you are in distress."

I guess she saw the genuine empathy in my eyes, as she proceeded to ❹ _____ _____ (쏟아 내다) her story. Her sister, who was relatively young, had just lost her husband, and this woman had spent the week being the rock upon which her sister could lean. Only now that she was leaving did she allow the ❺ _____ _____ _____ (슬픔의 홍수) for her sister to deluge her, to the point where she abandoned her inhibitions and ❻ _____ _____ _____ _____ (가슴이 미어지게 소리 내어 울었다) in such a public place. She spoke to me for just a few minutes, but I sensed that she parted from me a little comforted; for somebody else had just for a moment reached out to her and provided a shoulder for her to cry on, ❼ _____ _____ _____ _____ (~와 반대로) her usual role. I am often afraid of rejection and assume that no one would want me specifically to comfort them. But it's not true — where there is real emotion, there can never be enough warm hands to hold, empathetic eyes to reflect the pain, and shoulders to cry on.

*elicit (정보나 반응 등을 어렵게)끌어내다 **rebuttal 항변 *deluge 밀려들다

01 Test1 1번

(A), (B), (C)의 각 네모 안에서 문맥에 맞는 낱말로 가장 적절한 것은?

I am a graduate student majoring in political science. I am writing this letter to tell you about the (A) convenience / inconvenience students experience on campus. An increasing number of students are riding their bicycles to school. However, since there are not enough bicycle racks on campus, students have trouble finding places to park their bicycles. Often we spend a lot of time looking for a place for our bicycles, which often leads us to be late for class. It gets even (B) worse / better on rainy or snowy days. Last month, I heard that five bicycles parked on the roadside due to the lack of bicycle facilities on campus had been stolen. So I hope you take this matter very seriously and take necessary action to (C) resolve / dissolve it. More than anything, I ask you to create more bicycle racks.

	(A)	(B)	(C)
①	convenience	worse	resolve
②	convenience	better	resolve
③	inconvenience	worse	resolve
④	inconvenience	better	dissolve
⑤	inconvenience	worse	dissolve

02 Test1 2번

주어진 글 다음에 이어질 글의 순서로 가장 적절한 것은?

I was working through college selling children's books door to door in Florida. One particularly blistering day nothing was going right. I had knocked on every door without a single answer; I was hot, tired, and felt like a total failure.

(A) Then, I looked down the street at a small white house and was drawn toward it. I had barely knocked on the door when an older woman opened it and immediately asked me in. She gave me a drink and invited me to share a meal with her and her husband. It was obvious that they did not have much money.

(B) As I left, the man gave me money and said he just wanted to help me out and that he had no need for my books. As I walked back down the street I broke into tears and kept crying for blocks. These people who at first seemed to have so little had given me more than I could ever have asked for.

(C) During the two hours I was there, the woman and her husband shared stories of the hardships and experiences in their lives and told me that it was very important to always love and care deeply about others — even strangers.

*blistering 지독히 더운

① (A) – (C) – (B)
② (B) – (A) – (C)
③ (B) – (C) – (A)
④ (C) – (A) – (B)
⑤ (C) – (B) – (A)

다음 빈칸에 들어갈 말로 가장 적절한 것은?

It's probably worth mentioning that Socrates was put to death for his beliefs — and for spreading those beliefs too widely to the youth of Athens. So it's safe to say that challenging established thinking doesn't always sit well with people. But I'd argue it's not only a good idea to harness constructive conflict, it's critical to the decision-making process. You can't effectively set a strategy or decide direction if you're unwilling to grapple with tough questions and have some disagreement over ideas. Thoughtful leaders thrive on disagreement because it gives them the information they need to improve their ideas before they reach the world. We all have our own personal threshold of comfort around conflict. Some people thrive on lively debate; others find it deeply stressful. But if the boss can't be challenged safely, then no one can. I believe it's your job as a leader _____. By constructively harnessing disagreements within your team, you improve ideas and fuel productivity.

*harness 활용하다 **grapple with ~을 해결하려고 노력하다
***threshold 한계점

① to invite good criticism
② to wisely resolve conflict
③ to lead a constructive conversation
④ to motivate your team and reach a goal
⑤ to have a strong bond with your team members

다음 글의 내용을 한 문장으로 요약하고자 한다. 빈칸 (A), (B)에 들어갈 말로 가장 적절한 것은?

Antiracist educator and author Debby Irving uses an often-cited headwinds and tailwinds metaphor to explain the invisibility of the systemic, group-level differences that treat different groups of people differently. Headwinds are the challenges — some big, some small, some visible, some invisible — that make life harder for some people, but not for all people. When you run against a headwind, your speed slows down and you have to push harder. You can feel the headwind. When you have a tailwind pushing you, it is a force that propels you forward. It is consequential but easily unnoticed or forgotten. In fact, if you are like me when I jog with a tailwind, you may glow with pride at your great running time that day, as if it were your own athletic prowess. When you have the tailwind, you will not notice that some runners are running into headwinds. They may be running as hard as, or even harder than, you, but they will appear lazier and slower to you. When some of them grow tired and stop trying, they will appear self-destructive to you.

*prowess 기량, 훌륭한 솜씨

↓

When we are in a more ___(A)___ position compared to others, it's hard to be aware of our privileges and realize that there are some people facing ___(B)___ social conditions.

	(A)		(B)
①	favorable	......	ideal
②	favorable	......	adverse
③	unfavorable	......	challenging
④	unfavorable	......	ideal
⑤	urgent	......	adverse

다음 글에서 전체 흐름과 관계 <u>없는</u> 문장은?

Like in the early days of industrialization, workers today are no longer reaping the gains of progress. Worse, many have been left behind in the backwaters of progress. In the same way that opportunity dried up for middle-income artisans as a consequence of the industrialization process, the age of automation has meant diminishing opportunities for the American middle class. ① Like the victims of the early factories, many Americans have adjusted to the computerization of work by unwillingly shifting into lower-paying jobs or have failed to adjust and dropped out of the workforce completely. ② The computerization of work has been an important basis for the growth of the postindustrial, knowledge-based economy. ③ And similar to the victims of the factories, the losers to automation have primarily been men in the prime of life. ④ Up until the 1980s, manufacturing jobs allowed ordinary working men to attain a middle-class lifestyle without going to college. ⑤ As employment opportunities in manufacturing receded, a path of upward mobility was closed to many citizens.

*artisan 장인 **recede 줄다

글의 흐름으로 보아, 주어진 문장이 들어가기에 가장 적절한 곳은?

Change the Stor, Change the Future, Korten proclaims in his book on creating more sustainable and just earth economies.

We do not have an environmental problem so much as we have a *story* problem. Or so says David Korten, who argues that the grave environmental challenges we face today have been set in motion by the predominating cultural lens of what he calls the "sacred money and markets story." This has been a story with catastrophic outcomes, contends Korten. (①) Is there a way to fix it? (②) Korten thinks there is: intervene. (③) Intervening in the "sacred money and markets story" and supplanting it with the "sacred life and living earth story" as the prevailing story of our time, he argues, will result in changing the human cognition and behavior that got us into our current environmental mess. (④) Change the story, and we will climb our way out of destruction and despair and begin the repair and recovery of life systems on the planet. (⑤) Permit the dominant "sacred money and markets story" instead to proceed on its current trajectory uninterrupted, with *no* effective intervention, and we seal our own doom.

*catastrophic 파멸적인 **trajectory 궤도

(A), (B), (C)의 각 네모 안에서 어법에 맞는 표현으로 가장 적절한 것은?

Imagination often *seems* unbounded and without constraint. However, if this (A) were / had been the case then it would be *more* likely to generate falsehoods than truths. Imagination must be constrained in order to provide knowledge. On the other hand, if we want to generate any new knowledge, what we imagine cannot be entirely "up to us," as it must go beyond what we already know. The knowledge-generating capacity of the imagination can be explained by suggesting (B) that / whether some constraints on the imagination are fixed and within our control, allowing for exploratory activity within these constraints. For example, if one wants to know whether a sofa will fit through a door, one must constrain one's imagination to keep the relevant shapes and sizes and the laws of physics (C) fixing / fixed, while allowing for exploration of various possible ways of manipulating the sofa.

	(A)	(B)	(C)
①	were	that	fixed
②	were	whether	fixed
③	were	that	fixing
④	had been	whether	fixing
⑤	had been	that	fixing

다음 도표의 내용과 일치하지 <u>않는</u> 것은?

Average Rainfall and Total Water Consumption in Australia

Financial Year	Average Rainfall(mm)	Total Water Consumption(gigaliter)
2014-2015	416	14,877
2015-2016	453	13,669
2016-2017	580	14,303
2017-2018	433	15,386
2018-2019	347	13,288
2019-2020	347	11,231

The table above shows the average rainfall and the total water consumption in Australia in six financial years. ① During these six financial years, the highest average rainfall was recorded in financial year 2016-2017, and total water consumption reached its peak in financial year 2017-2018, with more than 15,000 gigaliters used. ② From financial year 2014-2015 to 2015-2016, the average rainfall increased, but during the same period, the total amount of water used fell by more than 1,000 gigaliters. ③ However, from financial year 2016-2017 to 2017-2018, the total water consumption showed an increase, whereas average rainfall dropped by 147 millimeters. ④ From financial year 2017-2018 to 2019-2020, the total amount of water consumed in Australia steadily declined. ⑤ The average rainfall in financial years 2018-2019 and 2019-2020 was just above 350 millimeters in both periods.

*gigaliter 기가리터(10억 리터)

Zhang Heng에 관한 다음 글의 내용과 일치하는 것은?

Zhang Heng was born in Henan, China in 78 CE. In his youth, he traveled to Chang'an and Luoyang to receive his education. Zhang Heng showed an early aptitude for literary pursuits and achieved fame for his poetry in his 20s. His work *To Live in Seclusion* is considered a masterpiece of the late Han dynasty. While most educated young men in China at the time sought to obtain government posts, Zhang Heng spent many years learning mathematics and astronomy instead. His accomplishments in these fields are extremely noteworthy and rival his literary fame. He was able to create an accurate chart of the stars, which assisted in keeping the imperial calendar accurate. He also invented a flying machine, which was able to leave the ground, though only for a few moments. In 132, he invented the first seismograph, which traced the direction of earthquakes and their seismic waves. It was only later in his life that Zhang Heng held a series of important government positions in the capital and remote regions, beginning in 116 and continuing until his death.

*aptitude 소질, 재능 **seismograph 지진계

① 중국 Henan으로 가서 교육을 받았다.
② 20대에 소설로 명성을 얻었다.
③ 이륙할 수 없는 비행 장치를 발명했다.
④ 132년에 최초의 지진계를 발명했다.
⑤ 말년이 되어서도 관직을 맡지 않았다.

2023 Westland Student Art Contest에 관한 다음 안내문의 내용과 일치하는 것은?

2023 Westland Student Art Contest

Do you want to see your artwork displayed at an exhibition?
If so, sign up for the 2023 Westland Student Art Contest

Contest Theme: Our Growing Community
• All fine art media allowed (oils, acrylics, watercolours, pastels, pencils, collage, etc.)
• All submitted pieces must be A3 in size.
• Two age groups: 7-12 and 13-18 years old

Prizes for Each Age Group
► First Place (1 person)
– A $200 gift card to use at Westland Shopping Center
► Second Place (3 persons)
– A $150 gift card to use at Westland Shopping Center
► Third Place (5 persons)
– A $100 gift card to use at Westland Shopping Center
※ All entries will be displayed at our exhibition.
The contest will run from June 5th to July 7th.
Find terms and conditions on our website: www.westsac.org.

① 아크릴 물감과 수채화 물감은 허용되지 않는다.
② 제출 작품의 크기에는 제한이 없다.
③ 1등 수상자는 150달러 기프트 카드를 받는다.
④ 수상한 작품만이 전시회에서 전시된다.
⑤ 이 대회는 6월 5일부터 7월 7일까지 진행된다.

2023 Happy Mall Dance Challenge with Your Dad에 관한 다음 안내문의 내용과 일치하지 <u>않는</u> 것은?

2023 Happy Mall Dance Challenge with Your Dad

In partnership with the trendy short-video platform ShortClip, we want to level up the "home date" fun this Father's Day. We invite kids and dads to show their dance moves and take on the dance challenge!

The challenge has three super easy steps:
1. Together with your dad, record a ShortClip video dancing to your favorite song.
2. Your video should be 15-30 seconds long.
3. Post it only on ShortClip with the hashtags #FathersDayDanceChallenge and #happymall by June 12.
※ Make sure your account is set to public to validate your entry.

The top 5 most viewed videos from June 12 to 18 will get a special prize from Happy Mall. So join now!

For more information, scan the QR code below.

---

① 가장 좋아하는 노래에 맞춰 댄스 동영상을 찍어야 한다.
② 동영상의 길이는 15~30초여야 않아야 한다.
③ 6월 12일까지 출품작에 해시태그를 달아 이메일로 보내야 한다.
④ 참가자의 계정을 공개로 설정해야 한다.
⑤ 가장 많이 시청된 다섯 편의 동영상에 특별 상품이 주어진다.

다음 빈칸에 들어갈 말로 가장 적절한 것은?

When we are young, we see our parents as people who always know the answers. That's probably why as soon as we can think independently, around the ages of 4-5, we start asking a lot of questions. Parents try to answer these questions in a way that a young mind can comprehend. However, when it comes to learning lessons about money, our parents' answers to these questions _____. Even worse, a passing comment about money in the kitchen or at the dinner table can have a lasting effect. For example, a common phrase used by parents in response to a child's request for something is "No, we can't afford that." Think for a moment about how a young mind might interpret that. The message could be interpreted as "we don't have enough money" or "there isn't enough money." These beliefs about money can lead to an entire life designed around making sure there is always enough money through an obsession around work. It could lead to someone feeling deprived and a propensity for overspending in adulthood to avoid the feeling of deprivation.

*obsession 집착 **propensity 경향

① get written into a money blueprint
② are taken as a joke and often ignored
③ reinforce our positive thoughts about money
④ help us live a life of simplicity and frugality
⑤ result in a belief that money can buy everything

13

다음 글의 밑줄 친 부분 중, 어법상 틀린 것은?

The idea that zebra stripes work to confuse predators while the zebra is in motion is a relatively early theory. This is a plausible possibility; zebras have the high-contrast patterning generally thought ① to promote dazzle effects, and as herd animals they might benefit from an interaction between dazzle effects and confusion effects created when targeting individuals in groups. They also have visually oriented lions and hyenas as their main predators, and as large animals that live in the open, they might find camouflaging via other mechanisms ② difficult. The motion dazzle hypothesis has been studied in zebras by modelling the motion signals created by moving zebra stripes. This analysis shows that zebra stripes create strong motion signals in directions other than the true direction of movement, supporting the hypothesis ③ that zebra stripes make movement processing difficult. While most recent work focuses on whether zebra stripes function as protection against biting insects rather than mammalian carnivores, this idea is not necessarily ④ mutually exclusive with the dazzle hypothesis. Rather than (or in addition to) lions and hyenas, stripes may target the motion processing of much smaller but no less ⑤ fitness-reduced flies instead.

*dazzle 현혹 **camouflage 위장하다 ***carnivore 육식 동물

14

다음 글에서 전체 흐름과 관계 없는 문장은?

It is interesting to reflect on the possible connection between increasing individualism and rising mental ill-health. ① This is discussed at length in Oliver James's book *Affluenza*, in which he points out that the United States, the world's most individualist society, is also on the top of the league for mental disorders (as recorded by the World Health Organization's World Mental Health Survey). ② Several other countries that rate highly on individualism also figure highly in this league table. ③ Comparing just 14 countries, including New Zealand (2nd), France (4th) and the Netherlands (7th), James defines 'affluenza' as 'the placing of a high value on money, possessions, appearances (physical and social) and fame', and he attributes this to what he calls 'selfish capitalism'. ④ It could certainly be argued that the relative importance attached to materialistic factors related to self-esteem is particularly important in cultures where 'selfish capitalism' is strong. ⑤ Generally, people living in an affluent country tend to feel prouder, more confident, and less afraid than people in a poor country, but they are not necessarily more compassionate or loving.

15 Test 1 15번

다음 글의 제목으로 가장 적절한 것은?

Sensors are opening vast new windows on the cosmos. Thanks to the constant advance of sensors and effectors in the form of adaptive optics, discovery of extrasolar planets moved from science fiction to commonplace with breathtaking speed. In the near future, sensor advances will allow us to analyze exoplanetary atmospheres and look for signatures of civilization. The same trends will open new horizons for amateur astronomers, who will soon enjoy affordable technical means to match the *Kepler* space telescope in planet-finding skills. Sensors are thus as much about democratizing amateur science as the creation of ever more powerful instruments. The *Kepler* satellite imaged a field of 115°, or a mere 0.25 percent of the sky. Planet-finding amateurs using digitally empowered backyard scopes could put a serious dent in the 99.75 percent of the sky yet to be examined.

*effector 이펙터(영상이나 음성 신호 등을 전기 신호로 바꿔 다양한 효과를 연출하는 장치) **optics 광학 ***dent (초기 단계의) 진척, 영향

① Sensors Open New Horizons for Astronomy
② The Mysteries of the Cosmos and Planet Earth
③ Sensors Accelerate the Pace of Physics Discoveries
④ Sensors Play a Decisive Role in Analyzing Alien Civilization
⑤ Role of The *Kepler* Space Telescope in a New Era of Astronomy

16 Test 1 16번

다음 글의 내용을 한 문장으로 요약하고자 한다. 빈칸 (A), (B)에 들어갈 말로 가장 적절한 것은?

Basic manners fit into the category of fundamentally important social phenomena we tend to overlook. When I moved to Vancouver from California, one of the first things that struck me was that the natives, when exiting public buses through the back door, always shouted out a loud and cheerful *Thank you*! to the bus driver. It initially struck me as a bit excessive, but I've since come to see it not only as an expression of a fundamentally more pleasant populace but also as a ritual that probably helps to create more pleasant people. The bus driver, whether she realizes it or not, feels better having been thanked; she is now more inclined to drive courteously, or to remain at the stop that extra second to allow someone running late to hop on the bus. This behavior ripples out across my rainy city in subtle waves, inclining people toward virtue like wind blowing over the grass.

*populace 대중 **courteously 친절하게 ***ripple 파문처럼 퍼지다

↓

Seemingly trivial social manners such as saying *Thank You*! has a(n) ___(A)___ effect in creating a generally more pleasant populace, so it does both people and the community a lot of ___(B)___.

	(A)		(B)
①	positive	......	harm
②	positive	......	good
③	negative	......	harm
④	insignificant	......	good
⑤	negative	......	wrong

다음 글의 주제로 가장 적절한 것은?

It matters to us how things are. But how things are not can be equally important. It matters when something you want is not there. In a variety of circumstances, it matters that a drink is sugar-free. A migraine sufferer might want any pudding as long as it is not chocolate. Anyone with an allergy or intolerance will have a similar type of negative preference. It could matter to someone that a particular train does not stop in Wakefield, if they were planning to get off there. Bereavement matters too. When a loved one is no longer around, the feeling of their absence is profound. Some fear their own non-existence more than anything else. In other cases, things not being a certain way can be entirely mundane. Someone might regret not being six-feet tall or not being a better chess player. But some cases of what is not are of great, even cosmic importance. It matters enormously that the planet Earth is not closer to the sun than it is. It is likely that there would be no human life on the planet if it were.

*migraine 편두통 **bereavement 사별 ***mundane 평범한, 세속적인

① the importance of how things are not
② consequences of what you eat and drink
③ the influence of what you think on your behavior
④ reasons why things are not going as expected
⑤ differences between what you want and how things are in reality

다음 글의 밑줄 친 부분 중, 문맥상 낱말의 쓰임이 적절하지 않은 것은?

'Mindreading' refers to the cognitive ability to attribute psychological states to other people. It is distinct from 'social cognition' which has the ① wider referent base of 'the cognitive structures that facilitate our ability to navigate the social world'. Social cognition is a broader category than mindreading because it is ② possible to successfully interact with other people without attributing psychological states to them. One might have a perfectly successful social interaction with another by responding to their behaviours, without giving any thought to the psychological states that caused them. Alternatively, one might ③ anticipate the behaviours of another person based on social protocols about how one ought to behave in a particular situation, for example, at a pedestrian crossing or waiting in line to get on a bus. Such social protocols ④ extend to how we expect people in different roles to behave, for example, the behaviours we expect of a bus driver and a fellow passenger. These are all instances of interacting with others which do not obviously ⑤ exclude reasoning about their psychological states.

*protocol 관습, (군대·궁전 등의) 의례

19 Test 1 19번

다음 글의 밑줄 친 부분 중, 문맥상 낱말의 쓰임이 적절하지 <u>않은</u> 것은?

The problem of free will has real-world implications for our self-understanding, our interpersonal relationships, and our moral and legal practices. The assumption that we have free will lurks behind the ① justification of many of our everyday attitudes and judgments. For instance, when someone morally wrongs us, not only do we experience resentment and moral anger; we typically feel that we are *justified* in doing so, since we assume that, absent any excusing conditions, people are free and morally responsible for what they do and are therefore ② appropriate targets for such responses. We also typically assume that when individuals "act of their own free will," they *justly* ③ <u>deserve</u> to be praised and blamed, punished and rewarded for their actions since they are morally responsible for what they do. ④ <u>Similar</u> assumptions are made in the criminal law. The US Supreme Court, for instance, has asserted: "A 'universal and persistent' foundation stone in our system of law, and particularly in our approach to punishment, sentencing, and incarceration, is the '⑤ <u>disbelief</u> in freedom of the human will and a consequent ability and duty of the normal individual to choose between good and evil.'"

*lurk 잠재하다   **incarceration 감금, 투옥

20 Test 1 20번

글의 흐름으로 보아, 주어진 문장이 들어가기에 가장 적절한 곳은?

> Furthermore, as new computational requirements emerged, they had to be implemented with the current hardware.

An aeronautical engineer who sets about the task of developing a new airplane will start by performing theoretical analyses involving thrust, lift, and drag. Next, she will build models and run experiments. And most important, as the plane is built, its components will be assembled, adjusted, and tested while the plane is safely on the ground. Evolution has no such luxury. (①) As a species evolves it always has to be done "in flight." (②) Every sequential modification has to be fully functional and competitive. (③) The neuroscientist David Linden has described the human brain as the progressive accumulation of evolutionary kludges, or quick-and-dirty fixes. (④) During brain evolution, new structures were placed on top of the older functional structures, leading to redundancy, waste of resources, unnecessary complexity, and sometimes competing solutions to the same problem. (⑤) There is no switching from analog to digital along the way.

*aeronautical 항공학의   **kludge 클루지(컴퓨터 속어) (호환성 없는 요소로 이루어진 장치 혹은 못쓰게 된 프로그램)   ***redundancy 불필요한 중복

21 Test 1 21번

다음 빈칸에 들어갈 말로 가장 적절한 것은?

Self-presentation and/or impression management have been long identified as motivators for SNS use. Specific to image sharing, Facebook users choose certain profile pictures to portray themselves as attractive or fun-loving, as popular, or to show their relationship status, which aim to create a particular image of the individual and to shape others' impressions of them. Instagram users also report posting images to express themselves or present a particular image to others. In line with this, Facebook users also report untagging themselves from images posted by others if those photos are unattractive or portray them doing something they don't want others to know about. However, this is not to say that Facebook identities are completely divorced from who the person is offline. Researchers compared self-ratings of individuals' actual personality and their idealized self with ratings made by observers of their Facebook profile. Observer ratings corresponded more closely with actual personality than idealized personality, suggesting that although people can use social media to influence others' perceptions of them, the images presented _____ .

① reinforce their narcissism and envy
② are not wildly different from their actual selves
③ are not an illusion but a true reflection of their identity
④ increase their popularity and potentially showcase their creativity
⑤ help them support and sustain relationships with other members on SNS

22 Test 1 22번

주어진 글 다음에 이어질 글의 순서로 가장 적절한 것은?

> Researchers like Blau, Scott, and Evan acknowledge that the concept of organization set was developed by analogy from Robert K. Merton's concept of role set.

(A) The fundamental idea is a simple one, but its implications are quite rich. One is led to ask questions regarding, for example, the relative size of the organization set, the extent to which one group of role partners is aware of the demands made by another, and the extent to which expectations held by partners coincide.

(B) Similarly, a given organization participates in a variety of relations depending on the identity of its specific partners and competitors. For example, a small grocery store will relate in one manner with its suppliers, another with its customers, yet another with city officials, and so on.

(C) Merton noted that a single position such as

"mother" is associated with not one, but a cluster of different roles depending on the identity of the counterpositions. Thus, a mother has specific role obligations toward her children, others toward the father, still others toward the child's teachers, and so on.

*organization set 조직 집합

① (A) – (C) – (B) ② (B) – (A) – (C)
③ (B) – (C) – (A) ④ (C) – (A) – (B)
⑤ (C) – (B) – (A)

23 Test 1 23번

다음 글의 밑줄 친 부분 중, 어법상 틀린 것은?

There are arguments about why faith in 'more education' might be misplaced. The entrepreneur Peter Thiel offers the most provocative version of that case. He claims that higher education is a 'bubble', ① arguing that it is 'overpriced' because people do not get 'their money's worth' but go to college 'simply because that's what everybody's doing.' Thiel does not deny that ② those who are better educated tend to earn more on average. Instead, he is suspicious that we never get to see the counterfactual: how these students would have done without their education. His sense is that many of ③ whom would have earned just as much, and that universities are 'just good at identifying talented people rather than adding value'. Thiel now offers $100,000 grants to young students who ④ choose to 'skip or stop out of college' to start companies instead. The Thiel Foundation, which manages the grants, points out that its recipients have started sixty companies ⑤ worth a combined total of over $1.1 billion.

*provocative 도발적인

다음 글을 읽고 물음에 답하시오.

To illustrate the connection between thought and feeling, consider a soft drink dispenser in a self-service restaurant. Our particular model has a row of labeled buttons at the top and spouts underneath that dispense the desired beverage (A) if / whether the corresponding button is pushed. In our case, the buttons represent our interpretations — *Wrong, Unfortunate, Terrible, Right* and *Shameful* (or "*I am wrong*"). Should I, in any given situation, arrive at the interpretation that something is wrong and consequently push the soda fountain button for "*I am wrong*," then the machine would ideally dispense the corresponding beverage, namely anger.

As long as I have awareness of pushing a certain button, the buttons (B) labeled / are labeled correctly and they are properly connected to the corresponding beverage container, the machine will function without a hitch. Unfortunately, most of us are unaware of the connections between interpretations on the mental level and our corresponding reactions on the emotional level, however. Because of this, we often behave like people who continuously push buttons on a soda machine and watch in desperation as the cup overflows. We do not notice that we are pushing the button since we are completely unaware of its existence. We are oblivious to the fact that a particular interpretation is made before anger, for example, arises in our system — namely, "*This is wrong*." When we become aware of this interpretation, it is like suddenly watching our own thumb continuously (C) push / pushed the soda button despite the fact that we have already filled up our cup or would actually prefer lemonade or water instead.

*dispenser 자판기, 디스펜서 **spout (주전자 등의) 주둥이
***hitch 문제, 장애

24

윗글의 요지로 가장 적절한 것은?

① 이성적 사고를 통해 감정을 제어할 수 있어야 한다.
② 자제력을 발휘해 분노를 통제해야 성공적인 사회 생활이 가능하다.
③ 무언가가 잘못되었다는 사실을 알아차리고 나서 분노하는 것은 소용없다.
④ 정신적인 관점에서의 해석과 감정적인 관점에서의 반응은 서로 관련이 없다.
⑤ 우리가 생각과 느낌의 연관성에 대해 알지 못해서 부정적인 결과가 초래된다.

25

윗글의 (A), (B), (C)의 각 네모 안에서 어법에 맞는 표현으로 가장 적절한 것은?

	(A)	(B)	(C)
①	if	labeled	push
②	if	labeled	pushed
③	if	are labeled	push
④	whether	are labeled	pushed
⑤	whether	labeled	push

다음 글을 읽고 물음에 답하시오.

I was once sitting in Ben Gurion Airport, waiting for my flight to be announced. Suddenly I heard a strange, almost animal-like noise. I looked around and realized that a woman sitting a few rows in front of me was weeping loudly. I was a little thrown and did not know what to do. Should I allow (a) her privacy? Should I approach her? My heart went out to her crying alone in an airport.

An older woman, who had also noticed her, went up to her and said something, but then moved away again and I guessed that (b) she had refused an offer of help, She continued with her aching crying, and I continued to wonder if I should do something nonetheless. Eventually I took my courage and went over. Rather than asking if everything was OK, which would probably have elicited a polite rebuttal as in the case of the other woman, I sat down next to her and said, "I don't want to bother you, but I couldn't help noticing that (c) you are in distress."

I guess she saw the genuine empathy in my eyes, as she proceeded to pour out her story. Her sister, who was relatively young, had just lost (d) her husband, and this woman had spent the week being the rock upon which her sister could lean. Only now that she was leaving did she allow the flood of ____(A)____ for her sister to deluge her, to the point where she abandoned her inhibitions and cried her heart out in such a public place.

She spoke to me for just a few minutes, but I sensed that she parted from me a little comforted; for somebody else had just for a moment reached out to her and provided a shoulder for (e) her to cry on, in a reversal of her usual role. I am often afraid of rejection and assume that no one would want me specifically to comfort them. But it's not true — where there is real emotion, there can never be enough warm hands to hold, ____(B)____ eyes to reflect the pain, and shoulders to cry on.

*elicit (정보나 반응 등을 어렵게)끌어내다 **rebuttal 항변
*deluge 밀려들다

26

밑줄 친 (a)~(e)중에서 가리키는 대상이 나머지 넷과 다른 것은?

① (a)　　　　② (b)　　　　③ (c)
④ (d)　　　　⑤ (e)

27

윗글에 필자에 관한 내용으로 적절하지 않은 것은?

① 공항에 앉아 비행편이 방송으로 공지되기를 기다리고 있었다.
② 공항에서 여자가 큰 소리로 울고 있는 것을 알아차렸다.
③ 공항에서 울던 여자에게 다가가 괜찮냐고 물었다.
④ 공항에서 울던 여자가 자신의 눈에서 진심어린 공감을 봤다고 생각한다.
⑤ 상대방에게 도움을 주려다가 거절당하는 것을 자주 두려워한다.

28

윗글의 빈칸 (A), (B)에 들어갈 말로 가장 적절한 것은?

	(A)		(B)
①	grief	......	envious
②	regret	......	revengeful
③	grief	......	empathetic
④	regret	......	revengeful
⑤	joyfulness	......	empathetic

29 Test1 1번

글의 흐름으로 보아, 주어진 문장이 들어가기에 가장 적절한 곳은?

> However, since there are not enough bicycle racks on campus, students have trouble finding places to park their bicycles.

I am a graduate student majoring in political science. I am writing this letter to tell you about the inconvenience students experience on campus. An increasing number of students are riding their bicycles to school. (①) Often we spend a lot of time looking for a place for our bicycles, which often leads us to be late for class. (②) It gets even worse on rainy or snowy days. (③) Last month, I heard that five bicycles parked on the roadside due to the lack of bicycle facilities on campus had been stolen. (④) So I hope you take this matter very seriously and take necessary action to resolve it. (⑤) More than anything, I ask you to create more bicycle racks.

30 Test1 2번

다음 글의 밑줄 친 부분 중, 어법상 틀린 것은?

I was working through college selling children's books door to door in Florida. One particularly blistering day nothing was going ① right. I had knocked on every door without a single answer; I was hot, tired, and felt like a total failure. Then, I looked down the street at a small white house and was drawn toward it. I had ② barely knocked on the door when an older woman opened it and immediately asked me in. She gave me a drink and invited me to share a meal with her and her husband. It was obvious that they did not have ③ much money. During the two hours I was there, the woman and her husband shared stories of the hardships and experiences in their lives and told

me that ④ this was very important to always love and care deeply about others — even strangers. As I left, the man gave me money and said he just wanted to help me out and that he had no need for my books. As I walked back down the street I broke into tears and kept ⑤ crying for blocks. These people who at first seemed to have so little had given me more than I could ever have asked for.

*blistering 지독히 더운

31 Test1 3번

다음 글의 밑줄 친 부분 중, 문맥상 낱말의 쓰임이 적절하지 않은 것은?

It's probably worth mentioning that Socrates was put to death for his beliefs — and for spreading those beliefs too widely to the youth of Athens. So it's safe to say that ① challenging established thinking doesn't always sit well with people. But I'd argue it's not only a good idea to harness constructive conflict, it's ② critical to the decision-making process. You can't effectively set a strategy or decide direction if you're ③ willing to grapple with tough questions and have some disagreement over ideas. Thoughtful leaders thrive on disagreement because it gives them the information they need to improve their ideas before they reach the world. We all have our own personal ④ threshold of comfort around conflict. Some people thrive on lively debate; others find it deeply stressful. But if the boss can't be challenged safely, then no one can. I believe it's your job as a leader to invite good criticism. By constructively harnessing disagreements within your team, you improve ideas and ⑤ fuel productivity.

*harness 활용하다 **grapple with ~을 해결하려고 노력하다
***threshold 한계점

Antiracist educator and author Debby Irving uses an often-cited headwinds and tailwinds metaphor to explain the invisibility of the systemic, group-level differences that treat different groups of people differently. Headwinds are the challenges — some big, some small, some visible, some invisible — that make life harder for some people, but not for all people. When you run against a headwind, your speed slows down and you have to push harder. You can feel the headwind. When you have a tailwind pushing you, it is _____ _____. It is consequential but easily unnoticed or forgotten. In fact, if you are like me when I jog with a tailwind, you may glow with pride at your great running time that day, as if it were your own athletic prowess. When you have the tailwind, you will not notice that some runners are running into headwinds. They may be running as hard as, or even harder than, you, but they will appear lazier and slower to you. When some of them grow tired and stop trying, they will appear self-destructive to you.

*prowess 기량, 훌륭한 솜씨

① a compass guiding your direction
② a force that propels you forward
③ a challenge that you should face head on
④ a good rival who you should compete with together
⑤ a mentor inspiring you to be the best version of yourself

Like in the early days of industrialization, workers today are no longer reaping the gains of progress. Worse, many have been left behind in the backwaters of progress. In the same way that opportunity dried up for middle-income artisans as a consequence of the industrialization process, the age of automation has meant diminishing opportunities for the American middle class. Like the victims of the early factories, many Americans have adjusted to the computerization of work by unwillingly shifting into lower-paying jobs or have failed to adjust and dropped out of the workforce completely. And similar to the victims of the factories, the losers to automation have primarily been men in the prime of life. Up until the 1980s, manufacturing jobs allowed ordinary working men to attain a middle-class lifestyle without going to college. As employment opportunities in manufacturing receded, a path of upward mobility was closed to many citizens.

*artisan 장인 **recede 줄다

① A Brief History of Industrial Progress across America
② The Rise and Fall of the American Middle Class
③ Why Mechanization No Longer Worked after the 1980s
④ The Material Affluence of the Middle Class in American History
⑤ The Automation Trap: How It Adversely Affects the American Middle Class

34 Test 1 6번

밑줄 친 we seal our own doom이 다음 글에서 의미하는 바로 가장 적절한 것은?

We do not have an environmental problem so much as we have a *story* problem. Or so says David Korten, who argues that the grave environmental challenges we face today have been set in motion by the predominating cultural lens of what he calls the "sacred money and markets story." This has been a story with catastrophic outcomes, contends Korten. Is there a way to fix it? Korten thinks there is: intervene. *Change the Story, Change the Future*, Korten proclaims in his book on creating more sustainable and just earth economies. Intervening in the "sacred money and markets story" and supplanting it with the "sacred life and living earth story" as the prevailing story of our time, he argues, will result in changing the human cognition and behavior that got us into our current environmental mess. Change the story, and we will climb our way out of destruction and despair and begin the repair and recovery of life systems on the planet. Permit the dominant "sacred money and markets story" instead to proceed on its current trajectory uninterrupted, with *no* effective intervention, and we seal our own doom.

*catastrophic 파멸적인 **trajectory 궤도

① nobody will care about our partnership with nature
② our efforts to address environmental ills will pay off
③ the repair and recovery of life systems will occur by themselves
④ we make our downfall and death inevitable on our own
⑤ fundamental social transformation will be beyond our control

35 Test 1 7번

다음 글에서 전체 흐름과 관계 없는 문장은?

Imagination often *seems* unbounded and without constraint. However, if this were the case then it would be *more* likely to generate falsehoods than truths. ① Imagination must be constrained in order to provide knowledge. ② On the other hand, if we want to generate any new knowledge, what we imagine cannot be entirely "up to us," as it must go beyond what we already know. ③ Knowledge generation can occur formally through direct research and experimental development in academic institutions, firms, and public institutions. ④ The knowledge-generating capacity of the imagination can be explained by suggesting that some constraints on the imagination are fixed and within our control, allowing for exploratory activity within these constraints. ⑤ For example, if one wants to know whether a sofa will fit through a door, one must constrain one's imagination to keep the relevant shapes and sizes and the laws of physics fixed, while allowing for exploration of various possible ways of manipulating the sofa.

36 Test 1 9번

글의 흐름으로 보아, 주어진 문장이 들어가기에 가장 적절한 곳은?

> While most educated young men in China at the time sought to obtain government posts, Zhang Heng spent many years learning mathematics and astronomy instead.

Zhang Heng was born in Henan, China in 78 CE. In his youth, he traveled to Chang'an and Luoyang to receive his education. Zhang Heng showed an early aptitude for literary pursuits and achieved fame for his poetry in his 20s. His work *To Live in Seclusion* is considered a masterpiece of the late Han dynasty. (①) His accomplishments in these fields are extremely noteworthy and rival his literary fame. (②) He was able to create an accurate chart of the stars, which assisted in keeping the imperial calendar accurate. (③) He also invented a flying machine, which was able to leave the ground, though only for a few moments. (④) In 132, he invented the first seismograph, which traced the direction of earthquakes and their seismic waves. (⑤) It was only later in his life that Zhang Heng held a series of important government positions in the capital and remote regions, beginning in 116 and continuing until his death.

*aptitude 소질, 재능 **seismograph 지진계

37 Test 1 12번

고난도

다음 글의 내용을 한 문장으로 요약하고자 한다. 빈칸 (A), (B)에 들어갈 말로 가장 적절한 것은?

When we are young, we see our parents as people who always know the answers. That's probably why as soon as we can think independently, around the ages of 4-5, we start asking a lot of questions. Parents try to answer these questions in a way that a young mind can comprehend. However, when it comes to learning lessons about money, our parents' answers to these questions get written into a money blueprint. Even worse, a passing comment about money in the kitchen or at the dinner table can have a lasting effect. For example, a common phrase used by parents in response to a child's request for something is "No, we can't afford that." Think for a moment about how a young mind might interpret that. The message could be interpreted as "we don't have enough money" or "there isn't enough money." These beliefs about money can lead to an entire life designed around making sure there is always enough money through an obsession around work. It could lead to someone feeling deprived and a propensity for overspending in adulthood to avoid the feeling of deprivation.

*obsession 집착 **propensity 경향

> Since our beliefs and behaviors about money are ___(A)___ by our parents, their comments about money can become a(n) ___(B)___ for our financial decision-making or consumption habits in adulthood.

	(A)		(B)
①	shaped	······	basis
②	shaped	······	burden
③	reflected	······	basis
④	scolded	······	burden
⑤	scolded	······	asset

38 Test 1 13번

주어진 글 다음에 이어질 글의 순서로 가장 적절한 것은?

The idea that zebra stripes work to confuse predators while the zebra is in motion is a relatively early theory.

(A) The motion dazzle hypothesis has been studied in zebras by modelling the motion signals created by moving zebra stripes. This analysis shows that zebra stripes create strong motion signals in directions other than the true direction of movement, supporting the hypothesis that zebra stripes make movement processing difficult.

(B) This is a plausible possibility; zebras have the high-contrast patterning generally thought to promote dazzle effects, and as herd animals they might benefit from an interaction between dazzle effects and confusion effects created when targeting individuals in groups. They also have visually oriented lions and hyenas as their main predators, and as large animals that live in the open, they might find camouflaging via other mechanisms difficult.

(C) While most recent work focuses on whether zebra stripes function as protection against biting insects rather than mammalian carnivores, this idea is not necessarily mutually exclusive with the dazzle hypothesis. Rather than (or in addition to) lions and hyenas, stripes may target the motion processing of much smaller but no less fitness-reducing flies instead.

*dazzle 현혹 **camouflage 위장하다 ***carnivore 육식 동물

① (A) – (C) – (B)
② (B) – (A) – (C)
③ (B) – (C) – (A)
④ (C) – (A) – (B)
⑤ (C) – (B) – (A)

39 Test 1 14번

(A), (B), (C)의 각 네모 안에서 문맥에 맞는 낱말로 가장 적절한 것은?

It is interesting to reflect on the possible connection between increasing individualism and rising mental ill-health. This is discussed at length in Oliver James's book *Affluenza*, in which he points out that the United States, the world's most individualist society, is also on the (A) top / bottom of the league for mental disorders (as recorded by the World Health Organization's World Mental Health Survey). Several other countries that rate highly on individualism also figure highly in this league table. Comparing just 14 countries, including New Zealand (2nd), France (4th) and the Netherlands (7th), James defines 'affluenza' as 'the placing of a high value on money, possessions, appearances (physical and social) and fame', and he (B) attributes / contributes this to what he calls 'selfish capitalism'. It could certainly be argued that the relative importance attached to (C) spiritual / materialistic factors related to self-esteem is particularly important in cultures where 'selfish capitalism' is strong.

(A)	(B)	(C)
① top	attributes	spiritual
② top	contributes	spiritual
③ top	attributes	materialistic
④ bottom	contributes	materialistic
⑤ bottom	attributes	materialistic

40 Test 1 15번

다음 글에서 전체 흐름과 관계 <u>없는</u> 문장은?

Sensors are opening vast new windows on the cosmos. Thanks to the constant advance of sensors and effectors in the form of adaptive optics, discovery of extrasolar planets moved from science fiction to commonplace with breathtaking speed. In the near future, sensor advances will allow us to analyze exoplanetary atmospheres and look for signatures of civilization. ① The same trends will open new horizons for amateur astronomers, who will soon enjoy affordable technical means to match the *Kepler* space telescope in planet-finding skills. ② Sensors are thus as much about democratizing amateur science as the creation of ever more powerful instruments. ③ Democratizing science does not mean settling questions about nature by voting; it means creating institutions and practices that fully incorporate principles of accessibility, transparency, and accountability. ④ The *Kepler* satellite imaged a field of 115°, or a mere 0.25 percent of the sky. ⑤ Planet-finding amateurs using digitally empowered backyard scopes could put a serious dent in the 99.75 percent of the sky yet to be examined.

*effector 이펙터(영상이나 음성 신호 등을 전기 신호로 바꿔 다양한 효과를 연출하는 장치) **optics 광학 ***dent (초기 단계의) 진척, 영향

41 Test 1 16번

다음 글의 주제로 가장 적절한 것은?

Basic manners fit into the category of fundamentally important social phenomena we tend to overlook. When I moved to Vancouver from California, one of the first things that struck me was that the natives, when exiting public buses through the back door, always shouted out a loud and cheerful *Thank you!* to the bus driver. It initially struck me as a bit excessive, but I've since come to see it not only as an expression of a fundamentally more pleasant populace but also as a ritual that probably helps to create more pleasant people. The bus driver, whether she realizes it or not, feels better having been thanked; she is now more inclined to drive courteously, or to remain at the stop that extra second to allow someone running late to hop on the bus. This behavior ripples out across my rainy city in subtle waves, inclining people toward virtue like wind blowing over the grass.

*populace 대중 **courteously 친절하게 ***ripple 파문처럼 퍼지다

① risks and outcomes of social exclusion
② the necessity of learning virtue in everyday life
③ the infectious nature of unkindness and rudeness
④ the significance of basic manners in various social contexts
⑤ the positive ripple effect of basic manners on others and community

42 Test 1 17번

주어진 글 다음에 이어질 글의 순서로 가장 적절한 것은?

> It matters to us how things are. But how things are not can be equally important. It matters when something you want is not there.

(A) When a loved one is no longer around, the feeling of their absence is profound. Some fear their own non-existence more than anything else. In other cases, things not being a certain way can be entirely mundane. Someone might regret not being six-feet tall or not being a better chess player.

(B) But some cases of what is not are of great, even cosmic importance. It matters enormously that the planet Earth is not closer to the sun than it is. It is likely that there would be no human life on the planet if it were.

(C) In a variety of circumstances, it matters that a drink is sugar-free. A migraine sufferer might want any pudding as long as it is not chocolate. Anyone with an allergy or intolerance will have a similar type of negative preference. It could matter to someone that a particular train does not stop in Wakefield, if they were planning to get off there. Bereavement matters too.

*mundane 평범한, 세속적인 **migraine 편두통 ***bereavement 사별

① (A) – (C) – (B)
② (B) – (A) – (C)
③ (B) – (C) – (A)
④ (C) – (A) – (B)
⑤ (C) – (B) – (A)

43 Test 1 18번

다음 빈칸에 들어갈 말로 가장 적절한 것은?

'Mindreading' refers to the cognitive ability to attribute psychological states to other people. It is distinct from 'social cognition' which has the broader referent base of 'the cognitive structures that facilitate our ability to navigate the social world'. Social cognition is a broader category than mindreading because it is possible to successfully interact with other people without attributing psychological states to them. One might have a perfectly successful social interaction with another by responding to their behaviours, without giving any thought to the psychological states that caused them. Alternatively, one might anticipate the behaviours of another person based on social protocols about how one ought to behave in a particular situation, for example, at a pedestrian crossing or waiting in line to get on a bus. Such social protocols extend to how we expect people in different roles to behave, for example, the behaviours we expect of a bus driver and a fellow passenger. These are all instances of interacting with others which do not obviously involve _____.

*protocol 관습, (군대·궁전 등의) 의례

① reasoning about their psychological states
② anticipation about the consequence of their actions
③ our cognitive thinking process and mental efforts
④ observance of social convention and social norms
⑤ intentional thinking of mindreading and social cognition

44 Test 1 19번

다음 글의 제목으로 가장 적절한 것은?

The problem of free will has real-world implications for our self-understanding, our interpersonal relationships, and our moral and legal practices. The assumption that we have free will lurks behind the justification of many of our everyday attitudes and judgments. For instance, when someone morally wrongs us, not only do we experience resentment and moral anger; we typically feel that we are *justified* in doing so, since we assume that, absent any excusing conditions, people are free and morally responsible for what they do and are therefore appropriate targets for such responses. We also typically assume that when individuals "act of their own free will," they *justly deserve* to be praised and blamed, punished and rewarded for their actions since they are morally responsible for what they do. Similar assumptions are made in the criminal law. The US Supreme Court, for instance, has asserted: "A 'universal and persistent' foundation stone in our system of law, and particularly in our approach to punishment, sentencing, and incarceration, is the 'belief in freedom of the human will and a consequent ability and duty of the normal individual to choose between good and evil.'"

*lurk 잠재하다 **incarceration 감금, 투옥

① There's No Such Thing as Free Will
② Free Will Is Not Without Its Limits and Problems
③ The Criminal Justice System in the Light of Free Will
④ Free Will as the Cornerstone of Our Attitudes and Judgments
⑤ Believing in Free Will Makes You Feel More Like Your True Self

45 Test 1 20번

다음 빈칸에 들어갈 말로 가장 적절한 것은?

An aeronautical engineer who sets about the task of developing a new airplane will start by performing theoretical analyses involving thrust, lift, and drag. Next, she will build models and run experiments. And most important, as the plane is built, its components will be assembled, adjusted, and tested while the plane is safely on the ground. Evolution has no such _____. As a species evolves it always has to be done "in flight." Every sequential modification has to be fully functional and competitive. The neuroscientist David Linden has described the human brain as the progressive accumulation of evolutionary kludges, or quick-and-dirty fixes. During brain evolution, new structures were placed on top of the older functional structures, leading to redundancy, waste of resources, unnecessary complexity, and sometimes competing solutions to the same problem. Furthermore, as new computational requirements emerged, they had to be implemented with the current hardware. There is no switching from analog to digital along the way.

*aeronautical 항공학의 **kludge 클루지(컴퓨터 속어)(호환성 없는 요소로 이루어진 장치 혹은 못쓰게 된 프로그램) ***redundancy 불필요한 중복

① luxury
② repetition
③ flexibility
④ complexity
⑤ adaptation

46 Test 1 21번

다음 글의 제목으로 가장 적절한 것은?

Self-presentation and/or impression management have been long identified as motivators for SNS use. Specific to image sharing, Facebook users choose certain profile pictures to portray themselves as attractive or fun-loving, as popular, or to show their relationship status, which aim to create a particular image of the individual and to shape others' impressions of them. Instagram users also report posting images to express themselves or present a particular image to others. In line with this, Facebook users also report untagging themselves from images posted by others if those photos are unattractive or portray them doing something they don't want others to know about. However, this is not to say that Facebook identities are completely divorced from who the person is offline. Researchers compared self-ratings of individuals' actual personality and their idealized self with ratings made by observers of their Facebook profile. Observer ratings corresponded more closely with actual personality than idealized personality, suggesting that although people can use social media to influence others' perceptions of them, the images presented are not wildly different from their actual selves.

① Limits of Self-Presentation on SNS
② What Types of Images Appears on SNS?
③ Little Deviation Between the True and Shown Self on SNS
④ Relationship Building: A Motivation for Image Sharing on SNS
⑤ Social Media: A Great Stage for Both Self-Presentation and Self-Disclosure

47 Test 1 22번

다음 빈칸에 들어갈 말로 가장 적절한 것은?

Researchers like Blau, Scott, and Evan acknowledge that the concept of organization set was developed by analogy from Robert K. Merton's concept of role set. Merton noted that a single position such as "mother" is associated with not one, but a cluster of different roles depending on the identity of the counterpositions. Thus, a mother has specific role obligations toward her children, others toward the father, still others toward the child's teachers, and so on. Similarly, a given organization _____ _____ depending on the identity of its specific partners and competitors. For example, a small grocery store will relate in one manner with its suppliers, another with its customers, yet another with city officials, and so on. The fundamental idea is a simple one, but its implications are quite rich. One is led to ask questions regarding, for example, the relative size of the organization set, the extent to which one group of role partners is aware of the demands made by another, and the extent to which expectations held by partners coincide.

*organization set 조직 집합

① sets specific task guidelines
② divides roles among its members
③ participates in a variety of relations
④ clearly defines its goals and objectives
⑤ decides its range of products and services

48 Test 1 23번

다음 글의 주제로 가장 적절한 것은?

There are arguments about why faith in 'more education' might be misplaced. The entrepreneur Peter Thiel offers the most provocative version of that case. He claims that higher education is a 'bubble', arguing that it is 'overpriced' because people do not get 'their money's worth' but go to college 'simply because that's what everybody's doing.' Thiel does not deny that those who are better educated tend to earn more on average. Instead, he is suspicious that we never get to see the counterfactual: how these students would have done without their education. His sense is that many of them would have earned just as much, and that universities are 'just good at identifying talented people rather than adding value'. Thiel now offers $100,000 grants to young students who choose to 'skip or stop out of college' to start companies instead. The Thiel Foundation, which manages the grants, points out that its recipients have started sixty companies worth a combined total of over $1.1 billion.

*provocative 도발적인

① challenges facing the education sector
② doubt and suspicion on the cost-effectiveness of higher education
③ a way of estimating the cost-effectiveness of higher education
④ a solution for addressing the current crisis of public education
⑤ a need for a systematic retraining program for school dropouts

Test 1 1번

I am a graduate student majoring in political science. I am writing this letter to tell you about the inconvenience students experience on campus. An increasing number of students ① is riding their bicycles to school. However, since there are not enough bicycle racks on campus, students have trouble ② finding places to park their bicycles. Often we spend a lot of time looking for a place for our bicycles, which often ③ lead us to be late for class. It gets ④ even worse on rainy or snowy days. Last month, I heard that five bicycles parked on the roadside due to the lack of bicycle _____ on campus had been stolen. So I hope you take this matter very ⑤ seriously and take necessary action to resolve it. More than anything, I ask you to create more bicycle racks.

49 윗글의 밑줄 친 부분 중 어법상 틀린 것을 2개 찾아 그 번호를 쓰고 고쳐 쓰시오.

(1) _____ → _____

(2) _____ → _____

50 윗글의 빈칸에 들어갈 단어를 영영 뜻풀이를 참고하여 쓰시오. (단, 주어진 글자로 시작하고, 필요시 어형을 바꿔 쓸 것)

> something such as a room or piece of equipment that is provided at a place for people to use

f_____

I was working through college selling children's books door to door in Florida. One particularly blistering day nothing was going right. I had knocked on every door without a single answer; I was hot, tired, and felt like a total failure. Then, I looked down the street at a small white house and was drawn toward it. 내가 문을 노크하자마자 한 연로한 여성이 문을 열어주었다 and immediately asked me in. She gave me a drink and invited me to share a meal with her and her husband. It was obvious that they did not have much money. During the two hours I was there, the woman and her husband shared stories of the hardships and experiences in their lives and told me that it was very important to always love and care deeply about others — even strangers. As I left, the man gave me money and said he just wanted to help me out and that he had no need for my books. As I walked back down the street I broke into tears and kept crying for blocks. These people who at first seemed to have so little had given me more than I could ever have asked for.

*blistering 지독히 더운

51 다음 질문에 대한 대답을 우리말로 간단히 쓰시오. (30글자 내외)

Q: Why did the writer break into tears while he or she was walking down the street?

A: _____

_____

52 윗글의 밑줄 친 우리말의 의미와 일치하도록 [보기]의 단어를 활용하여 [조건]에 맞게 문장을 완성하시오.

> [보기]   knock / the / door / older / woman / barely / on / open / when

> [조건]   · Barely를 문두에 사용할 것
> · 총 13단어로 쓰고 필요시 어형을 바꿔 쓸 것

소크라테스가 자신의 신념 때문에 죽임을 당했다는 것은 아마도 언급할 만한 가치가 있다. — and for spreading those beliefs too widely to the youth of Athens. So it's safe to say that ① challenging established thinking doesn't always sit well with people. But I'd argue it's not only a good idea to harness constructive conflict, it's critical to the decision-making process. You can't effectively set a strategy or decide direction if you're ② unwilling to grapple with tough questions and have some disagreement over ideas. Thoughtful leaders thrive on ③ agreement because it gives them the information they need to improve their ideas before they reach the world. We all have our own personal ④ threshold of comfort around conflict. Some people thrive on lively debate; others find it deeply stressful. But if the boss can't be challenged safely, then no one can. I believe it's your job as a leader to invite good criticism. By constructively ⑤ harnessing disagreements within your team, you improve ideas and fuel productivity.

*harness 활용하다   **grapple with ~을 해결하려고 노력하다
***threshold 한계점

53 윗글의 밑줄 친 부분 중 문맥상 어색한 것을 찾아 그 번호를 쓰고 고쳐 쓰시오.

_____ → _____

고난도

54 윗글의 밑줄 친 우리말의 의미와 일치하도록 [보기]의 단어를 활용하여 [조건]에 맞게 문장을 완성하시오.

> [보기]   probably / Socrates / put / mention / for / his / beliefs / to / worth / death

> [조건]   · 진주어-가주어 구문을 사용할 것
> · 필요시 어형을 바꿔 쓸 것
> · 총 14단어로 쓸 것

Antiracist educator and author Debby Irving uses an often-cited headwinds and tailwinds metaphor to explain the invisibility of the systemic, group-level differences that treat different groups of people differently. Headwinds are the challenges — some big, some small, some visible, some invisible ? that make life harder for some people, but not for all people. When you run against a headwind, your speed slows down and you have to push harder. You can feel the headwind. When you have a tailwind pushing you, it is a force that propels you forward. It is _____ but easily unnoticed or forgotten. In fact, if you are like me when I jog with a tailwind, you may glow with pride at your great running time that day, 마치 그것이 여러분 자신의 운동 기량인 것처럼. When you have the tailwind, you will not notice that some runners are running into headwinds. They may be running as hard as, or even harder than, you, but they will appear lazier and slower to you. When some of them grow tired and stop trying, they will appear self-destructive to you.

*prowess 기량, 훌륭한 솜씨

55 윗글의 빈칸에 들어갈 단어를 영영 뜻풀이를 참고하여 쓰시오. (단, 주어진 글자로 시작할 것)

having significant results or effects

c_____

56 윗글의 밑줄 친 우리말의 의미와 일치하도록 **보기** 의 단어를 활용하여 문장을 완성하시오. (8단어로 쓸 것)

보기 as / if / prowess / athletic

Like in the early days of industrialization, workers today are no longer reaping the gains of progress. Worse, many (A) have left behind in the backwaters of progress. In the same way that opportunity dried up for middle-income artisans as a consequence of the industrialization process, the age of automation has meant diminishing opportunities for the American middle class. Like the victims of the early factories, many Americans have adjusted to the computerization of work by unwillingly shifting into lower-paying jobs or have failed to adjust and dropped out of the workforce completely. And similar to the victims of the factories, the losers to automation have primarily been men in the prime of life. Up until the 1980s, manufacturing jobs allowed ordinary working men (B) attain a middle-class lifestyle without going to college. As employment opportunities in manufacturing receded, a path of upward mobility was closed to many citizens.

*artisan 장인 **recede 줄다

57 윗글의 밑줄 친 (A), (B)를 어법상 알맞은 형태로 고쳐 쓰시오.

(A) have left → _____

(B) attain → _____

고난도

58 윗글의 내용을 아래와 같이 요약하려고 한다. 빈칸 (A)와 (B)에 들어갈 알맞은 말을 지문에서 찾아 쓰시오.

Workers in the age of automation are going through a similar experience to those in the days of industrialization in that they have decreasing _____(A)_____, are reduced to working for lower wages while adapting to the new age or forced to drop out of the workforce, and are beginning to lose the opportunity for _____(B)_____ movement.

(A) _____   (B) _____

우리는 환경 문제를 가지고 있다기보다 '이야기' 문제를 가지고 있다. Or so says David Korten, who argues that the grave environmental challenges we face today have been set in motion by the predominating cultural lens of what he calls the "sacred money and markets story." This has been a story with ① catastrophic outcomes, contends Korten. Is there a way to fix it? Korten thinks there is: intervene. *Change the Story, Change the Future*, Korten proclaims in his book on creating more sustainable and just earth economies. ② Intervening in the "sacred money and markets story" and supplanting it with the "sacred life and living earth story" as the prevailing story of our time, he argues, will result in changing the human cognition and behavior that got us into our current environmental ③ mess. ④ Change the story, and we will climb our way out of destruction and despair and begin the repair and recovery of life systems on the planet. Permit the dominant "sacred money and markets story" instead to proceed on its current trajectory ⑤ interrupted, with *no* effective intervention, and we seal our own doom.

*catastrophic 파멸적인 **trajectory 궤도

59 윗글의 밑줄 친 우리말의 의미와 일치하도록 **보기**의 단어를 활용하여 문장을 영작하시오. (15단어로 쓸 것)

> **보기** so / an / enviroment / *story* / much / problem / as

_____

_____.

60 윗글의 밑줄 친 ①~⑤ 중 문맥상 어색한 것을 1개 찾아 그 번호를 쓰고 알맞은 말을 **보기**에서 골라 쓰시오.

> **보기** desirable / maintaining / challenge / protect / uninterrupted / economy /

_____ → _____

Imagination often *seems* unbounded and without _____. However, if this (A) is the case then it would be *more* likely to generate falsehoods than truths. Imagination must be constrained in order to provide knowledge. On the other hand, if we want to generate any new knowledge, what we imagine cannot be entirely "up to us," as it must go beyond (B) which we already know. The knowledge-generating capacity of the imagination can be explained by suggesting that some constraints on the imagination are fixed and within our control, allowing for exploratory activity within these constraints. For example, if one wants to know whether a sofa will fit through a door, one must constrain one's imagination to keep the relevant shapes and sizes and the laws of physics fixed, while (C) allowed for exploration of various possible ways of manipulating the sofa.

61 윗글의 빈칸에 들어갈 말을 본문에서 찾아 한 단어로 쓰시오. (필요시 어형을 바꿔 쓸 것)

_____

62 윗글의 밑줄 친 부분을 어법상 알맞은 형태로 고쳐 쓰시오.

(A) is → _____

(B) which → _____

(C) allowed → _____

Average Rainfall and Total Water Consumption in Australia

Financial Year	Average Rainfall(mm)	Total Water Consumption(gigaliter)
2014-2015	416	14,877
2015-2016	453	13,669
2016-2017	580	14,303
2017-2018	433	15,386
2018-2019	347	13,288
2019-2020	347	11,231

The table above shows the average rainfall and the total water consumption in Australia in six financial years. During these six financial years, the highest average rainfall was recorded in financial year 2016-2017, and total water consumption reached its (A) _____ in financial year 2017-2018, 15,000 기가리터 넘게 사용되며. From financial year 2014-2015 to 2015-2016, the average rainfall increased, but during the same period, the total amount of water used (B) _____ by more than 1,000 gigaliters. However, from financial year 2016-2017 to 2017-2018, the total water consumption showed an increase, whereas average rainfall dropped by 147 millimeters. From financial year 2017-2018 to 2019-2020, the total amount of water consumed in Australia steadily declined. The average rainfall in financial years 2018-2019 and 2019-2020 was just (C) _____ 350 millimeters in both periods.

*gigaliter 기가리터(10억 리터)

63 윗글의 (A)~(C)에 들어갈 문맥상 알맞은 말을 쓰시오. (단, 반드시 주어진 철자로 시작할 것)

(A) p _____

(B) f _____

(C) b _____

64 윗글의 밑줄 친 우리말의 의미와 일치하도록 보기 의 단어를 활용하여 문장을 영작하시오.

> 보기   gigaliter / with / than / use

_____

Zhang Heng was born in Henan, China in 78 CE. In his youth, he traveled to Chang'an and Luoyang to receive his education. Zhang Heng showed an early aptitude for literary pursuits and achieved fame for his poetry in his 20s. His work *To Live in Seclusion* is considered a masterpiece of the late Han dynasty. While most educed young men in China at the time sought to obtain government posts, Zhang Heng spent many years learning mathematics and astronomy instead. <u>His accomplishments in these fields</u> are extremely noteworthy and rival his literary fame. He was able to create an accurate chart of the stars, which assisted in keeping the imperial calendar accurate. He also invented a flying machine, which was able to leave the ground, though only for a few moments. In 132, he invented the first seismograph, which traced the direction of earthquakes and their seismic waves. 말년이 되어서야 비로소 Zhang Heng은 일련의 중요한 관직을 맡았다 in the capital and remote regions, beginning in 116 and continuing until his death.

*aptitude 소질, 재능 **seismograph 지진계

65 윗글의 밑줄 친 His accomplishments in these fields가 가리키는 것을 본문에서 모두 찾아 영어로 쓰시오.

_____

_____

66 윗글의 밑줄 친 우리말의 의미와 일치하도록 보기 의 단어를 활용하여 조건 에 맞게 문장을 완성하시오.

보기   later in his life / a series of / only / government / important / positions / hold

조건   · 부사구 도치 구문을 사용할 것
      · 총 15단어로 쓸 것(Zhang Heng 포함)

_____

_____

2023 Westland Student Art Contest

여러분의 미술 작품이 전시회에 전시되는 것을 보고 싶나요?
If so, sign up for the 2023 Westland Student Art Contest

Contest Theme: Our Growing Community
· All fine art media allowed (oils, acrylics, watercolours, pastels, pencils, collage, etc.)
· All submitted pieces must be A3 in size.
· Two age groups: 7-12 and 13-18 years old

Prizes for Each Age Group
► First Place (1 person)
– A $200 gift card to use at Westland Shopping Center
► Second Place (3 persons)
– A $150 gift card to use at Westland Shopping Center
► Third Place (5 persons)
– A $100 gift card to use at Westland Shopping Center

※ All entries will be displayed at our exhibition.
The contest will run from June 5th to July 7th.
Find terms and conditions on our website: www.westsac.org.

67 윗글의 밑줄 친 우리말의 의미와 일치하도록 보기 의 단어를 활용하여 문장을 영작하시오. (11단어로 쓸 것)

보기   want / at / artwork / exhibition / see / displayed / an / your

_____

_____ ?

68 윗글에서 다음 질문에 대한 답을 찾아 우리말로 쓰시오. (20글자 내외)

Q: How many people can win the prizes according to the passage? And how many artworks are displayed after the contest?

A: _____

2023 Happy Mall Dance Challenge with Your Dad

In partnership with the trendy short-video platform ShortClip, we want to level up the "home date" fun this Father's Day. We invite kids and dads to show their dance moves and take on the dance challenge!

The challenge has three super easy steps:
1. Together with your dad, record a ShortClip video dancing to your favorite song.
2. Your video should be 15-30 seconds long.
3. Post it only on ShortClip with the hashtags #FathersDayDanceChallenge and #happymall by June 12.
※ Make sure your account is set to public to _____ your entry.

The top 5 most viewed videos from June 12 to 18 will get a special prize from Happy Mall. So join now!

For more information, scan the QR code below.

69 다음 질문에 대한 대답을 윗글에서 찾아 쓰시오.

Q: Who is the event organizer according to the passage?

A: _____

70 윗글의 빈칸에 들어갈 단어를 영영 뜻풀이를 참고하여 쓰시오. (단, 주어진 글자로 시작할 것)

> to officially prove that something is true or correct

→ v_____

When we are young, we see our parents as people who always know the answers. That's probably why as soon as we can think independently, around the ages of 4-5, we start asking a lot of questions. Parents try to answer these questions in a way that a young mind can comprehend. However, when it comes to learning lessons about money, our parents' answers to these questions get written into a money blueprint. Even (A) better / worse, a passing comment about money in the kitchen or at the dinner table can have a lasting effect. For example, a common phrase used by parents in response to a child's request for something is "No, we can't afford that." Think for a moment about how a young mind might interpret that. The message could be interpreted as "we don't have enough money" or "there isn't enough money." These beliefs about money can lead to an entire life designed around making sure there is always enough money through a(n) (B) obsession / negligence around work. It could lead to someone feeling deprived and a propensity for overspending in adulthood to avoid the feeling of (C) deprivation / satisfaction.

*obsession 집착 **propensity 경향

71 윗글의 (A)~(C)의 각 네모 안에서 문맥상 알맞은 것을 골라 쓰시오.

(A) _____   (B) _____

(C) _____

🚩 고난도

72 윗글의 내용을 한 문장으로 요약하려고 한다. 빈칸 (A)와 (B)에 들어갈 알맞은 말을 본문에서 찾아 쓰시오.

> In terms of learning lessons about money, not only the answers considerate enough for our children to ___(A)___ but also the passing comments about money can have a lifelong effect on their money ___(B)___.

(A) _____   (B) _____

The idea that zebra stripes work to confuse predators while the zebra is in motion is a relatively early theory. This is a plausible possibility; zebras have the high-contrast patterning generally ① thought to promote dazzle effects, and as herd animals they might benefit from an interaction between dazzle effects and confusion effects ② creating when targeting individuals in groups. They also have visually oriented lions and hyenas as their main predators, and as large animals that live in the open, they might find ③ camouflaging via other mechanisms difficult. The motion dazzle hypothesis has been studied in zebras by modelling the motion signals created by moving zebra stripes. This analysis shows that zebra stripes create strong motion signals in directions other than the true direction of movement, supporting the hypothesis that zebra stripes make movement processing ④ difficultly. While most recent work focuses on whether zebra stripes function as protection against biting insects rather than mammalian carnivores, this idea is not necessarily mutually exclusive with the dazzle hypothesis. Rather than (or in addition to) lions and hyenas, stripes may target the motion processing of ⑤ much smaller but no less fitness-reducing flies instead.

*dazzle 현혹 **camouflage 위장하다 ***carnivore 육식 동물

73 윗글의 밑줄 친 ①~⑤ 중 어법상 틀린 것 2개를 찾아 그 번호를 쓰고 고쳐 쓰시오.

(1) _____ → _____

(2) _____ → _____

74 윗글의 내용을 한 문장으로 요약하려고 한다. 빈칸 (A)와 (B)에 들어갈 알맞은 말을 본문에서 찾아 쓰시오.

Zebra stripes may serve as ____(A)____ against both predators such as lions and hyenas and biting insects by creating strong motion signals in directions different from the true directions of movement, making motion ____(B)____ difficult.

(A) _____ (B) _____

It is interesting to reflect on the possible connection between increasing individualism and rising mental ill-health. This is discussed at length in Oliver James's book *Affluenza*, (A) which he points out that the United States, the world's most individualist society, is also on the top of the league for mental disorders (as recorded by the World Health Organization's World Mental Health Survey). Several other countries that rate highly on individualism also (B) figures highly in this league table. Comparing just 14 countries, including New Zealand (2nd), France (4th) and the Netherlands (7th), James defines 'affluenza' as 'the placing of a high value on money, possessions, appearances (physical and social) and fame', and he attributes this to (C) which he calls 'selfish capitalism'. It could certainly be argued that the relative importance attached to materialistic factors related to self-esteem is particularly important in cultures where 'selfish capitalism' is strong.

75 윗글의 밑줄 친 부분을 어법상 알맞은 형태로 고쳐 쓰시오.

(A) which → _____

(B) figures → _____

(C) which → _____

76 윗글을 읽고 다음 질문에 대한 답을 본문에서 찾아 쓰시오. (2단어)

Q: What does Oliver James think is the cause of affluenza?

A: _____

Sensors are opening vast new windows on the cosmos. Thanks to the constant advance of sensors and effectors in the form of adaptive optics, discovery of extrasolar planets moved from science fiction to _____ with breathtaking speed. In the near future, sensor advances will allow us to analyze exoplanetary atmospheres and look for signatures of civilization. The same trends will open new horizons for amateur astronomers, who will soon enjoy affordable technical means to match the Kepler space telescope in planet-finding skills. Sensors are thus as much about democratizing amateur science as the creation of ever more powerful instruments. The Kepler satellite imaged a field of 115°, or a mere 0.25 percent of the sky. Planet-finding amateurs using digitally empowered backyard scopes could put a serious dent in the 99.75 percent of the sky yet to be examined.

*effector 이펙터(영상이나 음성 신호 등을 전기 신호로 바꿔 다양한 효과를 연출하는 장치) **optics 광학 ***dent (초기 단계의) 진척, 영향

77 윗글의 빈칸에 들어갈 단어를 영영 뜻풀이를 참고하여 쓰시오. (단, 주어진 글자로 시작할 것)

something that happens or appears in many places and is not unusual

c_____

78 윗글의 내용을 한 문장으로 요약하려고 한다. 빈칸 (A)와 (B)에 들어갈 알맞은 말을 보기 에서 찾아 쓰시오.

The advance of sensors not only ___(A)___ various aspects of space exploration, but also will lead to the democratization of science in its contribution to amateur astronomers' ___(B)___ of new planets.

보기 analyzes / enables / hinders / creation / discovery /

(A) _____ (B) _____

Basic manners fit into the category of fundamentally important social phenomena we tend to overlook. When I moved to Vancouver from California, one of the first things that struck me was that the natives, when (A) exit public buses through the back door, always shouted out a loud and cheerful *Thank you*! to the bus driver. 그것은 처음에는 나에게는 조금 과하다는 느낌이 들었다, but I've since come to see it not only as an expression of a fundamentally more pleasant populace but also as a ritual that probably helps to create more pleasant people. The bus driver, whether she realizes it or not, feels better (B) be thanked; she is now more inclined to drive courteously, or to remain at the stop that extra second to allow someone running late to hop on the bus. This behavior ripples out across my rainy city in subtle waves, inclining people toward virtue like wind (C) blow over the grass.

*populace 대중 **courteously 친절하게 ***ripple 파문처럼 퍼지다

79 윗글의 밑줄 친 부분을 어법상 알맞은 형태로 맞게 고쳐 쓰시오.

(A) exit → _____

(B) be → _____

(C) blow → _____

80 윗글의 밑줄 친 우리말의 의미와 일치하도록 보기 의 단어를 배열하여 문장을 완성하시오. (필요시 어형을 바꿔 쓸 것)

> 보기 it / excessive / strike / initially / a / bit / me / as

_____

It matters to us how things are. But how things are not can be equally ① underline{important}. It matters when something you want is not there. In a variety of circumstances, it matters that a drink is sugar-free. A migraine sufferer might want any pudding as long as it is not chocolate. Anyone with an allergy or intolerance will have a similar type of ② positive preference. It could matter to someone that a particular train does not stop in Wakefield, if they were planning to get off there. Bereavement matters too. When a loved one is no longer around, the feeling of their ③ presence is profound. Some fear their own non-existence more than anything else. In other cases, things not being a certain way can be entirely mundane. Someone might ④ regret not being six-feet tall or not being a better chess player. But some cases of what is not are of great, even cosmic importance. It ⑤ matters enormously that the planet Earth is not closer to the sun than it is. It is likely that 만일 그렇다면(지구가 더 가까이에 있다면) 지구에는 어떤 인간 생명체도 없게 될 것이다.

*migraine 편두통 **bereavement 사별 ***mundane 평범한, 세속적인

81 윗글의 밑줄 친 부분 중 문맥상 어색한 것을 2개 찾아 그 번호를 쓰고 고쳐 쓰시오.

(1) _____ → _____

(2) _____ → _____

82 윗글의 밑줄 친 우리말의 의미와 일치하도록 보기 의 단어를 조건 에 맞게 영작하시오.

> 보기 there / human / on / it / the planet / life / be

> 조건 · 가정법을 사용하되, there로 시작할 것
> · 총 12단어로 쓸 것

_____ .

'Mindreading' refers to the cognitive ability to (A) <u>attribute psychological states to other people</u>. It is distinct from 'social cognition' which has the broader referent base of 'the cognitive structures that facilitate our ability to navigate the social world'. Social cognition is a broader category than mindreading because it is possible to successfully interact with other people without attributing psychological states to them. One might have a perfectly successful social interaction with another by responding to their behaviours, without giving any thought to the psychological states that caused them. Alternatively, one might anticipate the behaviours of another person based on social protocols about how one ought to behave in a particular situation, for example, at a pedestrian crossing or waiting in line to get on a bus. Such social protocols extend to how we expect people in different roles to behave, for example, the behaviours we expect of a bus driver and a fellow passenger. These are all instances of interacting with others which do not obviously involve reasoning about their psychological states.

*protocol 관습, (군대·궁전 등의) 의례

고난도

83 윗글의 밑줄 친 (A)와 같은 의미를 나타내는 어구 표현을 본문에서 찾아 영어로 쓰시오. (2곳을 찾아 쓸 것)

(1) _____

(2) _____

고난도

84 윗글의 내용을 한 문장으로 요약하려고 한다. 빈칸 (A)와 (B)에 들어갈 알맞은 말을 본문에서 찾아 쓰시오. (단, 필요시 어형을 바꿔 쓸 것)

> While mindreading means the cognitive ability to ____(A)____ about the psychological states of other people, social cognition has the broader meaning, in that there is a successful social interaction with others with the ____(B)____ of their behaviors based on social protocols about a certain situation or role without the process of mindreading.

(A) _____ (B) _____

The problem of free will has real-world implications for our self-understanding, our interpersonal relationships, and our moral and legal practices. The assumption ① which we have free will lurks behind the _____ of many of our everyday attitudes and judgments. For instance, when someone morally wrongs us, not only ② we experience resentment and moral anger; we typically feel that we ③ are *justified* in doing so, since we assume that, absent any excusing conditions, people are free and morally responsible for what they do and are therefore appropriate targets for such responses. We also typically assume that when individuals "act of their own free will," they *justly deserve* to be praised and blamed, punished and rewarded for their actions since they are morally responsible for ④ what they do. Similar assumptions are made in the criminal law. The US Supreme Court, for instance, has asserted: "A 'universal and persistent' foundation stone in our system of law, and particularly in our approach to punishment, sentencing, and incarceration, ⑤ are the 'belief in freedom of the human will and a consequent ability and duty of the normal individual to choose between good and evil.'"

*lurk 잠재하다 **incarceration 감금, 투옥

85 윗글의 빈칸에 들어갈 단어를 영영 뜻풀이를 참고하여 본문에서 찾아 쓰시오. (단, 필요시 어형을 바꿔 쓸 것.)

a reason why something is correct and morally right

_____

86 윗글의 밑줄 친 부분 중 어법상 틀린 것 3개를 찾아 그 번호를 쓰고 고쳐 쓰시오.

(1) _____ → _____

(2) _____ → _____

(3) _____ → _____

An aeronautical engineer who sets about the task of developing a new airplane will start by performing theoretical analyses involving thrust, lift, and drag. Next, she will build models and run experiments. And most important, as the plane is built, its components will be assembled, adjusted, and tested while the plane is safely on the ground. Evolution has no such luxury. As a species evolves it always has to be done "in flight." Every sequential modification has to be fully functional and competitive. The neuroscientist David Linden has described the human brain as the progressive _____ of evolutionary kludges, or quick-and-dirty fixes. During brain evolution, new structures were placed on top of the older functional structures, leading to redundancy, waste of resources, unnecessary complexity, and sometimes competing solutions to the same problem. Furthermore, as new computational requirements emerged, they had to be implemented with the current hardware. There is no switching from analog to digital along the way.

*aeronautical 항공학의 **kludge 클루지(컴퓨터 속어)(호환성 없는 요소로 이루어진 장치 혹은 못쓰게 된 프로그램) ***redundancy 불필요한 중복

87 윗글의 빈칸에 들어갈 단어를 영영 뜻풀이를 참고하여 쓰시오. (단, 주어진 철자로 시작할 것)

the process by which something increases in amount or is collected together over time

a_____

88 윗글의 내용을 한 문장으로 요약하려고 한다. 빈칸 (A)와 (B)에 들어갈 알맞은 말을 본문에서 찾아 쓰시오.

While the task of developing a new airplane goes through a series of processes on the ground before flight, evolution demands functional and competitive _____(A)_____ due to the ongoing accumulation of evolutionary fixes, causing inefficiency and difficulty in incorporationg new _____(B)_____ with the current hardware.

(A) _____ (B) _____

Test 1 21번

Self-presentation and/or impression management have been long identified as ① motivators for SNS use. Specific to image sharing, Facebook users choose certain profile pictures to portray themselves as attractive or fun-loving, as popular, or to show their relationship status, which aim to create a particular image of the individual and to shape others' ② impressions of them. Instagram users also report posting images to express (A) them or present a particular image to others. In line with this, Facebook users also report ③ tagging themselves from images posted by others if those photos are unattractive or portray (B) themselves doing something they don't want others to know about. However, this is not to say that Facebook identities are completely ④ divorced from who the person is offline. Researchers compared self-ratings of individuals' actual personality and their idealized self with ratings made by observers of their Facebook profile. Observer ratings ⑤ differentiated more closely with actual personality than idealized personality, suggesting that although people can use social media to influence others' perceptions of them, the images (C) present are not wildly different from their actual selves.

89 윗글의 밑줄 친 ①~⑤ 중 문맥상 낱말의 쓰임이 적절하지 않은 것을 2개 찾아 그 번호를 쓰고 보기 에서 골라 쓰시오.

보기   obstacles / prejudice / untagging / accorded / corresponded

(1) _____ → _____

(2) _____ → _____

90 윗글의 밑줄 친 (A)~(C)를 어법상 알맞은 형태로 고쳐 쓰시오.

(A) them   → _____

(B) themselves → _____

(C) present   → _____

Researchers like Blau, Scott, and Evan acknowledge that the concept of organization set was developed by _____ from Robert K. Merton's concept of role set. Merton noted that a single position such as "mother" is associated with not one, but a cluster of different roles depending on the identity of the counterpositions. Thus, a mother has specific role obligations toward her children, others toward the father, still others toward the child's teachers, and so on. ___(A)___, a given organization participates in a variety of relations depending on the identity of its specific partners and competitors. ___(B)___, a small grocery store will relate in one manner with its suppliers, another with its customers, yet another with city officials, and so on. The fundamental idea is a simple one, but its implications are quite rich. ___(C)___, one is led to ask questions regarding the relative size of the organization set, the extent to which one group of role partners is aware of the demands made by another, and the extent to which expectations held by partners coincide.

*organization set 조직 집합

91 윗글의 빈칸에 들어갈 단어를 영영 뜻풀이를 참고하여 쓰시오. (단, 주어진 글자로 시작할 것)

a comparison between two situations, processes, etc., that is intended to show that the two are similar

a _____

92 윗글의 빈칸 (A)~(C)에 들어갈 알맞은 말을 보기 에서 골라 쓰시오. (단, 중복 사용 가능)

보기   Similarly / However / Moreover / Therefore / For example / In fact

(A) _____

(B) _____

(C) _____

There are arguments about why faith in 'more education' might be (A) _____. The entrepreneur Peter Thiel offers the most provocative version of that case. He claims that higher education is a 'bubble', arguing that it is '(B) _____' because people do not get 'their money's worth' but go to college 'simply because that's what everybody's doing.' Thiel does not deny that those who are better educated tend to earn more on average. Instead, he is suspicious that we never get to see the counterfactual: 이 학생들이 교육이 없었다면 어떻게 했을지. His sense is that many of them would have earned just as much, and that universities are 'just good at identifying talented people rather than adding value'. Thiel now offers $100,000 grants to young students who (C) _____ to 'skip or stop out of college' to start companies instead. The Thiel Foundation, which manages the grants, points out that its recipients have started sixty companies worth a combined total of over $1.1 billion.

*provocative 도발적인

93 윗글의 빈칸 (A)~(C)에 들어갈 알맞은 말을 〔보기〕에서 골라 쓰시오.

> **보기** overpriced / reject / misplaced / organized / choose / inexpensive

(A) _____

(B) _____

(C) _____

94 윗글의 밑줄 친 우리말의 의미와 일치하도록 〔보기〕의 단어를 활용하여 영작하시오.

> **보기** how / do / students / their / these / education

> **조건**
> · without 가정법을 사용하되 주절 뒤에 둘 것
> · 간접 의문문을 사용할 것
> · 총 9단어로 쓸 것

→ _____ .

Test 1 24~25번

To illustrate the connection between thought and feeling, consider a soft drink dispenser in a self-service restaurant. Our particular model has a row of labeled buttons at the top and spouts underneath that dispense ① the desired beverage if the corresponding button is pushed. In our case, the buttons represent our interpretations — *Wrong, Unfortunate, Terrible, Right* and *Shameful* (or "*I am wrong*"). 만약 내가 어떤 특정한 상황에서 무언가가 잘못되었다는 해석에 도달해서 결과적으로 내가 틀렸다는 탄산음료가 나오는 버튼을 누르면, 그 기계는 그에 해당하는 음료, 즉 분노를 완벽하게 내놓을 것이다.

As long as I have awareness of pushing a certain button, the buttons are labeled correctly and they are properly connected to the corresponding beverage container, the machine will function without a hitch. Unfortunately, most of us are unaware of the connections between interpretations on the mental level and ② our corresponding reactions on the emotional level, however. Because of this, we often behave like people who continuously push buttons on a soda machine and watch in desperation as the cup overflows. We do not notice that we are pushing ③ the button since we are completely unaware of its existence. We are oblivious to the fact that a particular interpretation is made before ④ anger, for example, arises in our system — namely, "*This is wrong.*" When we become aware of ⑤ this interpretation, it is like suddenly watching our own thumb continuously push the soda button despite the fact that we have already filled up our cup or would actually prefer lemonade or water instead.

*dispenser 자판기, 디스펜서 **spout (주전자 등의) 주둥이
***hitch 문제, 장애

95 윗글의 밑줄 친 ①~⑤중, 의미하는 바가 다른 2개를 고르고, 이것들이 공통으로 가리키는 바를 본문에서 찾아 쓰시오.

_____ , _____ → _____

96 윗글의 밑줄 친 우리말의 의미와 일치하도록 〔보기〕의 단어를 빈칸에 넣어 문장을 완성하시오.

> **보기** arrive / dispense / I / would / ideally / the interpretation / should / at /

In any given situation, _____ _____ _____ _____ _____ _____ that something is wrong and consequently push the soda fountain button for "*I am wrong*," then the machine _____ _____ _____ the corresponding beverage, namely anger.

I was once sitting in Ben Gurion Airport, waiting for my flight to ① be announced. Suddenly I heard a strange, almost animal-like noise. I looked around and realized that a woman sitting a few rows in front of me was weeping loudly. I was a little thrown and did not know what to do. Should I allow her privacy? Should I approach her? My heart went out to her crying alone in an airport.

An older woman, who had also noticed her, went up to her and said something, but then moved away again and I guessed that she had refused an offer of help. She continued with her aching crying, and I continued to wonder if I should do something nonetheless. Eventually I took my courage and went over. Rather than asking if everything was OK, which would probably ② elicit a polite rebuttal as in the case of the other woman, I sat down next to her and said, "I don't want to bother you, but I couldn't help ③ notice that you are in distress."

I guess she saw (A) the genuine empathy in my eyes, as she proceeded to pour out her story. Her sister, who was relatively young, had just lost her husband, and this woman had spent the week being the rock upon which her sister could lean. she was leaving did she allow the flood of grief, to the point ④ where she abandoned her inhibitions and cried her heart out in such a public place.

She spoke to me for just a few minutes, but I sensed that she parted from me a little ⑤ comforting; for somebody else had just for a moment reached out to her and provided a shoulder for her to cry on, in a reversal of her usual role. I am often afraid of rejection and assume that no one would want me specifically to comfort them. But it's not true — where there is real emotion, there can never be enough warm hands to hold, empathetic eyes to reflect the pain, and shoulders to cry on.

*elicit (정보나 반응 등을 어렵게)끌어내다   **rebuttal 항변
*deluge 밀려들다

97 윗글의 밑줄 친 ①~⑤ 중 어법상 틀린 것 3개를 찾아 그 번호를 쓰고 고쳐 쓰시오.

(1) _____ → _____

(2) _____ → _____

(3) _____ → _____

98 윗글의 밑줄 친 (A)의 구체적 행위 사례들을 본문에서 찾아 우리말로 쓰시오. (30글자 내외)

_____

_____

❶ Do you enjoy water activities on rivers? ❷ With the year coming to a close, make 2024 your year to leave the ordinary behind and venture into extraordinary adventures. ❸ Enter the 2024 River Lottery for the chance to be awarded river permits for access to rafting, kayaking, and paddling on some of the most scenic and exciting waterways in the country. ❹ The permit lottery process is used for popular destinations and activities. ❺ It helps manage the large volume of interest and ensures an enhanced experience on the river. ❻ You can submit your application through the Lotteries page on our website or through the "Lotteries" section in the publicwaters.net mobile app.

❶ 하천에서의 수상 활동을 즐기시나요? ❷ 한 해가 마무리되어 가는데, 2024년을 여러분의 해로 만들어 일상의 것은 뒤로하고 특별한 모험을 감행하세요. ❸ 국내에서 가장 경치가 좋고 흥미진진한 몇몇 물길에서의 래프팅과 카야킹과 패들링 이용을 위한 하천 허가증을 받을 기회를 위해 '2024년 하천 추첨'에 참여하세요. ❹ 인기 있는 여행지와 활동에는 허가증 추첨 과정이 사용됩니다. ❺ 그것은 많은 관심을 다루는 데 도움을 주고, 하천에서의 더 나은 경험을 보장합니다. ❻ 저희 웹 사이트의 추첨 페이지를 통해서나 publicwaters.net 이동 전화 앱의 '추첨' 부문을 통해 여러분의 신청서를 제출하실 수 있습니다.

Word List

□ activity 활동　□ come to a close 끝나다　□ venture into ~을 감행하다　□ extraordinary 특별한, 보기 드문　□ lottery 추첨, 복권
□ award (상을) 수여하다　□ permit 허가증, 허가　□ access 접근, 이용　□ paddling 패들링(카누에서 패들로 저어 나가는 일)
□ scenic 경치가 좋은　□ waterway (강, 운하 등의) 물길, 수로　□ destination (여행 등의) 목적지　□ volume 분량　□ ensure 보장하다
□ enhanced 향상된, 개선된　□ mobile 이동 전화; 이동하는

• Word Test

1	lottery	_____	9	접근, 이용	_____
2	waterway	_____	10	경치가 좋은	_____
3	paddling	_____	11	이동 전화; 이동하는	_____
4	permit	_____	12	특별한, 보기 드문	_____
5	enhanced	_____	13	(상을) 수여하다	_____
6	volume	_____	14	보장하다	_____
7	venture into	_____	15	(여행 등의) 목적지	_____
8	activity	_____	16	끝나다	_____

Do you enjoy water activities on rivers? ❶ With / To the year coming to a close, make 2024 your year to leave the ordinary ❷ front / behind and venture into extraordinary adventures. Enter the 2024 River Lottery for the chance to be awarded river permits for access to rafting, kayaking, and paddling on some of the most ❸ scenic / scenery and exciting waterways in the country. The permit lottery process is used for popular destinations and activities. It helps manage the large volume of interest and ensures an enhanced experience on the river. You can submit your ❹ applicant / application through the Lotteries page on our website or through the "Lotteries" section in the publicwaters.net mobile app.

Do you enjoy water activities on rivers? With the year ❶ _____ (come) to a close, make 2024 your year to leave the ordinary behind and venture into extraordinary adventures. Enter the 2024 River Lottery for the chance ❷ _____ (be) awarded river permits for access to rafting, kayaking, and paddling on some of the most scenic and exciting waterways in the country. The permit lottery process ❸ _____ (use) for popular destinations and activities. It helps manage the large volume of interest and ensures an ❹ _____ (enhance) experience on the river. You can submit your application through the Lotteries page on our website or through the "Lotteries" section in the publicwaters.net mobile app.

Do you enjoy ❶ _____ _____ (수상 활동들) on rivers? With the year coming to a close, make 2024 your year to leave the ordinary behind and ❷ _____ _____ _____ _____ (특별한 모험들을 감행하다). Enter the 2024 River Lottery for the chance to be awarded river permits for access to rafting, kayaking, and paddling on some of ❸ _____ _____ _____ (가장 경치가 좋은) and exciting waterways in the country. The permit lottery process is used for popular destinations and activities. It helps manage the large volume of interest and ensures an ❹ _____ _____ (더 나은 경험) on the river. You can submit your application through the Lotteries page on our website or through the "Lotteries" section in the publicwaters.net mobile app.

❶ I pitched my tent in the dark and the pouring rain, hoping I'd scrambled far enough up the slope to be out of the range of flash floods. ❷ Crawling inside was like entering a washing machine on spin cycle — wind dashed against the wet fabric inches from my up-turned face, spraying me with a fine mist. ❸ As my sleeping bag slowly soaked through, tiredness slowly overcame me. ❹ As my eyelids began to feel heavy, I began to second-guess my choice of activities for the spring break holiday. ❺ I could have joined friends on a fishing trip, partaking in the sort of beery camaraderie that is more or less expected of college students during the final term of their final year. ❻ Instead, I decided at the last minute to throw my camping gear into a backpack, and head out to explore a remote corner of the Southern California desert. ❼ It never occurred to me to prepare for a storm!

*camaraderie 우정, 동지애

❶ 나는 갑작스러운 홍수의 범위를 벗어날 만큼 충분히 멀리 비탈을 기어올랐기를 바라면서 어둠 속에서 마구 쏟아지는 빗속에서 텐트를 쳤다. ❷ 안으로 기어들어 가는 것은 탈수 사이클에 맞춰진 세탁기에 들어가는 것과 비슷해, 바람이 위쪽을 향한 내 얼굴에서 몇 인치 떨어진 젖은 직물에 세게 부딪히며, 나에게 미세한 안개를 뿌렸다. ❸ 내 침낭이 천천히 완전히 젖으면서, 피로가 천천히 나를 압도하였다. ❹ 내 눈꺼풀이 무겁게 느껴지기 시작했을 때, 나는 봄 방학 휴일을 위한 나의 활동 선택을 비판하기 시작했다. ❺ 나는 낚시 여행에 친구들과 함께하여 대학생들에게 마지막 학년의 마지막 학기 동안 대체로 기대되는 맥주에 취한 우정 같은 그런 종류의 것에 참여할 수도 있었을 것이다. ❻ 대신에 나는 마지막 순간에, 캠핑 장비를 배낭에 던져 넣고 남부 캘리포니아 사막의 외딴곳을 탐험하기 위해 출발하기로 결심했다. ❼ 폭풍우에 대비하는 것은 나에게 전혀 떠오르지 않았다!

Word List

□ pitch (텐트를) 치다, 설치하다　□ scramble (손발을 써서) 기어가다　□ slope 비탈, 경사　□ range 범위　□ flash flood 갑작스러운 홍수
□ crawl 기어가다　□ spin cycle 탈수 사이클　□ dash 끼얹다, 돌진하다　□ fabric 직물, 천　□ spray 뿌리다　□ fine 미세한
□ mist 미세한[옅은] 안개, 이슬비　□ soak 젖다　□ through 완전히, 줄곧　□ overcome 압도하다
□ second-guess (결정 등을 사후에) 비판하다　□ spring break 봄 방학　□ partake 참여[참가]하다
□ beery 맥주에 취한, 맥주 냄새가 나는　□ more or less 대체로, 대략

• Word Test

1	soak		9	(결정 등을 사후에) 비판하다
2	pitch		10	완전히, 줄곧
3	slope		11	뿌리다
4	fine		12	범위
5	fabric		13	끼얹다, 돌진하다
6	overcome		14	대체로, 대략
7	partake		15	(손발을 써서) 기어가다
8	crawl		16	미세한[옅은] 안개, 이슬비

I pitched my tent in the dark and the pouring rain, hoping I'd scrambled ❶ enough far / far enough up the slope to be out of the range of flash floods. Crawling inside was like entering a washing machine on spin cycle — wind dashed against the wet fabric inches from my up-turned face, spraying me with a fine mist. As my sleeping bag slowly soaked through, tiredness slowly overcame me. As my eyelids began to feel ❷ heavy / heavily , I began to second-guess my choice of activities for the spring break holiday. I could ❸ join / have joined friends on a fishing trip, partaking in the sort of beery camaraderie that is more or less expected of college students during the final term of their final year. Instead, I decided at the last minute to throw my camping gear into a backpack, and head out to explore a remote corner of the Southern California desert. It never occurred ❹ for / to me to prepare for a storm!

*camaraderie 우정, 동지애

I pitched my tent in the dark and the pouring rain, hoping I'd ❶ _____ (scramble) far enough up the slope to be out of the range of flash floods. Crawling inside was like entering a washing machine on spin cycle — wind dashed against the wet fabric inches from my up-turned face, ❷ _____ (spray) me with a fine mist. As my sleeping bag slowly soaked through, tiredness slowly overcame me. As my eyelids began ❸ _____ (feel) heavy, I began to second-guess my choice of activities for the spring break holiday. I could have joined friends on a fishing trip, partaking in the sort of beery camaraderie that is more or less expected of college students during the final term of their final year. Instead, I decided at the last minute ❹ _____ (throw) my camping gear into a backpack, and head out to explore a remote corner of the Southern California desert. It never occurred to me ❺ _____ (prepare) for a storm!

*camaraderie 우정, 동지애

I pitched my tent in the dark and the pouring rain, hoping I'd scrambled far enough up the slope to be out of the range of flash floods. Crawling inside was like entering a(n) ❶ _____ _____ (세탁기) on spin cycle — wind dashed against the wet fabric inches from my up-turned face, spraying me with a ❷ _____ _____ (미세한 안개). As my sleeping bag slowly soaked through, tiredness slowly overcame me. As my eyelids began to feel heavy, I began to second-guess my choice of activities for the spring break holiday. I could have joined friends on a fishing trip, partaking in the sort of beery camaraderie that is ❸ _____ _____ _____ (대략) expected of college students during the final term of their final year. Instead, I decided ❹ _____ _____ _____ _____ (마지막 순간에) to throw my camping gear into a backpack, and head out to explore a remote corner of the Southern California desert. It never ❺ _____ _____ _____ (나에게 ~ 생각이 떠올랐다) to prepare for a storm!

*camaraderie 우정, 동지애

❶ You help other people understand you by creating a secure arena for communication — on their terms. ❷ Then the listener can use his energy to understand rather than to consciously or unconsciously react to your manner of communicating. ❸ All of us need to develop our flexibility and so be able to vary our style of communication, adapting it when we speak to people who are different from us. ❹ Here we find another truth: ❺ No matter what method you choose to communicate with, as an individual, you will always be in the minority. ❻ No matter what kind of behavior you have, the majority of people around you will function differently from you. ❼ You can't just base your method of communication on your own preferences. ❽ Flexibility and the ability to interpret other people's needs is what characterizes a good communicator. ❾ Knowing and understanding another person's style of behavior and method of communication will result in more educated guesses about how a person may possibly react in various situations. ❿ This understanding will also dramatically increase your ability to get through to the person in question.

❶ 여러분은 다른 사람의 방식에 따라 안심되는 의사소통의 장을 만듦으로써 그들이 여러분을 이해하도록 돕는다. ❷ 그러면 듣는 사람은 의식적으로 혹은 무의식적으로 여러분의 의사소통 방식에 반응하기보다는 이해하기 위해 자신의 에너지를 사용할 수 있다. ❸ 우리 모두는 유연성을 길러서, 우리와 다른 사람들에게 말할 때 우리의 의사소통 방식을 조정하면서 우리의 의사소통 방식을 달리할 수 있을 필요가 있다. ❹ 여기서 우리는 또 하나의 사실을 발견한다. ❺ 즉 여러분이 어떤 방법을 선택하여 소통하든지 간에, 개인으로서 여러분은 항상 소수일 것이다. ❻ 여러분이 어떤 행동을 하든지 간에, 여러분 주변 대부분의 사람은 여러분과 다르게 움직일 것이다. ❼ 여러분은 자신의 의사소통 방법의 근거를 단지 여러분 자신의 선호에만 둘 수 없다. ❽ 유연성과 다른 사람들의 요구를 이해하는 능력이 바로 훌륭한 소통가의 특징이다. ❾ 다른 사람의 행동 양식과 의사소통 방법을 알고 이해하는 것은 어떤 사람이 다양한 상황에서 아마도 어떻게 반응할 수도 있는지에 대한 더 근거 있는 추측을 하게 할 것이다. ❿ 이러한 이해는 또한 (대화의) 당사자를 이해시킬 수 있는 여러분의 능력을 극적으로 증가시킬 것이다.

Word List

□ **secure** 안심되는, 신뢰할 수 있는   □ **arena** 장(場), 영역   □ **on one's terms** ~의 방식에 따라   □ **consciously** 의식적으로
□ **manner** 방식   □ **flexibility** 유연성   □ **vary** 달리하다, 변화를 주다   □ **adapt** 조정하다, 적응하다   □ **minority** 소수   □ **majority** 다수
□ **function** 움직이다, 기능하다   □ **base ~ on ...** ~의 근거를 …에 두다   □ **preference** 선호, 기호   □ **interpret** 이해하다, 해석하다
□ **characterize** ~을 특징짓다, ~의 특징이 되다   □ **communicator** 소통가, 전달자   □ **educated** 근거 있는, 교육받은
□ **possibly** 아마, 혹시   □ **dramatically** 극적으로   □ **get through to** ~을 이해시키다, ~과 말이 통하다
□ **in question** 문제의, 논의가 되고 있는

• Word Test

1	communicator		10	의식적으로
2	interpret		11	유연성
3	minority		12	근거 있는, 교육받은
4	vary		13	아마, 혹시
5	secure		14	조정하다, 적응하다
6	on one's terms		15	선호, 기호
7	characterize		16	극적으로
8	function		17	다수
9	manner		18	장(場), 영역

You help other people ❶ understand / understanding you by creating a secure arena for communication — on their terms. Then the listener can use his energy to understand rather than to consciously or unconsciously react to your manner of communicating. All of us need to develop our ❷ flexibility / inflexibility and so be able to vary our style of communication, adapting it when we speak to people who are different from us. Here we find another truth: No matter what method you choose to communicate with, as an individual, you will always be in the ❸ minority / majority . No matter what kind of behavior you have, the majority of people around you will function differently from you. You can't just base your method of communication on your own preferences. Flexibility and the ability to interpret other people's needs is ❹ that / what characterizes a good communicator. Knowing and understanding another person's style of behavior and method of communication will result ❺ in / from more educated guesses about how a person may possibly react in various situations. This understanding will also dramatically increase your ability to get through to the person in question.

You help other people understand you by ❶ _____ (create) a secure arena for communication — on their terms. Then the listener can use his energy to understand rather than to consciously or unconsciously react to your manner of communicating. All of us need to develop our flexibility and so be able ❷ _____ (vary) our style of communication, ❸ _____ (adapt) it when we speak to people who are different from us. Here we find another truth: No matter what method you choose ❹ _____ (communicate) with, as an individual, you will always be in the minority. No matter what kind of behavior you have, the majority of people around you will function differently from you. You can't just base your method of communication on your own preferences. Flexibility and the ability to interpret other people's needs is what ❺ _____ (characterize) a good communicator. Knowing and understanding another person's style of behavior and method of communication will result in more educated guesses about how a person may possibly react in various situations. This understanding will also dramatically increase your ability to get through to the person in question.

You help other people understand you by creating a secure arena for communication — on their terms. Then the listener can use his energy to understand ❶ _____ _____ (~하기 보다는) to consciously or unconsciously react to your manner of communicating. All of us need to develop our flexibility and so be able to vary our style of communication, adapting it when we speak to people who ❷ _____ _____ _____ (~와 다르다) us. Here we find another truth: ❸ _____ _____ _____ _____ _____ _____ (당신이 어떤 방법을 선택하든지) to communicate with, as an individual, you will always be in the minority. No matter what kind of behavior you have, the majority of people around you will function differently from you. You can't just base your method of communication on your own preferences. Flexibility and the ability to interpret other people's needs is what characterizes a good communicator. Knowing and understanding another person's style of behavior and method of communication will result in ❹ _____ _____ _____ (더 근거있는 추측들) about how a person may possibly react in various situations. This understanding will also dramatically increase your ability to get through to the person in question.

❶ Seven-tenths of the earth's surface lies under water. ❷ The great world ocean represents the vast majority of our planet's habitable space, and we depend on it in ways we may never have paused to reflect on. ❸ It is home to perhaps two million species, the bulk of them still unknown to science. ❹ But despite all that, anyone keeping track of contemporary politics could be forgiven for wondering if the ocean is there at all. ❺ Remarkably few of our governments contain Ministries for the Ocean (South Korea and Canada are rare exceptions), and our politicians rarely campaign on ocean-related issues (though fishing did emerge as an issue during the 2016 Brexit referendum). ❻ The ocean is governed by a complex body of international law which the average citizen probably knows little about. ❼ Going about your busy life, you might be tempted to file the ocean, its politics and the Law of the Sea in a mental box along with gravity or the internet. ❽ Its immense size, and its permanence, might fool you into believing that the ocean is immune to degradation.

*referendum 국민 투표

❶ 지표의 7/10은 수면 아래에 있다. ❷ 거대한 세계 해양은 우리 행성에서 살기에 적합한 공간의 대부분에 해당하는데, 우리는 우리가 멈추어 깊이 생각해 본 적이 결코 없을 수도 있는 방식으로 그것에 의존한다. ❸ 그것은 대략 200만 종의 서식지인데, 그 종들의 대부분은 아직도 과학계에 알려져 있지 않다. ❹ 하지만 그 모든 것에도 불구하고, 현대의 정치를 따라가고 있는 사람은 누구나 해양이 도대체 거기에 있기나 한 것인지 의아해하는 것도 무리가 아니다. ❺ 우리 정부들 중 놀랄 정도로 극소수만이 '해양부'를 갖고 있고(대한민국과 캐나다는 드문 예외이다), (어업이 2016년 Brexit 국민 투표 동안에 쟁점으로 정말 부각되긴 했지만) 우리 정치가들은 해양 관련 사안에 관해 운동을 벌이는 일이 거의 없다. ❻ 해양은 보통의 시민이 아마 거의 알지 못하는 많은 복잡한 국제법에 의해 통제를 받는다. ❼ 계속 바쁜 생활을 하면서 여러분은 중력이나 인터넷과 마찬가지로 해양과 그것의 정치와 '해양법'을 마음 상자에 보관하고 싶어질지도 모른다. ❽ 그것의 어마어마한 크기와 그것의 영속성은 여러분을 속여 해양이 악화의 영향을 받지 [황폐화되지] 않는다고 믿게 할지도 모른다.

Word List

□ surface 표면   □ represent 해당[상당]하다, 나타내다, 대표하다   □ the vast majority of ~의 대다수   □ habitable 살기에 적합한
□ pause 잠시 멈추다   □ reflect on 되돌아보다, 반성하다   □ bulk 대부분, 큰 규모
□ keep track of ~을 따라가다, ~에 대해 계속 파악하고 있다   □ contemporary 현대의   □ could be forgiven for ~하는 것도 무리가 아니다
□ remarkably 놀랍게도   □ rare 드문   □ campaign 운동을 벌이다   □ go about 계속 ~을 하다   □ file (정리하여) 보관하다
□ gravity 중력   □ immense 어마어마한, 막대한   □ permanence 영속성   □ fool 속이다, 기만하다   □ immune to ~에 영향을 받지 않는
□ degradation 악화, 퇴화

Word Test

1	permanence		
2	represent		
3	go about		
4	bulk		
5	pause		
6	rare		
7	surface		
8	gravity		
9	immune to		
10	keep track of		

11	되돌아보다, 반성하다		
12	놀랍게도		
13	악화, 퇴화		
14	속이다, 기만하다		
15	살기에 적합한		
16	어마어마한, 막대한		
17	(정리하여) 보관하다		
18	~의 대다수		
19	현대의		
20	운동을 벌이다		

Seven-tenths of the earth's surface ❶ lays / lies under water. The great world ocean represents the vast majority of our planet's ❷ habitable / habitual space, and we depend on it in ways we may never have paused to reflect on. It is home to perhaps two million species, the bulk of them still unknown to science. But despite all that, anyone keeping track of ❸ contemporary / permanent politics could be forgiven for wondering if the ocean is there at all. Remarkably few of our governments contain Ministries for the Ocean (South Korea and Canada are rare exceptions), and our politicians rarely campaign on ocean-related issues (though fishing did emerge as an issue during the 2016 Brexit referendum). The ocean is governed by a complex body of international law ❹ what / which the average citizen probably knows ❺ few / little about. Going about your busy life, you might be tempted to file the ocean, its politics and the Law of the Sea in a mental box along with gravity or the internet. Its immense size, and its permanence, might fool you into believing ❻ which / that the ocean is immune to degradation.

*referendum 국민 투표

Seven-tenths of the earth's surface lies under water. The great world ocean represents the vast majority of our planet's habitable space, and we depend on it in ways we may never have paused to reflect on. It is home to perhaps two million species, the bulk of them still unknown to science. But despite all that, anyone ❶ _____ (keep) track of contemporary politics could be forgiven for wondering if the ocean is there at all. Remarkably few of our governments ❷ _____ (contain) Ministries for the Ocean (South Korea and Canada are rare exceptions), and our politicians rarely campaign on ocean-related issues (though fishing did emerge as an issue during the 2016 Brexit referendum). The ocean is governed by a complex body of international law which the average citizen probably ❸ _____ (know) little about. ❹ _____ (Go) about your busy life, you might be tempted to file the ocean, its politics and the Law of the Sea in a mental box along with gravity or the internet. Its immense size, and its permanence, might fool you into ❺ _____ (believe) that the ocean is immune to degradation.

*referendum 국민 투표

Seven-tenths of the earth's surface lies under water. The great world ocean represents the vast majority of our planet's habitable space, and we ❶ _____ _____ (~에 의존하다) it in ways we may never have paused to ❷ _____ _____ (~을 깊게 생각하다). It is home to perhaps two million species, the bulk of them still unknown to science. But ❸ _____ _____ _____ (그 모든 것에도 불구하고), anyone keeping track of contemporary politics could be forgiven for wondering if the ocean is there at all. Remarkably few of our governments contain Ministries for the Ocean (South Korea and Canada are rare exceptions), and our politicians rarely campaign on ocean-related issues (though fishing did emerge as an issue during the 2016 Brexit referendum). The ocean is governed by a complex body of international law which the average citizen probably knows little about. Going about your busy life, you might be tempted to file the ocean, its politics and the Law of the Sea in a mental box ❹ _____ _____ (~과 마찬가지로) gravity or the internet. Its immense size, and its permanence, might fool you into believing that the ocean is immune to degradation.

*referendum 국민 투표

❶ The nature of the task can matter more than the nature of the person. **❷** Most of us have heard the theory that we each have a preferred learning style, and the more we can use the one that fits, the more we'll remember. **❸** Unfortunately, virtually no evidence supports that theory. **❹** That doesn't mean that all approaches to studying are equally effective — it's just that the strategy that works best often depends more on the task than on the person. **❺** Similarly, different parts of our personalities can serve different types of goals. **❻** We act extraverted when we want to connect with others or seize an opportunity, and we become disciplined when we want to get something done or avoid mistakes. **❼** In one study, conscientiousness especially emerged when the things that needed to get done were difficult and urgent — even for people who were not especially organized and hardworking in general.

*extraverted 외향성의   **conscientiousness 성실성

❶ 업무의 본질이 사람의 본성보다 더 중요할 수 있다. ❷ 우리 대부분은 우리 각자가 선호하는 학습 방식을 가지고 있으며, 잘 맞는 것을 더 많이 사용할 수 있을수록, 더 많이 기억할 것이라는 이론을 들어 왔다. ❸ 안타깝게도 그 이론을 뒷받침하는 증거는 거의 없다. ❹ 그것은 학습에 대한 모든 접근법이 동등하게 효과적이라는 것을 의미하는 것이 아니라, 다만 가장 효과가 있는 전략은 흔히 사람보다는 과제에 더 달려 있다는 것이다. ❺ 비슷하게, 우리의 성격의 서로 다른 부분은 서로 다른 유형의 목적에 도움이 될 수 있다. ❻ 우리는 다른 사람들과 친해지고 싶거나 기회를 잡고 싶을 때는 외향적으로 행동하고, 어떤 일을 마무리하거나 실수를 피하고 싶을 때는 통제된 방식으로 행동하게 된다. ❼ 한 연구에서, 처리해야 할 일이 어렵고 긴급할 때 특히 성실성이 나타났는데, 대체로 특별히 체계적이지도 않고 근면하지도 않은 사람의 경우에도 심지어 그랬다.

Word List	
□ nature 본질, 본성　□ task 과제, 업무　□ matter 중요하다　□ theory 이론　□ fit (모양이) 맞다　□ virtually 거의, 사실상	
□ evidence 증거　□ support 뒷받침하다　□ approach 접근법　□ equally 동일하게　□ effective 효과적인　□ strategy 전략	
□ seize 잡다, 장악하다　□ disciplined 통제된 방식으로 행동하는　□ emerge 나타나다, 드러나다　□ urgent 긴급한	
□ organized 체계적인, 조직적인	

• Word Test

1	strategy	9	증거
2	equally	10	체계적인, 조직적인
3	virtually	11	(모양이) 맞다
4	nature	12	효과적인
5	theory	13	접근법
6	urgent	14	잡다, 장악하다
7	disciplined	15	중요하다
8	support	16	나타나다, 드러나다

The nature of the task can matter more than the nature of the person. Most of us have heard the theory ❶ [that / which] we each have a preferred learning style, and the more we can use the one that fits, ❷ [the less / the more] we'll remember. Unfortunately, virtually no evidence supports that theory. That doesn't mean that all approaches to studying are equally effective — it's just that the strategy that works best often depends more on the task ❸ [as / than] on the person. Similarly, different parts of our personalities can serve different types of goals. We act extraverted when we want to connect ❹ [by / with] others or seize an opportunity, and we become disciplined when we want to get something done or avoid mistakes. In one study, conscientiousness especially emerged when the things ❺ [that / what] needed to get done were difficult and urgent — even for people who were not especially organized and hardworking in general.

*extraverted 외향성의   **conscientiousness 성실성

The nature of the task can matter more than the nature of the person. Most of us ❶ _____ (have) heard the theory that we each have a preferred learning style, and the more we can use the one that fits, the more we'll remember. Unfortunately, virtually no evidence ❷ _____ (support) that theory. That doesn't mean that all approaches to ❸ _____ (study) are equally effective — it's just that the strategy that works best often depends more on the task than on the person. Similarly, different parts of our personalities can serve different types of goals. We act extraverted when we want to connect with others or seize an opportunity, and we become ❹ _____ (discipline) when we want to get something done or avoid mistakes. In one study, conscientiousness especially emerged when the things that ❺ _____ (need) to get done were difficult and urgent — even for people who were not especially organized and hardworking in general.

*extraverted 외향성의   **conscientiousness 성실성

The nature of the task can matter more than the nature of the person. Most of us have heard the theory that we each have a(n) ❶ _____ _____ _____ (선호하는 학습 방식), and the more we can use the one that fits, the more we'll remember. Unfortunately, virtually no evidence supports that theory. That doesn't mean that all approaches to studying are ❷ _____ _____ (똑같이 효과적인) — it's just that the strategy that works best often depends more on the task than on the person. Similarly, different parts of our personalities can serve different types of goals. We act extraverted when we want to connect with others or ❸ _____ _____ _____ (기회를 잡다), and we become disciplined when we want to get something done or avoid mistakes. In one study, conscientiousness especially emerged when the things that needed to get done were difficult and urgent — even for people who were not especially organized and hardworking ❹ _____ _____ (대개).

*extraverted 외향성의   **conscientiousness 성실성

❶ Gifts are one way of defining a private world of love and ritual which is different from, and in contrast to, the impersonal capitalist economy. ❷ Yet gift giving in modern society is affected by that economy. ❸ This is most obvious in the case of monetary gifts, whose value lies entirely in the capacity to purchase things in the marketplace. ❹ However, it also exists in the case of gifts of things where those gifts consist, as most do, of things that are purchased. ❺ There is a problem here. ❻ In advanced capitalist societies, consumption by individuals of things that they do not produce is a massive activity. ❼ There is a danger here that purchased gifts will lose their significance in the face of all the things that individuals purchase for themselves. ❽ Gift giving separates a world of love and ritual from the capitalist economy, but in the end the two systems of meaning cannot be entirely separated because they are interconnected.

❶ 선물은 비인격적인 자본주의 경세와 다르고 그것과 대조되는 사랑과 의식의 사적 세계를 분명하게 보여 주는 한 가지 방법이다. ❷ 하지만 현대 사회에서 선물을 주는 것은 그 경제의 영향을 받는다. ❸ 이것은 금전적 선물의 경우에 가장 명백하게 드러나는데, 금전적 선물의 가치는 전적으로 시장에서 물건을 구매하는 능력에 있다. ❹ 그러나 그것은 대부분의 선물이 그렇듯이, 그러한 선물이 구입된 물건으로 구성된 경우에도 존재한다. ❺ 여기에 문제가 있다. ❻ 선진 자본주의 사회에서 자신들이 생산하지 않는 물건을 개인이 소비하는 것은 대규모 활동이다. ❼ 구매한 선물은 사람들이 스스로 구매하는 모든 것들 앞에서 그 의미를 잃을 것이라는 위험성이 여기에 있다. ❽ 선물을 주는 것은 사랑과 의식의 세계를 자본주의 경제로부터 분리하지만, 결국 그 두 의미 체제는 그것들이 서로 연결되어 있기 때문에 완전히 분리될 수는 없다.

Word List
□ define 분명하게 보여 주다, 규정하다   □ ritual 의식[절차], 의례   □ in contrast to ~와 대조되는   □ impersonal 비인격적인, 인간미 없는
□ capitalist 자본주의의   □ affect 영향을 미치다   □ monetary 금전의, 화폐의   □ capacity 능력   □ consumption 소비
□ massive 대규모의, 대량의   □ significance 의미, 중요성   □ separate 분리하다   □ interconnected 서로 연결된

• **Word** **Test**

1	impersonal		7	의미, 중요성
2	separate		8	소비
3	affect		9	자본주의의
4	massive		10	서로 연결된
5	define		11	의식[절차], 의례
6	capacity		12	금전의, 화폐의

Gifts are one way of defining a private world of love and ritual which is different from, and in contrast to, the impersonal capitalist economy. Yet gift giving in modern society is affected by that economy. This is most ❶ ambiguous / obvious in the case of monetary gifts, ❷ which / whose value lies entirely in the capacity to purchase things in the marketplace. However, it also exists in the case of gifts of things ❸ which / where those gifts consist, as most do, of things that are purchased. There is a problem here. In advanced capitalist societies, consumption by individuals of things ❹ that / what they do not produce is a massive activity. There is a danger here that purchased gifts will lose their significance in the face of all the things that individuals purchase for themselves. Gift giving ❺ connectes / separates a world of love and ritual from the capitalist economy, but in the end the two systems of meaning cannot be entirely separated because they are interconnected.

Gifts are one way of ❶ _____ (define) a private world of love and ritual which is different from, and in contrast to, the impersonal capitalist economy. Yet gift giving in modern society is affected by that economy. This is most obvious in the case of monetary gifts, whose value ❷ _____ (lie) entirely in the capacity to purchase things in the marketplace. However, it also exists in the case of gifts of things where those gifts consist, as most do, of things that ❸ _____ (purchase). There is a problem here. In advanced capitalist societies, consumption by individuals of things that they do not produce ❹ _____ (be) a massive activity. There is a danger here that purchased gifts will lose their significance in the face of all the things that individuals purchase for themselves. Gift giving separates a world of love and ritual from the capitalist economy, but in the end the two systems of meaning cannot be entirely separated because they are interconnected.

Gifts are one way of defining a private world of love and ritual which is different from, and ❶ _____ _____ _____ (~와 대조적으로), the impersonal capitalist economy. Yet gift giving ❷ _____ _____ _____ (현대 사회에서) is affected by that economy. This is most obvious in the ❸ _____ _____ _____ _____ (금전적 선물의 경우), whose value lies entirely in the capacity to purchase things in the marketplace. However, it also exists in the case of gifts of things where those gifts consist, as most do, of things that are purchased. There is a problem here. In advanced capitalist societies, consumption by individuals of things that they do not produce is a ❹ _____ _____ (대규모 활동). There is a danger here that purchased gifts will lose their significance in the face of all the things that individuals purchase for themselves. Gift giving separates a world of love and ritual from the capitalist economy, but in the end the two systems of meaning cannot ❺ _____ _____ _____ (완전히 분리되다) because they are interconnected.

❶ We argue that a transition towards more sustainable lifestyles will come from re-visioning the human place in nature, realizing ourselves not as separate, but as part of the whole, with a responsibility to nurture the biosphere forever. ❷ It will not occur because we are afraid of weathering the 'perfect storm' of unsustainability. ❸ Instead, we believe that what is needed is a deeper and more positive process: a re-visioning of the relationship between people and planet, undertaken in different ways by individuals, families, communities and nations. ❹ Such visions will show the potential for reconnection to bring about not just planetary health, but also personal well-being, joy, health and flourishing. ❺ There is strong evidence to show that well-being — the 'good stuff' of life — is brought about by such reconnection of the human and the natural. ❻ It is a vision to find a way towards reconciling our aspirations with the finitudes of our planet.

*biosphere 생물권   **reconcile 조화시키다   ***finitude 유한성

❶ 우리는 더 지속 가능한 생활 양식으로의 전환이 우리 자신을 분리된 존재가 아니라 영원히 생물권을 보살필 책임이 있는 전체의 일부임을 깨달으면서 자연 속에서 인간의 위치를 다시 그려 보는 것으로부터 비롯될 거라고 주장한다. ❷ 우리가 지속 불가능이라는 '최악의 상황'을 헤쳐 나가는 것을 두려워한다고 해서 그런 일이 일어나는 것은 아닐 것이다. ❸ 대신에, 우리는 더 깊고 더 긍정적인 과정, 즉 개인, 가족, 사회, 국가에 의해 여러 가지 방법으로 시도되는, 사람과 지구 간의 관계를 다시 그려 보기가 필요하다고 믿는다. ❹ 그러한 비전은 지구의 건강뿐만이 아니라 개인의 행복, 기쁨, 건강 그리고 번영도 가져올 (지구와의) 재연결의 잠재력을 보여 줄 것이다. ❺ 인간과 자연의 그러한 재연결에 의해 행복, 즉 삶의 '좋은 것'이 생겨난다는 것을 보여 주는 강력한 증거가 있다. ❻ 그것은 우리의 열망을 우리 지구의 유한성과 조화시키는 방법을 찾기 위한 비전이다.

Word List	
□ transition 전환 □ sustainable 지속 가능한 □ re-vision 다시 그려 보다, 다시 상상하다 □ whole 전체 □ nurture 보살피다	
□ weather (역경 등을) 헤쳐 나가다, 견디다 □ perfect storm 최악의 상황 □ unsustainability 지속 불가능성 □ positive 긍정적인	
□ planet 지구, 행성 □ undertake 시도하다, 착수하다 □ potential 잠재력, 가능성 □ reconnection 재연결	
□ bring about ~을 가져오다, ~이 생기게 하다 □ planetary 지구의, 행성의 □ flourish 번영하다 □ aspiration 열망	

• Word Test

1	bring about	_____	8	지속 불가능성	_____
2	whole	_____	9	지구의, 행성의	_____
3	flourish	_____	10	지구, 행성	_____
4	undertake	_____	11	잠재력, 가능성	_____
5	positive	_____	12	지속 가능한	_____
6	transition	_____	13	열망	_____
7	weather	_____	14	보살피다	_____

We argue that a ❶ transition / translation towards more sustainable lifestyles will come from re-visioning the human place in nature, realizing ourselves not as separate, but as part of the whole, with a responsibility to nurture the biosphere forever. It will not occur because we are afraid of weathering the 'perfect storm' of unsustainability. Instead, we believe that ❷ which / what is needed is a deeper and more ❸ positive / negative process: a re-visioning of the relationship between people and planet, undertaken in different ways by individuals, families, communities and nations. Such visions will show the potential for reconnection to bring about not just planetary health, ❹ as well / but also personal well-being, joy, health and flourishing. There is strong evidence to show that well-being — the 'good stuff' of life — is brought about by such reconnection of the human and the natural. It is a vision to find a way towards reconciling our aspirations with the finitudes of our planet.

*biosphere 생물권 **reconcile 조화시키다 ***finitude 유한성

We argue that a transition towards more sustainable lifestyles will come from re-visioning the human place in nature, ❶ _____ (realize) ourselves not as separate, but as part of the whole, with a responsibility ❷ _____ (nurture) the biosphere forever. It will not occur because we are afraid of ❸ _____ (weather) the 'perfect storm' of unsustainability. Instead, we believe that what is needed ❹ _____ (be) a deeper and more positive process: a re-visioning of the relationship between people and planet, undertaken in different ways by individuals, families, communities and nations. Such visions will show the potential for reconnection to bring about not just planetary health, but also personal well-being, joy, health and flourishing. There is strong evidence to show that well-being — the 'good stuff' of life — is brought about by such reconnection of the human and the natural. It is a vision ❺ _____ (find) a way towards reconciling our aspirations with the finitudes of our planet.

*biosphere 생물권 **reconcile 조화시키다 ***finitude 유한성

We argue that a transition towards more sustainable lifestyles will ❶ _____ _____ _____ (다시 그려 보는 것으로부터 비롯되다) the human place in nature, realizing ourselves not as separate, but as part of the whole, with a responsibility to nurture the biosphere forever. It will not occur because we ❷ _____ _____ _____ _____ (헤쳐 나가기를 두려워하다) the 'perfect storm' of unsustainability. Instead, we believe that what is needed is a deeper and ❸ _____ _____ _____ (더 긍정적인 과정): a re-visioning of the relationship between people and planet, undertaken in different ways by individuals, families, communities and nations. Such visions will show the potential for reconnection to ❹ _____ _____ (~을 생기게 하다) not just planetary health, but also personal well-being, joy, health and flourishing. There is ❺ _____ _____ (강력한 증거) to show that well-being — the 'good stuff' of life — is brought about by such reconnection of the human and the natural. It is a vision to find a way towards reconciling our aspirations with the finitudes of our planet.

*biosphere 생물권 **reconcile 조화시키다 ***finitude 유한성

What Makes a Story Shareable, per Journalists

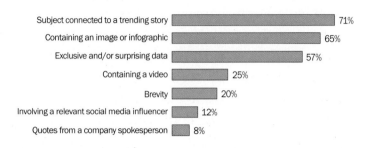

Subject connected to a trending story	71%
Containing an image or infographic	65%
Exclusive and/or surprising data	57%
Containing a video	25%
Brevity	20%
Involving a relevant social media influencer	12%
Quotes from a company spokesperson	8%

Based on a January 2022 survey of 2,547 journalists including full-time journalists, editorial writers, and bloggers

❶ The above graph shows the 2022 survey results of more than 2,500 journalists on what they think makes a story shareable. ❷ According to the survey, the factor that was most likely to help make a story shareable was the subject, with 71% saying that a shareable piece is one in which the subject is connected to a trending story. ❸ Containing an image or infographic was the second most cited factor in making a story shareable at 65%, with exclusive and/or surprising data (57%) next on the list. ❹ A quarter of the journalists who participated in the survey considered containing a video to be the factor that makes a story shareable. ❺ Journalists who said that involving a relevant social media influencer makes a story shareable accounted for 12%. ❻ The percentage of journalists who responded that including quotes from a company spokesperson is what makes a story shareable was less than half of the percentage of those who said that brevity will do the job.

❶ 위의 도표는 2,500명이 넘는 언론인을 대상으로 그들이 생각하기에 기사를 공유하기에 적절하게 만드는 것이 무엇인지에 관한 2022년 설문 조사 결과를 보여 준다. ❷ 설문 조사에 따르면, 기사를 공유하기에 적절하게 만드는 것에 도움이 될 가능성이 가장 많은 요인은 주제였으며, 71퍼센트가 공유하기에 적절한 기사는 그 주제가 사람들의 입에 많이 오르내리는 기사와 연결된 것이라고 말했다. ❸ 이미지 또는 인포그래픽을 포함하는 것을 기사를 공유하기에 적절하게 만드는 것에 있어 두 번째로 많이 인용되는 요인으로 65퍼센트를 기록했고, 독점적인 그리고/또는 놀라운 데이터(57퍼센트)가 목록에서 그 다음을 차지했다. ❹ 설문 조사에 참여한 언론인의 4분의 1이 넘는 사람들이 영상을 포함하는 것이 기사를 공유하기에 적절하게 만드는 요인이라고 여겼다. ❺ 관련된 소셜 미디어 인플루언서를 끌어들이는 것이 기사를 공유하기에 적절하게 만든다고 말한 언론인은 12퍼센트를 차지했다. ❻ 회사 대변인의 인용문을 포함하는 것이 기사를 공유하기에 적절하게 만든다고 응답한 언론인의 비율은, 간결함이 효과가 있을 거라고 말한 사람들의 비율의 절반에도 미치지 못했다.

Word List

□ survey 설문 조사　□ journalist 언론인　□ shareable 공유하기에 적절한　□ factor 요인, 요소
□ trending 사람들의 입에 많이 오르내리는, 유행하는　□ contain 포함하다　□ infographic 인포그래픽, 데이터 시각화　□ cited 인용되는
□ exclusive 독점적인　□ relevant 관련된　□ account for ~을 차지하다　□ quote 인용구　□ spokesperson 대변인
□ brevity 간결함　□ do the job 효과가 있다

• Word Test

1	quote	_____
2	brevity	_____
3	relevant	_____
4	survey	_____
5	shareable	_____
6	cited	_____

7	독점적인	_____	_____
8	요인, 요소	_____	_____
9	대변인	_____	_____
10	포함하다	_____	_____
11	언론인	_____	_____
12	~을 차지하다	_____	_____

The above graph shows the 2022 survey results of more than 2,500 journalists on ❶ that / what they think makes a story shareable. According to the survey, the factor ❷ that / what was most likely to help make a story shareable was the subject, with 71% saying that a shareable piece is one in which the subject is connected to a trending story. Containing an image or infographic was the second most ❸ cited / sited factor in making a story shareable at 65%, with exclusive and/or surprising data (57%) next on the list. A quarter of the journalists who participated in the survey considered containing a video to be the factor that makes a story shareable. Journalists who said that involving a ❹ relevant / reluctant social media influencer makes a story shareable accounted for 12%. The percentage of journalists who responded ❺ that / which including quotes from a company spokesperson is what makes a story shareable was less than half of the percentage of those who said that brevity will do the job.

The above graph shows the 2022 survey results of more than 2,500 journalists on what they think ❶ _____ (make) a story shareable. According to the survey, the factor that was most likely to help make a story shareable ❷ _____ (be) the subject, with 71% saying that a shareable piece is one in which the subject is connected to a trending story. ❸ _____ (Contain) an image or infographic was the second most cited factor in making a story shareable at 65%, with exclusive and/or surprising data (57%) next on the list. A quarter of the journalists who participated in the survey considered containing a video to be the factor that makes a story shareable. Journalists who said that ❹ _____ (involve) a relevant social media influencer makes a story shareable accounted for 12%. The percentage of journalists who responded that including quotes from a company spokesperson ❺ _____ (be) what makes a story shareable was less than half of the percentage of those who said that brevity will do the job.

The above graph shows the 2022 survey results of more than 2,500 journalists on what they think makes a story shareable. According to the survey, the factor that was most likely to help make a story shareable was the subject, with 71% saying that a shareable piece is one in which the subject ❶ _____ _____ _____ (~와 연결되다) a trending story. ❷ _____ _____ _____ (이미지를 포함하는 것) or infographic was the second most cited factor in making a story shareable at 65%, with exclusive and/or surprising data (57%) next on the list. A quarter of the journalists who ❸ _____ _____ (~에 참여했던) the survey considered containing a video to be the factor that makes a story shareable. Journalists who said that involving a relevant social media influencer makes a story shareable accounted for 12%. The percentage of journalists who responded that including quotes from a company spokesperson is what makes a story shareable was less than half of the percentage of those who said that ❹ _____ _____ _____ _____ _____ (간결함이 효과가 있을 것이다).

❶ Art Tatum (born in 1909 in Toledo, Ohio and died in 1956 in Los Angeles), is considered one of the greatest jazz pianists of all time. ❷ His performances were praised for their technical skills and creativity, which set a new standard for jazz piano virtuosity. ❸ Tatum, who was visually impaired from childhood, displayed an early talent for music. ❹ Although Tatum gained some formal piano training at the Toledo School of Music, he was largely self-taught. ❺ At age 13, after starting on the violin, Tatum concentrated on the piano and was soon performing on local radio programs. ❻ At 21 he moved to New York City, where he made his most impressive recordings during the 1930s and '40s. ❼ In 1943 he organized a trio with guitarist Tiny Grimes and bassist Slam Stewart, and he played mostly in the trio format for the rest of his life. ❽ Although Tatum was admired by many jazz musicians, his popularity faded in the mid to late 1940s with the advent of bebop — a movement that Tatum did not embrace.

*virtuosity (고도의) 기교 **bebop 비밥(재즈의 일종)

❶ (1909년에 오하이오주 톨레도에서 태어나 1956년에 로스앤젤레스에서 사망한) Art Tatum은 역사상 가장 위대한 재즈 피아니스트 중 한 명으로 여겨진다. ❷ 그의 연주는 그 기교와 창의성으로 찬사를 받았고, 이것은 재즈 피아노 기교에 새로운 기준을 세웠다. ❸ 어린 시절부터 시각 장애가 있었던 Tatum은 음악에 대한 조기 재능을 보였다. ❹ Tatum은 톨레도 음악학교에서 어느 정도의 정식 피아노 교육을 받기는 했지만, 주로 독학했다. ❺ 13세에, 바이올린을 시작한 후, Tatum은 피아노에 집중했고 머지않아 지역 라디오 프로그램에서 연주를 하고 있었다. ❻ 21세에 그는 뉴욕 시로 이주하여 거기서 1930년대와 40년대에 자신의 가장 인상적인 음반을 만들었다. ❼ 1943년에 그는 기타리스트 Tiny Grimes와 베이시스트 Slam Stewart와 함께 3인조를 결성했고, 남은 생애 동안 주로 3인조 체재로 연주했다. ❽ Tatum이 많은 재즈 음악가들에게 존경을 받기는 했으나, 그의 인기는 1940년대 중후반에 비밥의 등장과 함께 시들해졌는데, 이 동향을 Tatum은 받아들이지 않았다.

Word List

□ performance 연주 □ praise 찬사를 보내다 □ creativity 창의성 □ standard 기준 □ impaired 장애가 있는, 손상된
□ display 보이다 □ talent 재능 □ gain 얻다, 받다 □ formal 정식의 □ self-taught 독학한 □ impressive 인상적인
□ organize 결성하다, 조직하다 □ trio 3인조, 트리오 □ format 체재 □ admire 존경하다 □ popularity 인기 □ fade 시들해지다
□ advent 등장, 도래 □ movement 동향, 변화, 움직임 □ embrace 받아들이다

• Word Test

1	impressive	11	받아들이다
2	impaired	12	얻다, 받다
3	formal	13	체재
4	movement	14	찬사를 보내다
5	performance	15	인기
6	talent	16	기준
7	fade	17	독학한
8	trio	18	결성하다, 조직하다
9	creativity	19	등장, 도래
10	admire	20	보이다

Art Tatum (born in 1909 in Toledo, Ohio and died in 1956 in Los Angeles), is considered one of the ❶ greater / greatest jazz pianists of all time. His performances were praised for their technical skills and creativity, ❷ that / which set a new standard for jazz piano virtuosity. Tatum, who was visually ❸ impaired / impacted from childhood, displayed an early talent for music. Although Tatum gained some ❹ formal / informal piano training at the Toledo School of Music, he was largely self-taught. At age 13, after starting on the violin, Tatum concentrated on the piano and was soon performing on local radio programs. At 21 he moved to New York City, where he made his most ❺ impressive / compressive recordings during the 1930s and '40s. In 1943 he organized a trio with guitarist Tiny Grimes and bassist Slam Stewart, and he played mostly in the trio format for the rest of his life. Although Tatum was admired by many jazz musicians, his popularity faded in the mid to late 1940s with the advent of bebop — a movement that Tatum did not embrace.

*virtuosity (고도의) 기교   **bebop 비밥 (재즈의 일종)

Art Tatum (born in 1909 in Toledo, Ohio and died in 1956 in Los Angeles), ❶ _____ (consider) one of the greatest jazz pianists of all time. His performances were praised for their technical skills and creativity, which set a new standard for jazz piano virtuosity. Tatum, who was visually impaired from childhood, ❷ _____ (display) an early talent for music. Although Tatum gained some formal piano training at the Toledo School of Music, he was largely self-taught. At age 13, after ❸ _____ (start) on the violin, Tatum concentrated on the piano and was soon ❹ _____ (perform) on local radio programs. At 21 he moved to New York City, where he made his most impressive recordings during the 1930s and '40s. In 1943 he organized a trio with guitarist Tiny Grimes and bassist Slam Stewart, and he played mostly in the trio format for the rest of his life. Although Tatum ❺ _____ (admire) by many jazz musicians, his popularity faded in the mid to late 1940s with the advent of bebop — a movement that Tatum did not embrace.

*virtuosity (고도의) 기교   **bebop 비밥(재즈의 일종)

Art Tatum (born in 1909 in Toledo, Ohio and died in 1956 in Los Angeles), is considered one of the greatest jazz pianists ❶ _____ _____ _____ (역사상). His performances were praised for their technical skills and creativity, which ❷ _____ _____ _____ _____ (새로운 기준을 세우다) for jazz piano virtuosity. Tatum, who was visually impaired from childhood, displayed an ❸ _____ _____ _____ _____ (음악에 대한 조기 재능). Although Tatum gained some formal piano training at the Toledo School of Music, he was largely self-taught. At age 13, after starting on the violin, Tatum ❹ _____ _____ (~에 집중했다) the piano and was soon performing on local radio programs. At 21 he moved to New York City, where he made his most impressive recordings during the 1930s and '40s. In 1943 he organized a trio with guitarist Tiny Grimes and bassist Slam Stewart, and he played mostly in the trio format for the rest of his life. Although Tatum was admired by many jazz musicians, his popularity faded in the mid to late 1940s with ❺ _____ _____ _____ (~의 출현) bebop — a movement that Tatum did not embrace.

*virtuosity (고도의) 기교   **bebop 비밥 (재즈의 일종)

❶ High-Frequency Facial Device
❷ User Manual

❸ Effects and Benefits

❹ This high-frequency facial device is an effective beauty instrument.
❺ Effects and benefits include: acceleration of blood circulation, reduction of wrinkles and tightening of the skin.

❻ Usage Information

1. ❼ Do not use on one part of the skin for over 10 seconds.
2. ❽ Do not use if pregnant or intending to become pregnant.
3. ❾ For sensitive skin, place a piece of soft, light fabric on the skin before use to avoid excess stimulation.

❿ Important Safety Information

1. ⓫ Do not assemble or operate this device with wet hands.
2. ⓬ Remove the power cable after use.
3. ⓭ Do not insert any unnecessary items into the device's jack, as this may cause a fire. ⓮ If anything gets into the jack, contact the manufacturer. ⓯ Do not attempt to remove it yourself.

⓰ Warranty

⓱ Included with the purchase of this device is a 1-year limited warranty.

❶ 고주파 얼굴 마사지 기기
❷ 사용 설명서
❸ 효과 및 이점
❹ 이 고주파 얼굴 마사지 기기는 효과적인 미용 기구입니다. ❺ 효과와 이점은 혈액 순환 촉진, 주름 감소, 피부 조임을 포함합니다.
❻ 사용 정보
1. ❼ 피부의 한 부분에 10초 넘게 사용하지 마십시오.
2. ❽ 임신 중이거나 임신 계획이 있는 경우 사용하지 마십시오.
3. ❾ 민감한 피부의 경우, 과도한 자극을 피하기 위해 사용 전에 피부 위에 부드럽고 가벼운 천을 대십시오.
❿ 중요 안전 정보
1. ⓫ 젖은 손으로 본 기기를 조립하거나 조작하지 마십시오.
2. ⓬ 사용 후에는 전원 케이블을 뽑으십시오.
3. ⓭ 화재를 일으킬 수 있으므로 기기의 (플러그를 연결하는) 잭에 어떠한 불필요한 것도 넣지 마십시오. ⓮ 잭 안으로 무언가가 들어갈 경우 제조 업체로 연락하십시오. ⓯ 스스로 그것을 꺼내려고 하지 마십시오.
⓰ 품질 보증
⓱ 이 기기의 구매에는 1년간의 품질 보증서가 포함되어 있습니다.

Word List

□ high-frequency 고주파의　□ device 기기　□ effect 효과　□ benefit 이점, 혜택　□ instrument 기구　□ acceleration 촉진, 가속
□ circulation 순환　□ reduction 감소　□ wrinkle 주름　□ tighten 팽팽하게 하다　□ pregnant 임신한　□ sensitive 민감한
□ fabric 천　□ excess 초과한; 과도　□ stimulation 자극　□ assemble 조립하다　□ operate 작동하다　□ insert 넣다, 끼우다
□ manufacturer 제조업체　□ warranty 품질 보증(서)　□ purchase 구매

• Word Test

1	tighten	11	작동하다
2	device	12	자극
3	insert	13	천
4	acceleration	14	구매
5	benefit	15	제조업체
6	sensitive	16	임신한
7	assemble	17	효과
8	excess	18	주름
9	warranty	19	기구
10	reduction	20	순환

High-Frequency Facial Device
User Manual

Effects and Benefits

This high-frequency facial ❶ device / revise is an effective beauty instrument. Effects and benefits include: acceleration of blood circulation, ❷ deduction / reduction of wrinkles and tightening of the skin.

Usage Information

1. Do not use on one part of the skin for over 10 seconds.

2. Do not use if pregnant or intending to become pregnant.

3. For ❸ sensible / sensitive skin, place a piece of soft, light fabric on the skin before use to avoid excess stimulation.

Important Safety Information

1. Do not assemble or operate this device with ❹ dry / wet hands.

2. Remove the power cable after use.

3. Do not insert any unnecessary items into the device's jack, as this may cause a fire. If ❺ anything / something gets into the jack, contact the manufacturer. Do not attempt to remove it yourself.

Warranty

Included with the purchase of this device is a 1-year limited warranty.

High-Frequency Facial Device
User Manual

Effects and Benefits

This high-frequency facial device is an effective beauty instrument. Effects and benefits include: acceleration of blood circulation, reduction of wrinkles and tightening of the skin.

Usage Information

1. Do not use on one part of the skin for over 10 seconds.

2. Do not use if pregnant or intending ❶ _____ (become) pregnant.

3. For sensitive skin, place a piece of soft, light fabric on the skin before use ❷_____ (avoid) excess stimulation.

Important Safety Information

1. Do not assemble or operate this device with wet hands.

2. Remove the power cable after use.

3. Do not insert any unnecessary items into the device's jack, as this may cause a fire. If anything ❸ _____ (get) into the jack, contact the manufacturer. Do not attempt ❹ _____ (remove) it yourself.

Warranty

❺ _____ (Include) with the purchase of this device is a 1-year limited warranty.

High-Frequency Facial Device
User Manual

❶ _____ _____ _____ (효과들과 이점들)

This high-frequency facial device is an effective beauty instrument. Effects and benefits include:

❷ _____ _____ _____ _____ (혈액 순환 촉진), reduction of wrinkles and tightening of the skin.

❸ _____ _____ (사용 정보)

1. Do not use on one part of the skin for over 10 seconds.

2. Do not use if pregnant or intending to become pregnant.

3. For ❹ _____ _____ (민감한 피부), place a piece of soft, light fabric on the skin before use to avoid excess stimulation.

Important Safety Information

1. Do not assemble or operate this device with wet hands.

2. Remove the power cable after use.

3. Do not insert any unnecessary items into the device's jack, as this may cause a fire. If anything gets into the jack, contact the manufacturer. Do not ❺ _____ _____ (~하려고 시도하다) remove it yourself.

Warranty

Included with the purchase of this device is a 1-year limited warranty.

❶ Eco-Friendly Turtle Spotting Boat Tour

❷ Our unique eco-friendly turtle spotting tour allows you to watch the sea turtles and to swim in the most extraordinary turquoise waters around Turtle Island.

❸ The tour includes:

- ❹ a guided boat trip to Turtle Island
- ❺ two swim stops at caves and beaches, where you can relax and enjoy swimming with brightly-colored fish
- ❻ a snack bar on board with coffee, ice cream, sandwiches and snacks.

❼ **Available Days/Times:** Tuesdays, Wednesdays, Fridays and Sunday mornings

❽ **Departure & Arrival:** The pick-up time at your resort will be around 8:30 a.m. ❾ The drop-off time will be around 1:45 p.m., depending on the resort you are staying at.

❿ **Prices:** €23 per adult, €17 per child

(*⓫ Lunch is not included. ⓬ You're welcome to bring your own packed lunch, which can be consumed on board.)

⓭ Call us at 789-5213 to book this tour.

*turquoise 청록색(의)

❶ 거북이 찾기 친환경 보트 관광 여행
❷ 저희의 독특한 거북이 찾기 친환경 보트 관광 여행을 통해 여러분은 바다거북을 보고 거북섬 주변의 가장 색다른 청록색 바다에서 수영할 수 있습니다.
❸ 여행에 포함되는 사항:
- ❹ 가이드가 동행하는 거북섬행 보트 여행
- ❺ 휴식을 취하고 밝은 색깔의 물고기와 함께 수영을 즐길 수 있는 동굴과 해변에서의 수영을 위한 두 차례의 잠시 멈춤
- ❻ 커피, 아이스크림, 샌드위치, 간식이 제공되는 선상 스낵바
❼ 이용 요일/시간: 화요일, 수요일, 금요일, 일요일 오전
❽ 출발 및 도착: 리조트 픽업 시간은 오전 8시 30분경입니다. ❾ 내려 드리는 시간은 오후 1시 45분경으로, 머물고 계신 리조트에 따라 결정됩니다.
❿ 요금: 성인 1인당 23유로, 어린이 1인당 17유로
(*⓫ 점심 식사는 포함되어 있지 않습니다. ⓬ 선상에서 드실 수 있는 도시락을 직접 싸 오셔도 됩니다.)
⓭ 이 관광 여행을 예약하려면 789-5213으로 전화하십시오.

Word List

□ eco-friendly 친환경의   □ turtle 거북   □ spot 발견하다, 탐지하다   □ extraordinary 색다른, 비범한   □ cave 동굴
□ on board 선상의; 선상에서   □ available 이용 가능한   □ packed lunch 도시락   □ consume 먹다   □ book 예약하다

• Word Test

1	spot	_____	
2	available	_____	
3	consume	_____	
4	eco-friendly	_____	
5	cave	_____	

6	색다른, 비범한	_____	
7	선상의; 선상에서	_____	
8	예약하다	_____	
9	거북	_____	
10	도시락	_____	

Eco-Friendly Turtle Spotting Boat Tour

Our unique eco-friendly turtle spotting tour allows you to watch the sea turtles and to swim in the most ❶ ordinary / extraordinary turquoise waters around Turtle Island.

The tour includes:

- a guided boat trip to Turtle Island
- two swim stops at caves and beaches, ❷ where / which you can relax and enjoy swimming with brightly-colored fish
- a snack bar on board with coffee, ice cream, sandwiches and snacks.

Available Days/Times: Tuesdays, Wednesdays, Fridays and Sunday mornings

Departure & Arrival: The pick-up time at your resort will be around 8:30 a.m. The drop-off time will be around 1:45 p.m., depending ❸ in / on the resort you are staying at.

Prices: €23 per adult, €17 per child

(*Lunch is not included. You're welcome to bring your own packed lunch, ❹ which / where can be consumed on board.)

Call us at 789-5213 to book this tour.

*turquoise 청록색(의)

Eco-Friendly Turtle Spotting Boat Tour

Our unique eco-friendly turtle spotting tour allows you ❶ _____ (watch) the sea turtles and to swim in the most extraordinary turquoise waters around Turtle Island.

The tour includes:

- a guided boat trip to Turtle Island
- two swim stops at caves and beaches, where you can relax and enjoy ❷ _____ (swim) with brightly-colored fish
- a snack bar on board with coffee, ice cream, sandwiches and snacks.

Available Days/Times: Tuesdays, Wednesdays, Fridays and Sunday mornings

Departure & Arrival: The pick-up time at your resort will be around 8:30 a.m. The drop-off time will be around 1:45 p.m., ❸ _____ (depend) on the resort you are staying at.

Prices: €23 per adult, €17 per child

(*Lunch is not ❹ _____ (include). You're welcome to bring your own packed lunch, which can be consumed on board.)

Call us at 789-5213 to book this tour.

*turquoise 청록색(의)

Eco-Friendly Turtle Spotting Boat Tour

Our unique eco-friendly turtle spotting tour allows you to watch the sea turtles and to swim in

❶ _____ _____ _____ (가장 색다른) turquoise waters around Turtle Island.

❷ _____ _____ _____ (여행에 포함되는 사항들):

- a guided boat trip to Turtle Island
- two swim stops at caves and beaches, where you can relax and enjoy swimming with brightly-colored fish
- a ❸ _____ _____ _____ _____ (선상 스낵바) with coffee, ice cream, sandwiches and snacks.

Available Days/Times: Tuesdays, Wednesdays, Fridays and Sunday mornings

Departure & Arrival: The pick-up time at your resort will be around 8:30 a.m. The drop-off time will be around 1:45 p.m., depending on the resort you are staying at.

Prices: €23 per adult, €17 per child

(*❹ _____ _____ _____ _____ (점심 식사는 포함되지 않습니다). You're welcome to bring your own packed lunch, which can be consumed on board.)

Call us at 789-5213 to book this tour.

*turquoise 청록색(의)

❶ Conventional and nuclear weapons exist in physical space, where their deployments can be perceived and their capabilities at least roughly calculated. ❷ By contrast, cyber weapons derive an important part of their utility from their opacity; ❸ their disclosure may effectively degrade some of their capabilities. ❹ Their intrusions exploit previously undisclosed flaws in software, obtaining access to a network or system without the authorized user's permission or knowledge. ❺ In the case of distributed denial-of-service (DDoS) attacks (as on communication systems), a large number of seemingly valid information requests may be used to overwhelm systems and make them unavailable for their intended use. ❻ In such cases, the true sources of the attack may be masked, making it difficult or impossible to determine (at least in the moment) who is attacking. ❼ Even one of the most famous instances of cyber-enabled industrial sabotage — the Stuxnet disruption of manufacturing control computers used in Iranian nuclear efforts — has not been formally acknowledged by any government.

*deployment 배치 **opacity 불투명성 ***sabotage (고의적인) 파괴 행위

❶ 재래식 무기와 핵무기는 물리적 공간에 존재하는데 그곳에서 그것들의 배치는 인식될 수 있고, 그것들의 능력은 적어도 대략적으로나마 계산될 수 있다. ❷ 대조적으로 사이버 무기는 그 불투명성으로부터 그 유용성의 중요한 부분을 얻는다. ❸ 그래서 그것들을 공개하는 것은 실제로 그 능력 중 일부를 저하시킬 수도 있다. ❹ 그것[사이버 무기]의 침입은 이전에는 드러나지 않았던 소프트웨어의 결함을 이용하여 권한을 부여받은 사용자의 허락이나 인지 없이 네트워크나 시스템에 대한 접근 권한을 얻는다. ❺ (통신 시스템에 대한 것과 같은) 분산 서비스 거부(DDoS) 공격의 경우, 겉보기에 유효한 다수의 정보 요청이 시스템을 제압해서 그것들을 [시스템]이 원래 의도된 그 용도에 맞게 이용될 수 없도록 하는 데 이용될 수도 있다. ❻ 그런 경우 공격의 진짜 근원은 감춰질 수도 있어서, (적어도 그 순간에는) 누가 공격하고 있는지를 알아내는 것을 어렵거나 불가능하게 만들 수 있다. ❼ 심지어 사이버로 구동되는 산업 파괴 행위의 가장 유명한 예의 하나, 곧 Stuxnet이 이란의 핵 개발 활동에 사용된 제조 통제 컴퓨터를 붕괴시킨 것에 대해 어느 정부도 공식적으로 인정하지 않았다.

Word List

□ conventional 재래식의, 비핵의 □ nuclear 핵의 □ physical 물리적인 □ perceive 인식하다 □ capability 능력
□ roughly 대략적으로 □ calculate 계산하다 □ derive 얻다, 끌어내다 □ utility 유용성 □ disclosure 공개
□ degrade 저하시키다 □ intrusion 침입, 침범 □ exploit (부당하게) 이용하다 □ flaw 결함, 결점 □ access 접근 권한, 접근
□ authorized 권한을 부여받은
□ distributed denial-of-service (DDoS) attack 분산 서비스 거부 공격(여러 대의 공격자를 분산적으로 배치해서 동시에 하는 서비스 거부공격)
□ valid 유효한 □ overwhelm 제압하다, 전복시키다 □ mask 감추다, 가리다
□ Stuxnet 스틱스넷(발전소 · 공항 철도 등 기반 시설을 파괴할 목적으로 제작된 컴퓨터 바이러스로, 2010년 6월 벨라루스에서 처음으로 발견됨)
□ disruption 붕괴, 방해 □ acknowledge 인정하다

• Word Test

1	exploit		11	인정하다	
2	capability		12	인식하다	
3	calculate		13	침입, 침범	
4	access		14	결함, 결점	
5	degrade		15	권한을 부여받은	
6	disruption		16	공개	
7	physical		17	얻다, 끌어내다	
8	conventional		18	핵의	
9	valid		19	제압하다, 전복시키다	
10	utility		20	대략적으로	

Conventional and nuclear weapons exist in physical space, ❶ [where / which] their deployments can be perceived and their capabilities at least roughly calculated. By contrast, cyber weapons derive an important part of their utility ❷ [from / in] their opacity; their disclosure may effectively ❸ [degrade / upgrade] some of their capabilities. Their intrusions exploit previously undisclosed flaws in software, obtaining access to a network or system without the authorized user's permission or knowledge. In the case of distributed denial-of-service (DDoS) attacks (as on communication systems), a large number of seemingly ❹ [invalid / valid] information requests may be used to overwhelm systems and make them unavailable for their intended use. In such cases, the true sources of the attack may be masked, making ❺ [it / them] difficult or impossible to determine (at least in the moment) who is attacking. Even one of the most famous instances of cyber-enabled industrial sabotage — the Stuxnet disruption of manufacturing control computers used in Iranian nuclear efforts — has not been formally acknowledged by any government.

*deployment 배치   **opacity 불투명성   ***sabotage (고의적인) 파괴 행위

Conventional and nuclear weapons exist in physical space, where their deployments can be perceived and their capabilities at least roughly ❶ _____ (calculate). By contrast, cyber weapons derive an important part of their utility from their opacity; their disclosure may effectively degrade some of their capabilities. Their intrusions exploit previously undisclosed flaws in software, ❷ _____ (obtain) access to a network or system without the authorized user's permission or knowledge. In the case of distributed denial-of-service (DDoS) attacks (as on communication systems), a large number of seemingly valid information requests may be used to overwhelm systems and ❸ _____ (make) them unavailable for their intended use. In such cases, the true sources of the attack may be masked, making it difficult or impossible ❹ _____ (determine) (at least in the moment) who is attacking. Even one of the most famous instances of cyber-enabled industrial sabotage — the Stuxnet disruption of manufacturing control computers used in Iranian nuclear efforts — ❺ _____ (have) not been formally acknowledged by any government.

*deployment 배치   **opacity 불투명성   ***sabotage (고의적인) 파괴 행위

Conventional and nuclear weapons exist in physical space, where their deployments can be perceived and their capabilities at least roughly calculated. ❶ _____ _____ (대조적으로), cyber weapons derive an important part of their utility from their opacity; their disclosure may effectively degrade some of their capabilities. Their intrusions exploit ❷ _____ _____ _____ (이전에 들어나지 않았던 결함들) in software, obtaining access to a network or system without the authorized user's permission or knowledge. In the case of distributed denial-of-service (DDoS) attacks (as on communication systems), a large number of ❸ _____ _____ _____ _____ (겉보기에 유효한 정보 요청들) may be used to overwhelm systems and make them unavailable for their intended use. In such cases, the true sources of the attack may be masked, making it difficult or impossible to determine (at least in the moment) who is attacking. Even ❹ _____ _____ _____ _____ _____ (가장 유명한 보기들 중에 하나) of cyber-enabled industrial sabotage — the Stuxnet disruption of manufacturing control computers used in Iranian nuclear efforts — has not been formally acknowledged by any government.

*deployment 배치   **opacity 불투명성   ***sabotage (고의적인) 파괴 행위

❶ In cultures based on a rigid social hierarchy, with strict adherence to rules, visual art tends to adopt well-ordered, conventional, rigid and stereotypical forms. ❷ Ancient Egyptian art does not attempt to depict depth or distance, or the layout of objects in a scene. ❸ The same drawing system persisted for almost 3,000 years. ❹ Objects were arranged in a flat picture plane along lines drawn on walls. ❺ Objects and their parts were observed with great precision, but depicted in a way that conveyed shape in the most simplified manner. ❻ In human figures the torso was drawn from the front, but the head, waist and limbs were drawn in profile. ❼ Medieval artists revived the Egyptian reluctance to record the natural world faithfully, favouring instead depictions of the human form that conform to a strict formula involving expressionless, flat figures without individuality. ❽ This system of depiction was driven by religious concerns to avoid glorifying the attributes of individuals and their unique viewpoint on the world. ❾ There was little attempt to portray realistic depth, and the depicted stature of figures tended to reflect their social status.

*torso 몸통   **profile 옆모습   ***stature 신장

❶ 강직된 사회적 위계에 기반을 둔, 엄격한 규칙 고수가 존재하는 문화에서, 시각 예술은 질서정연하고, 관습적이며, 경직되고, 그리고 정형화된 형태를 취하는 경향이 있다. ❷ 고대 이집트 예술은 한 장면에서 입체감이나 거리감, 또는 사물의 배치를 묘사하려고 시도하지 않는다. ❸ 동일한 그림 방식이 거의 3,000년 동안 지속되었다. ❹ 벽에 그려진 선들을 따라 물체들이 평평한 화면(畵面)에 배열되어 있었다. ❺ 물체와 그것의 부분들은 매우 정밀하게 관찰되었지만, 가장 단순화된 방법으로 형태를 표현하는 방식으로 묘사되었다. ❻ 인물상에서 몸통은 앞모습으로 그려졌지만, 머리, 허리, 그리고 팔다리는 옆모습으로 그려졌다. ❼ 중세 예술가들은 자연계를 정확하게 표현하는 것에 대한 이집트인들의 꺼림을 부활시켰고, 대신 개성이 없는 무표정하고 생기 없는 인물상이 포함된 엄격한 방식에 부합하는 인간 형태의 묘사를 선호했다. ❽ 이 묘사 체계는 개인의 특성과 세상에 대한 그들의 독특한 관점을 미화하는 것을 피하려는 종교적 우려에서 비롯된 것이었다. ❾ 사실적인 입체감을 표현하려는 시도는 거의 없었고, 묘사된 인물들의 신장이 그들의 사회적 지위를 반영하는 경향이 있었다.

Word List

□ **rigid** 경직된, 엄격한   □ **hierarchy** 위계, 계급   □ **adherence** 고수, 충실   □ **adopt** 채택하다   □ **conventional** 관습적인
□ **stereotypical** 정형화된, 진부한   □ **adopt** 채택하다   □ **depth** 입체감, 깊이   □ **layout** 배치   □ **persist** 지속되다, 계속되다
□ **arrange** 배열하다, 정리하다   □ **flat** 평평한, 생기가 없는, 무미건조한   □ **picture plane** 화면(畵面)(그림을 그린 면)
□ **precision** 정밀(성), 정확(성)   □ **convey** 표현하다, 전달하다   □ **waist** 허리   □ **limb** 팔다리   □ **reluctance** 꺼림, (마음) 내키지 않음
□ **faithfully** 정확하게, 충실하게   □ **favour** 선호하다, 편들다   □ **conform to** ~에 부합하다[들어맞다], ~을 따르다   □ **formula** 방식, 공식
□ **expressionless** 무표정한   □ **glorify** 미화하다, 찬미하다   □ **attribute** 특성, 속성   □ **portray** 표현하다, 묘사하다

1	layout	_____	13	방식, 공식	_____
2	flat	_____	14	입체감, 깊이	_____
3	attribute	_____	15	정형화된, 진부한	_____
4	expressionless	_____	16	표현하다, 묘사하다	_____
5	conform to	_____	17	관습적인	_____
6	favour	_____	18	지속되다, 계속되다	_____
7	adherence	_____	19	표현하다, 전달하다	_____
8	precision	_____	20	미화하다, 찬미하다	_____
9	waist	_____	21	위계, 계급	_____
10	rigid	_____	22	정확하게, 충실하게	_____
11	reluctance	_____	23	팔다리	_____
12	arrange	_____	24	채택하다	_____

• 유형 1 네모 안에서 옳은 어법·어휘를 고르시오.

In cultures based on a rigid social hierarchy, with strict adherence ❶ to / for rules, visual art tends to adopt well-ordered, conventional, rigid and stereotypical forms. Ancient Egyptian art does not attempt to depict depth or distance, or the layout of objects in a scene. The same drawing system persisted for almost 3,000 years. Objects were arranged in a flat picture plane along lines drawn on walls. Objects and their parts were observed with great precision, but depicted in a way that conveyed shape in the most ❷ complicated / simplified manner. In human figures the torso was drawn from the front, but the head, waist and limbs were drawn in profile. Medieval artists revived the Egyptian reluctance to record the natural world faithfully, favouring instead depictions of the human form ❸ that / who conform to a strict formula involving expressionless, flat figures without individuality. This system of depiction was driven by religious concerns to avoid glorifying the attributes of individuals and their ❹ normal / unique viewpoint on the world. There was ❺ few / little attempt to portray realistic depth, and the depicted stature of figures tended to reflect their social status.

*torso 몸통 **profile 옆모습 ***stature 신장

In cultures based on a rigid social hierarchy, with strict adherence to rules, visual art tends ❶ _____ (adopt) well-ordered, conventional, rigid and stereotypical forms. Ancient Egyptian art does not attempt ❷ _____ (depict) depth or distance, or the layout of objects in a scene. The same drawing system persisted for almost 3,000 years. Objects were arranged in a flat picture plane along lines ❸ _____ (draw) on walls. Objects and their parts were observed with great precision, but depicted in a way that conveyed shape in the most simplified manner. In human figures the torso was drawn from the front, but the head, waist and limbs were drawn in profile. Medieval artists revived the Egyptian reluctance to record the natural world faithfully, favouring instead depictions of the human form that conform to a strict formula ❹ _____ (involve) expressionless, flat figures without individuality. This system of depiction was driven by religious concerns to avoid ❺ _____ (glorify) the attributes of individuals and their unique viewpoint on the world. There was little attempt to portray realistic depth, and the depicted stature of figures tended to reflect their social status.

*torso 몸통 **profile 옆모습 ***stature 신장

In cultures based on a ❶ _____ _____ _____ (경직된 사회적 위계), with strict adherence to rules, visual art tends to adopt well-ordered, conventional, rigid and stereotypical forms. Ancient Egyptian art does not ❷ _____ _____ (~하려고 시도하다) depict depth or distance, or the layout of objects in a scene. The same drawing system persisted for almost 3,000 years. Objects were arranged in a flat picture plane along lines drawn on walls. Objects and their parts were observed with great precision, but depicted in a way that conveyed shape ❸ _____ _____ _____ _____ _____ (가장 단순화된 방법으로). In human figures the torso was drawn from the front, but the head, waist and limbs were drawn in profile. Medieval artists revived the Egyptian reluctance to record the natural world faithfully, favouring instead depictions of the human form that ❹ _____ _____ _____ _____ _____ (엄격한 방식에 부합하다) involving expressionless, flat figures without individuality. This system of depiction was driven by religious concerns to avoid glorifying the attributes of individuals and their ❺ _____ _____ (독특한 관점) on the world. There was little attempt to portray realistic depth, and the depicted stature of figures tended to reflect their social status.

*torso 몸통 **profile 옆모습 ***stature 신장

257

❶ The search for publicity is, at heart, a quest for a shortcut to friendship. ❷ Yet real kindness is never available in a public sphere. ❸ It is the fruit of a few intimate and reciprocal connections. ❹ It cannot be won remotely or one-sidedly. ❺ If it is safety one seeks, one must definitively and immediately cease to strive to be known to people one doesn't know and concentrate instead on building up genuine bonds that can survive one's errors and endure for life. ❻ Paradoxically and poignantly, it is most often the very anxious who feel a particular longing for the embrace of fame; ❼ but it is especially they (given their fragility) who should be warned away from its ultimately always revengeful arms. ❽ Being entirely forgotten by the world is no curse or sign of failure; ❾ it is the very basis for a contented and safe life in which one swaps the prospect of followers and mean-minded detractors for the deeper satisfaction of true friends.

*reciprocal 호혜적인 **poignantly 통렬하게 ***detractor 비방하는 사람

❶ 널리 알려짐을 추구하는 것은 본질적으로 교우 관계로 가는 지름길을 얻기 위한 탐색이다. ❷ 그러나 진정한 호의는 대중의 영역에서 결코 구할 수 없다. ❸ 그것은 소수의 친밀하고 호혜적인 관계의 결실이다. ❹ 그것은 멀리 떨어져서 혹은 일방적으로는 얻을 수 없다. ❺ 어떤 사람이 얻고자 하는 것이 무사(無事)라면, 그는 분명히 그리고 즉시 자신이 모르는 사람에게 알려지기 위해 애쓰는 것을 중단하고, 그 대신 자신의 실수에도 불구하고 존속되어 평생 지속될 수 있는 진정한 유대감을 구축하는 데 집중해야 한다. ❻ 역설적으로 그리고 통렬하게, 명성의 수용에 대한 특별한 갈망을 느끼는 사람은 대체로 매우 불안한 사람들이다. ❼ 그러나 궁극적으로 항상 앙심에 찬 그것 [명성]의 팔에 접근하지 않도록 경고되어야 하는 대상은 (그들의 연약함을 고려할 때) 특히 그들 [매우 불안한 사람들]이다. ❽ 세상에 의해 완전히 잊힌다는 것은 저주나 실패의 징후가 아니다. ❾ 그것은 추종자들과 심술궂은 마음을 가진 비방하는 사람들의 [사람들을 만날] 가능성을 진정한 친구한테서 오는 더 깊은 만족으로 교환하는 만족스러우며 안전한 삶을 위한 바로 그 기반이다.

Word List

□ publicity 널리 알려짐 □ at heart 본질적으로, 근본적으로 □ quest 탐색, 탐구 □ sphere 영역, 분야 □ intimate 친밀한
□ remotely 멀리 떨어져서, 원격으로 □ definitively 분명히, 확실하게 □ strive to do ~하기 위해 애쓰다[힘쓰다] □ genuine 진정한
□ survive (~에도 불구하고) 존속하다, 살아남다 □ paradoxically 역설적으로 □ anxious 불안한 □ longing 갈망, 열망
□ embrace 수용, 포용 □ fragility 연약함 □ warn ~ away from ... ~이 …에 접근하지 않도록 경고하다 □ ultimately 궁극적으로
□ revengeful 앙심에 찬, 복수심에 불타는 □ contented 만족스러운 □ swap - for... ~을 …으로 교환하다 □ prospect 가능성, 전망
□ mean-minded 심술궂은 마음을 가진

• Word Test

1	embrace	10	멀리 떨어져서, 원격으로
2	quest	11	본질적으로, 근본적으로
3	anxious	12	역설적으로
4	survive	13	진정한
5	definitively	14	가능성, 전망
6	intimate	15	갈망, 열망
7	revengeful	16	연약함
8	contented	17	궁극적으로
9	publicity	18	영역, 분야

The search for publicity is, at heart, a quest for a shortcut to friendship. Yet real kindness is never ❶ available / valuable in a public sphere. It is the fruit of a few intimate and reciprocal connections. It cannot be won remotely or one-sidedly. If it is safety one seeks, one must ❷ definitively / infinitively and immediately cease to strive to be known to people one doesn't know and concentrate instead on building up genuine bonds that can survive one's errors and endure for life. Paradoxically and poignantly, it is most often the very anxious ❸ who / which feel a particular longing for the embrace of fame; but it is especially ❹ they / them (given their fragility) who should be warned away from its ultimately always revengeful arms. Being entirely forgotten by the world is no curse or sign of failure; it is the very basis for a contented and safe life in which one swaps the ❺ prospect / prosperity of followers and mean-minded detractors for the deeper satisfaction of true friends.

*reciprocal 호혜적인　**poignantly 통렬하게　***detractor 비방하는 사람

The search for publicity is, at heart, a quest for a shortcut to friendship. Yet real kindness is never available in a public sphere. It is the fruit of a few intimate and reciprocal connections. It cannot be ❶ _____ (win) remotely or one-sidedly. If it is safety one seeks, one must definitively and immediately cease ❷ _____ (strive) to be known to people one doesn't know and concentrate instead on ❸ _____ (build) up genuine bonds that can survive one's errors and endure for life. Paradoxically and poignantly, it is most often the very anxious who ❹ _____ (feel) a particular longing for the embrace of fame; but it is especially they (given their fragility) who should be warned away from its ultimately always revengeful arms. ❺ _____ (Be) entirely forgotten by the world is no curse or sign of failure; it is the very basis for a contented and safe life in which one swaps the prospect of followers and mean-minded detractors for the deeper satisfaction of true friends.

*reciprocal 호혜적인　**poignantly 통렬하게　***detractor 비방하는 사람

The search for publicity is, at heart, a quest for a ❶ _____ _____ _____ (교우 관계로 가는 지름길). Yet real kindness is never available in a public sphere. It is the fruit of a few intimate and reciprocal connections. It cannot be won remotely or one-sidedly. If it is safety one seeks, one must definitively and immediately cease to strive to be known to people one doesn't know and concentrate instead on ❷ _____ _____ _____ _____ (진정한 유대감을 구축하는 것) that can survive one's errors and endure for life. Paradoxically and poignantly, it is most often the very anxious who feel a particular ❸ _____ _____ (~에 대한 갈망) the embrace of fame; but it is especially they (given their fragility) who should be warned away from its ultimately always revengeful arms. Being entirely forgotten by the world is no curse or ❹ _____ _____ _____ (실패의 징후); it is the very basis for a contented and safe life in which one swaps the prospect of followers and mean-minded detractors for the deeper satisfaction of true friends.

*reciprocal 호혜적인　**poignantly 통렬하게　***detractor 비방하는 사람

❶ It is important to understand the distinction between indicators of market or nonmarket activity and well-defined measures of benefit or cost. ❷ While economic values are often related to human activities, simple indicators viewed in isolation (e.g., number of beach visits) can sometimes provide misleading perspectives. ❸ For example, simple activity indicators ignore values realized by nonusers or benefits related to unmeasured activities (i.e., activities not captured by the indicator in question). ❹ Because of these and other limitations, indicators of economic activity sometimes increase due to negative changes in the environment. ❺ Suppose that closing local beach A due to pollution causes more people to visit neighboring unpolluted beach B. ❻ An analyst looking solely at visitor numbers for beach B might incorrectly conclude that this represents a positive change at beach B, when in fact more visitors to beach B simply reflects the closure of beach A (a substitute beach). ❼ Using the appropriate economic frameworks for analysis can prevent such misleading conclusions. ❽ Simple behavioral (and other) indicators can sometimes provide a cost-effective means to help guide policy — but they can also contribute to incorrect conclusions if not paired with more comprehensive economic analysis.

❶ 시장 또는 비시장 활동의 지표와 이익 또는 비용에 대한 명확한 척도 사이의 차이를 이해하는 것이 중요하다. ❷ 경제적 가치는 인간의 활동과 관련이 있을 때가 많지만, 분리해서 보는 단순한 지표(예를 들어, 해변 방문 횟수)는 때때로 오해를 일으키는 관점을 제공할 수 있다. ❸ 예를 들어, 단순 활동 지표는 비사용자에 의해 실현된 값이나 측정되지 않은 활동과 관련된 이익(즉, 해당 지표에 포착되지 않은 활동)을 무시한다. ❹ 이것들과 다른 이런저런 한계들 때문에, 경제 활동 지표는 환경 내의 부정적인 변화 때문에 때때로 증가한다. ❺ 오염으로 인해 지역의 A 해수욕장이 폐쇄되면 더 많은 사람이 이웃한 오염되지 않은 B 해수욕장을 방문하게 된다고 가정해 보라. ❻ 오로지 B 해수욕장에 대한 방문자 수만을 바라보는 분석가는 실제로는 B 해수욕장의 더 많은 방문객이 단순히 A 해수욕장(대체 해수욕장)의 폐쇄를 반영하고 있는데도, 이것이 B 해수욕장의 긍정적인 변화를 나타낸다는 잘못된 결론을 내릴 수도 있다. ❼ 적절한 경제 분석 틀을 사용하면 오해를 일으키는 그러한 결론을 방지할 수 있다. ❽ 단순한 행동 (그리고 기타) 지표가 때로는 정책을 이끄는 데 도움이 되는 비용 효과가 높은 수단을 제공할 수 있지만, 만약 더 포괄적인 경제 분석과 결합하지 않으면 그것들은 또한 잘못된 결론의 원인이 될 수 있다.

Word List

□ distinction 차이, 구별 □ indicator 지표 □ well-defined (범위가 잘 정해져서) 명확한, 알기 쉬운 □ measure 척도
□ in isolation 고립되어 □ misleading 오해를 일으키는 □ perspective 관점 □ capture 포착하다 □ limitation 한계, 제한
□ pollution 오염 □ analyst 분석가 □ solely 오로지 □ conclude 결론을 내리다 □ represent 나타내다 □ reflect 반영하다
□ closure 폐쇄 □ substitute 대체물 □ appropriate 적절한 □ framework 틀, 체제 □ analysis 분석
□ contribute to ~의 원인이 되다

• Word Test

1 represent _____
2 closure _____
3 measure _____
4 misleading _____
5 capture _____
6 analysis _____
7 distinction _____
8 solely _____
9 appropriate _____
10 pollution _____

11 반영하다 _____
12 틀, 체제 _____
13 결론을 내리다 _____
14 대체물 _____
15 관점 _____
16 분석가 _____
17 ~의 원인이 되다 _____
18 고립되어 _____
19 지표 _____
20 한계, 제한 _____

It is important to understand the ❶ distinction / distribution between indicators of market or nonmarket activity and well-defined measures of benefit or cost. While economic values are often related to human activities, simple indicators viewed in isolation (e.g., number of beach visits) can sometimes provide misleading perspectives. For example, simple activity indicators ignore values realized by nonusers or benefits related to unmeasured activities (i.e., activities not captured by the indicator in question). ❷ Because / Because of these and other limitations, indicators of economic activity sometimes increase due to negative changes in the environment. Suppose ❸ that / which closing local beach A due to pollution causes more people to visit neighboring unpolluted beach B. An analyst looking solely at visitor numbers for beach B might incorrectly conclude that this represents a positive change at beach B, when in fact more visitors to beach B simply reflects the closure of beach A (a substitute beach). Using the ❹ appreciative / appropriate economic frameworks for analysis can prevent such misleading conclusions. Simple behavioral (and other) indicators can sometimes provide a cost-effective means to help guide policy — but they can also contribute to incorrect conclusions if not paired with more ❺ compressive / comprehensive economic analysis.

It is important ❶ _____ (understand) the distinction between indicators of market or nonmarket activity and well-defined measures of benefit or cost. While economic values are often related to human activities, simple indicators ❷ _____ (view) in isolation (e.g., number of beach visits) can sometimes provide misleading perspectives. For example, simple activity indicators ignore values ❸ _____ (realize) by nonusers or benefits related to unmeasured activities (i.e., activities not captured by the indicator in question). Because of these and other limitations, indicators of economic activity sometimes increase due to negative changes in the environment. Suppose that closing local beach A due to pollution causes more people ❹ _____ (visit) neighboring unpolluted beach B. An analyst looking solely at visitor numbers for beach B might incorrectly conclude that this represents a positive change at beach B, when in fact more visitors to beach B simply reflects the closure of beach A (a substitute beach). ❺ _____ (Use) the appropriate economic frameworks for analysis can prevent such misleading conclusions. Simple behavioral (and other) indicators can sometimes provide a cost-effective means to help guide policy — but they can also contribute to incorrect conclusions if not paired with more comprehensive economic analysis.

It is important to understand the distinction between indicators of market or nonmarket activity and ❶ _____ _____ (명확한 척도들) of benefit or cost. While economic values are often related to human activities, simple indicators viewed in isolation (e.g., number of beach visits) can sometimes provide misleading perspectives. For example, simple activity indicators ignore values realized by nonusers or benefits ❷ _____ _____ (~와 관련된) unmeasured activities (i.e., activities not captured by the indicator in question). Because of these and other limitations, indicators of economic activity sometimes increase due to ❸ _____ _____ (부정적인 변화들) in the environment. Suppose that closing local beach A due to pollution causes more people to visit neighboring unpolluted beach B. An analyst looking solely at visitor numbers for beach B might incorrectly conclude that this represents a positive change at beach B, when in fact more visitors to beach B simply reflects the closure of beach A (a substitute beach). Using the appropriate economic frameworks for analysis can prevent such misleading conclusions. Simple behavioral (and other) indicators can sometimes provide a cost-effective means to help guide policy — but they can also ❹ _____ _____ (~에 기여하다) incorrect conclusions if not paired with more ❺ _____ _____ _____ (포괄적인 경제 분석).

❶ When you look at the photos of an expert like Malick Sidibé, you are looking at a small fraction of the portraits he chose to show his viewers. ❷ Photos with closed eyes, crooked clothing, unflattering expressions, or those with a poor exposure, were surely edited out and hidden from his audience. ❸ Street photographers like Joel Meyerowitz make thousands of photos that are never seen by fans. ❹ His discriminating eye chooses exactly what he wants his audience to see. ❺ Any digital image that doesn't meet Meyerowitz's personal expectations is put in a folder that may never be opened again. ❻ Most of the photographs anyone makes will likely end up in a digital junk heap on a forgotten hard drive. ❼ The point is that photographers put a lot of creative energy, time, and expense into making photographs, most of which don't represent the quality the creator expects. ❽ Yet, those hidden photos are critically important to the process of image-making. ❾ They represent the stages of failure and experimentation needed to arrive at a creative breakthrough. ❿ Those *in-between* photos are part of the step-by-step development process that leads you from one successful image to the next.

*crooked 비뚤어진

❶ Malick Sidibé와 같은 전문가의 사진을 볼 때, 여러분은 그가 자신의 관람객들에게 보여 주기로 결정한 작은 일부의 인물 사진들을 보고 있는 것이다. ❷ 눈을 감고 있는, 옷차림이 비뚤어진, 실물보다 못 나온 표정의 사진들, 또는 노출이 좋지 않은 사진들은 틀림없이 편집 중에 삭제되어 그의 관람객에게 숨겨졌다. ❸ Joel Meyerowitz와 같은 거리 사진작가들은 팬들이 못 보는 수천 장의 사진을 제작한다. ❹ 판단력이 뛰어난 그의 안목은 정확히 그가 자신의 관람객이 보기를 원하는 것을 선택한다. ❺ Meyerowitz의 개인적인 기대에 미치지 못하는 디지털 이미지는 무엇이든 다시는 열리지 않을 수도 있는 폴더에 저장된다. ❻ 누가 제작하는 사진이든 대부분은 아마 결국 잊혀진 하드 드라이브 상의 디지털 쓰레기 더미에 들어가게 될 것이다. ❼ 요점은 사진작가들이 사진을 제작하는 데 많은 창조적 에너지와 시간 및 비용을 투자하지만, 대부분은 제작자가 기대하는 품질을 나타내지 못한다는 것이다. ❽ 하지만, 그러한 숨겨진 사진들은 이미지 제작 과정에 결정적으로 중요하다. ❾ 그것들은 창조적 대성공에 도달하는 데 필요한 실패와 실험의 단계들을 나타낸다. ❿ 그러한 '중간에 있는' 사진들은 여러분을 하나의 성공적 이미지에서 그 다음 성공적 이미지로 이끄는 단계별 발전 과정의 일부이다.

Word List

□ **expert** 전문가　□ **fraction** 일부, 부분　□ **portrait** 인물 사진　□ **viewer** 관람객　□ **unflattering** 실물보다 못 나온
□ **exposure** 노출　□ **edit out** (편집 중에) ~을 삭제하다　□ **photographer** 사진작가　□ **discriminating** 판단력이 뛰어난
□ **exactly** 정확히　□ **junk** 쓰레기　□ **heap** 더미, 무더기　□ **critically** 결정적으로　□ **represent** 나타내다　□ **experimentation** 실험
□ **breakthrough** 대성공　□ **in-between** 중간의

• Word Test

1	exactly		9	실험
2	expert		10	쓰레기
3	breakthrough		11	결정적으로
4	portrait		12	중간의
5	represent		13	관람객
6	heap		14	판단력이 뛰어난
7	photographer		15	일부, 부분
8	unflattering		16	노출

When you look at the photos of an expert like Malick Sidibé, you are looking at a small fraction of the portraits he chose to show his viewers. Photos with closed eyes, crooked clothing, unflattering expressions, or those with a poor exposure, were surely edited out and hidden from his audience. Street photographers like Joel Meyerowitz make thousands of photos ❶ that / who are never seen by fans. His discriminating eye chooses exactly ❷ that / what he wants his audience to see. Any digital image that doesn't meet Meyerowitz's personal expectations is put in a folder that may never be opened again. Most of the photographs anyone makes will likely end up in a digital junk heap on a forgotten hard drive. The point is ❸ that / which photographers put a lot of creative energy, time, and expense into making photographs, most of which don't represent the ❹ quantity / quality the creator expects. Yet, those hidden photos are critically important to the process of image-making. They represent the stages of failure and experimentation needed to arrive at a creative breakthrough. Those *in-between* photos are part of the step-by-step development process that leads you from one ❺ successful / successive image to the next.

*crooked 비뚤어진

When you look at the photos of an expert like Malick Sidibé, you are looking at a small fraction of the portraits he chose ❶ _____ (show) his viewers. Photos with closed eyes, crooked clothing, unflattering expressions, or those with a poor exposure, were surely edited out and hidden from his audience. Street photographers like Joel Meyerowitz ❷ _____ (make) thousands of photos that are never seen by fans. His ❸ _____ (discriminate) eye chooses exactly what he wants his audience to see. Any digital image that doesn't meet Meyerowitz's personal expectations ❹ _____ (be) put in a folder that may never be opened again. Most of the photographs anyone makes will likely end up in a digital junk heap on a forgotten hard drive. The point is that photographers put a lot of creative energy, time, and expense into making photographs, most of which don't represent the quality the creator expects. Yet, those hidden photos are critically important to the process of image-making. They represent the stages of failure and experimentation ❺ _____ (need) to arrive at a creative breakthrough. Those *in-between* photos are part of the step-by-step development process that leads you from one successful image to the next.

*crooked 비뚤어진

When you look at the photos of an expert like Malick Sidibé, you are looking at a small fraction of the portraits he chose to show his viewers. Photos with closed eyes, crooked clothing, unflattering expressions, or those ❶ _____ _____ _____ _____ (노출이 좋지 않은), were surely edited out and hidden from his audience. Street photographers like Joel Meyerowitz make thousands of photos that are never seen by fans. His ❷ _____ _____ (식별력이 있는 안목) chooses exactly what he wants his audience to see. Any digital image that doesn't meet Meyerowitz's personal expectations is put in a folder that may never be opened again. Most of the photographs anyone makes will likely ❸ _____ _____ _____ (결국 ~로 끝나다) a digital junk heap on a forgotten hard drive. The point is that photographers put a lot of ❹ _____ _____ (창조적 에너지), time, and expense into making photographs, most of which don't represent the quality the creator expects. Yet, those hidden photos are critically important to the process of image-making. They represent the stages of failure and experimentation needed to arrive at a creative breakthrough. Those *in-between* photos are ❺ _____ _____ _____ _____ _____ (단계별 발전의 일부) process that leads you from one successful image to the next.

*crooked 비뚤어진

❶ Plans need to have a degree of flexibility under changing circumstances, but settling on clear deadlines and tasks helps to avoid opening up the problematic flexibility that can open the door to interpreting delay as something other than that. ❷ To take an illustration from the context of health, consider Gary, who has noticed that he has been getting colds quite frequently and thinks that it would be good to make an appointment with a primary care physician soon to get some medical tests done. ❸ And yet, he finds himself putting it off. ❹ Gary thinks of himself as conscientious and certainly not someone who would fail to take care of himself. ❺ As he considers, at a certain point, whether to phone the doctor or put it off for a day, the lack of specificity in his intention affords him plenty of wiggle room for thinking that he is still going to make the appointment "soon." ❻ In such contexts, by entering into his calendar a specific time for making the call and an automatic reminder, Gary can create an attentional structure that makes it difficult for him to overlook the fact that failing to make the call at the appointed time is a case of delay.

*conscientious 성실한 **wiggle room 여지

❶ 계획은 변화하는 상황에서 어느 정도의 유연성을 가질 필요가 있지만, 명확한 기한과 과제를 정하는 것이 지연을 그것이 아닌 어떤 것으로 해석하는 길을 열어 줄 수도 있는 문제가 있는 유연성을 가능하게 하는 것을 피하는 데 도움이 된다. ❷ 건강이라는 상황에서 예를 들자면, Gary를 생각해 보라. 그는 자신이 감기에 상당히 자주 걸리고 있다는 것을 알아채고는 곧 1차 진료 의사에게 진료를 예약하여 몇 가지 의학적 검사를 받는 것이 좋을 것이라고 생각한다. ❸ 그렇지만, 그는 자신이 그것을 미루고 있음을 깨닫는다. ❹ Gary는 자신을 성실하고, 분명 스스로를 돌보지 않을 사람이 아니라고 생각한다. ❺ 특정 시점에서 그가 의사에게 전화를 해야 할지 아니면 그것을 하루 미뤄야 할지 고민하고 있을 때, 그의 계획에서 구체성이 결여된 것이 그에게 자신이 여전히 '곧' 예약을 할 것이라고 생각할 수 있는 충분한 여지를 준다. ❻ 그러한 상황에서 자신의 캘린더에 전화를 걸기 위한 구체적인 시간과 자동 알림을 입력함으로써, Gary는 정해진 시간에 전화를 걸지 않는 것이 지연의 경우에 해당한다는 사실을 자신이 간과하기 어렵게 하는 주의 구조를 만들 수 있다.

Word List

□ a degree of 어느 정도의   □ flexibility 유연성, 융통성   □ settle on ~을 정하다   □ open up ~을 가능하게 하다
□ open the door to ~로 가는 길[기회]을 열어 주다   □ interpret 해석하다   □ delay 지연   □ illustration 사례
□ appointment 예약, 약속   □ primary care physician 1차 진료 의사, 주치의   □ put off ~을 미루다   □ specificity 구체성
□ intention 계획, 의도   □ afford 주다, 제공하다   □ context 맥락, 전후 사정   □ enter 입력하다, 적어넣다   □ automatic 자동의
□ reminder (생각나게 하는) 신호, 메모   □ overlook 간과하다, 못 보고 넘어가다

• Word Test

1	enter	9	사례
2	open up	10	~을 미루다
3	reminder	11	~을 정하다
4	appointment	12	맥락, 전후 사정
5	specificity	13	계획, 의도
6	afford	14	간과하다, 못 보고 넘어가다
7	flexibility	15	해석하다
8	delay	16	자동의

Plans need to have a degree of ❶ flexibility / rigidity under changing circumstances, but settling on clear deadlines and tasks helps to avoid opening up the problematic flexibility that can open the door to interpreting delay as something other than that. To take an illustration from the context of health, consider Gary, ❷ which / who has noticed that he has been getting colds quite frequently and thinks that it would be good to make an appointment with a primary care ❸ physicist / physician soon to get some medical tests done. And yet, he finds himself putting it off. Gary thinks of himself ❹ as / for conscientious and certainly not someone who would fail to take care of himself. As he considers, at a certain point, whether to phone the doctor or put it off for a day, the lack of specificity in his intention affords him plenty of wiggle room for thinking that he is still going to make the ❺ appointment / disappointment "soon." In such contexts, by entering into his calendar a specific time for making the call and an automatic reminder, Gary can create an attentional structure that makes it difficult for him to overlook the fact that failing to make the call at the appointed time is a case of delay.

*conscientious 성실한 **wiggle room 여지

Plans need to have a degree of flexibility under changing circumstances, but settling on clear deadlines and tasks helps to avoid ❶ _____ (open) up the problematic flexibility that can open the door to interpreting delay as something other than that. To take an illustration from the context of health, consider Gary, who has noticed that he has been getting colds quite frequently and thinks that it would be good ❷ _____ (make) an appointment with a primary care physician soon to get some medical tests ❸ _____ (do). And yet, he finds himself putting it off. Gary thinks of himself as conscientious and certainly not someone who would fail to take care of himself. As he considers, at a certain point, whether ❹ _____ (phone) the doctor or put it off for a day, the lack of specificity in his intention affords him plenty of wiggle room for thinking that he is still going to make the appointment "soon." In such contexts, by entering into his calendar a specific time for making the call and an automatic reminder, Gary can create an attentional structure that makes it difficult for him ❺ _____ (overlook) the fact that failing to make the call at the appointed time is a case of delay.

*conscientious 성실한 **wiggle room 여지

Plans need to have ❶ _____ _____ _____ (어느 정도의) flexibility under changing circumstances, but settling on clear deadlines and tasks helps to avoid opening up the problematic flexibility that can open the door to interpreting delay as something other than that. To take an illustration from the context of health, consider Gary, who has noticed that he has been getting colds quite frequently and thinks that it would be good to ❷ _____ _____ _____ _____ (~와 약속을 하다) a primary care physician soon to get some medical tests done. And yet, he finds himself putting it off. Gary thinks of himself as conscientious and certainly not someone who would fail to ❸ _____ _____ _____ _____ (스스로를 돌보다). As he considers, at a certain point, whether to phone the doctor or put it off for a day, the ❹ _____ _____ _____ (구체성의 결여) in his intention affords him plenty of wiggle room for thinking that he is still going to make the appointment "soon." In such contexts, by entering into his calendar a specific time for making the call and an automatic reminder, Gary can create a(n) ❺ _____ _____ (주의 구조) that makes it difficult for him to overlook the fact that failing to make the call at the appointed time is a case of delay.

*conscientious 성실한   **wiggle room 여지

268

❶ Even the care we take for nature is motivated by a certain goal-oriented striving under the heading of "conservation." ❷ We treat nature as a scarce resource to be preserved for the health of the planet and the security of future generations. ❸ But rarely do we attempt to appreciate and protect nature for its own sake, as a source of wonder and awe in the face of which we stand to gain new perspectives on ourselves and the goals we pursue. ❹ When pressed to articulate why biodiversity matters, for example, we turn almost automatically to some account of how, when one species goes extinct, others will suffer, including, in the end, ourselves. ❺ We lack the vocabulary in which to understand the diversity of nature as intrinsically meaningful and as worthy of our engagement.

*articulate 분명히 설명하다 **intrinsically 본질적으로

❶ 우리가 자연에 내해 하는 돌봄조차도 '보존'이라는 제목 아래 특정한 목표 지향적인 노력으로 동기 부여가 된다. ❷ 우리는 자연을 지구의 건강과 미래 세대의 안전을 위해 보존되어야 할 희소한 자원으로 취급한다. ❸ 그러나 우리는 자연 그 자체를 위해, 즉 우리가 직면했을 때 우리 자신 그리고 우리가 추구하는 목표에 관한 새로운 관점을 얻을 것 같은 경이로움과 경외심의 원천으로서 자연의 진가를 인정하고 보호하려는 시도를 거의 하지 않는다. ❹ 예를 들어, 생물 다양성이 왜 중요한지 분명히 설명하라는 압력을 받을 때, 우리는 거의 무의식적으로 한 종이 멸종할 때, 결국 우리 자신을 포함하여 다른 종들이 어떻게 고통받을지에 대한 어떤 설명에 의존한다. ❺ 우리에게는 자연의 다양성을 본질적으로 의미 있고 우리가 관여할 가치가 있는 것으로 이해하는 어휘가 없다.

Word List

□ motivate 동기를 부여하다 □ goal-oriented 목표 지향적인 □ striving 노력 □ heading 제목 □ conservation 보존
□ scarce 희소한 □ preserve 보존하다 □ security 안전 □ appreciate 진가를 인정하다 □ for one's own sake ~ 자체를 위해
□ awe 경외심 □ stand to do ~할 것 같다 □ perspective 관점 □ pursue 추구하다 □ biodiversity 생물 다양성 □ account 설명
□ extinct 멸종한 □ vocabulary 어휘 □ engagement 관여

• **Word Test**

1	extinct	9	희소한
2	heading	10	노력
3	appreciate	11	어휘
4	perspective	12	경외심
5	engagement	13	설명
6	motivate	14	보존
7	biodiversity	15	안전
8	preserve	16	추구하다

Even the care we take for nature is motivated by a certain goal-oriented striving under the heading of "conservation." We treat nature ❶ as / in a scarce resource to be preserved for the health of the planet and the security of future generations. But rarely ❷ we do / do we attempt to appreciate and protect nature for its own sake, as a source of wonder and awe in the face of which we stand to gain new ❸ perspectives / prospective on ourselves and the goals we pursue. When pressed to articulate why biodiversity matters, for example, we turn almost ❹ automatic / automatically to some account of how, when one species goes ❺ existing / extinct, others will suffer, including, in the end, ourselves. We lack the vocabulary in which to understand the diversity of nature as intrinsically meaningful and as worthy of our engagement.

*articulate 분명히 설명하다   **intrinsically 본질적으로

Even the care we take for nature is motivated by a certain goal-oriented striving under the heading of "conservation." We treat nature as a scarce resource ❶ _____ (be) preserved for the health of the planet and the security of future generations. But rarely do we attempt ❷ _____ (appreciate) and protect nature for its own sake, as a source of wonder and awe in the face of which we stand to gain new perspectives on ourselves and the goals we pursue. When ❸ _____ (press) to articulate why biodiversity matters, for example, we turn almost automatically to some account of how, when one species ❹ _____ (go) extinct, others will suffer, ❺ _____ (include), in the end, ourselves. We lack the vocabulary in which to understand the diversity of nature as intrinsically meaningful and as worthy of our engagement.

*articulate 분명히 설명하다   **intrinsically 본질적으로

Even the care we take for nature is motivated by a certain goal-oriented striving under the heading of "conservation." We treat nature as a ❶ _____ _____ (희소한 자원) to be preserved for the health of the planet and the security of future generations. But rarely do we attempt to appreciate and protect ❷ _____ _____ _____ _____ _____ (자연 그 자체를 위해), as a source of wonder and awe in the face of which we stand to gain new perspectives on ourselves and the goals we pursue. When pressed to articulate why biodiversity matters, for example, we turn almost automatically to some account of how, when one species ❸ _____ _____ (멸종하다), others will suffer, including, in the end, ourselves. We lack the vocabulary in which to understand the ❹ _____ _____ _____ (자연의 다양성) as intrinsically meaningful and as worthy of our engagement.

*articulate 분명히 설명하다   **intrinsically 본질적으로

❶ Sport does not require architecture. ❷ A field can serve as the grounds for footraces, ball games, and other modes of sporting activity. ❸ Early football games in England famously, or perhaps notoriously, took place without fixed dimensions and across the townscape. ❹ Swimming, boating, surfing all can take place in natural, undesigned sites. ❺ The exterior wall of a building can be the backboard for handball or tennis. ❻ Nevertheless, the architecture of sport stretches back through history to the earliest exemplars of built forms. ❼ This is notable for both sporting and architectural reasons. ❽ In order to design and build sport architecture, there must already be in place some degree of codification of the rules of the game to be played and the minimum spatial dimensions necessary to undertake that activity. ❾ Thus the precursor of our modern stadia, the stadion, was both the place where a footrace was run and a unit of measurement. ❿ Sport architecture therefore emerges at the intersection of the codification of the rules of various games and means and mode of design and construction.

*codification 체계화, 집대성 **precursor 전신 ***stadium 육상 경기장(*pl.* stadia)

❶ 스포츠에는 건축불이 필요하지 않다. ❷ 들판이 도보 경주, 구기(종목), 그리고 다른 방식의 스포츠 활동을 위한 장소의 역할을 할 수 있다. ❸ 영국의 초창기 축구 경기는 유명하게도 혹은 어쩌면 악명 높게도 고정된 크기 없이, 그리고 도시 경관 전체에 걸쳐 열렸다. ❹ 수영, 보트 타기, 서핑은 모두 자연의, 설계되지 않은 장소에서 이루어질 수 있다. ❺ 건물의 외벽은 핸드볼이나 테니스의 백보드가 될 수 있다. ❻ 그런데도, 스포츠의 건축물은 건축된 형태의 가장 초기 사례까지 역사를 통해 거슬러 올라간다. ❼ 이것은 스포츠상의 그리고 건축상의 이유 양면에서 주목할 만하다. ❽ 스포츠 건축물을 설계하고 짓기 위해서는 열리게 될 경기의 규칙과 그 활동을 수행하는 데 필요한 최소한의 공간의 크기에 대한 어느 정도의 체계화가 이미 마련되어 있어야 한다. ❾ 그러므로 우리의 현대 육상 경기장의 전신인 stadion은 도보 경주하는 장소이자 측정 단위이기도 했다. ❿ 따라서 스포츠 건축물은 다양한 경기 규칙의 체계화와 설계 및 건축의 수단과 양식이 교차하는 지점에서 나타난다.

Word List

□ architecture 건축물, 건축   □ footrace 도보 경주   □ mode 방식   □ notoriously 악명 높게   □ townscape 도시 경관
□ exterior 외부의   □ exemplar 사례   □ notable 주목할 만한   □ spatial 공간의   □ dimension 크기, 규모, 범위
□ undertake 수행하다   □ measurement 측정   □ emerge 나타나다   □ intersection 교차하는 지점, 교차점

• Word Test

1	undertake	_____	8	주목할 만한	_____
2	exemplar	_____	9	도보 경주	_____
3	emerge	_____	10	크기, 규모, 범위	_____
4	architecture	_____	11	악명 높게	_____
5	spatial	_____	12	측정	_____
6	townscape	_____	13	외부의	_____
7	mode	_____	14	교차하는 지점, 교차점	_____

Sport does not require architecture. A field can serve as the grounds for footraces, ball games, and other modes of sporting activity. Early football games in England famously, or perhaps notoriously, took place ❶ | with / without | fixed dimensions and across the townscape. Swimming, boating, surfing all can take place in natural, undesigned sites. The exterior wall of a building can be the backboard for handball or tennis. ❷ | Nevertheless / Therefore |, the architecture of sport stretches back through history to the earliest exemplars of built forms. This is notable for both sporting ❸ | and / or | architectural reasons. In order to design and build sport architecture, there must already be in place some degree of codification of the rules of the game to be played and the ❹ | maximum / minimum | spatial dimensions necessary to undertake that activity. Thus the precursor of our modern stadia, the stadion, was both the place ❺ | when / where | a footrace was run and a unit of measurement. Sport architecture therefore emerges at the intersection of the codification of the rules of various games and means and mode of design and construction. *codification 체계화, 집대성 **precursor 전신 ***stadium 육상 경기장(*pl.* stadia)

Sport does not require architecture. A field can serve as the grounds for footraces, ball games, and other modes of sporting activity. Early football games in England famously, or perhaps notoriously, took place without ❶ _____ (fix) dimensions and across the townscape. Swimming, boating, surfing all can take place in natural, undesigned sites. The exterior wall of a building can be the backboard for handball or tennis. Nevertheless, the architecture of sport stretches back through history to the earliest exemplars of built forms. This is notable for both sporting and architectural reasons. In order ❷ _____ (design) and build sport architecture, there must already be in place some degree of codification of the rules of the game to ❸ _____ (play) and the minimum spatial dimensions necessary ❹ _____ (undertake) that activity. Thus the precursor of our modern stadia, the stadion, ❺ _____ (be) both the place where a footrace was run and a unit of measurement. Sport architecture therefore emerges at the intersection of the codification of the rules of various games and means and mode of design and construction. *codification 체계화, 집대성 **precursor 전신 ***stadium 육상 경기장(*pl.* stadia)

Sport does not require architecture. A field can serve as the grounds for footraces, ball games, and other modes of sporting activity. Early football games in England famously, or perhaps notoriously, took place without fixed dimensions and across the townscape. Swimming, boating, surfing all can ❶ _____ _____ _____ (~에서 열리다) natural, undesigned sites. The ❷ _____ _____ _____ _____ _____ (건물의 외벽) can be the backboard for handball or tennis. Nevertheless, the architecture of sport stretches back through history to the earliest exemplars of built forms. This is notable for both sporting and architectural reasons. In order to design and build sport architecture, there must already be in place some degree of codification of the rules of the game to be played and the minimum spatial dimensions necessary to undertake that activity. Thus the precursor of our modern stadia, the stadion, was both the place where a footrace was run and ❸ _____ _____ _____ _____ (측정의 단위). Sport architecture therefore emerges ❹ _____ _____ _____ (교차점에서) of the codification of the rules of various games and means and mode of design and construction. *codification 체계화, 집대성 **precursor 전신 ***stadium 육상 경기장(*pl.* stadia)

❶ Great fairytales are full of suspense and emotional ups and downs, with the hero or heroine fighting and then overcoming antagonists and obstacles. ❷ The bigger the difficulties and the greater the suspense, the more interesting the story. ❸ Cinderella had no clothes, no carriage, and a rigid deadline. ❹ She had lost her shoe. ❺ Cinderella was sad, then happy because of the fairy Godmother, then scared again when the clock struck 12. ❻ An interviewee faced an employer going bankrupt, saw her superiors resign, and was left with a weak team. ❼ Both of these examples have a central character: Cinderella and the interviewee. ❽ Audiences generally identify more with people and characters in the stories than with abstract discussion. ❾ In business storytelling, when there is no one central character, characters can be woven into the body of the story. ❿ For example: "In the next 10 minutes, I will show you five reasons why our business will disappear within five years if we continue with business as usual." ⓫ Then, one reason could include the story of how a big customer was disappointed and another reason could include the story of how a group of salesmen felt helpless.

*antagonist (주인공과 대립되는) 적대역

❶ 훌륭한 동화는 긴장감과 감정적 기복으로 가득 차 있으며, 남녀 주인공이 적대역 및 장애물과 싸우다가 이를 이겨 낸다. ❷ 어려움이 클수록, 그리고 긴장감이 굉장할수록 이야기가 더 흥미진진하다. ❸ 신데렐라는 옷과 마차가 없었고 엄격한 시한이 있었다. ❹ 그녀는 자신의 신발 한 짝을 잃어버렸다. ❺ 신데렐라는 슬펐고 그 후 요정 대모 덕분에 행복했다가 시계가 12시를 치자 다시 겁을 먹었다. ❻ 한 인터뷰 대상자는 고용주가 파산하는 것에 직면했고, 자신의 상관들이 사직하는 것을 보았으며, 약한 팀과 함께 남겨졌다. ❼ 이 두 가지 예에는 중심인물이 있는데, 신데렐라와 인터뷰 대상자이다. ❽ 청중은 일반적으로 추상적 논의보다 이야기 속 사람들과 인물들과 더 동질감을 갖는다. ❾ 비지니스 스토리텔링에서 중심인물이 한 명도 없을 때 인물들이 이야기의 본문에 엮어질 수 있다. ❿ 다음과 같이 예를 들어 보자. "앞으로 10분 안에, 우리가 평소대로 사업을 계속한다면 5년 안에 우리의 사업이 사라질 5가지 이유를 보여 드리겠습니다." ⓫ 그런 다음 한 가지 이유에는 거물 고객이 어떻게 실망했는지에 대한 이야기가 포함될 수 있을 것이고 또 다른 이유에는 한 무리의 영업 사원들이 어떻게 무력감을 느꼈는지에 대한 이야기가 포함될 수 있을 것이다.

• Word Test

1 superior	_____	9 장애(물)	_____
2 fairytale	_____	10 엮다, 짜다	_____
3 overcome	_____	11 사직하다, 사임하다	_____
4 include	_____	12 무력한	_____
5 godmother	_____	13 긴장감	_____
6 ups and downs	_____	14 여주인공	_____
7 abstract	_____	15 파산한	_____
8 carriage	_____	16 엄격한, 고정된	_____

Great fairytales are full of suspense and emotional ups and downs, with the hero or heroine fighting and then overcoming ❶ antagonists / colleague and obstacles. The bigger the difficulties and the ❷ greater / greatest the suspense, the more interesting the story. Cinderella had no clothes, no carriage, and a rigid deadline. She had lost her shoe. Cinderella was sad, then happy ❸ because / because of the fairy Godmother, then scared again when the clock struck 12. An interviewee faced an employer going bankrupt, saw her superiors resign, and was left with a weak team. Both of these examples have a central character: Cinderella and the interviewee. Audiences generally identify more with people and characters in the stories than with ❹ abstract / concrete discussion. In business storytelling, when there is no one central character, characters can be woven into the body of the story. For example: "In the next 10 minutes, I will show you five reasons ❺ which / why our business will disappear within five years if we continue with business as usual." Then, one reason could include the story of how a big customer was disappointed and another reason could include the story of how a group of salesmen felt helpless.

*antagonist (주인공과 대립되는) 적대역

Great fairytales are full of suspense and emotional ups and downs, with the hero or heroine fighting and then ❶ _____ (overcome) antagonists and obstacles. The bigger the difficulties and the greater the suspense, the more interesting the story. Cinderella had no clothes, no carriage, and a rigid deadline. She had lost her shoe. Cinderella was sad, then happy because of the fairy Godmother, then scared again when the clock struck 12. An interviewee faced an employer ❷ _____ (go) bankrupt, saw her superiors ❸ _____ (resign), and was left with a weak team. Both of these examples have a central character: Cinderella and the interviewee. Audiences generally identify more with people and characters in the stories than with abstract discussion. In business storytelling, when there is no one central character, characters can ❹ _____ (weave) into the body of the story. For example: "In the next 10 minutes, I will show you five reasons why our business will disappear within five years if we continue with business as usual." Then, one reason could include the story of how a big customer ❺ _____ (disappoint) and another reason could include the story of how a group of salesmen felt helpless.

*antagonist (주인공과 대립되는) 적대역

Great fairytales ❶ _____ _____ _____ (~로 가득차다) suspense and emotional ups and downs, with the hero or heroine fighting and then overcoming antagonists and obstacles. The bigger the difficulties and the greater the suspense, the more interesting the story. Cinderella had no clothes, no carriage, and a rigid deadline. She had lost her shoe. Cinderella was sad, then happy because of the fairy Godmother, then scared again when the clock struck 12. An interviewee ❷ _____ _____ _____ _____ _____ (고용주가 파산하는 것에 직면했다), saw her superiors resign, and was left with a weak team. Both of these examples have a central character: Cinderella and the interviewee. Audiences generally identify more with people and characters in the stories than with ❸ _____ _____ (추상적 논의). In business storytelling, when there is no one central character, characters can be woven into the body of the story. For example: "In the next 10 minutes, I will show you five reasons why our business will disappear within five years if we continue with business ❹ _____ _____ (평상시처럼)." Then, one reason could include the story of how a big customer was disappointed and another reason could include the story of how a group of salesmen ❺ _____ _____ (무력감을 느꼈다).

*antagonist (주인공과 대립되는) 적대역

❶ Throughout history, people have pooled their resources to varying degrees in order to enjoy the benefits and manage the risks that come from living in large groups. ❷ These benefits include specialisation of labour, mutual defence and shared infrastructure. ❸ As groups get larger — from family to village to major cities and nation states — the mutual obligations become more abstract and are often mediated through institutions and the political process. ❹ Rather than 'owe' something to our family or community, our obligations morph into solidarity with fellow citizens or duty to our country. ❺ In the past, for example, families educated their children, cared for the sick and unemployed at home; today most rely on schools, medical facilities and (in some countries) unemployment benefits paid by the state. ❻ That is why today people are expected to contribute to the common good when they are productive adults and, in exchange, get an education when they are young and support when they are sick, unemployed or old. ❼ The exact nature of these expectations varies according to the cultural norms, institutions, policies and laws that define the rights and obligations of individuals relative to those of the wider society, but the existence of such expectations is universal.

*morph 변하다

❶ 역사를 통틀어 사람들은 대규모 집단으로 사는 데에서 오는 이득을 누리고 거기서 오는 위험을 관리하기 위해 다양한 정도로 자신들의 자원을 공동 관리해 왔다. ❷ 이 이득에는 노동의 전문화, 공동 방위, 그리고 기반 시설 공유가 포함된다. ❸ 가족에서 마을, 대도시, 국민 국가로 집단이 더 커지면서, 상호 간의 의무는 더 추상적이 되어 흔히 제도와 정치 과정을 통해 중재된다. ❹ 우리 의무는 우리 가족이나 공동체에 무언가를 '빚지고 있기'보다는 동료 시민과의 연대나 국가에 대한 임무로 변한다. ❺ 예를 들어, 과거에는 가족이 집에서 자기 아이를 교육했고 병자와 실직자를 돌보았지만, 오늘날은 대부분이 국가가 비용을 대는 학교, 의료 시설, 그리고 (몇몇 나라에서는) 실업 수당에 의존한다. ❻ 그 때문에 오늘날 사람들은 생산적인 성인일 때 공익에 기여하고, 그 대가로 어릴 때는 교육을, 아프거나 실직하거나 늙었을 때는 부양을 받을 것으로 기대된다. ❼ 이런 기대의 정확한 속성은 더 넓은 사회의 그것들[권리와 의무]에 견주어 개인의 권리와 의무를 규정하는 문화적 규범, 제도, 정책과 법에 따라 다르지만, 그런 기대가 존재하는 것은 보편적이다.

• Word Test

1	contribute to	11	정확한
2	degree	12	이득, 수당[보조금]
3	abstract	13	보편적인
4	specialisation	14	다양한
5	existence	15	공익
6	institution	16	노동
7	solidarity	17	빚지고 있다, 갚아야 한다
8	relative to	18	의무
9	pool	19	중재하다
10	mutual	20	의료 시설

Throughout history, people have pooled their resources to varying degrees in order to enjoy the benefits and manage the risks ❶ that / who come from living in large groups. These benefits include specialisation of labour, mutual ❷ defence / offence and shared infrastructure. As groups get larger — from family to village to major cities and nation states — the mutual obligations become more abstract and are often mediated through institutions and the political process. Rather than 'owe'something to our family or community, our obligations morph into ❸ solitude / solidarity with fellow citizens or duty to our country. In the past, for example, families educated their children, cared for the sick and unemployed at home; today most rely on schools, medical facilities and (in some countries) unemployment benefits paid by the state. That is ❹ which / why today people are expected to contribute to the common good when they are productive adults and, in exchange, get an education when they are young and support when they are sick, unemployed or old. The exact nature of these expectations varies according to the cultural norms, institutions, policies and laws that define the rights and obligations of individuals relative to ❺ it / those of the wider society, but the existence of such expectations is universal.

*morph 변하다

Throughout history, people have pooled their resources to varying degrees in order to enjoy the benefits and manage the risks that come from ❶ _____ (live) in large groups. These benefits include specialisation of labour, mutual defence and shared infrastructure. As groups get larger — from family to village to major cities and nation states — the mutual obligations become more abstract and are often ❷ _____ (mediate) through institutions and the political process. Rather than 'owe' something to our family or community, our obligations morph into solidarity with fellow citizens or duty to our country. In the past, for example, families educated their children, cared for the sick and unemployed at home; today most rely on schools, medical facilities and (in some countries) unemployment benefits ❸ _____ (pay) by the state. That is why today people are expected ❹ _____ (contribute) to the common good when they are productive adults and, in exchange, get an education when they are young and support when they are sick, unemployed or old. The exact nature of these expectations ❺ _____ (vary) according to the cultural norms, institutions, policies and laws that define the rights and obligations of individuals relative to those of the wider society, but the existence of such expectations is universal.

*morph 변하다

Throughout history, people have pooled their resources ❶ _____ _____ _____ (다양한 정도로) in order to enjoy the benefits and manage the risks that come from living in large groups. These benefits include specialisation of labour, mutual defence and shared infrastructure. As groups get larger — from family to village to major cities and nation states — the mutual obligations become more abstract and are often mediated through institutions and the political process. Rather than 'owe' something to our family or community, our obligations morph into ❷ _____ _____ _____ _____ (동료 시민들과의 연대) or duty to our country. In the past, for example, families educated their children, cared for the sick and unemployed at home; today most rely on schools, medical facilities and (in some countries) unemployment benefits paid by the state. That is why today people ❸ _____ _____ _____ (~으로 예상되다) contribute to the common good when they are productive adults and, in exchange, get an education when they are young and support when they are sick, unemployed or old. The exact nature of these expectations varies according to the cultural norms, institutions, policies and laws that define the rights and obligations of individuals relative to those of the wider society, but the ❹ _____ _____ _____ _____ _____ _____ (그런 기대의 존재는 보편적이다).

*morph 변하다

278

❶ Natural processes in soils in many places on the planet concentrate potentially hazardous geologic materials. ❷ The health hazards posed by these elements depend on the way humans interact with their environment, which can vary significantly among different cultures. ❸ Primitive cultures that live off the land are more susceptible to hazards and diseases associated with contaminated or poor water quality, toxic elements in plants harvested from contaminated soils, and insect- and animal-borne diseases associated with unsanitary environments. ❹ In contrast, more developed societies are more likely to be affected by air pollution, different types of water pollution, and indoor pollution such as radon exposure. ❺ Some diseases reflect a complex interaction among humans, insects or animals, climate, and the natural concentration of certain elements in the environment. ❻ For instance, schistosomiasis-bearing snails are abundant in parts of Africa and Asia where natural waters are rich in calcium derived from soils, but in similar climates in South America, the condition is rare. ❼ It is thought that this difference is because the waters in South America are calcium-poor, whereas disease-bearing snails need calcium to build their shells.

*schistosomiasis 주혈흡충증

❶ 지구상의 많은 장소에 있는 토양에서의 자연적 과정은 잠재적으로 위험한 지질 물질을 한 곳에 집중시킨다. ❷ 이러한 요소들에 의해 제기되는 건강 위험은 인간이 자신의 환경과 상호 작용하는 방식에 따라 좌우되는데, 이것은 서로 다른 문화 사이에서 상당히 다양할 수 있다. ❸ 토지에 의지해서 살아 나가는 낙후한 문화는 오염되거나 열악한 수질과 관련된 위험과 질병, 오염된 토양에서 수확한 식물의 독성 요소, 그리고 비위생적인 환경과 관련된 곤충과 동물을 매개로 하는 질병에 더 취약하다. ❹ 이와는 대조적으로, 더 선진화된 사회는 대기 오염, 갖가지 종류의 수질 오염, 그리고 라돈 노출과 같은 실내 오염에 의해 영향을 받을 가능성이 더 크다. ❺ 어떤 질병들은 인간, 곤충 혹은 동물, 기후, 그리고 환경에 있는 특정 요소들의 자연적인 집중 사이의 복잡한 상호 작용을 반영한다. ❻ 예를 들어, 주혈흡충증을 유발하는 달팽이는 토양에서 나오는 칼슘이 자연 수역에 풍부한 아프리카와 아시아 일부 지역에 많지만, 남아메리카의 비슷한 기후 지역에서는 그 질병이 희귀하다. ❼ 이러한 차이는 질병을 유발하는 달팽이가 껍질을 만들기 위해 칼슘을 필요로 하는 반면, 남아메리카의 수역은 칼슘이 부족하기 때문이라고 여겨진다.

• Word Test

1	susceptible to	_____	11	비위생적인	_____
2	exposure	_____	12	(~에서) 나오다	_____
3	soil	_____	13	상호 작용	_____
4	toxic	_____	14	껍질	_____
5	hazardous	_____	15	지질의	_____
6	vary	_____	16	오염시키다	_____
7	rich	_____	17	잠재적으로	_____
8	element	_____	18	집중, 농도	_____
9	condition	_____	19	낙후한, 원시적인	_____
10	climate	_____	20	수역, 영해	_____

Natural processes in soils in many places on the planet concentrate potentially hazardous geologic materials. The health hazards posed by these elements depend on the way humans interact with their environment, ❶ that / which can vary significantly among different cultures. ❷ Primary / Primitive cultures that live off the land are more susceptible to hazards and diseases associated with contaminated or poor water quality, toxic elements in plants harvested from contaminated soils, and insect- and animal-borne ❸ deceases / diseases associated with unsanitary environments. In contrast, more developed societies are more likely to be affected by air pollution, different types of water pollution, and indoor pollution such as radon exposure. Some diseases reflect a complex interaction among humans, insects or animals, climate, and the natural concentration of certain elements in the environment. For instance, schistosomiasis-bearing snails are abundant in parts of Africa and Asia ❹ which / where natural waters are rich in calcium derived from soils, but in similar climates in South America, the condition is rare. It is thought ❺ that / which this difference is because the waters in South America are calcium-poor, whereas disease-bearing snails need calcium to build their shells.

*schistosomiasis 주혈흡충증

Natural processes in soils in many places on the planet concentrate potentially hazardous geologic materials. The health hazards ❶ _____ (pose) by these elements depend on the way humans interact with their environment, which can vary significantly among different cultures. Primitive cultures that live off the land ❷ _____ (be) more susceptible to hazards and diseases associated with contaminated or poor water quality, toxic elements in plants ❸ _____ (harvest) from contaminated soils, and insect- and animal-borne diseases associated with unsanitary environments. In contrast, more ❹ _____ (develope) societies are more likely to be affected by air pollution, different types of water pollution, and indoor pollution such as radon exposure. Some diseases reflect a complex interaction among humans, insects or animals, climate, and the natural concentration of certain elements in the environment. For instance, schistosomiasis-bearing snails are abundant in parts of Africa and Asia where natural waters are rich in calcium derived from soils, but in similar climates in South America, the condition is rare. It is thought that this difference is because the waters in South America ❺ _____ (be) calcium-poor, whereas disease-bearing snails need calcium to build their shells.

*schistosomiasis 주혈흡충증

Natural processes in soils in many places on the planet concentrate ❶ _____ _____ (잠재적으로 위험한) geologic materials. The health hazards posed by these elements depend on the way humans interact with their environment, which can vary significantly among different cultures. Primitive cultures that ❷ _____ _____ _____ _____ (토지에 의지해서 살다) are more susceptible to hazards and diseases associated with contaminated or poor water quality, toxic elements in plants harvested from contaminated soils, and insect- and animal-borne diseases associated with unsanitary environments. ❸ _____ _____ (대조적으로), more developed societies are more likely to be affected by air pollution, different types of water pollution, and indoor pollution such as radon exposure. Some diseases reflect a ❹ _____ _____ (복잡한 상호작용) among humans, insects or animals, climate, and the natural concentration of certain elements in the environment. For instance, schistosomiasis-bearing snails are abundant in parts of Africa and Asia where natural waters are rich in calcium ❺ _____ _____ _____ (토양에서 나오는), but in similar climates in South America, the condition is rare. It is thought that this difference is because the waters in South America are calcium-poor, whereas disease-bearing snails need calcium to build their shells.

*schistosomiasis 주혈흡충증

❶ The United States lags in some sustainability indicators because it has already developed unsustainably. ❷ It's easier to start from scratch and develop sustainably than to fix all of the mistakes we've made. ❸ It will be very expensive to rebuild our infrastructure to be more sustainable. ❹ Leapfrogging allows developing countries to skip the implementation of old, inefficient technologies used in developed countries, thereby avoiding the environmentally harmful stages of economic development. ❺ For example, developing countries can build mobile phone networks that require much less raw materials and construction than land lines. ❻ They can deploy decentralized renewable energy systems such as PV panels, while in the United States we will be stuck for some time with old coal-fired power plants and an aging, inefficient electrical grid. ❼ U.S. cities and suburbs were built when energy was cheap and there were no concerns about global warming, so we are forced to drive great distances to accomplish everyday tasks. ❽ Developing countries can concentrate development in cities where people can live more sustainably, and preserve green space around the cities.

*leapfrogging 립프로깅(등 짚고 뛰어넘기) **deploy 효율적으로 사용하다, 배치하다
***PV (photovoltaic) 광발전의

❶ 미국은 이미 지속 가능하지 않게 발전했기 때문에 일부 지속 가능성 지표에서 뒤처져 있다. ❷ 우리가 저지른 모든 실수를 고치는 것보다 처음부터 시작해서 지속 가능하게 발전하는 것이 더 쉽다. ❸ 우리의 사회 기반 시설을 더 지속 가능하게 다시 짓는 것은 매우 비용이 많이 들 것이다. ❹ 립프로깅을 통해 개발 도상국은 선진국에서 사용되었던 낡고 비효율적인 기술의 이행을 건너뛸 수 있게 되고, 그렇게 함으로써 환경에 해로운 경제 개발 단계를 피할 수 있게 된다. ❺ 예를 들어, 개발 도상국은 지상 통신선보다 훨씬 더 적은 원자재와 공사를 필요로 하는 휴대 전화 네트워크를 구축할 수 있다. ❻ 이 국가들은 광발전 패널과 같은 분산형 재생 에너지 시스템을 효율적으로 사용할 수 있는 반면, 미국에서 우리는 석탄을 때는 오래된 발전소와 노후화되고 있는 비효율적 전력망에서 한동안 꼼짝 못 할 것이다. ❼ 미국의 도시와 교외는 에너지가 저렴하고 지구 온난화에 대한 우려가 없을 때 세워졌기 때문에, 우리는 일상의 과업을 수행하기 위해 어쩔 수 없이 먼 거리를 운전할 수밖에 없다. ❽ 개발 도상국들은 사람들이 더 지속 가능하게 살 수 있는 도시에 개발을 집중시켜 도시 주변의 녹지 공간을 보존할 수 있다.

Word List

□ lag 뒤처지다 □ sustainability 지속 가능성 □ indicator 지표 □ from scratch 처음부터 □ infrastructure 사회 기반 시설
□ skip 건너뛰다 □ implementation 이행, 실행 □ harmful 해로운 □ raw material 원자재 □ land line 지상 통신선
□ decentralized 분산형의, 분권화된 □ renewable 재생 가능한 □ stuck 꼼짝 못 하는, 빠져나갈 수가 없는 □ coal-fired 석탄을 때는
□ aging 노후화되고 있는 □ electrical grid 전력망 □ suburb 교외

• **Word Test**

1	infrastructure	9	건너뛰다
2	electrical grid	10	교외
3	indicator	11	노후화되고 있는
4	stuck	12	재생 가능한
5	lag	13	처음부터
6	decentralized	14	지상 통신선
7	raw material	15	지속 가능성
8	implementation	16	해로운

• 유형 1 네모 안에서 옳은 어법·어휘를 고르시오.

The United States lags in some sustainability indicators because it has already developed unsustainably. It's easier to start from scratch and develop sustainably ❶ as / than to fix all of the mistakes we've made. It will be very ❷ cheap / expensive to rebuild our infrastructure to be more sustainable. Leapfrogging allows developing countries to skip the implementation of old, ❸ efficient / inefficient technologies used in developed countries, thereby avoiding the environmentally harmful stages of economic development. For example, developing countries can build mobile phone networks that require ❹ much / very less raw materials and construction than land lines. They can deploy decentralized renewable energy systems such as PV panels, ❺ when / while in the United States we will be stuck for some time with old coal-fired power plants and an aging, inefficient electrical grid. U.S. cities and suburbs were built when energy was cheap and there were no concerns about global warming, so we are forced to drive great distances to accomplish everyday tasks. Developing countries can concentrate development in cities ❻ where / which people can live more sustainably, and preserve green space around the cities.

*leapfrogging 립프로깅(등 짚고 뛰어넘기) **deploy 효율적으로 사용하다, 배치하다 ***PV (photovoltaic) 광발전의

• 유형 2 괄호 안의 동사를 알맞은 형태로 쓰시오.

The United States lags in some sustainability indicators because it has already developed unsustainably. It's easier to start from scratch and develop sustainably than ❶ _____ (fix) all of the mistakes we've made. It will be very expensive ❷ _____ (rebuild) our infrastructure to be more sustainable. Leapfrogging allows developing countries ❸ _____ (skip) the implementation of old, inefficient technologies used in developed countries, thereby avoiding the environmentally harmful stages of economic development. For example, ❹ _____ (develop) countries can build mobile phone networks that require much less raw materials and construction than land lines. They can deploy decentralized renewable energy systems such as PV panels, while in the United States we will be stuck for some time with old coal-fired power plants and an aging, inefficient electrical grid. U.S. cities and suburbs were built when energy was cheap and there ❺ _____ (be) no concerns about global warming, so we are forced ❻ _____ (drive) great distances to accomplish everyday tasks. Developing countries can concentrate development in cities where people can live more sustainably, and preserve green space around the cities.

*leapfrogging 립프로깅(등 짚고 뛰어넘기) **deploy 효율적으로 사용하다, 배치하다 ***PV (photovoltaic) 광발전의

The United States lags in some sustainability indicators because it has already developed unsustainably. It's easier to start ❶ _____ _____ (처음부터) and develop sustainably than to fix all of the mistakes we've made. It will be very expensive to rebuild our infrastructure to be more sustainable. Leapfrogging allows developing countries to skip the implementation of old, inefficient technologies used in developed countries, thereby avoiding the environmentally harmful ❷ _____ _____ _____ _____ (경제 개발의 단계들). For example, developing countries can build mobile phone networks that require much less raw materials and construction than land lines. They can deploy ❸ _____ _____ _____ _____ (분산형 재생 에너지 시스템들) such as PV panels, while in the United States we will ❹ _____ _____ (꼼짝 못하다) for some time with old coal-fired power plants and an aging, ❺ _____ _____ _____ (비효율적인 전력망). U.S. cities and suburbs were built when energy was cheap and there were no concerns about global warming, so we ❻ _____ _____ _____ (어쩔 수 없이 ~하다) drive great distances to accomplish everyday tasks. Developing countries can concentrate development in cities where people can live more sustainably, and preserve green space around the cities.

*leapfrogging 립프로깅(등 짚고 뛰어넘기) **deploy 효율적으로 사용하다, 배치하다 ***PV (photovoltaic) 광발전의

❶ The debate about how to understand social life has ancient roots and can be traced at least as far back as Plato, who analyzed the differing worldviews of poetry and philosophy (which was at the time an approximation of science). ❷ Echoes of this debate are still heard today in the endless dialogue between the humanities and the sciences regarding how the world may best be comprehended. ❸ Some thinkers argue that the internal states of humans cannot be examined scientifically at all and must instead be understood nonscientifically via intuitive, interpretive, or even religious methods. ❹ Even some scientists devoted to strong empiricism adopt this view. ❺ B. F. Skinner, the leading twentieth-century advocate of behaviorism and the author of *Walden Two*, famously reasoned that internal mental states are unobservable and unquantifiable subjectivities and thus belong outside the range of objective scientific scrutiny, in contrast to observable (individual and collective) behaviors. ❻ Some philosophers and theologians continue to embrace the age-old dualistic separation between the material world and the mental world. ❼ The underlying claim is that we cannot use science to fully understand the soul or even feelings, thoughts, morals, or beauty. ❽ While the issue of the soul is a matter unto itself, feelings, thoughts, morals, and even beauty — and their evolutionary origins — are, in fact, yielding increasingly to science in the twenty-first century with techniques as diverse as MRI imaging and behavior genetics.

*empiricism 경험주의 **scrutiny 면밀한 조사[검증] ***theologian 신학자

❶ 사회생활을 이해하는 방법에 관한 논쟁은 고대에 기원을 두고 있고 적어도 플라톤까지 멀리 거슬러 올라갈 수 있는데, 플라톤은 시와 철학(그 당시에는 과학에 가까운 것이었다)의 서로 다른 세계관을 분석했다. ❷ 세계가 어떻게 가장 잘 이해될 수 있을지에 관한 인문학과 과학 사이의 끝없는 의견 교환에서 이 논쟁의 반향은 오늘날에도 여전히 들리고 있다. ❸ 몇몇 사상가들은 인간의 내적 상태는 과학적으로 결코 조사될 수 없으며 대신에 직관적, 해석적, 혹은 심지어는 종교적 방법을 통해 비과학적으로 이해되어야 한다고 주장한다. ❹ 심지어 강력한 경험주의에 전념했던 몇몇 과학자들조차 이 견해를 받아들인다. ❺ 20세기의 선도적인 행동주의 옹호자이자 *Walden Two*의 저자인 B.F. Skinner는 내적 정신 상태는 관찰할 수 있는 (개인적이고 집단적인) 행동과는 대조적으로 관찰이 불가능하고 수량화할 수 없는 주관성을 지닌 것이며, 따라서 객관적인 과학적 면밀한 조사의 범위 밖에 속한다고 추론한 것으로 유명했다. ❻ 몇몇 철학자들과 신학자들은 물질세계와 정신세계 간의 아주 오래된 이원론적 분리를 계속해서 받아들인다. ❼ 근본적인 주장은 우리가 과학을 이용해 영혼 혹은 심지어 감정, 사고, 도덕, 혹은 미를 완전히 이해할 수 없다는 것이다. ❽ 영혼의 문제는 그 자신만이 갖고 있는 문제이지만, 감정, 사고, 도덕, 그리고 미조차, 그리고 그것들의 진화적 기원도 사실상 자기 공명 영상법을 이용한 영상과 행동 유전학과 같은 다양한 기술을 가진 21세기 과학에 점점 더 굴복하고 있다.

Word List

□ trace (역사적으로) 거슬러 올라가다 □ approximation 가까운 것, 근사치 □ echo 반향 □ humanities 인문학
□ comprehend 이해하다 □ internal 내적인, 내부의 □ intuitive 직관적인 □ interpretive 해석적인 □ devote 전념하다, 바치다
□ adopt 받아들이다, 채택하다 □ advocate 옹호자, 지지자 □ behaviorism 행동주의 □ reason 추론하다
□ unquantifiable 수량화할 수 없는 □ subjectivity 주관성 □ objective 객관적인 □ dualistic 이원론의 □ separation 분리
□ underlying 근본적인, 근원적인 □ soul 영혼 □ moral 도덕 □ unto itself 그 자신만이 갖고 있는 □ evolutionary 진화의
□ yield 굴복하다, 양보하다 □ MRI (magnetic resonance imaging) 자기 공명 영상법 □ genetics 유전학

1	intuitive	13	객관적인
2	trace	14	내적인, 내부의
3	underlying	15	받아들이다, 채택하다
4	echo	16	영혼
5	reason	17	분리
6	dualistic	18	유전학
7	yield	19	수량화할 수 없는
8	advocate	20	행동주의
9	moral	21	해석적인
10	subjectivity	22	인문학
11	devote	23	가까운 것, 근사치
12	comprehend	24	진화의

• 유형 1 네모 안에서 옳은 어법·어휘를 고르시오.

The debate about how to understand social life has ancient roots and can be traced at least as far back as Plato, ❶ who / whom analyzed the differing worldviews of poetry and philosophy (which was at the time an approximation of science). Echoes of this debate are still heard today in the endless dialogue between the humanities and the sciences regarding how the world may best be comprehended. Some thinkers argue ❷ that / which the internal states of humans cannot be examined scientifically at all and must instead be understood nonscientifically via intuitive, interpretive, or even religious methods. Even some scientists devoted to strong empiricism ❸ adapt / adopt this view. B. F. Skinner, the leading twentieth-century advocate of behaviorism and the author of *Walden Two*, famously reasoned ❹ that / which internal mental states are unobservable and unquantifiable subjectivities and thus belong ❺ inside / outside the range of objective scientific scrutiny, in contrast to observable (individual and collective) behaviors. Some philosophers and theologians continue to embrace the age-old dualistic separation between the material world ❻ and / or the mental world. The underlying claim is ❼ that / which we cannot use science to fully understand the soul or even feelings, thoughts, morals, or beauty. While the issue of the soul is a matter unto itself, feelings, thoughts, morals, and even beauty — and their evolutionary origins — are, in fact, yielding increasingly to science in the twenty-first century with techniques as diverse as MRI imaging and behavior genetics.

*empiricism 경험주의 **scrutiny 면밀한 조사[검증] ***theologian 신학자

The debate about how ❶ _____ (understand) social life has ancient roots and can be traced at least as far back as Plato, who ❷ _____ (analyze) the differing worldviews of poetry and philosophy (which was at the time an approximation of science). Echoes of this debate are still heard today in the endless dialogue between the humanities and the sciences regarding how the world may best be comprehended. Some thinkers argue that the internal states of humans cannot be examined scientifically at all and must instead ❸ _____ (understand) nonscientifically via intuitive, interpretive, or even religious methods. Even some scientists ❹ _____ (devote) to strong empiricism adopt this view. B. F. Skinner, the leading twentieth-century advocate of behaviorism and the author of *Walden Two*, famously reasoned that internal mental states are unobservable and unquantifiable subjectivities and thus belong outside the range of objective scientific scrutiny, in contrast to observable (individual and collective) behaviors. Some philosophers and theologians continue ❺ _____ (embrace) the age-old dualistic separation between the material world and the mental world. The underlying claim is that we cannot use science to fully ❻ _____ (understand) the soul or even feelings, thoughts, morals, or beauty. While the issue of the soul is a matter unto itself, feelings, thoughts, morals, and even beauty — and their evolutionary origins — are, in fact, ❼ _____ (yield) increasingly to science in the twenty-first century with techniques as diverse as MRI imaging and behavior genetics.

*empiricism 경험주의 **scrutiny 면밀한 조사[검증] ***theologian 신학자

The debate about how to understand social life has ancient roots and can be traced at least as far back as Plato, who analyzed the differing worldviews of poetry and philosophy (which was at the time an approximation of science). ❶ _____ _____ _____ _____ (이 논쟁의 반향들) are still heard today in the endless dialogue between the humanities and the sciences regarding how the world may best be comprehended. Some thinkers argue that the internal states of humans cannot be examined scientifically at all and must instead be understood nonscientifically via intuitive, interpretive, or even ❷ _____ _____ (종교적인 방법들). Even some scientists ❸ _____ _____ (~에 전념했던) strong empiricism adopt this view. B. F. Skinner, the leading twentieth-century advocate of behaviorism and the author of *Walden Two*, famously reasoned that internal mental states are unobservable and unquantifiable subjectivities and thus belong outside the range of objective scientific scrutiny, in contrast to observable (individual and collective) behaviors. Some philosophers and theologians continue to embrace the age-old ❹ _____ _____ (이원론적 분리) between the material world and the mental world. The ❺ _____ _____ (근본적인 주장) is that we cannot use science to fully understand the soul or even feelings, thoughts, morals, or beauty. While the issue of the soul is a matter unto itself, feelings, thoughts, morals, and even beauty — and their evolutionary origins — are, in fact, yielding increasingly to science in the twenty-first century with techniques as diverse as MRI imaging and behavior genetics.

*empiricism 경험주의 **scrutiny 면밀한 조사[검증] ***theologian 신학자

❶ Emily was the youngest of three daughters in a family of great soccer players. ❷ Her mother played soccer in high school and college, as did her two older sisters. ❸ Following in their footsteps, Emily began her freshman year of high school as a star player on the soccer team. ❹ Soon, however, Emily's coach noticed that while Emily had great skills, she just didn't show the kind of passion for the game she had seen in other great players she'd coached. ❺ She noticed something else about Emily: she had an unusually graceful stride as she ran up and down the field. ❻ And to her coach's surprise, Emily seemed to absolutely love the running drills that the other players hated during practice. ❼ One day, the coach called her over after practice. ❽ "Emily, why do you play soccer?" she asked. ❾ Somewhat puzzled, she responded, "Because everyone in my family plays soccer. ❿ And because I'm really good at it." ⓫ Then the coach asked, "But do you love it?" ⓬ With a somewhat dejected look, she shook her head. ⓭ "Playing soccer was really fun when I was younger. ⓮ But now it feels like something I *have* to do. ⓯ Everyone expects me to be like my mom and sisters. ⓰ I don't want to let them down." ⓱ That's when she realized that her job as Emily's coach had, in an important way, just begun. ⓲ Rather than continue to try to get her to fit in as a soccer player, the coach asked Emily about her true interests. ⓳ She wasn't surprised to learn that Emily had a passion for running. ⓴ Running was effortless for her, she said. ㉑ When running long distances, she felt relaxed and free from all the worries and cares in her life. ㉒ After several more conversations with Emily and then an initially difficult discussion with her family, the coach and her family allowed Emily to leave the soccer team and switch to running track for the spring semester. ㉓ By her junior year, Emily was the number one runner on the girls' cross-country team, and as a senior, she led the team to the state finals. ㉔ While she lost one of her better players, the coach knew she'd done the right thing. ㉕ In the process, she helped Emily find her true passion.

*stride 달리는 모습, 보폭 *dejected 낙심한, 기가 죽은

❶ Emily는 훌륭한 축구 선수들로 이루어진 가족에서 세 딸 중 막내였다. ❷ 그녀의 어머니는 고등학교와 대학에서 축구를 했고, 그녀의 두 언니도 그러했다. ❸ 그들의 선례를 따라, Emily는 축구팀의 스타 선수로서 고등학교 1학년을 시작했다. ❹ 하지만 곧, Emily의 코치는 Emily가 훌륭한 기술을 가지고 있지만, 자신이 코치했던 다른 훌륭한 선수들에게서 보았던 게임에 대한 열정을 전혀 보여 주지 않는다는 것을 알아챘다. ❺ 그녀는 Emily에 대해 또 다른 것을 알아챘는데, 그것은, 그녀는 경기장을 이리저리 뛰어다닐 때 몹시 우아한 모습으로 달린다는 것이었다. ❻ 그리고 그녀의 코치에게 놀랍게도, Emily는 다른 선수들이 연습하는 동안 싫어했던 달리기 훈련을 굉장히 좋아하는 것처럼 보였다. ❼ 어느 날, 코치는 연습 후에 그녀를 불렀다. ❽ "Emily, 넌 왜 축구를 하니?"라고 그녀가 물었다. ❾ 그녀는 다소 어리둥절하며 "우리 가족 모두가 축구를 하기 때문입니다. ❿ 그리고 제가 그것을 정말 잘하기 때문입니다."라고 대답했다. ⓫ 그러자 코치가 물었다. "하지만 너는 그것을 좋아하니?" ⓬ 그녀는 다소 낙심한 표정으로 고개를 저었다. ⓭ "제가 더 어렸을 때는 축구를 하는 것이 정말 재미있었습니다. ⓮ 하지만 이제는 그것이 제가 해야만 '하는' 일처럼 느껴집니다. ⓯ 모든 사람이 제가 어머니나 언니들처럼 되기를 기대합니다. ⓰ 저는 그들을 실망시키고 싶지 않습니다." ⓱ 그때 그녀는 Emily의 코치로서의 자신의 역할이 중요한 면에서 이제 막 시작되었음을 깨달았다. ⓲ 코치는 그녀가 축구 선수로서 적응하게 하려고 계속 노력하기보다 Emily의 진정한 관심사에 관해 물었다. ⓳ 그녀는 Emily가 달리기에 열정이 있다는 것을 알고 놀라지 않았다. ⓴ 달리기가 그녀에게는 수월하다고 그녀는 말했다. ㉑ 장거리 달리기를 할 때, 그녀는 편안하고 삶의 모든 걱정과 염려로부터 해방된 느낌이었다. ㉒ Emily와 몇 번 더 대화를 나누고, 이후 그녀의 가족과 처음에는 어려웠던 논의 후에, 코치와 그녀의 가족은 Emily가 봄 학기에 축구팀을 떠나 트랙 달리기로 옮기는 것을 허락했다. ㉓ 3학년이었을 때 Emily는 여자 크로스컨트리 팀에서 최고의 주자가 되었고, 마지막 학년 때 그녀는 팀을 주 결승전으로 이끌었다. ㉔ 비록 우수한 선수 중 한 명을 잃었지만, 코치는 자신이 옳은 일을 했다는 것을 알고 있었다. ㉕ 그 과정에서 그녀는 Emily가 자신의 진정한 열정을 찾도록 도와주었다.

Word
List

□ follow in one's footsteps ~의 선례를 따르다 □ freshman 1학년, 신입생 □ notice 알아차리다 □ passion 열정
□ unusually 몹시, 대단히 □ graceful 우아한, 품위 있는 □ to one's surprise ~에게 놀랍게도 □ drill 훈련
□ puzzled 어리둥절한, 당혹스러운 □ let ~ down ~을 실망시키다 □ fit in (~에) 적응하다 □ interest 관심사, 흥미 □ relaxed 편안한
□ care 염려, 돌봄, 주의 □ initially 처음에 □ switch 옮기다, 바꾸다

• Word Test

1	puzzled	_____	9	1학년, 신입생	_____
2	to one's surprise	_____	10	열정	_____
3	relaxed	_____	11	관심사, 흥미	_____
4	notice	_____	12	옮기다, 바꾸다	_____
5	graceful	_____	13	~을 실망시키다	_____
6	fit in	_____	14	염려, 돌봄, 주의	_____
7	unusually	_____	15	훈련	_____
8	initially	_____	16	~의 선례를 따르다	_____

• 유형 1 네모 안에서 옳은 어법·어휘를 고르시오.

Emily was ❶ the younger / the youngest of three daughters in a family of great soccer players. Her mother played soccer in high school and college, as did her two older sisters. Following in their footsteps, Emily began her freshman year of high school as a star player on the soccer team. Soon, however, Emily's coach noticed that ❷ while / when Emily had great skills, she just didn't show the kind of passion for the game she ❸ saw / had seen in other great players she'd coached. She noticed something else about Emily: she had an unusually graceful stride as she ran up and down the field. And to her coach's surprise, Emily seemed to absolutely love the running drills ❹ what / that the other players hated during practice. One day, the coach called her over after practice. "Emily, why do you play soccer?" she asked. Somewhat puzzled, she responded, "Because everyone in my family plays soccer. And because I'm really good at it." Then the coach asked, "But do you love it?" With a somewhat dejected look, she ❺ nodded / shook her head. "Playing soccer was really fun when I was younger. But now it feels like something I *have* to do. Everyone expects me to be like my mom and sisters. I don't want to let them down." That's ❻ when / where she realized that her job as Emily's coach had, in an important way, just begun. Rather than continue to try to get her ❼ fit / to fit in as a soccer player, the coach asked Emily about her true interests. She wasn't surprised to learn that Emily had a passion for running. Running was effortless for her, she said. When running long distances, she felt relaxed and free from all the worries and cares in her life. After several more conversations with Emily and then an initially difficult discussion with her family, the coach and her family allowed Emily to leave the soccer team and switch to running track for the spring semester. By her junior year, Emily was the number one runner on the girls' cross-country team, and as a senior, she led the team to the state finals. While she lost one of her better players, the coach knew she'd done the right thing. In the process, she helped Emily ❽ find / finding her true passion.

*stride 달리는 모습, 보폭 *dejected 낙심한, 기가 죽은

Emily was the youngest of three daughters in a family of great soccer players. Her mother played soccer in high school and college, as did her two older sisters. ❶ _____ (Follow) in their footsteps, Emily began her freshman year of high school as a star player on the soccer team. Soon, however, Emily's coach noticed that while Emily had great skills, she just didn't show the kind of passion for the game she had seen in other great players she'd coached. She noticed something else about Emily: she had an unusually graceful stride as she ran up and down the field. And to her coach's surprise, Emily seemed to absolutely ❷ _____ (love) the running drills that the other players hated during practice. One day, the coach called her over after practice. "Emily, why do you play soccer?" she asked. Somewhat puzzled, she responded, "Because everyone in my family ❸ _____ (play) soccer. And because I'm really good at it." Then the coach asked, "But do you love it?" With a somewhat dejected look, she shook her head. "Playing soccer was really fun when I was younger. But now it feels like something I *have* to do. Everyone expects me ❹ _____ (be) like my mom and sisters. I don't want to let them down." That's when she realized that her job as Emily's coach had, in an important way, just begun. Rather than continue to try ❺ _____ (get) her to fit in as a soccer player, the coach asked Emily about her true interests. She wasn't surprised to learn that Emily had a passion for running. Running was effortless for her, she said. When ❻ _____ (run) long distances, she felt ❼ _____ (relax) and free from all the worries and cares in her life. After several more conversations with Emily and then an initially difficult discussion with her family, the coach and her family allowed Emily ❽ _____ (leave) the soccer team and switch to running track for the spring semester. By her junior year, Emily was the number one runner on the girls' cross-country team, and as a senior, she led the team to the state finals. While she lost one of her better players, the coach knew she'd done the right thing. In the process, she helped Emily find her true passion.

*stride 달리는 모습, 보폭 *dejected 낙심한, 기가 죽은

Emily was ❶ _____ _____ _____ _____ _____ (세 명의 딸들 중에 막내) in a family of great soccer players. Her mother played soccer in high school and college, as did her two older sisters. Following in their footsteps, Emily began her freshman year of high school as a star player on the soccer team. Soon, however, Emily's coach noticed that while Emily had great skills, she just didn't show the kind of passion for the game she had seen in other great players she'd coached. She noticed something else about Emily: she had an unusually graceful stride as she ran up and down the field. And to her coach's surprise, Emily ❷ _____ _____ _____ _____ (굉장히 좋아하는 것처럼 보였다) the running drills that the other players hated during practice. One day, the coach called her over after practice. "Emily, why do you play soccer?" she asked. ❸ _____ _____ (다소 어리둥절하며), she responded, "Because everyone in my family plays soccer. And because I'm really good at it." Then the coach asked, "But do you love it?" With a somewhat dejected look, she ❹ _____ _____ _____ (그녀의 고개를 가로저었다). "Playing soccer was really fun when I was younger. But now it feels like something I *have* to do. Everyone expects me to be like my mom and sisters. I don't want to ❺ _____ _____ _____ (그들을 실망시키다)." That's when she realized that her job as Emily's coach had, in an important way, just begun. Rather than continue to try to get her to ❻ _____ _____ (적응하다) as a soccer player, the coach asked Emily about her true interests. She wasn't surprised to learn that Emily had a passion for running. Running was effortless for her, she said. When running long distances, she felt relaxed and free from all the worries and cares in her life. After several more conversations with Emily and then an initially difficult discussion with her family, the coach and her family allowed Emily to leave the soccer team and switch to running track for the spring semester. By her junior year, Emily was the number one runner on the girls' cross-country team, and as a senior, she led the team to the state finals. While she lost one of her better players, the coach knew she'd done the right thing. ❼ _____ _____ _____ (그 과정에서), she helped Emily find her true passion.

*stride 달리는 모습, 보폭   *dejected 낙심한, 기가 죽은

01 Test 2 1번

글의 흐름으로 보아, 주어진 문장이 들어가기에 가장 적절한 곳은?

> With the year coming to a close, make 2024 your year to leave the ordinary behind and venture into extraordinary adventures.

Do you enjoy water activities on rivers? (①) Enter the 2024 River Lottery for the chance to be awarded river permits for access to rafting, kayaking, and paddling on some of the most scenic and exciting waterways in the country. (②) The permit lottery process is used for popular destinations and activities. (③) It helps manage the large volume of interest and ensures an enhanced experience on the river. (④) You can submit your application through the Lotteries page on our website or through the "Lotteries" section in the publicwaters.net mobile app. (⑤) Don't miss this opportunity to enjoy various water activities on the most beautiful rivers in the country.

02 Test 2 2번

주어진 글 다음에 이어질 글의 순서로 가장 적절한 것은?

> I pitched my tent in the dark and the pouring rain, hoping I'd scrambled far enough up the slope to be out of the range of flash floods.

(A) Instead, I decided at the last minute to throw my camping gear into a backpack, and head out to explore a remote corner of the Southern California desert. It never occurred to me to prepare for a storm!

(B) Crawling inside was like entering a washing machine on spin cycle — wind dashed against the wet fabric inches from my up-turned face, spraying me with a fine mist. As my sleeping bag slowly soaked through, tiredness slowly overcame me.

(C) As my eyelids began to feel heavy, I began to second-guess my choice of activities for the spring break holiday. I could have joined friends on a fishing trip, partaking in the sort of beery camaraderie that is more or less expected of college students during the final term of their final year.

*camaraderie 우정, 동지애

① (A) – (C) – (B)
② (B) – (A) – (C)
③ (B) – (C) – (A)
④ (C) – (A) – (B)
⑤ (C) – (B) – (A)

03 Test 2 3번

다음 글의 제목으로 가장 적절한 것은?

You help other people understand you by creating a secure arena for communication — on their terms. Then the listener can use his energy to understand rather than to consciously or unconsciously react to your manner of communicating. All of us need to develop our flexibility and so be able to vary our style of communication, adapting it when we speak to people who are different from us. Here we find another truth: No matter what method you choose to communicate with, as an individual, you will always be in the minority. No matter what kind of behavior you have, the majority of people around you will function differently from you. You can't just base your method of communication on your own preferences. Flexibility and the ability to interpret other people's needs is what characterizes a good communicator. Knowing and understanding another person's style of behavior and method of communication will result in more educated guesses about how a person may possibly react in various situations. This understanding will also dramatically increase your ability to get through to the person in question.

① The Challenge of Speaking Your Mind
② The Importance of Communication Skills in Everyday Life
③ Adjust Your Communication Style to the Listener's Terms
④ What Communication Barriers Are and How to Overcome Them
⑤ Lack of Communication: How It Affects Us and Ways to Improve It

04 Test 2 4번

다음 글의 밑줄 친 부분 중, 문맥상 낱말의 쓰임이 적절하지 않은 것은?

Seven-tenths of the earth's surface lies under water. The great world ocean represents the vast majority of our planet's ① habitable space, and we depend on it in ways we may never have paused to reflect on. It is home to perhaps two million species, the bulk of them still unknown to science. But despite all that, anyone keeping track of contemporary politics could be ② forgiven for wondering if the ocean is there at all. Remarkably few of our governments contain Ministries for the Ocean (South Korea and Canada are rare exceptions), and our politicians ③ rarely campaign on ocean-related issues (though fishing did emerge as an issue during the 2016 Brexit referendum). The ocean is governed by a complex body of international law which the average citizen probably knows ④ little about. Going about your busy life, you might be tempted to file the ocean, its politics and the Law of the Sea in a mental box along with gravity or the internet. Its immense size, and its permanence, might fool you into believing that the ocean is ⑤ susceptible to degradation.

*referendum 국민 투표

다음 빈칸에 들어갈 말로 가장 적절한 것은?

The nature of the task can matter more than the nature of the person. Most of us have heard the theory that we each have a preferred learning style, and the more we can use the one that fits, the more we'll remember. Unfortunately, virtually no evidence supports that theory. That doesn't mean that all approaches to studying are equally effective — it's just that the strategy that works best _____.
Similarly, different parts of our personalities can serve different types of goals. We act extraverted when we want to connect with others or seize an opportunity, and we become disciplined when we want to get something done or avoid mistakes. In one study, conscientiousness especially emerged when the things that needed to get done were difficult and urgent — even for people who were not especially organized and hardworking in general.

*extraverted 외향성의 **conscientiousness 성실성

① is variable and subject to fluctuation
② makes the most of the nature of the person
③ often depends more on the task than on the person
④ places the emphasis on harmony among the members
⑤ always considers all the personality types of the members

다음 글의 내용을 한 문장으로 요약하고자 한다. 빈칸 (A), (B)에 들어갈 말로 가장 적절한 것은?

Gifts are one way of defining a private world of love and ritual which is different from, and in contrast to, the impersonal capitalist economy. Yet gift giving in modern society is affected by that economy. This is most obvious in the case of monetary gifts, whose value lies entirely in the capacity to purchase things in the marketplace. However, it also exists in the case of gifts of things where those gifts consist, as most do, of things that are purchased. There is a problem here. In advanced capitalist societies, consumption by individuals of things that they do not produce is a massive activity. There is a danger here that purchased gifts will lose their significance in the face of all the things that individuals purchase for themselves. Gift giving separates a world of love and ritual from the capitalist economy, but in the end the two systems of meaning cannot be entirely separated because they are interconnected.

↓

The meaning of gift giving is strongly ___(A)___ by the capitalist economy because the private world of love and ritual clearly expressed by gift giving cannot be completely ___(B)___ it.

	(A)		(B)
①	denied	......	attached to
②	damaged	......	detached from
③	damaged	......	independent from
④	influenced	......	attached to
⑤	influenced	......	detached from

07 Test 2 7번

다음 글에서 전체 흐름과 관계 없는 문장은?

We argue that a transition towards more sustainable lifestyles will come from re-visioning the human place in nature, realizing ourselves not as separate, but as part of the whole, with a responsibility to nurture the biosphere forever. It will not occur because we are afraid of weathering the 'perfect storm' of unsustainability. ① Instead, we believe that what is needed is a deeper and more positive process: a re-visioning of the relationship between people and planet, undertaken in different ways by individuals, families, communities and nations. ② Such visions will show the potential for reconnection to bring about not just planetary health, but also personal well-being, joy, health and flourishing. ③ Specifically, the field of planetary health focuses on social movements that analyze and address the impacts of human disruptions to Earth's natural systems on human health and all life on Earth. ④ There is strong evidence to show that well-being — the 'good stuff' of life — is brought about by such reconnection of the human and the natural. ⑤ It is a vision to find a way towards reconciling our aspirations with the finitudes of our planet.

*biosphere 생물권 **reconcile 조화시키다 ***finitude 유한성

08 Test 2 8번

다음 도표의 내용과 일치하지 않는 것은?

What Makes a Story Shareable, per Journalists

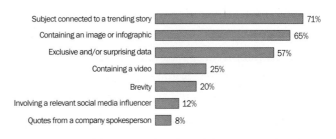

Based on a January 2022 survey of 2,547 journalists including full-time journalists, editorial writers, and bloggers

The above graph shows the 2022 survey results of more than 2,500 journalists on what they think makes a story shareable. ① According to the survey, the factor that was most likely to help make a story shareable was the subject, with 71% saying that a shareable piece is one in which the subject is connected to a trending story. ② Containing an image or infographic was the second most cited factor in making a story shareable at 65%, with exclusive and/or surprising data (57%) next on the list. ③ A quarter of the journalists who participated in the survey considered containing a video to be the factor that makes a story shareable. ④ Journalists who said that involving a relevant social media influencer makes a story shareable accounted for 12%. ⑤ The percentage of journalists who responded that including quotes from a company spokesperson is what makes a story shareable was more than half of the percentage of those who said that brevity will do the job.

다음 글의 밑줄 친 부분 중, 어법상 틀린 것은?

Art Tatum (born in 1909 in Toledo, Ohio and died in 1956 in Los Angeles), ① is considered one of the greatest jazz pianists of all time. His performances were praised for their technical skills and creativity, which ② set a new standard for jazz piano virtuosity. Tatum, who was visually impaired from childhood, displayed an early talent for music. Although Tatum gained some formal piano training at the Toledo School of Music, he was largely self-taught. At age 13, after ③ starting on the violin, Tatum concentrated on the piano and was soon performing on local radio programs. At 21 he moved to New York City, where he made his most impressive recordings during the 1930s and '40s. In 1943 he organized a trio with guitarist Tiny Grimes and bassist Slam Stewart, and he played ④ mostly in the trio format for the rest of his life. Although Tatum was admired by many jazz musicians, his popularity faded in the mid to late 1940s with the advent of bebop — a movement ⑤ what Tatum did not embrace.

*virtuosity (고도의) 기교   **bebop 비밥(재즈의 일종)

High-Frequency Facial Device에 관한 다음 안내문의 내용과 일치하는 것은?

High-Frequency Facial Device
User Manual

Effects and Benefits

This high-frequency facial device is an effective beauty instrument. Effects and benefits include: acceleration of blood circulation, reduction of wrinkles and tightening of the skin.

Usage Information

1. Do not use on one part of the skin for over 10 seconds.
2. Do not use if pregnant or intending to become pregnant.
3. For sensitive skin, place a piece of soft, light fabric on the skin before use to avoid excess stimulation.

Important Safety Information

1. Do not assemble or operate this device with wet hands.
2. Remove the power cable after use.
3. Do not insert any unnecessary items into the device's jack, as this may cause a fire. If anything gets into the jack, contact the manufacturer. Do not attempt to remove it yourself.

Warranty

Included with the purchase of this device is a 1-year limited warranty.

① 혈액 순환을 촉진하나 주름 감소에는 효과가 없다.
② 피부의 한 부분에 10초 넘게 사용할 수 있다.
③ 임신 중이거나 임신 계획이 있는 경우에도 사용가능하다.
④ 잭 안으로 무언가가 들어갈 경우 제조 업체로 연락해야 한다.
⑤ 구매 후 1년이 지나도 품질 보증을 받을 수 있다.

11 Test 2 11번

Eco-Friendly Turtle Spotting Boat Tour에 관한 다음 안내문의 내용과 일치하지 <u>않는</u> 것은?

Eco-Friendly Turtle Spotting Boat Tour

Our unique eco-friendly turtle spotting tour allows you to watch the sea turtles and to swim in the most extraordinary turquoise waters around Turtle Island.

The tour includes:
o a guided boat trip to Turtle Island
o two swim stops at caves and beaches, where you can relax and enjoy swimming with brightly-colored fish
o a snack bar on board with coffee, ice cream, sandwiches and snacks.

Available Days/Times: Tuesdays, Wednesdays, Fridays and Sunday mornings

Departure & Arrival: The pick-up time at your resort will be around 8:30 a.m. The drop-off time will be around 1:45 p.m., depending on the resort you are staying at.

Prices: €23 per adult, €17 per child
(* Lunch is not included. You're welcome to bring your own packed lunch, which can be consumed on board.)
Call us at 789-5213 to book this tour.

*turquoise 청록색(의)

① 수영할 수 있는 시간을 두 번 제공한다.
② 스낵바에서 간식과 음료를 제공한다.
③ 리조트 픽업 시간은 오전 8시 30분경이다.
④ 성인은 1인당 23유로의 요금을 낸다.
⑤ 점심 식사로 도시락을 제공한다.

12 Test 2 12번

다음 글의 밑줄 친 부분 중, 문맥상 낱말의 쓰임이 적절하지 <u>않은</u> 것은?

Conventional and nuclear weapons exist in physical space, where their deployments can be perceived and their capabilities at least roughly ① calculated. By contrast, cyber weapons derive an important part of their utility from their opacity; their disclosure may effectively ② degrade some of their capabilities. Their intrusions exploit previously undisclosed flaws in software, obtaining access to a network or system without the authorized user's permission or knowledge. In the case of distributed denial-of-service (DDoS) attacks (as on communication systems), a large number of seemingly valid information requests may be used to overwhelm systems and make them ③ available for their intended use. In such cases, the true sources of the attack may be ④ masked, making it difficult or impossible to determine (at least in the moment) who is attacking. Even one of the most famous instances of cyber-enabled industrial sabotage — the Stuxnet disruption of manufacturing control computers used in Iranian nuclear efforts — has not been formally ⑤ acknowledged by any government.

*deployment 배치 **opacity 불투명성 ***sabotage (고의적인) 파괴 행위

13 Test 2 13번

다음 글의 제목으로 가장 적절한 것은?

In cultures based on a rigid social hierarchy, with strict adherence to rules, visual art tends to adopt well-ordered, conventional, rigid and stereotypical forms. Ancient Egyptian art does not attempt to depict depth or distance, or the layout of objects in a scene. The same drawing system persisted for almost 3,000 years. Objects were arranged in a flat picture plane along lines drawn on walls. Objects and their parts were observed with great precision, but depicted in a way that conveyed shape in the most simplified manner. In human figures the torso was drawn from the front, but the head, waist and limbs were drawn in profile. Medieval artists revived the Egyptian reluctance to record the natural world faithfully, favouring instead depictions of the human form that conform to a strict formula involving expressionless, flat figures without individuality. This system of depiction was driven by religious concerns to avoid glorifying the attributes of individuals and their unique viewpoint on the world. There was little attempt to portray realistic depth, and the depicted stature of figures tended to reflect their social status.

*torso 몸통 **profile 옆모습 ***stature 신장

① What Makes Ancient Egyptian Art Great?
② Art as a Form of One's Unique Viewpoint
③ How Is Medieval Art Different from Ancient Egyptian Art?
④ Realistic Depth: A Distinctive Characteristic of Medieval Art
⑤ Medieval Art as a Faithful Successor to Ancient Egyptian Art

14 Test 2 14번

다음 글에서 전체 흐름과 관계 <u>없는</u> 문장은?

The search for publicity is, at heart, a quest for a shortcut to friendship. Yet real kindness is never available in a public sphere. It is the fruit of a few intimate and reciprocal connections. ① It cannot be won remotely or one-sidedly. ② If it is safety one seeks, one must definitively and immediately cease to strive to be known to people one doesn't know and concentrate instead on building up genuine bonds that can survive one's errors and endure for life. ③ Communication skills and stress management techniques are essential not only in managing conflict but also in building trust, bonds, and a sense of safety in the relationships. ④ Paradoxically and poignantly, it is most often the very anxious who feel a particular longing for the embrace of fame; but it is especially they (given their fragility) who should be warned away from its ultimately always revengeful arms. ⑤ Being entirely forgotten by the world is no curse or sign of failure; it is the very basis for a contented and safe life in which one swaps the prospect of followers and mean-minded detractors for the deeper satisfaction of true friends.

*reciprocal 호혜적인 **poignantly 통렬하게 ***detractor 비방하는 사람

15 Test 2 15번

다음 글의 요지로 가장 적절한 것은?

It is important to understand the distinction between indicators of market or nonmarket activity and well-defined measures of benefit or cost. While economic values are often related to human activities, simple indicators viewed in isolation (e.g., number of beach visits) can sometimes provide misleading perspectives. For example, simple activity indicators ignore values realized by nonusers or benefits related to unmeasured activities (i.e., activities not captured by the indicator in question). Because of these and other limitations, indicators of economic activity sometimes increase due to negative changes in the environment. Suppose that closing local beach A due to pollution causes more people to visit neighboring unpolluted beach B. An analyst looking solely at visitor numbers for beach B might incorrectly conclude that this represents a positive change at beach B, when in fact more visitors to beach B simply reflects the closure of beach A (a substitute beach). Using the appropriate economic frameworks for analysis can prevent such misleading conclusions. Simple behavioral (and other) indicators can sometimes provide a cost-effective means to help guide policy — but they can also contribute to incorrect conclusions if not paired with more comprehensive economic analysis.

① 단순 활동 지표에 근거할수록 경제적 예측의 정확성은 떨어지게 마련이다.
② 단순한 지표가 아닌 포괄적인 시각에서 경제적 현상을 바라볼 필요가 있다.
③ 단순 행동 지표를 활용하여 특정 경제 활동의 이익과 비용을 정확히 측정할 수 있다.
④ 적절한 경제 분석 틀을 사용하면 측정되지 않은 활동과 관련된 이익을 고려할 수 있다.
⑤ 방문자들의 행동 양식에 대한 고찰을 통해 특정 장소의 경제적 가치를 판단할 수 있다.

16 Test 2 16번

글의 흐름으로 보아, 주어진 문장이 들어가기에 가장 적절한 곳은?

Yet, those hidden photos are critically important to the process of image-making.

When you look at the photos of an expert like Malick Sidibé, you are looking at a small fraction of the portraits he chose to show his viewers. Photos with closed eyes, crooked clothing, unflattering expressions, or those with a poor exposure, were surely edited out and hidden from his audience. Street photographers like Joel Meyerowitz make thousands of photos that are never seen by fans. His discriminating eye chooses exactly what he wants his audience to see. (①) Any digital image that doesn't meet Meyerowitz's personal expectations is put in a folder that may never be opened again. (②) Most of the photographs anyone makes will likely end up in a digital junk heap on a forgotten hard drive. (③) The point is that photographers put a lot of creative energy, time, and expense into making photographs, most of which don't represent the quality the creator expects. (④) They represent the stages of failure and experimentation needed to arrive at a creative breakthrough. (⑤) Those *in-between* photos are part of the step-by-step development process that leads you from one successful image to the next.

*crooked 비뚤어진

17 Test 2 17번

주어진 글 다음에 이어질 글의 순서로 가장 적절한 것은?

Plans need to have a degree of flexibility under changing circumstances, but settling on clear deadlines and tasks helps to avoid opening up the problematic flexibility that can open the door to interpreting delay as something other than that.

(A) And yet, he finds himself putting it off. Gary thinks of himself as conscientious and certainly not someone who would fail to take care of himself. As he considers, at a certain point, whether to phone the doctor or put it off for a day, the lack of specificity in his intention affords him plenty of wiggle room for thinking that he is still going to make the appointment "soon."

(B) To take an illustration from the context of health, consider Gary, who has noticed that he has been getting colds quite frequently and thinks that it would be good to make an appointment with a primary care physician soon to get some medical tests done.

(C) In such contexts, by entering into his calendar a specific time for making the call and an automatic reminder, Gary can create an attentional structure that makes it difficult for him to overlook the fact that failing to make the call at the appointed time is a case of delay.

*conscientious 성실한 **wiggle room 여지

① (A) – (C) – (B)
② (B) – (A) – (C)
③ (B) – (C) – (A)
④ (C) – (A) – (B)
⑤ (C) – (B) – (A)

18 Test 2 18번

다음 글의 요지로 가장 적절한 것은?

Even the care we take for nature is motivated by a certain goal-oriented striving under the heading of "conservation." We treat nature as a scarce resource to be preserved for the health of the planet and the security of future generations. But rarely do we attempt to appreciate and protect nature for its own sake, as a source of wonder and awe in the face of which we stand to gain new perspectives on ourselves and the goals we pursue. When pressed to articulate why biodiversity matters, for example, we turn almost automatically to some account of how, when one species goes extinct, others will suffer, including, in the end, ourselves. We lack the vocabulary in which to understand the diversity of nature as intrinsically meaningful and as worthy of our engagement.

*articulate 분명히 설명하다 **intrinsically 본질적으로

① 자연의 다양성에 대한 이해를 돕는 어휘의 개발이 필요하다.
② 지속 가능한 발전을 위해 생물 다양성을 유지하는 것이 중요하다.
③ 우리는 자연의 본질을 이해하고 보호하려는 시도를 거의 하지 않는다.
④ 자연은 지구의 건강과 미래 세대의 안전을 위해 적극적으로 보존되어야 한다.
⑤ 목표 지향적인 노력으로 동기부여 되어 자연을 보존하는 것은 바람직하지 않다.

19

(A), (B), (C)의 각 네모 안에서 문맥에 맞는 낱말로 가장 적절한 것은?

Sport does not require architecture. A field can serve as the grounds for footraces, ball games, and other modes of sporting activity. Early football games in England famously, or perhaps notoriously, took place without (A) fixed / unfixed dimensions and across the townscape. Swimming, boating, surfing all can take place in natural, undesigned sites. The exterior wall of a building can be the backboard for handball or tennis. Nevertheless, the architecture of sport stretches back through history to the earliest exemplars of built forms. This is notable for both sporting and architectural reasons. In order to design and build sport architecture, there must already be in place some degree of codification of the rules of the game to be played and the minimum spatial dimensions necessary to (B) overtake / undertake that activity. Thus the precursor of our modern stadia, the stadion, was both the place where a footrace was run and a unit of measurement. Sport architecture therefore (C) emerges / disappears at the intersection of the codification of the rules of various games and means and mode of design and construction.

*codification 체계화, 집대성 **precursor 전신
***stadium 육상 경기장(*pl.* stadia)

	(A)		(B)		(C)
①	fixed	······	overtake	······	emerges
②	fixed	······	undertake	······	emerges
③	fixed	······	overtake	······	disappears
④	unfixed	······	undertake	······	disappears
⑤	unfixed	······	overtake	······	emerges

20

다음 빈칸에 들어갈 말로 가장 적절한 것은?

Great fairytales are full of suspense and emotional ups and downs, with the hero or heroine fighting and then overcoming antagonists and obstacles. The bigger the difficulties and the greater the suspense, the more interesting the story. Cinderella had no clothes, no carriage, and a rigid deadline. She had lost her shoe. Cinderella was sad, then happy because of the fairy Godmother, then scared again when the clock struck 12. An interviewee faced an employer going bankrupt, saw her superiors resign, and was left with a weak team. Both of these examples have a central character: Cinderella and the interviewee. Audiences generally _____.
In business storytelling, when there is no one central character, characters can be woven into the body of the story. For example: "In the next 10 minutes, I will show you five reasons why our business will disappear within five years if we continue with business as usual." Then, one reason could include the story of how a big customer was disappointed and another reason could include the story of how a group of salesmen felt helpless.

*antagonist (주인공과 대립되는) 적대역

① do not want to be kept in suspense while they listen to a story
② like the characters tailored to stimulate their own fantasy and imagination
③ understand and follow the logic of a story when it starts with conclusions first
④ pay attention to the fairytales with a happy ending, with the good getting rewarded
⑤ identify more with people and characters in the stories than with abstract discussion

21 Test 2 21번

주어진 글 다음에 이어질 글의 순서로 가장 적절한 것은?

> Throughout history, people have pooled their resources to varying degrees in order to enjoy the benefits and manage the risks that come from living in large groups.

(A) The exact nature of these expectations varies according to the cultural norms, institutions, policies and laws that define the rights and obligations of individuals relative to those of the wider society, but the existence of such expectations is universal.

(B) In the past, for example, families educated their children, cared for the sick and unemployed at home; today most rely on schools, medical facilities and (in some countries) unemployment benefits paid by the state. That is why today people are expected to contribute to the common good when they are productive adults and, in exchange, get an education when they are young and support when they are sick, unemployed or old.

(C) These benefits include specialisation of labour, mutual defence and shared infrastructure. As groups get larger — from family to village to major cities and nation states — the mutual obligations become more abstract and are often mediated through institutions and the political process. Rather than 'owe' something to our family or community, our obligations morph into solidarity with fellow citizens or duty to our country.

*morph 변하다

① (A) – (C) – (B)　　② (B) – (A) – (C)
③ (B) – (C) – (A)　　④ (C) – (A) – (B)
⑤ (C) – (B) – (A)

22 Test 2 22번

다음 빈칸에 들어갈 말로 가장 적절한 것은?

Natural processes in soils in many places on the planet concentrate potentially hazardous geologic materials. The health hazards posed by these elements depend on the way humans interact with their environment, which can vary significantly among different cultures. Primitive cultures that live off the land are more susceptible to hazards and diseases associated with contaminated or poor water quality, toxic elements in plants harvested from contaminated soils, and insect- and animal-borne diseases associated with unsanitary environments. In contrast, more developed societies are more likely to be affected by air pollution, different types of water pollution, and indoor pollution such as radon exposure. Some diseases reflect a complex interaction among humans, insects or animals, climate, and the natural _____ of certain elements in the environment. For instance, schistosomiasis-bearing snails are abundant in parts of Africa and Asia where natural waters are rich in calcium derived from soils, but in similar climates in South America, the condition is rare. It is thought that this difference is because the waters in South America are calcium-poor, whereas disease-bearing snails need calcium to build their shells.

*schistosomiasis 주혈흡충증

① decline　　　　② extinction
③ evolution　　　④ reproduction
⑤ concentration

23 Test 2 23번

다음 글의 주제로 가장 적절한 것은?

The United States lags in some sustainability indicators because it has already developed unsustainably. It's easier to start from scratch and develop sustainably than to fix all of the mistakes we've made. It will be very expensive to rebuild our infrastructure to be more sustainable. Leapfrogging allows developing countries to skip the implementation of old, inefficient technologies used in developed countries, thereby avoiding the environmentally harmful stages of economic development. For example, developing countries can build mobile phone networks that require much less raw materials and construction than land lines. They can deploy decentralized renewable energy systems such as PV panels, while in the United States we will be stuck for some time with old coal-fired power plants and an aging, inefficient electrical grid. U.S. cities and suburbs were built when energy was cheap and there were no concerns about global warming, so we are forced to drive great distances to accomplish everyday tasks. Developing countries can concentrate development in cities where people can live more sustainably, and preserve green space around the cities.

*leapfrogging 립프로깅(등 짚고 뛰어넘기)
**deploy 효율적으로 사용하다, 배치하다   ***PV (photovoltaic) 광발전의

① a universal approach to sustainable development
② the key role of the U.S. in environmentally sustainable development
③ a comparison of the current infrastructure status of many countries
④ a way of preventing the use of environmentally harmful technologies
⑤ the main reason the U.S. is being left behind in sustainable development

Test 2 24-25번

다음 글을 읽고 물음에 답하시오.

The debate about how to understand social life has ancient roots and can be traced at least as far back as Plato, who analyzed the differing worldviews of poetry and philosophy (which was at the time an approximation of science). Echoes of this debate are still heard today in the endless dialogue between the humanities and the sciences regarding how the world may best be comprehended. Some thinkers argue that the internal states of humans cannot be examined scientifically at all and must instead be understood nonscientifically via intuitive, interpretive, or even religious methods. Even some scientists devoted to strong empiricism

adopt this view. B. F. Skinner, the leading twentieth-century advocate of behaviorism and the author of *Walden Two*, famously reasoned that internal mental states are unobservable and unquantifiable subjectivities and thus belong outside the range of objective scientific scrutiny, in contrast to observable (individual and collective) behaviors. Some philosophers and theologians continue to embrace the age-old _____ between the material world and the mental world. The underlying claim is that we cannot use science to fully understand the soul or even feelings, thoughts, morals, or beauty. While the issue of the soul is a matter unto itself, feelings, thoughts, morals, and even beauty — and their evolutionary origins — are, in fact, yielding increasingly to science in the twenty-first century with techniques as diverse as MRI imaging and behavior genetics.

*empiricism 경험주의 **scrutiny 면밀한 조사[검증]
***theologian 신학자

24 윗글의 요지로 가장 적절한 것은?

① 현대 과학 기술은 건강한 정신 상태를 유지하는 데 도움을 준다.
② 정신세계와 물질세계의 조화를 추구하면서 살아가는 것이 중요하다.
③ 과학은 관찰 가능하고 수량화할 수 있는 대상만을 조사 대상으로 삼는다.
④ 인간의 정신세계는 과학적으로 조사될 수 없으며 비과학적으로 이해되어야 한다.
⑤ 직관적이고 해석적인 방법을 통해 인간의 정신세계를 이해하는 것은 불가능하다.

25 윗글의 빈칸에 들어갈 말로 가장 적절한 것은?

① potential conflict
② constant harmony
③ rational integration
④ dualistic separation
⑤ unnatural coexistence

다음 글을 읽고 물음에 답하시오.

Emily was the youngest of three daughters in a family of great soccer players. Her mother played soccer in high school and college, as did her two older sisters. Following in their footsteps, Emily began her freshman year of high school as a star player on the soccer team. Soon, however, Emily's coach noticed that while Emily had great skills, she just didn't show the kind of passion for the game she had seen in other great players she'd coached. She noticed something else about Emily: (a) she had an unusually graceful stride as she ran up and down the field.

And to her coach's surprise, Emily seemed to absolutely love the running drills that the other players hated during practice. One day, the coach called her over after practice. "Emily, why do (b) you play soccer?" she asked. Somewhat puzzled, she responded, "Because everyone in my family plays soccer. And because I'm really good at it." Then the coach asked, "But do you love it?"

With a somewhat dejected look, she shook her head. "Playing soccer was really fun when I was younger. But now it feels like something I *have* to do. Everyone expects (c) me to be like my mom and sisters. I don't want to let them down." That's when she realized that her job as Emily's coach had, in an important way, just begun. Rather than continue to try to get her to fit in as a soccer player, the coach asked Emily about her true interests. She wasn't surprised to learn that Emily had a passion for running. Running was effortless for (d) her, she said. When running long distances, she felt relaxed and free from all the worries and cares in her life.

After several more conversations with Emily and then an initially difficult discussion with her family, the coach and her family allowed Emily to leave the soccer team and switch to running track for the spring semester. By her junior year, Emily was the number one runner on the girls' cross-country team, and as a senior, she led the team to the state finals. While she lost one of (e) her better players, the coach knew she'd done the right thing. In the process, she _____.

*stride 달리는 모습, 보폭 *dejected 낙심한, 기가 죽은

26 밑줄 친 (a)~(e)중에서 가리키는 대상이 나머지 넷과 다른 것은?

① (a)　　　② (b)　　　③ (c)
④ (d)　　　⑤ (e)

27 윗글에 관한 내용으로 적절하지 않은 것은?

① Emily는 축구 선수들로 이루어진 가족 출신이었다.
② Emily는 축구팀의 스타 선수로서 고등학교 1학년을 시작했다.
③ Emily는 축구 연습 중 달리기 훈련을 굉장히 좋아하는 것처럼 보였다.
④ Emily의 코치는 Emily가 달리기에 열정이 있다는 것을 알고 놀랐다.
⑤ Emily는 3학년이었을 때 여자 크로스컨트리 팀에서 최고의 주자가 되었다.

28 다음 빈칸에 들어갈 말로 가장 적절한 것은?

① helped Emily find her true passion
② left the soccer team to join the running club
③ had a hard time persuading Emily's family
④ was disappointed at Emily's lack of enthusiasm
⑤ found a way to rebuild a relationship with Emily

29 Test 2 1번

(A), (B), (C)의 각 네모 안에서 어법에 맞는 표현으로 가장 적절한 것은?

Do you enjoy water activities on rivers? With the year (A) come / coming to a close, make 2024 your year to leave the ordinary behind and venture into extraordinary adventures. Enter the 2024 River Lottery for the chance to (B) award / be awarded river permits for access to rafting, kayaking, and paddling on some of the most scenic and exciting waterways in the country. The permit lottery process is used for popular destinations and activities. It helps (C) manage / managed the large volume of interest and ensures an enhanced experience on the river. You can submit your application through the Lotteries page on our website or through the "Lotteries" section in the publicwaters.net mobile app.

	(A)	(B)	(C)
①	come	award	manage
②	come	be awarded	managed
③	coming	award	manage
④	coming	be awarded	managed
⑤	coming	be awarded	manage

30 Test 2 2번

글의 흐름으로 보아, 주어진 문장이 들어가기에 가장 적절한 곳은?

As my eyelids began to feel heavy, I began to second-guess my choice of activities for the spring break holiday.

I pitched my tent in the dark and the pouring rain, hoping I'd scrambled far enough up the slope to be out of the range of flash floods. (①) Crawling inside was like entering a washing machine on spin cycle — wind dashed against the wet fabric inches from my up-turned face, spraying me with a fine mist. (②) As my sleeping bag slowly soaked through, tiredness slowly overcame me. (③) I could have joined friends on a fishing trip, partaking in the sort of beery camaraderie that is more or less expected of college students during the final term of their final year. (④) Instead, I decided at the last minute to throw my camping gear into a backpack, and head out to explore a remote corner of the Southern California desert. (⑤) It never occurred to me to prepare for a storm!

*camaraderie 우정, 동지애

31 Test 2 3번

다음 빈칸에 들어갈 말로 가장 적절한 것은?

You help other people understand you by creating a secure arena for communication — on their terms. Then the listener can use his energy to understand rather than to consciously or unconsciously react to your manner of communicating. All of us need to develop our flexibility and so be able to vary our style of communication, adapting it when we speak to people who are different from us. Here we find another truth: No matter what method you choose to communicate with, as an individual, you will always be in the minority. No matter what kind of behavior you have, the majority of people around you will function differently from you. You can't just base your method of communication on your own preferences. _____ _____ is what characterizes a good communicator. Knowing and understanding another person's style of behavior and method of communication will result in more educated guesses about how a person may possibly react in various situations. This understanding will also dramatically increase your ability to get through to the person in question.

① Winning the hearts of the audience members
② Using appropriate body language and facial expressions
③ Flexibility and the ability to interpret other people's needs
④ The skill to convey your points in a simple, concise manner
⑤ Authenticity and creating a comfortable atmosphere for listeners

32 Test 2 4번

다음 글의 요지로 가장 적절한 것은?

Seven-tenths of the earth's surface lies under water. The great world ocean represents the vast majority of our planet's habitable space, and we depend on it in ways we may never have paused to reflect on. It is home to perhaps two million species, the bulk of them still unknown to science. But despite all that, anyone keeping track of contemporary politics could be forgiven for wondering if the ocean is there at all. Remarkably few of our governments contain Ministries for the Ocean (South Korea and Canada are rare exceptions), and our politicians rarely campaign on ocean-related issues (though fishing did emerge as an issue during the 2016 Brexit referendum). The ocean is governed by a complex body of international law which the average citizen probably knows little about. Going about your busy life, you might be tempted to file the ocean, its politics and the Law of the Sea in a mental box along with gravity or the internet. Its immense size, and its permanence, might fool you into believing that the ocean is immune to degradation.

*referendum 국민 투표

① 해양 자원의 지속 가능한 이용 방식을 모색해야 한다.
② 해양 생태계를 있는 그대로 보존하기 위해 노력해야 한다.
③ 해양에 관한 복잡한 국제법의 통제와 규제를 완화해야 한다.
④ 해양의 중요성에도 불구하고 현대의 정치는 여전히 홀대하고 있다.
⑤ 해양의 거대한 크기와 영속성으로 인해 해양은 쉽게 황폐화되지 않는다.

33 Test 2 5번

다음 글에서 전체 흐름과 관계 없는 문장은?

The nature of the task can matter more than the nature of the person. Most of us have heard the theory that we each have a preferred learning style, and the more we can use the one that fits, the more we'll remember. Unfortunately, virtually no evidence supports that theory. ① That doesn't mean that all approaches to studying are equally effective — it's just that the strategy that works best often depends more on the task than on the person. ② Similarly, different parts of our personalities can serve different types of goals. ③ We act extraverted when we want to connect with others or seize an opportunity, and we become disciplined when we want to get something done or avoid mistakes. ④ That is, when acting extraverted, people report high levels of happiness, and this applies to both introverts and extraverts equally. ⑤ In one study, conscientiousness especially emerged when the things that needed to get done were difficult and urgent — even for people who were not especially organized and hardworking in general.

*extraverted 외향성의   **conscientiousness 성실성

34 Test 2 6번

다음 글의 밑줄 친 부분 중, 문맥상 낱말의 쓰임이 적절하지 않은 것은?

Gifts are one way of defining a private world of love and ritual which is ① different from, and in contrast to, the impersonal capitalist economy. Yet gift giving in modern society is ② affected by that economy. This is most obvious in the case of monetary gifts, whose value lies entirely in the capacity to purchase things in the marketplace. However, it also exists in the case of gifts of things where those gifts consist, as most do, of things that are purchased. There is a ③ problem here. In advanced capitalist societies, consumption by individuals of things that they do not produce is a massive activity. There is a danger here that purchased gifts will ④ lose their significance in the face of all the things that individuals purchase for themselves. Gift giving separates a world of love and ritual from the capitalist economy, but in the end the two systems of meaning cannot be entirely separated because they are ⑤ independent.

35 Test 2 7번

(A), (B), (C)의 각 네모 안에서 어법에 맞는 표현으로 가장 적절한 것은?

We argue that a transition towards more sustainable lifestyles will come from re-visioning the human place in nature, realizing (A) us / ourselves not as separate, but as part of the whole, with a responsibility to nurture the biosphere forever. It will not occur because we are afraid of weathering the 'perfect storm' of unsustainability. Instead, we believe that what is needed is a deeper and more positive process: a re-visioning of the relationship between people and planet, undertaken in different ways by individuals, families, communities and nations. Such visions will show the potential for reconnection to (B) bring / bringing about not just planetary health, but also personal well-being, joy, health and flourishing. There is strong evidence to show that well-being — the 'good stuff' of life — (C) is / being brought about by such reconnection of the human and the natural. It is a vision to find a way towards reconciling our aspirations with the finitudes of our planet.

*biosphere 생물권 **reconcile 조화시키다 ***finitude 유한성

	(A)	(B)	(C)
①	us	bring	is
②	ourselves	bring	being
③	ourselves	bring	is
④	ourselves	bringing	being
⑤	us	bringing	is

36 Test 2 9번

Art Tatum에 관한 다음 글의 내용과 일치하지 않는 것은?

Art Tatum (born in 1909 in Toledo, Ohio and died in 1956 in Los Angeles), is considered one of the greatest jazz pianists of all time. His performances were praised for their technical skills and creativity, which set a new standard for jazz piano virtuosity. Tatum, who was visually impaired from childhood, displayed an early talent for music. Although Tatum gained some formal piano training at the Toledo School of Music, he was largely self-taught. At age 13, after starting on the violin, Tatum concentrated on the piano and was soon performing on local radio programs. At 21 he moved to New York City, where he made his most impressive recordings during the 1930s and '40s. In 1943 he organized a trio with guitarist Tiny Grimes and bassist Slam Stewart, and he played mostly in the trio format for the rest of his life. Although Tatum was admired by many jazz musicians, his popularity faded in the mid to late 1940s with the advent of bebop — a movement that Tatum did not embrace.

*virtuosity (고도의) 기교 **bebop 비밥(재즈의 일종)

① 역사상 가장 유명한 재즈 피아니스트 중 한 명이다.
② 어린 시절부터 시각 장애가 있었지만 음악에 대한 조기 재능을 보였다.
③ 톨레도 음악학교에서 정식으로 피아노 교육을 어느 정도 받았다.
④ 21세에 뉴욕 시로 이주하여 자신의 가장 인상적인 음반을 만들었다.
⑤ 1940년대 중후반에 인기가 절정에 이르렀다.

37 Test 2 12번

주어진 글 다음에 이어질 글의 순서로 가장 적절한 것은?

Conventional and nuclear weapons exist in physical space, where their deployments can be perceived and their capabilities at least roughly calculated.

(A) Their intrusions exploit previously undisclosed flaws in software, obtaining access to a network or system without the authorized user's permission or knowledge. In the case of distributed denial-of-service (DDoS) attacks (as on communication systems), a large number of seemingly valid information requests may be used to overwhelm systems and make them unavailable for their intended use.

(B) By contrast, cyber weapons derive an important part of their utility from their opacity; their disclosure may effectively degrade some of their capabilities.

(C) In such cases, the true sources of the attack may be masked, making it difficult or impossible to determine (at least in the moment) who is attacking. Even one of the most famous instances of cyber-enabled industrial sabotage — the Stuxnet disruption of manufacturing control computers used in Iranian nuclear efforts — has not been formally acknowledged by any government.

*deployment 배치   **opacity 불투명성   *** sabotage (고의적인) 파괴 행위

① (A) – (C) – (B)
② (B) – (A) – (C)
③ (B) – (C) – (A)
④ (C) – (A) – (B)
⑤ (C) – (B) – (A)

38 Test 2 13번

다음 빈칸에 들어갈 말로 가장 적절한 것은?

In cultures based on a rigid social hierarchy, with strict adherence to rules, visual art tends to adopt well-ordered, conventional, rigid and stereotypical forms. Ancient Egyptian art does not attempt to depict depth or distance, or the layout of objects in a scene. The same drawing system persisted for almost 3,000 years. Objects were arranged in a flat picture plane along lines drawn on walls. Objects and their parts were observed with great precision, but depicted in a way that conveyed shape in the most simplified manner. In human figures the torso was drawn from the front, but the head, waist and limbs were drawn in profile. Medieval artists revived the Egyptian reluctance to record the natural world faithfully, favouring instead depictions of the human form that _____ involving expressionless, flat figures without individuality. This system of depiction was driven by religious concerns to avoid glorifying the attributes of individuals and their unique viewpoint on the world. There was little attempt to portray realistic depth, and the depicted stature of figures tended to reflect their social status.

*torso 몸통   **profile 옆모습   ***stature 신장

① refuse religious ideals
② conform to a strict formula
③ are reverse representations of reality
④ do not directly reveal humanity
⑤ are without regard to formality

다음 글의 제목으로 가장 적절한 것은?

The search for publicity is, at heart, a quest for a shortcut to friendship. Yet real kindness is never available in a public sphere. It is the fruit of a few intimate and reciprocal connections. It cannot be won remotely or one-sidedly. If it is safety one seeks, one must definitively and immediately cease to strive to be known to people one doesn't know and concentrate instead on building up genuine bonds that can survive one's errors and endure for life. Paradoxically and poignantly, it is most often the very anxious who feel a particular longing for the embrace of fame; but it is especially they (given their fragility) who should be warned away from its ultimately always revengeful arms. Being entirely forgotten by the world is no curse or sign of failure; it is the very basis for a contented and safe life in which one swaps the prospect of followers and mean-minded detractors for the deeper satisfaction of true friends.

*reciprocal 호혜적인 **poignantly 통렬하게 ***detractor 비방하는 사람

① What is Better, Fame or Friendship?
② A True Friend Does Not Care about What People Think
③ Genuine Satisfaction Comes from a Few True Friends
④ The Search for Publicity: A Shortcut to Real Friendship
⑤ *The More The Better* Is Always Right When It Comes to Friendship

글의 흐름으로 보아, 주어진 문장이 들어가기에 가장 적절한 곳은?

> An analyst looking solely at visitor numbers for beach B might incorrectly conclude that this represents a positive change at beach B, when in fact more visitors to beach B simply reflects the closure of beach A (a substitute beach).

It is important to understand the distinction between indicators of market or nonmarket activity and well-defined measures of benefit or cost. While economic values are often related to human activities, simple indicators viewed in isolation (e.g., number of beach visits) can sometimes provide misleading perspectives. (①) For example, simple activity indicators ignore values realized by nonusers or benefits related to unmeasured activities (i.e., activities not captured by the indicator in question). (②) Because of these and other limitations, indicators of economic activity sometimes increase due to negative changes in the environment. (③) Suppose that closing local beach A due to pollution causes more people to visit neighboring unpolluted beach B. (④) Using the appropriate economic frameworks for analysis can prevent such misleading conclusions. (⑤) Simple behavioral (and other) indicators can sometimes provide a cost-effective means to help guide policy — but they can also contribute to incorrect conclusions if not paired with more comprehensive economic analysis.

41 Test 2 16번

(A), (B), (C)의 각 네모 안에서 문맥에 맞는 낱말로 가장 적절한 것은?

When you look at the photos of an expert like Malick Sidibé, you are looking at a small (A) fraction / friction of the portraits he chose to show his viewers. Photos with closed eyes, crooked clothing, unflattering expressions, or those with a poor exposure, were surely edited out and hidden from his audience. Street photographers like Joel Meyerowitz make thousands of photos that are never seen by fans. His (B) discriminating / indiscriminate eye chooses exactly what he wants his audience to see. Any digital image that doesn't meet Meyerowitz's personal expectations is put in a folder that may never be opened again. Most of the photographs anyone makes will likely end up in a digital junk heap on a forgotten hard drive. The point is that photographers put a lot of creative energy, time, and expense into making photographs, most of which don't represent the quality the creator expects. Yet, those hidden photos are critically (C) important / unimportant to the process of image-making. They represent the stages of failure and experimentation needed to arrive at a creative breakthrough. Those *in-between* photos are part of the step-by-step development process that leads you from one successful image to the next.

*crooked 비뚤어진

	(A)	(B)	(C)
①	fraction	discriminating	important
②	friction	discriminating	important
③	fraction	discriminating	unimportant
④	friction	indiscriminate	unimportant
⑤	fraction	indiscriminate	unimportant

42 Test 2 17번

다음 글의 내용을 한 문장으로 요약하고자 한다. 빈칸 (A), (B)에 들어갈 말로 가장 적절한 것은?

Plans need to have a degree of flexibility under changing circumstances, but settling on clear deadlines and tasks helps to avoid opening up the problematic flexibility that can open the door to interpreting delay as something other than that. To take an illustration from the context of health, consider Gary, who has noticed that he has been getting colds quite frequently and thinks that it would be good to make an appointment with a primary care physician soon to get some medical tests done. And yet, he finds himself putting it off. Gary thinks of himself as conscientious and certainly not someone who would fail to take care of himself. As he considers, at a certain point, whether to phone the doctor or put it off for a day, the lack of specificity in his intention affords him plenty of wiggle room for thinking that he is still going to make the appointment "soon." In such contexts, by entering into his calendar a specific time for making the call and an automatic reminder, Gary can create an attentional structure that makes it difficult for him to overlook the fact that failing to make the call at the appointed time is a case of delay.

*conscientious 성실한 **wiggle room 여지

↓

By   (A)   structures that steer our attention toward tasks and away from distractions, we can resist the temptation to arbitrarily interpret our   (B)   .

	(A)	(B)
①	avoiding	laziness
②	avoiding	failure
③	designing	procrastination
④	designing	failure
⑤	prioritizing	procrastination

43 Test 2 18번

다음 빈칸에 들어갈 말로 가장 적절한 것은?

Even the care we take for nature is motivated by a certain goal-oriented striving under the heading of "conservation." We treat nature as a scarce resource to be preserved for the health of the planet and the security of future generations. But rarely do we attempt to _____ _____, as a source of wonder and awe in the face of which we stand to gain new perspectives on ourselves and the goals we pursue. When pressed to articulate why biodiversity matters, for example, we turn almost automatically to some account of how, when one species goes extinct, others will suffer, including, in the end, ourselves. We lack the vocabulary in which to understand the diversity of nature as intrinsically meaningful and as worthy of our engagement.

*articulate 분명히 설명하다　**intrinsically 본질적으로

① take full advantage of nature
② take pleasure in every aspect of nature
③ engage with nature out of pure curiosity
④ appreciate and protect nature for its own sake
⑤ think that nature might have something to teach us

44 Test 2 19번

다음 글에서 전체 흐름과 관계 <u>없는</u> 문장은?

Sport does not require architecture. A field can serve as the grounds for footraces, ball games, and other modes of sporting activity. Early football games in England famously, or perhaps notoriously, took place without fixed dimensions and across the townscape. Swimming, boating, surfing all can take place in natural, undesigned sites. The exterior wall of a building can be the backboard for handball or tennis. Nevertheless, the architecture of sport stretches back through history to the earliest exemplars of built forms. ① This is notable for both sporting and architectural reasons. ② In order to design and build sport architecture, there must already be in place some degree of codification of the rules of the game to be played and the minimum spatial dimensions necessary to undertake that activity. ③ The tensions involved in the globalization of sport and sport architecture increasingly revolve around how big money affects long-standing relationships between fans and the game. ④ Thus the precursor of our modern stadia, the stadion, was both the place where a footrace was run and a unit of measurement. ⑤ Sport architecture therefore emerges at the intersection of the codification of the rules of various games and means and mode of design and construction.

*codification 체계화, 집대성　**precursor 전신
***stadium 육상 경기장(*pl.* stadia)

45 [Test 2 20번]

다음 글의 제목으로 가장 적절한 것은?

Great fairytales are full of suspense and emotional ups and downs, with the hero or heroine fighting and then overcoming antagonists and obstacles. The bigger the difficulties and the greater the suspense, the more interesting the story. Cinderella had no clothes, no carriage, and a rigid deadline. She had lost her shoe. Cinderella was sad, then happy because of the fairy Godmother, then scared again when the clock struck 12. An interviewee faced an employer going bankrupt, saw her superiors resign, and was left with a weak team. Both of these examples have a central character: Cinderella and the interviewee. Audiences generally identify more with people and characters in the stories than with abstract discussion. In business storytelling, when there is no one central character, characters can be woven into the body of the story. For example: "In the next 10 minutes, I will show you five reasons why our business will disappear within five years if we continue with business as usual." Then, one reason could include the story of how a big customer was disappointed and another reason could include the story of how a group of salesmen felt helpless.

*antagonist (주인공과 대립되는) 적대역

① Common Characteristics of Great Fairytales
② Small Talk Can Bring the Business Setting to Life
③ Pros and Cons of Factual Storytelling in Business
④ Start with Your Own Story When Negotiating Something
⑤ Include Characters for Effective Business Storytelling

 고난도
46 [Test 2 21번]

다음 글의 밑줄 친 부분 중, 어법상 틀린 것은?

Throughout history, people have pooled their resources to varying degrees in order to enjoy the benefits and manage the risks ① that come from living in large groups. These benefits include specialisation of labour, mutual defence and shared infrastructure. As groups get larger — from family to village to major cities and nation states — the mutual obligations become more ② abstract and are often mediated through institutions and the political process. Rather than 'owe' something to our family or community, our obligations morph into solidarity with fellow citizens or duty to our country. In the past, for example, families educated their children, cared for the sick and unemployed at home; today most rely on schools, medical facilities and (in some countries) unemployment benefits ③ paid by the state. That is why today people are expected to contribute to the common good when they are productive adults and, in exchange, ④ get an education when they are young and support when they are sick, unemployed or old. The exact nature of these expectations varies according to the cultural norms, institutions, policies and laws that define the rights and obligations of individuals relative to ⑤ them of the wider society, but the existence of such expectations is universal.

*morph 변하다

주어진 글 다음에 이어질 글의 순서로 가장 적절한 것은?

> Natural processes in soils in many places on the planet concentrate potentially hazardous geologic materials.

(A) The health hazards posed by these elements depend on the way humans interact with their environment, which can vary significantly among different cultures. Primitive cultures that live off the land are more susceptible to hazards and diseases associated with contaminated or poor water quality, toxic elements in plants harvested from contaminated soils, and insect- and animal-borne diseases associated with unsanitary environments.

(B) For instance, schistosomiasis-bearing snails are abundant in parts of Africa and Asia where natural waters are rich in calcium derived from soils, but in similar climates in South America, the condition is rare. It is thought that this difference is because the waters in South America are calcium-poor, whereas disease-bearing snails need calcium to build their shells.

(C) In contrast, more developed societies are more likely to be affected by air pollution, different types of water pollution, and indoor pollution such as radon exposure. Some diseases reflect a complex interaction among humans, insects or animals, climate, and the natural concentration of certain elements in the environment.

*schistosomiasis 주혈흡충증

① (A) – (C) – (B)
② (B) – (A) – (C)
③ (B) – (C) – (A)
④ (C) – (A) – (B)
⑤ (C) – (B) – (A)

다음 빈칸 (A), (B)에 들어갈 말로 가장 적절한 것은?

The United States lags in some sustainability indicators because it has already developed unsustainably. It's easier to start from scratch and develop sustainably than to fix all of the mistakes we've made. It will be very expensive to rebuild our infrastructure to be more sustainable. Leapfrogging allows developing countries to skip the implementation of old, inefficient technologies used in developed countries, thereby ___(A)___ the environmentally harmful stages of economic development. For example, developing countries can build mobile phone networks that require much less raw materials and construction than land lines. They can deploy decentralized renewable energy systems such as PV panels, while in the United States we will be stuck for some time with old coal-fired power plants and an aging, inefficient electrical grid. U.S. cities and suburbs were built when energy was cheap and there were no concerns about global warming, so we are forced to drive great distances to accomplish everyday tasks. Developing countries can concentrate development in cities where people can live more sustainably, and ___(B)___ green space around the cities.

*leapfrogging 립프로깅(등 짚고 뛰어넘기)
**deploy 효율적으로 사용하다, 배치하다   ***PV (photovoltaic) 광발전의

	(A)		(B)
①	avoiding	......	reduce
②	avoiding	......	preserve
③	regulating	......	damage
④	regulating	......	preserve
⑤	undergoing	......	damage

Test 2 1번

Do you enjoy water activities on rivers? <u>한 해가 마무리되어 가는 데</u>, make 2024 your year to leave the ordinary behind and venture into extraordinary adventures. Enter the 2024 River Lottery for the chance to be awarded river permits for access to rafting, kayaking, and paddling on some of the most scenic and exciting waterways in the country. The permit lottery process is used for popular destinations and activities. It helps manage the large volume of interest and _____ an enhanced experience on the river. You can submit your application through the Lotteries page on our website or through the "Lotteries" section in the publicwaters.net mobile app.

49 윗글의 밑줄 친 우리말 의미와 일치하도록 보기 의 단어 를 활용하여 조건 에 맞게 영작하시오.

> 보기   come / the year / a close / to

> 조건   · with를 사용한 분사구문을 사용할 것
>   · 필요시 어형을 바꿔 쓸 것

→ _____ .

50 윗글의 빈칸에 들어갈 단어를 영영 뜻풀이를 참고하여 쓰 시오. (단, 주어진 글자로 시작하고, 필요시 어형을 바꿔 쓸 것)

> to make certain that something happens or is done

→ e_____

Test 2 2번

I pitched my tent in the dark and the pouring rain, hoping I'd scrambled far enough up the slope to be out of the range of flash floods. Crawling inside was like entering a washing machine on spin cycle — wind dashed against the wet fabric inches from my up-turned face, spraying me with a fine mist. As my sleeping bag slowly soaked through, tiredness slowly overcame me. As my eyelids began to feel heavy, I began to second-guess <u>my choice of activities</u> for the spring break holiday. I could have joined friends on a fishing trip, partaking in the sort of beery camaraderie that is more or less expected of college students during the final term of their final year. Instead, I decided at the last minute to throw my camping gear into a backpack, and head out to explore a remote corner of the Southern California desert. <u>폭풍우에 대비하는 것은 나에게 전혀 떠오르지 않았다!</u>

*camaraderie 우정, 동지애

51 윗글의 밑줄 친 **my choice of activities**가 가리키는 것을 본문에서 찾아 우리말로 쓰시오. (20자 내외)

→ _____

52 윗글의 밑줄 친 우리말 의미와 일치하도록 보기 의 단 어를 활용하여 조건 에 맞게 영작하시오.

> 보기   prepare for / occur to / a storm / never / me

> 조건   · 진주어-가주어 구문을 활용할 것
>   · 필요시 어형을 바꿔 쓸 것

→ _____

→ _____

You help other people understand you by creating a secure arena for communication — on their terms. Then the listener can use his energy to understand rather than to consciously or unconsciously react to your manner of communicating. All of us need to develop our flexibility and so be able to vary our style of communication, adapting it (A) <u>what</u> we speak to people who are different from us. Here we find another truth: No matter what method you choose to communicate with, as an individual, you will always be in the minority. 여러분이 어떤 행동을 하든지 간에, 여러분 주변의 대부분의 사람들은 여러분과 다르게 움직일 것이다. You can't just base your method of communication on your own preferences. Flexibility and the ability to interpret other people's needs is (B) <u>that</u> characterizes a good communicator. Knowing and understanding another person's style of behavior and method of communication will result in more educated guesses about (C) <u>why</u> a person may possibly react in various situations. This understanding will also dramatically increase your ability to get through to the person in question.

53 윗글의 밑줄 친 (A)~(C)를 어법상 알맞은 형태로 고쳐 쓰시오.

(A) what → _____

(B) that → _____

(C) why → _____

54 윗글의 밑줄 친 우리말 의미와 일치하도록 보기 의 단어를 순서대로 배열하여 문장을 완성하시오.

> 보기 matter / the majority / what / differently / no / from / function / kind / of

_____ _____ _____ _____

of behavior you have, _____ _____

_____ people around you will _____

_____ _____ you.

Seven-tenths of the earth's surface ① <u>lies</u> under water. The great world ocean represents the vast majority of our planet's habitable space, and we depend on it in ways we may never have paused to reflect on. It is home to perhaps two million species, the bulk of them still unknown to science. But despite all that, anyone keeping track of contemporary politics could ② <u>be forgiven</u> for wondering if the ocean is there at all. Remarkably few of our governments ③ <u>contains</u> Ministries for the Ocean (South Korea and Canada are rare exceptions), and our politicians rarely campaign on ocean-related issues (though fishing ④ <u>did</u> emerge as an issue during the 2016 Brexit referendum). The ocean is governed by a complex body of international law which the average citizen probably knows little about. Going about your busy life, you might be tempted ⑤ <u>filing</u> the ocean, its politics and the Law of the Sea in a mental box along with gravity or the internet. Its immense size, and its permanence, might fool you into believing that the ocean is immune to degradation.

*referendum 국민 투표

55 윗글의 밑줄 ①~⑤ 중, 어법상 틀린 것을 2개 찾아 그 번호를 쓰고 고쳐 쓰시오.

(1) _____ → _____

(2) _____ → _____

56 윗글에서 다음 질문에 대한 답을 찾아 우리말로 쓰시오. (30자 내외)

Q: What shows that governmental figures are apathetic towards the ocean?

A: _____

The nature of the task can matter more than the nature of the person. Most of us have heard the theory that we each have a preferred learning style, and ① the more we can use the one that fits, the more we'll remember. Unfortunately, virtually no evidence ② supports that theory. That doesn't mean that all approaches to studying are equally effective — it's just that the strategy that works best often depends more on the task that on the person. Similarly, different parts of our ③ personalities can serve different types of goals. We act extraverted when we want to connect with others or seize an opportunity, and we become ④ disciplined when we want to get something done or avoid mistakes. In one study, conscientiousness especially ⑤ vanished when the things that needed to get done were difficult and urgent — even for people who were not especially organized and hardworking in general.

*extraverted 외향성의 **conscientiousness 성실성

57 윗글의 밑줄 친 ①~⑤ 중 문맥상 어색한 것을 1개 찾아 그 번호를 쓰고 고쳐 쓰시오.

_____ → _____

고난도

58 윗글의 내용을 한 문장으로 요약하려고 한다. 빈칸 (A)와 (B)에 들어갈 알맞은 말을 본문에서 찾아 쓰시오.

No one learning style is the most effective approach to success, rather, the strategy that works best can depend more on the nature of the ___(A)___ than the nature of the person, and different parts of our character can ___(B)___ different types of goals.

(A) _____ (B) _____

Gifts are one way of defining a private world of love and ritual which is different from, and in contrast to, the impersonal capitalist economy. Yet gift giving in modern society is affected by that economy. This is most obvious in the case of monetary gifts, 그것의 가치는 전적으로 시장에서 물건을 구매하는 능력에 달려 있다. However, it also exists in the case of gifts of things where those gifts consist, as most do, of things that are purchased. There is a problem here. In advanced capitalist societies, _____ by individuals of things that they do not produce is a massive activity. There is a danger here that purchased gifts will lose their significance in the face of all the things that individuals purchase for themselves. Gift giving separates a world of love and ritual from the capitalist economy, but in the end the two systems of meaning cannot be entirely separated because they are interconnected.

59 윗글의 밑줄 친 우리말 의미와 일치하도록 보기 의 단어를 활용하여 조건 에 맞게 문장을 완성하시오.

| 보기 | things / lie / the capacity / entirely / value / purchase / in |

| 조건 | · 소유격 관계대명사를 사용할 것
· 필요시 어형을 바꿔 쓸 것
· 총 10단어로 쓸 것 |

_____

_____ in the marketplace

60 윗글의 빈칸에 들어갈 단어를 영영 뜻풀이를 참고하여 쓰시오. (단, 주어진 글자로 시작할 것)

the use of something such as fuel or energy, or the amount that people use

c_____

We argue that a transition towards more sustainable lifestyles will come from re-visioning the human place in nature, realizing ourselves not as separate, but as part of the whole, with a responsibility to _____ the biosphere forever. It will not occur because we are afraid of weathering the 'perfect storm' of unsustainability. Instead, we believe that what is needed is a deeper and more positive process: a re-visioning of the relationship between people and planet, undertaken in different ways by individuals, families, communities and nations. Such visions will show the potential for reconnection (A) to bring about not just planetary health, but also personal well-being, joy, health and flourishing. There is strong evidence to show that well-being — the 'good stuff' of life — is brought about by such reconnection of the human and the natural. It is a vision to find a way towards reconciling our aspirations with the finitudes of our planet.

*biosphere 생물권 **reconcile 조화시키다 ***finitude 유한성

61 윗글의 빈칸에 들어갈 단어를 영영 뜻풀이를 참고하여 쓰시오. (단, 주어진 글자로 시작할 것)

> to provide the care and attention necessary for a young child, animal, or plant to grow and develop

n_____

62 윗글의 밑줄 친 (A)를 as well as를 사용해 다시 쓰시오.

_____

_____

What Makes a Story Shareable, per Journalists

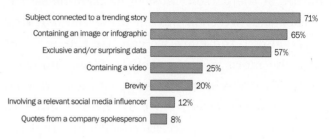

Based on a January 2022 survey of 2,547 journalists including full-time journalists, editorial writers, and bloggers

The above graph shows the 2022 survey results of more than 2,500 journalists on what they think makes a story shareable. 설문 조사에 따르면, 기사를 공유하기에 적절하게 만드는 것에 도움이 될 가능성이 많은 요인은 주제였는데, with 71% saying that a shareable piece is one in which the subject is connected to a trending story. Containing an image or infographic was the second most (A) citing factor in making a story shareable at 65%, with exclusive and/or surprising data (57%) next on the list. A quarter of the journalists who (B) participating in the survey considered containing a video to be the factor that makes a story shareable. Journalists who said that involving a relevant social media influencer makes a story shareable accounted for 12%. The percentage of journalists who responded that including quotes from a company spokesperson (C) are what makes a story shareable was less than half of the percentage of those who said that brevity will do the job.

63 윗글의 밑줄 친 우리말 의미와 일치하도록 보기 의 단어를 활용하여 조건 에 맞게 문장을 완성하시오.

> 보기 likely / was / the factor / the subject / most / help / to

> 조건 · 관계대명사 that을 사용할 것
> · 필요시 단어 중복 사용 가능

According to the survey, _____

_____

make a story shareable _____,

64 윗글의 밑줄 친 (A)~(C)를 어법상 알맞은 형태로 고쳐 쓰시오.

(A) citing → _____
(B) participating → _____
(C) are → _____

Test 2 9번

Art Tatum (born in 1909 in Toledo, Ohio and died in 1956 in Los Angeles), 역사상 가장 위대한 재즈 피아니스트 중 한 명으로 여겨진다. His performances were praised for their technical skills and creativity, which set a new ① standard for jazz piano virtuosity. Tatum, who was ② visually impaired from childhood, displayed an early talent for music. Although Tatum gained some formal piano training at the Toledo School of Music, he was largely ③ self-taught. At age 13, after starting on the violin, Tatum concentrated on the piano and was soon performing on local radio programs. At 21 he ④ moved to New York City, where he made his most impressive recordings during the 1930s and '40s. In 1943 he organized a trio with guitarist Tiny Grimes and bassist Slam Stewart, and he played mostly in the trio format for the rest of his life. Although Tatum was admired by many jazz musicians, his popularity ⑤ soared in the mid to late 1940s with the advent of bebop — a movement that Tatum did not embrace.

*virtuosity (고도의) 기교   **bebop 비밥(재즈의 일종)

65 윗글의 밑줄 친 ①~⑤ 중 문맥상 어색한 것을 1개 찾아 그 번호를 쓰고 고쳐 쓰시오.

_____ → _____

66 윗글의 밑줄 친 우리말 의미와 일치하도록 보기 의 단어를 활용하여 조건 에 맞게 영작하시오.

> 보기 jazz pianist / of all time / consider / great / one

> 조건 · 최상급 표현을 사용할 것
> · 필요시 어형을 바꿔 쓰고 단어를 추가할 것
> · 총 11단어로 쓸 것

_____

_____

High-Frequency Facial Device
User Manual

Effects and Benefits

This high-frequency facial device is an effective beauty instrument. Effects and benefits include: acceleration of blood circulation, reduction of _____ and tightening of the skin.

Usage Information

1. Do not use on one part of the skin for over 10 seconds.
2. Do not use if pregnant or intending to become pregnant.
3. For sensitive skin, place a piece of soft, light fabric on the skin before use to avoid excess stimulation.

Important Safety Information

1. 젖은 손으로 본 기기를 조립하거나 조작하지 마시오.
2. Remove the power cable after use.
3. Do not insert any unnecessary items into the device's jack, as this may cause a fire. If anything gets into the jack, contact the manufacturer. Do not attempt to remove it yourself.

Warranty

Included with the purchase of this device is a 1-year limited warranty.

67 윗글의 빈칸에 들어갈 단어를 영영 뜻풀이를 참고하여 쓰시오. (단, 주어진 글자로 시작하고, 필요시 어형을 바꿔 쓸 것)

> a line that appears on your skin when you get older

w_____

68 윗글의 밑줄 친 우리말 의미와 일치하도록 보기의 단어를 활용하여 조건에 맞게 영작하시오.

> **보기**   this device / operate / with / assemble / hands / or / wet

> **조건**   · 명령문을 사용할 것
> · 축약형은 쓰지 말 것

_____

_____

Eco-Friendly Turtle Spotting Boat Tour

저희의 독특한 거북이 찾기 친환경 보트 관광 여행을 통해 여러분은 바다거북을 보고 거북섬 주변의 가장 색다른 청록색 바다에서 수영할 수 있습니다.

The tour includes:

o a ① guided boat trip to Turtle Island
o two swim stops at caves and beaches, where you can relax and enjoy ② to swim with brightly-colored fish
o a snack bar on board with coffee, ice cream, sandwiches and snacks

Available Days/Times: Tuesdays, Wednesdays, Fridays and Sunday mornings

Departure & Arrival: The pick-up time at your resort will be around 8:30 a.m. The drop-off time will be around 1:45 p.m., ③ depending on the resort you are staying at.

Prices: €23 per adult, €17 per child
(* Lunch is not ④ including. You're welcome to bring your own packed lunch, ⑤ which can be consumed on board.)
Call us at 789-5213 to book this tour.

*turquoise 청록색(의)

69

윗글의 밑줄 친 ①~⑤ 중, 어법상 **틀린** 것을 2개 찾아 그 번호를 쓰고 고쳐 쓰시오.

(1) _____ → _____

(2) _____ → _____

70

윗글의 밑줄 친 우리말 의미와 일치하도록 〔보기〕의 단어를 활용하여 〔조건〕에 맞게 문장을 완성하시오.

〔보기〕 you / watch / swim / the most / and the sea turtles / in / extraordinary

〔조건〕
· 〈allow+목적어+to 부정사〉구문을 사용할 것
· 필요시 어형을 바꿔 쓸 것
· 총 14단어로 쓸 것

Our unique eco-friendly turtle spotting tour

_____

_____

turquoise waters around Turtle Island.

〔Test 2 12번〕

Conventional and nuclear weapons exist in physical space, where their deployments can be perceived and their capabilities at least roughly calculated. By contrast, cyber weapons derive an important part of their utility from their opacity; their _____ may effectively degrade some of their capabilities. Their intrusions exploit previously undisclosed flaws in software, obtaining access to a network or system without the authorized user's permission or knowledge. In the case of distributed denial-of-service (DDoS) attacks (as on communication systems), a large number of seemingly valid information requests may be used to overwhelm systems and make them unavailable for their intended use. In such cases, the true sources of the attack may be masked, (적어도 그 순간에는) 누가 공격하고 있는지 알아내는 것을 어렵거나 불가능하게 만든다, Even one of the most famous instances of cyber-enabled industrial sabotage — the Stuxnet disruption of manufacturing control computers used in Iranian nuclear efforts — has not been formally acknowledged by any government.

*deployment 배치 **opacity 불투명성 ***sabotage (고의적인) 파괴 행위

71

윗글의 빈칸에 들어갈 알맞은 말을 〔보기〕에서 골라 쓰시오.

〔보기〕 undisclose / permission / disclosure / secret / closure

→ _____ .

72

윗글의 밑줄 친 우리말 의미와 일치하도록 〔보기〕의 단어를 활용하여 〔조건〕에 맞게 문장을 완성하시오.

〔보기〕 determine / impossible / difficult / attack / or / is / it / to

〔조건〕
· 가목적어를 사용할 것
· 필요시 어형을 바꿔 쓸 것

making _____

_____ (at least at the

moment) who _____ .

In cultures based on a rigid social hierarchy, with strict adherence to rules, visual art tends to adopt well-ordered, conventional, rigid and stereotypical forms. Ancient Egyptian art does not attempt to depict depth or distance, or the layout of objects in a scene. The same drawing system persisted for almost 3,000 years. Objects were arranged in a flat picture plane along lines drawn on walls. Objects and their parts were observed with great precision, but depicted in a way that conveyed shape in the most simplified manner. In human figures the torso was drawn from the front, but the head, waist and limbs were drawn in profile. Medieval artists 자연계를 정확하게 표현하는 것에 대한 이집트인들의 꺼림을 부활시켰다, favouring instead depictions of the human form that conform to a strict formula involving expressionless, flat figures without individuality. This system of depiction was driven by religious concerns to avoid glorifying the attributes of individuals and their unique viewpoint on the world. There was little attempt to portray realistic depth, and the depicted stature of figures tended to reflect their social status.

*torso 몸통   **profile 옆모습   ***stature 신장

73 윗글의 밑줄 친 우리말 의미와 일치하도록 보기 의 단어를 배열하여 문장을 완성하시오.

> 보기   record / the Egyptian / the natural / world / reluctance / revived / to

_____

_____ faithfully

74 윗글에서 다음 질문에 대한 답을 찾아 우리말로 쓰시오. (20자 내외)

Q; What were the characteristics of human figures drawn by ancient Egyptian?

A: _____

The search for publicity is, at heart, a quest for a shortcut to friendship. Yet real kindness is never available in a public sphere. It is the fruit of a few intimate and reciprocal connections. It cannot be won remotely or one-sidedly. If it is safety one seeks, one must definitively and immediately cease to strive (A) to know to people one doesn't know and concentrate instead on building up genuine bonds that can survive one's errors and endure for life. Paradoxically and poignantly, it is most often the very anxious (B) what feel a particular longing for the embrace of fame; but it is especially they (given their fragility) who should be warned away from its ultimately always revengeful arms. Being entirely forgotten by the world is no curse or sign of failure; it is the very basis for a contented and safe life (C) which one swaps the prospect of followers and mean-minded detractors for the deeper satisfaction of true friends.

*reciprocal 호혜적인   **poignantly 통렬하게   *** detractor 비방하는 사람

75 윗글의 밑줄 친 it이 가리키는 것을 본문에서 찾아 쓰시오. (2단어)

_____

76 윗글의 밑줄 친 (A)~(C)를 어법상 알맞은 형태로 고쳐 쓰시오.

(A) to know → _____

(B) what   → _____

(C) which → _____

It is important to understand the distinction between indicators of market or nonmarket activity and well-defined measures of benefit or cost. While economic values are often related to human activities, simple indicators viewed in ① isolation (e.g., number of beach visits) can sometimes provide misleading perspectives. For example, simple activity indicators ② reflect values realized by nonusers or benefits related to unmeasured activities (i.e., activities not captured by the indicator in question). Because of these and other limitations, indicators of economic activity sometimes increase due to ③ negative changes in the environment. 오염으로 인해 지역의 A 해수욕장이 폐쇄되면 더 많은 사람이 이웃한 오염되지 않은 B 해수욕장을 방문하게 된다고 가정해 보라. An analyst looking solely at visitor numbers for beach B might incorrectly conclude that this represents a ④ positive change at beach B, when in fact more visitors to beach B simply reflects the closure of beach A (a substitute beach). Using the appropriate economic frameworks for analysis can prevent such ⑤ misleading conclusions. Simple behavioral (and other) indicators can sometimes provide a cost-effective means to help guide policy — but they can also contribute to incorrect conclusions if not paired with more comprehensive economic analysis.

77 윗글의 밑줄 친 ①~⑤ 중 문맥상 어색한 것을 1개 찾아 그 번호를 쓰고 고쳐 쓰시오.

_____ → _____

78 윗글의 밑줄 친 우리말 의미와 일치하도록 보기 의 단어를 순서대로 배열하여 문장을 완성하시오

> 보기 local beach A / due to / more people / causes / visit / closing / to / pollution

Suppose that _____

_____

neighboring unpolluted beach B.

When you look at the photos of an expert like Malick Sidibé, you are looking at a small fraction of the portraits he chose (A) showing his viewers. Photos with closed eyes, crooked clothing, unflattering expressions, or those with a poor exposure, were surely edited out and hidden from his audience. Street photographers like Joel Meyerowitz make thousands of photos that are never seen by fans. His discriminating eye chooses exactly what he wants his audience to see. Any digital image that doesn't meet Meyerowitz's personal expectations is put in a folder that may never be (B) opening again. Most of the photographs anyone makes will likely end up in a digital junk heap on a forgotten hard drive. The point is that photographers put a lot of creative energy, time, and expense into making photographs, most of which don't represent the quality the creator expects. Yet, those hidden photos are critically important to the process of image-making. They represent the stages of failure and experimentation (C) need to arrive at a creative breakthrough. Those (a) *in-between photos* are part of the step-by-step development process that leads you from one successful image to the next.

*crooked 비뚤어진

79 윗글의 밑줄 친 (A)~(C)를 어법상 알맞은 형태로 고쳐 쓰시오.

(A) showing → _____

(B) opening → _____

(C) need → _____

80 윗글의 밑줄 친 (a)와 의미가 같은 말을 본문에서 찾아 쓰시오. (2단어로 쓸 것)

Plans need to have a degree of flexibility under changing circumstances, but settling on clear deadlines and tasks helps to avoid opening up the problematic flexibility that 지연을 그것과는 다른 어떤 것으로 해석할 수 있는 길을 열어 줄 수 있는. To take an illustration from the context of health, consider Gary, who has noticed that he has been getting colds quite frequently and thinks that it would be good to make an appointment with a primary care physician soon to get some medical tests done. And yet, he finds himself putting it off. Gary thinks of himself as conscientious and certainly not someone who would fail to take care of himself. As he considers, at a certain point, whether to phone the doctor or put it off for a day, the lack of specificity in his intention affords him plenty of wiggle room for thinking that he is still going to make the appointment "soon." In such contexts, by entering into his calendar a specific time for making the call and an automatic reminder, Gary can create an attentional structure that makes it difficult for him to _____ the fact that failing to make the call at the appointed time is a case of delay.

*conscientious 성실한 **wiggle room 여지

81 윗글의 밑줄 친 우리말 의미와 일치하도록 **보기** 의 단어를 순서대로 배열하여 문장을 완성하시오. (단, 필요시 어형을 바꿔 쓸 것)

| 보기 | something / that / as / other / interpret / delay / than |

can open the door to _____

_____

82 윗글의 빈칸에 들어갈 단어를 영영 뜻풀이를 참고하여 쓰시오. (단, 주어진 글자로 시작할 것)

| to fail to notice or do something |

o _____

Even the care we take for nature is motivated by a certain goal-oriented striving under the heading of "conservation." We treat nature as a scarce resource to be preserved for the health of the planet and the security of future generations. But 우리는 자연 그 자체를 위해 자연의 진가를 인정하고 보호하려는 시도를 거의 하지 않는다, as a source of wonder and awe in the face of which we stand to gain new perspectives on ourselves and the goals we pursue. When pressed to articulate why biodiversity matters, for example, we turn almost automatically to some account of how, when one species goes extinct, others will suffer, including, in the end, ourselves. We lack the vocabulary in which to understand the diversity of nature as intrinsically meaningful and as worthy of our engagement.

*articulate 분명히 설명하다 **intrinsically 본질적으로

83 윗글의 밑줄 친 우리말 의미와 일치하도록 **보기** 의 단어를 활용하여 **조건** 에 맞게 문장을 완성하시오.

| 보기 | attempt / nature / protect / appreciate and / we |

| 조건 | · 〈to부정사〉를 사용할 것
· 필요시 단어를 추가할 것
· 총 8단어로 쓸 것 |

rarely _____

_____ for its own sake

84 윗글의 내용을 한 문장으로 요약하려고 한다. 빈칸에 공통으로 들어갈 알맞을 말을 본문에서 찾아 쓰시오.

| We regard _____ as a scarce resource to be preserved and try to make efforts towards such goal, but we rarely attempt to understand the _____, as a source of wonder and awe. |

_____

Sport does not require architecture. A field can serve as the grounds for footraces, ball games, and other modes of sporting activity. Early football games in England famously, or perhaps notoriously, took place without (A) fixing dimensions and across the townscape. Swimming, boating, surfing all can take place in natural, undesigned sites. The exterior wall of a building can be the backboard for handball or tennis. Nevertheless, the architecture of sport stretches back through history to the earliest exemplars of built forms. This is notable for both ____(a)____ and ____(b)____ reasons. In order to design and build sport architecture, there must already be in place some degree of codification of the rules of the game (B) to play and the minimum spatial dimensions necessary to undertake that activity. Thus the precursor of our modern stadia, the stadion, was both the place where a footrace was run and a unit of measurement. Sport architecture therefore emerges at the intersection of the codification of the rules of various games and (C) mean and mode of design and construction.

*codification 체계화, 집대성 **precursor 전신
***stadium 육상 경기장(*pl.* stadia)

85 윗글의 빈칸 (a)와 (b)에 알맞은 말을 본문에서 찾아 쓰시오. (필요시 어형을 바꿔 쓸 것)

(a) _____   (b) _____

86 윗글의 밑줄 친 (A)~(C)를 어법상 알맞은 형태로 고쳐 쓰시오.

(A) fixing → _____

(B) to play → _____

(C) mean → _____

Great fairytales are full of suspense and emotional ups and downs, with the hero or heroine fighting and then overcoming antagonists and obstacles. The bigger the difficulties and the greater the suspense, ① the more interesting the story. Cinderella had no clothes, no carriage, and a rigid deadline. She had lost her shoe. Cinderella was sad, then happy because of the fairy Godmother, then ② scaring again when the clock struck 12. An interviewee faced an employer going bankrupt, saw her superiors resign, and was left with a weak team. Both of these examples ③ has a central character: Cinderella and the interviewee. Audiences generally identify more with people and characters in the stories than with abstract discussion. In business storytelling, when there is no one central character, characters can be woven into the body of the story. For example: "In the next 10 minutes, I will show you ④ five reasons why our business will disappear within five years if we continue with business as usual." Then, one reason could include the story of how a big customer was ⑤ disappointing and another reason could include the story of how a group of salesmen felt helpless.

*antagonist (주인공과 대립되는) 적대역

87 윗글의 밑줄 친 ①~⑤ 중, 어법상 틀린 것을 3개 찾아 그 번호를 쓰고 고쳐 쓰시오.

(1) _____ → _____

(2) _____ → _____

(3) _____ → _____

88 윗글을 읽고 요지에 해당하는 문장을 찾아 쓰시오.

_____

_____

Throughout history, people have pooled their resources to varying degrees in order to enjoy the benefits and manage the risks that come from living in large groups. These benefits include specialisation of labour, mutual defence and shared infrastructure. As groups get larger — from family to village to major cities and nation states — the mutual obligations become more abstract and are often _____ through institutions and the political process. Rather than 'owe' something to our family or community, our obligations morph into solidarity with fellow citizens or duty to our country. In the past, for example, families educated their children, cared for the sick and unemployed at home; today most rely on schools, medical facilities and (in some countries) unemployment benefits paid by the state. That is why today people are expected to contribute to the common good when they are productive adults and, in exchange, get an education when they are young and support when they are sick, unemployed or old. The exact nature of these expectations varies according to the cultural norms, institutions, policies and laws that define the rights and obligations of individuals relative to those of the wider society, but the existence of such expectations is universal.

*morph 변하다

89 윗글의 빈칸에 들어갈 단어를 영영 뜻풀이를 참고하여 쓰시오. (단, 주어진 글자로 시작하고, 어형을 바꿔 쓸 것)

> to try to end a disagreement between two people or groups

m_____

90 윗글의 밑줄 친 such expectations의 내용을 본문에서 찾아 우리말로 쓰시오. (50자 내외)

_____

_____

Natural processes in soils in many places on the planet concentrate potentially hazardous geologic materials. The health hazards posed by these elements depend on (A) the way how humans interact with their environment, which can vary significantly among different cultures. Primitive cultures that live off the land are more susceptible to hazards and diseases associated with contaminated or poor water quality, toxic elements in plants harvested from contaminated soils, and insect- and animal-borne diseases associated with unsanitary environments. In contrast, 더 선진화된 사회는 대기 오염, 갖가지 종류의 수질 오염, 그리고 라돈 노출과 같은 실내 오염에 영향을 받을 가능성이 더 크다. Some diseases reflect a complex interaction among humans, insects or animals, climate, and the natural concentration of certain elements in the environment. For instance, schistosomiasis-bearing snails are abundant in parts of Africa and Asia (B) which natural waters are rich in calcium derived from soils, but in similar climates in South America, the condition is rare. It is thought that this difference is (C) because of the waters in South America are calcium-poor, whereas disease-bearing snails need calcium to build their shells.

*schistosomiasis 주혈흡충증

91 윗글의 밑줄 친 (A)~(C)를 어법상 알맞은 형태로 고쳐 쓰시오.

(A) the way how → _____

(B) which → _____

(C) because of → _____

92 윗글의 밑줄 친 우리말 의미와 일치하도록 보기 의 단어를 순서대로 배열하여 문장을 완성하시오.

> 보기 such / to / affected / likely / be / as / by / more / are

more developed societies _____ _____

_____ _____ _____ _____

_____ air pollution, different types of

water pollution, and indoor pollution _____

_____ radon exposure

Test 2 23번

The United States ① lags in some sustainability indicators because it has already developed unsustainably. It's easier to start from scratch and develop sustainably than to fix all of the mistakes we've made. It will be very expensive to rebuild our infrastructure to be more sustainable. Leapfrogging allows developing countries to ② skip the implementation of old, inefficient technologies used in developed countries, thereby avoiding the environmentally harmful stages of economic development. For example, ③ developing countries can build mobile phone networks that require much less raw materials and construction than land lines. They can deploy decentralized renewable energy systems such as PV panels, while in the United States we will be stuck for some time with old coal-fired power plants and an aging, inefficient electrical grid. U.S. cities and suburbs were built when energy was cheap and there were no concerns about global warming, so we are ④ free to drive great distances to accomplish everyday tasks. Developing countries can ⑤ concentrate development in cities where people can live more sustainably, and preserve green space around the cities.

*leapfrogging 립프로깅(등 짚고 뛰어넘기)
**deploy 효율적으로 사용하다, 배치하다   ***PV (photovoltaic) 광발전의

93 윗글의 밑줄 친 ①~⑤ 중, 문맥상 어색한 것을 1개 찾아 그 번호를 쓰고 고쳐 쓰시오.

_____ → _____

94 윗글에서 다음 질문에 대한 답을 찾아 우리말로 쓰시오. (30자 내외)

Q: According to the passage, why is the United States lagging behind in sustainability indicators?

A: _____

The debate about how to understand social life 고대에 기원을 두고 있고 적어도 플라톤까지 멀리 거슬러 올라갈 수 있는데, who analyzed the differing worldviews of poetry and philosophy (which was at the time an approximation of science). Echoes of this debate are still heard today in the endless dialogue between the humanities and the sciences regarding how the world may best be comprehended. Some thinkers argue that the internal states of humans cannot be examined scientifically at all and must instead be understood nonscientifically via intuitive, interpretive, or even religious methods. Even some scientists devoted to strong empiricism adopt this view. B. F. Skinner, the leading twentieth-century advocate of behaviorism and the author of *Walden Two*, famously reasoned that internal mental states are unobservable and unquantifiable subjectivities and thus belong outside the range of objective scientific scrutiny, in contrast to observable (individual and collective) behaviors. Some philosophers and theologians continue to embrace the age-old dualistic separation between the material world and the mental world. The underlying claim is that we cannot use science to fully understand the soul or even feelings, thoughts, morals, or beauty. While the issue of the soul is a matter unto itself, feelings, thoughts, morals, and even beauty — and their evolutionary origins — are, in fact, yielding increasingly to science in the twenty-first century with techniques as diverse as MRI imaging and behavior genetics.

*empiricism 경험주의   **scrutiny 면밀한 조사[검증]
***theologian 신학자

95 윗글의 밑줄 친 우리말 의미와 일치하도록 보기 의 단어를 순서대로 배열하여 문장을 완성하시오.

보기 as / can / back / traced / far / as / be

has ancient roots and _____ _____

_____ at least _____ _____

_____ _____ Plato

96 밑줄 친 this view의 문맥상 의미를 우리말로 설명하시오. (30자 내외)

_____

_____

Emily was the youngest of three daughters in a family of great soccer players. Her mother played soccer in high school and college, as did her two older sisters. Following in their footsteps, Emily began her freshman year of high school as a star player on the soccer team. Soon, however, Emily's coach noticed that while Emily had great skills, she just didn't show the kind of passion for the game she had seen in other great players she'd coached. She noticed something else about Emily: she had an unusually graceful stride as she ran up and down the field.

And to her coach's surprise, Emily seemed to absolutely love the running drills that the other players hated during practice. One day, the coach called her over after practice. "Emily, why do you play soccer?" she asked. Somewhat puzzled, she responded, "Because everyone in my family plays soccer. And because I'm really good at it." Then the coach asked, "But do you love it?"

With a somewhat dejected look, she shook her head. "Playing soccer was really fun when I was younger. But now it feels like something I *have* to do. Everyone expects me to be like my mom and sisters. I don't want to let them down." That's when she realized that her job as Emily's coach had, in an important way, just begun. Rather than continue to try to get her to fit in as a soccer player, the coach asked Emily about her true interests. She wasn't surprised to learn that Emily had a passion for running. Running was effortless for her, she said. When running long distances, she felt relaxed and free from all the worries and cares in her life.

After several more conversations with Emily and then an initially difficult discussion with her family, the coach and her family allowed Emily to leave the soccer team and switch to running track for the spring semester. By her junior year, Emily was the number one runner on the girls' cross-country team, and as a senior, she led the team to the state finals. While she lost one of her better players, the coach knew she'd done the right thing. In the process, she helped Emily find her true passion.

*stride 달리는 모습, 보폭   *dejected 낙심한, 기가 죽은

97 윗글의 밑줄 친 부분을 it으로 시작하는 문장이 되도록 빈칸에 쓰시오. (5단어)

it _____ the running drills that the other players hated during practice

98 윗글의 내용을 한 문장으로 요약하려고 한다. 빈칸 (A)와 (B)에 들어갈 알맞은 말을 본문에서 찾아 쓰시오.

> Despite giving up the great soccer player, the coach was able to help Emily discover her true _____(A)_____ as a(n) _____(B)_____.

(A) _____   (B) _____

❶ Your insurance adjuster recently submitted the assessment for the wind damage to our roof. ❷ There are specific errors within the claim that you need to address. ❸ The damage was to the dormer on the north side of the house. ❹ High winds from last month's storms had lifted many of the tiles from the roof and caused a leak. ❺ This caused water damage to the internal ceiling of an upstairs bedroom. ❻ When the adjuster examined the dormer, he looked only at the roofing on the dormer's south side, where damage was minimal. ❼ The true damage was on the north side. ❽ He awarded damages based on what he saw, and it seems that he did not look very closely at the extent of the damage. ❾ A specialist from Caesar Roofing estimates repairs to both the roof and the water-damaged ceiling at $968. ❿ Your check for $232 arrived today. ⓫ I am holding the check until I receive your response to this letter. ⓬ Please contact me as soon as possible about this matter.

*dormer 지붕창, 천창

❶ 귀사의 손해 사정인이 최근에 우리 지붕의 바람 피해에 대한 사정액을 제출했습니다. ❷ 청구액에는 처리되어야 할 명백한 오류가 있습니다. ❸ 그 피해는 집 북쪽에 있는 지붕창에 있었습니다. ❹ 지난달의 폭풍으로 인한 강풍이 지붕에서 많은 타일들을 들뜨게 하여 누수를 일으켰습니다. ❺ 이것이 위층 침실의 내부 천장에 물 피해를 일으켰습니다. ❻ 사정인이 지붕창을 검사할 때, 그는 지붕창 남쪽에 있는 지붕 재료만 보았는데, 그곳은 피해가 아주 적었습니다. ❼ 진짜 피해는 북쪽에 있었습니다. ❽ 그는 자신이 본 것을 토대로 손해 보상액 판정을 내렸는데, 피해 규모를 별로 자세히 살피지 않은 것 같습니다. ❾ Caesar Roofing의 한 전문가는 지붕과 물에 피해를 입은 천장 둘 다의 수리 비용을 968달러로 추산하고 있습니다. ❿ 귀사의 232달러 수표가 오늘 도착했습니다. ⓫ 저는 이 편지에 대한 귀사의 답장을 받을 때까지 수표를 보관하고 있겠습니다. ⓬ 이 문제에 대해 가능한 한 빨리 연락 주십시오.

Word List

☐ **insurance** 보험 ☐ **adjuster** 손해 사정인 ☐ **submit** 제출하다 ☐ **assessment** 사정액, 평가액
☐ **damage** 피해, (*pl.*) 손해액, 손해 보상액 ☐ **specific** 구체적인, 특정한 ☐ **claim** (보상 등에 대한) 청구(액) ☐ **address** 처리하다, 다루다
☐ **high wind** 강풍 ☐ **lift** 들어올리다 ☐ **leak** 누수 ☐ **internal** 내부의 ☐ **ceiling** 천장 ☐ **minimal** 아주 적은, 최소의
☐ **award** 수여[지급] 판정을 내리다 ☐ **extent** 규모, 범위 ☐ **specialist** 전문가 ☐ **estimate** 추산하다

• Word Test

1	specialist	9	아주 적은, 최소의
2	submit	10	내부의
3	leak	11	추산하다
4	award	12	손해 사정인
5	address	13	들어올리다
6	insurance	14	규모, 범위
7	specific	15	(보상 등에 대한) 청구(액)
8	ceiling	16	사정액, 평가액

Your insurance adjuster recently submitted the assessment for the wind damage to our roof. There are specific errors within the claim ❶ what / that you need to address. The damage was to the dormer on the north side of the house. High winds from last month's storms had lifted many of the tiles from the roof and caused a leak. This caused water damage to the internal ceiling of an upstairs bedroom. When the adjuster examined the dormer, he looked only at the roofing on the dormer's south side, ❷ which / where damage was minimal. The true damage was on the north side. He awarded damages based on ❸ what / that he saw, and it seems that he did not look very closely at the extent of the damage. A specialist from Caesar Roofing estimates repairs to ❹ both / either the roof and the water-damaged ceiling at $968. Your check for $232 arrived today. I am holding the check ❺ by / until I receive your response to this letter. Please contact me as soon as possible about this matter.

*dormer 지붕창, 천창

Your insurance adjuster recently submitted the assessment for the wind damage to our roof. There are specific errors within the claim that you need ❶ _____ (address). The damage was to the dormer on the north side of the house. High winds from last month's storms ❷ _____ (lift) many of the tiles from the roof and caused a leak. This caused water damage to the internal ceiling of an upstairs bedroom. When the adjuster examined the dormer, he looked only at the roofing on the dormer's south side, where damage was minimal. The true damage was on the north side. He awarded damages ❸ _____ (base) on what he saw, and it seems that he did not look very closely at the extent of the damage. A specialist from Caesar Roofing estimates repairs to both the roof and the water-damaged ceiling at $968. Your check for $232 ❹ _____ (arrive) today. I am ❺ _____ (hold) the check until I receive your response to this letter. Please contact me as soon as possible about this matter.

*dormer 지붕창, 천창

Your ❶ _____ _____ (보험 손해사정인) recently submitted the assessment for the wind damage to our roof. There are ❷ _____ _____ (명백한 오류들) within the claim that you need to address. The damage was to the dormer on the north side of the house. High winds from last month's storms had lifted many of the tiles from the roof and caused a leak. This caused water damage to the internal ceiling of an upstairs bedroom. When the adjuster examined the dormer, he looked only at the roofing on the dormer's south side, where damage was minimal. The true damage was on the north side. He awarded damages ❸ _____ _____ _____ _____ _____ (그가 본 것을 토대로), and it seems that he did not look very closely at the ❹ _____ _____ _____ _____ (피해의 범위). A specialist from Caesar Roofing estimates repairs to both the roof and the water-damaged ceiling at $968. Your check for $232 arrived today. I am holding the check until I receive your response to this letter. Please contact me ❺ _____ _____ _____ _____ (가능한 한 빨리) about this matter.

*dormer 지붕창, 천창

❶ In 2004, my son Noah was turning one year old and I had a problem: ❷ How do I make him a birthday cake? ❸ He was seriously allergic to dairy, soy, and egg. ❹ A memory of an incident unsettled me — a bite of bakery cake at daycare sent us to the emergency room. ❺ I had never made a birthday cake myself. ❻ But Noah was turning one — I wanted him to have birthday cake. ❼ I found a website called foodallergickids.org, and asked on the forum there: ❽ Did anyone have a dairy-, soy- and egg-free cake recipe? ❾ In response to my question, I got a shower of warm welcomes from parents on the site. ❿ They shared an excellent safe cake recipe, and provided a host of other support. ⓫ Parents on the site helped me figure out how to make a clear and effective allergy-awareness sheet for his daycare teachers. ⓬ They shared tips for how to safely order food in a restaurant. ⓭ Their experience was invaluable, and they also were emotionally supportive in a way no one else could be.

❶ 2004년 내 아들 Noah는 막 한 살이 되어 가고 있었는데, 나에게 문제 하나가 있었다. ❷ 어떻게 아들에게 생일 케이크를 만들어 주지? ❸ 그는 유제품, 콩, 그리고 계란에 대해 심각한 알레르기가 있었다. ❹ 한 사건의 기억이 나를 불안하게 했는데, 어린이집에서 제과점 케이크를 한입 먹은 것으로 우리는 응급실에 갔었다. ❺ 나는 직접 생일 케이크를 만들어 본 적이 없었다. ❻ 하지만 Noah는 한 살이 되어 가고 있었고, 나는 그가 생일 케이크를 먹기를 원했다. ❼ 나는 foodallergickids.org라는 웹 사이트를 발견했고, 그곳의 포럼에서 물었다. ❽ 유제품과 콩과 계란이 없는 케이크 조리법을 갖고 있으신 분 있으세요? ❾ 내 질문에 대한 반응으로, 나는 그 사이트의 부모들로부터 많은 따뜻한 환영을 받았다. ❿ 그들은 훌륭하고 안전한 케이크 조리법을 공유해 주었고 많은 다른 지원도 해 주었다. ⓫ 그 사이트의 부모들은 내가 그의 어린이집 선생님들에게 명료하고 효과적인 알레르기 주의표를 만들어 주는 방법을 생각해 내는 데 도움을 주었다. ⓬ 그들은 식당에서 음식을 안전하게 주문하는 방법에 관한 조언을 공유했다. ⓭ 그들의 경험은 매우 귀중했고, 그들은 또한 다른 어느 누구도 그럴 수 없는 방식으로 정서적으로 도움이 되었다.

Word List

□ turn (어떤 나이가) 되다 □ seriously 심각하게, 진지하게 □ allergic 알레르기가 있는 □ dairy 유제품; 유제품의 □ soy 콩
□ incident 사건, 일 □ unsettle 불안하게 하다 □ bite 한입, 소량의 음식 □ daycare 어린이집, 탁아소 □ emergency room 응급실
□ forum 포럼, 공개 토론(의 장) □ recipe 조리법 □ shower 다량, 소나기 □ a host of 많은 □ invaluable 매우 귀중한
□ supportive 지지하는

• Word Test

1	turn		9	사건, 일	
2	shower		10	유제품; 유제품의	
3	allergic		11	지지하는	
4	daycare		12	응급실	
5	invaluable		13	많은	
6	soy		14	한입, 소량의 음식	
7	forum		15	조리법	
8	unsettle		16	심각하게, 진지하게	

In 2004, my son Noah was turning one year old and I had a problem: How do I make him a birthday cake? He was ❶ serious / seriously allergic to dairy, soy, and egg. A memory of an incident unsettled me — a bite of bakery cake at daycare sent us to the emergency room. I had never made a birthday cake myself. But Noah was turning one — I wanted him to have birthday cake. I found a website called foodallergickids.org, and asked on the forum there: Did ❷ anyone / someone have a dairy-, soy- and egg-free cake recipe? In response to my question, I got a shower of warm welcomes from parents on the site. They shared an excellent safe cake recipe, and provided a host of other support. Parents on the site helped me ❸ figure / figuring out how to make a clear and effective allergy-awareness sheet for his daycare teachers. They shared tips for how to ❹ safe / safely order food in a restaurant. Their experience was ❺ invaluable / valueless, and they also were emotionally supportive in a way no one else could be.

In 2004, my son Noah was turning one year old and I had a problem: How do I make him a birthday cake? He was seriously allergic to dairy, soy, and egg. A memory of an incident unsettled me — a bite of bakery cake at daycare sent us to the emergency room. I ❶ _____ (have) never made a birthday cake myself. But Noah was turning one — I wanted him ❷ _____ (have) birthday cake. I found a website ❸ _____ (call) foodallergickids.org, and asked on the forum there: Did anyone have a dairy-, soy- and egg-free cake recipe? In response to my question, I got a shower of warm welcomes from parents on the site. They shared an excellent safe cake recipe, and provided a host of other support. Parents on the site helped me figure out how ❹ _____ (make) a clear and effective allergy-awareness sheet for his daycare teachers. They shared tips for how to safely ❺ _____ (order) food in a restaurant. Their experience was invaluable, and they also were emotionally supportive in a way no one else could be.

In 2004, my son Noah was turning one year old and I had a problem: How do I make him a birthday cake? He ❶ _____ _____ _____ _____ (~에 대해 심각한 알레르기가 있었다) dairy, soy, and egg. A memory of an incident unsettled me — a bite of bakery cake at daycare sent us to the ❷ _____ _____ (응급실). I had never made a birthday cake myself. But Noah was turning one — I wanted him to have birthday cake. I found a website called foodallergickids.org, and asked on the forum there: Did anyone have a dairy-, soy- and egg-free cake recipe? ❸ _____ _____ _____ (~에 대해 반응하여) my question, I got a shower of warm welcomes from parents on the site. They shared an excellent safe cake recipe, and provided a host of other support. Parents on the site helped me ❹ _____ _____ (생각해 내다) how to make a clear and effective allergy-awareness sheet for his daycare teachers. They shared tips for how to safely order food in a restaurant. Their experience was invaluable, and they also ❺ _____ _____ _____ (정서적으로 도움이 되었다) in a way no one else could be.

333

❶ Did you know that fluoridated toothpaste, magnetic resonance imaging (MRI) technology, N-95 masks, and blood banking all have origins in academic research labs? ❷ The discoveries that contributed to these successful innovations may well have remained of purely academic interest had researchers not taken active steps to move those discoveries into the realm of invention. ❸ By doing so, those inventors changed the world. ❹ You as a researcher want your work to matter. ❺ You spend long hours designing, conducting, and analyzing experiments, and then you think hard about how and where to disseminate the results. ❻ Researchers present their work via seminars, conference posters and presentations, book chapters, and journal publications — primarily targeting other academic researchers. ❼ We now challenge you to think more broadly about taking your messages to additional audiences, especially those that have commercial capabilities.

*fluoridate 불소를 넣다　**resonance 공명　***disseminate 전파하다

❶ 불소를 넣은 치약, 자기 공명 영상(MRI) 기술, N-95 마스크, 그리고 혈액은행이 모두 대학 연구실에서 기원했다는 것을 알고 있었는가? ❷ 이 성공한 혁신들에 기여한 발견들은 연구자들이 그 발견들을 발명의 영역으로 옮겨 갈 적극적 조치를 취하지 않았다면 아마도 순전히 학문적으로 흥미로운 것으로 남았을 것이다. ❸ 그렇게 함으로써 그 발명가들은 세상을 바꾸었다. ❹ 연구자로서 여러분은 여러분의 연구가 중요하기를 원한다. ❺ 실험을 설계하고 실시하고 분석하느라 오랜 시간을 보내고, 그리고 나서는 어떻게 어디로 그 결과를 전파할 것인지에 관해 골똘히 생각한다. ❻ 연구자는 세미나, 학회 포스터와 발표, 저서의 장(章), 그리고 학술지 출판물을 통해 자기 연구를 공개하는데, 주로 다른 학술 연구자를 대상으로 한다. ❼ 우리는 지금 여러분에게 여러분의 메시지를 그 밖의 독자들, 특히 상업적 역량이 있는 사람들에게 가져가는 것에 관해 더 폭넓게 생각해 보라고 요구한다.

Word List

□ toothpaste 치약　□ magnetic 자기의, 자석의　□ academic 대학의, 학문의　□ lab 실험실　□ contribute to ~에 기여하다
□ innovation 혁신　□ purely 순전히　□ realm 영역, 왕국　□ conduct 실시하다, 행하다　□ analyze 분석하다　□ experiment 실험
□ via ~을 통하여　□ conference 학회, 회의　□ publication 출판물, 출판　□ primarily 주로　□ target 대상으로 하다
□ challenge (상대방에게 도전이 될 일을) 요구하다　□ audience 독자, 청중　□ capability 역량, 능력

Word Test

1	realm		10	혁신	
2	audience		11	출판물, 출판	
3	conduct		12	자기의, 자석의	
4	contribute to		13	대상으로 하다	
5	primarily		14	역량, 능력	
6	toothpaste		15	~을 통하여	
7	conference		16	분석하다	
8	academic		17	실험실	
9	experiment		18	순전히	

Did you know that fluoridated toothpaste, magnetic resonance imaging (MRI) technology, N-95 masks, and blood banking all have origins in academic research labs? The discoveries ❶ | that / what | contributed to these ❷ | successful / successive | innovations may well have remained of purely academic interest had researchers not taken active steps to move those discoveries into the realm of invention. By doing so, those inventors changed the world. You as a researcher want your work to matter. You spend long hours designing, conducting, and analyzing experiments, and then you think ❸ | hard / hardly | about how and where to disseminate the results. Researchers present their work via seminars, conference posters and presentations, book chapters, and journal publications — ❹ | primarily / primitively | targeting other academic researchers. We now challenge you to think more broadly about taking your messages to additional audiences, especially those ❺ | that / what | have commercial capabilities.

*fluoridate 불소를 넣다   **resonance 공명   ***disseminate 전파하다

Did you know that fluoridated toothpaste, magnetic resonance imaging (MRI) technology, N-95 masks, and blood banking all ❶ _____ (have) origins in academic research labs? The discoveries that contributed to these successful innovations may well have remained of purely academic interest had researchers not taken active steps ❷ _____ (move) those discoveries into the realm of invention. By ❸ _____ (do) so, those inventors changed the world. You as a researcher ❹ _____ (want) your work to matter. You spend long hours designing, conducting, and analyzing experiments, and then you think hard about how and where ❺ _____ (disseminate) the results. Researchers present their work via seminars, conference posters and presentations, book chapters, and journal publications — primarily targeting other academic researchers. We now challenge you to think more broadly about taking your messages to additional audiences, especially those that have commercial capabilities.

*fluoridate 불소를 넣다   **resonance 공명   ***disseminate 전파하다

Did you know that fluoridated toothpaste, magnetic resonance imaging (MRI) technology, N-95 masks, and ❶ _____ _____ (혈액 은행) all have origins in academic research labs? The discoveries that ❷ _____ _____ (~에 기여했던) these successful innovations may well have remained of purely academic interest had researchers not taken active steps to move those discoveries into the ❸ _____ _____ _____ (발명의 영역). By doing so, those inventors changed the world. You as a researcher want your work to matter. You ❹ _____ _____ _____ (오랜 시간들을 보내다) designing, conducting, and analyzing experiments, and then you think hard about how and where to disseminate the results. Researchers present their work via seminars, conference posters and presentations, book chapters, and journal publications — primarily targeting ❺ _____ _____ _____ (다른 학술 연구자들). We now challenge you to think more broadly about taking your messages to additional audiences, especially those that have commercial capabilities.

*fluoridate 불소를 넣다   **resonance 공명   ***disseminate 전파하다

❶ It is rumored that Michael Jordan practiced more than anyone else, was always up for another practice game, or a card game, a round of golf, shooting baskets far into the night while his teammates were done and gone. ❷ Ericsson and Pool reference this continued energy as maintenance, yet in light of Jordan's remarkable level of energy throughout the night following a demanding game, it was far beyond maintenance. ❸ It was self-invigorating and self-renewing. ❹ It was a self-fulfilling prophecy that flowed like a humming mantra: "The more one does, the more one can do." ❺ To put this into terms for invigorating the students in our classrooms, it is easy to rally students with a similar trigger. ❻ By planning a show or exhibition of their work or a demonstration of their performances, students are motivated with renewed energy as they prepare to showcase their work. ❼ The invitation to show their artwork, or perform in the PE demonstration, or participate in the school musical performance or the school poetry fest seems to do the trick. ❽ Humans are motivated to act by enticements that matter to them: endeavors that are relevant and raise the bar on the mundane routines of the everyday class work.

*mantra 주문 **enticement 유인책 ***mundane 평범한

❶ Michael Jordan은 팀 동료들이 끝내고 가 버린 동안에 밤늦게까지 바스켓을 향해 슈팅 연습을 하면서, 다른 누구보다 연습을 더 많이 했으며 늘 기꺼이 또 한 번의 연습 게임, 혹은 카드 게임이나 골프 한 라운드를 하려고 했다는 소문이 있다. ❷ Ericsson과 Pool은 이러한 지속적인 활력을 유지 관리라고 언급하지만, 힘든 경기 후 밤새도록 지속된 Jordan의 놀랄 만한 수준의 활력을 고려해 볼 때 그것은 유지 관리를 훨씬 넘어서는 것이었다. ❸ 그것은 스스로 활기를 불어넣는 것이고 스스로 새롭게 하는 것이었다. ❹ 그것은 "많이 하면 할수록 더 많이 할 수 있다"라는 흥얼거리는 주문처럼 흘러나오는 자기 충족적인 예언이었다. ❺ 이를 우리 교실에서 학생들에게 활기를 불어넣기 위한 말로 설명하자면, 비슷한 유인으로 학생들을 고무하는 것은 쉬운 일이다. ❻ 자기 작품의 품평회나 전시회, 또는 자신의 성과에 대한 발표회를 계획함으로써 학생들은 자신의 작품을 소개할 준비를 하는 동안 새로운 활기로 동기를 부여받는다. ❼ 자기 미술 작품을 전시하거나, 체육 발표에서 실연하거나, 학교의 뮤지컬 공연이나 학교 시 축제에 참여하도록 권유하는 것이 효과가 있는 것 같다. ❽ 인간은 자신에게 중요한 유인책, 곧 유의미하면서 매일의 교실 수업의 평범한 일과에 대한 기준을 높이는 시도에 의해 행동의 동기를 부여받는다.

Word List

□ rumor 소문을 내다　□ up for (어떤 활동을) 기꺼이 하려고 하는　□ shoot a basket (농구에서) 득점을 하다　□ maintenance 유지 (관리)
□ in light of ~에 비추어　□ remarkable 놀랄 만한, 현저한　□ demanding 힘든, 고된　□ self-invigorating 스스로 활기를 불어넣는
□ self-fulfilling (예언이) 자기 충족적인　□ prophecy 예언　□ humming 흥얼거리는, 콧노래를 부르는　□ invigorate 고무하다
□ rally 고무하다, 자극하다　□ trigger 유인, 동기　□ exhibition 전시(회)　□ showcase 소개하다　□ PE (physical education) 체육
□ poetry 시　□ fest 축제, 파티　□ do the trick 효과가 있다　□ endeavor 시도, 노력　□ relevant 유의미한, 관련된
□ raise the bar 기준[기대치]을 높이다

• Word Test

1　maintenance _____

2　prophecy _____

3　showcase _____

4　remarkable _____

5　rumor _____

6　trigger _____

7　endeavor _____

8　fest _____

9　invigorate _____

10　전시(회) _____

11　효과가 있다 _____

12　시 _____

13　힘든, 고된 _____

14　고무하다, 자극하다 _____

15　~에 비추어 _____

16　흥얼거리는, 콧노래를 부르는 _____

17　유의미한, 관련된 _____

18　기꺼이 하려고 하는 _____

It is rumored ❶ that / which Michael Jordan practiced more than anyone else, was always up for another practice game, or a card game, a round of golf, shooting baskets far into the night ❷ during / while his teammates were done and gone. Ericsson and Pool reference this continued energy as maintenance, yet in light of Jordan's remarkable level of energy throughout the night following a demanding game, it was far beyond maintenance. It was self-invigorating and self-renewing. It was a self-fulfilling prophecy that flowed like a humming mantra: "The more one does, the ❸ more / most one can do." To put this into terms for invigorating the students in our classrooms, it is easy to rally students with a similar trigger. By planning a show or exhibition of their work or a demonstration of their performances, students are motivated with renewed energy as they prepare to showcase their work. The invitation to show their artwork, or perform in the PE demonstration, or participate in the school musical performance or the school poetry fest seems to do the trick. Humans are motivated to act by enticements ❹ that / what matter to them: endeavors that are ❺ relevant / reluctant and raise the bar on the mundane routines of the everyday class work.

*mantra 주문   **enticement 유인책   ***mundane 평범한

It is rumored that Michael Jordan practiced more than anyone else, was always up for another practice game, or a card game, a round of golf, ❶ _____ (shoot) baskets far into the night while his teammates were done and gone. Ericsson and Pool reference this ❷ _____ (continue) energy as maintenance, yet in light of Jordan's remarkable level of energy throughout the night following a demanding game, it was far beyond maintenance. It was self-invigorating and self-renewing. It was a self-fulfilling prophecy that flowed like a humming mantra: "The more one does, the more one can do." To put this into terms for invigorating the students in our classrooms, it is easy ❸ _____ (rally) students with a similar trigger. By planning a show or exhibition of their work or a demonstration of their performances, students are motivated with renewed energy as they prepare ❹ _____ (showcase) their work. The invitation to show their artwork, or perform in the PE demonstration, or participate in the school musical performance or the school poetry fest seems ❺ _____ (do) the trick. Humans are motivated to act by enticements that matter to them: endeavors that are relevant and raise the bar on the mundane routines of the everyday class work.

*mantra 주문   **enticement 유인책   ***mundane 평범한

It is rumored that Michael Jordan practiced more than anyone else, was always up for another practice game, or a card game, a round of golf, shooting baskets far into the night while his teammates were done and gone. Ericsson and Pool reference this continued energy as maintenance, yet ❶ _____ _____ _____ (~에 비추어) Jordan's remarkable level of energy throughout the night following a demanding game, it was ❷ _____ _____ _____ (유지 관리를 훨씬 넘어서는). It was self-invigorating and self-renewing. It was a self-fulfilling prophecy that flowed like a humming mantra: "The more one does, the more one can do." To put this into terms for invigorating the students in our classrooms, it is easy to rally students with a similar trigger. By planning a show or exhibition of their work or a demonstration of their performances, students are motivated with renewed energy as they ❸ _____ _____ _____ _____ _____ (그들의 작품을 소개할 준비를 하다). The invitation to show their artwork, or perform in the PE demonstration, or participate in the school musical performance or the school poetry fest seems to do the trick. Humans are motivated to act by enticements that matter to them: endeavors that are relevant and ❹ _____ _____ _____ (기준을 높이다) on the mundane routines of the everyday class work.

*mantra 주문 **enticement 유인책 ***mundane 평범한

❶ I have been teaching a course on leadership for many years and have concluded that the main way you can distinguish good from not so good leaders is in who they are looking out for. ❷ Bad leaders always have one person in mind — themselves. ❸ They may say they care about others; they may do things that seem to show care for others; they even may appear to be sad when hearing about the misfortunes of others. ❹ But in the end, they always look out for #1 — themselves. ❺ When they help others, it is to help themselves or merely to demonstrate overtly but falsely how caring and considerate they are. ❻ When they listen to others, it is to figure out what's in it for them. ❼ When they act in ways to benefit others, they always have themselves in mind first. ❽ Just as criminologists sometimes say that to figure out the perpetrators of a crime, you should follow the money, to figure out who is a good leader, you should follow the benefits — ❾ whom is the leader trying to benefit, and in particular, is it anyone beyond him- or herself, or those who immediately can benefit him- or herself?

*overtly 공공연하게   **criminologist 범죄학자   ***perpetrator 가해자

❶ 나는 여러 해 동안 리더십에 대한 강의를 해 왔는데, 좋은 지도자들을 그다지 좋지 않은 지도자들과 구별할 수 있는 주요한 방법은 그들이 누구의 이익을 생각하는가에 있다고 결론을 내렸다. ❷ 나쁜 지도자들은 늘 한 사람만 염두에 두고 있는데, 바로 자신이다. ❸ 그들은 자신이 다른 사람들에 대해 배려한다고 말할지도 모르고, 다른 사람들에 대한 배려를 보여 주는 것처럼 보이는 일을 할지도 모르고, 심지어 다른 사람들의 불행에 관해 들을 때 슬퍼하고 있는 것처럼 보일지도 모른다. ❹ 그러나 결국 늘 그들은 첫째가는 사람, 즉 자기 자신의 이익을 생각한다. ❺ 그들이 다른 사람들을 도울 때, 그것은 자기 자신을 돕기 위해서이거나 그저 자기가 얼마나 배려하고 사려 깊은지를 공공연하지만 그릇되게 보여 주기 위해서이다. ❻ 그들이 다른 사람들에게 귀 기울일 때, 그것은 거기에 자기에게 이익이 되는 무엇이 있는지 알아내기 위해서이다. ❼ 그들이 다른 사람들에게 이득을 주는 방식으로 일할 때, 그들은 늘 자기 자신을 먼저 염두에 두고 있다. ❽ 마치 가끔 범죄학자들이 범죄의 가해자를 알아내기 위해 돈을 주시해야 한다고 말하는 것과 꼭 마찬가지로, 누가 훌륭한 지도자인지를 알아내기 위해서는 이득을 주시해야 한다. ❾ 즉, 지도자가 이득을 주려고 애쓰는 사람이 누구인가, 그리고 특히 그 사람이 자신이 아닌 어떤 사람인가, 아니면 자신에게 직접 이득을 줄 수 있는 사람들인가?

Word List

□ conclude 결론을 내리다   □ distinguish 구별하다   □ look out for ~의 이익을 생각하다, ~을 보살피다   □ merely 그저, 단지
□ demonstrate (행동으로) 보여 주다, 실증하다   □ falsely 그릇되게   □ caring 배려하는   □ considerate 사려 깊은
□ figure out 알아내다   □ immediately 직접, 즉시

• Word Test

1 look out for _____
2 conclude _____
3 caring _____
4 figure out _____
5 demonstrate _____

6 사려 깊은 _____
7 그릇되게 _____
8 구별하다 _____
9 직접, 즉시 _____
10 그저, 단지 _____

I have been teaching a course on leadership for many years and have concluded ❶ that / which the main way you can distinguish good ❷ from / to not so good leaders is in who they are looking out for. Bad leaders always have one person in mind — themselves. They may say they care about others; they may do things that seem to show care for others; they even may appear to be sad when hearing about the misfortunes of others. But in the end, they always look out for #1 — themselves. When they help others, it is to help themselves or merely to demonstrate overtly but falsely how caring and ❸ considerable / considerate they are. When they listen to others, it is to figure out what's in it for them. When they act in ways to benefit others, they always have themselves in mind first. Just as criminologists ❹ sometime / sometimes say that to figure out the perpetrators of a crime, you should follow the money, to figure out who is a good leader, you should follow the benefits — ❺ who / whom is the leader trying to benefit, and in particular, is it anyone beyond him- or herself, or those who immediately can benefit him- or herself?   *overtly 공공연하게   **criminologist 범죄학자   ***perpetrator 가해자

I have been ❶ _____ (teach) a course on leadership for many years and have concluded that the main way you can distinguish good from not so good leaders ❷ _____ (be) in who they are looking out for. Bad leaders always have one person in mind — themselves. They may say they care about others; they may do things that seem ❸ _____ (show) care for others; they even may appear to be sad when ❹ _____ (hear) about the misfortunes of others. But in the end, they always look out for #1 — themselves. When they help others, it is to help themselves or merely to demonstrate overtly but falsely how caring and considerate they are. When they listen to others, it is to figure out what's in it for them. When they act in ways ❺ _____ (benefit) others, they always have themselves in mind first. Just as criminologists sometimes say that to figure out the perpetrators of a crime, you should follow the money, to figure out who is a good leader, you should follow the benefits — whom is the leader trying to benefit, and in particular, is it anyone beyond him- or herself, or those who immediately can benefit him- or herself?   *overtly 공공연하게   **criminologist 범죄학자   ***perpetrator 가해자

I have been teaching a course on leadership for many years and have concluded that the main way you can ❶ _____ _____ _____ _____ _____ _____ _____ (좋은 지도자들을 그렇지 않은 지도자들과 구별하다) is in who they are looking out for. Bad leaders always have one person in mind — themselves. They may say they ❷ _____ _____ _____ (다른 사람을 배려하다); they may do things that seem to show care for others; they even may appear to be sad when hearing about the misfortunes of others. But in the end, they always look out for #1 — themselves. When they help others, it is to help themselves or merely to ❸ _____ _____ (공공연하게 보여 주다) but falsely how caring and considerate they are. When they listen to others, it is to ❹ _____ _____ (알아내다) what's in it for them. When they act in ways to benefit others, they always ❺ _____ _____ _____ _____ (그들 자신을 먼저 염두에 두다). Just as criminologists sometimes say that to figure out the perpetrators of a crime, you should follow the money, to figure out who is a good leader, you should follow the benefits — whom is the leader trying to benefit, and in particular, is it anyone beyond him- or herself, or those who immediately can benefit him- or herself?   *overtly 공공연하게   **criminologist 범죄학자   ***perpetrator 가해자

❶ In Ise, Japan, the Shinto Grand Shrine is disassembled every twenty years and an exact replica, rebuilt of similar materials, is assembled in the same place. ❷ In this form of preservation, perpetuating the building techniques and the ritual act of re-creation matters more than the physical continuity of the structure. ❸ Similarly, the ancient White Horse of Uffington in England was "re-created" for centuries by locals, who scraped the chalk figure every seven years to keep it from being obscured by growing vegetation. ❹ Likewise, cultures that rely on oral traditions retain their sense of cultural heritage without any tangible objects at all, but rather by retelling stories from the past. ❺ These and other traditional or "folk" ways of retaining heritage bring the past and present together, fused in a repeating, cyclical sense of custom through use and interaction in everyday life.

*replica 복제품 **perpetuate 영구화하다 ***scrape 긁어내다

❶ 일본의 Ise에 있는 Shinto Grand Shrine은 20년마다 해체되어 유사한 재료로 다시 만든 정확한 복제품이 같은 장소에 조립된다. ❷ 이런 형태의 보존에서 건축 기법과 재창조의 의식 행위를 영구화하는 것이 구조물의 물리적인 연속성보다 더 중요하다. ❸ 비슷하게 영국의 고대 White Horse of Uffington은 지역 주민들에 의해 수 세기 동안 '재창조되었는데' 지역 주민들은 자라는 초목에 (그것이) 보이지 않게 되는 것을 막기 위해 백악 형상을 7년마다 긁어냈다. ❹ 마찬가지로, 구전에 의존하는 문화는 어떤 유형의 물체가 전혀 없이, 오히려 과거로부터 내려오는 이야기를 다시 함으로써, 문화유산에 대한 자신들의 감각을 유지한다. ❺ 유산을 유지하는 이런 그리고 여타 전통적이거나 '민속적인' 방법들은 일상 생활에서의 활용과 상호 작용을 통해 반복적이고 순환되는 관습이라는 느낌으로 융합되어 과거와 현재를 결합시킨다.

Word List

□ disassemble 해체하다, 분해하다 □ exact 정확한 □ assemble 조립하다 □ preservation 보존 □ ritual 의식상의, 의식을 위한
□ physical 물리적인 □ continuity 연속성 □ local 지역 주민 □ chalk 백악(백색의 연토질 석회암) □ obscure 보이지 않게 하다
□ vegetation 초목, 식물 □ rely on ~에 의존하다 □ oral 구전의 □ retain 유지하다 □ heritage 유산 □ tangible 유형의
□ folk 민속적인, 민간의 □ fuse 융합시키다, 결합시키다 □ cyclical 순환되는, 주기적인

• Word Test

1	assemble		10	보존	
2	obscure		11	정확한	
3	ritual		12	순환되는, 주기적인	
4	fuse		13	유산	
5	disassemble		14	구전의	
6	tangible		15	물리적인	
7	retain		16	민속적인, 민간의	
8	rely on		17	지역 주민	
9	continuity		18	초목, 식물	

In Ise, Japan, the Shinto Grand Shrine is disassembled every twenty years and an exact replica, rebuilt of ❶ different / similar materials, is assembled in the same place. In this form of preservation, perpetuating the building techniques and the ritual act of re-creation matters more than the physical ❷ continuity / intermittent of the structure. Similarly, the ancient White Horse of Uffington in England was "re-created" for centuries by locals, ❸ who / that scraped the chalk figure every seven years to keep it ❹ for / from being obscured by growing vegetation. Likewise, cultures that rely on oral traditions retain their sense of cultural heritage without any ❺ tangible / intangible objects at all, but rather by retelling stories from the past. These and other traditional or "folk" ways of retaining heritage bring the past and present together, fused in a repeating, cyclical sense of custom through use and interaction in everyday life.

*replica 복제품 **perpetuate 영구화하다 ***scrape 긁어내다

In Ise, Japan, the Shinto Grand Shrine is disassembled every twenty years and an exact replica, rebuilt of similar materials, is assembled in the same place. In this form of preservation, ❶ _____ (perpetuate) the building techniques and the ritual act of re-creation ❷ _____ (matter) more than the physical continuity of the structure. Similarly, the ancient White Horse of Uffington in England was "re-created" for centuries by locals, who scraped the chalk figure every seven years to keep it from ❸ _____ (be) obscured by growing vegetation. Likewise, cultures that rely on oral traditions retain their sense of cultural heritage without any tangible objects at all, but rather by retelling stories from the past. These and other traditional or "folk" ways of ❹ _____ (retain) heritage bring the past and present together, ❺ _____ (fuse) in a repeating, cyclical sense of custom through use and interaction in everyday life.

*replica 복제품 **perpetuate 영구화하다 ***scrape 긁어내다

In Ise, Japan, the Shinto Grand Shrine is disassembled ❶ _____ _____ _____ (20년 마다) and an exact replica, rebuilt of similar materials, is assembled in the same place. In this form of preservation, perpetuating the building techniques and the ritual act of re-creation matters more than the physical continuity of the structure. Similarly, the ancient White Horse of Uffington in England was "re-created" for centuries by locals, who scraped the chalk figure every seven years to keep it from being obscured by growing vegetation. Likewise, cultures that ❷ _____ _____ _____ _____ (구전에 의존하다) retain their sense of ❸ _____ _____ (문화유산) without any ❹ _____ _____ (유형의 물체들) at all, but rather by retelling stories from the past. These and other traditional or "folk" ways of retaining heritage bring the past and present together, fused in a repeating, cyclical sense of custom through use and interaction in everyday life.

*replica 복제품 **perpetuate 영구화하다 ***scrape 긁어내다

❶ Students bring energy and creativity to solving campus environmental problems, finding resources, and collecting detailed information. ❷ They are eager and energetic and contribute a unique perspective to the process of environmental action, although they are often overlooked as a resource by staff and administrators. ❸ Students' own systems of governance can be effective vehicles for promoting environmental change. ❹ Students across the country have advocated for recycling programs and other environmental initiatives at many schools. ❺ Commonly, they provide the volunteer labor to begin and promote a program. ❻ The most successful and lasting programs are partnerships between students and university staff and administrators. ❼ At Tufts University, student pressure and activism led to divestment from a utility company because its planned hydroelectric plant threatened sensitive ecosystems and indigenous people. ❽ A student lawsuit at UCLA forced improved ventilation in the art studios.

*divestment 투자 회수　**indigenous 토착의, 지역 고유의　***ventilation 환기

❶ 학생들은 캠퍼스의 한경 문제를 해결하고, 자원을 찾고, 상세한 정보를 수집하는 데 힘과 창의력을 발휘한다. ❷ 비록 직원과 관리자에 의해 자주 재원(財源)으로 무시되기는 하지만, 그들은 열정적이고 활력이 넘치며 환경 행동 과정에 독특한 관점을 제공한다. ❸ 학생들 자신의 관리 체계는 환경 변화를 촉진하는 데 효과적인 수단이 될 수 있다. ❹ 전국의 학생들은 많은 학교에서 재활용 프로그램과 여타의 환경 관련 계획들을 지지해왔다. ❺ 일반적으로, 그들은 프로그램을 시작하고 홍보하기 위해 자원봉사를 제공한다. ❻ 가장 성공적이고 지속적인 프로그램은 학생과 대학 직원 및 관리자 간의 협력이다. ❼ Tufts 대학교에서는 학생들의 압력과 행동 주의로 인해 한 전기 공급 회사는 투자를 회수하게 되었는데, 그 이유는 그 회사가 계획한 수력 발전소가 민감한 생태계와 토착민들을 위협했기 때문이다. ❽ UCLA의 학생 소송은 화실의 환기를 개선하도록 강제했다.

Word List

□ creativity 창의력　□ detailed 상세한　□ eager 열정적인　□ contribute ~ to ... ~에 …을 제공하다　□ unique 독특한
□ perspective 관점　□ overlook 무시하다, 간과하다　□ administrator 관리자　□ governance 관리　□ vehicle 수단
□ advocate 지지하다　□ initiative 계획　□ commonly 일반적으로　□ activism 행동주의
□ utility company 전기, 가스 등을 공급하는 회사　□ hydroelectric plant 수력 발전소　□ threaten 위협하다　□ lawsuit 소송

• Word Test

1	advocate	_____	9	독특한	_____
2	threaten	_____	10	행동주의	_____
3	governance	_____	11	관점	_____
4	contribute ~ to ...	_____	12	계획	_____
5	eager	_____	13	관리자	_____
6	overlook	_____	14	수단	_____
7	commonly	_____	15	소송	_____
8	creativity	_____	16	상세한	_____

Students bring energy and creativity ❶ for / to solving campus environmental problems, finding resources, and collecting detailed information. They are eager and energetic and contribute a unique perspective to the process of environmental action, ❷ although / unless they are often overlooked as a resource by staff and administrators. Students' own systems of governance can be ❸ affective / effective vehicles for promoting environmental change. Students across the country have advocated for recycling programs and other environmental initiatives at many schools. Commonly, they provide the volunteer labor to begin and promote a program. The most ❹ successful / successive and lasting programs are partnerships between students and university staff and administrators. At Tufts University, student pressure and activism led to divestment from a utility company because its planned hydroelectric plant threatened ❺ sensitive / sensual ecosystems and indigenous people. A student lawsuit at UCLA forced improved ventilation in the art studios.

*divestment 투자 회수   **indigenous 토착의, 지역 고유의   ***ventilation 환기

Students bring energy and creativity to ❶ _____ (solve) campus environmental problems, finding resources, and collecting detailed information. They are eager and energetic and contribute a unique perspective to the process of environmental action, although they are often ❷ _____ (overlook) as a resource by staff and administrators. Students' own systems of governance can be effective vehicles for ❸ _____ (promote) environmental change. Students across the country have advocated for recycling programs and other environmental initiatives at many schools. Commonly, they provide the volunteer labor ❹ _____ (begin) and promote a program. The most successful and lasting programs ❺ _____ (be) partnerships between students and university staff and administrators. At Tufts University, student pressure and activism led to divestment from a utility company because its planned hydroelectric plant threatened sensitive ecosystems and indigenous people. A student lawsuit at UCLA forced improved ventilation in the art studios.

*divestment 투자 회수   **indigenous 토착의, 지역 고유의   ***ventilation 환기

Students bring energy and creativity to solving campus environmental problems, finding resources, and collecting ❶ _____ _____ (상세한 정보). They are eager and energetic and contribute a ❷ _____ _____ (독특한 관점) to the process of environmental action, although they are often overlooked as a resource by staff and administrators. Students' own ❸ _____ _____ _____ (관리 체계들) can be effective vehicles for promoting environmental change. Students across the country have advocated for recycling programs and other environmental initiatives at many schools. Commonly, they provide the volunteer labor to begin and promote a program. The most successful and ❹ _____ _____ (지속적인 프로그램들) are partnerships between students and university staff and administrators. At Tufts University, student pressure and activism led to divestment from a utility company because its planned hydroelectric plant ❺ _____ _____ _____ (민감한 생태계들을 위협했다) and indigenous people. A student lawsuit at UCLA forced improved ventilation in the art studios.

*divestment 투자 회수   **indigenous 토착의, 지역 고유의   ***ventilation 환기

EU-28 Population by Age Group and Participation in Tourism, 2017

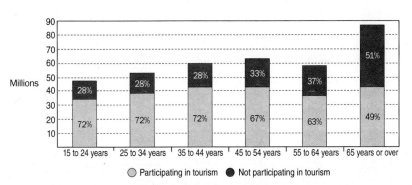

❶ 위의 도표는 2017년 연령대별 EU 28의 인구와 관광 여행 참여를 보여 준다. ❷ 모든 연령 집단에서 관광 여행에 참여한 사람의 수는 3천만 명이 넘었다. ❸ 35~44세의 연령 집단에서, 관광 여행에 참여한 사람들의 수는 4천만 명을 넘었다. ❹ 관광 여행에 참여한 25~34세 사람들의 비율은 관광 여행에 참여한 55~64세 사람들의 비율보다 더 높았다. ❺ 45~54세의 인구 집단에서 관광 여행에 참여한 인구의 비율은 그렇지 않은 인구 비율의 2배가 넘었다. ❻ 65세 이상의 연령 집단에서만, 관광 여행에 참여하지 않은 사람들의 비율이 관광 여행에 참여한 사람들의 비율보다 더 높았다.

❶ The above graph shows EU-28 population by age group and participation in tourism in 2017. ❷ In all of the age groups, the number of people who participated in tourism was over 30 million. ❸ In the 35-44 age group, the number of people who participated in tourism was more than 40 million. ❹ The percentage of people aged 25-34 who participated in tourism was higher than that of people aged 55-64 who participated in tourism. ❺ In the 45-54 age group, the percentage of the population who participated in tourism was more than double the percentage of the population who did not. ❻ Only in the 65 years or over age group was the percentage of people who did not participate in tourism higher than that of people who participated in tourism.

• Word Test

| 1 | million | _____ | 3 | 인구 | _____ |
| 2 | participation | _____ | 4 | 관광 여행 | _____ |

네모 안에서 옳은 어법·어휘를 고르시오.

The above graph shows EU-28 population by age group and participation in tourism in 2017. In all of the age ❶ group / groups , the number of people ❷ who / whom participated in tourism was over 30 million. In the 35-44 age group, the number of people who participated in tourism was more than 40 million. The percentage of people aged 25-34 who participated in tourism was ❸ higher / lower than that of people aged 55-64 who participated in tourism. In the 45-54 age group, the percentage of the population who participated in tourism was more than double the percentage of the population who did not. Only in the 65 years or over age group was the percentage of people who did not participate in tourism higher than ❹ this / that of people who participated in tourism.

• 유형 2 괄호 안의 동사를 알맞은 형태로 쓰시오.

The above graph ❶ _____ (show) EU-28 population by age group and participation in tourism in 2017. In all of the age groups, the number of people who participated in tourism ❷ _____ (be) over 30 million. In the 35-44 age group, the number of people who participated in tourism was more than 40 million. The percentage of people aged 25-34 who participated in tourism was higher than that of people ❸ _____ (age) 55-64 who participated in tourism. In the 45-54 age group, the percentage of the population who participated in tourism was more than double the percentage of the population who did not. Only in the 65 years or over age group was the percentage of people who did not participate in tourism higher than that of people who ❹ _____ (participate) in tourism.

• 유형 3 우리말에 맞게 빈칸에 알맞은 말을 쓰시오.

The above graph shows EU-28 population by age group and participation in tourism in 2017. In all of the age groups, the number of people who ❶ _____ _____ _____ (관광에 참여했다) was over 30 million. In the 35-44 age group, the ❷ _____ _____ _____ (사람들의 수) who participated in tourism was more than 40 million. The percentage of people aged 25-34 who participated in tourism was ❸ _____ _____ (~보다 더 높은) that of people aged 55-64 who participated in tourism. In the 45-54 age group, the percentage of the population who participated in tourism was more than double the percentage of the population who did not. Only in the 65 years or over age group was the percentage of people who did not participate in tourism higher than that of people who participated in tourism.

❶ The Philippine eagle lives in the forests of the Philippines. ❷ It is one of the rarest and most powerful birds in the world, with a wingspan of over 7 feet. ❸ Its main diet is monkeys and medium-sized mammals, a fact that has earned it a second name, "monkey-eating eagle." ❹ It hunts during the day, beginning at the top of a mountain and moving down from tree to tree. ❺ This allows it to soar from one location to another, conserving energy since it doesn't have to flap its wings. ❻ Two eagles will sometimes hunt together, one soaring overhead to distract a group of monkeys while the other swoops in for the kill. ❼ Because of habitat destruction, the Philippine eagle is critically endangered, with fewer than 750 left in the wild. ❽ Mating pairs have only one chick every two years, making the population slow to recover. ❾ Luckily, the only known predators of the eagle are humans. ❿ The birds have been protected as the national bird of the Philippines since 1995. ⓫ Killing one is punishable by 12 years in jail!

*swoop 급습[기습]하다

❶ 필리핀 독수리는 필리핀의 숲에서 산다. ❷ 그것은 날개의 폭이 7피트가 넘는, 세계에서 가장 희귀하고 강한 새 중 하나이다. ❸ 그것의 주식은 원숭이와 중간 크기의 포유동물인데, 이 사실로 '원숭이를 먹는 독수리'라는 두 번째 이름을 얻었다. ❹ 그것은 산꼭대기에서 시작하여 나무에서 나무로 내려오면서 낮 동안 사냥한다. ❺ 이렇게 하면, 날개를 퍼덕거릴 필요가 없기 때문에 에너지를 절약하면서, 한 곳에서 다른 곳으로 날아오를 수 있다. ❻ 가끔 독수리 두 마리가 함께 사냥을 하곤 하는데, 한 마리는 원숭이 무리의 주의를 분산시키기 위해서 머리 위로 활공하고, 그 동안에 다른 한 마리는 사냥감을 잡으려고 급습하여 들어온다. ❼ 서식지 파괴로 인해, 필리핀 독수리는 심각한 멸종 위기에 처해 있는데, 야생에서 남은 것은 750마리가 채 안 된다. ❽ 짝짓기를 하는 쌍은 2년마다 새끼 한 마리만 가져서 개체 수의 회복을 더디게 한다. ❾ 다행히도, 독수리의 유일한 포식자로 알려진 것은 인간이다. ❿ 이 새들은 1995년부터 필리핀의 국조로 보호되어 왔다. ⓫ 한 마리를 죽이면 징역 12년형의 처벌을 받을 수 있다!

Word List

□ rare 희귀한   □ wingspan 날개폭   □ main 주된   □ diet 식단   □ mammal 포유동물   □ soar 날아오르다, 활공하다
□ conserve 절약하다, 보존하다   □ flap 퍼덕거리다   □ overhead 머리 위에   □ distract 주의를 분산시키다   □ habitat 서식지
□ destruction 파괴   □ critically 심각하게   □ endangered 멸종 위기의   □ mate 짝짓기를 하다   □ chick (새의) 새끼
□ predator 포식자   □ punishable 처벌을 받을 수 있는, 형에 처해질 수 있는   □ in jail 수감되어

• Word Test

1	overhead		10	날아오르다, 활공하다	
2	conserve		11	날개폭	
3	rare		12	(새의) 새끼	
4	habitat		13	식단	
5	main		14	주의를 분산시키다	
6	mate		15	퍼덕거리다	
7	critically		16	파괴	
8	predator		17	멸종 위기의	
9	punishable		18	포유동물	

The Philippine eagle lives in the forests of the Philippines. It is one of the rarest and most powerful ❶ bird / birds in the world, with a wingspan of over 7 feet. Its main diet is monkeys and medium-sized mammals, a fact that has earned it a second name, "monkey-eating eagle." It hunts ❷ during / while the day, beginning at the top of a mountain and moving down from tree to tree. This allows it to soar from one location to another, conserving energy since it doesn't have to flap its wings. Two eagles will sometimes hunt together, one soaring overhead to distract a group of monkeys while ❸ another / the other swoops in for the kill. Because of ❹ habitat / habitant destruction, the Philippine eagle is critically endangered, with ❺ fewer / less than 750 left in the wild. Mating pairs have only one chick every two years, making the population slow to recover. Luckily, the only known predators of the eagle are humans. The birds have been protected as the national bird of the Philippines since 1995. Killing one is punishable by 12 years in jail!

*swoop 급습[기습]하다

The Philippine eagle lives in the forests of the Philippines. It is one of the rarest and most powerful birds in the world, with a wingspan of over 7 feet. Its main diet is monkeys and medium-sized mammals, a fact that has earned it a second name, "monkey-eating eagle." It hunts during the day, ❶ _____ (begin) at the top of a mountain and moving down from tree to tree. This allows it ❷ _____ (soar) from one location to another, ❸ _____ (conserve) energy since it doesn't have to flap its wings. Two eagles will sometimes hunt together, one soaring overhead ❹ _____ (distract) a group of monkeys while the other swoops in for the kill. Because of habitat destruction, the Philippine eagle is critically endangered, with fewer than 750 left in the wild. Mating pairs have only one chick every two years, making the population slow ❺ _____ (recover). Luckily, the only known predators of the eagle are humans. The birds have been protected as the national bird of the Philippines since 1995. Killing one is punishable by 12 years in jail!

*swoop 급습[기습]하다

The Philippine eagle lives in the forests of the Philippines. It is one of the rarest and most powerful birds in the world, with a wingspan of over 7 feet. Its ❶ _____ _____ (주식) is monkeys and medium-sized mammals, a fact that has earned it a second name, "monkey-eating eagle." It hunts during the day, beginning ❷ _____ _____ _____ _____ _____ _____ (산꼭대기에서) and moving down from tree to tree. This allows it to soar from one location to another, conserving energy since it doesn't have to flap its wings. Two eagles will sometimes hunt together, one soaring overhead to distract a group of monkeys while the other swoops in for the kill. Because of ❸ _____ _____ (서식지 파괴), the Philippine eagle is critically endangered, with fewer than 750 left in the wild. Mating pairs have only one chick ❹ _____ _____ _____ (2년 마다), making the population slow to recover. Luckily, the only known predators of the eagle are humans. The birds have been protected as the national bird of the Philippines since 1995. Killing one is punishable by 12 years in jail!

*swoop 급습[기습]하다

❶ **Summer Adventure Camps**

❷ Come and experience challenge and adventure this summer. ❸ Our summer camps offer a range of fun outdoor activities — kayaking, rock climbing, seashore explorations, team games and challenges.

❹ **Junior Explorer Camp (June 29th-July 1st)**

- ❺ Age: 8-10 years
- ❻ Cost: $120 per person, max 15 participants

❼ **Adventure Camp (July 5th-8th)**

- ❽ Age: 10-14 years
- ❾ Cost: $140 per person, max 15 participants

■ ❿ **PLEASE NOTE**

⓫ We provide all specialized equipment. ⓬ You should bring the following:

- ⓭ Sunscreen and towel
- ⓮ A large plastic bag for taking home wet clothes
- ⓯ Several sets of warm clothes suitable for outdoors (NOT jeans/denim)
- ⓰ Sturdy shoes or boots, hat and gloves

※ ⓱ Spaces are very limited and fill up fast. ⓲ For questions, call us at 231-5467.

*sturdy 튼튼한

❶ 여름모험 캠프

❷ 이번 여름에 도전과 모험을 경험하러 오세요. ❸ 저희 여름 캠프는 카약 타기, 암벽 등반, 해안 탐험, 팀 경기 및 도전과 같은 다양한 즐거운 야외 활동을 제공합니다.

❹ 주니어 탐험가 캠프 (6월 29일~7월 1일)

- ❺ 연령: 8~10세
- ❻ 비용: 1인당 120달러, 참가 인원 최대 15명

❼ 모험 캠프 (7월 5일~8일)

- ❽ 연령: 10~14세
- ❾ 비용: 1인당 140달러, 참가 인원 최대 15명

■ ❿ 주목해 주세요

⓫ 저희는 모든 전문적인 장비를 제공합니다. ⓬ 여러분은 다음을 가져와야 합니다.

- ⓭ 선크림과 수건
- ⓮ 젖은 옷을 집으로 가져가기 위한 대형 비닐봉지
- ⓯ 야외에 적합한 따뜻한 옷 몇 벌(청바지/데님 불가)
- ⓰ 튼튼한 신발이나 부츠, 모자, 장갑

※ ⓱ 자리는 매우 한정되어 있고 빨리 채워집니다. ⓲ 질문이 있으시면 231-5467로 연락해 주세요.

Word List

□ a range of 다양한　□ outdoor 야외의　□ activity 활동　□ seashore 해안　□ exploration 탐험　□ max 최대한
□ participant 참가자　□ specialized 전문적인　□ equipment 장비　□ suitable for ~에 적합한　□ limited 제한된

• Word Test

1	specialized	_____	6	탐험	_____
2	max	_____	7	활동	_____
3	suitable for	_____	8	제한된	_____
4	seashore	_____	9	참가자	_____
5	outdoor	_____	10	장비	_____

Summer Adventure Camps

Come and experience challenge and ❶ advent / adventure this summer. Our summer camps offer a range of fun outdoor activities — kayaking, rock climbing, seashore explorations, team games and challenges.

Junior Explorer Camp (June 29th-July 1st)
- Age: 8-10 years
- Cost: $120 per person, max 15 ❷ participant / participants

Adventure Camp (July 5th-8th)
- Age: 10-14 ❸ year / years
- Cost: $140 per person, max 15 participants

■ PLEASE NOTE

We provide all specialized equipment. You should bring the following:
- Sunscreen and towel
- A large plastic bag for taking home wet clothes
- Several sets of warm clothes suitable ❹ for / of outdoors (NOT jeans/denim)
- Sturdy shoes or boots, hat and gloves

※ Spaces are very limited and fill up fast. For questions, call us at 231-5467.

*sturdy 튼튼한

Summer Adventure Camps

Come and experience challenge and adventure this summer. Our summer camps ❶ _____ (offer) a range of fun outdoor activities — kayaking, rock climbing, seashore explorations, team games and challenges.

Junior Explorer Camp (June 29th-July 1st)
- Age: 8-10 years
- Cost: $120 per person, max 15 participants

Adventure Camp (July 5th-8th)
- Age: 10-14 years
- Cost: $140 per person, max 15 participants

■ PLEASE NOTE

We provide all ❷ _____ (specialize) equipment. You should bring the ❸ _____ (follow):
- Sunscreen and towel
- A large plastic bag for taking home wet clothes
- Several sets of warm clothes suitable for outdoors (NOT jeans/denim)
- Sturdy shoes or boots, hat and gloves

※ Spaces are very ❹ _____ (limit) and fill up fast. For questions, call us at 231-5467.

*sturdy 튼튼한

Summer Adventure Camps

Come and experience challenge and adventure this summer. Our summer camps offer a range of fun ❶ ＿＿＿＿＿ ＿＿＿＿＿ (야외 활동들) — kayaking, ❷ ＿＿＿＿＿ ＿＿＿＿＿ (암벽 등반), seashore explorations, team games and challenges.

Junior Explorer Camp (June 29th-July 1st)

- Age: 8-10 years
- Cost: $120 per person, max 15 participants

Adventure Camp (July 5th-8th)

- Age: 10-14 years
- Cost: $140 per person, max 15 participants

■ PLEASE NOTE

We provide all ❸ ＿＿＿＿＿ ＿＿＿＿＿ (전문화된 장비). You should bring the following:

- Sunscreen and towel
- A large plastic bag for taking home wet clothes
- Several sets of warm clothes suitable for outdoors (NOT jeans/denim)
- Sturdy shoes or boots, hat and gloves

※ Spaces are very limited and ❹ ＿＿＿＿＿ ＿＿＿＿＿ ＿＿＿＿＿ (빨리 채워지다). For questions, call us at 231-5467.

*sturdy 튼튼한

❶ Green Medical Transport Chair

❷ The Green Medical Transport Chair is specially designed to transport patients short distances. ❸ It is not to be used as a regular wheelchair.

• ❹ **Operating Tips**

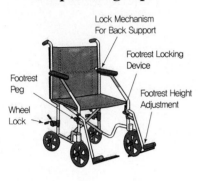

Lock Mechanism For Back Support

Footrest Locking Device

Footrest Peg

Footrest Height Adjustment

Wheel Lock

1. ❺ To open the chair, tilt to one side and push down on the seat rails.
2. ❻ Lift the back support to an upright position. ❼ The lock to secure the back will engage automatically.
3. ❽ The lowest part of the footrest should not be less than 2 1/2 inches from the ground to permit proper clearance.

❾ Note: The transport chair should not be operated without the assistance of an attendant.

• ❿ **Safety Tips**

1. ⓫ Before entering or leaving the chair, engage the wheel locks against the tires on both rear wheels.
2. ⓬ Do not move forward on the seat while leaning forward out of the chair.
3. ⓭ Do not step on the foot plates when transferring.

*tilt 기울이다

❶ Green 의료용 이동 의자
❷ Green 의료용 이동 의자는 환자들을 단거리로 이동시키기 위해 특별히 고안되어 있습니다. ❸ 그것은 보통의 휠체어로 사용되지 않습니다.
• ❹ 조작 팁
1. ❺ 의자를 펴기 위해서는, 한쪽으로 기울여 좌석 걸이를 누르세요.
2. ❻ 등받이 지지대를 수직이 되도록 들어올리세요. ❼ 등받이를 고정하는 잠금장치가 자동으로 채워질 것입니다.
3. ❽ 적절한 여유 공간이 있게 하려면 발 받침대의 가장 낮은 부분은 지면으로부터 2.5 인치보다 적게 떨어져서는 안 됩니다.
❾ 참고: 이동용 의자는 간병인의 도움 없이 작동되어서는 안 됩니다.
• ❿ 안전 팁
1. ⓫ 의자에 타고 내리기 전에, 양쪽 뒷바퀴의 타이어에 바퀴 잠금장치를 채우세요.
2. ⓬ 몸을 앞으로 숙여 몸이 의자 밖으로 나가게 한 상태에서 좌석에 앉아 앞으로 이동하지 마세요.
3. ⓭ 이동 시 발판을 밟지 마세요.

Word List

□ transport 이동; 이동시키다   □ distance 거리   □ regular 보통의   □ operate 조작하다, 작동하다   □ rail 걸이   □ support 지지대
□ upright 수직의   □ secure 고정하다   □ footrest 발 받침대   □ proper 적절한   □ clearance 여유 공간   □ assistance 도움
□ attendant 간병인, 간호인   □ rear 뒤쪽의   □ lean 기대다

• Word Test

1 rear _____
2 support _____
3 assistance _____
4 proper _____
5 transport _____
6 regular _____
7 secure _____

8 기대다 _____
9 거리 _____
10 발 받침대 _____
11 간병인, 간호인 _____
12 여유 공간 _____
13 조작하다, 작동하다 _____
14 수직의 _____

Green Medical Transport Chair

The Green Medical Transport Chair is specially designed to transport patients short distances. It is not to be used ❶ as / by a regular wheelchair.

- **Operating Tips**
1. To open the chair, tilt to one side and push down on the seat rails.
2. Lift the back support to an upright position. The lock to secure the back will engage automatically.
3. The lowest part of the footrest should not be ❷ fewer / less than 2 1/2 inches from the ground to permit ❸ proper / prosper clearance.

Note: The transport chair should not be operated without the assistance of an ❹ attendance / attendant .

- **Safety Tips**
1. Before entering or leaving the chair, engage the wheel locks against the tires on both rear wheels.
2. Do not move forward on the seat while leaning forward out of the chair.
3. Do not step on the foot plates when transferring.

*tilt 기울이다

Green Medical Transport Chair

The Green Medical Transport Chair is specially designed ❶ _____ (transport) patients short distances. It is not to be used as a regular wheelchair.

- **Operating Tips**
1. ❷ _____ (open) the chair, tilt to one side and push down on the seat rails.
2. Lift the back support to an upright position. The lock ❸ _____ (secure) the back will engage automatically.
3. The lowest part of the footrest should not be less than 2 1/2 inches from the ground to permit proper clearance.

Note: The transport chair should not be operated without the assistance of an attendant.

- **Safety Tips**
1. Before ❹ _____ (enter) or leaving the chair, engage the wheel locks against the tires on both rear wheels.
2. Do not move forward on the seat while leaning forward out of the chair.
3. Do not step on the foot plates when ❺ _____ (transfer).

*tilt 기울이다

Green Medical Transport Chair

The Green Medical Transport Chair is specially designed to transport patients short distances. It is not to be used as a regular wheelchair.

• **Operating Tips**

1. To open the chair, tilt to one side and push down on the seat rails.
2. Lift the back support to an upright position. The lock to secure the back will engage automatically.
3. The lowest part of the footrest should not be ❶ _____ _____ (~보다 적은) 2 1/2 inches from the ground to permit proper clearance.

Note: The transport chair should not be operated without the assistance of an attendant.

• **Safety Tips**

1. Before entering or leaving the chair, engage the wheel locks against the tires on both ❷ _____ _____ (뒷바퀴들).
2. Do not ❸ _____ _____ (앞으로 이동하다) on the seat while leaning forward out of the chair.
3. Do not ❹ _____ _____ (~을 밟다) the foot plates when transferring.

*tilt 기울이다

❶ People consume a range of ingredients to attain a balanced diet. ❷ And yet, people can tire of the sameness and out of curiosity desire to experience new tastes and textures. ❸ This taste dilemma has developed throughout mammalian history, as humans evolved to adapt to many habitats. ❹ Humans are omnivores. ❺ Being omnivorous requires exploration and innovation. ❻ Yet, as Paul Rozin sees it, exploration and testing can lead to anxiety because of a fear of eating new, foreign food, not knowing whether it will be disgusting or tasty. ❼ Rozin has written about this hypothesis of food selection that humans (and rats!) have an aversion to consuming new foods yet at the same time have a drive to do so. ❽ He proposes that there is a paradox surrounding our food choice habits, a form of cognitive dissonance. ❾ This dilemma drives humans to eat beyond our biological imperative as we eat more and more variety than is needed for survival.

*omnivore 잡식 동물 **aversion 반감 ***biological imperative 생명 유지의 필수 요소

❶ 사람들은 균형 잡힌 식단을 얻기 위해 다양한 재료를 섭취한다. ❷ 그럼에도 불구하고, 사람들은 같은 것에 싫증을 느낄 수 있고 호기심으로 인해 새로운 맛과 질감을 경험하고 싶어 한다. ❸ 이 미각 딜레마는 포유류 역사 전반에 걸쳐 발생해 왔는데 인간이 많은 거주 환경에 적응하도록 진화했기 때문이다. ❹ 인간은 잡식 동물이다. ❺ 잡식성이 되는 데는 탐색과 혁신이 필요하다. ❻ 그러나 Paul Rozin이 생각하듯이, 새롭고 익숙하지 않은 음식이 역겨울지 맛있을지 알지 못하므로 그것을 먹는 데 대한 두려움 때문에, 탐색과 시험은 불안으로 이어질 수도 있다. ❼ Rozin은 인간(그리고 쥐!)이 새로운 음식을 섭취하는 것에 대해 반감을 가지고 있지만, 동시에 그렇게 하려는 욕구가 있다는 음식 선택의 이 가설에 관한 글을 썼다. ❽ 그는 인지 부조화의 한 형태로, 우리의 음식 선택 습관을 둘러싼 역설이 있다는 점을 제시한다. ❾ 우리가 생존에 필요한 것보다 점점 더 다양한 음식을 먹게 되면서, 이 딜레마는 인간을 생명 유지의 필수 요소 이상으로 먹도록 몰아간다.

Word List

□ consume 섭취하다, 소비하다 □ a range of 다양한 □ ingredient 재료 □ attain 얻다, 획득하다 □ balanced 균형 잡힌
□ diet 식단 □ texture (음식이 입안에서 느껴지는) 질감 □ mammalian 포유류의 □ evolve 진화하다 □ adapt 적응하다
□ habitat 거주 환경, 서식지 □ omnivorous 잡식성의 □ exploration 탐험 □ innovation 혁신 □ disgusting 역겨운
□ hypothesis 가설 □ drive 욕구; (사람을 특정한 방식의 행동을 하도록) 몰아붙이다[만들다] □ paradox 역설 □ cognitive 인지의, 인식의
□ dissonance 부조화

• Word Test

1	innovation		10	부조화
2	hypothesis		11	탐험
3	mammalian		12	역겨운
4	cognitive		13	식단
5	consume		14	거주 환경, 서식지
6	attain		15	역설
7	adapt		16	균형 잡힌
8	texture		17	재료
9	omnivorous		18	진화하다

People consume a range of ingredients to attain a balanced diet. And yet, people can tire of the ❶ sameness / variety and out of curiosity desire to experience new tastes and textures. This taste dilemma has developed throughout mammalian history, as humans evolved to adapt to many habitats. Humans are omnivores. Being omnivorous requires exploration and innovation. Yet, as Paul Rozin sees it, exploration and testing can lead to anxiety ❷ because / because of a fear of eating new, foreign food, not knowing ❸ though / whether it will be disgusting or tasty. Rozin has written about this hypothesis of food selection that humans (and rats!) have an aversion to consuming new foods yet at the same time have a drive to do so. He proposes ❹ that / which there is a paradox surrounding our food choice habits, a form of cognitive dissonance. This dilemma drives humans to eat beyond our biological imperative as we eat more and more variety ❺ as / than is needed for survival.

*omnivore 잡식 동물 **aversion 반감 ***biological imperative 생명 유지의 필수 요소

People consume a range of ingredients ❶ _____ (attain) a balanced diet. And yet, people can tire of the sameness and out of curiosity desire to experience new tastes and textures. This taste dilemma has developed throughout mammalian history, as humans evolved ❷ _____ (adapt) to many habitats. Humans are omnivores. Being omnivorous requires exploration and innovation. Yet, as Paul Rozin sees it, exploration and testing can lead to anxiety because of a fear of ❸ _____ (eat) new, foreign food, not knowing whether it will be disgusting or tasty. Rozin has written about this hypothesis of food selection that humans (and rats!) have an aversion to consuming new foods yet at the same time have a drive to do so. He proposes that there is a paradox ❹ _____ (surround) our food choice habits, a form of cognitive dissonance. This dilemma drives humans ❺ _____ (eat) beyond our biological imperative as we eat more and more variety than is needed for survival.

*omnivore 잡식 동물 **aversion 반감 ***biological imperative 생명 유지의 필수 요소

People consume a range of ingredients to attain a balanced diet. And yet, people can ❶ _____ _____ _____ _____ (같은 것에 싫증나다) and out of curiosity desire to experience new tastes and textures. This taste dilemma has developed throughout mammalian history, as humans evolved to adapt to many habitats. Humans are omnivores. Being omnivorous requires exploration and innovation. Yet, as Paul Rozin sees it, exploration and testing can ❷ _____ _____ _____ (불안으로 이어지다) because of a fear of eating new, foreign food, not knowing whether it will be disgusting or tasty. Rozin has written about this hypothesis of food selection that humans (and rats!) ❸ _____ _____ _____ _____ (~을 혐오하다) consuming new foods yet ❹ _____ _____ _____ (동시에) have a drive to do so. He proposes that there is a paradox surrounding our food choice habits, a form of ❺ _____ _____ (인지 부조화). This dilemma drives humans to eat beyond our biological imperative as we eat more and more variety than is needed for survival.

*omnivore 잡식 동물 **aversion 반감 ***biological imperative 생명 유지의 필수 요소

❶ Like an addiction to anything, when the craving for certainty is met, there is a sensation of reward. ❷ At low levels, for example, when predicting where your foot will land as you walk, the reward is often unnoticeable (except when your foot doesn't land the way you predicted, which equates with uncertainty). ❸ The pleasure of prediction is more acute when you listen to music based on repeating patterns. ❹ The ability to predict, and then obtain data that meets those predictions, generates an overall *toward* response. ❺ It's part of the reason that games such as solitaire, Sudoku, and crossword puzzles are enjoyable. ❻ They give you a little rush from creating more certainty in the world, in a safe way. ❼ Entire industries are devoted to resolving larger uncertainties: from shop-front palm readers, to the mythical "black boxes" that can supposedly predict stock trends and make investors millions. ❽ Some parts of accounting and consulting make their money by helping executives experience a perception of increasing certainty, through strategic planning and "forecasting". ❾ While the financial markets of 2008 showed once again that the future is inherently uncertain, the one thing that's certain is that people will always pay lots of money at least to *feel* less uncertain. ❿ That's because uncertainty feels, to the brain, like a threat to your life.

*craving 갈망, 열망

❶ 무엇이든지 그것에 대한 중독처럼, 확실성에 대한 갈망이 충족될 때에도, 보상의 느낌이 있다. ❷ 낮은 수준에서는, 예를 들어, 걸으면서 발이 어디에 착지할지를 예측할 때는, (발이 예측대로 착지하지 않는 경우는 그것이 불확실성과 동일하므로 제외하고) 보상은 눈에 띄지 않는 경우가 많다. ❸ 반복되는 패턴을 바탕으로 한 음악을 들을 때 예측의 즐거움은 더 강하다. ❹ 예측한 다음 그러한 예측을 충족하는 데이터를 얻을 수 있는 능력은 전체적으로 '순조로운' 반응을 생성한다. ❺ 그것은 솔리테르(혼자서 하는 카드놀이), 스도쿠, 크로스워드 퍼즐과 같은 게임이 즐거운 이유의 일부이다. ❻ 그것들은 세상에서 더 많은 확실성을 안전한 방식으로 만드는 것으로부터 오는 약간의 쾌감을 제공한다. ❼ 상점 앞에서 손금을 보는 사람에서부터 주식 동향을 예측하고 어쩌면 투자자가 한밑천 잡을 수 있게 해 줄 수 있다고 하는 신화에나 나옴직한 '블랙박스'에 이르기까지 전체 산업이 더 큰 불확실성을 해결하는 데 전념하고 있다. ❽ 회계 및 컨설팅의 일부분은 전략적인 계획과 '예측'을 통해 경영 간부들이 증가하는 확실성에 대한 인식을 경험할 수 있도록 도움으로써 수익을 창출한다. ❾ 2008년의 금융 시장은 미래가 본질적으로 불확실하다는 것을 다시 한번 보여 주었지만, 한 가지 확실한 것은 사람들이 적어도 불확실성을 덜 '느끼기' 위해 항상 많은 돈을 지불하려 한다는 점이다. ❿ 왜냐하면 불확실성이 뇌에는 삶에 대한 위협처럼 느껴지기 때문이다.

Word List

□ addiction 중독　□ sensation 느낌　□ reward 보상　□ unnoticeable 눈에 띄지 않는　□ equate 동일하다
□ acute 아주 강한, 격렬한　□ obtain 얻다, 획득하다　□ solitaire 솔리테르(혼자서 하는 카드놀이)　□ rush 쾌감, 황홀감
□ be devoted to ~에 전념하다　□ shop-front 상점 앞의　□ palm reader 손금 보는 사람　□ mythical 신화에나 나옴직한, 가공의
□ supposedly 아마도, 추측건대　□ make ~ millions ~을 한밑천 잡게 하다　□ investor 투자자　□ accounting 회계
□ executive 경영 간부, 임원, 중역　□ strategic 전략적인　□ inherently 본질적으로

1	strategic	10	쾌감, 황홀감
2	accounting	11	투자자
3	equate	12	신화에나 나옴직한, 가공의
4	palm reader	13	본질적으로
5	addiction	14	상점 앞의
6	reward	15	느낌
7	be devoted to	16	눈에 띄지 않는
8	obtain	17	경영 간부, 임원, 중역
9	supposedly	18	아주 강한, 격렬한

• 유형 1 네모 안에서 옳은 어법·어휘를 고르시오.

Like an addiction to anything, when the craving for certainty is met, there is a sensation of reward. At low levels, for example, when predicting ❶ [where / which] your foot will land as you walk, the reward is often unnoticeable (except when your foot doesn't land the way you predicted, ❷ [that / which] equates with uncertainty). The pleasure of prediction is more acute when you listen to music based on repeating patterns. The ability to predict, and then obtain data that meets those predictions, generates an overall *toward* response. It's part of the reason that games ❸ [as such / such as] solitaire, Sudoku, and crossword puzzles are enjoyable. They give you ❹ [a few / a little] rush from creating more certainty in the world, in a safe way. Entire industries are devoted to resolving larger uncertainties: from shop-front palm readers, to the mythical "black boxes" that can supposedly predict stock trends and make investors millions. Some parts of accounting and consulting make their money by helping executives experience a ❺ [perception / perfection] of increasing certainty, through strategic planning and "forecasting". While the financial markets of 2008 showed once again that the future is inherently uncertain, the one thing that's certain is that people will always pay lots of money at least to *feel* less uncertain. That's because uncertainty feels, to the brain, like a threat to your life.

*craving 갈망, 열망

Like an addiction to anything, when the craving for certainty ❶ _____ (meet), there is a sensation of reward. At low levels, for example, when predicting where your foot will land as you walk, the reward is often unnoticeable (except when your foot doesn't land the way you predicted, which ❷ _____ (equate) with uncertainty). The pleasure of prediction is more acute when you listen to music based on repeating patterns. The ability ❸ _____ (predict), and then obtain data that meets those predictions, generates an overall *toward* response. It's part of the reason that games such as solitaire, Sudoku, and crossword puzzles are enjoyable. They give you a little rush from creating more certainty in the world, in a safe way. Entire industries are devoted to ❹ _____ (resolve) larger uncertainties: from shop-front palm readers, to the mythical "black boxes" that can supposedly predict stock trends and make investors millions. Some parts of accounting and consulting make their money by helping executives ❺ _____ (experience) a perception of increasing certainty, through strategic planning and "forecasting". While the financial markets of 2008 showed once again that the future is inherently uncertain, the one thing that's certain is that people will always pay lots of money at least to *feel* less uncertain. That's because uncertainty feels, to the brain, like a threat to your life.

*craving 갈망, 열망

Like an addiction to anything, when the craving for certainty is met, there is a sensation of reward. At low levels, for example, when predicting where your foot will land as you walk, the reward is often unnoticeable (except when your foot doesn't land the way you predicted, which equates with uncertainty). The ❶ _____ _____ _____ (예측의 즐거움) is more acute when you listen to music based on repeating patterns. The ability to predict, and then obtain data that meets those predictions, generates an overall *toward* response. It's part of the reason that games ❷ _____ _____ (~와 같은) solitaire, Sudoku, and crossword puzzles are enjoyable. They give you a little rush from creating more certainty in the world, in a safe way. Entire industries ❸ _____ _____ _____ (~에 전념하다) resolving larger uncertainties: from shop-front palm readers, to the mythical "black boxes" that can supposedly predict stock trends and make investors millions. Some parts of accounting and consulting make their money by helping executives experience a perception of increasing certainty, through strategic planning and "forecasting". While the financial markets of 2008 showed once again that the future is ❹ _____ _____ (본질적으로 불확실한), the one thing that's certain is that people will always ❺ _____ _____ _____ _____ (많은 돈을 지불하다) at least to *feel* less uncertain. That's because uncertainty feels, to the brain, like a threat to your life.

*craving 갈망, 열망

❶ One of the earliest experiments investigating the distortions caused by categorization was a simple study in which subjects were asked to estimate the lengths of a set of eight line segments. ❷ The longest of those lines was 5 percent longer than the next in the bunch, which, in turn, was 5 percent longer than the third longest, and so on. ❸ The researchers asked half their subjects to estimate the lengths of each of the lines, in centimeters. ❹ But before asking the other subjects to do the same, they artificially grouped the lines into two sets — the longer four lines were labeled "Group A," the shorter four labeled "Group B." ❺ The experimenters found that once the lines were thought of as belonging to a group, the subjects perceived them differently. ❻ They judged the lines within each group as being closer in length to one another than they really were, and the length difference between the two groups as being greater than it actually was.

*segment 토막

❶ 범주화로 인한 왜곡을 연구한 가장 초창기의 실험 중 하나는 피험자에게 한 묶음으로 된 여덟 개의 끈 토막의 길이를 추정하도록 요청한 간단한 연구였다. ❷ 그중 가장 긴 줄은 그 꾸러미에 있는 다음 줄보다 5퍼센트 더 길었고, 그것은 다시 세 번째 긴 끈보다 5퍼센트 더 길었으며, 그런 식으로 계속되었다. ❸ 연구원들은 피험자 절반에게 각 끈의 길이를 센티미터 단위로 추정하도록 요청했다. ❹ 하지만 다른 피험자들에게 똑같이 하도록 요청하기 전에, 그들은 인위적으로 끈을 두 묶음으로 분류했는데, 더 긴 네 개의 끈은 '그룹 A'로 불렸고, 더 짧은 네 개는 '그룹 B'로 불렸다. ❺ 실험자들은 그 끈이 어떤 그룹에 속한다고 생각되면, 그 피험자들은 그것들을 다르게 인식한다는 것을 발견했다. ❻ 그들은 각 그룹 내의 끈이 실제보다 길이가 서로 더 비슷하고, 두 그룹 간의 길이 차이는 실제보다 더 크다고 판단했다.

• Word Test

1	subject	8	범주화
2	distortion	9	인식하다
3	belonging	10	인위적으로
4	judge	11	실제로
5	group	12	추정하다
6	experiment	13	(~이라고) 부르다
7	bunch	14	조사하다

One of the earliest ❶ experiment / experiments investigating the distortions caused by categorization was a simple study ❷ in which / of which subjects were asked to estimate the lengths of a set of eight line segments. The longest of those lines was 5 percent longer than the next in the bunch, which, in turn, was 5 percent longer than the third longest, and so on. The researchers asked half their subjects to estimate the lengths of each of the lines, in centimeters. But before asking the other subjects to do the same, they artificially grouped the lines ❸ by / into two sets — the longer four lines were labeled "Group A," the shorter four labeled "Group B." The experimenters found ❹ that / which once the lines were thought of as belonging to a group, the subjects perceived them ❺ different / differently . They judged the lines within each group as being closer in length to one another than they really were, and the length difference between the two groups as being greater than it actually was.

*segment 토막

One of the earliest experiments investigating the distortions ❶ _____ (cause) by categorization ❷ _____ (be) a simple study in which subjects were asked to estimate the lengths of a set of eight line segments. The longest of those lines was 5 percent longer than the next in the bunch, which, in turn, was 5 percent longer than the third longest, and so on. The researchers asked half their subjects ❸ _____ (estimate) the lengths of each of the lines, in centimeters. But before ❹ _____ (ask) the other subjects to do the same, they artificially grouped the lines into two sets — the longer four lines were labeled "Group A," the shorter four labeled "Group B." The experimenters found that once the lines were thought of as belonging to a group, the subjects perceived them differently. They judged the lines within each group as ❺ _____ (be) closer in length to one another than they really were, and the length difference between the two groups as being greater than it actually was.

*segment 토막

One of the earliest experiments investigating the distortions caused by categorization was a simple study in which subjects were asked to estimate the lengths of ❶ _____ _____ _____ (한 묶음의) eight line segments. The longest of those lines was 5 percent longer than the next in the bunch, which, in turn, was 5 percent longer than the third longest, and so on. The researchers asked half their subjects to estimate the lengths of each of the lines, in centimeters. But before asking the other subjects to ❷ _____ _____ _____ (똑같이 하다), they artificially ❸ _____ _____ _____ _____ _____ _____ (끈들을 두 묶음으로 분류했다) — the longer four lines were labeled "Group A," the shorter four labeled "Group B." The experimenters found that once the lines were thought of as belonging to a group, the subjects perceived them differently. They judged the lines within each group as being closer in length to ❹ _____ _____ (서로) than they really were, and the length difference between the two groups as being greater than it actually was.

*segment 토막

❶ In my research with Liane Young and James Dungan of Boston College, we studied the effects of loyalty on people using Amazon's Mechanical Turk, an online marketplace where users earn money for completing tasks. ❷ At the beginning of the study, we asked some participants to write an essay about loyalty and others to write about fairness. ❸ Later in the study, they were each exposed to poor work by someone else. ❹ Those who had received the loyalty nudge were less willing to blow the whistle on a fellow user for inferior performance. ❺ This finding complements research showing that bribery is more common in countries that prize collectivism. ❻ The sense of group belonging and interdependence among members often leads people to tolerate the offense. ❼ It makes them feel less accountable for it, diffusing responsibility to the collective whole instead of assigning it to the individual. ❽ In short, empathy for those within one's immediate circle can conflict with justice for all.

*nudge (가벼운) 자극, (팔꿈치로) 슬쩍 찌르기 **blow the whistle on ~을 고자질하다 ***bribery 뇌물

❶ Boston 대학의 Liane Young 및 James Dungan과 함께한 나의 연구에서, 우리는 이용자들이 과업을 완수한 것에 대해 돈을 버는 온라인 시장인 Amazon의 Mechanical Turk를 이용하는 사람들에게 충성도가 미치는 영향을 연구했다. ❷ 연구를 시작할 때, 우리는 몇몇 참가자들에게 충성도에 관한 에세이를 쓰도록 요청했고, 다른 참가자들에게는 공정성에 관한 에세이를 쓰도록 했다. ❸ 그 연구의 후반부에서, 그들은 각각 다른 사람이 한 서투른 작업을 접했다. ❹ 충성도 자극을 받은 사람들은 열등한 수행 능력에 대해 동료 이용자를 기꺼이 고자질하려는 마음이 덜했다. ❺ 이 연구 결과는 집단주의를 높이 평가하는 나라에서 뇌물이 더 흔하다는 것을 보여 주는 연구를 보완한다. ❻ 구성원들 사이의 집단 소속감과 상호 의존성이 흔히 사람들로 하여금 그 범죄를 용인하도록 한다. ❼ 그것은 그들이 그것에 대해 책임감을 덜 느끼도록 만들고, 책임을 개인의 탓으로 돌리는 대신에 집단 전체에 분산시킨다. ❽ 간단히 말해서, 자신의 가장 가까운 범위 안에 있는 사람들에 대한 공감은 모두를 위한 정의와 충돌할 수 있다.

Word List

□ effect 영향   □ loyalty 충성도   □ complete 완수하다   □ task 과제   □ fairness 공정성   □ expose 노출시키다
□ inferior 열등한   □ complement 보완하다   □ prize 높이 평가하다   □ collectivism 집단주의   □ interdependence 상호 의존성
□ tolerate 용인하다   □ offense 범죄   □ accountable 책임감을 느끼는   □ diffuse 분산시키다
□ assign (동가·이유 따위를) (~ 탓으로) 돌리다, ~의 것[탓]으로 하다   □ empathy 공감   □ immediate 가장 가까운, 인접한
□ conflict 충돌하다

• Word Test

1	interdependence		10	집단주의	
2	complete		11	공감	
3	prize		12	충돌하다	
4	immediate		13	용인하다	
5	effect		14	노출시키다	
6	inferior		15	과제	
7	offense		16	책임감을 느끼는	
8	diffuse		17	충성도	
9	fairness		18	보완하다	

In my research with Liane Young and James Dungan of Boston College, we studied the effects of ❶ loyalty / royalty on people using Amazon's Mechanical Turk, an online marketplace ❷ where / which users earn money for completing tasks. At the beginning of the study, we asked some participants to write an essay about loyalty and others to write about fairness. Later in the study, they were each exposed to poor work by someone else. Those who had received the loyalty nudge were ❸ fewer / less willing to blow the whistle on a fellow user for inferior performance. This finding ❹ complements / compliments research showing that bribery is more common in countries that prize collectivism. The sense of group belonging and interdependence among members often leads people to tolerate the offense. It makes them feel less accountable for ❺ it / them , diffusing responsibility to the collective whole instead of assigning it to the individual. In short, empathy for those within one's immediate circle can conflict with justice for all.

*nudge (가벼운) 자극, (팔꿈치로) 슬쩍 찌르기 **blow the whistle on ~을 고자질하다 ***bribery 뇌물

In my research with Liane Young and James Dungan of Boston College, we studied the effects of loyalty on people using Amazon's Mechanical Turk, an online marketplace where users earn money for ❶ _____ (complete) tasks. At the beginning of the study, we asked some participants ❷ _____ (write) an essay about loyalty and others to write about fairness. Later in the study, they were each exposed to poor work by someone else. Those who ❸ _____ (receive) the loyalty nudge were less willing ❹ _____ (blow) the whistle on a fellow user for inferior performance. This finding complements research showing that bribery is more common in countries that prize collectivism. The sense of group belonging and interdependence among members often ❺ _____ (lead) people to tolerate the offense. It makes them feel less accountable for it, diffusing responsibility to the collective whole instead of assigning it to the individual. In short, empathy for those within one's immediate circle can conflict with justice for all.

*nudge (가벼운) 자극, (팔꿈치로) 슬쩍 찌르기 **blow the whistle on ~을 고자질하다 ***bribery 뇌물

In my research with Liane Young and James Dungan of Boston College, we studied the effects of loyalty on people using Amazon's Mechanical Turk, an online marketplace where users earn money for completing tasks. At the beginning of the study, we asked some participants to write an essay about loyalty and others to write about fairness. Later in the study, they were each exposed to poor work by someone else. Those who had received the loyalty nudge were less willing to blow the whistle on a fellow user for ❶ _____ _____ (열등한 실적). This finding complements research showing that bribery is more common in countries that prize collectivism. The ❷ _____ _____ _____ _____ (집단 소속감) and interdependence among members often leads people to tolerate the offense. It makes them feel less accountable for it, diffusing responsibility to the collective whole ❸ _____ _____ (~대신에) assigning it to the individual. ❹ _____ _____ (간단히 말해서), empathy for those within one's immediate circle can ❺ _____ _____ _____ (정의와 충돌하다) for all.

*nudge (가벼운) 자극, (팔꿈치로) 슬쩍 찌르기 **blow the whistle on ~을 고자질하다 ***bribery 뇌물

363

❶ Social engineering is a method of gaining access to systems, data, or buildings through the exploitation of the human psychology. ❷ As foolish as it may sound, some companies and organizations think that they are resistant to the threat of social engineering. ❸ On the contrary, no organization is immune to social engineering, not even the White House or any other prominent system. ❹ For instance, a contest was held at a security conference wherein the participants were asked to obtain information from target companies, which could be utilized for a hypothetical attack. ❺ Out of the 140 phone calls that were made to employees of the target companies, almost all the employees divulged information except for five, who refused to give out anything. ❻ In addition, 90% of the employees clicked on a URL, which was sent to them by the participants. ❼ These employees did not even bother knowing the person who sent it. ❽ This security conference concluded on how wide and dangerous the scope of social engineering is for all systems and organizations.

*social engineering 사회 공학   **divulge (비밀을) 누설하다

❶ 사회 공학은 인간의 심리를 이용하여 시스템, 정보, 또는 건물에 접근하는 방법이다. ❷ 어리석게 들릴지 모르지만, 일부 회사와 조직은 그들이 사회 공학의 위협에 저항력이 있다고 생각한다. ❸ 이와 반대로, 사회 공학에 영향을 받지 않는 조직은 없으며, 심지어 백악관이나 다른 어떤 탁월한 시스템도 마찬가지이다. ❹ 예를 들어, 한 보안 학회에서 대회가 열렸는데, 거기에서 참가자들은 가상 공격에 활용될 수 있는 정보를 표적 회사로부터 얻어 낼 것을 요구받았다. ❺ 표적 회사의 직원들에게 걸었던 140통의 전화 통화에서 아무것도 내놓지 않았던 다섯 명을 제외하고는 거의 모든 직원이 정보를 누설했다. ❻ 게다가, 직원의 90퍼센트는 참가자가 그들에게 보낸 URL을 클릭했다. ❼ 이 직원들은 심지어 그것을 보낸 사람을 알려고도 하지 않았다. ❽ 이 보안 학회는 모든 시스템과 조직에게 있어 사회 공학의 범위가 참으로 광범위하고 위험하다고 결론지었다.

Word List

□ engineering 공학   □ method 방법   □ gain access to ~에 접근하다   □ exploitation (부당한) 이용   □ psychology 심리
□ resistant to ~에 저항력이 있는   □ threat 위협   □ on the contrary 그와 반대로   □ immune to ~에 영향을 받지 않는
□ prominent 탁월한   □ contest 대회, 시합   □ security 보안   □ obtain 얻다   □ utilize 활용하다, 이용하다
□ hypothetical 가상의, 가상적인   □ conclude 결론짓다, 끝나다   □ scope 범위

• Word Test

1	gain access to	9	~에 영향을 받지 않는
2	threat	10	범위
3	conclude	11	방법
4	engineering	12	~에 저항력이 있는
5	utilize	13	가상의, 가상적인
6	psychology	14	대회, 시합
7	security	15	(부당한) 이용
8	prominent	16	얻다

Social engineering is a method of gaining access to systems, data, or buildings through the exploitation of the human psychology. As ❶ foolish / more foolish as it may sound, some companies and organizations think ❷ that / which they are resistant to the threat of social engineering. On the contrary, no organization is immune to social engineering, not even the White House or any other ❸ prominent / promising system. For instance, a contest was held at a security conference wherein the participants were asked to obtain information from target companies, ❹ who / which could be utilized for a hypothetical attack. Out of the 140 phone calls that were made to employees of the target companies, almost all the employees divulged information except for five, ❺ who / whom refused to give out anything. In addition, 90% of the employees clicked on a URL, which was sent to them by the participants. These employees did not even bother knowing the person who sent it. This security conference concluded on how wide and dangerous the scope of social engineering is for all systems and organizations.

*social engineering 사회 공학   **divulge (비밀을) 누설하다

Social engineering is a method of gaining access to systems, data, or buildings through the exploitation of the human psychology. As foolish as it may sound, some companies and organizations think that they are resistant to the threat of social engineering. On the contrary, no organization ❶ _____ (be) immune to social engineering, not even the White House or any other prominent system. For instance, a contest was held at a security conference wherein the participants ❷ _____ (ask) to obtain information from target companies, which could be utilized for a hypothetical attack. Out of the 140 phone calls that were made to employees of the target companies, almost all the employees divulged information except for five, who refused ❸ _____ (give) out anything. In addition, 90% of the employees clicked on a URL, which was sent to them by the participants. These employees did not even bother ❹ _____ (know) the person who sent it. This security conference concluded on how wide and dangerous the scope of social engineering ❺ _____ (be) for all systems and organizations.

*social engineering 사회 공학   **divulge (비밀을) 누설하다

Social engineering is a method of ❶ _____ _____ _____ (~에 접근하는) systems, data, or buildings through the exploitation of the human psychology. ❷ _____ _____ _____ _____ _____ _____ (어리석게 들릴지 모르지만), some companies and organizations think that they are resistant to the threat of social engineering. On the contrary, no organization is ❸ _____ _____ (~에 영향을 받지 않는) social engineering, not even the White House or any other prominent system. For instance, a contest was held at a security conference wherein the participants were asked to obtain information from target companies, which could be utilized for a hypothetical attack. Out of the 140 phone calls that were made to employees of the target companies, almost all the employees divulged information ❹ _____ _____ (~을 제외하고) five, who refused to give out anything. In addition, 90% of the employees clicked on a URL, which was sent to them by the participants. These employees did not even bother knowing the person who sent it. This security conference concluded on how wide and dangerous the scope of social engineering is for all systems and organizations.

*social engineering 사회 공학   **divulge (비밀을) 누설하다

❶ More often than not, key environmental influences on personality occur during a person's early life, so it would require a time machine to fix things — think *Back to the Future*. ❷ It is also quite common for nurture to act in concert with nature, accentuating predispositions or enhancing existing potential. ❸ For example, ambitious people tend to have competitive jobs, and as their jobs become more competitive they tend to become more ambitious as a result. ❹ Likewise, extraverts may choose jobs that require a great deal of networking and interpersonal schmoosing. ❺ Yet adaptation to those jobs tends to increase their extraversion even further. ❻ And so personal qualities, including talent-related traits, are always influenced by both nature and nurture, but often in the same direction, such that nurture ends up amplifying characteristics that were already there to begin with. ❼ In that sense, the more people change, the more they become like themselves. ❽ By and large, as we grow older we all become exaggerated versions of our earlier selves.

*extravert 외향적인 사람   **schmoose (환심을 사려고) 한담을 나누다

❶ 대개 성격에 미치는 주요한 환경적 영향은 한 개인의 어린 시절 동안 발생하므로, 상황을 고치기 위해서는 타임머신이 필요할 텐데, 영화 *Back to the Future*를 생각해 보라. ❷ 또한 후천성은 성향을 두드러지게 하거나 기존의 잠재력을 향상시키면서 선천성과 함께 작용하는 경우가 아주 흔하다. ❸ 예를 들어, 야심을 가진 사람들은 경쟁하는 직업을 갖는 경향이 있고, 그들의 직업이 더 경쟁적으로 될수록 그들은 결과적으로 더 야심을 가지게 되는 경향이 있다. ❹ 마찬가지로 외향적인 사람들은 많은 인적 네트워크 형성과 개인 간의 한담을 나누는 것을 필요로 하는 직업을 선택할 수도 있다. ❺ 하지만 그러한 직업에 대한 적응은 그들의 외향성을 훨씬 더 증가시키는 경향이 있다. ❻ 그래서 재능과 관련된 특성을 포함하여 개인적 자질은 항상 선천성과 후천성 양쪽 모두에 의해서, 하지만 흔히 같은 방향으로 영향을 받는데, 후천성이 결국 이미 처음부터 존재했던 특성을 증폭했던 방식이다. ❼ 그런 면에서 사람들은 더 많이 변할수록 그만큼 더 자신처럼 된다. ❽ 대체로, 우리가 나이가 들면서 우리는 모두 우리의 초기 모습의 부풀려진 형태가 된다.

Word List

□ more often than not 대개, 자주   □ personality 성격   □ fix 고치다   □ nurture 후천성, 양육
□ in concert with ~과 함께, ~과 협력하여   □ nature 선천성, 본성   □ accentuate 두드러지게 하다, 강조하다
□ predisposition 성향, 경향   □ enhance 강화하다   □ ambitious 야심을 가진   □ competitive 경쟁적인
□ networking 인적 네트워크[정보망] 형성   □ interpersonal 개인 간의, 대인 관계의   □ adaptation 적응, 순응
□ amplify 증폭시키다, ~을 확대하다   □ by and large 대체로, 일반적으로   □ version 형태[판], 버전

• Word Test

1	adaptation	9	형태[판], 버전
2	accentuate	10	성격
3	competitive	11	후천성, 양육
4	more often than not	12	선천성, 본성
5	fix	13	성향, 경향
6	in concert with	14	야심을 가진
7	enhance	15	개인 간의, 대인 관계의
8	by and large	16	증폭시키다, ~을 확대하다

More often than not, key environmental influences on personality occur ❶ during / while a person's early life, so it would require a time machine to fix things — think *Back to the Future*. It is also quite common for nurture to act in concert with nature, accentuating predispositions or ❷ enhancing / reducing existing potential. For example, ambitious people tend to have ❸ comparative / competitive jobs, and as their jobs become more competitive they tend to become more ambitious as a result. Likewise, extraverts may choose jobs that require a great deal of networking and interpersonal schmoosing. Yet adaptation to those jobs tends to increase their ❹ introversion / extraversion even further. And so personal qualities, including talent-related traits, are always influenced by both nature and nurture, but often in the same direction, such that nurture ends up amplifying characteristics ❺ that / who were already there to begin with. In that sense, the more people change, the more they become like themselves. By and large, as we grow older we all become exaggerated versions of our earlier selves.

*extravert 외향적인 사람 **schmoose (환심을 사려고) 한담을 나누다

More often than not, key environmental influences on personality occur during a person's early life, so it would require a time machine to fix things — think *Back to the Future*. It is also quite common for nurture ❶ _____ (act) in concert with nature, accentuating predispositions or enhancing existing potential. For example, ambitious people tend to have competitive jobs, and as their jobs become more competitive they tend to become more ambitious as a result. Likewise, extraverts may choose jobs that require a great deal of networking and interpersonal schmoosing. Yet adaptation to those jobs tends to increase their extraversion even further. And so personal qualities, ❷ _____ (include) talent-related traits, ❸ _____ (be) always influenced by both nature and nurture, but often in the same direction, such that nurture ❹ _____ (end) up amplifying characteristics that were already there to begin with. In that sense, the more people change, the more they become like themselves. By and large, as we grow older we all become ❺ _____ (exaggerate) versions of our earlier selves.

*extravert 외향적인 사람 **schmoose (환심을 사려고) 한담을 나누다

❶ _____ _____ _____ _____ (대개), key environmental influences on personality occur during a person's early life, so it would require a time machine to fix things — think *Back to the Future*. It is also quite common for nurture to act in concert with nature, accentuating predispositions or enhancing ❷ _____ _____ (기존의 잠재력). For example, ambitious people tend to have competitive jobs, and as their jobs become more competitive they tend to become more ambitious ❸ _____ _____ _____ (결과적으로). Likewise, extraverts may choose jobs that require a great deal of networking and interpersonal schmoosing. Yet ❹ _____ _____ _____ _____ (그러한 직업들에 대한 적응) tends to increase their extraversion even further. And so personal qualities, including talent-related traits, are always influenced by both nature and nurture, but often in the same direction, such that nurture ends up amplifying characteristics that were already there to begin with. In that sense, the more people change, the more they become like themselves. By and large, as we grow older we all become exaggerated versions of our earlier selves.

*extravert 외향적인 사람 **schmoose (환심을 사려고) 한담을 나누다

❶ People often confuse two different standards for thinking, which we might call the "good thinker" (active open-mindedness) and the "expert." ❷ Because experts *know* the answer to most questions, they usually do not have to consider alternatives or counterevidence. ❸ If we admire experts, we may come to admire people who are "decisive" in the sense of being rigid. ❹ When a news commentator criticizes a political candidate for waffling and being unsure (as might befit a good thinker faced with many of the issues that politicians must face), the implication is that the candidate is not expert enough to have figured out the right answer. ❺ Similarly, a person who adopts a know-it-all tone — speaking without qualification or doubt — is giving a sign of expertise. ❻ Some parents (perhaps because they *are* experts about the matter under discussion) talk this way to their children, who come to think of it as a "grown-up" way to talk.

*waffle 모호한 태도를 보이다   **befit ~에 걸맞다

❶ 사람들은 흔히 생각에 대한 두 가지 다른 기준을 혼동하는데, 우리는 그것을 '훌륭한 사색가'(적극적인 열린 마음)와 '전문가'라고 부를 수도 있을 것이다. ❷ 전문가들은 대부분의 질문에 대한 답을 '알고' 있기 때문에, 그들은 보통 대안이나 반증을 고려할 필요가 없다. ❸ 우리가 만약 전문가들을 존경한다면, 우리는 완고하다는 의미에서 '결단력 있는' 사람들을 존경하게 될지도 모른다. ❹ 뉴스 해설자가 정치 후보자가 모호한 태도를 보이고 확신이 없다고 (그것은 정치인이 반드시 직면해야 하는 문제 중 많은 것에 직면한 훌륭한 사색가에게 걸맞을 수도 있겠지만) 비판할 때, 이것이 내포하는 것은 그 후보자는 올바른 답을 생각해 냈을 만큼 충분히 전문적이지는 않다는 것이다. ❺ 마찬가지로, 무조건적으로 또는 의심의 여지 없이 말하면서 모든 것을 다 아는 듯한 어조를 취하는 사람은 전문성의 신호를 주고 있는 것이다. ❻ 어떤 부모들은 (아마도 그들이 논의 중인 사안에 대하여 '정말로' 전문가이기 때문에) 자녀들에게 이런 방식으로 이야기하는데, 그들은 그것을 '어른스러운' 말하기 방식으로 여기게 된다.

• Word Test

1	confuse		9	대안	
2	expert		10	내포, 암시, 결과	
3	decisive		11	확신이 없는	
4	counterevidence		12	무조건적으로	
5	know-it-all		13	완고한, 경직된	
6	candidate		14	~하게 되다	
7	figure out		15	열린 마음, 편견 없음	
8	faced with		16	어조, 말투	

People often confuse two different standards for thinking, ❶ which / that we might call the "good thinker" (active open-mindedness) and the "expert." Because experts *know* the answer to most questions, they usually do not have to consider alternatives or counterevidence. If we admire experts, we may come to admire people who are "decisive" in the sense of being ❷ flexible / rigid . When a news commentator criticizes a political ❸ candid / candidate for waffling and being unsure (as might befit a good thinker faced with many of the issues that politicians must face), the ❹ explication / implication is that the candidate is not expert enough to have figured out the right answer. Similarly, a person who adopts a know-it-all tone — speaking without qualification or doubt — is giving a sign of expertise. Some parents (perhaps because they *are* experts about the matter under discussion) talk this way to their children, who come to think of it ❺ as / to a "grown-up" way to talk.

*waffle 모호한 태도를 보이다 **befit ~에 걸맞다

People often confuse two different standards for thinking, which we might call the "good thinker" (active open-mindedness) and the "expert." Because experts *know* the answer to most questions, they usually do not have to consider alternatives or counterevidence. If we ❶ _____ (admire) experts, we may come to admire people who are "decisive" in the sense of being rigid. When a news commentator criticizes a political candidate for waffling and being unsure (as might befit a good thinker ❷ _____ (face) with many of the issues that politicians must face), the implication is that the candidate is not expert enough ❸ _____ (have) figured out the right answer. Similarly, a person who adopts a know-it-all tone — ❹ _____ (speak) without qualification or doubt — ❺ _____ (be) giving a sign of expertise. Some parents (perhaps because they *are* experts about the matter under discussion) talk this way to their children, who come to think of it as a "grown-up" way to talk.

*waffle 모호한 태도를 보이다 **befit ~에 걸맞다

People often confuse two different standards for thinking, which we might call the "good thinker" (active open-mindedness) and the "expert." Because experts *know* the answer to most questions, they usually do not have to consider alternatives or counterevidence. If we admire experts, we may ❶ _____ _____ _____ _____ (사람들을 존경하게 되다) who are "decisive" in the sense of being rigid. When a ❷ _____ _____ (뉴스 해설자) criticizes a political candidate for waffling and being unsure (as might befit a good thinker ❸ _____ _____ (~에 직면한) many of the issues that politicians must face), the implication is that the candidate is not expert enough to have figured out the right answer. Similarly, a person who adopts a know-it-all tone — speaking without qualification or doubt — is giving a ❹ _____ _____ _____ (전문성의 신호). Some parents (perhaps because they *are* experts about the matter under discussion) talk this way to their children, who come to think of it as a "grown-up" way to talk.

*waffle 모호한 태도를 보이다 **befit ~에 걸맞다

❶ Any object will experience a temperature decrease if it emits more radiation than it absorbs. ❷ At night, the Earth's surface emits infra-red radiation, but since the Sun is not shining, it absorbs very little radiation ❸ (in fact, it only absorbs the infra-red that is emitted by the atmosphere downward toward the surface). ❹ Thus, the Earth's surface cools all night long. ❺ When the sun finally peaks over the horizon, the Earth is still emitting a good amount of infra-red radiation. ❻ In fact, it is still emitting more than it absorbs from the first faint rays of sunshine at dawn. ❼ Not until the incoming solar radiation grows larger, some time after sunrise, does the incoming radiation finally equal the outgoing infra-red radiation. ❽ At that precise moment, the temperature will have reached its minimum value, for in the next minute, the incoming solar radiation will be larger than the outgoing infra-red, and so absorption will exceed emission and the temperature will rise as a consequence.

*radiation 복사 에너지, 복사   **infra-red 적외선의; 적외선

❶ 어떤 물체든 흡수하는 것보다 더 많은 복사 에너지를 방사하면 온도의 하락을 겪게 될 것이다. ❷ 밤에 지구의 표면은 적외선 복사 에너지를 방사하지만, 태양이 비치고 있지 않기 때문에, 그것은 아주 적은 양의 복사 에너지를 흡수한다. ❸ (실제로 그것[지구의 표면]은 대기에 의해 지표면을 향하여 아래 방향으로 방사되는 적외선만 흡수한다.) ❹ 따라서, 지구의 표면은 밤새도록 식는다. ❺ 태양이 마침내 지평선 위로 우뚝 솟을 때, 지구는 여전히 상당한 양의 적외선 복사 에너지를 방사하고 있다. ❻ 사실 지구는 여전히 희미한 새벽 첫 햇살로부터 흡수하는 것보다 더 많이 방사하고 있다. ❼ 일출 후 어느 정도 시간이 지나서, 들어오는 태양 복사 에너지가 더 커지게 되어서야 비로소 들어오는 복사 에너지가 나가는 적외선 복사 에너지와 결국 같아지게 된다. ❽ 바로 그 순간에 온도는 최솟값에 도달하게 될 것인데, 왜냐하면 다음 순간에, 들어오는 태양 복사 에너지는 나가는 적외선보다 더 커질 것이고, 따라서 흡수량이 방사량을 초과하게 되어, 그 결과로 온도가 상승하게 될 것이다.

Word List

□ temperature 온도   □ emit 방사하다, 방출하다   □ absorb 흡수하다   □ atmosphere 대기, 분위기   □ surface 표면   □ cool 식다
□ peak 우뚝 솟다, 최고 한도에 이르다   □ horizon 지평선, 수평선   □ faint 희미한, 약한   □ ray 빛살, 광선   □ dawn 새벽
□ incoming 들어오는   □ equal ~과 같다   □ outgoing 나가는, 떠나는   □ precise 정확한, 틀림없는   □ exceed ~을 초과하다
□ as a consequence 그 결과로

• Word Test

1 dawn	_____	9 식다	_____
2 absorb	_____	10 빛살, 광선	_____
3 peak	_____	11 방사하다, 방출하다	_____
4 precise	_____	12 ~을 초과하다	_____
5 temperature	_____	13 들어오는	_____
6 equal	_____	14 대기, 분위기	_____
7 faint	_____	15 지평선, 수평선	_____
8 surface	_____	16 나가는, 떠나는	_____

Any object will experience a temperature ❶ increase / decrease if it emits more radiation than it absorbs. At night, the Earth's surface emits infra-red radiation, but since the Sun is not shining, it absorbs very ❷ few / little radiation (in fact, it only absorbs the infra-red that is emitted by the atmosphere downward toward the surface). Thus, the Earth's surface cools all night long. When the sun finally peaks over the horizon, the Earth is still emitting a good amount of infra-red radiation. In fact, it is still emitting more than it absorbs from the first ❸ faint / strong rays of sunshine at dawn. Not until the incoming solar radiation grows larger, some time after sunrise, ❹ does the incoming radiation / the incoming radiation does finally equal the outgoing infra-red radiation. At that precise moment, the temperature will have reached its minimum value, for in the next minute, the incoming solar radiation will be larger ❺ as / than the outgoing infra-red, and so absorption will exceed emission and the temperature will rise as a consequence.

*radiation 복사 에너지, 복사   **infra-red 적외선의; 적외선

Any object will experience a temperature decrease if it emits more radiation than it absorbs. At night, the Earth's surface emits infra-red radiation, but since the Sun is not ❶ _____ (shine), it absorbs very little radiation (in fact, it only absorbs the infra-red that is emitted by the atmosphere downward toward the surface). Thus, the Earth's surface cools all night long. When the sun finally peaks over the horizon, the Earth is still ❷ _____ (emit) a good amount of infra-red radiation. In fact, it is still emitting more than it absorbs from the first faint rays of sunshine at dawn. Not until the incoming solar radiation ❸ _____ (grow) larger, some time after sunrise, does the incoming radiation finally ❹ _____ (equal) the outgoing infra-red radiation. At that precise moment, the temperature will have reached its minimum value, for in the next minute, the incoming solar radiation will be larger than the outgoing infra-red, and so absorption will exceed emission and the temperature will rise as a consequence.

*radiation 복사 에너지, 복사   **infra-red 적외선의; 적외선

Any object will experience a temperature decrease if it emits more radiation than it absorbs. At night, the Earth's surface emits infra-red radiation, but since the Sun is not shining, it absorbs very little radiation (in fact, it only absorbs the infra-red that is emitted by the atmosphere downward toward the surface). Thus, the Earth's surface cools ❶ _____ _____ _____ (밤새도록). When the sun finally peaks over the horizon, the Earth is still emitting a good amount of infra-red radiation. ❷ _____ _____ (사실), it is still emitting more than it absorbs from the first faint rays of sunshine ❸ _____ _____ (새벽에). Not until the incoming ❹ _____ _____ (태양 복사) grows larger, some time after sunrise, does the incoming radiation finally equal the outgoing infra-red radiation. At that precise moment, the temperature will have reached its minimum value, for in the next minute, the incoming solar radiation will be larger than the outgoing infra-red, and so absorption will exceed emission and the temperature will rise as a consequence.

*radiation 복사 에너지, 복사   **infra-red 적외선의; 적외선

❶ Some experts argue that until the world's distribution of wealth is altered, population will not be controlled. ❷ For example, Piel proposed that population control closely follows economic development, which enables people to escape from the poverty cycle. ❸ In other words, as poverty lessens, birth rates also decrease because women have better educational and professional opportunities as well as access to birth control. ❹ Lowered infant mortality accompanies economic development, and improved nutrition and medical care also helps to reduce birth rates. ❺ But unfortunately, poverty has been growing. ❻ More than one billion people in the world live in desperate poverty without the basic resources of clean water, adequate food, shelter, or sanitation. ❼ Even in developed countries such as the United States, more than one person in nine (11.3%) fell below the official poverty line in 2000. ❽ If current practices continue, one half of the world's population will live in absolute poverty by 2050, meaning too poor to grow or buy enough food, or maintain a job.

❶ 몇몇 전문가들은 세계의 부의 분배가 바뀌기 전까지는 인구가 억제되지 않을 것이라고 주장한다. ❷ 예를 들어, Piel은 인구 억제가 경제 발전을 밀접하게 뒤따르는데, 이것은 사람들이 빈곤의 순환에서 벗어날 수 있게 해준다고 제언했다. ❸ 다시 말해서, 빈곤이 줄어듦에 따라 출산율도 감소하는데, 이는 여성들이 피임을 더 쉽게 이용하는 것과 더불어 더 나은 교육 및 직업의 기회를 가지기 때문이다. ❹ 영아 사망률 저하가 경제 발전에 동반되며, 영양과 의료 서비스의 개선 또한 출산율을 낮추는데 도움이 된다. ❺ 하지만 불행하게도, 빈곤은 증가해 오고 있다. ❻ 세계의 10억이 넘는 사람들이 깨끗한 물, 적절한 음식, 주거지, 또는 위생 시설이라는 기초 자원 없이 극심한 빈곤 속에서 살고 있다. ❼ 심지어 미국과 같은 선진국에서도, 2000년에 9명 중 1명이 넘는 수(11.3퍼센트)가 공식적인 빈곤선 아래로 떨어졌다. ❽ 만약 현재의 관행이 계속된다면, 세계 인구의 절반이 2050년이 되면 절대적 빈곤 속에서 살게 될 것이고, 이것은 너무 가난해서 충분한 식량을 재배하거나 구입할 수 없는 것 혹은 직업을 유지할 수 없는 것을 의미한다.

Word List
□ argue 주장하다 □ distribution 분배 □ wealth 부 □ alter 바꾸다 □ poverty 빈곤, 가난 □ lessen 줄다 □ birth rate 출산율 □ professional 직업의 □ access 접근, 이용 □ birth control 산아 제한 □ mortality 사망률 □ accompany ~에 동반되다 □ nutrition 영양 □ desperate 극심한 □ adequate 적절한 □ shelter 거처 □ sanitation 위생 시설 □ official 공식적인 □ poverty line 빈곤선(최저 한도의 생활을 유지하는 데 필요한 수입 수준) □ absolute 절대적인 □ maintain 유지하다

• Word Test

1 wealth
2 access
3 mortality
4 argue
5 birth rate
6 adequate
7 poverty
8 absolute
9 sanitation
10 nutrition

11 분배
12 ~에 동반되다
13 바꾸다
14 거처
15 산아 제한
16 극심한
17 줄다
18 공식적인
19 직업의
20 유지하다

Some experts argue that until the world's distribution of wealth is altered, ❶ popularity / population will not be controlled. For example, Piel proposed that population control closely follows economic development, ❷ that / which enables people to escape from the poverty cycle. In other words, as poverty lessens, birth rates also decrease because women have better educational and professional opportunities as well as access to birth control. Lowered infant ❸ morality / mortality accompanies economic development, and improved nutrition and medical care also helps to reduce birth rates. But unfortunately, poverty has been growing. More than one billion people in the world live in desperate poverty without the basic resources of clean water, ❹ adequate / inadequate food, shelter, or sanitation. Even in developed countries such as the United States, more than one person in nine (11.3%) fell below the official poverty line in 2000. If current practices continue, one half of the world's population will live in absolute poverty by 2050, meaning ❺ so / too poor to grow or buy enough food, or maintain a job.

Some experts argue that until the world's distribution of wealth ❶ _____ (alter), population will not be controlled. For example, Piel proposed that population control closely follows economic development, which enables people ❷ _____ (escape) from the poverty cycle. In other words, as poverty lessens, birth rates also decrease because women have better educational and professional opportunities as well as access to birth control. Lowered infant mortality accompanies economic development, and ❸ _____ (improve) nutrition and medical care also helps to reduce birth rates. But unfortunately, poverty has been ❹ _____ (grow). More than one billion people in the world live in desperate poverty without the basic resources of clean water, adequate food, shelter, or sanitation. Even in developed countries such as the United States, more than one person in nine (11.3%) fell below the official poverty line in 2000. If current practices continue, one half of the world's population will live in absolute poverty by 2050, meaning too poor ❺ _____ (grow) or buy enough food, or maintain a job.

Some experts argue that until the world's distribution of wealth is altered, population will not be controlled. For example, Piel proposed that population control closely follows ❶ _____ _____ (경제 발전), which enables people to escape from the poverty cycle. ❷ _____ _____ _____ (다시 말해서), as poverty lessens, birth rates also decrease because women have better educational and professional opportunities as well as access to birth control. Lowered infant mortality accompanies economic development, and improved nutrition and medical care also helps to reduce birth rates. But unfortunately, poverty has been growing. ❸ _____ _____ _____ _____ (10억이 넘는) people in the world live in ❹ _____ _____ (극심한 빈곤) without the basic resources of clean water, adequate food, shelter, or sanitation. Even in developed countries ❺ _____ _____ (~와 같은) the United States, more than one person in nine (11.3%) fell below the official poverty line in 2000. If current practices continue, one half of the world's population will live in absolute poverty by 2050, meaning too poor to grow or buy enough food, or maintain a job.

❶ The introduction of digital technology has presented customers with transparency and new ways to search for information about products. ❷ Consumers are increasingly relying on online reviews on the internet or "word of mouth" from friends. ❸ The change in consumer behavior has likewise presented firms with a new way to connect with its customer base. ❹ Firms that are the most effective at connecting information regarding the customer's path to purchase (supporting the buying process) are able to position themselves strongly in the future market. ❺ Several large organizations have realized that competitive advantage is no longer derived from low cost or product differentiation. ❻ Instead, competitive advantage is gained and sustained through a platform offering a system of connected and complementary products that raise consumer's switching costs through strong network effects, meaning the higher the value of the platform is, the more people use it. ❼ Network effects and knowledge of customer behavior and needs provide the driving force behind any successful organization and platform, together with a demand-driven approach (what will customers want and why?).

*switching cost 전환 비용(한 제품에서 경쟁사의 다른 제품으로 전환하는 데 드는 비용)

❶ 디지털 기술의 도입은 고객들에게 투명성과 제품에 대한 정보를 검색하는 새로운 방법을 제공했다. ❷ 소비자들은 점점 더 인터넷 상의 온라인 후기나 친구들의 '입소문'에 의존하고 있다. ❸ 소비자 행동의 변화는 마찬가지로 기업에게 자사의 고객층과 연결될 수 있는 새로운 방법을 제공하였다. ❹ 고객의 구매로 이어지는 길에 관한 정보를 연결하는 (구매 과정을 지원하는) 데 가장 효과적인 기업은 미래 시장에서 확고하게 자신의 자리를 잡을 수 있다. ❺ 몇몇 대기업은 경쟁 우위가 더 이상 낮은 비용이나 제품 차별화로부터 얻어지지 않는다는 것을 깨달았다. ❻ 대신에, 강력한 네트워크 효과를 통해 소비자의 전환 비용을 높이는 연결된 상호 보완적인 제품의 체계를 제공하는 플랫폼을 통해 경쟁 우위가 확보되고 유지되는데, 이는 플랫폼의 가치가 더 높을수록 사람들이 그것을 더 많이 이용한다는 것을 의미한다. ❼ 네트워크 효과와 고객의 행동 및 욕구에 대한 지식이 수요 주도적 접근 방식(고객은 무엇을 원할 것이며 그 이유는 무엇인가?)과 함께 모든 성공적인 조직 및 플랫폼을 뒷받침하는 원동력을 제공한다.

Word List

□ present 제공하다 □ transparency 투명성 □ word of mouth 입소문 □ likewise 마찬가지로 □ customer base 고객층
□ effective 효과적인 □ regarding ~에 관한 □ purchase 구매 □ position ~의 자리를 잡다 □ derive - from ... …으로부터 ~을 얻다
□ differentiation 차별화 □ competitive advantage 경쟁 우위 □ sustain 유지하다 □ complementary 상호 보완적인
□ driving force 원동력 □ together with ~과 함께 □ demand-driven 수요 주도적인 □ approach 접근

• Word Test

1	customer base	9	차별화
2	present	10	구매
3	sustain	11	상호 보완적인
4	word of mouth	12	~과 함께
5	demand-driven	13	투명성
6	driving force	14	접근
7	position	15	마찬가지로
8	regarding	16	효과적인

The introduction of digital technology has presented customers with ❶ transparency / translation and new ways to search for information about products. Consumers are increasingly relying ❷ in / on online reviews on the internet or "word of mouth" from friends. The change in consumer behavior has likewise presented firms with a new way to connect with its customer base. Firms ❸ that / what are the most effective at connecting information regarding the customer's path to purchase (supporting the buying process) are able to position themselves strongly in the future market. Several large organizations have realized that competitive advantage is no longer derived ❹ from / to low cost or product differentiation. Instead, competitive advantage is gained and sustained through a platform offering a system of connected and complementary products that raise consumer's switching costs through strong network effects, meaning the higher the value of the platform is, the more people use it. Network effects and knowledge of customer behavior and needs provide the driving force behind any ❺ successful / successive organization and platform, together with a demand-driven approach (what will customers want and why?).

*switching cost 전환 비용(한 제품에서 경쟁사의 다른 제품으로 전환하는 데 드는 비용)

The introduction of digital technology has presented customers with transparency and new ways ❶ _____ (search) for information about products. Consumers are increasingly ❷ _____ (rely) on online reviews on the internet or "word of mouth" from friends. The change in consumer behavior has likewise presented firms with a new way to connect with its customer base. Firms that are the most effective at connecting information regarding the customer's path to purchase (supporting the buying process) ❸ _____ (be) able to position themselves strongly in the future market. Several large organizations have realized that competitive advantage is no longer ❹ _____ (derive) from low cost or product differentiation. Instead, competitive advantage is gained and sustained through a platform ❺ _____ (offer) a system of connected and complementary products that raise consumer's switching costs through strong network effects, meaning the higher the value of the platform is, the more people use it. Network effects and knowledge of customer behavior and needs provide the driving force behind any successful organization and platform, together with a demand-driven approach (what will customers want and why?).

*switching cost 전환 비용(한 제품에서 경쟁사의 다른 제품으로 전환하는 데 드는 비용)

The introduction of digital technology has presented customers with transparency and new ways to search for information about products. Consumers are increasingly relying on online reviews on the internet or "word of mouth" from friends. The change in ❶ _____ _____ (소비자 행동) has likewise presented firms with a new way to connect with its customer base. Firms that are the most effective at connecting information regarding the ❷ _____ _____ _____ _____ (고객의 구매로 이어지는 길) (supporting the buying process) are able to position themselves strongly in the future market. Several large organizations have realized that competitive advantage is no longer derived from low cost or ❸ _____ _____ (제품 차별화). Instead, competitive advantage is gained and sustained through a platform offering a system of connected and ❹ _____ _____ (상호 보완적인 제품들) that raise consumer's switching costs through strong network effects, meaning the higher the value of the platform is, the more people use it. Network effects and knowledge of customer behavior and needs provide the driving force behind any successful organization and platform, together with a demand-driven approach (what will customers want and why?).

*switching cost 전환 비용(한 제품에서 경쟁사의 다른 제품으로 전환하는 데 드는 비용)

❶ Adapted to life in the icy environment in the Antarctic Ocean, where their bodies are at the same glacial temperature as the seas around them, krill are reliant on an unusual internal chemistry. ❷ For instance, they possess some of the most powerful and unusual digestive enzymes known in nature. ❸ Enzymes are biological catalysts, vastly accelerating processes such as digestion. ❹ Our own enzyme processes, and those of most other animals, slow down dramatically as the temperature drops. ❺ Krill enzymes, though, have some extreme working conditions to cope with, and consequently, they've evolved to be superpowerful. ❻ The amazing characteristics of krill enzymes have recently been used for human medicine, to treat wounds and infections, bedsores, gastrointestinal disorders, and blood clots, to name but a few applications. ❼ Scientific advances on this scale are rare. ❽ When they do occur, it's amazing how often they emerge in the most unlikely circumstances, from research into what might be regarded as unpromising animals. ❾ It's another reason to make sure that we do our utmost not only to safeguard krill but to value all the biological wealth of the planet.

*catalyst 촉매 **bedsore 욕창 ***gastrointestinal 위장의

❶ 크릴은 남극해의 차가운 환경에서의 생활에 적응해 있고, 그곳에서는 그들의 몸도 주변의 바다와 같이 빙하의 온도이므로, 특이한 체내 화학 작용에 의존한다. ❷ 예를 들어, 그들은 자연에서 알려진 가장 강력하고 특이한 소화 효소 중 일부를 가지고 있다. ❸ 효소는 생물학적 촉매이며, 소화와 같은 과정을 크게 가속한다. ❹ 우리 자신의 효소 작용, 그리고 대부분의 다른 동물의 그것은 온도가 떨어짐에 따라 급격하게 느려진다. ❺ 하지만 크릴 효소는 대처해야 할 몇몇 극한의 작용 환경을 가지고 있고, 결과적으로, 그것은 진화하여 매우 강력해졌다. ❻ 크릴 효소의 놀라운 특징들은 몇 가지 적용 사례만 예로 들자면, 부상과 감염, 욕창, 위장 장애 및 혈전 등을 치료하기 위하여 최근에 인간의 의약품에 사용되어 왔다. ❼ 이러한 규모의 과학적 발전은 흔치 않다. ❽ 그러한 발전이 일어날 때, 가망이 없는 동물로 여겨질 수도 있는 것에 대한 연구로부터, 가장 예상 밖의 환경에서 그러한 발전이 참으로 자주 출현하는 것은 놀라운 일이다. ❾ 그것이 바로 우리가 크릴을 보호하기 위해서뿐만 아니라 지구의 모든 생물학적 재산을 소중하게 여기기 위해서 반드시 최선을 다해야 하는 또 다른 이유이다.

Word List

□ adapt oneself to ~에 적응하다 □ glacial 빙하의 □ reliant on ~에 의존하는 □ internal 체내의 □ chemistry 화학 작용
□ possess 가지다 □ digestive 소화의 □ enzyme 효소 □ accelerate 가속하다 □ extreme 극한의 □ cope with ~에 대처하다
□ consequently 결과적으로 □ infection 염증 □ disorder 장애, 질환 □ blood clot 혈전 □ application 적용, 응용
□ scale 규모 □ rare 드문 □ emerge 출현하다 □ circumstance 환경 □ unpromising 가망이 없는
□ do one's utmost ~의 최선을 다하다 □ safeguard 보호하다

• Word Test

1	emerge		12	장애, 질환
2	scale		13	빙하의
3	adapt oneself to		14	보호하다
4	reliant on		15	체내의
5	blood clot		16	드문
6	chemistry		17	극한의
7	digestive		18	환경
8	unpromising		19	적용, 응용
9	accelerate		20	가지다
10	cope with		21	결과적으로
11	infection		22	효소

Adapted to life in the icy environment in the Antarctic Ocean, ❶ where / which their bodies are at the same glacial temperature as the seas around them, krill are reliant ❷ in / on an unusual internal chemistry. For instance, they possess some of the most powerful and unusual digestive enzymes known in nature. Enzymes are biological catalysts, vastly accelerating processes such as digestion. Our own enzyme processes, and those of most other animals, slow down ❸ dramatic / dramatically as the temperature drops. Krill enzymes, though, have some extreme working conditions to cope with, and consequently, they've evolved to be superpowerful. The amazing characteristics of krill enzymes have recently been used for human medicine, to treat wounds and infections, bedsores, gastrointestinal disorders, and blood clots, to name but ❹ a few / a little applications. Scientific advances on this scale are rare. When they do occur, it's amazing how often they emerge in the most unlikely circumstances, from research into what might be regarded as unpromising animals. It's another reason to make sure that we do our utmost not only to safeguard krill ❺ and / but to value all the biological wealth of the planet.

*catalyst 촉매 **bedsore 욕창 ***gastrointestinal 위장의

❶ _____ (Adapt) to life in the icy environment in the Antarctic Ocean, where their bodies are at the same glacial temperature as the seas around them, krill are reliant on an unusual internal chemistry. For instance, they possess some of the most powerful and unusual digestive enzymes known in nature. Enzymes are biological catalysts, vastly ❷ _____ (accelerate) processes such as digestion. Our own enzyme processes, and those of most other animals, slow down dramatically as the temperature drops. Krill enzymes, though, have some extreme working conditions ❸ _____ (cope) with, and consequently, they've evolved to be superpowerful. The amazing characteristics of krill enzymes have recently been used for human medicine, ❹ _____ (treat) wounds and infections, bedsores, gastrointestinal disorders, and blood clots, to name but a few applications. Scientific advances on this scale ar e rare. When they do occur, it's amazing how often they emerge in the most unlikely circumstances, from research into what might be regarded as unpromising animals. It's another reason ❺ _____ (make) sure that we do our utmost not only to safeguard krill but to value all the biological wealth of the planet.

*catalyst 촉매 **bedsore 욕창 ***gastrointestinal 위장의

Adapted to life in the icy environment in the Antarctic Ocean, where their bodies are at the same glacial temperature as the seas around them, krill ❶ _____ _____ _____ (~에 의지하다) an unusual internal chemistry. For instance, they possess some of the most powerful and unusual digestive enzymes ❷ _____ _____ _____ (자연에서 알려진). Enzymes are biological catalysts, vastly accelerating processes such as digestion. Our own enzyme processes, and those of most other animals, slow down dramatically ❸ _____ _____ _____ _____ (온도가 떨어짐에 따라). Krill enzymes, though, have some extreme working conditions to ❹ _____ _____ (~에 대처하다), and consequently, they've evolved to be superpowerful. The amazing characteristics of krill enzymes have recently been used for human medicine, to treat wounds and infections, bedsores, gastrointestinal disorders, and blood clots, to name but a few applications. Scientific advances on this scale are rare. When they do occur, it's amazing how often they emerge ❺ _____ _____ _____ _____ _____ (가장 예상 밖의 환경들에서), from research into what might be regarded as unpromising animals. It's another reason to make sure that we do our utmost not only to safeguard krill but to value all the biological wealth of the planet.

*catalyst 촉매 **bedsore 욕창 ***gastrointestinal 위장의

❶ Cultural values are fundamental within a workplace because they define the terms of the psychological contracts that an employee holds with the organization. ❷ Unlike formal contracts of employment, psychological contracts are unwritten, often unarticulated, and usually only exist as assumptions. ❸ In a culturally homogeneous setting, assumptions are generally understood and shared, so the psychological contracts in play may be relatively clear: ❹ rewards are dependent on how well you do, the employee expects to stay in the organization for many years or for just a few years, the corporate ethos reflects the ethos of that particular society, and so on. ❺ However, in a culturally diverse workforce people may have very different expectations of the psychological contract. ❻ For example, in some cultures an organization may reward people because of their family connections rather than on the basis of their performance, or, in the case of transnational corporations, the overall corporate ethos is very different to that of the host nation.

*unarticulated 분명히 표현되지 않은   **homogeneous 동질의   ***ethos 정신, 기풍

❶ 문화적 가치는 직원이 조직과 맺고 있는 심리적 계약의 조건을 규정하기 때문에 직장 내에서 핵심적이다. ❷ 정식 고용 계약과는 달리, 심리적 계약은 성문화되지 않고, 흔히 분명히 표현되지 않으며, 보통 추정으로만 존재한다. ❸ 문화적으로 동질한 환경에서는 추정되는 것이 일반적으로 이해되고 공유되므로, 작동 중인 심리적 계약이 비교적 명확할 수 있다. ❹ 즉 보상이 여러분이 얼마나 잘 하느냐에 달려 있다는 것, 직원은 여러 해 동안 또는 단지 몇 년 동안만 조직 내에 머물기를 기대한다는 것, 기업 정신이 그 특정한 사회의 정신을 반영한다는 것 기타 등등이다. ❺ 그러나 문화적으로 다양한 직원들 속에서는 사람들이 심리적 계약에 대해 서로 매우 다른 기대를 가질 수도 있다. ❻ 예를 들어, 어떤 문화에서는 조직이 사람들의 성과에 근거해서가 아니라 그들의 가족 연줄 때문에 그들에게 보상을 할 수도 있고, 혹은 다국적 기업의 경우, 전반적인 기업 정신이 현지국의 그것과는 매우 다르기도 하다.

Word List

□ value 가치   □ fundamental 핵심적인, 근원적인   □ workplace 직장   □ define 정의하다, 규정하다   □ term (계약의) 조건
□ psychological 심리적   □ contract 계약   □ formal 정식의   □ exist 존재하다   □ assumption 추정, 전제, 가정
□ in play 작동 중인   □ dependent on ~에 달려 있는   □ diverse 다양한   □ workforce (모든) 직원, 노동 인구   □ expectation 기대
□ on the basis of ~에 근거하여   □ performance 성과   □ transnational corporation 다국적 기업
□ host nation 현지국, 다국적 기업의 자회사 소재국

• Word Test

1	workplace		10 (모든) 직원, 노동 인구	
2	in play		11 심리적	
3	exist		12 ~에 달려 있는	
4	diverse		13 정식의	
5	term		14 ~에 근거하여	
6	value		15 정의하다, 규정하다	
7	expectation		16 다국적 기업	
8	performance		17 핵심적인, 근원적인	
9	contract		18 추정, 전제, 가정	

Cultural values are fundamental within a workplace because they ❶ define / refine the terms of the psychological contracts that an employee holds with the organization. Unlike formal contracts of employment, psychological contracts are unwritten, often unarticulated, and usually only exist as assumptions. In a culturally homogeneous setting, assumptions are generally understood and shared, so the psychological contracts in play may be relatively clear: rewards are dependent on how well you do, the ❷ employee / employer expects to stay in the organization for many years or for just a few years, the corporate ethos reflects the ethos of that particular society, and so on. ❸ However / Therefore , in a culturally diverse workforce people may have very different expectations of the psychological contract. For example, in some cultures an organization may reward people ❹ because / because of their family connections rather than on the basis of their performance, or, in the case of transnational corporations, the overall corporate ethos is very different to ❺ this / that of the host nation.

*unarticulated 분명히 표현되지 않은   **homogeneous 동질의   ***ethos 정신, 기풍

Cultural values are fundamental within a workplace because they define the terms of the psychological contracts that an employee holds with the organization. Unlike formal contracts of employment, psychological contracts are unwritten, often unarticulated, and usually only exist as assumptions. In a culturally homogeneous setting, assumptions are generally ❶ _____ (understand) and ❷ _____ (share), so the psychological contracts in play may be relatively clear: rewards are dependent on how well you do, the employee expects ❸ _____ (stay) in the organization for many years or for just a few years, the corporate ethos ❹ _____ (reflect) the ethos of that particular society, and so on. However, in a culturally diverse workforce people may have very different expectations of the psychological contract. For example, in some cultures an organization may reward people because of their family connections rather than on the basis of their performance, or, in the case of transnational corporations, the overall corporate ethos ❺ _____ (be) very different to that of the host nation.

*unarticulated 분명히 표현되지 않은   **homogeneous 동질의   ***ethos 정신, 기풍

Cultural values are fundamental within a workplace because they define the terms of the psychological contracts that an employee holds with the organization. Unlike ❶ _____ _____ _____ _____ (정식 고용 계약), psychological contracts are unwritten, often unarticulated, and usually only exist as assumptions. In a culturally homogeneous setting, assumptions are generally understood and shared, so the psychological contracts ❷ _____ _____ (작동 중인) may be relatively clear: rewards are ❸ _____ _____ (~에 달려있는) how well you do, the employee expects to stay in the organization for many years or for just a few years, the corporate ethos reflects the ethos of that particular society, and so on. However, in a culturally diverse workforce people may have very different expectations of the ❹ _____ _____ (심리적 계약). For example, in some cultures an organization may reward people because of their family connections rather than on the basis of their performance, or, in the case of transnational corporations, the overall corporate ethos is very different to that of the host nation.

*unarticulated 분명히 표현되지 않은   **homogeneous 동질의   ***ethos 정신, 기풍

381

❶ In his endlessly amusing book, *A Mathematician Plays the Stock Market*, John Allen Paulos points out that we tend to misunderstand the role chance plays in the outcomes of apparently even games. ❷ Imagine that two people — I will call them George Soros and George Bozos — flip a fair coin 1,000 times each, competing to see who can come up with the most heads. ❸ We tend to imagine that, after that many flips, the outcome would almost always come out very even, with Soros and Bozos each getting about 500 heads and 500 tails. ❹ We infer from that conclusion that if one of the players actually ends up well ahead of the other, that outcome must be due either to an unfair coin or to the special skill of one of the players.

❺ In fact, as Paulos points out, there is a far greater probability that after 1,000 fair coin flips, Soros or Bozos would be well ahead of the other, having flipped 525 heads to, say, 475 heads. ❻ We might call this the law of small numbers; ❼ that is, 1,000 flips may seem like a lot, but actually it's not enough observations to ensure that Soros and Bozos will come out even. ❽ Thus, if 10,000 people all flipped a fair coin 1,000 times, the aggregate results would tend to be that a goodly number would end up with pretty good records and an equal number would end up with pretty sorry records. ❾ A very few would have spectacular records and a very few would have abysmal records. ❿ Far less than we might expect would have even records.

*aggregate 합계의 **abysmal 최악의

❶ 한없이 재미있는 자신의 책 *A Mathematician Plays the Stock Market*(수학자, 주식 시장을 가지고 놀다)에서 John Allen Paulos는 우리가 확률이 반반으로 보이는 게임의 결과에서 우연이 행하는 역할을 잘못 이해하는 경향이 있다고 지적한다. ❷ 두 사람이-George Soros와 George Bozos라고 부르겠는데-공정한 동전을 각각 1,000번 던지며 누가 가장 많은 앞면을 낼 수 있는지 보기 위해 겨룬다고 상상해 보라. ❸ 우리는 그렇게 많은 던지기 후에 Soros와 Bozos가 각각 약 500번의 앞면과 500번의 뒷면을 얻어서 결과가 거의 항상 매우 대등하게 나올 것이라고 상상하는 경향이 있다. ❹ 우리는 그 결론으로부터 만약 선수 중 한 명이 다른 한 명보다 실제로 훨씬 앞서게 된다면, 그 결과는 틀림없이 불공정한 동전이나 선수 중 한 명의 특별한 기술 때문일 것이라고 추론한다. ❺ 실제로는, Paulos가 지적하는 것처럼. 1,000번의 공정한 동전의 던지기 후에 Soros 또는 Bozos가 가령 475번의 앞면에 비하여 525번의 앞면을 던져서 상대보다 훨씬 앞서 있을 확률이 훨씬 더 크다. ❻ 우리는 이것을 작은 수의 법칙이라고 부를 수도 있을 것이다. ❼ 바꾸어 말하면, 1,000번의 던지기가 많은 것처럼 보일 수 있지만, 그것은 실제로 Soros와 Bozos가 대등하게 끝날 것이라는 것을 확실하게 하기에 충분한 관찰이 아니다. ❽ 따라서 만약 10,000명의 사람이 모두 공정한 동전을 1,000번 던진다면 합한 결과는 상당한 수의 사람이 꽤 좋은 기록으로 끝날, 그리고 같은 수의 사람이 꽤 아쉬운 기록으로 끝날 경향을 보일 것이다. ❾ 극소수는 굉장한 기록을 낼 것이고 극소수는 최악의 기록을 낼 것이다. ❿ 우리가 예상할 수 있는 것보다 훨씬 더 적은 사람들이 반반의 기록을 낼 것이다.

1	infer	_____	9	결과
2	amusing	_____	10	관찰
3	flip	_____	11	~보다 훨씬 앞선
4	probability	_____	12	상당한, 꽤 큰
5	apparently	_____	13	대등한, 동등한
6	spectacular	_____	14	공정한, 공평한
7	ensure	_____	15	(동전의) 앞면
8	compete	_____	16	(동전의) 뒷면

• 유형 **1** 네모 안에서 옳은 어법·어휘를 고르시오.

In his endlessly amusing book, *A Mathematician Plays the Stock Market*, John Allen Paulos points out that we tend to misunderstand the role chance plays in the outcomes of apparently even games. Imagine ❶ | that / which | two people — I will call them George Soros and George Bozos — flip a fair coin 1,000 times each, competing to see who can come up with the most heads. We tend to imagine that, after that many flips, the outcome would almost always come out very even, with Soros and Bozos each getting about 500 heads and 500 tails. We ❷ | infer / induce | from that conclusion that if one of the players actually ends up well ahead of ❸ | another / the other |, that outcome must be due ❹ | both / either | to an unfair coin or to the special skill of one of the players.

In fact, as Paulos points out, there is a ❺ | far / very | greater probability that after 1,000 fair coin flips, Soros or Bozos would be well ahead of the other, having flipped 525 heads to, say, 475 heads. We might call this the law of small numbers; that is, 1,000 flips may seem like a lot, but actually it's not enough observations to ensure ❻ | that / what | Soros and Bozos will come out even. Thus, if 10,000 people all flipped a fair coin 1,000 times, the aggregate results would tend to be that a goodly number would end up with pretty good records and an equal number would end up with pretty sorry records. A very few would have spectacular records and a very few would have abysmal records. Far less than we might expect would have even records.

*aggregate 합계의 **abysmal 최악의

In his endlessly amusing book, *A Mathematician Plays the Stock Market*, John Allen Paulos points out that we tend ❶ _____ (misunderstand) the role chance plays in the outcomes of apparently even games. Imagine that two people — I will call them George Soros and George Bozos — flip a fair coin 1,000 times each, ❷ _____ (compete) to see who can come up with the most heads. We tend to imagine that, after that many flips, the outcome would almost always come out very even, with Soros and Bozos each ❸ _____ (get) about 500 heads and 500 tails. We infer from that conclusion that if one of the players actually ❹ _____ (end) up well ahead of the other, that outcome must be due either to an unfair coin or to the special skill of one of the players.

In fact, as Paulos points out, there is a far greater probability that after 1,000 fair coin flips, Soros or Bozos would be well ahead of the other, ❺ _____ (have) flipped 525 heads to, say, 475 heads. We might call this the law of small numbers; that is, 1,000 flips may seem like a lot, but actually it's not enough observations ❻ _____ (ensure) that Soros and Bozos will come out even. Thus, if 10,000 people all flipped a fair coin 1,000 times, the aggregate results would tend to be that a goodly number would end up with pretty good records and an equal number would end up with pretty sorry records. A very few would have spectacular records and a very few would have abysmal records. Far less than we might expect would have even records.

*aggregate 합계의   **abysmal 최악의

In his endlessly amusing book, *A Mathematician Plays the Stock Market*, John Allen Paulos ❶ _____ _____ (지적하다) that we tend to misunderstand the role chance plays in the outcomes of apparently even games. Imagine that two people — I will call them George Soros and George Bozos — flip a fair coin 1,000 times each, competing to see who can ❷ _____ _____ _____ (~을 내놓다) the most heads. We tend to imagine that, after that many flips, the outcome would almost always come out very even, with Soros and Bozos each getting about 500 heads and 500 tails. We ❸ _____ _____ (~로부터 추론하다) that conclusion that if one of the players actually ends up well ahead of the other, that outcome must be due either to an unfair coin or to the special skill of one of the players.

In fact, as Paulos points out, there is a ❹ _____ _____ _____ (훨씬 더 큰 확률) that after 1,000 fair coin flips, Soros or Bozos would be well ahead of the other, having flipped 525 heads to, say, 475 heads. We might call this the law of small numbers; that is, 1,000 flips may seem like a lot, but actually it's not enough observations to ensure that Soros and Bozos will come out even. Thus, if 10,000 people all flipped a fair coin 1,000 times, the aggregate results would tend to be that a goodly number would ❺ _____ _____ _____ (결국 ~하게 되다) pretty good records and an equal number would end up with pretty sorry records. A very few would have spectacular records and a very few would have abysmal records. Far less than we might expect would have even records.

*aggregate 합계의   **abysmal 최악의

❶ Once, a girl in my class called Emma decided to do a research paper on a particular political group. ❷ Her father was an active member of the group, as she herself was soon to become, so this major research paper of hers was a rite of passage as well. ❸ Perhaps because I was so enthusiastic over her choice of a topic, she assumed I was also sympathetic to her political point of view. ❹ Almost conspiratorially she expressed to me her worries about a history teacher who would also be reading her paper and giving it a grade.

❺ "Ms. Maples is quite open about her political views, and hers differ from my father's. ❻ I am worried how she'll mark my paper," she said. ❼ I assured her that Ms. Maples would insist, as I would, on an objective presentation of factual material and on sources other than publications of the political group in question, but that our insistence did not in any way imply a prejudice against her or her work. ❽ "As far as politics go," I told her, "mine are probably similar to those of Ms. Maples', and look how excited I am about your paper."

❾ I had meant to put her at ease, but my mistake was immediately evident from the blood leaving her face. ❿ I smiled with great kindness. ⓫ "It's going to be a wonderful paper," I said. ⓬ *It's going to be the end of my life*, Emma thought. ⓭ As to the final outcome, it was a wonderful paper, and working on it with her was the beginning of one of the warmest relationships I ever enjoyed with a student. ⓮ I tried not only to help her see different points of view, but also to give depth to her own.

⓯ To achieve that, I introduced her to the novels of Ayn Rand and a few other books. ⓰ What I saw in this girl was the ability to believe in something more than survival, gratification, and success. ⓱ It was her having some conviction, aside from any content of the conviction itself, that I strove to reinforce. ⓲ I think it was Toynbee who said that the values of Sparta and Valhalla are preferable to no values at all. ⓳ And a misfired challenge to the young may be preferable to allowing their need for challenge and commitment to go unmet.

*rite of passage 통과 의례 **conspiratorially 공모하는 듯이

❶ 언젠가 내 수업에 Emma라고 불리는 한 소녀가 특정한 정치적 집단에 대한 연구 논문을 쓰기로 했다. ❷ 그녀의 아버지는 그 집단에서 활동하는 회원이었고, 그녀 자신도 곧 그렇게 될 것이었기 때문에, 그녀의 이번 주요 연구 논문은 통과 의례이기도 했다. ❸ 아마도 내가 그녀의 주제 선택에 너무 열광했기 때문인지, 그녀는 나도 역시 그녀의 정치적 관점에 동조한다고 지레짐작했다. ❹ 거의 공모하는 듯이 그녀는 자신의 논문을 또한 읽고 점수를 매길 한 역사 선생님에 대한 자신의 걱정을 나에게 표현했다.

❺ "Maples 선생님은 자신의 정치적 견해에 대해 상당히 솔직하신 편인데, 그녀의 정치적 견해는 제 아버지의 견해와 달라요. ❻ 저는 그녀가 제 논문을 어떻게 채점하실지 걱정돼요."라고 그녀는 말했다. ❼ Maples 선생님은 내가 그럴 것처럼 사실적인 자료의 객관적인 제시와 해당 정치적 집단의 출판물이 아닌 다른 자료를 요구하겠지만, 우리의 요구가 어떤 식으로든 그녀 또는 그녀의 결과물에 대한 선입견을 의미하는 것은 아니라고 안심시켰다. ❽ "정치적 견해에 관한 한, 나의 것이 아마도 Maples 선생님의 것과 유사할 것 같은데, 내가 너의 논문에 대해 얼마나 신이 나 있는지 보아라."라고 나는 그녀에게 말했다.

❾ 나는 그녀를 안심시키려 한 것인데, 그녀의 얼굴에서 핏기가 가시는 것으로부터 내가 실수했다는 것이 즉시 분명해졌다. ❿ 나는 매우 친절하게 미소를 지었다. ⓫ "멋진 논문이 될 거야."라고 나는 말했다. ⓬ Emma는, '이것이 내 인생의 마지막이 될 거야.'라고 생각했다. ⓭ 최종 결과물에 관해 말하자면, 그것은 멋진 논문이었고, 그녀와 함께 논문 작업을 한 것은 내가 학생과 누렸던 가장 따뜻한 관계 중 하나의 시작이었다. ⓮ 나는 그녀가 다른 관점을 볼 수 있도록 도왔을 뿐만 아니라 그녀 자신의 관점에 깊이를 더해 주려고 노력했다.

⓯ 그것을 이루기 위해, 나는 그녀에게 Ayn Rand의 소설과 몇 권의 다른 책들을 소개해 주었다. ⓰ 내가 이 소녀에게서 본 것은 생존, 만족, 성공보다 더 큰 어떤 것을 믿는 능력이었다. ⓱ 내가 강화하려고 노력한 것은 확신 자체에 담긴 어떠한 내용 외에도 그녀가 어떤 확신을 갖는 것이었다. ⓲ 내 생각에 Toynbee가 이렇게 말했던 것 같은데, Sparta와 Valhalla의 가치가 아무런 가치도 없는 것보다 낫다. ⓳ 그리고 젊은이에게 실패에 그친 도전이 그들의 도전과 헌신에 대한 욕구를 충족시키지 않은 채로 두는 것보다 더 나을지도 모른다.

Word List

□ sympathetic 동조하는   □ point of view 관점   □ mark 채점하다   □ assure 안심시키다   □ insist on ~을 요구하다[고집하다]
□ objective 객관적인   □ presentation 제시   □ factual 사실적인   □ source (연구를 위한) 자료   □ publication 출판물
□ imply 의미하다   □ prejudice 선입견, 편견   □ put - at ease ~을 안심시키다   □ evident 분명히 알 수 있는
□ give depth to ~에 깊이를 더하다   □ novel 소설   □ gratification 만족   □ conviction 확신   □ aside from ~ 외에도
□ content 내용   □ strive 노력하다   □ reinforce 강화하다   □ preferable to ~보다 더 나은   □ misfired 실패에 그친, 불발의
□ unmet 충족되지 않은, 채워지지 않은

1	presentation	12	확신
2	mark	13	사실적인
3	gratification	14	안심시키다
4	preferable to	15	내용
5	source	16	선입견, 편견
6	aside from	17	출판물
7	sympathetic	18	강화하다
8	imply	19	실패에 그친, 불발의
9	strive	20	소설
10	evident	21	객관적인
11	insist on	22	관점

• 유형 1 네모 안에서 옳은 어법·어휘를 고르시오.

Once, a girl in my class ❶ [calling / called] Emma decided to do a research paper on a particular political group. Her father was an active member of the group, as she herself was soon to become, so this major research paper of ❷ [her / hers] was a rite of passage as well. Perhaps because I was so enthusiastic over her choice of a topic, she assumed I was also sympathetic to her political point of view. Almost conspiratorially she expressed to me her worries about a history teacher who ❸ [will / would] also be reading her paper and giving it a grade.

"Ms. Maples is quite open about her political views, and hers differ from my father's, I am worried how she'll mark my paper," she said. I assured her ❹ [that / what] Ms. Maples would insist, as I would, on an objective presentation of factual material and on sources other than publications of the political group in question, but that our insistence did not in any way imply a ❺ [prejudice / prelude] against her or her work. "As far as politics go," I told her, "mine are probably similar to those of Ms. Maples', and look how excited I am about your paper."

I had meant to put her at ease, but my mistake was immediately evident from the blood leaving her face. I smiled with great kindness. "It's going to be a wonderful paper," 1 said. *It's going to be the end of my life*, Emma thought. As to the final outcome, it was a wonderful paper, and working on it with her was the beginning of one of the warmest relationships I ever enjoyed with a student. I tried not only to help her see different points of view, ❻ [and also / but also] to give depth to her own.

To achieve that, I introduced her to the novels of Ayn Rand and a few other books. ❼ [That / What] I saw in this girl was the ability to believe in something more than survival, gratification, and success. It was her having some conviction, aside from any content of the conviction itself, that I strove to reinforce. I think it was Toynbee ❽ [who / whom] said that the values of Sparta and Valhalla are preferable to no values at all. And a misfired challenge to the young may be preferable to allowing their need for challenge and commitment to go unmet.

*rite of passage 통과 의례 **conspiratorially 공모하는 듯이

Once, a girl in my class called Emma decided ❶ _____ (do) a research paper on a particular political group. Her father was an active member of the group, as she herself was soon to become, so this major research paper of hers was a rite of passage as well. Perhaps because I was so enthusiastic over her choice of a topic, she assumed I was also sympathetic to her political point of view. Almost conspiratorially she expressed to me her worries about a history teacher who would also be ❷ _____ (read) her paper and giving it a grade.

"Ms. Maples is quite open about her political views, and hers differ from my father's, I am ❸ _____ (worry) how she'll mark my paper," she said. I assured her that Ms. Maples would insist, as I would, on an objective presentation of factual material and on sources other than publications of the political group in question, but that our insistence did not in any way imply a prejudice against her or her work. "As far as politics go," I told her, "mine are probably similar to those of Ms. Maples', and look how ❹ _____ (excite) I am about your paper."

I ❺ _____ (mean) to put her at ease, but my mistake was immediately evident from the blood ❻ _____ (leave) her face. I smiled with great kindness. "It's going to be a wonderful paper," I said. *It's going to be the end of my life*, Emma thought. As to the final outcome, it was a wonderful paper, and working on it with her was the beginning of one of the warmest relationships I ever enjoyed with a student. I tried not only to help her see different points of view, but also ❼ _____ (give) depth to her own.

To achieve that, I introduced her to the novels of Ayn Rand and a few other books. What I saw in this girl was the ability to believe in something more than survival, gratification, and success. It was her having some conviction, aside from any content of the conviction itself, that I strove ❽ _____ (reinforce). I think it was Toynbee who said that the values of Sparta and Valhalla are preferable to no values at all. And a misfired challenge to the young may be preferable to ❾ _____ (allow) their need for challenge and commitment to go unmet.

*rite of passage 통과 의례   **conspiratorially 공모하는 듯이

387

Once, a girl in my class called Emma ❶ _____ _____ (~하기로 결정했다) do a research paper on a particular political group. Her father was an active member of the group, as she herself was soon to become, so this major research paper of hers was a rite of passage as well. Perhaps because I was so ❷ _____ _____ (~에 열광적인) her choice of a topic, she assumed I was also sympathetic to her political point of view. Almost conspiratorially she expressed to me her worries about a history teacher who would also be reading her paper and giving it a grade.

"Ms. Maples is quite open about her political views, and hers differ from my father's, I am worried how she'll mark my paper," she said. I assured her that Ms. Maples would insist, as I would, on an objective presentation of factual material and on sources other than publications of the political group in question, but that our insistence did not in any way imply a prejudice against her or her work. "As far as politics go," I told her, "mine are probably ❸ _____ _____ (~와 유사한) those of Ms. Maples', and look how excited I am about your paper."

I had meant to put her at ease, but my mistake was immediately evident from the blood leaving her face. I smiled with great kindness. "It's going to be a wonderful paper," I said. *It's going to be the end of my life*, Emma thought. ❹ _____ _____ _____ _____ _____ (최종 결과물에 관해 말하자면), it was a wonderful paper, and working on it with her was the beginning of one of the warmest relationships I ever enjoyed with a student. I tried not only to help her see different points of view, but also to ❺ _____ _____ _____ (~에 깊이를 더하다) her own.

To achieve that, I introduced her to the novels of Ayn Rand and a few other books. What I saw in this girl was the ability to believe in something more than survival, gratification, and success. It was her having some conviction, ❻ _____ _____ (~외에도) any content of the conviction itself, that I strove to reinforce. I think it was Toynbee who said that the values of Sparta and Valhalla are ❼ _____ _____ (~보다 더 나은) no values at all. And a misfired challenge to the young may be preferable to allowing their need for challenge and commitment to go unmet.

*rite of passage 통과 의례   **conspiratorially 공모하는 듯이

01 Test 3 1번

다음 글의 밑줄 친 부분 중, 문맥상 낱말의 쓰임이 적절하지 않은 것은?

Your insurance adjuster recently submitted the assessment for the wind damage to our roof. There are specific ① errors within the claim that you need to address. The damage was to the dormer on the north side of the house. High winds from last month's storms had lifted many of the tiles from the roof and caused a leak. This caused ② water damage to the internal ceiling of an upstairs bedroom. When the adjuster examined the dormer, he looked only at the roofing on the dormer's south side, where damage was ③ maximal. The true damage was on the north side. He awarded damages based on what he saw, and it seems that he did not look very closely at the ④ extent of the damage. A specialist from Caesar Roofing estimates repairs to both the roof and the water-damaged ceiling at $968. Your check for $232 arrived today. I am holding the check until I receive your response to this letter. Please contact me as soon as possible about this ⑤ matter.

*dormer 지붕창, 천창

02 Test 3 2번

글의 흐름으로 보아, 주어진 문장이 들어가기에 가장 적절한 곳은?

> They shared an excellent safe cake recipe, and provided a host of other support.

In 2004, my son Noah was turning one year old and I had a problem: How do I make him a birthday cake? He was seriously allergic to dairy, soy, and egg. A memory of an incident unsettled me — a bite of bakery cake at daycare sent us to the emergency room. I had never made a birthday cake myself. But Noah was turning one — I wanted him to have birthday cake. (①) I found a website called foodallergickids.org, and asked on the forum there: Did anyone have a dairy-, soy- and egg-free cake recipe? (②) In response to my question, I got a shower of warm welcomes from parents on the site. (③) Parents on the site helped me figure out how to make a clear and effective allergy-awareness sheet for his daycare teachers. (④) They shared tips for how to safely order food in a restaurant. (⑤) Their experience was invaluable, and they also were emotionally supportive in a way no one else could be.

03 Test 3 3번

다음 글의 밑줄 친 부분 중, 어법상 틀린 것은?

Did you know that fluoridated toothpaste, magnetic resonance imaging (MRI) technology, N-95 masks, and blood banking all have origins in academic research labs? The discoveries that contributed to these successful innovations may well have remained of purely academic interest ① had researchers not taken active steps to move those discoveries into the realm of invention. By doing so, those inventors changed the world. You as a researcher want your work ② to matter. You spend long hours designing, conducting, and ③ analyzing experiments, and then you think hard about how and where to disseminate the results. Researchers present their work via seminars, conference posters and presentations, book chapters, and journal publications — primarily ④ targets other academic researchers. We now challenge you to think more broadly about taking your messages to additional audiences, especially ⑤ those that have commercial capabilities.

*fluoridate 불소를 넣다 **resonance 공명 ***disseminate 전파하다

389

04 Test 3 4번

다음 글의 제목으로 가장 적절한 것은?

It is rumored that Michael Jordan practiced more than anyone else, was always up for another practice game, or a card game, a round of golf, shooting baskets far into the night while his teammates were done and gone. Ericsson and Pool reference this continued energy as maintenance, yet in light of Jordan's remarkable level of energy throughout the night following a demanding game, it was far beyond maintenance. It was self-invigorating and self-renewing. It was a self-fulfilling prophecy that flowed like a humming mantra: "The more one does, the more one can do." To put this into terms for invigorating the students in our classrooms, it is easy to rally students with a similar trigger. By planning a show or exhibition of their work or a demonstration of their performances, students are motivated with renewed energy as they prepare to showcase their work. The invitation to show their artwork, or perform in the PE demonstration, or participate in the school musical performance or the school poetry fest seems to do the trick. Humans are motivated to act by enticements that matter to them: endeavors that are relevant and raise the bar on the mundane routines of the everyday class work.

*mantra 주문 **enticement 유인책 ***mundane 평범한

① Unlocking Student Talent for Life
② Persistence: The Road to Success
③ Self-Fulfilling Prophecies of Athletes
④ Challenges to Undefeated Conquests
⑤ Quests that Breathe Life into Students

05 Test 3 5번

다음 빈칸에 들어갈 말로 가장 적절한 것은?

I have been teaching a course on leadership for many years and have concluded that the main way you can distinguish good from not so good leaders is in who they are looking out for. Bad leaders always have one person in mind — themselves. They may say they care about others; they may do things that seem to show care for others; they even may appear to be sad when hearing about the misfortunes of others. But in the end, they always look out for #1 — themselves. When they help others, it is to help themselves or merely to demonstrate overtly but _____ how caring and considerate they are. When they listen to others, it is to figure out what's in it for them. When they act in ways to benefit others, they always have themselves in mind first. Just as criminologists sometimes say that to figure out the perpetrators of a crime, you should follow the money, to figure out who is a good leader, you should follow the benefits — whom is the leader trying to benefit, and in particular, is it anyone beyond him- or herself, or those who immediately can benefit him- or herself?

*overtly 공공연하게 **criminologist 범죄학자 ***perpetrator 가해자

① truly
② firmly
③ falsely
④ secretly
⑤ selflessly

06 고난도 Test 3 6번

다음 글의 내용을 한 문장으로 요약하고자 한다. 빈칸 (A), (B)에 들어갈 말로 가장 적절한 것은?

In Ise, Japan, the Shinto Grand Shrine is disassembled every twenty years and an exact replica, rebuilt of similar materials, is assembled in the same place. In this form of preservation, perpetuating the building techniques and the ritual act of re-creation matters more than the physical continuity of the structure. Similarly, the ancient White Horse of Uffington in England was "re-created" for centuries by locals, who scraped the chalk figure every seven years to keep it from being obscured by growing vegetation. Likewise, cultures that rely on oral traditions retain their sense of cultural heritage without any tangible objects at all, but rather by retelling stories from the past. These and other traditional or "folk" ways of retaining heritage bring the past and present together, fused in a repeating, cyclical sense of custom through use and interaction in everyday life.

*replica 복제품 **perpetuate 영구화하다 ***scrape 긁어내다

↓

Countries, though having different cultural heritage,   (A)   both their tangible and intangible cultural assets by using and interacting with those assets on a   (B)   throughout their lives for centuries.

	(A)		(B)
①	sustain	······	temporary
②	combine	······	regular
③	revive	······	temporary
④	conserve	······	regular
⑤	establish	······	permanent

07 Test 3 7번

(A), (B), (C)의 각 네모 안에서 문맥에 맞는 낱말로 가장 적절한 것은?

Students bring energy and creativity to solving campus environmental problems, finding resources, and collecting detailed information. They are eager and energetic and (A) contribute / discourage a unique perspective to the process of environmental action, although they are often overlooked as a resource by staff and administrators. Students' own systems of governance can be (B) effective / ineffective vehicles for promoting environmental change. Students across the country have advocated for recycling programs and other environmental initiatives at many schools. Commonly, they provide the volunteer labor to begin and promote a program. The most successful and lasting programs are partnerships between students and university staff and administrators. At Tufts University, student pressure and activism led to divestment from a utility company because its planned hydroelectric plant (C) threatened / protected sensitive ecosystems and indigenous people. A student lawsuit at UCLA forced improved ventilation in the art studios.

*divestment 투자 회수 **indigenous 토착의, 지역 고유의
***ventilation 환기

	(A)		(B)		(C)
①	contribute	······	effective	······	threatened
②	contribute	······	ineffective	······	threatened
③	contribute	······	effective	······	protected
④	discourage	······	ineffective	······	protected
⑤	discourage	······	effective	······	threatened

EU-28 인구의 관광 여행 참여도에 관한 다음 글의 내용과 일치하지 <u>않는</u> 것은?

EU-28 Population by Age Group and Participation in Tourism, 2017

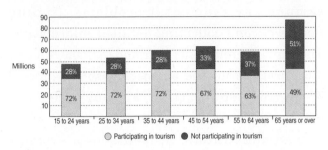

The above graph shows EU-28 population by age group and participation in tourism in 2017. In all of the age groups, the number of people who participated in tourism was over 30 million. In the 35-44 age group, the number of people who participated in tourism was more than 40 million. The percentage of people aged 25-34 who participated in tourism was higher than that of people aged 55-64 who participated in tourism. In the 45-54 age group, the percentage of the population who participated in tourism was more than double the percentage of the population who did not. Only in the 65 years or over age group was the percentage of people who did not participate in tourism higher than that of people who participated in tourism.

① 2017년 실시된 관광 여행 관련 설문에 참여한 사람은 3천만 명 이상이다.

② 관광 여행을 가 본 35~44세 연령층의 수는 4천만 명 이상이다.

③ 관광 여행을 가 본 25~34세 그룹 비율이 55~64세 그룹보다 높다.

④ 45~54세 그룹 내 관광 참여자 비율이 비참여자 비율의 2배 이상이다.

⑤ 관광 비참여자 비율이 참여자 비율보다 유일하게 높은 연령대는 65세 이상이다.

다음 글의 제목으로 가장 적절한 것은?

The Philippine eagle lives in the forests of the Philippines. It is one of the rarest and most powerful birds in the world, with a wingspan of over 7 feet. Its main diet is monkeys and medium-sized mammals, a fact that has earned it a second name, "monkey-eating eagle." It hunts during the day, beginning at the top of a mountain and moving down from tree to tree. This allows it to soar from one location to another, conserving energy since it doesn't have to flap its wings. Two eagles will sometimes hunt together, one soaring overhead to distract a group of monkeys while the other swoops in for the kill. Because of habitat destruction, the Philippine eagle is critically endangered, with fewer than 750 left in the wild. Mating pairs have only one chick every two years, making the population slow to recover. Luckily, the only known predators of the eagle are humans. The birds have been protected as the national bird of the Philippines since 1995. Killing one is punishable by 12 years in jail!

*swoop 급습[기습]하다

① Hunting Techniques of Birds
② Hidden Identity of Monkey Predators
③ Human Beings: Future Friend or Foe?
④ Something Special about Birds of Prey
⑤ Rescues of Endangered Philippine Eagles

10 Test 3 10번

Summer Adventure Camps에 관한 다음 안내문의 내용과 일치하지 <u>않는</u> 것은?

Summer Adventure Camps

Come and experience challenge and adventure this summer. Our summer camps offer a range of fun outdoor activities — kayaking, rock climbing, seashore explorations, team games and challenges.

Junior Explorer Camp (June 29th-July 1st)
· Age: 8-10 years
· Cost: $120 per person, max 15 participants

Adventure Camp (July 5th-8th)
· Age: 10-14 years
· Cost: $140 per person, max 15 participants

■ PLEASE NOTE
We provide all specialized equipment. You should bring the following:
· Sunscreen and towel
· A large plastic bag for taking home wet clothes
· Several sets of warm clothes suitable for outdoors (NOT jeans/denim)
· Sturdy shoes or boots, hat and gloves

※ Spaces are very limited and fill up fast. For questions, call us at 231-5467.

*sturdy 튼튼한

① 6월 29부터 7월 1일까지 진행될 캠프 참가 연령대는 8세에서 10세까지다.
② 7월 5일부터 8일까지 진행될 캠프의 최대 참가자 수는 15명이다.
③ 모든 참가자에게는 전문적인 장비가 제공될 예정이다.
④ 참가자들이 챙겨가야 할 물품에는 청바지가 포함되어 있지 않다.
⑤ 유선상으로만 캠프 등록을 받고 있으며, 참가자 인원수는 정해져 있다.

11 Test 3 11번

Green Medical Transport Chair에 관한 다음 안내문의 내용과 일치하지 <u>않는</u> 것은?

Green Medical Transport Chair

The Green Medical Transport Chair is specially designed to transport patients short distances. It is not to be used as a regular wheelchair.

· Operating Tips
1. To open the chair, tilt to one side and push down on the seat rails.
2. Lift the back support to an upright position. The lock to secure the back will engage automatically.
3. The lowest part of the footrest should not be less than 2 1/2 inches from the ground to permit proper clearance.

Note: The transport chair should not be operated without the assistance of an attendant.

· Safety Tips
1. Before entering or leaving the chair, engage the wheel locks against the tires on both rear wheels.
2. Do not move forward on the seat while leaning forward out of the chair.
3. Do not step on the foot plates when transferring.

*tilt 기울이다

① 환자들의 단거리 이동을 돕는 수단이다.
② 등받이를 고정하는 잠금장치는 수동 장치다.
③ 간병인의 도움 없이 작동해서는 안 된다.
④ 양쪽 뒷바퀴에는 바퀴 잠금장치가 있다.
⑤ 이동할 때 발판을 밟으면 안전하지 않다.

12 Test 3 12번

다음 빈칸에 들어갈 말로 가장 적절한 것은?

People consume a range of ingredients to attain a balanced diet. And yet, people can tire of the sameness and out of curiosity desire to experience new tastes and textures. This taste dilemma has developed throughout mammalian history, as humans evolved to adapt to many habitats. Humans are omnivores. Being omnivorous requires exploration and innovation. Yet, as Paul Rozin sees it, exploration and testing can lead to anxiety because of a fear of eating new, foreign food, not knowing whether it will be disgusting or tasty. Rozin has written about this hypothesis of food selection that humans (and rats!) have an aversion to consuming new foods yet at the same time have a drive to do so. He proposes that there is a(n) _____ surrounding our food choice habits, a form of cognitive dissonance. This dilemma drives humans to eat beyond our biological imperative as we eat more and more variety than is needed for survival.

*omnivore 잡식 동물 **aversion 반감
***biological imperative 생명 유지의 필수 요소

① paradox
② objective
③ principle
④ uniformity
⑤ intentionality

13 Test 3 13번

다음 글의 제목으로 가장 적절한 것은?

Like an addiction to anything, when the craving for certainty is met, there is a sensation of reward. At low levels, for example, when predicting where your foot will land as you walk, the reward is often unnoticeable (except when your foot doesn't land the way you predicted, which equates with uncertainty). The pleasure of prediction is more acute when you listen to music based on repeating patterns. The ability to predict, and then obtain data that meets those predictions, generates an overall *toward* response. It's part of the reason that games such as solitaire, Sudoku, and crossword puzzles are enjoyable. They give you a little rush from creating more certainty in the world, in a safe way. Entire industries are devoted to resolving larger uncertainties: from shop-front palm readers, to the mythical "black boxes" that can supposedly predict stock trends and make investors millions. Some parts of accounting and consulting make their money by helping executives experience a perception of increasing certainty, through strategic planning and "forecasting". While the financial markets of 2008 showed once again that the future is inherently uncertain, the one thing that's certain is that people will always pay lots of money at least to *feel* less uncertain. That's because uncertainty feels, to the brain, like a threat to your life.

*craving 갈망, 열망

① Comfort of Unusual Threats
② Foreseeing the Future for All
③ Strategies to Cope with the Unknown
④ The Pleasure and Pain of Uncertainties
⑤ Understanding Our Addiction to Predictability

14 Test 3 14번

다음 글의 밑줄 친 부분 중, 어법상 틀린 것은?

One of the earliest experiments investigating the distortions caused by categorization ① was a simple study in which subjects were asked to estimate the lengths of a set of eight line segments. The longest of those lines was 5 percent longer than the next in the bunch, ② which, in turn, was 5 percent longer than the third longest, and so on. The researchers asked half their subjects ③ to estimate the lengths of each of the lines, in centimeters. But before asking the other subjects to do the same, they artificially grouped the lines into two sets — the longer four lines were labeled "Group A," the shorter four labeled "Group B." The experimenters found that once the lines were thought of as belonging to a group, the subjects ④ perceive them differently. They judged the lines within each group as ⑤ being closer in length to one another than they really were, and the length difference between the two groups as being greater than it actually was.

*segment 토막

15 Test 3 15번

다음 글의 밑줄 친 부분 중, 어법상 틀린 것은?

In my research with Liane Young and James Dungan of Boston College, we studied the effects of loyalty on people using Amazon's Mechanical Turk, an online marketplace ① where users earn money for completing tasks. At the beginning of the study, we asked some participants to write an essay about loyalty and others to write about fairness. Later in the study, they were each exposed to poor work by someone else. Those who ② had received the loyalty nudge were less willing to blow the whistle on a fellow user for inferior performance. This finding complements research showing ③ that bribery is more common

in countries that prize collectivism. The sense of group belonging and interdependence among members often ④ lead people to tolerate the offense. It makes them feel less accountable for it, ⑤ diffusing responsibility to the collective whole instead of assigning it to the individual. In short, empathy for those within one's immediate circle can conflict with justice for all.

*nudge (가벼운) 자극, (팔꿈치로) 슬쩍 찌르기
**blow the whistle on ~을 고자질하다   ***bribery 뇌물

16 Test 3 16번

글의 흐름으로 보아, 주어진 문장이 들어가기에 가장 적절한 곳은?

These employees did not even bother knowing the person who sent it.

Social engineering is a method of gaining access to systems, data, or buildings through the exploitation of the human psychology. As foolish as it may sound, some companies and organizations think that they are resistant to the threat of social engineering. (①) On the contrary, no organization is immune to social engineering, not even the White House or any other prominent system. (②) For instance, a contest was held at a security conference wherein the participants were asked to obtain information from target companies, which could be utilized for a hypothetical attack. (③) Out of the 140 phone calls that were made to employees of the target companies, almost all the employees divulged information except for five, who refused to give out anything. (④) In addition, 90% of the employees clicked on a URL, which was sent to them by the participants. (⑤) This security conference concluded on how wide and dangerous the scope of social engineering is for all systems and organizations.

*social engineering 사회 공학   **divulge (비밀을) 누설하다

17 Test 3 17번

밑줄 친 nurture to act in concert with nature가 다음 글에서 의미하는 바로 가장 적절한 것은?

More often than not, key environmental influences on personality occur during a person's early life, so it would require a time machine to fix things — think *Back to the Future*. It is also quite common for <u>nurture to act in concert with nature</u>, accentuating predispositions or enhancing existing potential. For example, ambitious people tend to have competitive jobs, and as their jobs become more competitive they tend to become more ambitious as a result. Likewise, extraverts may choose jobs that require a great deal of networking and interpersonal schmoosing. Yet adaptation to those jobs tends to increase their extraversion even further. And so personal qualities, including talent-related traits, are always influenced by both nature and nurture, but often in the same direction, such that nurture ends up amplifying characteristics that were already there to begin with. In that sense, the more people change, the more they become like themselves. By and large, as we grow older we all become exaggerated versions of our earlier selves.

*extravert 외향적인 사람 **schmoose (환심을 사려고) 한담을 나누다

① One's potential can be developed through education.
② Cultivated traits are more powerful than genetic factors.
③ Genetically predetermined traits influence nonhereditary traits.
④ Adaptability plays a dominant role in molding a person's character.
⑤ Genetics are in play with environmental factors in shaping a person.

18 Test 3 18번

다음 글의 제목으로 가장 적절한 것은?

People often confuse two different standards for thinking, which we might call the "good thinker" (active open-mindedness) and the "expert." Because experts *know* the answer to most questions, they usually do not have to consider alternatives or counterevidence. If we admire experts, we may come to admire people who are "decisive" in the sense of being rigid. When a news commentator criticizes a political candidate for waffling and being unsure (as might befit a good thinker faced with many of the issues that politicians must face), the implication is that the candidate is not expert enough to have figured out the right answer. Similarly, a person who adopts a know-it-all tone — speaking without qualification or doubt — is giving a sign of expertise. Some parents (perhaps because they *are* experts about the matter under discussion) talk this way to their children, who come to think of it as a "grown-up" way to talk.

*waffle 모호한 태도를 보이다 **befit ~에 걸맞다

① Politician's Distortion of Beliefs
② How Should We Think and Speak?
③ Confusing Good Thinking with Expertise
④ The Pitfalls of Admiring Decision-Makers
⑤ Rigid Standard of Cognition and Rationality

19 Test 3 19번

다음 글의 밑줄 친 부분 중, 어법상 틀린 것은?

Any object will experience a temperature decrease if it emits more radiation than it absorbs. At night, the Earth's surface emits infra-red radiation, but since the Sun is not shining, it absorbs very ① <u>little</u> radiation (in fact, it only absorbs the infra-red that is emitted by the atmosphere downward toward the surface). Thus, the Earth's surface cools all night long. When the sun finally peaks over the horizon, the Earth is still ② emitting a good amount of infra-red radiation. In fact, it is still emitting more than it absorbs from the first faint rays of sunshine at dawn. Not until the incoming solar radiation grows larger, some time after sunrise, ③ do the incoming radiation finally equal the outgoing infra-red radiation. At that precise moment, the temperature ④ will have reached its minimum value, for in the next minute, the incoming solar radiation will be larger than the outgoing infra-red, and so absorption will exceed emission and the temperature will rise ⑤ as a consequence.

*radiation 복사 에너지, 복사   **infra-red 적외선의; 적외선

20 Test 3 20번

다음 글의 밑줄 친 부분 중, 어법상 틀린 것은?

Some experts argue that until the world's distribution of wealth is altered, population will not be controlled. For example, Piel proposed that population control ① closely follows economic development, which enables people to escape from the poverty cycle. In other words, as poverty lessens, birth rates also decrease ② because women have better educational and professional opportunities as well as access to birth control. Lowered infant mortality accompanies economic development, and improved nutrition and medical care also helps ③ to reduce birth rates. But unfortunately, poverty has been growing. More than one billion people in the world ④ live in desperate poverty without the basic resources of clean water, adequate food, shelter, or sanitation. Even in developed countries such as the United States, more than one person in nine (11.3%) fell below the official poverty line in 2000. If current practices continue, one half of the world's population will live in absolute poverty by 2050, meaning too poor to grow or buy enough food, or ⑤ maintaining a job.

21 Test 3 21번

다음 빈칸에 들어갈 말로 가장 적절한 것은?

The introduction of digital technology has presented customers with transparency and new ways to search for information about products. Consumers are increasingly relying on online reviews on the internet or "word of mouth" from friends. The change in consumer behavior has likewise presented firms with a new way to connect with its customer base. Firms that are the most effective at connecting information regarding the customer's path to purchase (supporting the buying process) are able to position themselves strongly in the future market. Several large organizations have realized that competitive advantage is no longer derived from low cost or product differentiation. Instead, competitive advantage is gained and sustained through a platform offering a system of connected and complementary products that raise consumer's switching costs through strong network effects, meaning the higher the value of the platform is, the more people use it. Network effects and knowledge of customer behavior and needs provide _____ behind any successful organization and platform, together with a demand-driven approach (what will customers want and why?).

*switching cost 전환 비용(한 제품에서 경쟁사의 다른 제품으로 전환하는 데 드는 비용)

① exclusive rights
② the driving force
③ product awareness
④ an economic insight
⑤ invisible competitive edge

22 Test 3 22번

다음 글의 밑줄 친 부분 중, 문맥상 낱말의 쓰임이 적절하지 않은 것은?

Adapted to life in the icy environment in the Antarctic Ocean, where their bodies are at the same glacial temperature as the seas around them, krill are reliant on an unusual internal chemistry. For instance, they possess some of the most powerful and unusual digestive enzymes known in nature. Enzymes are biological catalysts, vastly ① accelerating processes such as digestion. Our own enzyme processes, and those of most other animals, slow down dramatically as the temperature drops. Krill enzymes, though, have some ② extreme working conditions to cope with, and consequently, they've evolved to be superpowerful. The amazing characteristics of krill enzymes have recently been used for human medicine, to treat wounds and infections, bedsores, gastrointestinal disorders, and blood clots, to name but a few ③ applications. Scientific advances on this scale are rare. When they do occur, it's amazing how often they emerge in the most ④ unlikely circumstances, from research into what might be regarded as unpromising animals. It's another reason to make sure that we do our utmost not only to safeguard krill but to ⑤ overlook all the biological wealth of the planet.

*catalyst 촉매 **bedsore 욕창 ***gastrointestinal 위장의

23 Test 3 23번

다음 글에서 전체 흐름과 관계 없는 문장은?

Cultural values are fundamental within a workplace because they define the terms of the psychological contracts that an employee holds with the organization. ① Unlike formal contracts of employment, psychological contracts are unwritten, often unarticulated, and usually only exist as assumptions. ② In a culturally homogeneous setting, assumptions are generally understood and shared, so the psychological contracts in play may be relatively clear: rewards are dependent on how well you do, the employee expects to stay in the organization for many years or for just a few years, the corporate ethos reflects the ethos of that particular society, and so on. ③ However, in a culturally diverse workforce people may have very different expectations of the psychological contract. ④ Due to globalization and major advances in technology, such as the workforce being replaced by artificial intelligence, there has been a change in defining the importance of psychological contract. ⑤ For example, in some cultures an organization may reward people because of their family connections rather than on the basis of their performance, or, in the case of transnational corporations, the overall corporate ethos is very different to that of the host nation.

*unarticulated 분명히 표현되지 않은 **homogeneous 동질의
***ethos 정신, 기풍

In his endlessly amusing book, A *Mathematician Plays the Stock Market*, John Allen Paulos points out that we tend to misunderstand the role chance plays in the (a) outcomes of apparently even games. Imagine that two people — I will call them George Soros and George Bozos — flip a fair coin 1,000 times each, competing to see who can come up with the most heads. We tend to imagine that, after that many flips, the outcome would almost always come out very (b) even, with Soros and Bozos each getting about 500 heads and 500 tails. We infer from that conclusion that if one of the players actually ends up well ahead of the other, that outcome must be due either to an unfair coin or to the special skill of one of the players.

In fact, as Paulos points out, there is a far greater (c) probability that after 1,000 fair coin flips, Soros or Bozos would be well ahead of the other, having flipped 525 heads to, say, 475 heads. We might call this the law of small numbers; that is, 1,000 flips may seem like a lot, but actually it's not (d) enough observations to ensure that Soros and Bozos will come out even. Thus, if 10,000 people all flipped a fair coin 1,000 times, the aggregate results would tend to be that a goodly number would end up with pretty good records and a (e) greater number would end up with pretty sorry records. A very few would have spectacular records and a very few would have abysmal records. Far less than we might expect would have even records.

*aggregate 합계의 **abysmal 최악의

24

윗글의 제목으로 가장 적절한 것은?

① Coin Flip: How Fair Is the Game?
② High Risk and Return of Coin Flipping
③ Challenging Our Perception of Chance
④ The Law of Probability in the Gaming World
⑤ Mathematical Anatomy of a Gambler's Fallacy

25

밑줄 친 (a)~(e)중에서 문맥상 낱말의 쓰임이 적절하지 않은 것은?

① (a)   ② (b)   ③ (c)
④ (d)   ⑤ (e)

(A)

Once, a girl in my class called Emma decided to do a research paper on a particular political group. Her father was an active member of the group, as she herself was soon to become, so this major research paper of hers was a rite of passage as well. Perhaps because I was so enthusiastic over her choice of a topic, she assumed I was also (a) sympathetic to her political point of view.

*rite of passage 통과 의례

(B)

I tried not only to help her see different points of view, but also to give depth to her own. To achieve that, I introduced her to the novels of Ayn Rand and a few other books. What I saw in this girl was the ability to believe in something more than survival, gratification, and success. It was her having some conviction, aside from any content of the conviction itself, that I strove to (b) reinforce. I think it was Toynbee who said that the values of Sparta and Valhalla are preferable to no values at all. And a misfired challenge to the young may be preferable to allowing their need for challenge and commitment to go unmet.

(C)

Almost conspiratorially she expressed to me her worries about a history teacher who would also be reading her paper and giving it a grade. "Ms. Maples is quite open about her political views, and hers differ from my father's, I am (c) excited how she'll mark my paper," she said. I assured her that Ms. Maples would insist, as I would, on an objective presentation of factual material and on sources other than publications of the political group in question, but that our insistence did not in any way imply a prejudice against her or her work.

**conspiratorially 공모하는 듯이

(D)

"As far as politics go," I told her, "mine are probably similar to those of Ms. Maples', and look how excited I am about your paper." I had meant to put her at ease, but my mistake was immediately (d) evident from the blood leaving her face. I smiled with great kindness. "It's going to be a wonderful paper," I said. *It's going to be the end of my life*, Emma thought. As to the final outcome, it was a wonderful paper, and working on it with her was the (e) beginning of one of the warmest relationships I ever enjoyed with a student.

26

주어진 글 다음에 이어질 글의 순서로 가장 적절한 것은?

① (B) — (D) — (C)　　② (C) — (B) — (D)
③ (C) — (D) — (B)　　④ (D) — (B) — (C)
⑤ (D) — (C) — (B)

27

밑줄 친 (a)~(e) 중에서 문맥상 낱말의 쓰임이 적절하지 않은 것은?

① (a)　　② (b)　　③ (c)
④ (d)　　⑤ (e)

28

윗글에 관한 내용으로 적절하지 않은 것은?

① 필자는 소녀의 논문 주제에 관심을 보였다.
② 필자는 Maples 선생님과 다른 정치적 관점을 갖고 있다.
③ 필자는 소녀를 위로하는 데 크게 실패했다.
④ 소녀는 최종적으로 논문에 좋은 결과를 받았다.
⑤ 필자는 소녀에게 몇 권의 책을 추천해 주었다.

29 Test 3 1번

다음 글의 밑줄 친 부분 중, 어법상 틀린 것은?

Your insurance adjuster recently submitted the assessment for the wind damage to our roof. There are specific errors within the claim that you need ① to address. The damage was to the dormer on the north side of the house. High winds from last month's storms ② had lifted many of the tiles from the roof and caused a leak. ③ This caused water damage to the internal ceiling of an upstairs bedroom. When the adjuster examined the dormer, he looked only at the roofing on the dormer's south side, ④ where damage was minimal. The true damage was on the north side. He awarded damages based on ⑤ that he saw, and it seems that he did not look very closely at the extent of the damage. A specialist from Caesar Roofing estimates repairs to both the roof and the water-damaged ceiling at $968. Your check for $232 arrived today. I am holding the check until I receive your response to this letter. Please contact me as soon as possible about this matter.

*dormer 지붕창, 천창

30 Test 3 2번

필자 'I'에 관한 다음 글의 내용과 일치하지 않는 것은?

In 2004, my son Noah was turning one year old and I had a problem: How do I make him a birthday cake? He was seriously allergic to dairy, soy, and egg. A memory of an incident unsettled me — a bite of bakery cake at daycare sent us to the emergency room. I had never made a birthday cake myself. But Noah was turning one — I wanted him to have birthday cake. I found a website called foodallergickids.org, and asked on the forum there: Did anyone have a dairy-, soy- and egg-free cake recipe? In response to my question, I got a shower of warm welcomes from parents on the site. They shared an excellent safe cake recipe, and provided a host of other support. Parents on the site helped me figure out how to make a clear and effective allergy-awareness sheet for his daycare teachers. They shared tips for how to safely order food in a restaurant. Their experience was invaluable, and they also were emotionally supportive in a way no one else could be.

① 첫돌을 맞이할 아들에게 생일 케이크를 만들어 주고 싶었다.
② 음식 알레르기를 가진 아들을 응급실에 데리고 간 적이 있었다.
③ 본인이 직접 누군가의 생일 케이크를 만들어 본 경험이 없었다.
④ 유제품, 콩과 계란이 없는 케이크 조리법을 친구로부터 공유받았다.
⑤ 인터넷을 통해 알레르기에 관한 다양한 정보와 정서적인 응원을 받았다.

31 Test 3 3번

주어진 글 다음에 이어질 글의 순서로 가장 적절한 것은?

Did you know that fluoridated toothpaste, magnetic resonance imaging (MRI) technology, N-95 masks, and blood banking all have origins in academic research labs?

(A) By doing so, those inventors changed the world. You as a researcher want your work to matter. You spend long hours designing, conducting, and analyzing experiments, and then you think hard about how and where to disseminate the results.

(B) The discoveries that contributed to these successful innovations may well have remained of purely academic interest had researchers not taken active steps to move those discoveries into the realm of invention.

(C) Researchers present their work via seminars, conference posters and presentations, book chapters, and journal publications — primarily targeting other academic researchers. We now challenge you to think more broadly about taking your messages to additional audiences, especially those that have commercial capabilities.

*fluoridate 불소를 넣다 **resonance 공명 ***disseminate 전파하다

① (A) — (C) — (B) 　② (B) — (A) — (C)
③ (B) — (C) — (A) 　④ (C) — (A) — (B)
⑤ (C) — (B) — (A)

32 Test 3 4번

다음 빈칸에 들어갈 말로 가장 적절한 것은?

It is rumored that Michael Jordan practiced more than anyone else, was always up for another practice game, or a card game, a round of golf, shooting baskets far into the night while his teammates were done and gone. Ericsson and Pool reference this continued energy as maintenance, yet in light of Jordan's remarkable level of energy throughout the night following a demanding game, it was far beyond maintenance. It was self-invigorating and self-renewing. It was a self-fulfilling prophecy that flowed like a humming mantra: "The more one does, the more one can do." To put this into terms for invigorating the students in our classrooms, it is easy to rally students with a similar trigger. By planning a show or exhibition of their work or a demonstration of their performances, students are _____ as they prepare to showcase their work. The invitation to show their artwork, or perform in the PE demonstration, or participate in the school musical performance or the school poetry fest seems to do the trick. Humans are motivated to act by enticements that matter to them: endeavors that are relevant and raise the bar on the mundane routines of the everyday class work.

*mantra 주문 **enticement 유인책 ***mundane 평범한

① reframing fear into growth
② hindered by fear of failing
③ motivated with renewed energy
④ pressured to meet expectations
⑤ ready to leave their comfort zone

33 Test 3 5번

다음 글의 밑줄 친 부분 중, 어법상 틀린 것은?

I have been teaching a course on leadership for many years and have concluded that the main way you can distinguish good from not so good leaders ① is in who they are looking out for. Bad leaders always have one person in mind — themselves. They may say they care about others; they may do things that seem to show care for others; they even may appear to be sad when ② heard about the misfortunes of others. But in the end, they always look out for #1 — themselves. When they help others, it is to help ③ themselves or merely to demonstrate overtly but falsely how caring and considerate they are. When they listen to others, it is to figure out what's in it for them. When they act in ways ④ to benefit others, they always have themselves in mind first. Just as criminologists sometimes say ⑤ that to figure out the perpetrators of a crime, you should follow the money, to figure out who is a good leader, you should follow the benefits — whom is the leader trying to benefit, and in particular, is it anyone beyond him- or herself, or those who immediately can benefit him- or herself?

*overtly 공공연하게 **criminologist 범죄학자 ***perpetrator 가해자

34 Test 3 6번

다음 글에서 전체 흐름과 관계 <u>없는</u> 문장은?

In Ise, Japan, the Shinto Grand Shrine is disassembled every twenty years and an exact replica, rebuilt of similar materials, is assembled in the same place. ① In this form of preservation, perpetuating the building techniques and the ritual act of re-creation matters more than the physical continuity of the structure. ② Similarly, the ancient White Horse of Uffington in England was "re-created" for centuries by locals, who scraped the chalk figure every seven years to keep it from being obscured by growing vegetation. ③ Likewise, cultures that rely on oral traditions retain their sense of cultural heritage without any tangible objects at all, but rather by retelling stories from the past. ④ Oral tradition helps the younger generation make sense of the world by teaching them about important aspects of their culture such as wisdom of their ancestors

and knowledgeable philosophy of life. ⑤ These and other traditional or "folk" ways of retaining heritage bring the past and present together, fused in a repeating, cyclical sense of custom through use and interaction in everyday life.

*replica 복제품 **perpetuate 영구화하다 ***scrape 긁어내다

35 Test 3 7번

다음 빈칸에 들어갈 말로 가장 적절한 것은?

Students bring energy and creativity to _____, finding resources, and collecting detailed information. They are eager and energetic and contribute a unique perspective to the process of environmental action, although they are often overlooked as a resource by staff and administrators. Students' own systems of governance can be effective vehicles for promoting environmental change. Students across the country have advocated for recycling programs and other environmental initiatives at many schools. Commonly, they provide the volunteer labor to begin and promote a program. The most successful and lasting programs are partnerships between students and university staff and administrators. At Tufts University, student pressure and activism led to divestment from a utility company because its planned hydroelectric plant threatened sensitive ecosystems and indigenous people. A student lawsuit at UCLA forced improved ventilation in the art studios.

*divestment 투자 회수 **indigenous 토착의, 지역 고유의 ***ventilation 환기

① introducing student body government
② illustrating exemplar student leadership
③ solving campus environmental problems
④ uniting social activists with social beliefs
⑤ promoting environmental volunteer programs

36 Test 3 9번

다음 글의 밑줄 친 부분 중, 어법상 틀린 것은?

The Philippine eagle lives in the forests of the Philippines. It is one of the rarest and most powerful birds in the world, with a wingspan of over 7 feet. Its main diet is monkeys and medium-sized mammals, a fact ① that has earned it a second name, "monkey-eating eagle." It hunts during the day, beginning at the top of a mountain and moving down from tree to tree. This allows it ② to soar from one location to another, conserving energy since it doesn't have to flap its wings. Two eagles will sometimes hunt together, one soaring overhead to distract a group of monkeys while the other swoops in for the kill. ③ Because of habitat destruction, the Philippine eagle is critically endangered, with fewer than 750 left in the wild. Mating pairs have only one chick every two years, making the population slow to recover. Luckily, the only known predators of the eagle ④ are humans. The birds ⑤ were protected as the national bird of the Philippines since 1995. Killing one is punishable by 12 years in jail!

*swoop 급습[기습]하다

37 Test 3 12번

다음 글의 주제로 가장 적절한 것은?

People consume a range of ingredients to attain a balanced diet. And yet, people can tire of the sameness and out of curiosity desire to experience new tastes and textures. This taste dilemma has developed throughout mammalian history, as humans evolved to adapt to many habitats. Humans are omnivores. Being omnivorous requires exploration and innovation. Yet, as Paul Rozin sees it, exploration and testing can lead to anxiety because of a fear of eating new, foreign food, not knowing whether it will be disgusting or tasty. Rozin has written about this hypothesis of food selection that humans (and rats!) have an aversion to consuming new foods yet at the same time have a drive to do so. He proposes that there is a paradox surrounding our food choice habits, a form of cognitive dissonance. This dilemma drives humans to eat beyond our biological imperative as we eat more and more variety than is needed for survival.

*omnivore 잡식 동물 **aversion 반감
***biological imperative 생명 유지의 필수 요소

① curiosity of the human taste bud
② benefits of consuming various foods
③ need for maintaining a balanced diet
④ factors affecting our food choices habits
⑤ role of our biological system to eat healthy

38 Test 3 13번

다음 빈칸에 들어갈 말로 가장 적절한 것은?

Like an addiction to anything, when the craving for certainty is met, there is a sensation of reward. At low levels, for example, when predicting where your foot will land as you walk, the reward is often unnoticeable (except when your foot doesn't land the way you predicted, which equates with uncertainty). The pleasure of prediction is more acute when you listen to music based on repeating patterns. The ability to predict, and then obtain data that meets those predictions, generates an overall *toward* response. It's part of the reason that games such as solitaire, Sudoku, and crossword puzzles are enjoyable. They give you a little rush from creating more certainty in the world, in a safe way. Entire industries are devoted to resolving larger uncertainties: from shop-front palm readers, to the mythical "black boxes" that can supposedly predict stock trends and make investors millions. Some parts of accounting and consulting make their money by helping executives experience a perception of increasing certainty, through strategic planning and "forecasting". While the financial markets of 2008 showed once again that the future is inherently uncertain, the one thing that's certain is that people will always pay lots of money at least to _____. That's because uncertainty feels, to the brain, like a threat to your life.

*craving 갈망, 열망

① notice outliers
② feel less uncertain
③ find order in chaos
④ satisfy their senses
⑤ solve unsolved mysteries

39 Test 3 14번

범주화로 인한 왜곡에 관한 다음 글의 내용과 일치하지 <u>않는</u> 것은?

Onc of the earliest experiments investigating the distortions caused by categorization was a simple study in which subjects were asked to estimate the lengths of a set of eight line segments. The longest of those lines was 5 percent longer than the next in the bunch, which, in turn, was 5 percent longer than the third longest, and so on. The researchers asked half their subjects to estimate the lengths of each of the lines, in centimeters. But before asking the other subjects to do the same, they artificially grouped the lines into two sets — the longer four lines were labeled "Group A," the shorter four labeled "Group B." The experimenters found that once the lines were thought of as belonging to a group, the subjects perceived them differently. They judged the lines within each group as being closer in length to one another than they really were, and the length difference between the two groups as being greater than it actually was.

*segment 토막

① 피실험자들은 실험에서 잘린 여덟 개의 끈 길이를 추정하도록 요청받았다.
② 실험에 사용된 끈 중에서 가장 긴 것은 2번째로 긴 것보다 5퍼센트 길었다.
③ 잘린 여덟 개의 끈은 피실험자들에 의해서 길이별로 두 묶음으로 분류되었다.
④ 피실험자들은 두 묶음의 선들이 실제보다 서로 더 비슷한 길이로 인식했다.
⑤ 피실험자들은 두 묶음 사이의 길이 차이도 실제보다 더 큰 것으로 인식했다.

40 Test 3 15번

글의 흐름으로 보아, 주어진 문장이 들어가기에 가장 적절한 곳은?

It makes them feel less accountable for it, diffusing responsibility to the collective whole instead of assigning it to the individual.

In my research with Liane Young and James Dungan of Boston College, we studied the effects of loyalty on people using Amazon's Mechanical Turk, an online marketplace where users earn money for completing tasks. At the beginning of the study, we asked some participants to write an essay about loyalty and others to write about fairness. (①) Later in the study, they were each exposed to poor work by someone else. (②) Those who had received the loyalty nudge were less willing to blow the whistle on a fellow user for inferior performance. (③) This finding complements research showing that bribery is more common in countries that prize collectivism. (④) The sense of group belonging and interdependence among members often leads people to tolerate the offense. (⑤) In short, empathy for those within one's immediate circle can conflict with justice for all.

*nudge (가벼운) 자극, (팔꿈치로) 슬쩍 찌르기
**blow the whistle on ~을 고자질하다   ***bribery 뇌물

41 Test 3 16번

다음 글의 밑줄 친 부분 중, 어법상 틀린 것은?

Social engineering is a method of gaining access to systems, data, or buildings through the exploitation of the human psychology. As foolish as it may sound, some companies and organizations think ① that they are resistant to the threat of social engineering. On the contrary, no organization is immune to social engineering, not even the White House or any other prominent system. For instance, a contest was held at a security conference wherein the participants were asked to obtain information from target companies, which could be ② utilized for a hypothetical attack. Out of the 140 phone calls that were made to employees of the target companies, almost all the employees divulged information except for five, who refused ③ to give out anything. In addition, 90% of the employees clicked on a URL, which was sent to them by the participants. These employees did not even bother knowing the person who sent ④ them. This security conference concluded on ⑤ how wide and dangerous the scope of social engineering is for all systems and organizations.

*social engineering 사회 공학   **divulge (비밀을) 누설하다

42 Test 3 17번

글의 흐름으로 보아, 주어진 문장이 들어가기에 가장 적절한 곳은?

> Yet adaptation to those jobs tends to increase their extraversion even further.

More often than not, key environmental influences on personality occur during a person's early life, so it would require a time machine to fix things — think *Back to the Future*. (①) It is also quite common for nurture to act in concert with nature, accentuating predispositions or enhancing existing potential. (②) For example, ambitious people tend to have competitive jobs, and as their jobs become more competitive they tend to become more ambitious as a result. (③) Likewise, extraverts may choose jobs that require a great deal of networking and interpersonal schmoosing. (④) And so personal qualities, including talent-related traits, are always influenced by both nature and nurture, but often in the same direction, such that nurture ends up amplifying characteristics that were already there to begin with. (⑤) In that sense, the more people change, the more they become like themselves. By and large, as we grow older we all become exaggerated versions of our earlier selves.

*extravert 외향적인 사람   **schmoose (환심을 사려고) 한담을 나누다

43 Test 3 18번

다음 글의 밑줄 친 부분 중, 어법상 틀린 것은?

People often confuse two different standards for thinking, ① which we might call the "good thinker" (active open-mindedness) and the "expert." Because experts *know* the answer to most questions, they usually do not have to consider alternatives or counterevidence. If we admire experts, we may come to admire people who are "decisive" in the sense of ② being rigid. When a news commentator criticizes a political candidate for waffling and being unsure (as might befit a good thinker faced with many of the issues that politicians must face), the implication is that the candidate is not expert enough ③ to have figured out the right answer. Similarly, a person who adopts a know-it-all tone — speaking without qualification or doubt — ④ are giving a sign of expertise. Some parents (perhaps because they *are* experts about the matter under discussion) talk this way to their children, ⑤ who come to think of it as a "grown-up" way to talk.

*waffle 모호한 태도를 보이다   **befit ~에 걸맞다

44 Test 3 19번

다음 글에서 전체 흐름과 관계 <u>없는</u> 문장은?

Any object will experience a temperature decrease if it emits more radiation than it absorbs. At night, the Earth's surface emits infra-red radiation, but since the Sun is not shining, it absorbs very little radiation (in fact, it only absorbs the infra-red that is emitted by the atmosphere downward toward the surface). Thus, the Earth's surface cools all night long. ① When the sun finally peaks over the horizon, the Earth is still emitting a good amount of infra-red radiation. ② Not only the Earth but other objects, including stars, emit and absorb radiation regardless of their temperature. ③ In fact, it is still emitting more than it absorbs from the first faint rays of sunshine at dawn. ④ Not until the incoming solar radiation grows larger, some time after sunrise, does the incoming radiation finally equal the outgoing infra-red radiation. ⑤ At that precise moment, the temperature will have reached its minimum value, for in the next minute, the incoming solar radiation will be larger than the outgoing infra-red, and so absorption will exceed emission and the temperature will rise as a consequence.

*radiation 복사 에너지, 복사   **infra-red 적외선의; 적외선

45 Test 3 20번

다음 글의 요지로 가장 적절한 것은?

Some experts argue that until the world's distribution of wealth is altered, population will not be controlled. For example, Piel proposed that population control closely follows economic development, which enables people to escape from the poverty cycle. In other words, as poverty lessens, birth rates also decrease because women have better educational and professional opportunities as well as access to birth control. Lowered infant mortality accompanies economic development, and improved nutrition and medical care also helps to reduce birth rates. But unfortunately, poverty has been growing. More than one billion people in the world live in desperate poverty without the basic resources of clean water, adequate food, shelter, or sanitation. Even in developed countries such as the United States, more than one person in nine (11.3%) fell below the official poverty line in 2000. If current practices continue, one half of the world's population will live in absolute poverty by 2050, meaning too poor to grow or buy enough food, or maintain a job.

① 경제 발전과 인구 변화는 빈곤의 문제와 강한 상관관계가 있다.
② 부의 분배에 영향을 미치는 것은 사회·경제적 조건과 정치력이다.
③ 빈곤율의 감소는 저출산의 원인이라기보다는 결과에 가깝다.
④ 빈곤율을 낮추기 위해서 우선적으로 중요한 것이 경제 발전이다.
⑤ 부의 분배와 인구 조절이 이루어진 선진국에서도 빈곤은 증가하고 있다.

46 Test 3 21번

다음 글의 밑줄 친 부분 중, 문맥상 낱말의 쓰임이 적절하지 <u>않은</u> 것은?

The introduction of digital technology has presented customers with transparency and new ways to search for information about products. Consumers are increasingly relying on online reviews on the internet or "word of mouth" from friends. The ① change in consumer behavior has likewise presented firms with a new way to connect with its customer base. Firms that are the most effective at ② connecting information regarding the customer's path to purchase (supporting the buying process) are able to position themselves strongly in the future market. Several large organizations have realized that competitive ③ advantage is no longer derived from low cost or product differentiation. Instead, competitive advantage is gained and sustained through a platform offering a system of connected and complementary products that ④ raise consumer's switching costs through strong network effects, meaning the higher the value of the platform is, the more people use it. Network effects and knowledge of customer behavior and needs ⑤ limit the driving force behind any successful organization and platform, together with a demand-driven approach (what will customers want and why?).

*switching cost 전환 비용(한 제품에서 경쟁사의 다른 제품으로 전환하는 데 드는 비용)

47 Test 3 22번

크릴에 관한 다음 글의 내용과 일치하지 않는 것은?

Adapted to life in the icy environment in the Antarctic Ocean, where their bodies are at the same glacial temperature as the seas around them, krill are reliant on an unusual internal chemistry. For instance, they possess some of the most powerful and unusual digestive enzymes known in nature. Enzymes are biological catalysts, vastly accelerating processes such as digestion. Our own enzyme processes, and those of most other animals, slow down dramatically as the temperature drops. Krill enzymes, though, have some extreme working conditions to cope with, and consequently, they've evolved to be superpowerful. The amazing characteristics of krill enzymes have recently been used for human medicine, to treat wounds and infections, bedsores, gastrointestinal disorders, and blood clots, to name but a few applications. Scientific advances on this scale are rare. When they do occur, it's amazing how often they emerge in the most unlikely circumstances, from research into what might be regarded as unpromising animals. It's another reason to make sure that we do our utmost not only to safeguard krill but to value all the biological wealth of the planet.

*catalyst 촉매 **bedsore 욕창 ***gastrointestinal 위장의

① 크릴이 극한의 추운 환경에서 살 수 있는 비결은 효소이다.
② 크릴이 가진 효소는 대부분의 다른 동물의 것과 유사하여 활용도가 높다.
③ 크릴 효소의 가치는 인간의 의약품에서 두드러진다.
④ 인간은 가망이 없는 동물로부터도 유용한 과학적 발견을 할 수 있다.
⑤ 크릴처럼 지구의 모든 생물학적 재산은 중요한 역할을 할 수 있다.

48 Test 3 23번

다음 빈칸에 들어갈 말로 가장 적절한 것은?

Cultural values are fundamental within a workplace because they define the terms of the psychological contracts that an employee holds with the organization. Unlike formal contracts of employment, psychological contracts are unwritten, often unarticulated, and usually only exist as assumptions. In a culturally homogeneous setting, assumptions are generally understood and shared, so the psychological contracts in play may be relatively clear: rewards are dependent on how well you do, the employee expects to stay in the organization for many years or for just a few years, the corporate ethos reflects the ethos of that particular society, and so on. However, in a culturally diverse workforce people may have very different _____. For example, in some cultures an organization may reward people because of their family connections rather than on the basis of their performance, or, in the case of transnational corporations, the overall corporate ethos is very different to that of the host nation.

*unarticulated 분명히 표현되지 않은 **homogeneous 동질의
***ethos 정신, 기풍

① obligations that focus on making profits
② complaints on cultivating corporate culture
③ beliefs on the importance of relationships
④ expectations of the psychological contract
⑤ perceptions on how to contribute to society

Test 3 1번

Your insurance adjuster recently submitted the assessment for the wind damage to our roof. There are specific errors within the claim (A) what you need to address. The damage was to the dormer on the north side of the house. High winds from last month's storms had lifted many of the tiles from the roof and (B) causing a leak. This caused water damage to the internal ceiling of an upstairs bedroom. When the adjuster examined the dormer, he looked only at the roofing on the dormer's south side, where damage was minimal. The true damage was on the north side. He awarded damages based on (C) which he saw, and it seems that he did not look very closely at the extent of the damage. A specialist from Caesar Roofing estimates repairs to both the roof and the water-damaged ceiling at $968. Your check for $232 arrived today. I am holding the check until I receive your response to this letter. Please contact me as soon as possible about this matter.

*dormer 지붕창, 천창

49 윗글의 밑줄 친 부분을 어법상 알맞은 형태로 고쳐 쓰시오.

(A) what → _____

(B) causing → _____

(C) which → _____

50 윗글의 밑줄 친 This가 가리키는 내용을 본문에서 찾아 쓰시오.

_____

Test 3 2번

In 2004, my son Noah was turning one year old and I had a ① problem: How do I make him a birthday cake? He was seriously allergic to dairy, soy, and egg. A memory of an incident unsettled me — a bite of bakery cake at daycare sent us to the emergency room. I had ② always made a birthday cake myself. But Noah was turning one — I wanted him to have birthday cake. I found a website called foodallergickids.org, and asked on the forum there: Did anyone have a dairy-, soy- and egg-free cake _____? In response to my question, I got a ③ shower of warm welcomes from parents on the site. They shared an excellent safe cake recipe, and provided a host of other support. Parents on the site helped me figure out how to make a ④ clear and effective allergy-awareness sheet for his daycare teachers. They shared tips for how to safely order food in a restaurant. Their experience was ⑤ invaluable, and they also were emotionally supportive in a way no one else could be.

51 윗글의 빈칸에 들어갈 단어를 영영 뜻풀이를 참고하여 본문에서 찾아 쓰시오.

> a set of instructions for cooking or preparing a particular food

_____

52 윗글의 밑줄 친 ①~⑤ 중 문맥상 어색한 것을 1개 찾아 그 번호를 쓰고 고쳐 쓰시오.

_____ → _____

Did you know that fluoridated toothpaste, magnetic resonance imaging (MRI) technology, N-95 masks, and blood banking all have origins in academic research labs? The discoveries that contributed to these successful innovations may well have remained of purely academic interest had ____(A)____ not taken active steps to move those discoveries into the realm of invention. By doing so, those inventors changed the world. You as a researcher want your work to matter. You spend long hours designing, conducting, and analyzing experiments, and then you think hard about how and where to disseminate the results. ____(B)____ present their work via seminars, conference posters and presentations, book chapters, and journal publications — primarily targeting other academic researchers. We now challenge you to think more broadly about taking your messages to additional audiences, especially those that have commercial capabilities.

*fluoridate 불소를 넣다 **resonance 공명 ***disseminate 전파하다

53 윗글의 빈칸 (A), (B)에 공통으로 들어갈 말을 본문에서 찾아 쓰시오. (대·소문자 구분 없음)

_____

54 밑줄 친 By doing so가 가리키는 것을 본문에서 찾아 쓰시오. (14단어)

_____

_____

It is rumored that Michael Jordan practiced more than anyone else, was always up for another practice game, or a card game, a round of golf, shooting baskets far into the night (A) during his teammates were done and gone. Ericsson and Pool reference this continued energy as maintenance, yet in light of Jordan's remarkable level of energy throughout the night following a demanding game, it was far beyond maintenance. It was self-invigorating and self-renewing. It was a self-fulfilling prophecy (B) what flowed like a humming mantra: "The more one does, the more one can do." To put this into terms for invigorating the students in our classrooms, it is easy to rally students with a similar trigger. By planning a show or exhibition of their work or a demonstration of their performances, students are motivated with renewed energy as they prepare to showcase their work. The invitation to show their artwork, or perform in the PE demonstration, or (C) participating in the school musical performance or the school poetry fest seems to do the trick. Humans are motivated to act by enticements that matter to them: endeavors that are relevant and raise the bar on the mundane routines of the everyday class work.

*mantra 주문 **enticement 유인책 ***mundane 평범한

55 윗글의 밑줄 친 it이 가리키는 것을 본문에서 찾아 쓰시오. (12단어로 쓸 것)

_____

_____

56 윗글의 밑줄 친 부분을 어법상 알맞은 형태로 고쳐 쓰시오.

(A) during → _____

(B) what → _____

(C) participating → _____

I have been teaching a course on leadership for many years and have concluded that the main way you can distinguish good from ① not so good leaders is in who they are looking out for. Bad leaders always have one person in mind — themselves. They may say they ② care about others; they may do things that seem to show care for others; they even may appear to be sad when hearing about the misfortunes of others. But in the end, they always look out for #1 — themselves. When they help others, it is to help themselves or merely to demonstrate ③ overtly but falsely how caring and considerate they are. When they listen to others, it is to figure out what's in it for them. When they act in ways to ④ harm others, they always have themselves in mind first. Just as criminologists sometimes say that to figure out the perpetrators of a crime, you should follow the money, to figure out who is a good leader, you should follow the benefits — whom is the leader trying to benefit, and in particular, is it anyone ⑤ beyond him- or herself, or those who immediately can benefit him- or herself?

*overtly 공공연하게 **criminologist 범죄학자 ***perpetrator 가해자

57 윗글의 밑줄 친 ①~⑤ 중 문맥상 어색한 것을 1개 찾아 그 번호를 쓰고 고쳐 쓰시오.

_____ → _____

58 윗글을 읽고 다음 질문에 대한 답을 본문에서 찾아 쓰시오. (2단어로 쓸 것)

Q: Just as criminologists should follow the money to figure out the perpetrator of a crime, what should we follow to figure out who are the bad leaders in the passage?

A: _____

In Ise, Japan, the Shinto Grand Shrine is disassembled every twenty years and an exact replica, rebuilt of similar materials, is assembled in the same place. In this form of preservation, perpetuating the building techniques and the ritual act of re-creation matters more than the physical continuity of the structure. Similarly, the ancient White Horse of Uffington in England was "re-created" for centuries by locals, 그들은 자라는 초목에 그것이 보이지 않게 되는 것을 막기 위해 백악 형상을 7년마다 긁어냈다. Likewise, cultures that rely on oral traditions retain their sense of cultural heritage without any tangible objects at all, but rather by retelling stories from the past. These and other traditional or "folk" ways of retaining heritage bring the past and present together, fused in a repeating, cyclical sense of custom through use and interaction in everyday life.

*replica 복제품 **perpetuate 영구화하다 ***scrape 긁어내다

59 윗글의 this form of preservation이 가리키는 것을 본문에서 찾아 우리말로 쓰시오. (35자 내외)

_____

_____

고난도

60 윗글의 밑줄 친 우리말의 의미와 일치하도록 보기의 단어를 순서대로 배열하여 조건에 맞게 문장을 완성하시오.

| 보기 | the chalk / seven years / figure / growing vegetation / it / every / who / being obscured / to keep / scraped / by / from |

| 조건 | · 관계대명사 who로 시작할 것 |

_____

_____

Students bring energy and creativity to ① solving campus environmental problems, finding resources, and collecting detailed information. They are eager and energetic and contribute a unique perspective to the process of environmental action, although they are often ② overlooked as a resource by staff and administrators. Students' own systems of governance can be effective vehicles for promoting environmental change. Students across the country have ③ advocated for recycling programs and other environmental initiatives at many schools. Commonly, they provide the volunteer labor to begin and promote a program. The most ④ successful and lasting programs are partnerships between students and university staff and administrators. At Tufts University, student pressure and activism led to divestment from a utility company because its planned hydroelectric plant ⑤ guarded sensitive ecosystems and indigenous people. A student lawsuit at UCLA forced improved ventilation in the art studios.

*divestment 투자 회수   **indigenous 토착의, 지역 고유의
***ventilation 환기

61 윗글의 밑줄 친 ①~⑤ 중 문맥상 어색한 것을 1개 찾아 그 번호를 쓰고 고쳐 쓰시오.

_____ → _____

62 윗글에서 다음 질문에 대한 답을 본문에서 찾아 쓰시오. (8단어로 쓸 것)

Q: According to the passage, what is the most successful and enduring programs mentioned above?

A: _____

EU-28 Population by Age Group and Participation in Tourism, 2017

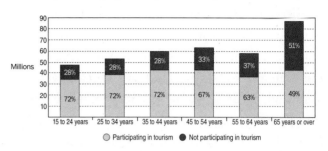

○ Participating in tourism ● Not participating in tourism

The above graph shows EU-28 population by age group and _____ in tourism in 2017. In all of the age groups, the number of people who participated in tourism was over 30 million. In the 35-44 age group, the number of people who participated in tourism was more than 40 million. The percentage of people aged 25-34 who participated in tourism was higher than that of people aged 55-64 who participated in tourism. In the 45-54 age group, the percentage of the population who participated in tourism was more than double the percentage of the population who did not. Only in the 65 years or over age group was the percentage of people who did not participate in tourism higher than that of people who participated in tourism.

63 윗글에서 다음 질문에 대한 답을 본문에서 찾아 쓰시오. (4단어로 쓸 것)

Q: In which age group has a higher percentage of people who did not participate in tourism than that of people who did?

A: _____

64 윗글의 빈칸에 들어갈 단어를 영영 뜻풀이를 참고하여 쓰시오. (단, 주어진 글자로 시작할 것)

the process of taking part in something

p_____

The Philippine eagle lives in the forests of the Philippines. It is one of the ① rarest and most powerful (A) bird in the world, with a wingspan of over 7 feet. Its main diet is monkeys and medium-sized mammals, a fact that has earned it a second name, "monkey-eating eagle." It hunts during the day, beginning at the ② top of a mountain and moving down from tree to tree. This allows it to soar from one location to another, (B) conserves energy since it doesn't have to flap its wings. Two eagles will sometimes hunt together, one soaring overhead to ③ attract a group of monkeys while (C) another swoops in for the kill. Because of habitat destruction, the Philippine eagle is critically endangered, with fewer than 750 left in the wild. Mating pairs have only one chick every two years, making the population ④ slow to recover. Luckily, the only known predators of the eagle are humans. The birds have been protected as the ⑤ national bird of the Philippines since 1995. Killing one is punishable by 12 years in jail!

*swoop 급습[기습]하다

65 윗글의 밑줄 친 ①~⑤ 중 문맥상 어색한 것을 1개 찾아 그 번호를 쓰고 고쳐 쓰시오.

_____ → _____

66 윗글의 밑줄 친 부분을 어법상 알맞은 형태로 고쳐 쓰시오.

(A) bird → _____

(B) conserves → _____

(C) another → _____

Summer Adventure Camps

Come and experience challenge and adventure this summer. Our summer camps offer a range of fun outdoor (A) activity — kayaking, rock climbing, seashore explorations, team games and challenges.

Junior Explorer Camp (June 29th-July 1st)
· Age: 8-10 years
· Cost: $120 per person, max 15 participants

Adventure Camp (July 5th-8th)
· Age: 10-14 years
· Cost: $140 per person, max 15 participants

■ **PLEASE NOTE**
We provide all (B) specialize equipment. You should bring the following:
· Sunscreen and towel
· A large plastic bag for taking home wet clothes
· Several sets of warm clothes _____ for outdoors (NOT jeans/denim)
· Sturdy shoes or boots, hat and gloves

※ Spaces are very limited and (C) filled up fast. For questions, call us at 231-5467.

*sturdy 튼튼한

67 윗글의 빈칸에 들어갈 단어를 영영 뜻풀이를 참고하여 쓰시오. (단, 주어진 글자로 시작할 것)

right for a particular purpose, person, or situation

s _____

68 윗글의 밑줄 친 부분을 어법상 알맞은 형태로 고쳐 쓰시오.

(A) activity → _____

(B) specialize → _____

(C) filled → _____

Green Medical Transport Chair

The Green Medical Transport Chair is specially designed to transport patients short distances. It is not (A) to use as a regular wheelchair.

Lock Mechanism For Back Support
Footrest Locking Device
Footrest Peg
Wheel Lock
Footrest Height Adjustment

· **Operating Tips**
1. To open the chair, tilt to one side and push down on the seat rails.
2. Lift the back support to an upright position. The lock to secure the back will engage automatically.
3. The lowest part of the footrest should not be less than 2 1/2 inches from the ground (B) permitting proper clearance.

Note: The transport chair should not be operated without the assistance of an _____.

· **Safety Tips**
1. Before entering or leaving the chair, (C) engaging the wheel locks against the tires on both rear wheels.
2. Do not move forward on the seat while leaning forward out of the chair.
3. Do not step on the foot plates when transferring.

*tilt 기울이다

69 윗글의 밑줄 친 부분을 어법상 알맞은 형태로 고쳐 쓰시오.

(A) to use → _____

(B) permitting → _____

(C) engaging → _____

70 윗글의 빈칸에 들어갈 단어를 영영 뜻풀이를 참고하여 쓰시오. (단, 주어진 글자로 시작할 것)

someone whose job is to look after another person, especially a person who is in an important position or one who is ill

a_____

People consume a range of ingredients to attain a balanced diet. And yet, people can tire of the sameness and out of curiosity desire to experience new tastes and textures. This taste dilemma has developed throughout mammalian history, as humans evolved to adapt to many habitats. Humans are omnivores. Being omnivorous requires exploration and innovation. Yet, as Paul Rozin sees it, exploration and testing can lead to anxiety because of a fear of eating new, foreign food, not knowing whether it will be disgusting or tasty. Rozin has written about this hypothesis of food selection that humans (and rats!) have an aversion to consuming new foods yet at the same time have a drive to do so. He proposes that there is (A) a paradox surrounding our food choice habits, a form of cognitive dissonance. 우리가 생존에 필요한 것보다 점점 더 다양한 음식을 먹게 되면서, 이 딜레마는 인간을 생명 유지의 필수 요소 이상으로 먹도록 몰아간다.

*omnivore 잡식 동물 **aversion 반감
***biological imperative 생명 유지의 필수 요소

71 윗글의 밑줄 친 (A)가 의미하는 바를 본문에서 찾아 쓰시오. (2단어로 쓸 것)

_____

고난도

72 윗글의 밑줄 친 우리말의 의미와 일치하도록 보기 의 단어를 순서대로 배열하여 문장을 완성하시오.

보기   eat / more and more / humans / to / variety / our / as / drives / we / beyond / eat / biological imperative

This dilemma _____

_____

than is needed for survival.

Like an addiction to anything, when the craving for certainty is met, there is a sensation of ① reward. At low levels, for example, when predicting where your foot will land as you walk, the reward is often unnoticeable (except when your foot doesn't land the way you predicted, which equates with uncertainty). The pleasure of prediction is ② more acute when you listen to music based on repeating patterns. The ability to predict, and then obtain data that meets those predictions, generates an overall *toward* response. It's part of the reason that games such as solitaire, Sudoku, and crossword puzzles are enjoyable. They give you a ③ little rush from creating more certainty in the world, in a safe way. Entire industries are devoted to resolving larger uncertainties: from shop-front palm readers, to the mythical "black boxes" that can supposedly predict stock trends and make investors millions. Some parts of accounting and consulting make their money by helping executives experience a perception of ④ decreasing certainty, through strategic planning and "forecasting". While the financial markets of 2008 showed once again that the future is inherently uncertain, the one thing that's certain is that people will always pay lots of money at least to *feel* less uncertain. That's because uncertainty feels, to the brain, like a ⑤ threat to your life.

*craving 갈망, 열망

73 윗글의 밑줄 친 ①~⑤ 중 문맥상 어색한 것을 1개 찾아 그 번호를 쓰고 고쳐 쓰시오.

_____ → _____

고난도

74 윗글의 내용을 한 문장으로 요약하려고 한다. 빈칸 (A)와 (B)에 들어갈 알맞은 말을 본문에서 찾아 쓰시오.

Our brain likes to be sure about things and feels good when it can ___(A)___ outcomes, but when we feel uncertain, it can feel scary, so people are willing to ___(B)___ to feel more sure.

(A) _____

(B) _____

One of the earliest experiments investigating the distortions caused by categorization was a ① simple study in which subjects were asked to estimate the lengths of a set of eight line segments. The longest of those lines was 5 percent longer than the next in the bunch, which, in turn, was 5 percent ② longer than the third longest, and so on. The researchers asked half their subjects to estimate the lengths of each of the lines, in centimeters. But before asking the other subjects to do the ③ same, they artificially grouped the lines into two sets — the longer four lines were labeled "Group A," the shorter four labeled "Group B." The experimenters found that once the lines were thought of as belonging to a group, the subjects perceived them ④ similarly. They judged the lines within each group as being closer in length to one another than they really were, and the length difference between the two groups as being ⑤ greater than it actually was.

*segment 토막

75 윗글에서 다음 질문에 대한 답을 찾아 본문의 표현 그대로 쓰시오. (5단어로 쓸 것)

Q: Why did the group of subjects who divided the length of the string into groups A and B feel that the length of the string in each group was closer?

A: It's because of _____ .

76 윗글의 밑줄 친 ①~⑤ 중 문맥상 어색한 것을 1개 찾아 그 번호를 쓰고 고쳐 쓰시오.

_____ → _____

In my research with Liane Young and James Dungan of Boston College, we studied the effects of ___(A)___ on people using Amazon's Mechanical Turk, an online marketplace where users earn money for completing tasks. At the beginning of the study, we asked some participants to write an essay about ___(B)___ and others to write about fairness. Later in the study, they were each exposed to poor work by someone else. Those who had received the loyalty nudge were less willing to blow the whistle on a fellow user for inferior performance. This finding complements research showing that bribery is more common in countries that prize collectivism. The sense of group belonging and interdependence among members often leads people to tolerate the offense. It makes them feel less accountable for it, diffusing responsibility to the collective whole instead of assigning it to the individual. In short, empathy for those within one's immediate circle can conflict with justice for all.

*nudge (가벼운) 자극, (팔꿈치로) 슬쩍 찌르기
**blow the whistle on ~을 고자질하다   ***bribery 뇌물

77 윗글의 빈칸 (A), (B)에 공통으로 들어갈 말을 본문에서 찾아 쓰시오.

_____

78 윗글의 밑줄 친 This finding이 가리키는 것을 본문에서 찾아 우리말로 쓰시오. (40자 내외)

_____

_____

Social engineering is a method of gaining access to systems, data, or buildings through the exploitation of the human psychology. As foolish as it may sound, some _____ and organizations think that they are resistant to the threat of social engineering. On the contrary, no organization is immune to social engineering, not even the White House or any other prominent system. For instance, a contest was held at a security conference wherein the participants were asked to obtain information from target companies, which could be utilized for a hypothetical attack. Out of the 140 phone calls that were made to employees of the target _____, almost all the employees divulged information except for five, who refused to give out anything. In addition, 90% of the employees clicked on a URL, which was sent to them by the participants. These employees did not even bother knowing the person who sent it. This security conference concluded on how wide and dangerous the scope of social engineering is for all systems and organizations.

*social engineering 사회 공학   **divulge (비밀을) 누설하다

79 윗글의 빈칸에 공통으로 들어갈 말을 본문에서 찾아 쓰시오.

_____

🚩 고난도

80 윗글의 내용을 한 문장으로 요약하려고 한다. 빈칸 (A)와 (B)에 들어갈 알맞은 말을 본문에서 찾아 쓰시오. (단, 필요시 어형을 바꿔 쓸 것)

While some companies and organizations mistakenly believe that they have _____(A)_____ to the threat of social engineering, virtually all employees of the target companies that were subjected to the hypothetical attack were forced to _____(B)_____ company information.

(A) _____

(B) _____

More often than not, key environmental influences on personality occur during a person's early life, so it would require a time machine to fix things — think *Back to the Future*. It is also quite common for nurture to act in concert with nature, accentuating predispositions or enhancing existing potential. For example, ambitious people tend to have competitive jobs, and as their jobs become more competitive they tend to become more ambitious as a result. Likewise, extraverts may choose jobs that require a great deal of networking and interpersonal schmoosing. Yet adaptation to those jobs tends to increase their extraversion even further. And so personal qualities, including talent-related traits, are always influenced by both nature and nurture, but often in the same direction, such that 후천성은 결국 이미 처음부터 존재했던 특성을 증폭시키는 것으로 끝난다. In that sense, the more people change, the more they become like themselves. By and large, as we grow older we all become exaggerated versions of our earlier selves.

*extravert 외향적인 사람   **schmoose (환심을 사려고) 한담을 나누다

81 윗글의 밑줄 친 우리말의 의미와 일치하도록 보기 의 단어를 순서대로 배열하여 문장을 완성하시오.

보기   characteristics / nurture / ends up / were / to begin / amplifying / with / that / already there

_____

_____

82 윗글에서 다음 질문에 대한 답을 찾아 쓰시오. (1단어로 쓸 것)

Q: Which personal qualities eventually amplify those that were already present from the start?

A: _____

People often confuse two ① different standards for thinking, which we might call the "good thinker" (active open-mindedness) and the "expert." Because experts *know* the answer to ② most questions, they usually do not have to consider alternatives or counterevidence. If we admire experts, we may come to admire people who are "decisive" in the sense of being ③ flexible. When a news commentator criticizes a political candidate for waffling and being unsure (as might befit a good thinker faced with many of the issues that politicians must face), the implication is that the candidate is not expert enough to have figured out the ④ right answer. Similarly, a person who adopts a ⑤ know-it-all tone — speaking without qualification or doubt — is giving a sign of expertise. Some parents (perhaps because they *are* experts about the matter under discussion) talk this way to their children, who come to think of it as a "grown-up" way to talk.

*waffle 모호한 태도를 보이다 **befit ~에 걸맞다

83 윗글의 밑줄 친 ①~⑤ 중 문맥상 어색한 것을 1개 찾아 그 번호를 쓰고 고쳐 쓰시오.

_____ → _____

84 윗글의 밑줄 친 this way가 가리키는 것을 본문에서 찾아 우리말로 쓰시오. (35자 내외)

_____

_____

Any object will experience a temperature decrease if it emits ① more radiation than it absorbs. At night, the Earth's surface emits infra-red radiation, but since the Sun is not shining, it absorbs very little radiation (in fact, it only absorbs the infra-red that is emitted by the atmosphere ② downward toward the surface). Thus, the Earth's surface cools all night long. When the sun finally peaks over the horizon, the Earth is still emitting a ③ good amount of infra-red radiation. In fact, it is still emitting more than it absorbs from the first faint rays of sunshine at dawn. Not until the incoming solar radiation grows ④ smaller, some time after sunrise, does the incoming radiation finally equal the outgoing infra-red radiation. At that precise moment, the temperature will have reached its ⑤ minimum value, for in the next minute, the incoming solar radiation will be larger than the outgoing infra-red, and so absorption will exceed emission and the temperature will rise as a consequence.

*radiation 복사 에너지, 복사 **infra-red 적외선의; 적외선

85 윗글에서 다음 질문에 대한 답을 찾아 우리말로 쓰시오. (25글자 내외)

Q: When does the temperature rise in terms of solar radiation energy and infra-red in the passage?

_____

86 윗글의 밑줄 친 ①~⑤ 중 문맥상 어색한 것을 1개 찾아 그 번호를 쓰고 고쳐 쓰시오.

_____ → _____

Some experts argue that until the world's distribution of wealth is altered, population will not be controlled. For example, Piel proposed that population control closely follows economic development, which enables people to escape from the poverty cycle. In other words, as poverty lessens, birth rates also decrease because women have better educational and professional opportunities as well as access to birth control. Lowered infant mortality accompanies economic development, and improved nutrition and medical care also helps to reduce birth rates. But unfortunately, poverty has been growing. More than one billion people in the world live in desperate poverty without the basic resources of clean water, adequate food, shelter, or sanitation. Even in developed countries such as the United States, more than one person in nine (11.3%) fell below the official poverty line in 2000. If current practices continue, one half of the world's population will live in absolute poverty by 2050, meaning too poor to grow or buy enough food, or maintain a job.

87 윗글에서 다음 질문에 대한 답을 찾아 본문의 표현 그대로 쓰시오. (2단어로 쓸 것)

Q: According to Piel's suggestion, what enables people to break out of the cycle of poverty and closely follows economic development?

A: _____

88 윗글의 내용을 한 문장으로 요약하려고 한다. 빈칸 (A)와 (B)에 들어갈 알맞은 말을 본문에서 찾아 쓰시오.

> Improving ____(A)____ distribution is essential for controlling population growth, but poverty is increasing with over a billion people lacking ____(B)____ needs

(A) _____

(B) _____

The introduction of digital technology has presented customers with ① transparency and new ways to search for information about products. Consumers are increasingly relying on online reviews on the internet or "word of mouth" from friends. The change in consumer behavior has likewise presented firms with a new way to ② connect with its customer base. Firms that are the most effective at connecting information regarding the customer's path to purchase (supporting the buying process) are able to position themselves ③ strongly in the future market. Several large organizations have realized that competitive advantage is no longer derived from low cost or product differentiation. Instead, competitive advantage is gained and sustained through a platform offering a system of connected and complementary products that ④ lower consumer's switching costs through strong network effects, meaning the higher the value of the platform is, the more people use it. Network effects and knowledge of customer behavior and needs provide the driving force ⑤ behind any successful organization and platform, together with a demand-driven approach (what will customers want and why?).

*switching cost 전환 비용(한 제품에서 경쟁사의 다른 제품으로 전환하는 데 드는 비용)

고난도

89 윗글의 내용을 한 문장으로 요약하려고 한다. 빈칸 (A)와 (B)에 들어갈 알맞은 말을 본문에서 찾아 쓰시오. (단, 필요시 어형을 바꿔 쓸 것)

> Digital tech and online reviews changed consumer behavior, prompting firms to offer a(n) ____(A)____ of complementary products with strong network effects to connect with customers and ____(B)____ competitive advantage.

(A) _____   (B) _____

90 윗글의 밑줄 친 ①~⑤ 중 문맥상 어색한 것을 1개 찾아 그 번호를 쓰고 고쳐 쓰시오.

_____ → _____

Test 3 22번

Adapted to life in the icy environment in the Antarctic Ocean, where their bodies are at the same glacial temperature as the seas around them, krill are reliant on an unusual internal chemistry. For instance, they possess some of the most powerful and unusual digestive ____(A)____ known in nature. Enzymes are biological catalysts, vastly accelerating processes such as digestion. Our own enzyme processes, and those of most other animals, slow down dramatically as the temperature drops. Krill enzymes, though, have some extreme working conditions to cope with, and consequently, they've evolved to be superpowerful. The amazing characteristics of krill ____(B)____ have recently been used for human medicine, to treat wounds and infections, bedsores, gastrointestinal disorders, and blood clots, to name but a few applications. Scientific advances on this scale are rare. When they do occur, it's amazing how often they emerge in the most unlikely circumstances, from research into what might be regarded as _____ animals. It's another reason to make sure that we do our utmost not only to safeguard krill but to value all the biological wealth of the planet.

*catalyst 촉매 **bedsore 욕창 ***gastrointestinal 위장의

91 윗글의 빈칸 (A), (B)에 공통으로 들어갈 말을 본문에서 찾아 쓰시오. (단, 필요시 어형을 바꿔 쓸 것)

_____

92 윗글의 빈칸에 들어갈 단어를 영영 뜻풀이를 참고하여 쓰시오. (단, 주어진 글자로 시작할 것)

unlikely to be satisfactory or successful

u_____

Cultural values are ① fundamental within a workplace because they define the terms of the psychological contracts that an employee holds with the organization. Unlike formal contracts of employment, psychological contracts are unwritten, often unarticulated, and usually only exist as ② assumptions. In a culturally homogeneous setting, assumptions are generally understood and shared, so the psychological contracts in play may be relatively ③ unclear: rewards are dependent on how well you do, the employee expects to stay in the organization for many years or for just a few years, the corporate ethos reflects the ethos of that ④ particular society, and so on. However, in a culturally diverse workforce people may have very different expectations of the psychological contract. For example, in some cultures an organization may reward people because of their family connections rather than on the basis of their performance, or, in the case of transnational corporations, the overall corporate ethos is very ⑤ different to that of the host nation.

*unarticulated 분명히 표현되지 않은 **homogeneous 동질의
***ethos 정신, 기풍

93 윗글의 밑줄 친 ①~⑤ 중 문맥상 어색한 것을 1개 찾아 그 번호를 쓰고 고쳐 쓰시오.

_____ → _____

94 윗글에서 다음 질문에 대한 답을 찾아 본문의 표현 그대로 쓰시오. (3단어)

Q: What makes culturally diverse employees have very different expectations among themselves?

A: _____

In his endlessly amusing book, *A Mathematician Plays the Stock Market*, John Allen Paulos points out that we tend to misunderstand the role chance plays in the outcomes of apparently even games. Imagine that two people — I will call them George Soros and George Bozos — flip a fair coin 1,000 times each, competing to see who can come up with the most heads. We tend to imagine that, after that many flips, the outcome would almost always come out very even, with Soros and Bozos each getting about 500 heads and 500 tails. We infer from that conclusion that if one of the players actually ends up well ahead of the other, that outcome must be due either to an unfair coin or to the special skill of one of the players.

In fact, as Paulos points out, there is a far greater probability that after 1,000 fair coin flips, Soros or Bozos would be well ahead of the other, having flipped 525 heads to, say, 475 heads. We might call this the law of small numbers; that is, 1,000 flips may seem like a lot, but actually it's not enough observations to ensure that Soros and Bozos will come out even. Thus, if 10,000 people all flipped a fair coin 1,000 times, the aggregate results would tend to be that a goodly number would end up with pretty good records and an equal number would end up with pretty sorry records. A very few would have spectacular records and a very few would have abysmal records. Far less than we might expect would have even records.

*aggregate 합계의 **abysmal 최악의

95 윗글에서 다음 질문에 대한 답을 찾아 영어로 쓰시오. (5단어)

Q: Write the name of the law that shows that it is difficult to obtain the probabilistic result we expect with a small number of trials.

A: _____

96

윗글의 밑줄 친 this가 가리키는 것을 본문에서 찾아 우리말로 쓰시오. (75자 내외)

_____

_____

Once, a girl in my class called Emma decided to do a research paper on a particular political group. Her father was an active member of the group, as she herself was soon to become, so this major research paper of hers was a rite of passage as well. Perhaps because I was so ① enthusiastic over her choice of a topic, she assumed I was also sympathetic to her political point of view. Almost conspiratorially she expressed to me her worries about a history teacher who would also be reading her paper and giving it a grade.

"Ms. Maples is quite open about her political views, and hers differ from my father's, I am ② worried how she'll mark my paper," she said. I assured her that Ms. Maples would insist, as I would, on an objective presentation of factual material and on sources other than publications of the political group in question, but that our insistence did not in any way imply a prejudice against her or her work. "As far as politics go," I told her, "mine are probably similar to those of Ms. Maples', and look how excited I am about your paper."

I had meant to put her at ease, but my mistake was immediately ③ evident from the blood leaving her face. I smiled with great kindness. "It's going to be a wonderful paper," I said. *It's going to be the end of my life*, Emma thought. As to the final outcome, it was a wonderful paper, and working on it with her was the beginning of one of the warmest relationships I ever enjoyed with a student. I tried not only to help her see ④ same points of view, but also to give depth to her own.

To achieve that, I introduced her to the novels of Ayn Rand and a few other books. What I saw in this girl was the ability to believe in something ⑤ more than survival, gratification, and success. It was her having some conviction, aside from any content of the conviction itself, that I strove to reinforce. I think it was Toynbee who said that the values of Sparta and Valhalla are preferable to no values at all. And a misfired challenge to the young may be preferable to allowing their need for challenge and commitment to go unmet.

*rite of passage 통과 의례   **conspiratorially 공모하는 듯이

97

윗글의 밑줄 친 ①~⑤ 중 문맥상 어색한 것을 1개 찾아 그 번호를 쓰고 고쳐 쓰시오.

_____ → _____

98

윗글의 내용을 한 문장으로 요약하려고 한다. 빈칸 (A)와 (B)에 들어갈 알맞은 말을 본문에서 찾아 쓰시오. (단, 필요시 어형을 바꿔 쓸 것)

> A teacher helps a student with a research paper on a political group, leading to a __(A)__ relationship and an attempt to reinforce the student's conviction in __(B)__ in something more than success.

(A) _____

(B) _____

지은이

NE능률 영어교육연구소

NE능률 영어교육연구소는 혁신적이며 효율적인 영어 교재를 개발하고
영어 학습의 질을 한 단계 높이고자 노력하는 NE능률의 연구조직입니다.

2024학년도 능률 EBS 수능특강 변형 문제 〈영어독해연습(하)〉

펴 낸 이   주민홍
펴 낸 곳   서울특별시 마포구 월드컵북로 396(상암동) 누리꿈스퀘어 비즈니스타워 10층
            ㈜NE능률 (우편번호 03925)
펴 낸 날   2023년 4월 10일 초판 제1쇄 발행
전   화   02 2014 7114
팩   스   02 3142 0356
홈 페 이 지 www.neungyule.com
등 록 번 호 제1-68호
I S B N   979-11-253-4165-9 53740
정   가   19,000원

NE 능률

고객센터

교재 내용 문의 : contact.nebooks.co.kr (별도의 가입 절차 없이 작성 가능)

제품 구매, 교환, 불량, 반품 문의 : 02-2014-7114

☎ 전화문의는 본사 업무시간 중에만 가능합니다.

NE능률 교재 MAP

아래 교재 MAP을 참고하여 본인의 현재 혹은 목표 수준에 따라 교재를 선택하세요.
NE능률 교재들과 함께 영어실력을 쑥쑥~ 올려보세요!
MP3 등 교재 부가 학습 서비스 및 자세한 교재 정보는 www.nebooks.co.kr 에서 확인하세요.

수능

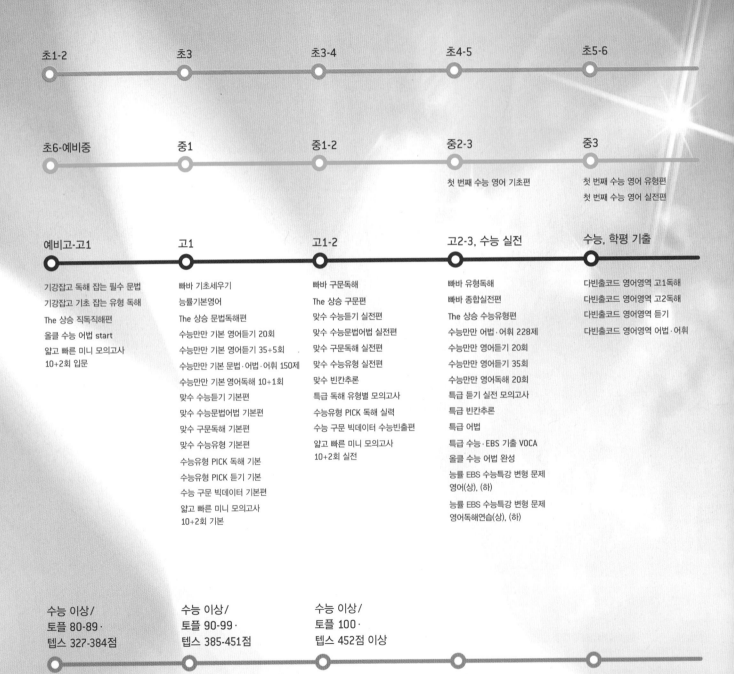

초1-2　　초3　　초3-4　　초4-5　　초5-6

초6·예비중　　중1　　중1-2　　중2-3　　중3

중2-3
첫 번째 수능 영어 기초편

중3
첫 번째 수능 영어 유형편
첫 번째 수능 영어 실전편

예비고-고1
기강잡고 독해 잡는 필수 문법
기강잡고 기초 잡는 유형 독해
The 상승 직독직해편
올클 수능 어법 start
얇고 빠른 미니 모의고사 10+2회 입문

고1
빠바 기초세우기
능률기본영어
The 상승 문법독해편
수능만만 기본 영어듣기 20회
수능만만 기본 영어듣기 35+5회
수능만만 기본 문법·어법·어휘 150제
수능만만 기본 영어독해 10+1회
맞수 수능듣기 기본편
맞수 수능문법어법 기본편
맞수 구문독해 기본편
맞수 수능유형 기본편
수능유형 PICK 독해 기본
수능유형 PICK 듣기 기본
수능 구문 빅데이터 기본편
얇고 빠른 미니 모의고사 10+2회 기본

고1-2
빠바 구문독해
The 상승 구문편
맞수 수능듣기 실전편
맞수 수능문법어법 실전편
맞수 구문독해 실전편
맞수 수능유형 실전편
맞수 빈칸추론
특급 독해 유형별 모의고사
수능유형 PICK 독해 실력
수능 구문 빅데이터 수능빈출편
얇고 빠른 미니 모의고사 10+2회 실전

고2-3, 수능 실전
빠바 유형독해
빠바 종합실전편
The 상승 수능유형편
수능만만 어법·어휘 228제
수능만만 영어듣기 20회
수능만만 영어듣기 35회
수능만만 영어독해 20회
특급 듣기 실전 모의고사
특급 빈칸추론
특급 어법
특급 수능·EBS 기출 VOCA
올클 수능 어법 완성
능률 EBS 수능특강 변형 문제 영어(상), (하)
능률 EBS 수능특강 변형 문제 영어독해연습(상), (하)

수능, 학평 기출
다빈출코드 영어영역 고1독해
다빈출코드 영어영역 고2독해
다빈출코드 영어영역 듣기
다빈출코드 영어영역 어법·어휘

수능 이상/
토플 80-89·
텝스 327-384점

수능 이상/
토플 90-99·
텝스 385-451점

수능 이상/
토플 100·
텝스 452점 이상

·2024학년도 수능 및 내신 대비·

능률
EBS 수능특강

변형 문제
영어독해
연습(하)

733제

정답 및 해설

능률
EBS 수능특강

변형 문제
영어독해
연습(하)

733제

정답 및 해설

10강 p.6

01 ③ 02 ③ 03 ③ 04 ③ 05 ② 06 ⑤ 07 ④ 08 ② 09 ⑤ 10 ④ 11 ④ 12 ④ 13 ② 14 ④ 15 ①
16 ② 17 ① 18 ④ 19 ③ 20 ② 21 only have you failed to help the athlete 22 선수가 과제를 완료하는 데 어느 정도 실패한다면 그것은 진전으로 여겨질 수 있다는 것 23 lest they be mistaken for self-appointed authorities over what society should do 24 (1) 기후 과학자가 기후에 적절한 조치를 취하지 않는 것 (2) 의사가 정기적인 암 검사 또는 태아기 영양 계획을 지지하지 않는 것 25 (A) conducted (B) which (C) were 26 activation 27 ③ → disastrous 28 one characteristic that helps entrepreneurs get started and also persist in their efforts to succeed 29 ① → During ③ → struggling[struggle] ⑥ → said 30 one day at a time 31 ② → invulnerable 32 (A) chemical (B) sound 33 ② → that of Richard Strauss 34 similarities 35 ① → been distinguished 36 (1) 무턱대고 암기하기 (2) 곰곰이 생각해 보기, 토론하기, 다양한 정보 출처 사용하기, 아이디어를 이전 지식과 연관시키기, 패턴 찾아보기, 증거 확인하기, 주장을 비판적으로 검토하기 37 the reason that merely having someone listen can be such a powerful experience 38 (A) manage (B) emotional 39 ③ → exchanged 40 (A) regret (B) share

11강 p.12

01 ③ 02 ④ 03 ④ 04 ③ 05 ④ 06 ③ 07 ④ 08 ⑤ 09 ⑤ 10 ③ 11 ① 12 ② 13 ③ 14 ⑤ 15 ②
16 ① 17 ⑤ 18 ② 19 ③ 20 ③ 21 ⑤ 22 ② 23 ③ → emergence 24 costs a mere third as much as shifting it by plane 25 reinforcement 26 공중위생 캠페인을 지원하는 필수적 시스템 및 서비스와 함께 대규모로 신속하게 강화하는 것 27 instead of relying on rules that you've been told will produce clear text 28 (1) 독자가 어떻게 반응할지를 아는 것 (2) 글쓰기에 규칙을 유연하게 적용하는 것 29 (1) alternating (2) crash (3) do 30 대량 결실이 없는 해 다음에는 일부 전문적으로 씨앗을 먹는 동물들의 개체수가 급감하여 많은 도토리가 살아남는다는 것 31 (1) ④ → filled (2) ⑤ → that 32 who had walked for more than two hours without complaining 33 ② → extensive 34 overload 35 (1) ③ → have (2) ④ → assign 36 knowledge transfer 37 cognitive 38 appears that these genes have a direct impact on dogs' intense ability and desire for social contact 39 (1) ① → how 생략 또는 that[in which] (2) ④ → Compared 40 (1) 강한 규범 (2) 일탈 행동에 대한 낮은 관용 (3) 약한 규범 (4) 일탈 행동에 대한 허용 범위가 넓음 41 (1) ③ → pondering (2) ⑤ → flying 42 (A) Roberto Clemente (B) Roberto Clemente

12강 p.18

01 ④ 02 ③ 03 ① 04 ③ 05 ④ 06 ④ 07 ② 08 ③ 09 ⑤ 10 ③ 11 ③ 12 ③ 13 ③ 14 ⑤ 15 ④
16 ③ 17 ④ 18 ④ 19 ④ 20 ② 21 ② 22 ④ 23 (A) is (B) scores (C) invigorated 24 학습자가 계속해서 도달 가능한 행동을 향해 앞으로 가게 하며 숙련도를 유지하고 지속하면서도 도달된 새로운 기록에 마음속으로 플러스 점수를 매기는 끊임없는 순환 25 (1) ② → the higher (2) ③ → necessarily 26 lifespan 27 힘든 장애물을 헤치고 다양한 능력을 갖추며 성공적으로 잘 성장해 왔다는 것 28 represents the entire developmental process, provides proof 29 (A) Othello (B) Hamlet 30 Hamlet처럼 철저해야 하고, Othello처럼 행동 지향적이되, 성급한 결론을 내리지 않고, 끝없는 질문의 고리에 갇히지 않는 사람들 31 (A) to acquire (B) exploring (C) them over (D) chase 32 새끼 토끼들이 Koa의 몸 위를 뛰어다니도록 하고, Koa의 다리 안쪽을 찾아가서 온기와 보호를 얻는 것 33 (A) the destabilizing effect this has on prices (B) to make it easier for customers to contact them 34 ④ → suppliers 35 ⑤ → independent 36 priorities 37 it, could 38 10년 전에는 많은 정보 수집에 초점을 두었지만, 요즘 검색 엔진은 인간의 행동에 기반을 두고 검색자의 선택 범위를 좁혀 준다. 39 (1) ② → scatter (2) ③ → absence 40 Dispersal 41 (1) ③ → scattered (2) ④ → must have read (3) ⑤ → deflated 42 Mom told the girl that the dog had just smelled the bone

Test 1 p.27

01 ③ 02 ① 03 ① 04 ② 05 ② 06 ③ 07 ① 08 ⑤ 09 ④ 10 ③ 11 ③ 12 ① 13 ⑤ 14 ⑤ 15 ①
16 ② 17 ① 18 ⑤ 19 ⑤ 20 ⑤ 21 ② 22 ⑤ 23 ③ 24 ⑤ 25 ③ 26 ④ 27 ③ 28 ⑤ 29 ① 30 ④
31 ③ 32 ② 33 ⑤ 34 ④ 35 ③ 36 ① 37 ① 38 ② 39 ③ 40 ③ 41 ⑤ 42 ④ 43 ① 44 ④ 45 ①
46 ③ 47 ③ 48 ② 49 (1) ① → are (2) ③ → leads 50 facilities 51 어렵게 사는 분들로부터 생각지도 못한 과분한 친절을 받은 것에 감동받아서 52 Barely had I knocked on the door when an older woman opened it 53 ③ → disagreement 54 It is probably worth mentioning that Socrates was put to death for his beliefs 55 consequential 56 as if it were your own athletic prowess 57 (A) → have been left (B) → to attain 58 (A) opportunities (B) upward 59 We do not have an environmental problem so much as we have a *story* problem 60 ⑤ → uninterrupted 61 constraint 62 (A) were (B) what (C) allowing 63 (A) peak (B) fell (C) below 64 with more than 15,000 gigaliters used 65 an accurate chart of the stars, a flying machine, the first seismograph 66 Only later in his life did Zhang Heng hold a series of important government positions 67 Do you want to see your artwork displayed at an exhibition 68 수여자는 총 18명이며, 모든 출품작이 전시된다. 69 Happy Mall 70 validate 71 (A) worse (B) obsession (C) deprivation 72 (A) comprehend (B) blueprint 73 (1) ② → created (2) ④ → difficult 74 (A) protection (B) processing 75 (A) in which (B) figure (C) what 76 selfish capitalism 77 commonplace 78 (A) enables (B) discovery 79 (A) exit → exiting (B) be → having been (C) blow → blowing 80 It initially struck me as a bit excessive 81 (1) ② →

negative ②③ → absence 82 there would be no human life on the planet if it were 83 (1) giving any thought to the psychological states that caused them (2) reasoning about their psychological states 84 (A) reason (B) anticipation 85 justification 86 (1) ① → that (2) ② → do we experience (3) ⑤ → is 87 accumulation 88 (A) modification (B) requirements 89 (1) ③ → untagging (2) ⑤ → corresponded 90 (A) themselves (B) them (C) presented 91 analogy 92 (A) Similarly (B) For example (C) For example 93 (A) misplaced (B) overpriced (C) choose 94 how these students would have done without their education 95 ③, ⑤ → thought 96 should I arrive at the interpretation / would ideally dispense 97 (1) ② → have elicited (2) ③ → noticing (3) ⑤ → comforted 98 잡을 수 있는 따뜻한 손, 고통을 비추는 공감하는 눈, 기대어 올 수 있는 어깨

Test 2 p.42

01 ① 02 ③ 03 ③ 04 ⑤ 05 ③ 06 ⑤ 07 ③ 08 ⑤ 09 ⑤ 10 ④ 11 ⑤ 12 ③ 13 ⑤ 14 ③ 15 ②
16 ④ 17 ② 18 ③ 19 ② 20 ⑤ 21 ⑤ 22 ⑤ 23 ⑤ 24 ④ 25 ④ 26 ⑤ 27 ④ 28 ① 29 ⑤ 30 ③
31 ③ 32 ④ 33 ④ 34 ⑤ 35 ③ 36 ⑤ 37 ② 38 ② 39 ③ 40 ④ 41 ① 42 ③ 43 ④ 44 ③ 45 ⑤
46 ⑤ 47 ① 48 ② 49 With the year coming to a close 50 ensures 51 남부 캘리포니아 사막의 외딴 곳을 탐험함 52 It never occurred to me to prepare for a storm! 53 (A) → when (B) → what (C) → how 54 No matter what kind, the majority of, function differently from 55 (1) ③ → contain (2) ⑤ → to file 56 정치가들이 해양 관련 사안에 관해 운동을 벌이는 일이 거의 없다 57 ⑤ → emerged 58 (A) task (B) serve 59 whose value lies entirely in the capacity to purchase things 60 consumption 61 nurture 62 to bring about personal well-being, joy, health and flourishing as well as planetary health 63 the factor that was most likely to help, was the subject 64 (A) → cited (B) → participated (C) → is 65 ⑤ → faded 66 is considered one of the greatest jazz pianists of all time 67 wrinkles 68 Do not assemble or operate this device with wet hands. 69 (1) ② → swimming (2) ④ → included 70 allows you to watch the sea turtles and to swim in the most extraordinary 71 disclosure 72 it difficult or impossible to determine, is attacking 73 revived the Egyptian reluctance to record the natural world 74 몸통은 정면을, 머리와 허리, 팔다리는 측면을 그렸다. 75 real kindness 76 (A) to be known (B) who[that] (C) in which[where] 77 ② → ignore 78 closing local beach A due to pollution causes more people to visit 79 (A) → to show (B) → opened (C) → needed 80 hidden photos 81 interpreting delay as something other than that 82 overlook 83 do we attempt to appreciate and protect nature 84 nature 85 (a) sporting (b) architectural 86 (A) fixed (B) to be played (C) means 87 (1) ② → scared (2) ③ → have (3) ⑤ → disappointed 88 Audiences generally identify more with people and characters in the stories than with abstract discussion. 89 mediated 90 생산적인 성인일 때 공익에 기여하고, 그 대가로 어릴 때는 교육을, 아프거나 실직하거나 늙었을 때는 부양을 받음 91 (A) → the way(that / in which)[how] (B) → where[in which] (C) → because 92 are more likely to be affected by, such as 93 ④ → forced 94 사회 기반 시설을 지속 가능하게 다시 짓는 것은 매우 많은 비용이 든다. 95 can be traced, as far back as 96 인간의 내적 상태는 과학적으로는 결코 조사될 수 없으며 직관적, 해석적, 심지어 종교적 방법을 통해 비과학적으로 이해되어야 한다는 견해 97 seemed that Emily absolutely loved 98 (A) passion (B) runner

Test 3 p.56

01 ③ 02 ③ 03 ④ 04 ⑤ 05 ③ 06 ④ 07 ① 08 ① 09 ③ 10 ⑤ 11 ② 12 ① 13 ⑤ 14 ④ 15 ④
16 ⑤ 17 ⑤ 18 ③ 19 ② 20 ⑤ 21 ② 22 ⑤ 23 ④ 24 ⑨ 25 ⑤ 26 ③ 27 ③ 28 ② 29 ⑤ 30 ④
31 ② 32 ③ 33 ② 34 ④ 35 ③ 36 ⑤ 37 ④ 38 ② 39 ③ 40 ⑤ 41 ④ 42 ④ 43 ④ 44 ② 45 ⑤
46 ⑤ 47 ② 48 ④ 49 (A) that[which] (B) caused[had caused] (C) what 50 a leak 51 recipe 52 ② → never 53 researchers 54 researchers had taken active steps to move those discoveries into the realm of invention 55 Jordan's remarkable level of energy throughout the night following a demanding game 56 (A) while (B) that[which] (C) participate 57 ④ → benefit 58 the benefits 59 20년마다 해체되어 유사한 재료로 다시 만든 정확한 복제품이 같은 장소에 조립되는 것 60 who scraped the chalk figure every seven years to keep it from being obscured by growing vegetation 61 ⑤ → threatened 62 partnerships between students and university staff and administrators 63 65 years or over 64 participation 65 ③ → distract 66 (A) birds (B) conserving (C) the other 67 suitable 68 (A) experience (B) specialized (C) fill 69 (A) to be used (B) to permit (C) engage 70 attendant 71 taste dilemma 72 drives humans to eat beyond our biological imperative as we eat more and more variety 73 ④ → increasing 74 (A) predict (B) pay 75 the distortions caused by categorization 76 ④ → differently 77 loyalty 78 충성도 자극을 받은 사람들은 열등한 수행 능력에 대해 동료 이용자를 기꺼이 고자질하려는 마음이 덜했다는 것 79 companies 80 (A) resistance (B) divulge 81 nurture ends up amplifying characteristics that were already there to begin with 82 nurture 83 ③ → rigid 84 무조건적으로 또는 의심의 여지 없이 말하면서 모든 것을 다 아는 듯한 어조를 취하는 것 85 들어오는 태양 복사 에너지가 나가는 적외선보다 더 커질 때 86 ④ → larger 87 population control 88 (A) wealth (B) basic 89 (A) platform (B) (to) gain 90 ④ → raise 91 enzymes 92 unpromising 93 ③ → clear 94 the psychological contract 95 the law of small numbers 96 1000번의 공정한 동전의 던지기 후에 Soros 또는 Bozos가 가령 475번의 앞면에 비하여 525번의 앞면을 던져서 상대보다 훨씬 앞서 있을 확률이 훨씬 더 큰 것 97 ④ → different 98 (A) warmest (B) believing

1번 ───────────────── p.6

• Word Test

1 유지하다   2 치료사   3 굳게 결심한, 단호한
4 완벽주의적인   5 강화하다   6 중요한, 결정적인
7 ~을 수행하다   8 어느 정도   9 ~을 해결하기 위해 노력하다
10 속이다, 기만하다   11 explore   12 smoothly
13 intervention   14 subtle   15 apparent
16 assignment   17 unknowingly   18 dialog
19 athlete   20 progress

유형 1
❶ subtle   ❷ smoothly   ❸ however
❹ have you   ❺ progress

유형 2
❶ are   ❷ agreed
❸ being reinforced   ❹ be deceived
❺ be considered   ❻ to discuss

유형 3
❶ once determined to work on
❷ important to be aware of
❸ might very well feel like
❹ continually exploring their goals

2번 ───────────────── p.8

• Word Test

1 권위자, 권한   2 ~에 대해 생각해 보다   3 상황
4 논쟁, 논란   5 천문학자   6 객관적인; 목적   7 특정한
8 윤리적인   9 검사, 상영   10 경우, 기회   11 late
12 take sides   13 respect   14 routine
15 principle   16 initiative   17 reasonably
18 speak out   19 mistaken   20 appropriate

유형 1
❶ objective   ❷ public   ❸ what
❹ irresponsible   ❺ as

유형 2
❶ is   ❷ appear   ❸ to avoid
❹ be seen   ❺ supporting

유형 3
❶ take sides on policy controversies
❷ have risked losing the respect
❸ lest they be mistaken for
❹ appropriate action on climate

3번 ───────────────── p.11

• Word Test

1 활성화   2 수치, 숫자   3 고급스러운, 호화로운
4 행동의   5 얻다, 획득하다   6 친환경의   7 ~에 비해
8 평범한, 중립적인   9 수행하다, 처리하다   10 cue

11 high-status   12 hypothetical   13 performance
14 promote   15 respectively   16 corresponding
17 household cleaner   18 colleague

유형 1
❶ who   ❷ neutral   ❸ which
❹ in which   ❺ respectively

유형 2
❶ was   ❷ had   ❸ was
❹ occurred   ❺ were

유형 3
❶ relative to others
❷ hypothetical consumer products
❸ equal in price
❹ activation of status motives

4번 ───────────────── p.13

• Word Test

1 거의, 사실상   2 벤처 사업, (사업상의) 모험
3 성취하다, 달성하다   4 착수하다, 맡다
5 근거가 없는, 정당하지 않은   6 지속하다, 계속하다
7 확대하다   8 변인, 변수; 변하기 쉬운   9 set out to *do*
10 disastrous   11 characteristic
12 entrepreneur   13 optimism   14 guaranteed
15 downside   16 ultimately

유형 1
❶ distinguish   ❷ despite   ❸ downside
❹ that   ❺ deadly

유형 2
❶ found   ❷ is   ❸ needed
❹ leading   ❺ guaranteed
❻ be magnified

유형 3
❶ whatever they set out to accomplish
❷ the odds being highly stacked against
❸ persist in their efforts to succeed
❹ what can be disastrous results
❺ high level of optimism

5-7번 ───────────────── p.15

• Word Test

1 막대   2 (서서히) 지나가다, (녹듯이) 사라지다   3 놀라다
4 소모하다, 소비하다   5 좌우명, 처세훈
6 힘든 일; 힘들어하다, 고투하다   7 기숙사
8 ~을 갑자기 끝내다   9 편입하다, 전학하다
10 말하다, 함께 나누다   11 assignment   12 theory
13 hip   14 enforcement   15 all at once
16 pressure   17 endure   18 tense
19 overcome with   20 community

유형 1
❶ consumed   ❷ struggle   ❸ positive
❹ coped   ❺ through   ❻ so
❼ herself

유형 2

① were **②** had endured **③** was left
④ melted **⑤** found **⑥** has carried

유형 3

① felt pressure all around **②** was cut short
③ day in and day out **④** made little sense to
⑤ stayed in touch **⑥** overcome with major anxiety

8번 ————————————— p.19

• Word Test

1 유전의　　2 분자　　3 막　　4 필수적인, 중요한
5 ~을 안전하게 막아 주는, ~에 손상되지 않는　　6 노출시키다
7 화학 물질　　8 solitary　　9 sonic　　10 cluster
11 cell　　12 means　　13 in a fraction of a second
14 biochemical

유형 1

① Given **②** tightly
③ invulnerable **④** ill-suited **⑤** another

유형 2

① is **②** are **③** depends
④ exchanging **⑤** exposed

유형 3

① communicate with one another
② a likely means of communication
③ But to date
④ in a fraction of a second

9번 ————————————— p.21

• Word Test

1 행렬　　2 상기시키다　　3 ~의 특징을 나타내다
4 불러일으키다　　5 ~을 추구하다, ~을 얻고자 하다
6 타오르다　　7 ~을 면하기 힘든　　8 해석　　9 chase
10 heavenly bodies　　11 aspect　　12 suspicion
13 funeral　　14 similarity　　15 value
16 heights

유형 1

① whose **②** that **③** of
④ similarities **⑤** were

유형 2

① to say **②** glows **③** moving
④ invoking **⑤** striving

유형 3

① among his closest friends
② across moonlit heights
③ aspects in common
④ would be subject to suspicion himself

10번 ————————————— p.23

• Word Test

1 외적인　　2 비판적으로　　3 활성화하다　　4 내용
5 분석　　6 상기하다, 재현하다　　7 접근법
8 comprehend　　9 conceptual　　10 subsequently
11 argument　　12 hurdle　　13 reflect
14 distinguish

유형 1

① external **②** clear
③ on the other hand **④** that
⑤ previous

유형 2

① been distinguished **②** sees **③** is
④ have **⑤** activating

유형 3

① as little time and effort as possible
② subsequently reproduce the material
③ can vary in terms of
④ critically examining arguments

11번 ————————————— p.25

• Word Test

1 토대　　2 인정하다, 확인하다　　3 드러내다
4 이해심 있는, 공감하는　　5 짐, 부담　　6 긍정하다
7 고개 끄덕임　　8 드러내다, 보여 주다　　9 therapist
10 triumph　　11 compassionate　　12 frightening
13 cling　　14 quality　　15 grief　　16 commute

유형 1

① saying **②** less **③** empathetic
④ even if **⑤** validate

유형 2

① to experience **②** build **③** relieves
④ lies **⑤** knowing

유형 3

① carrying the burden completely alone
② foundation to cling to
③ just being there
④ runs with it

12-14번 ————————————— p.27

• Word Test

1 떠내려가다　　2 ~을 깜짝 놀라게 하다　　3 중요한
4 관계, 연결　　5 결국　　6 겁쟁이　　7 열망　　8 야망
9 disquiet　　10 enthusiasm　　11 mature
12 decline　　13 belong　　14 bridesmaid
15 reach out　　16 revive

유형 1

① where **②** declined **③** whom
④ for **⑤** having **⑥** revive

01 ③　02 ③　03 ③　04 ③　05 ②　06 ⑤
07 ④　08 ②　09 ⑤　10 ④　11 ④　12 ④
13 ②　14 ③　15 ①　16 ②　17 ①　18 ③
19 ③　20 ②　21 only have you failed to help the
athlete　22 선수가 과제를 완료하는 데 어느 정도 실패한다면
그것은 진전으로 여겨질 수 있다는 것
23 lest they be mistaken for self-appointed
authorities over what society should do
24 (1) 기후 과학자가 기후에 적절한 조치를 취하지 않는 것
(2) 의사가 정기적인 암 검사 또는 태아기 영양 계획을 지지하지 않는 것
25 (A) conducted (B) which (C) were
26 activation　27 ③ → disastrous　28 one
characteristic that helps entrepreneurs get started
and also persist in their efforts to succeed
29 ① → During　③ → struggling[struggle]　⑥ → said
30 one day at a time　31 ② → invulnerable
32 (A) chemical (B) sound
33 ② → that of Richard Strauss　34 similarities
35 ① → been distinguished　36 (1) 무턱대고 암기하기
(2) 곰곰이 생각해 보기, 토론하기, 다양한 정보 출처 사용하기,
아이디어를 이전 지식과 연관시키기, 패턴 찾아보기, 증거 확인하기,
주장을 비판적으로 검토하기　37 the reason that merely
having someone listen can be such a powerful
experience　38 (A) manage (B) emotional
39 ③ → exchanged　40 (A) regret (B) share

01 ③

문제해설

이 글은 완벽주의 운동선수를 치료하거나 상담할 때 주의해야 할 점에 대한 것으로, 빈칸 앞에서 운동선수들이 겉으로 보기에 과제 수행을 너무 잘하고 있는 것을 보고 스스로 자신이 최고의 치료사라고 착각할 수도 있다고 언급하고 있고, 빈칸 뒤에서 이 시점에서 완벽주의 운동 선수를 돕지 못할 뿐만 아니라 해결하고자 했던 문제가 오히려 강화될 수도 있다는 내용이 나오므로, 빈칸에 들어갈 말로 가장 적절한 것은 ③ '운동선수에게 속지 않도록 해야 한다는 것'이다.

오답노트

① 당신의 고객의 비밀을 누설하지
② 결과에 실망하지
④ 상담 속도를 낮추지
⑤ 고객의 반응을 의심하지

02 ③

문제해설

보통의 상황에서는 과학자들이 객관성 유지를 위해 특정 정책을 옹호하는 것을 피하고자 하는 것이 당연할 수 있지만 과학자들도 정책 문제에 대한 목소리를 내는 것이 권리이자 의무일 수도 있으며 그렇지 않을 경우 오히려 책임을 다하지 않는 것이 될 수도 있다는 내용으로, '관여를 완전히 피하는 것 자체가 무책임한 것으로 보일 수 있다.'가 의미하는 것으로 가장 적절한 것은 ③ '과학자들은 더 큰 공공의 이익을 위해 필요할 때에 정책 문제에 대해 자신의 의견을 말할 수 있어야 한다.'이다.

오답노트

① 과학자는 무슨 일이 있어도 객관적이어야 한다.
② 과학자의 정치적 참여는 과학자로서의 권리 및 의무와 관련이 거의 없다.
④ 과학자가 정책을 옹호하게 되면 다른 과학자들의 존경을 받지 못할 수 있다.
⑤ 과학자들이 정책 이슈에 대해 발언하지 않는 것이 쉽지 않지만 관여하지 않도록 주의해야 한다.

03 ③

문제해설

Griskevicius와 그의 동료들의 실험에서 높은 사회적 지위의 직장을 얻어 빠르게 승진하는 것과 같이 지위 동기와 관련된 이야기를 읽었던 처치 집단의 대학생들이 평범한 이야기를 읽은 통제 집단의 대학생들보다 친환경 제품을 선택하는 비율이 높았다는 내용이므로, 글의 제목으로 가장 적절한 것은은 ③ '지위 동기의 자극: 친환경 선택의 변수'이다.

오답노트

① 친환경 제품: 득인가 실인가?
② 왜 일반 제품이 (친환경 제품보다) 기능이 좋은가
④ 친환경적 자세: 교육의 산물
⑤ 친환경 제품과 그렇지 않은 제품의 차이는 무엇인가?

04 ③

문제해설

성공하려고 나선 것을 성공적으로 성취할 수 있다는 개인적인 믿음인 자기 효능감이 사업가에게 미치는 긍정적인 영향과 부정적인 영향에 대한 내용이므로, 글의 주제로 가장 적절한 것은 ③ '자기 효능감이 사업자에게 미칠 수 있는 영향'이다.

오답노트

① 벤처 사업을 시작하는 것의 장점과 단점
② 자기 효능감과 낙관주의의 최적의 수준
④ 사업가에게 있어 자기 효능감의 중요성
⑤ 필요한 자원의 부족으로 인한 문제를 해결하는 방법

05 ②

문제해설

Krista는 학업과 보모 일을 병행하면서 힘들게 일하며 압박감을 느끼던 중 자신이 일하던 가족의 엄마였던 Delia가 고관절을 다쳐 수술을 받고 경력도 단절되었지만 "한 번에 하루씩"을 삶의 모토로 긍정적인 삶의 자세를 가지고 있었던 것을 보게 된다. 학교 기숙사에서 큰 걱정으로 압도되어 있던 자신이 어느 순간 Delia가 말했던 하루하루 헤쳐나간다는 것을 진심으로 믿고 있으며 자신이 스스로 그렇게 말하고 있었다는 것을 깨닫고 Delia에게 고마웠다는 내용으로, 이 글의 제목으로 가장 적절한 것은 ② 'Delia의 선물: 한 번에 하루씩'이다.

① 무기력을 극복하는 방법
③ 긍정: 언제나 바람이지만 현실에서 잘 안되는 것
④ 성공하기 위해서 필요한 올바른 자세는 무엇인가?
⑤ 수술을 받은 후 그녀에게 무슨 일이 일어났는가?

06 ⑤

Krista가 거울 속 자신을 바라보며 "괜찮아 오늘을 헤쳐나가기만 하자"라고 말하는 자신을 보고 깜짝 놀라며 처음으로 자신이 한 번에 하루씩 넘길 수 있다고 진정으로 믿었다는 것이 문맥상 자연스러우므로 ⑤의 give up(포기하다)을 survive(견디다, 넘기다) 등으로 고쳐야 한다.

07 ④

박테리아는 서로 네트워킹하며 협력적으로 공생하기 위해 끊임없이 소통하는 존재로 음성 신호가 그들에게 그럴싸한 수단처럼 보일 수도 있지만, 세포 내에서 수만 개의 분자를 사용하여 의사소통을 한다는 내용의 글이므로, '박테리아가 서로 계속 네트워킹하며 (A) 소통하는 존재이지만, (B) 소리는 그들의 사회에서 적정한 의사소통 수단이 아니다.'로 요약하는 것이 가장 적절하다.

① 내성적인 …… 소리   ② 내성적인 …… 화학 물질
③ 사교적인 …… 화학 물질   ⑤ 소통하는 …… 움직임

08 ②

듣는 사람에 따라 해석이 달라질 것인데, 브람스 교향곡 4번을 듣고 Herzogenberg은 해질 녘 아름다운 경치 속의 산책과 같다는 주어진 글 뒤에, 그녀(Herzogenberg)의 반응은 Strauss와 나란히 놓고 보면 더욱 흥미로운데 그는 달빛이 비치는 고원을 가로질러 이동하는 장례 행렬을 생각나게 했다는 (B)가 이어진 후, Strauss의 달빛이건 Herzogenberg의 일몰이건 중요하지 않고 둘 다 천체를 상기시키고 말로 나타낼 수 없는 표현을 추구하는 공통적인 특성을 나타낸다는 (A)가 온 후, 마지막으로 그 음악은 적어도 추격, 전투, 만화의 특성을 나타낼 수는 없을 것이며 누군가 그런 해석을 내놓는다면 그 자신이 의심을 면하기 어려울 것이라는 (C)로 이어지는 것이 자연스럽다.

09 ⑤

학습에 대한 두 가지 접근법에 관한 글로 학습에 대한 표면적 접근법을 취하는 학생은 학습을 강요된 일로 보아 무턱대고 암기하는 특성을 지니는 반면에 학습에 대해 심층 접근법을 취하는 학생은 자료를 이해하고 개념 분석을 활성화하려는 의도를 가지고 있다는 내용으로, 빈칸 부분에는 표면적 접근법에 대한 내용으로 이해하지 않고 무턱대고 암기한다는 내용이 되어야 하므로, 빈칸에 들어갈 말은 ⑤ '이해하기'이다.

① 만들기   ② 대체하기
③ 왜곡하기   ④ 발표하기

10 ④

감정을 드러낼 수 있기만 해도 감정을 관리하기 훨씬 쉬워질 수 있으므로

감정을 있는 그대로 인정해 주는 것이 중요하다는 내용의 글이므로, 글의 요지로 가장 적절한 것은 ④이다.

11 ④

Cheryl이 대학시절 친했던 Jen과 졸업 후에 다른 지역에서 살며 점점 연락이 뜸해지고 소원해진 이후 연락이 아예 끊긴 상황에 대해 자신이 끝까지 연락을 취하지 못했음을 후회하고 있으며 친구와 삶을 공유하고 성장을 함께 나누며 우정을 지속하지 못한 것을 안타까워하는 내용이므로, 글의 제목으로 가장 적절한 것은 ④ '관계: 소중하고 지킬만한 가치가 있는 것'이다.

① 재회: 행동보다 말이 더 쉽다
② 옛 친구와 관계를 회복하는 방법
③ 우정에 대한 올바른 태도는 무엇인가?
⑤ 우정의 끈은 쉽게 끊어지지 않는다.

12 ④

Cheryl은 Jen과 점점 연락이 뜸하고 소원해진 이후 연락이 아예 끊긴 상황을 후회하고 있으며 자신의 삶을 누군가와 공유하고 성장을 함께 나눌 수 있는 관계를 가지지 못한 것을 안타까워하는 상황으로 그러한 관계를 맺고 있는 사람이 없다는 것이 그녀를 불안하게 한다는 것이 글의 흐름으로 자연스러우므로 ④의 connection(관계, 연결)을 absence(부재)와 같은 말로 고쳐야 한다.

13 ②

'그러나 당신이 스스로 그 운동선수에게 속지 않도록 하는 것이 중요하다'는 주어진 문장에서 however로 글의 흐름이 전환되는데 ② 앞에서 운동선수들이 겉으로 과제 수행을 너무 잘하고 있는 것을 보고 스스로 자신이 최고의 치료사라고 착각할 수 있다는 내용이 오며, ② 뒤에서 이 시점에서 완벽주의 운동 선수를 돕지 못할 뿐만 아니라 해결하고자 했던 문제가 오히려 강화될 수도 있다는 내용이 이어지므로 주어진 문장이 들어갈 가장 적절한 곳은 ②이다.

14 ③

보통의 상황에서는 과학자들이 객관성 유지를 위해 특정 정책을 옹호하는 것을 피하고자 하는 것이 당연할 수 있지만 과학자들도 시민이며 시민으로서 정책 문제에 대한 목소리를 내는 것이 권리이자 의무일 수도 있다는 내용의 글이므로, 필자의 주장으로 가장 적절한 것은 ③이다.

15 ①

Griskevicius와 그의 동료들의 실험에서 높은 사회적 지위의 직장을 얻어 빠르게 승진하는 것과 같이 지위 동기와 관련된 이야기를 읽었던 처치 집단의 대학생들이 평범한 이야기를 읽은 통제집단의 대학생들보다 친환경 제품을 선택하는 비율이 높았다는 내용의 글이고, 빈칸이 있는 마지막 문장에서 이 글의 내용을 요약하고 있으므로 빈칸에 들어갈 말로 가장 적절한 것은 ① '지위 동기의 자극'이다.

② 고등 교육에 대한 갈망

③ 다양한 상품의 사용
④ 친환경 제품에 대한 경험
⑤ 친환경 실험에 참여

16 ②

문제해설

주어진 문장은 '그러나 자기 효능감은 부정적인 면도 가지고 있다'는 의미로 however 전후로 글의 흐름이 전환된다. ② 앞에서는 자기 효능감이 사업가가 사업을 시작하고 성공을 위해 지속적으로 노력할 수 있도록 해 주는 긍정적인 측면을 말하고, ② 뒤에서 사업에 대한 막연하고 근거 없는 믿음이 오히려 치명일 수 있다는 부정적인 측면을 언급하고 있으므로 주어진 문장이 들어갈 가장 적절한 곳은 ②이다.

17 ①

문제해설

이 글은 박테리아는 서로 네트워킹하며 협력적으로 공생하기 위해 끊임없이 소통하는 존재로 음성 신호가 그들에게 그럴싸한 수단처럼 보일 수도 있지만, 세포 내에서 수만 개의 분자를 사용한다는 내용이므로, '어떤 박테리아는 해롭지만 대부분의 경우 유용하게 활용될 수 있는데, 식물과 동물의 생명을 유지하며, 산업 및 의학적 과정에 이용된다'라고 서술하는 ①은 글의 전체 흐름과 관계가 없다.

18 ③

문제해설

③ that절의 주어 the same movement 뒤에 동사가 와야 하므로 evoking을 동사의 과거형 evoked로 바꾸어야 한다.

오답노트

① '~하자마자'의 의미로 전치사 on 뒤에 동명사를 쓰므로 동명사 hearing은 적절하다.
② 앞에 나온 response를 가리키는 대명사 that은 적절하다.
④ It ~ that 강조구문으로, 이 문장에서는 the similarities를 강조하고 있으며 주어 the similarities가 복수이므로 that 뒤에 오는 동사 tell은 적절하다.
⑤ 가정법 과거로 현재 그렇지 않은데 가정을 하는 상황이므로 if 절 안에서는 동사의 과거형을 사용한다. 따라서 be동사 were는 적절하다.

19 ③

문제해설

주어진 문장은 '반면에 학습에 대해 심층 접근법을 취하는 학생은 자료를 이해하고 개념 분석을 활성화하려는 의도를 가지고 있다'는 의미로, 'on the other hand'가 있으므로 주어진 문장 전후로 글의 내용이 전환되는데, ③ 앞에서는 표면 접근법의 예시로 내용을 이해하지 않고 무턱대고 암기하는 전략을 언급하고 있고, ③ 뒤에서는 심층 접근법을 가진 학생의 학습 전략 특성에 관한 내용이 오므로 주어진 문장이 들어갈 가장 적절한 곳은 ③이다.

20 ②

문제해설

감정을 드러낼 수 있기만 해도 감정을 관리하기 훨씬 쉬워질 수 있으므로 감정을 있는 그대로 인정해 주는 것이 중요하다는 내용이므로, '치료사가 무슨 일을 하는지 완벽하기 위해서는 다양한 치료의 접근법, 면허 제도, 그리고 명칭을 이해하는 것이 중요하다.'라고 서술하는 ②는 글의 전체 흐름과 관계가 없다.

21 only have you failed to help the athlete

문제해설

'~할 뿐만 아니라'라는 의미가 되도록 Not only ~ 구문으로 시작하며, 부정어형 부사가 문두에 오므로 〈부정어+조동사+주어+동사〉의 도치 구문이 되도록 하면 Not only have you failed가 된다. fail은 to부정사를 목적어로 취하므로 to help the athlete을 이어서 쓴다.

22 선수가 과제를 완료하는 데 어느 정도 실패한다면 그것은 진전으로 여겨질 수 있다는 것

문제해설

This는 바로 앞의 내용으로, 과제를 완료하지 못한 것이 실패를 논할 기회를 제공하기 때문에 진전으로 여겨질 수 있다는 내용이다.

23 lest they be mistaken for self-appointed authorities over what society should do

문제해설

'~하지 않도록'이라는 의미의 〈lest+주어+(should)+동사원형〉의 형태와 'A를 B로 오인하다'라는 의미의 〈mistake A for B〉의 형태를 결합하되 의미상 수동형이어야 하므로 be mistaken for를 쓴다. '사회가 무엇을 해야 하는지에 대해'는 over what society should do로 나타낸다.

24 (1) 기후 과학자가 기후에 적절한 조치를 취하지 않는 것
(2) 의사가 정기적인 암 검사 또는 태아기 영양 계획을 지지하지 않는 것

문제해설

밑줄 친 부분은 과학자로서 '무책임한 것으로 보일 수 있다'는 내용의 예시로 마지막 문장의 For a climate scientist ~ prenatal nutrition initiatives.에서 기후 과학자와 의사를 예로 들어 과학자로서의 무책임한 사례를 들고 있다.

25 (A) conducted (B) which (C) were

문제해설

(A) '수행된' 연구라는 의미이므로 수동의 의미가 있는 과거분사 conducted로 고쳐 써야 한다.
(B) 선행사가 the green product이며, 뒤에 이어지는 절이 불완전하므로 in which를 계속적 용법의 주격 관계대명사 which로 고쳐 써야 한다.
(C) 주어는 The corresponding figures이므로 복수형 동사 were로 고쳐 써야 한다.

26 activation

문제해설

'장비나 프로세스가 작동하고 있는 상태'라는 의미의 단어는 activation(활성화)이다.

27 ③ → disastrous

문제해설

사업 성공에 대한 개인의 믿음과 관련 있는 자기 효능감에 관한 글로서, 자기 효능감의 부정적 영향이 사업가로 하여금 비참한 결과로 이어질 과업에 착수하도록 하고, 이것이 흔히 근거 없는 낙관에 의해 확대될 수 있다고 했으므로, ③ fortunate(운 좋은)는 disastrous(비참한) 정도의 말로 고쳐야 한다.

28 one characteristic that helps entrepreneurs get started and also persist in their efforts to succeed

문제해설

'하나의 특징'을 주어의 보어로 쓰고 또 이것을 주격 관계대명사 that으로 연결해 주는 형태가 나와야 한다. 따라서 one characteristic that이라고 쓰고, 관계사절의 술부로 〈help+목적어+동사원형〉 구조를 이용하되 and로 병렬하면 helps entrepreneurs get started and also persist in their efforts가 된다. 즉 get과 persist가 목적격 보어로 병렬되도록 한다. '성공하기 위한 노력'은 efforts 뒤에 to부정사의 형용사적 용법으로 to succeed를 쓴다.

29 ① → During
③ → struggling[struggle]
⑥ → said

문제해설

① '~하는 동안'의 의미로 While 다음엔 절이나 분사(구)가 와야 하는데, 명사구가 왔으므로 During으로 고쳐야 한다.
③ 〈지각동사 see+목적어+동사원형/현재분사〉의 형태여야 하므로 struggled를 현재분사 struggling 혹은 struggle로 고쳐야 한다.
⑥ took, looked와 접속사 and로 병렬되어 있으므로 saying을 said로 고쳐 써야 한다.

오답노트

② 주어가 앞에 있는 These이므로 과거형 복수 동사 were는 적절하다.
④ 동사 seemed의 보어로 nice와 병렬을 이루는 형용사 impossible은 적절하다.
⑤ Krista가 큰 걱정으로 압도된 자신을 발견한 것이므로 목적어로 쓰인 재귀대명사 herself는 적절하다.

30 one day at a time

문제해설

Delia가 삶에 대처하는 방법이지만 자신에게는 불가능한 것처럼 보였던 신념에 대해 학교 기숙사에서 처음으로, 그리고 진정으로 믿게 되었던 것을 a gift(선물)로 표현한 것이다. 그 신념의 내용은 바로 앞 문장에 있는 one day at a time(한 번에 하루씩)이다.

31 ② → invulnerable

문제해설

박테리아는 매우 촘촘하게 짜여서, 화학적, 물리적 공격에 쉽게 당하지 않는 얇은 막과 무리 속에서 산다고 했으므로 vulnerable(취약한)이 아닌 invulnerable(안전하게 막아 주는, 상처받지 않는)이 되어야 한다.

32 (A) chemical (B) sound

문제해설

빈칸 부분이 글의 핵심 부분으로 '박테리아에게 (B) 음파보다는 (A) 화학적 교신이 더 낫다는 것'이라는 내용이다. 따라서 (A) chemical(화학적인)과 (B) sound(음파, 소리)가 들어가야 한다.

33 ② → that of Richard Strauss

문제해설

이 문장의 경우 Elisabeth von Herzogenberg의 반응(response)과 Richard Strauss의 반응(response)이 비교가 되어야 한다. 즉 주어인 Her response에 대한 대응이 되어야 하고 response가 단수이므로 that of Richard Strauss로 고쳐 주어야 한다.

오답노트

① '~하자마자'라는 의미로 〈On+v-ing〉가 쓰이므로 On은 적절하다.
③ 고요히 '이동하는' 장례 행렬이라는 의미이므로 능동의 의미를 갖는 현재분사 moving은 적절하다.
④ 가주어-진주어 구문에서 진주어 역할을 하는 명사절을 이끄는 접속사 that은 적절하다.
⑤ 가정법 과거의 주절에는 〈조동사 과거형(would)+동사원형〉의 형태가 와야 하므로 be는 적절하다.

34 similarities

문제해설

영영 뜻풀이는 "어떤 것이 다른 것과 비슷한 정도 또는 그들이 유사하다는 사실"이라는 의미로 빈칸에는 문장 끝에 나오는 differences와 대조되도록 similarity(유사)의 복수형 similarities가 들어가야 한다.

35 ① → been distinguished

문제해설

① 학습에 대한 두 가지 접근법이 '구분되어 왔다'라고 하는 것이 문맥상 적절하고, 또 동사 distinguish의 목적어가 나와 있지 않으므로 수동형 been distinguished로 고쳐야 한다.

오답노트

② '가능한 한 ~'이라는 의미의 as ~ as possible에 쓰인 as possible은 적절하다.
③ 전치사 without은 목적어로 명사나 동명사를 취하므로 동명사 understanding은 적절하다.
④ 앞에 있는 have intention of에 comprehending과 and로 병렬되는 activating은 적절하다.
⑤ Possible strategies의 보어로서 reflecting, discussing, using, ralating, looking, checking과 병렬 연결되고 있는 examining은 적절하다.

36 (1) 무턱대고 암기하기
(2) 곰곰이 생각해 보기, 토론하기, 다양한 정보 출처 사용하기, 아이디어를 이전 지식과 연관시키기, 패턴 찾아보기, 증거 확인하기, 주장을 비판적으로 검토하기

문제해설

표면 접근법의 학습 전략은 One of the most common strategies ~ reproduce the material.에 나와 있고, 심층 접근법의 학습 전략은 Possible strategies are ~ critically examining arguments.에 나와 있다.

37 the reason that merely having someone listen can be such a powerful experience

문제해설

가주어-진주어 구문을 이용하되, 의미상 '~것이 그 이유이다'라고 했으므로 It's the reason that을 쓴다. that절의 주어는 동명사구로 사역동사 have를 이용하여 having some listen으로 나타낼 수 있는데, 앞에 '단지'를 의미하는 merely를 덧붙여 준다. '매우 강력한 경험이 될 수 있다'는 〈such+a(n)+형용사+명사〉와 can을 이용하여 can be such a powerful experience로 나타내면 된다.

38 (A) manage (B) emotional

문제해설

감정을 있는 그대로 들어 주고 드러내는 것이 중요하다는 내용의 글이므로, '우리의 감정을 드러내는 것은 (A) 관리하기 더 쉽고 경험하기 더 재미

있게 만들어서, 이점을 이해하고 우리의 (B) <u>감정</u> 상태를 살펴 주는 누군가가 있는 것이 중요하다.'와 같이 요약하는 것이 적절하다.

39 ③ → exchanged

문제해설

③ 주어 Cheryl and Jen 다음의 living in different ~ widespread email은 분사구문으로 삽입된 형태이다. 따라서 동사가 와야 하는 자리이므로 exchanging을 동사 exchanged로 고쳐 써야 한다.

오답노트

① Drake university를 선행사로 하며, 뒤에 완전한 절이 이어지므로 관계부사 where는 적절하다.
② she thought 다음에 또 동사가 이어지므로 이는 삽입절이다. 따라서 she thought는 적절하다.
④ '~한 이상, ~이므로, ~ 때문에'의 의미를 갖는 접속사 now that은 적절하다.
⑤ 가정법 과거에 쓰인 be동사 were는 적절하다.

40 (A) regret (B) share

문제해설

(A) '자신이 한 말이나 행동에 대해 유감스럽게 생각하거나 슬퍼하다'라는 의미의 단어는 regret(후회하다)이다. (B) '다른 사람과 동시에 무언가를 사용하거나 갖다'라는 의미의 단어는 share(나누다, 공유하다)이다.

---

11 강

1번 ————————————————— p.48

• Word Test

1 양   2 거대한, 막대한   3 광범위한, 널리 퍼진
4 이동하다   5 물품, 상품   6 운하   7 수면, 지면, 표면
8 consequence   9 shipping   10 prompt
11 mere   12 bottleneck   13 weight
14 emergence

유형 1

❶ who   ❷ greatly   ❸ therefore
❹ fewer and fewer ❺ quantities

유형 2

❶ knows   ❷ required   ❸ costs
❹ has meant   ❺ was given

유형 3

❶ mere third as much as
❷ four-fifths of international trade
❸ in terms of total income
❹ prompting widespread concern

2번 ————————————————— p.50

• Word Test

1 보강, 강화   2 감염, 감염병   3 내놓다, 산출하다, 해내다
4 정책   5 환자   6 확인하다   7 근본적으로
8 차단하다, 가로막다   9 제거하다   10 입헌의, 헌법에 따르는
11 scholar   12 confront   13 precaution
14 mobilization   15 democracy   16 transmission
17 trace   18 buildup   19 scale   20 expert

유형 1

❶ unprepared   ❷ rapid   ❸ it
❹ infrastructure

유형 2

❶ hit   ❷ became   ❸ identified
❹ needed   ❺ to eliminate

유형 3

❶ fundamentally unprepared
❷ what was needed to confront it
❸ sticking to universal precautions
❹ while keeping the economy open

3번 ————————————————— p.53

• Word Test

1 도표, 도형   2 수반하다   3 부분   4 원칙적으로
5 간접적인   6 아주 명료한   7 quantity   8 oddly
9 compose   10 effective   11 authority
12 active voice

<table>
<tr><td colspan="3">유형 1</td></tr>
<tr><td>① which</td><td>② for example</td><td>③ Besides</td></tr>
<tr><td>④ them</td><td>⑤ indirect</td><td></td></tr>
</table>

<table>
<tr><td colspan="3">유형 2</td></tr>
<tr><td>① is</td><td>② be compared</td><td>③ makes</td></tr>
<tr><td>④ is</td><td>⑤ to understand</td><td></td></tr>
</table>

유형 3

① are most easily understood
② along these lines   ③ In principle
④ as the voice of authority
⑤ when to bend the rules

4번 ——————————— p.55

• Word Test

1 (생물의) 종   2 적응   3 향하다, 돌리다
4 동시에 발생하다, 시간대를 맞추다
5 급감하다, 붕괴하다, 추락하다   6 전문적인; 전문가
7 충격파   8 지리적   9 seed   10 incidence
11 alternate   12 range   13 population
14 agent   15 fluctuate   16 crop

유형 1

① adaption   ② survive   ③ through
④ that   ⑤ so

유형 2

① alternating   ② works   ③ serve
④ affected   ⑤ do

유형 3

① across a broad geographic range
② fluctuate dramatically across years
③ a wide variety of
④ direct their attention to

5-7번 ——————————— p.57

• Word Test

1 여행 가방   2 깔끔한   3 약   4 뚱한 표정을 짓다
5 (풀로) 붙이다   6 인사하다   7 초인종   8 faded
9 pack   10 cough   11 ungrateful   12 respect
13 invite   14 object

유형 1

① week   ② objected   ③ frowned
④ off   ⑤ Faded   ⑥ packed
⑦ respect

유형 2

① to take   ② to stop   ③ cut
④ greeted   ⑤ filled   ⑥ had walked

유형 3

① seems to be seriously ill
② far from where they lived
③ neat and clean
④ for being so ungrateful
⑤ without complaining

8번 ——————————— p.61

• Word Test

1 과부하   2 내용   3 상호 작용   4 ~을 야기하다
5 알고 있음   6 식별하다   7 분산된   8 요구 사항
9 발전, 진보   10 활용하다   11 impose
12 comprehension   13 arise from   14 electronic
15 prohibitively   16 risk   17 personalize
18 extensive   19 attempt   20 incorporation

유형 1

① However   ② that   ③ overload
④ incorporation   ⑤ address

유형 2

① spent   ② imposes   ③ is
④ to identify   ⑤ caused

유형 3

① gives rise to new challenges
② arise from
③ on acquaintance with and comprehension of
④ make decisions by themselves

9번 ——————————— p.63

• Word Test

1 이전, 이동   2 기업의   3 엄격하게   4 해외에서; 해외의
5 다시 모으다   6 법으로 처벌하다   7 자본   8 내용
9 생계 수단   10 심해지다   11 규제 완화   12 apply
13 catch-up   14 in pursuit of   15 barrier
16 strategy   17 circulate   18 liberalization
19 sophisticated   20 border   21 migrate
22 assign

유형 1

① that   ② less   ③ migrate
④ enabled   ⑤ as

유형 2

① is allowed   ② are criminalized
③ reassemble   ④ be performed
⑤ has intensified

유형 3

① in pursuit of a better livelihood
② The higher up the skills curve
③ into a meaningful whole
④ in discount offshore locations

10번 ——————————— p.66

• Word Test

1 비언어적인   2 특성   3 공존하다   4 접촉   5 가축화
6 진화하다   7 영향   8 상호 작용   9 유용한 것, 이점
10 언어적인, 언어의   11 definitely   12 advanced
13 intense   14 behavioral   15 transformation
16 gene   17 enhance   18 foster   19 capable
20 cognitive

유형 1

❶ that ❷ cognitive ❸ nonverbal
❹ Furthermore ❺ domestication

유형 2

❶ have developed ❷ have helped ❸ relied
❹ suggests ❺ to have

유형 3

❶ than previously thought
❷ not capable of understanding verbal communication
❸ in their interactions with humans
❹ due to two genes

11번 ─────────────────── p.68

• Word Test

1 되풀이되다　2 범위　3 관용, 참음　4 경직된
5 규범적인　6 조직화, 조화　7 포착하다
8 외부의, 외적인　9 conform to　10 constraint
11 restrict　12 dimension　13 permissible
14 order　15 norm　16 simultaneously

유형 1

❶ whereas ❷ which ❸ permissible
❹ simultaneously ❺ that

유형 2

❶ is captured ❷ is associated
❸ restricts ❹ affording ❺ conforming

유형 3

❶ regarding external societal constraints
❷ behavior deemed appropriate
❸ degree of order and coordination
❹ conforming to normative rules

12-14번 ─────────────────── p.70

• Word Test

1 통로, 활주로　2 꽉 쥐기[움켜잡기], 이해　3 애타게, 간절히
4 항공 대원　5 (기재된 서명, 날짜 등) 지니고 있다, 가지고 있다
6 (비행기로) 공수하다[실어 나르다]　7 (군인을) 배치하다[주둔시키다]
8 투수　9 autograph　10 thrilled
11 military personnel　12 victim　13 run into
14 proceed　15 relief supplies　16 marvel

유형 1

❶ thrilled ❷ Although ❸ hardly
❹ anxiously ❺ proceeded ❻ Despite
❼ had

유형 2

❶ stationed ❷ being ❸ bought
❹ coming ❺ headed ❻ been filled
❼ flying ❽ had helped

─────────────────────────────

유형 3

❶ at a discounted price
❷ just in case I ran into him
❸ in my best manners
❹ had brushed me off
❺ proudly bore the name
❻ played an important part

─────────────────────────────

p.74

01 ③　02 ④　03 ④　04 ③　05 ④　06 ③
07 ④　08 ⑤　09 ⑤　10 ③　11 ①　12 ②
13 ③　14 ⑤　15 ②　16 ①　17 ⑤　18 ②
19 ③　20 ③　21 ⑤　22 ②
23 ③ → emergence　24 costs a mere third as much as shifting it by plane
25 reinforcement　26 공중위생 캠페인을 지원하는 필수적 시스템 및 서비스와 함께 대규모로 신속하게 강화하는 것
27 instead of relying on rules that you've been told will produce clear text　28 (1) 독자가 어떻게 반응할지를 아는 것 (2) 글쓰기에 규칙을 유연하게 적용하는 것
29 (1) alternating (2) crash (3) do　30 대량 결실이 없는 해 다음에는 일부 전문적으로 씨앗을 먹는 동물들의 개체수가 급감하여 많은 도토리가 살아남는다는 것　31 (1) ④ → filled (2) ⑤ → that　32 who had walked for more than two hours without complaining　33 ② → extensive
34 overload　35 (1) ③ → have (2) ④ → assign
36 knowledge transfer　37 cognitive
38 appears that these genes have a direct impact on dogs' intense ability and desire for social contact　39 (1) ① → how 생략 또는 that[in which] (2) ④ → Compared
40 (1) 강한 규범 (2) 일탈 행동에 대한 낮은 관용 (3) 약한 규범 (4) 일탈 행동에 대한 허용 범위가 넓음
41 (1) ③ → pondering (2) ⑤ → flying
42 (A) Roberto Clemente (B) Roberto Clemente

01 ③

문제해설

대양은 수면으로서 대량의 해상 운송에 유리하며, 점점 더 해상 화물 운송에 대한 의존이 증가한다는 내용의 글이므로, '이 사실에도 불구하고, 해양을 통한 화물 수송의 주요 단점은 화물을 한 지점에서 다른 지점으로 나르는 데 필요한 시간일 것이다'라는 ③은 글의 전체 흐름과 관계가 없다.

02 ④

문제해설

④ such a public health campaign을 대신하는 대명사이므로 them을 it으로 바꿔야 한다.

오답노트

① 기본적으로 '준비되지 않은' 경제, 사회, 그리고 입헌 민주 국가를 타격했다고 하는 것이 자연스러우므로 수동의 의미를 지닌 과거분사 unprepared는 적절하다.
② 앞에 선행사가 없으므로 선행사를 포함하는 주격 관계대명사 what은 적절하다.

③ 전치사 of의 목적어로 쓰인 동명사 sticking은 적절하다.
⑤ 주어와 동사가 생략되고, 접속사와 함께 쓰인 분사구로 시간을 나타내는 〈while+v-ing〉이므로 현재분사 keeping은 적절하다.

03 ④

문제해설

독자의 반응 방식을 생각하며 글쓰기의 일반적인 규칙을 목록화해서 활용할 수 있지만, 좋은 글쓰기는 기계적이지 않고 규칙을 유연하게 적용하며 독자의 사고방식에 부합하는 글을 쓴다는 것이 글의 요지이므로, 정답은 ④이다.

04 ③

문제해설

주어진 문장은 '이것은 매우 잘 작용하지만, 여러 해에 걸쳐 도토리 수확량이 극적으로 변동할 때, 동물 군집 전체에 걸쳐 충격파를 보낼 수 있다'는 내용으로 This는 ③의 앞부분 내용 '대량 결실이 없는 해 다음에는 일부 전문적으로 씨앗을 먹는 동물들의 개체 수가 급감해 다음 번 대량 결실이 있는 해 더 많은 도토리가 살아남는다'는 내용을 가리킨다. 그리고, 도토리 열매가 도토리 분산의 행위자 역할을 하는 동물들을 훨씬 뛰어 넘어서 매우 다양한 동물들에게 군집 내의 중요한 자원이라는 내용의 문장 앞인 ③에 들어가는 것이 가장 적절하다.

05 ④

문제해설

아픈 엄마(Charity)의 약을 구하기 위해 어린 소년인 Washington이 Vera의 집을 방문하자, Vera의 엄마가 Washington을 집에 데려다주겠다고 말한 주어진 글에 이어, 함께 쇼핑몰에 가기로 했던 약속을 취소하고 Vera와 함께 빈민가에 위치한 Washington의 집으로 향한 엄마의 모습이 그려지는 (D)가 이어진 다음, 낡았지만 깔끔한 집에 병져 누운 Washington의 엄마에게 식료품과 약을 전하는 내용의 (B)가 이어지고, 자신의 잘못을 뉘우친 뒤, 집으로 돌아가 Washington을 위해 옷가지를 챙기는 (C)가 오는 것이 흐름상 자연스럽다.

06 ③

문제해설

(c)는 Vera를 가리키고 나머지는 모두 Vera의 엄마를 가리킨다.

07 ④

문제해설

집에 돌아온 후 Washington에게 줄 옷가지와 물건들을 여행 가방 가득 채운 사람은 Vera의 엄마가 아니라 Vera이므로 ④는 글의 내용과 일치하지 않는다.

08 ⑤

문제해설

최근 전자 미디어와 컴퓨터 네트워크의 발전으로 대규모 정보 분산 저장이 가능하게 되면서, 엄청난 정보가 즉각 가용해짐으로 인해 새로운 난제가 야기되었다는 주어진 글에 이어, 이용자들의 정보 과부하 위험이 정보를 다루는 소프트웨어 시스템에 새 과제를 부여했다는 (C)가 오고, 그중 하나가 인간과 컴퓨터의 상호 작용에 어려움을 겪거나 스스로 의사 결정을 내릴 수 있는 지식이 없을 때 그들에게 도움이 되는 메커니즘을 시스템에 통합하는 것이라는 (B)가 이어지고, 개인화된 추천 시스템은 정보 과부하로 인해 야기되는 문제 일부를 해결하려는 시도 중 하나라는 (A)가 오는 것이 자연스럽다.

09 ⑤

문제해설

점점 더 많은 나라들이 산업과 서비스의 상층부에 진입하기 위해 노력함에 따라 첨단 기술 투자를 유치하기 위한 경쟁이 '심해졌고', 따라서 이러한 기술 집약적인 부문이 이제 격차 해소 게임의 비결로 간주되고 있다는 흐름이 자연스러우므로 ⑤의 weakened(약해지다)는 intensified(심해졌다)와 같은 말로 고쳐야 한다.

10 ③

문제해설

주어진 문장은 '그러나 Andics와 Miklosi가 Science지에 보고한 바에 따르면, 연구는 이제 일부 개들이 1,000개가 넘는 단어를 인식할 수 있을지도 모른다는 것을 시사한다'는 내용이다. 그러므로, 이 문장은 한때는 개가 언어적 의사소통을 이해할 수 있는 능력이 있는 것이 아니라 인간의 몸짓과 행동을 이해하는 비언어적 능력에 의존한다고 믿어졌다는 내용 다음과 이 능력(1,000개 넘는 단어를 인식하는 능력)은 그들이 인간과 상호작용을 할 때 유용한 것이다는 내용의 문장 앞인 ③에 들어가는 것이 가장 적절하다.

11 ①

문제해설

경직된 문화에서는 강한 규범과 일탈 행동에 대한 낮은 관용을 보이고, 유연한 문화에서는 약한 규범과 일탈 행동에 대한 관용을 보인다는 내용의 글이므로, '외부의 (A) 사회적 제약에 관하여 문화가 상이한 방식은 해당 문화가 얼마나 (B) 경직되게 형성되어 있는가에 따라 포착된다'와 같이 요약하는 것이 가장 적절하다.

오답노트

② 경제적 …… 경직된   ③ 사회적 …… 강한
④ 경제적 …… 강한   ⑤ 종교적 …… 관용적인

12 ②

문제해설

'I'가 가장 좋아하던 야구 선수 중 한 명인 Roy Face의 사인을 받을 생각에 흥분된 상태로 야구장으로 향했다는 주어진 글 다음, 'I'가 Roy Face를 보고 다가가 정중하게 사인을 요청했으나, Roy Face가 이를 매정하게 무시하고 지나갔다는 내용인 (C)가 이어지고, 어떻게 해야 하나를 생각하고 있던 'I'에게 갑자기 등장한 Roberto Clemente가 대신 사인을 해줬다는 내용인 (B)가 이어진 뒤, Clemente가 그날 경기에서 중요한 역할을 하고, 그 이후로도 그가 1972년 비행기 사고로 죽을 때까지 그를 영웅으로 생각했다는 내용의 (D)가 오는 것이 자연스럽다.

13 ③

문제해설

(c)는 Roy Face를 가리키고 나머지는 모두 Roberto Clemente을 가리킨다.

14 ⑤

문제해설

지진 피해자들을 위한 구호물자를 공수하던 중 비행기 사고로 사망한 사람은 Roy Face가 아니라 Roberto Clemente이므로 ⑤는 글의 내용과 일치하지 않는다.

15 ②

문제해설

대양을 통한 수송은 중요한데 국제 상품 거래의 4/5가 해상 화물 운송을 이용하고 거대한 컨테이너선이 수에즈 운하를 막은 사건이 세계 무역에 광범위한 우려를 유발한 것만 봐도 그 중요성을 알 수 있다는 내용의 글이므로, 글의 주제로 가장 적절한 것은 ② '국제 무역에 있어 해상 운송의 중요성'이다.

오답노트

① 국제적인 운송이 지구에 해로운 이유
③ 현대 운송에서 수에즈 운하의 역할과 그 중요성
④ 국제 무역에서 항공 운송의 장점과 단점
⑤ 해상, 육상, 항공 운송의 차이점과 유사점

16 ①

문제해설

새로운 코로나바이러스가 미국에 등장했을 때, 그것은 준비되지 않은 경제, 사회, 민주 국가를 타격했다는 주어진 글에 이어, 국가는 별다른 조치 등을 전혀 내놓을 수가 없었고, 그저 신속한 검사, 접촉자 추적 등의 대책이었다고 설명하는 (C)가 오고, 그런 검사는 마스크 착용, 손 씻기, 그리고 보편적 예방책을 충실히 지키는 문화적 측면으로 보강해야 했다는 내용의 (B)가 이어지며, 그런 공중위생 캠페인을 대규모로 신속하게 강화했다면, 경제를 개방하면서도 바이러스를 제거할 만큼 충분히 전염을 차단했을 것이라는 내용의 (A)가 오는 것이 자연스럽다.

17 ⑤

문제해설

독자가 사고하는 방식을 이해하고 그 이해에 부합하게 글을 쓰는 것이 분명히 '더' 효과적이라고 하는 것이 자연스러우므로 ⑤의 less(덜)는 more(더)와 같은 말로 고쳐야 한다.

18 ②

문제해설

도토리 열매의 대량 결실 후에 도토리를 거의 생산하지 않는 것을 번갈아 할 경우, 도토리를 먹는 동물 개체 수를 줄여, 다음해에 생산량을 늘리는 데는 도움이 된다. 그러나 여러 해에 걸쳐 도토리 수확량이 극적으로 변동하면, 여러 동물에게 여파를 미칠 수 있는데, 그 대상은 도토리 분산의 행위자 역할을 하는 동물 뿐 아니라, 사람까지로 광범위하다는 내용의 글이므로, '분산은 자손들에게 특히 치명적인데, 그 이유는 분산 이후에 그들이 새로운 자원과 짝짓기 대상을 찾기 때문이다'라는 ②는 글의 전체 흐름과 관계가 없다.

19 ③

문제해설

최근 엄청난 정보가 즉각 가용해짐에 따라 정보의 양이 많아졌고, 이 내용을 알고 이해하는 데 엄청나게 긴 시간이 요구될 때 이용자가 자원을 효과적으로 활용하지 못하게 된다는 난제가 생겼다고 했으므로, 빈칸에 들어갈 말로 가장 적절한 것은 ③ '이용자들의 정보 과부하'이다.

오답노트

① 신원 도용
② 더욱 경쟁적인 압박감
④ 빅 데이터 분석 실수
⑤ 신용 사기 및 불법 혹은 허위 거래

20 ③

문제해설

Increasingly sophisticated work-flow technologies can now slice up the contents of a job into work tasks, assign them to different parts of the globe, and reassemble the results into a meaningful whole.에서 '점점 더 정교한 작업 흐름 기술이 이제 일의 내용을 업무 과제로 분할하고 그것들을 세계의 여러 지역으로 할당하고, 그 결과를 의미 있는 전체로 다시 모을 수 있도록 했다'라고 했으므로 ③은 글의 내용과 일치하지 않는다.

21 ⑤

문제해설

개의 행동적 특성은 그들이 인간과 조화로운 관계를 가질 수 있게 해 주며, 두 가지 기여 요인으로 그들의 인지 능력과 그들의 유전적 구성이라고 여겨진다는 글로, 개들의 일부 유전자는 개의 사회적 접촉에 대한 강한 열망과 능력에 직접적인 영향을 미치는 것으로 보이며, 그것은 '친절한' 유전자로 여겨지고, 사람들과의 긍정적인 상호 작용을 촉진하는 데 도움을 준다고 하는 것이 자연스러우므로 ⑤의 hostile(적대적인)은 friendly(우호적인)와 같은 말로 고쳐야 한다.

22 ②

문제해설

경직된 문화에서는 강한 규범과 일탈 행동에 대한 낮은 관용을 보이고, 유연한 문화에서는 약한 규범과 일탈 행동에 대한 관용을 보인다는 내용의 글이므로, '식민지 역사가 다르다는 점을 고려할 때, 라틴 아메리카와 아시아 유교 사회는 현재 문화적 다양성에서도 서로 상이하다'라는 ②는 글의 전체 흐름과 관계가 없다.

23 ③ → emergence

문제해설

물건을 운송하여 나른 것이 대양, 즉 바다를 통하는 것이 비용 면에서나 물동량 면에서 유리하다는 내용으로, 문맥상 거대한 컨테이너선들이 '출현'한다는 의미가 되어야 하므로 ③ emergency(비상, 비상사태)는 emergence(출현)과 같은 말로 고쳐야 한다.

24 costs a mere third as much as shifting it by plane

문제해설

문장의 주어는 Moving으로 시작하는 동명사구이고, '비용이 들다'라는 동사가 먼저 나와야 하므로 costs가 우선 나온다. 이어지는 내용은 〈배수사+as ~ as ...〉 구문을 이용하여, a third as much as ...로 나타내는데, '1/3밖에'는 a mere third로 써 준다. '그것을 비행기로 옮길 만큼 많이'은 as much as 뒤에 shifting it by plane을 쓴다.

25 reinforcement

문제해설

'생각, 신념, 또는 감정을 더 강하게 만드는 행위'라는 의미의 단어는 reinforcement(강화, 보강)이다.

26 공중위생 캠페인을 지원하는 필수적 시스템 및 서비스와 함께 대규모로 신속하게 강화하는 것

문제해설

this mobilization(이 동원)은 바로 앞 문장에서 언급한 바이러스 전염을 차단하는 방법을 가리킨다.

27 instead of relying on rules that you've been told will produce clear text

문제해설

'규칙에 의존하는 것 대신에'는 instead of relying on rules로 써 주고, 이어서 rules를 수식하는 관계절 that will produce clear text로 쓴다. 마지막으로 삽입어구로 주격 관계대명사와 will 사이에 you've been told(들었던)기 들어가면 자연스럽다. 주로 삽입어구의 경우 주격 관계대명사와 동사 사이에 들어간다.

28 (1) 독자가 어떻게 반응할지를 아는 것
(2) 글쓰기에 규칙을 유연하게 적용하는 것

문제해설

명료한 글쓰기를 위한 두 가지 방법은 The only way to produce ~ composing text and graphics.에서와 Besides, using them makes writing ~ instead of following them.에 나타나 있다.

29 (A) alternating (B) crash (C) do

문제해설

(1) 동사 is가 이미 있으므로 분사가 와야 하는 자리이다. 따라서 주어와 능동의 관계인 현재분사 alternating으로 고쳐 써야 한다.
(2) 앞에 동사가 없으므로 동사가 와야 하는 자리이다. 따라서 동사 crash로 고쳐 써야 한다.
(3) 〈so+동사+주어〉는 '~도 그렇다'라는 표현으로 앞에 있는 동사 increase를 대신 받으므로 are를 do로 고쳐 써야 한다.

30 대량 결실이 없는 해 다음에는 일부 전문적으로 씨앗을 먹는 동물들의 개체 수가 급감하여 많은 도토리가 살아남는다는 것

문제해설

바로 앞 문장 전체를 this로 받고 있는데, 즉 대량 결실이 없는 해 다음에는 일부 전문적으로 씨앗을 먹는 동물들의 개체 수가 급감하여 많은 도토리가 살아남는다는 것을 말한다.

31 (1) ④ → filled (2) ⑤ → that

문제해설

④ 식료품으로 가득 '채워진' 캐리어 가방이라는 수동의 의미이므로 filling을 과거분사 filled로 고쳐 써야 한다.
⑤ 선행사 things가 있고 이어지는 절에 목적어가 없으므로 what을 목적격 관계대명사 that으로 고쳐 써야 한다.

오답노트

① promise는 to부정사를 목적어로 취하므로 to take는 적절하다.
② '~하러 가다'라는 의미를 가진 〈go+v-ing〉이 사용된 것이므로 shopping은 적절하다.
③ 전치사 from 뒤에서 생략된 the place를 선행사로 하는 관계부사 where는 적절하다.

32 who had walked for more than two hours without complaining

문제해설

the young boy를 선행사로 하는 관계대명사 who가 먼저 오고, '두 시간 이상 걸었다'고 했으므로 had walked for more than two hours로 쓴다. '불평 없이'는 〈without+v-ing〉를 활용하여 without complaining으로 쓴다.

33 ② → extensive

문제해설

전자 미디어와 컴퓨터 네트워크의 발전으로 대규모의 분산된 정보 저장소가 생기게 되었고 이는 광범위한 자원의 일상에서 사용에 새로운 문제를 야기한다는 내용이므로 ② limited(제한된)를 extensive(광범위한)와 같은 말로 고쳐 써야 한다.

34 overload

문제해설

전자 미디어와 컴퓨터의 발전으로 인해 정보 이용자가 정보 과부하를 느끼거나 겪게 될 때에 소프트웨어 시스템을 통해 도움을 얻게 하는 방법을 제시하는 내용의 글이므로, 이 글의 주제는 '정보 과부하로 인해 컴퓨터 이용자가 직면한 문제에 대한 해결 방안'으로 나타낼 수 있다. 따라서 빈칸에 들어갈 말은 overload(과부하)가 가장 적절하다.

35 (1) ③ → have (2) ④ → assign

문제해설

③ 주어가 앞에 있는 corporate strategies이므로 has를 복수형 동사 have로 고쳐 써야 한다.
④ 조동사 can 뒤의 동사원형으로 slice, reassemble과 병렬 연결되고 있으므로 assigning은 assign으로 고쳐 써야 한다.

오답노트

① 재귀대명사 용법 중 '강조 용법'으로 쓰인 themselves는 적절하다.
② 가주어-진주어 구문으로 진주어로 쓰인 to separate는 적절하다.
⑤ '~의 비결'이라고 할 때 〈key to+명사(구)〉로 나타내므로 전치사 to는 적절하다.

36 knowledge transfer

문제해설

밑줄 친 부분은 무역 자유화로 인해 숙련된 전문적인 업무가 임금이 싼 해외의 지역, 예를 들면, 중국이나 인도와 같은 나라에서 이루어지고 있다는 것으로, 이는 이 글의 핵심 소재인 '지식 이전(knowledge transfer)'을 가리키는 내용이다.

37 cognitive

문제해설

'사고, 사유, 또는 기억과 같은 의식적인 지적 활동과 관련된'이라는 의미의 단어는 cognitive(인지의)이다.

38 appears that these genes have a direct impact on dogs' intense ability and desire for social contact

문제해설

〈주어+appear+to-v〉 구문은 〈It+appears+that+주어+동사〉 구문으로 전환할 수 있으므로 It appears that these genes have ~.로 바꾸면 된다.

39 (1) ① → how 생략 또는 that[in which]
(2) ④ → Compared

문제해설

① 방법을 나타내는 경우 the way 다음에 how를 쓰지 않는다. how 없이 쓰거나 that 또는 in which를 사용한다.
④ individuals in tight cultures를 의미상 주어로 하는 분사로, 의미상 수동이어야 하므로 Comparing은 Compared로 고쳐 써야 한다.

12 강

1번 ──────────── p.90

• Word Test

1 유지하다   2 넘어서다, 초과하다   3 정점, 최고 기록
4 고단한, 심신을 피로 [소모] 하게 하는   5 난공불락의, 무적의
6 열망, 갈망   7 두드리다   8 절정 [최고조] 에 이르다
9 noticeable   10 perceive   11 sustain
12 outing   13 stretch   14 tip   15 involve
16 persist

유형 1

❶ undefeatable   ❷ what   ❸ forward
❹ yearning   ❺ the other

유형 2

❶ is   ❷ involves   ❸ is
❹ scores   ❺ moving

유형 3

❶ anything done previously
❷ no matter how
❸ from passivity toward reachable action
❹ keep the learner moving ever forward

2번 ──────────── p.92

• Word Test

1 물질, 동인   2 (지속되는) 기간   3 크기, 규모
4 도포, 바르기, 적용   5 복잡성   6 보여 주다, 증명하다
7 실험   8 증식하다, 번식하다   9 paradox
10 exposure   11 dictate   12 topical
13 lifespan   14 multicellular   15 irrelevant
16 rate

유형 1

❶ when   ❷ increased   ❸ duration
❹ neither   ❺ irrelevant

유형 2

❶ is copied   ❷ was expected   ❸ to occur
❹ published   ❺ were exposed

유형 3

❶ lifespan got longer and longer
❷ this turned out not to be the case
❸ span of survival after the exposure
❹ as far as

3번 ──────────── p.95

• Word Test

1 포식자   2 기능, 능력   3 척도, 측정   4 공연, 연주
5 장애물, 장애   6 그 후에   7 명백한, 분명한   8 원숙한
9 레퍼토리, 연주 목록   10 secure   11 deficit
12 proficient   13 impair   14 forage
15 comprehensive   16 implicit   17 causal
18 parasite

유형 1

❶ Whatever ❷ evident ❸ varied
❹ more ❺ that

유형 2

❶ be acquired ❷ is ❸ lies
❹ tells ❺ displaying

유형 3

❶ in possession of
❷ keeps the bird from attending to
❸ direct causal reflection
❹ in a way impossible to counterfeit

유형 3

❶ went to pick out
❷ plenty of opportunity
❸ became obsessed with
❹ so intent on investigating
❺ stepped in to help
❻ was determined to protect

4번 ─────────── p.98

• Word Test

1 결론 2 철저한, 빈틈없는 3 지연, 지체
4 다루다, 씨름하다 5 분석 6 절약하다, 아끼다
7 기관, 단체 8 잘못 9 관료적인, 관료주의의
10 scarce 11 pile up 12 loop 13 investigation
14 widespread 15 frequent 16 reflection
17 paralysis 18 frustrate

유형 1

❶ While ❷ On the one hand ❸ thorough
❹ For ❺ latter

유형 2

❶ is ❷ taking
❸ to economize ❹ are ❺ solving

유형 3

❶ analysis paralysis
❷ widespread fault in individuals
❸ as action oriented as
❹ stuck in a loop of endless questioning

5-7번 ─────────── p.100

• Word Test

1 ~에 사로잡힌 2 망설임 3 정착하다
4 동료애, 우정 5 개입하다 6 아이를 돌봐 주다
7 파충류 8 ~에 열중하고 있는 9 주민 10 lizard
11 investigate 12 pursue 13 nurture 14 vet
15 integral 16 permission 17 suitable
18 shelter

유형 1

❶ permission ❷ who ❸ investigate
❹ checked ❺ nurture ❻ hesitation

유형 2

❶ to acquire ❷ knocking ❸ becoming
❹ providing ❺ were returned ❻ to exercise

8번 ─────────── p.104

• Word Test

1 접근법 2 매체 3 전문가 4 영향을 미치다
5 출현 6 거래, 매매 7 받아들이다, 흡수하다
8 ~을 고려할 때 9 확인[확증]하다, 입증하다
10 commodity 11 advocate 12 contact
13 supplier 14 added value 15 suit
16 entity 17 auction 18 destabilizing

유형 1

❶ destabilizing ❷ it ❸ as
❹ advocate

유형 2

❶ affects ❷ have embraced ❸ have used
❹ using ❺ decides

유형 3

❶ in the light of
❷ affects commodities more than brands
❸ as a passive entity to absorb
❹ given that

9번 ─────────── p.106

• Word Test

1 우선 사항, 우선권 2 관례, 관습 3 일관성 4 처음에
5 이해 6 측면 7 요소 8 주장 9 기능
10 relevance 11 primarily 12 interpret
13 agreeable 14 irrelevant 15 assume
16 disturb 17 wholeness 18 cognitive

유형 1

❶ up ❷ that ❸ that
❹ Although ❺ aspect

유형 2

❶ to contain ❷ have transferred ❸ are
❹ regards ❺ makes

유형 3

❶ related to economy of time
❷ at the outset
❸ leaves room for other priorities
❹ independent of coherence and relevance

10번 — p.108

p.108

• Word Test

1 이데올로기　2 주제　3 유명 디자이너 의류
4 (가격 등이) 저렴한, 알맞은　5 범위　6 후자　7 전자
8 implication　9 independent of　10 adopt
11 contemporary　12 initial　13 inquirer
14 alternative

유형 1

❶ independent　❷ former
❸ contemporary　❹ what　❺ adopting

유형 2

❶ were powered　❷ searched　❸ informed
❹ be presented　❺ taking　❻ knowing

유형 3

❶ collect as much information as possible
❷ by observed human behavior
❸ choosing from a range of options
❹ without ever knowing

11번 — p.110

p.110

• Word Test

1 씨앗　2 예외 없이, 변함없이　3 유기체　4 계속되다
5 (생물체 내에서 특정한 기능을 수행하는) 기제, 구조
6 빈약하게 하다, 저하시키다　7 자연 선택, 자연 도태
8 편승하다, 얻어 타고 이동하다　9 pollen　10 density
11 threatened　12 scatter　13 lack
14 a suite of　15 essential　16 favour

유형 1

❶ seldom　❷ exploratory　❸ invariably
❹ impoverished　❺ that

유형 2

❶ favours　❷ has found　❸ to scatter
❹ change　❺ limits

유형 3

❶ lack the capacity to
❷ spread from one place to another
❸ for a whole suite of reasons
❹ population densities within a local area

12-14번 — p.112

p.112

• Word Test

1 맞이하다　2 (물)방울이 떨어지는　3 찢다, 뜯어내다
4 (텔레비전·라디오의) 광고 (방송)　5 속삭이다, 소곤거리다
6 라벨을 붙이다　7 타격　8 용돈　9 damp
10 scatter　11 gasp　12 wrap　13 undo
14 deflated　15 exclaim　16 pool

유형 1

❶ besides　❷ ashamed　❸ allowance
❹ undo　❺ crouched　❻ till
❼ deflated

유형 2

❶ were　❷ had considered
❸ had forgotten　❹ standing　❺ scattered
❻ chewing　❼ smelled

유형 3

❶ chatting and laughing together
❷ really noticing him for the first time
❸ caved in
❹ as if all of them were still there
❺ must have read the gift tag
❻ break the news

---

p.116

01 ④　02 ③　03 ①　04 ③　05 ④　06 ④
07 ②　08 ③　09 ⑤　10 ③　11 ③　12 ③
13 ③　14 ⑤　15 ④　16 ③　17 ④　18 ④
19 ④　20 ③　21 ②　22 ④
23 (A) is (B) scores (C) invigorated　24 학습자가 계속해서 도달 가능한 행동을 향해 앞으로 가게 하며 숙련도를 유지하고 지속하면서도 도달된 새로운 기록에 마음속으로 플러스 점수를 매기는 끊임없는 순환　25 (1) ② → the higher (2) ③ → necessarily　26 lifespan　27 힘든 장애물을 헤치고 다양한 능력을 갖추며 성공적으로 잘 성장해 왔다는 것
28 represents the entire developmental process, provides proof　29 (A) Othello (B) Hamlet
30 Hamlet처럼 철저해야 하고, Othello처럼 행동 지향적이되, 성급한 결론을 내리지 않고, 끝없는 질문의 고리에 갇히지 않는 사람들
31 (A) to acquire (B) exploring (C) them over (D) chase　32 새끼 토끼들이 Koa의 몸 위를 뛰어다니도록 하고, Koa의 다리 안쪽을 찾아가서 온기와 보호를 얻는 것
33 (A) the destabilizing effect this has on prices (B) to make it easier for customers to contact them
34 ④ → suppliers　35 ⑤ → independent
36 priorities　37 it, could　38 10년 전에는 많은 정보 수집에 초점을 두었지만, 요즘 검색 엔진은 인간의 행동에 기반을 두고 검색자의 선택 범위를 좁혀 준다.
39 (1) ② → scatter (2) ③ → absence
40 Dispersal　41 (1) ③ → scattered (2) ④ → must have read (3) ⑤ → deflated　42 Mom told the girl that the dog had just smelled the bone

01 ④

문제해설

이전의 기록을 넘어 새로운 한계에 도달하고자 하는 도전 정신의 중요성을 강조한 글이므로, 글의 제목으로 가장 적절한 것은 ④ '한계를 넘어 새로운 정상에 이르는 도전을 찾으라'이다.

오답노트

① 코칭: 학습자에게서 비범한 우월함을 찾기
② 연습이 완벽을 만든다: 전문 지식을 쌓기 위해 노력하라
③ 성장을 일으키고 유지해 주는 결정적 순간을 설계하라
⑤ 성공은 성공을 낳는다: 성공 경험을 제공하는 것의 중요성

02 ③

유기체의 크기가 커지고 나이가 많아짐에 따라 암 발병 위험이 증가할 것으로 알려졌는데 실제로는 이것이 암 발병률과 상관관계가 없어 보인다는 내용이므로, Peto's paradox가 의미하는 바로 가장 적절한 것은 ③ '개체의 크기 및 나이와 암 발병 간의 상관관계는 없음'이다.

① 환경 호르몬이 종양에 미치는 해로운 영향
② 변이 축적으로 인한 노년의 질병으로서의 암
④ 작고 수명이 짧은 유기체의 높은 암 저항력
⑤ 영상 진단 촬영으로 인한 방사선과 관계된 암 위험성

03 ①

개별 새의 노래 숙달 수준은 그 노래하는 새가 잘 성장해 왔다는 것과, 기민성, 기억력, 먹이 찾기 능력, 포식자 경계력 같은 다양한 자질을 가지고 있다는 것을 보여 준다는 내용의 글로, 무엇이든지 부화 후 새의 노래 핵 체계 성장을 '손상시키는' 것과, 무엇이든 새가 노래에 주의를 기울이고 노래 연습하는 것을 방해하는 것은, 나중에 새의 원숙한 노래 레퍼토리 크기와 완벽성의 부족으로 명백히 드러난다고 하는 것이 자연스러우므로 ① assists(돕다)는 impairs(손상시키다)와 같은 말로 고쳐야 한다.

04 ③

주어진 문장은 '다른 한편으로는 복잡한 비즈니스 문제를 다루려면 느린 사고와 철저한 조사가 필요하지만, 심사숙고의 과정은 의사 결정에서 지연을 초래하고 행동을 방해할 수도 있을 것이다'는 내용이다. 그러므로, 빠르면서도 생각하는 데는 게으른 것은 우리의 부족하고 값비싼 정신적 자원을 절약하게 해 주지만, 그 결과로 나온 해결책은 부실하고 효과적이지 못하다는 내용 다음과 조직과 기관이 효율적이고 효과적이려면 복잡한 비즈니스 문제를 해결하는 것에 대한 이러한 도전을 극복할 수 있는 사람들이 필요하다는 내용의 앞인 ③에 들어가는 것이 가장 적절하다.

05 ④

글 (A)는 부모에게서 개 키우기를 허락 받은 Danielle이 돈을 모으려 일을 찾는 내용이다. Danielle이 돈을 충분히 모은 후 골든 리트리버 종인 Koa를 집으로 데려와서 새집과 가족의 일부로서 적응하며 뒤뜰에서 도마뱀을 쫓아다니기도 했는데, 그러다가 Koa가 집 주변에서 불쑥 솟아오른 흙더미를 발견했다는 (D)가 이어지고, 이를 지켜보던 Danielle이 거기서 새끼 토끼들을 발견했고, Danielle과 엄마는 직접 새끼들을 돌볼 준비가 되어 있었으나, 갑자기 Koa가 토끼들을 돌보는 데 개입했다는 (B)가 오고, 강아지가 토끼를 돌보는 것은 특이했지만, 엄마는 Koa에게 양육의 기회를 주기로 했다는 (C)가 이어지는 것이 흐름상 적절하다.

06 ④

(d)는 Danielle의 엄마를 가리키고 나머지는 모두 Danielle을 가리킨다.

07 ②

Koa가 먼저 집 주변의 솟아오른 흙더미를 발견했고, 이후 Danielle이 이를 보러왔으므로 ②는 글의 내용과 일치하지 않는다.

08 ③

③ 〈make+목적어+형용사〉의 구문으로, 현재 목적어는 to contact 이하의 내용이다. 따라서 가목적어 it을 make와 easier 사이에 넣어 make it easier로 고쳐 써야 한다. for customers는 to contact의 의미상의 주어가 된다.

① the destabilizing effect가 주어로 단수이므로 단수형 동사 affects는 적절하다. this has on prices는 삽입된 관계사절이다.
② 〈not just A but also B〉의 구조에서 A와 B는 같은 형식으로 병렬되어야 하므로 to create는 적절하다.
④ absorb의 목적어절을 이끄는 복합관계대명사로 whatever는 적절하다.
⑤ 앞에 있는 customers를 가리키는 복수형 대명사 them은 적절하다.

09 ⑤

통일성과 일관성에 관한 주장이 의미를 가지기 위해서는 인지적 기능을 가져야 하는데, 그 기능은 내용 전달 자체뿐 아니라 시간의 절약과도 관련이 있다는 주어진 글에 이어, 상관없는 요소들은 시간을 낭비하게 하고 이해를 방해하므로, 관련 있는 것만 담는 것이 논픽션(꾸며내지 않은 이야기)의 관례인데 문학에 대한 전통적 견해는 이 관례를 문학적 허구에 이입했다는 (C)가 오고, 허구의 문학은 다른 우선 사항들을 위한 여지를 남겨둔다며, 그 이유로 독자들은 정보를 얻기 위해 독서를 할 뿐만아니라, 오락이나 시간을 보내기 위해서도 독서를 한다는 점을 제시한 (B)가 이어지고, 결국 독자들은 독서를 시간을 보내는 방법으로 여기지, 인지로 여기지는 않는다는 내용인 (A)가 오는 것이 자연스럽다.

10 ③

과거 검색 엔진은 검색 용어에 따라 가능한 한 많은 정보를 수집하여 별개의 정보를 제공한 반면 오늘날에는 인간의 행동을 관찰하여 정보를 받은 모형에 따라 검색 결과가 제시되어 검색자의 선택 범위를 좁힌다는 내용의 글이므로, '사용자의 습관에 대한 정보를 수집하면, 흔히 검색 엔진이 수행하는 것은 사용자의 프로필을 만드는 것이며, 이는 검색 엔진이 그 사용자에게 어떤 광고를 목표로 삼을지를 결정하도록 돕는다'라는 ③은 글의 전체 흐름과 관계가 없다.

11 ③

장거리 분산이 일어나지 않으면, 동계 교배로 멸종의 위기에 처하게 되거나, 환경 조건의 변경 및 국지적 영역 안 개체군의 밀도 증가 시 개체군 존속에 위협을 받을 수 있다는 내용의 글이므로, 글의 주제로 가장 적절한 것은 ③ '동식물의 생존에 있어 분산의 중요성'이다.

① 새가 지구상 생명체들에게 있어 중요한 이유
② 다양한 씨앗 분산에 있어 동물의 역할
④ 멸종 위기에 처한 새 관리에 있어 분산 추정의 필요성
⑤ 장거리 분산 이후 동식물의 정착

12 ③

크리스마스 선물을 받는 데에만 신경쓰는 Sherry와 'I'에게 엄마가 가족

을 위한 선물을 준비했냐고 물으시는 주어진 글 다음, 이에 부끄러움을 느껴 Sherry와 함께 가족의 선물을 사러 갔다가, 가족 선물과 함께 애완견 Jaques에게 줄 선물까지 사온 뒤 포장을 해 나무 밑에 두고, 다음 날이 되어 비를 뚫고 교회에 다녀온 이야기가 나오는 (C)가 이어지고, 비에 젖은 Jaques를 집안으로 들인 후, 외출했다 돌아왔을 때 다른 선물은 그대로였지만 Jacques을 위해 준비한 뼈다귀 선물만 풀어져 있고, 그 뼈를 씹고 있는 Jacques을 발견한 내용의 (D)가 이어진 뒤, Jacques가 글을 읽는 능력이 있다고 생각해 텔레비전 프로그램에 출연까지 생각했으나, 강아지가 냄새를 맡고 뼈다귀 선물을 알아챈 것 같다는 엄마의 말에 실망하는 (B)로 이어지는 것이 자연스럽다.

13 ③

문제해설

(c)는 Sherry를 가리키고 나머지는 모두 Sherry의 엄마를 가리킨다.

14 ⑤

문제해설

거실 바닥에 찢어진 선물 포장지가 사방으로 흩어져 있는 상태였지만, 선물들의 개수는 그대로 있는 듯 보였고, 단지 Jacques가 자신의 선물만 풀었기 때문에 ⑤는 글의 내용과 일치하지 않는다.

15 ④

문제해설

④ '도달된' 새로운 기록이라는 의미이므로 수동형인 been reached로 고쳐 써야 한다.

오답노트

① '~하기 위해'라는 부사적 용법으로 앞에 있는 to exceed와 and로 병렬되는 to push는 적절하다.
② 선행사가 없고 불완전한 구조가 이어지므로 관계대명사 what은 적절하다.
③ 〈no matter how+형용사〉는 '아무리 ~ 하더라도'라는 의미를 갖는 구문이므로 how는 적절하다.
⑤ 앞의 successes를 선행사로 하는 주격 관계대명사 that은 적절하다.

16 ③

문제해설

기존에는 수명이 점점 길어짐에 따라 암의 위험이 정비례하여 증가할 것으로 예상했지만, 실험에 따르면 이는 사실이 아닌 것으로 밝혀졌는데, 쥐를 대상으로 한 실험 결과에 따르면 암 발병 위험을 결정하는 것은 발암 물질에 노출된 시간이지 노출된 쥐의 나이가 아니었다는 내용으로, 빈칸에 들어갈 말로 적절한 것은 ③ '연장된 수명 그 자체는 무관할 수 있다'이다.

오답노트

① 유기체의 신체 크기가 중요한 역할을 한다
② 각 개체의 성장률이 결정적이다
④ 각 개체의 유전적 구성은 무시해도 될 정도이다
⑤ 발암 물질에 노출된 기간이 중요하지 않을 수 있다

17 ④

문제해설

풍부한 레퍼토리와 능숙한 노래 솜씨는 새가 안전한 둥지에서 잘 자랐고, 그 후에 질병과 기생충의 방해가 없었고, 기민성, 기억력, 먹이 찾기 능력, 포식자 경계력 같은 다양한 사질을 가진 상태에서, 수백 시간의 성공적인

노래 연습을 했다는 것을 보여 주므로, 개별 새의 노래 숙달 수준이 그 새의 전체적인 발달 이력을 압축해서 보여 준다는 내용의 글이므로, '사실, 도시에 사는 몇몇 새의 종들은 인간이 만들어낸 소음에 대항하기 위해 그들의 노래 소리를 수정해 왔다.'라는 ④는 글의 전체 흐름과 관계가 없다.

18 ④

문제해설

문제를 해결하는 데 있어 생각의 속도는 빠르지만 행동이 신중하지 못한 Othello같은 유형이 있는가 하면, 너무 생각이 많고, 숙고하느라 분석 불능의 늪에 빠져버릴 수 있는 Hamlet같은 유형도 있다는 내용으로, 빈칸에 들어갈 말로 적합한 것은 ④ 'Hamlet처럼 철저하고 Othello처럼 행동 지향적인'이다.

오답노트

① Othello처럼 신중하고 Hamlet처럼 빠른
② Hamlet처럼 무모하고 Othello처럼 성급한
③ Othello처럼 빠르고 Hamlet처럼 활력 넘치는
⑤ Hamlet처럼 철저하고 Othello처럼 사고 지향적인

19 ④

문제해설

in the electronic age, given that customers today have as much information about suppliers as they have about them에서 보듯 '전자 시대에는 고객의 공급자 정보가, 공급자의 고객 정보에 필적한다'고 했으므로 ④는 글의 내용과 일치하지 않는다.

20 ③

문제해설

상관없는 요소들은 시간을 낭비하게 하고 이해를 방해하기 때문에 관련 있는 것만 담는 것이 논픽션의 관례였다는 것이 자연스러우므로 ③의 fiction(허구)은 non-fiction(꾸며내지 않은 이야기)과 같은 말로 고쳐야 한다.

21 ②

문제해설

과거 검색 엔진은 검색 용어에 따라 가능한 한 많은 정보를 수집한 후 별개의 정보를 제공한 반면, 요즘 검색 엔진은 인간의 행동을 관찰하여 정보를 받은 모형에 따라 검색 결과가 제시되어 검색자의 선택 범위를 좁힌다고 했으므로, 빈칸에 들어갈 말로 적합한 것은 ② '관찰된 사람의 행동'이다.

오답노트

① 개인의 구매 역사
③ 지역에 특화된 결과
④ 식당 선택 선호도
⑤ 공공기관의 빅 데이터

22 ④

문제해설

동식물의 생존에 있어 장거리 분산의 중요성을 강조한 글로 장거리 분산이 일어나지 않을 경우, 동식물은 동계 교배로 멸종의 위기에 처하게 되거나, 환경 조건의 변경이 생기거나 국지적 영역 안 개체군의 밀도가 증가할 때 개체군 존속에 위협을 받을 수 있다는 내용이므로, '하지만, 씨앗 분산의 거리상 증가가 항상 식물의 번식에 이득이 되지는 않는데, 설사 된다 하더라도 그 관계는 꽤 복잡하다.'라는 ④는 글의 전체 흐름과 관계가 없다.

23 (A) is (B) scores (C) invigorated

문제해설

(A) 주어가 Reaching beyond anything done previously 이므로 단수형 동사 is로 고쳐 써야 한다. always knocking ~ record와 a farther reach ~ before는 주어와 동격이고, what ~ "reachfulness"는 삽입절이다.
(B) 동사 maintains and sustains와 접속사 yet과 함께 병렬 연결되어 있는 구조이므로 scored는 scores로 고쳐 써야 한다.
(C) 앞에 있는 it is에 호응하여 '고무된다'라는 의미의 수동형이 되어야 하므로 invigorated로 고쳐 써야 한다.

24 학습자가 계속해서 도달 가능한 행동을 향해 앞으로 가게 하며 숙련도를 유지하고 지속하면서도 도달된 새로운 기록에 마음속으로 플러스 점수를 매기는 끊임없는 순환

문제해설

This는 앞에 있는 두 문장의 내용을 가리킨다.

25 (1) ② → the higher (2) ③ → necessarily

문제해설

② 〈the 비교급 ~, the 비교급 ...〉 구문이고, 등위접속사 and로 the higher its body와 병렬 연결되어 있으므로 high는 the higher로 고쳐 써야 한다.
③ 동사 mean을 수식하도록 형용사 necessary를 부사 necessarily로 고쳐 써야 한다. not necessarily는 '반드시 ~은 아니다'라는 의미이다.

오답노트

① 〈there is[are]+명사〉 구문이고 risk of an error가 단수이므로 단수형 동사 is는 적절하다.
④ 문맥상 '~와 관련 되었다'라는 수동형 의미이므로 was related는 적절하다.
⑤ the time of exposure to the carcinogen agent를 강조하는 〈It ~ that ...〉 강조 구문이므로 접속사 that은 적절하다.

26 lifespan

문제해설

'사람이나 동물이 살거나 살 것으로 예상되는 기간'이라는 의미의 단어는 lifespan(수명)이다.

27 힘든 장애물을 헤치고 다양한 능력을 갖추며 성공적으로 잘 성장해 왔다는 것

문제해설

'좋은 배경'이라는 것은 개별 새가 힘든 장애물을 헤치고 다양한 능력을 갖추며 성공적으로 잘 성장해 왔다는 것을 말한다.

28 represents the entire developmental process, provides proof

문제해설

개별 새의 풍부한 레퍼토리와 능숙한 노래 솜씨는 그 새가 장애물을 잘 헤치고 잘 성장해 왔다는 것과 다양한 자질을 갖고 있다는 것을 보여 준다는 내용의 글로서, '새의 노래의 능숙함은 노래하는 새의 전체적인 발달 과정을 나타내며, 개별 새의 다재다능한 자질과 능력에 대한 증거를 제공한다.'와 같이 요약할 수 있다.

29 (A) Othello (B) Hamlet

문제해설

the latter는 '후자'이므로 앞부분에서 언급한 두 사람 중 Othello를 가리키며, the former는 '전자'로 Hamlet을 가리킨다.

30 Hamlet처럼 철저해야 하고, Othello처럼 행동 지향적이되, 성급한 결론을 내리지 않고, 끝없는 질문의 고리에 갇히지 않는 사람들

문제해설

복잡한 비즈니스 문제를 해결하는 데 필요한 유형의 사람은 These people must be as thorough as Hamlet and as action oriented as Othello, without jumping to conclusions like the latter or being stuck in a loop of endless questioning like the former.에 잘 나타나 있다.

31 (A) to acquire (B) exploring (C) them over (D) chase

문제해설

(A) 〈allow+목적어+to-v〉이므로 acquiring을 to acquire로 고쳐 써야 한다.
(B) 〈전치사 with+명사(구)〉 구문으로, 뒤에 a raised spot of dirt alongside the house라는 목적어가 나오므로 동명사 exploring으로 고쳐 써야 한다.
(C) '~를 철저히 검사하다'라는 의미의 check over는 목적어를 취하는 동사구인데 목적어가 대명사일 경우, 〈동사+대명사+부사〉의 어순이 되어야 하므로 them over로 고쳐 써야 한다.
(D) '차라리 ~하겠다'라는 의미로 〈would rather+동사원형〉을 쓰므로 to chase를 chase로 고쳐 써야 한다.

32 새끼 토끼들이 Koa의 몸 위를 뛰어다니도록 하고, Koa의 다리 안쪽을 찾아가서 온기와 보호를 얻는 것

문제해설

Koa가 모성 본능을 발휘하는 것을 의미하며 맨 마지막 문장 They hop all over her and always find their way to the crook of her leg and find warmth and shelter.에 잘 드러나 있다.

33 (A) the destabilizing effect this has on prices
(B) to make it easier for customers to contact them

문제해설

(A) 우리말 뒤에 affects라는 동사가 이미 있으므로 주어진 우리말을 문장의 주어부가 되어야 한다. 따라서 주어는 the destabilizing effect(불안정한 효과)가 되고, 이것을 수식하는 관계절로 관계대명사가 생략된 형태를 이용하여 this has on price(이것이 가격에 주는)를 쓴다.
(B) '~할 수 있도록'이라는 의미가 되도록 부사적 용법의 to부정사로 시작하게 하며, 〈동사(make)+가목적어(it)+목적격 보어+for+의미상 주어+진목적어(to-v)〉 형태의 구문을 이용하여 to make it easier for customers to contact them으로 나타낸다.

34 ④ → suppliers

문제해설

④는 '공급 회사'를 가리키는 반면에, ① ② ③ ⑤는 모두 '고객'을 가리킨다.

35 ⑤ → independent

문제해설

우리는 불필요한 것에 시간을 낭비하고 싶지 않기 때문에 논리적 일관성과 통일성을 갈망하지만 허구의 문학에서는 다른 우선 사항을 위한 여지를 남긴다는 내용의 글로, 통일성과 일관성에 '상관없이' 기분 좋게 시간을 보내게 해 주는 작품의 모든 측면을 받아들일 준비가 되어 있다고 하는 것이 자연스러우므로 dependent(의지하는)를 independent(독자적인, 관련이 없는)와 같은 말로 고쳐 써야 한다.

36 priorities

문제해설

'가장 먼저 해야 하거나 다른 무엇보다 주의가 필요한 중요한 것'이라는 의미의 단어는 priority(우선 사항)인데, other 다음에는 주로 복수명사가 오므로 빈칸에는 복수형 priorities가 들어가야 적절하다.

37 it, could

문제해설

'가능한 한 ~한 …'라는 의미의 〈as+형용사+(명사)+as possible〉은 〈as+형용사+(명사)+as+주어+can〉으로 바꿔 쓸 수 있다.

38 10년 전에는 많은 정보 수집에 초점을 두었지만, 요즘 검색 엔진은 인간의 행동에 기반을 두고 검색자의 선택 범위를 좁혀 준다.

문제해설

10년 전과 요즘 검색 엔진의 분명한 차이점은 검색 엔진이 10년 전과 요즘 모두 많은 정보를 수집하는 것은 동일하지만, 요즘 검색 엔진은 사람의 행동 정보에 근거해서 선택 사항을 고르도록 하므로 예전보다 많이 선택 범위가 좁혀지도록 처리되고 있다.

39 (1) ② → scatter (2) ③ → absence

문제해설

② 동물에 편승하거나 바람을 이용해서 행해지는 것은 씨앗과 꽃가루를 모으기 위한 것이 아니라 퍼뜨리기 위한 것이므로 gather(모으다)를 scatter(뿌리다) 정도로 고쳐 써야 한다.
③ 장거리 분산이 '일어나지 않는 경우' 동계 교배에 대한 위협이 존재한다는 내용이 되어야 하므로 presence(존재)를 absence(부재) 정도로 고쳐 주어야 한다.

40 Dispersal

문제해설

'넓은 지역에 다른 방향으로 사물이나 사람들을 퍼뜨리는 과정'이라는 의미의 단어는 Dispersal(분산)이다.

41 (1) ③ → scattered (2) ④ → must have read
   (3) ⑤ → deflated

문제해설

③ 의미상 주어 gift paper와 scatter는 수동 관계이므로 scattered로 고쳐야 한다.
④ 뼈를 선물 꾸러미에서 찾아낸 것을 보고 한 말로 과거의 강한 추측을 나타내는 말이 필요하므로 must have read로 고쳐 써야 한다.
⑤ '위축된, 바람이 빠진'이라는 의미로 사람의 감정을 나타내며 주격 보어이므로, 과거분사형 deflated로 고쳐야 한다.

① 엄마가 물은 시점(asked)보다 이전에 이루어진 행위이므로 과거완료 had considered는 적절하다.
② 〈notice+목적어+v-ing〉하면 '~가 …하는 것을 알아차리다'라는 의미이므로 현재분사 standing은 적절하다.

42 Mom told the girl that the dog had just smelled the bone.

문제해설

그 강아지는 다른 선물들은 건드리지 않고 자신의 선물을 어떻게 찾았는지와 그 사실을 소녀는 어떻게 알게 되었는가는 글의 후반부의 It was quite a blow when she told me, "You know, he probably just smelled the bone."에 나타나 있다.

Test 1

1번 —————————————————————— p.132

• Word Test

1 심각하게　2 정치학　3 ~ 때문에　4 대학원생
5 시설　6 (결과적으로) ~에 이르다　7 자전거 보관대
8 lack　9 roadside　10 park　11 matter
12 resolve　13 inconvenience　14 major in

유형 1

① in　② are　③ However
④ which　⑤ resolve

유형 2

① majoring　② to park　③ looking
④ parked　⑤ been stolen

유형 3

① increasing number of students
② have trouble finding
③ leads us to be late for class
④ lack of bicycle facilities

2번 —————————————————————— p.134

• Word Test

1 울음을 터뜨리다　2 즉시　3 고난, 어려움　4 deeply
5 failure　6 obvious

유형 1

① failure　② obvious　③ hardships
④ As　⑤ little

유형 2

① selling　② was drawn　③ opened
④ crying　⑤ seemed

유형 3

① door to door
② I had barely knocked on the door
③ broke into tears
④ more than I could ever have asked for

3번 —————————————————————— p.136

• Word Test

1 언급하다　2 활기찬　3 도전하다　4 ~을 즐기다[잘하다]
5 갈등　6 효과적으로　7 fuel　8 strategy
9 disagreement　10 critical　11 established
12 spread

유형 1

① widely　② established　③ unwilling
④ Thoughtful　⑤ stressful

유형 2

① mentioning　② spreading　③ have
④ be challenged

유형 3

① was put to death for　② sit well with people
③ thrive on disagreement　④ invite good criticism

4번 —————————————————————— p.138

• Word Test

1 역풍　2 체계적인　3 간과되는　4 반인종주의의
5 나아가게 하다　6 비유　7 athletic
8 invisibility　9 cite　10 tailwind
11 slow down　12 consequential

유형 1

① invisibility　② that　③ slows down
④ as　⑤ appear

유형 2

① to explain　② treat　③ make
④ pushing　⑤ trying

유형 3

① but not for all people
② easily unnoticed or forgotten
③ glow with pride
④ appear self-destructive

5번 —————————————————————— p.140

• Word Test

1 마지못해　2 산업화　3 이득　4 전성기　5 이루다
6 희생자　7 ~에서 탈락하다, 낙오하다　8 ~의 결과로
9 변두리, 벽지　10 shift into　11 reap
12 mobility　13 progress　14 dry up
15 adjust to　16 manufacturing　17 primarily
18 diminish

유형 1

① reaping　② diminishing　③ unwillingly
④ primarily　⑤ As

유형 2

① dried　② has meant
③ have adjusted　④ shifting　⑤ was closed

유형 3

① many have been left behind
② dropped out of the workforce completely
③ men in the prime of life
④ path of upward mobility

6번 —————————————————————— p.142

• Word Test

1 주장하다　2 지배적인, 우세한　3 대체[대신]하다
4 확정하다, 결정하다　5 신성시되는, 성스러운
6 지배적인, 우세한　7 주장하다　8 선언하다
9 지배적인, 우세한　10 environmental　11 proceed
12 doom　13 outcome　14 cognition
15 sustainable　16 intervene　17 grave
18 mess

유형 1
1. so much as
2. predominating
3. proclaims
4. it
5. that

유형 2
1. argues
2. has been
3. Intervening
4. supplanting
5. got

유형 3
1. have been set in motion by
2. more sustainable and just
3. prevailing story of our time
4. out of destruction and despair

7번 ——————————— p.145

• Word Test
1. 능력　2. 물리학　3. 무한한　4. 탐색의, 탐구의
5. 제한[제약]하다　6. 만들어 내다　7. manipulate
8. relevant　9. fixed　10. falsehood
11. go beyond　12. constraint

유형 1
1. However
2. what
3. that
4. whether
5. manipulating

유형 2
1. be constrained
2. be explained
3. are
4. wants
5. allowing

유형 3
1. in order to provide knowledge
2. go beyond what we already know
3. within our control
4. exploration of various possible ways

8번 ——————————— p.147

• Word Test
1. 감소하다　2. 소비(량)　3. 표　4. 감소하다, 떨어지다
5. 도달하다　6. period　7. steadily　8. record
9. rainfall　10. peak

유형 1
1. During
2. peak
3. increased
4. more
5. whereas

유형 2
1. was recorded
2. used
3. dropped
4. consumed
5. was

유형 3
1. the highest average rainfall
2. during the same period
3. steadily declined
4. in both periods

9번 ——————————— p.149

• Word Test
1. 문학의　2. 성취하다　3. 도움이 되다　4. 업적
5. 추적하다; 흔적　6. ~에 필적하다[버금가다]　7. 관직, 벼슬
8. 걸작　9. obtain　10. chart　11. remote
12. imperial　13. noteworthy　14. pursuit
15. fame　16. astronomy

유형 1
1. pursuits
2. astronomy
3. accurate
4. which
5. that

유형 2
1. is considered
2. learning
3. keeping
4. held
5. beginning

유형 3
1. achieved fame for his poetry
2. sought to obtain government posts
3. rival his literary fame
4. though only for a few moments

10번 ——————————— p.151

• Word Test
1. 콜라주　2. 아크릴 물감　3. 작품　4. 미술 작품
5. 전시회　6. submit　7. display　8. entry
9. watercolour　10. community

유형 1
1. exhibition
2. Theme
3. fine
4. entries
5. run

유형 2
1. displayed
2. Growing
3. submitted
4. to use
5. be displayed

유형 3
1. sign up for
2. in size
3. Prizes for Each Age Group
4. terms and conditions

11번 ——————————— p.154

• Word Test
1. 계정　2. 아주, 특히　3. 동작, 움직임　4. 참가
5. ~과 협력하여　6. 게시하다　7. view　8. dance to
9. validate　10. take on　11. make sure
12. trendy

유형 1
1. moves
2. long
3. Post
4. validate
5. scan

유형 2
1. to show
2. has
3. dancing
4. is set
5. viewed

유형 3

❶ In partnership with
❷ take on the dance challenge
❸ most viewed videos
❹ For more information

12번 ——————————————— p.156

• Word Test

1 (~할) 여유가 있다 2 독립적으로 3 효과 4 ~에 관한 한
5 ~에 대응하여 6 과소비, 돈의 탕진 7 지나가는, 잠깐의
8 comprehend 9 deprivation 10 request
11 interpret 12 phrase 13 lasting
14 blueprint

유형 1

❶ independently ❷ comprehend ❸ worse
❹ as ❺ overspending

유형 2

❶ to answer ❷ learning ❸ used
❹ be interpreted ❺ designed

유형 3

❶ when it comes to
❷ get written into a money blueprint
❸ have a lasting effect
❹ avoid the feeling of deprivation

13번 ——————————————— p.158

• Word Test

1 그럴듯한 2 얼룩말 3 가설 4 혼란스럽게 만들다
5 촉진하다 6 대조, 차이 7 ~을 통하여 8 물다
9 움직이고 있는 10 mechanism 11 predator
12 herd 13 patterning 14 relatively
15 stripe 16 mammalian 17 possibility
18 analysis

유형 1

❶ plausible ❷ that ❸ difficult
❹ protection ❺ less

유형 2

❶ thought ❷ created
❸ been studied ❹ supporting ❺ biting

유형 3

❶ benefit from an interaction
❷ live in the open
❸ true direction of movement
❹ not necessarily mutually exclusive

14번 ——————————————— p.161

• Word Test

1 평가되다, 여겨지다 2 정신 질환 3 개인주의 4 요소
5 상세히, 길게 6 소유물 7 (두각을) 나타내다, 두드러지다

8 상대적인 9 ~에 관해 (곰곰이) 생각하다 10 개인주의의
11 ill-health 12 league 13 capitalism
14 appearance 15 connection 16 fame
17 self-esteem 18 point out 19 record
20 attach

유형 1

❶ in ❷ mental ❸ Several
❹ defines ❺ what

유형 2

❶ points ❷ rate ❸ Comparing
❹ be argued

유형 3

❶ reflect on the possible connection
❷ rate highly on individualism
❸ attributes this to
❹ attached to materialistic factors

15번 ——————————————— p.163

• Word Test

1 추세, 동향 2 표시, 특징 3 놀라운, 놀랄 만한
4 망원경 5 방대한 6 지속적인, 부단한
7 작동시키다, 권한을 주다 8 천문학자 9 행성
10 commonplace 11 horizon 12 civilization
13 extrasolar 14 scope 15 analyze
16 cosmos 17 instrument 18 affordable

유형 1

❶ Thanks to ❷ commonplace ❸ who
❹ affordable ❺ empowered

유형 2

❶ moved ❷ to analyze ❸ to match
❹ imaged ❺ using

유형 3

❶ in the form of ❷ with breathtaking speed
❸ democratizing amateur science
❹ yet to be examined

16번 ——————————————— p.165

• Word Test

1 현지인, 토착민 2 예절 3 간과하다 4 ~하고 싶어 하는
5 말투, 표현법 6 비가 많이 오는
7 특별한 인상을 주다, 느낌이 들게 하다 8 근본적으로
9 category 10 phenomenon 11 initially
12 subtle 13 excessive 14 ritual
15 exiting 16 hop

유형 1

❶ fundamentally ❷ that ❸ ritual
❹ whether ❺ virtue

유형 2

❶ struck ❷ helps ❸ feels
❹ to hop ❺ blowing

❶ we tend to overlook
❷ as a bit excessive
❸ feels better having been thanked
❹ in subtle waves

17번 ——————————— p.167

• Word Test

1 엄청나게   2 중요하다, 문제가 되다   3 (영향·느낌·경험 등이) 엄청난   4 (음식물·약에 대한) 과민증, 견딜 수 없음   5 선호
6 부정의(not 등의 부정어가 든), 음성의   7 환자   8 equally
9 as long as   10 cosmic   11 circumstances
12 around   13 a variety of   14 planet

유형 1

❶ equally   ❷ that   ❸ profound
❹ cosmic   ❺ if

유형 2

❶ is   ❷ planning   ❸ fear
❹ are   ❺ were

유형 3

❶ In a variety of circumstances
❷ as long as
❸ things not being a certain way
❹ even cosmic importance

18번 ——————————— p.169

• Word Test

1 항해하다, 돌아다니다   2 구조   3 확장되다, 미치다
4 예상하다   5 인지, 인식   6 심리적인   7 ~을 언급하다
8 뚜렷이 다른, 구별되는   9 facilitate   10 reason
11 alternatively   12 social   13 referent
14 pedestrian crossing   15 state   16 cognitive

유형 1

❶ distinct   ❷ broader   ❸ another
❹ extend   ❺ obviously

유형 2

❶ to navigate   ❷ interact   ❸ caused
❹ waiting   ❺ reasoning

유형 3

❶ refers to   ❷ broader referent base
❸ possible to successfully interact with
❹ behave in a particular situation
❺ instances of interacting with others

19번 ——————————— p.172

• Word Test

1 변명이 되다, 용서하다   2 윤리적   3 영향, 함의
4 보통, 전형적으로   5 상정, 추정   6 적절한
7 그에 따르는, 결과로서 일어나는   8 대인 관계의, 사람과 사람 사이의   9 부당하게 취급하다, 모욕하다   10 persistent

11 criminal law   12 responsible for   13 absent
14 justification   15 practice   16 sentence
17 foundation stone   18 resentment

유형 1

❶ For instance   ❷ do we   ❸ appropriate
❹ since   ❺ duty

유형 2

❶ wrongs   ❷ be praised   ❸ are made
❹ has asserted   ❺ is

유형 3

❶ our everyday attitudes and judgments
❷ free and morally responsible
❸ act of their own free will
❹ freedom of the human will

20번 ——————————— p.175

• Word Test

1 임시변통의   2 경쟁력 있는   3 분석   4 점진적인
5 부품, 요소   6 양력   7 변이, 수정   8 계산상의, 컴퓨터와 관련된   9 수행하다   10 호사, 사치   11 생기다, 나타나다   12 조정하다   13 neuroscientist
14 theoretical   15 evolution   16 fix
17 implement   18 functional   19 thrust
20 requirement   21 assemble   22 drag
23 sequential   24 accumulation

유형 1

❶ theoretical   ❷ assembled   ❸ As
❹ unnecessary   ❺ Furthermore

유형 2

❶ is built   ❷ evolves
❸ has described   ❹ were placed
❺ be implemented

유형 3

❶ sets about   ❷ Evolution has no such luxury
❸ older functional structures
❹ along the way

21번 ——————————— p.177

• Word Test

1 보여 주다, 제시하다   2 상태   3 동기를 부여하는 것
4 일치하다   5 분리하다, 단절시키다   6 자기표현, 자기 제시
7 나타내다, 보여 주다   8 shape   9 perception
10 fun-loving   11 in line with   12 specific
13 identify   14 observer

유형 1

❶ which   ❷ shape
❸ unattractive   ❹ divorced
❺ corresponded

유형 2

❶ aim   ❷ posted   ❸ to know
❹ suggesting   ❺ presented

유형 3

❶ have been long identified
❷ In line with this
❸ actual personality and their idealized self
❹ not wildly different from

22번 ──────────────── p.180

• Word Test

1 경쟁자　**2** ~에 관하여　**3** 인정하다　**4** 주목하다
5 군, 무리　**6** (보통 복수형으로) 영향, 결과　**7** ~에 참여하다
8 공무원　**9** supplier　**10** be associated with
11 obligation　**12** coincide　**13** identity
14 concept　**15** rich　**16** fundamental

유형 1

❶ analogy　　❷ Similarly
❸ For example　❹ another　　❺ to

유형 2

❶ was developed　❷ depending　　❸ is led
❹ is　　　　　　❺ held

유형 3

❶ depending on the identity
❷ relate in one manner
❸ its implications are quite rich

23번 ──────────────── p.182

• Word Test

1 너무 비싼　**2** ~이 아닐까 하고 생각하다　**3** 보조금
4 부적절한　**5** 견해, 생각　**6** recipient
7 on average　**8** entrepreneur　**9** bubble
10 talented

유형 1

❶ overpriced　❷ what　　❸ without
❹ value　　　❺ that

유형 2

❶ be misplaced　❷ arguing　　❸ have done
❹ adding　　　　❺ have started

유형 3

❶ tend to earn more on average
❷ good at identifying talented people
❸ skip or stop out of college
❹ worth a combined total of over

24-25번 ──────────────── p.184

• Word Test

1 작동하다　**2** 라벨이 부착된　**3** 절망하여　**4** 해석
5 인식, 지각　**6** 설명하다　**7** 발생하다　**8** 해당하는
9 식수대　**10** mental　**11** prefer
12 underneath　**13** namely　**14** properly
15 oblivious　**16** consequently　**17** connection
18 represent

유형 1

❶ corresponding　❷ that
❸ Unfortunately　❹ Because of　❺ oblivious
❻ despite

유형 2

❶ is pushed　　❷ arrive　　❸ are
❹ overflows　　❺ arises

유형 3

❶ a row of labeled buttons
❷ in any given situation
❸ I have awareness of
❹ in desperation
❺ completely unaware of its existence

26-28번 ──────────────── p.187

• Word Test

1 계속해서[이어서] ~을 하다　**2** 사생활　**3** 진정한
4 줄, 열　**5** 반대　**6** 공감하는　**7** 그만두다, 버리다
8 아픈, 쑤시는　**9** pour out　**10** empathy
11 reflect　**12** thrown　**13** notice　**14** distress
15 inhibition　**16** rejection

유형 1

❶ waiting　　❷ nonetheless　❸ distress
❹ upon　　　❺ where　　　　❻ rejection
❼ empathetic

유형 2

❶ be announced　❷ was　　　❸ had refused
❹ asking　　　　❺ proceeded　❻ being
❼ to hold

유형 3

❶ a few rows in front of me
❷ took my courage
❸ couldn't help noticing
❹ pour out
❺ flood of grief
❻ cried her heart out
❼ in a reversal of

---

p.191

01 ③　02 ①　03 ①　04 ②　05 ②　06 ③
07 ①　08 ⑤　09 ④　10 ⑤　11 ③　12 ①
13 ⑤　14 ⑤　15 ①　16 ②　17 ①　18 ⑤
19 ⑤　20 ⑤　21 ②　22 ⑤　23 ③　24 ⑤
25 ③　26 ④　27 ③　28 ③　29 ①　30 ④
31 ③　32 ②　33 ⑤　34 ④　35 ③　36 ①
37 ①　38 ②　39 ③　40 ③　41 ⑤　42 ④
43 ①　44 ④　45 ①　46 ③　47 ③　48 ②

49 (1) ① → are　(2) ③ → leads
50 facilities　**51** 어렵게 사는 분들로부터 생각지도 못한 과분한 친절을 받은 것에 감동받아서　**52** Barely had I knocked on the door when an older woman opened it
53 ③ → disagreement　**54** It is probably worth mentioning that Socrates was put to death for his beliefs　**55** consequential

56 as if it were your own athletic prowess
57 (A) → have been left (B) → to attain
58 (A) opportunities (B) upward   **59** We do not have an environmental problem so much as we have a *story* problem   **60** ⑤ → uninterrupted
61 constraint   **62** (A) were (B) what (C) allowing   **63** (A) peak (B) fell (C) below
64 with more than 15,000 gigaliters used
65 an accurate chart of the stars, a flying machine, the first seismograph   **66** Only later in his life did Zhang Heng hold a series of important government positions   **67** Do you want to see your artwork displayed at an exhibition
68 수여자는 총 18명이며, 모든 출품작이 전시된다.
69 Happy Mall   **70** validate   **71** (A) worse (B) obsession (C) deprivation   **72** (A) comprehend (B) blueprint   **73** (1) ② → created (2) ④ → difficult   **74** (A) protection (B) processing
75 (A) in which (B) figure (C) what   **76** selfish capitalism   **77** commonplace   **78** (A) enables (B) discovery   **79** (A) exit → exiting (B) be → having been (C) blow → blowing   **80** It initially struck me as a bit excessive   **81** (1) ② → negative (2) ③ → absence   **82** there would be no human life on the planet if it were   **83** (1) giving any thought to the psychological states that caused them (2) reasoning about their psychological states
84 (A) reason (B) anticipation   **85** justification
86 (1) ① → that (2) ② → do we experience (3) ⑤ → is   **87** accumulation   **88** (A) modification (B) requirements   **89** (1) ③ → untagging (2) ⑤ → corresponded   **90** (A) themselves (B) them (C) presented   **91** analogy   **92** (A) Similarly (B) For example (C) For example
93 (A) misplaced (B) overpriced (C) choose
94 how these students would have done without their education   **95** ③, ⑤ → thought
96 should I arrive at the interpretation / would ideally dispense   **97** (1) ② → have elicited (2) ③ → noticing (3) ⑤ → comforted
98 잡을 수 있는 따뜻한 손, 고통을 비추는 공감하는 눈, 기대어 울 수 있는 어깨

01 ③

문제해설

(A) 점점 더 많은 수의 학생이 자전거를 타고 등교하고 있지만 교정에 자전거 보관대가 충분하지 않아 불편함을 겪을 것이므로, inconvenience(불편함)가 적절하다. convenience는 '편안함'이라는 뜻이다.
(B) 자전거를 둘 장소를 찾느라 많은 시간을 보내서 수업에 늦는 결과가 초래되며 비가 오거나 눈이 오는 날에는 상황이 더 나빠질 것이므로 worse(더 나쁜)가 적절하다. better는 '더 좋은'이라는 뜻이다.
(C) 문제를 심각하게 받아들여 그것을 해결하는 데 필요한 조치를 해 달라고 부탁하는 문맥이 자연스러우므로, resolve(해결하다)가 적절하다. dissolve는 '녹이다'라는 뜻이다.

02 ①

문제해설

아동 도서를 판매하며 고학으로 대학을 다니던 필자가 지독히 더웠던 어느 날 어느 것도 제대로 되는 것이 없어 자신이 완전한 실패자처럼 느껴졌다는 내용의 주어진 글에 이어, 한 집에 이끌려 문을 노크하자 연로한 여성이 필자에게 마실 것을 주고 식사를 권했다는 내용의 (A)가 오고, 그 집에 있던 두 시간 동안 노부부가 필자에게 삶에서 겪었던 고난과 경험의 이야기를 해 주면서 다른 사람을 사랑하고 보살피는 것이 중요하다는 이야기를 해주었다는 내용의 (C)가 온 후, 집을 떠나면서 필자가 노부부의 친절에 감동하여 눈물을 흘렸다는 내용인 (B)로 마무리하는 것이 자연스럽다.

03 ①

문제해설

건설적인 갈등이 의사 결정 과정에서 중요하고, 사려 깊은 리더들은 의견 차이가 자신들의 아이디어들을 발전시키는 데 필요한 정보를 주기 때문에 그것을 즐긴다고 했으므로, 건전한 비판을 청하고 의견 차이를 건설적으로 활용하는 것이 리더의 역할임을 알 수 있다. 따라서 빈칸에 들어갈 말로 가장 적절한 것은 ① '건전한 비판을 청하는 것'이다.

오답노트

② 갈등을 현명하게 해결하는 것
③ 건설적인 대화를 주도하는 것
④ 팀에 동기를 부여하고 목표에 도달하는 것
⑤ 팀원들과 강한 유대감을 가지는 것

04 ②

문제해설

달리기를 할 때 순풍이 우리를 밀면 그것은 우리를 앞으로 나아가게 하는 힘이지만 우리는 그것을 쉽게 간과하거나 잊게 되고, 일부 주자가 역풍을 맞고 있다는 사실을 눈치채지 못하면서 그들을 더 게으르고 더 느리게 보거나 심지어 자멸적으로 보게 된다는 내용의 글로서, '우리가 다른 사람들에 비해 더 (A) 유리한 위치에 있을 때, 우리의 특권을 인식하고 (B) 불리한 사회적 조건에 직면한 일부 사람들이 있다는 것을 깨닫기 어렵다.'와 같이 요약하는 것이 가장 적절하다.

오답노트

① 유리한 …… 이상적인   ③ 불리한 …… 어려운
④ 불리한 …… 이상적인   ⑤ 급박한 …… 불리한

05 ②

문제해설

산업화 초기처럼 오늘날의 노동자들은 더 이상 진보의 이익을 거두지 못하고 있으며 자동화의 시대는 미국 중산층에게 기회의 감소를 의미했다는 내용이므로, '노동의 컴퓨터화는 탈공업화된, 지식 기반 경제의 성장을 위한 중요한 기초가 되어왔다.'는 ②는 글의 전체 흐름과 관계가 없다.

06 ③

문제해설

주어진 문장은 Korten이 더 지속 가능하고 공정한 지구 경제를 만드는 것에 관한 자신의 저서에서 '이야기를 바꾸고 미래를 바꾸라'고 선언했다는 내용으로, ③ 뒤 문장에서 '신성시되는 돈과 시장 이야기'를 '신성시되는 생명과 살아있는 지구 이야기'로 바꿈으로써 인간의 인식과 행동을 바꾸는 결과를 가져올 것이라는 Korten의 주장이 언급되고 있으므로, 주어진 문장이 들어가기에 가장 직절한 곳은 ③이다.

07 ①

문제해설

(A) 〈if+주어+동사의 과거형, 주어+조동사의 과거형+동사원형〉 구문을 통해 현재의 사실과 다르거나 반대되는 내용을 가정하는 상황을 나타내고 있으므로, if절의 동사로 과거동사 were는 적절하다.

(B) suggesting의 목적절이 확실한 상황과 관련된 사실적인 부분을 진술하고 있으므로, 명사절을 이끄는 접속사로 that은 적절하다.

(C) to keep의 목적격 보어 자리로 목적어 the relevant shapes and sizes and the laws of physics와 의미상 수동의 관계이므로, 과거분사 fixed는 적절하다.

08 ⑤

문제해설

2018~2019와 2019~2020 회계 연도의 평균 강수량은 두 기간 모두 347밀리리터로 350밀리미터를 약간 밑돌았으므로, ⑤는 도표의 내용과 일치하지 않는다.

09 ④

문제해설

In 132, he invented the first seismograph, which traced the direction of earthquakes and their seismic waves.에서 132년에 최초의 지진계를 발명했는데, 그것은 지진의 방향과 지진파를 추적할 수 있었다고 했으므로, ④가 글의 내용과 일치한다.

10 ⑤

문제해설

The contest will run from June 5th to July 7th.에서 대회는 6월 5일부터 7월 7일까지 진행된다고 했으므로, ⑤가 안내문의 내용과 일치한다.

11 ③

문제해설

세 번째 단계의 Post it only on ShortClip with the hashtags #FathersDayDanceChallenge and #happymall by June 12.에서 6월 12일까지 출품작에 해시태그를 달아 ShortClip에만 게시하라고 했으므로, ③은 안내문의 내용과 일치하지 않는다.

12 ①

문제해설

부모의 돈에 관한 가르침은 아이에게 지속적인 영향을 미쳐 돈을 중심으로 설계된 평생의 삶으로 이어지거나 돈에 대한 박탈감을 피하기 위해 성인이 되어 과소비하는 경향을 초래할 수도 있다는 내용이므로, 빈칸에 들어갈 말로 가장 적절한 것은 ① '돈의 청사진에 기록된다'이다.

오답노트

② 농담으로 받아들여지고 종종 무시당한다
③ 돈에 대한 우리의 긍정적인 생각을 강화한다
④ 우리가 간소하고 검소한 삶을 살게 돕는다
⑤ 돈으로 모든 것을 살 수 있다는 신념을 초래한다

13 ⑤

문제해설

⑤ 수식의 대상인 flies가 적응도를 감소시키는 주체가 되므로 수동의 과거분사 fitness-reduced를 능동의 현재분사 fitness-reducing으로 고쳐야 한다.

오답노트

① '~을 …라고 생각하다'는 〈think+목적어+목적격 보어(to부정사)〉 구문인데 이것이 수동태가 되면 능동태에서 목적격 보어였던 to부정사가 과거분사 thought 뒤에 이어지게 되므로, to promote를 쓰는 것은 적절하다.

② 동사 find의 목적격 보어 자리이므로 형용사 difficult를 쓰는 것은 적절하다.

③ the hypothesis를 구체화하는 절을 이끌며 완전한 구조가 이어지고 있으므로, 동격절을 이끄는 접속사 that을 쓰는 것은 적절하다.

④ 절의 주격 보어로 사용된 형용사 exclusive를 수식하는 자리이므로 부사 mutually를 쓰는 것은 적절하다.

14 ⑤

문제해설

증가하는 개인주의와 늘어나는 정신 질환 사이의 연관성과 그 이유에 관한 내용이므로, '일반적으로 부유한 나라에 사는 사람들은 가난한 나라에 사는 사람들보다 더 자랑스럽고, 더 자신감 있고, 덜 두려움을 느끼는 경향이 있지만, 그들이 반드시 더 인정이 있거나 애정이 있는 것은 아니다.'라는 ⑤는 글의 전체 흐름과 관계가 없다.

15 ①

문제해설

센서의 발전은 태양계 밖에 있는 행성의 대기를 분석하고 문명의 표시를 찾을 수 있게 하며, 적당한 가격의 기술적 수단을 갖게 되는 아마추어 천문학자들에게 새로운 지평을 열어 줄 것이라는 내용이므로, 글의 제목으로 가장 적절한 것은 ① '센서가 천문학에 새로운 지평을 연다'이다.

오답노트

② 우주와 지구라는 행성의 신비
③ 센서가 물리학 발견의 속도를 가속화한다
④ 센서는 외계 문명을 분석하는 데 결정적인 역할을 한다
⑤ 천문학의 새로운 시대에서 '케플러' 우주 망원경의 역할

16 ②

문제해설

버스에서 내리는 사람들이 운전기사에게 감사 인사를 함으로써 운전기사는 승객들을 좀 더 배려하고 싶은 마음이 드는 경우처럼, 감사 인사와 같은 우리가 간과하는 경향이 있는 기본 예절을 실천하는 것이 사회 전반에 긍정적인 영향을 미쳐 사람들이 착한 행동을 하게 만든다는 내용이므로, ''감사합니다!' 라고 말하는 것과 같은 겉보기에는 사소한 사회적 기본 예절이 일반적으로 더 즐거운 사람들을 만드는 데에 (A) 긍정적인 영향을 미쳐서, 그것은 사람들과 공동체 모두에게 많은 (B) 도움이 된다.'와 같이 요약하는 것이 가장 적절하다.

오답노트

① 긍정적인 …… 해   ③ 부정적인 …… 해
④ 대수롭지 않은 …… 도움   ⑤ 부정적인 …… 잘못

17 ①

문제해설

원하는 것이 거기에 있지 않을 때, 음료나 음식에 특정 성분이 들어 있지 않은 것, 기차가 특정 역에서 서지 않는 것, 사랑하는 사람이 더는 존재하지 않는 것 등 상황이 어떠하지 않다는 것이 중요할 수 있다는 내용이므로, 글의 주제로 가장 적절한 것은 ① '상황이 어떠하지 않은지의 중요성'이다.

오답노트

② 여러분이 먹고 마시는 것의 결과

③ 여러분이 생각하는 것이 여러분의 행동에 미치는 영향
④ 상황이 기대하는 것처럼 진행되지 않는 이유
⑤ 여러분이 원하는 것과 현실에서 상황이 어떠한지의 차이

18 ⑤

문제해설

사회 인지는 우리가 다른 사람의 심리 상태에 대해 생각하지 않고 사회적 관습을 토대로 다른 사람과 상호 작용할 수 있게 해 주는데, 사회적 관습은 서로 다른 역할을 하는 사람들이 어떻게 행동하리라고 우리가 기대하느냐에까지 확장된다고 했다. 따라서 이러한 사회적 관습에 기반해서 다른 사람의 심리적 상태에 대한 추론을 수반하지 않고 그들과 상호 작용하는 것이 가능할 것인데, 앞에 부정어 not이 있다는 것을 고려하여 ⑤ exclude(포함시키지 않다)를 involve(수반하다, 포함하다)와 같은 말로 바꿔야 한다.

19 ⑤

문제해설

자유 의지의 문제는 우리의 자기 이해, 대인 관계뿐만 아니라 도덕적, 법적 관행에 현실적인 영향을 미친다는 내용이다. 따라서 미국 연방 대법원은 인간 의지의 자유에 대한 믿음과 그와 관련한 개인의 능력과 의무에 대한 믿음을 미국 법체계의 토대로 삼을 것이므로, ⑤ disbelief(불신)를 belief(믿음)와 같은 말로 바꿔야 한다.

20 ⑤

문제해설

주어진 문장은 첨가의 연결어 Furthermore로 시작하여 새로운 계산상의 필요가 생겼을 때 그것들은 현재의 하드웨어를 가지고 실행되어야 했다는 내용으로, ⑤의 앞 문장에서 두뇌가 진화하는 동안 새로운 구조물이 더 오래된 기능적 구조물 위에 놓여 불필요한 중복, 자원의 낭비, 불필요한 복잡성 등의 문제점이 있었다는 내용이 언급되고 있고, ⑤의 뒤 문장에서 그 과정에서 아날로그에서 디지털로 바뀌는 것이 불가능하다는 주어진 문장의 내용에 대한 결론적 내용이 언급되고 있으므로, 주어진 문장이 들어가기에 가장 적절한 곳은 ⑤이다.

21 ②

문제해설

사람들이 자신들에 대한 다른 사람들의 인식에 영향을 주기 위해 소셜 미디어를 사용하지만, 소셜 미디어를 통해 제시된 이미지는 실제 그 사람의 모습과 동떨어져 있지 않다는 결론을 얻을 수 있으므로, 빈칸에 들어갈 말로 가장 적절한 것은 ② '실제 자신과 크게 다르지 않다'이다.

오답노트

① 그들의 나르시시즘과 시기심을 강화한다
③ 환상이 아니라 그들의 정체성에 대한 진정한 반영이다
④ 그들의 인기를 높이고 잠재적으로 그들의 창의성을 보여 준다
⑤ 그들이 SNS에서 다른 구성원들과 관계를 유지하고 지지하도록 돕는다

22 ⑤

문제해설

Blau, Scott, 그리고 Evan과 같은 연구자는 조직 집합이라는 개념이 Merton의 역할 군이라는 개념에서 유추되어 개발되었다는 것을 인정한다는 주어진 글에 이어, '어머니'라는 가족 관계 내의 지위가 상대 지위의 정체성에 따라 다양한 역할군과 연관된다는 Merton의 역할 군 개념을 구체화한 내용의 (C)가 오고, Similarly라는 연결어로 시작하여 마찬가지로 특정 조직도 특정 파트너와 경쟁자의 정체성에 따라 다양한 관계에 참여한다는 점을 작은 식료품점의 예시로 제시하는 (B)가 온 후, 근본적인

개념은 간단하지만, 그것이 미치는 영향력은 상당히 다채롭다는 내용인 (A)로 마무리하는 것이 자연스럽다.

23 ③

문제해설

③ 문장의 주격 보어 역할을 하는 that절 안에서 주어와 동사가 한 번만 사용되었고 선행사가 없으므로 관계대명사 whom을 일반대명사 them으로 고쳐야 한다.

오답노트

① 주어 He의 부수적 동작을 나타내는 분사구문을 이끄는 자리로 뒤에 목적어 that절이 이어지고 있으므로, 능동의 현재분사 arguing을 쓰는 것은 적절하다.
② '사람들'을 의미하면서 관계대명사 who의 수식을 받는 자리이므로 대명사 those를 쓰는 것은 적절하다.
④ 주격 관계대명사 who 관계사절 안에서 선행사 young students에 대한 동사 자리이므로 복수형 동사 choose를 쓰는 것은 적절하다.
⑤ '가치가 있는'이라는 의미로 명사구 sixty companies를 수식하는, 형용사 worth를 쓰는 것은 적절하다.

24 ⑤

문제해설

생각과 느낌 사이의 연관성은 청량 음료 자판기에 비유될 수 있는데, 우리들 대부분은 정신적인 관점에서의 해석과 감정적인 관점에서 그에 해당하는 반응 사이의 연관성에 대해 잘 알지 못하기 때문에 부정적인 결과가 초래된다는 내용이므로, 글의 요지로 가장 적절한 것은 ⑤이다.

25 ③

문제해설

(A) '만약 ~하면'이라는 의미의 조건 부사절을 이끄는 접속사 자리이므로 if가 적절하다. whether는 조건 부사절을 이끄는 접속사로 사용될 수 없다.
(B) '버튼에 올바르게 표시가 되어 있다'라는 수동의 의미가 되어야 하므로, 수동태 are labeled가 적절하다.
(C) 지각동사로 동명사인 watching의 목적어 our own thumb과 목적격 보어가 의미상 능동의 관계이므로 동사원형 push가 적절하다.

26 ④

문제해설

(a), (b), (c), (e)는 모두 공항에서 울고 있던 여자를 가리키고 (d)는 공항에서 울고 있던 여자의 동생을 가리킨다.

27 ③

문제해설

Rather than asking if everything was OK, ~ but I couldn't help noticing that you are in distress."에서 모든 것이 괜찮은지 묻기보다는 "당신을 성가시게 하고 싶지는 않지만, 저는 당신이 비탄에 빠져 있다는 것을 눈치챌 수밖에 없었어요."라고 말했다고 했으므로, ③은 글의 내용과 일치하지 않는다.

28 ③

문제해설

(A) 여자는 남편을 잃은 지 얼마 되지 않은 자신의 여동생이 기댈 수 있는 바위가 되어 주며 그 주를 보낸 후 공항에서 큰 소리로 울고 있었던 것이므로, grief(슬픔)가 적절하다.
(B) 다른 사람을 위로하는 데 있어서 잡을 수 있는 따뜻한 손, 고통을 비추

는 공감하는 눈, 기대어 울 수 있는 어깨는 아무리 충분해도 지나치지 않다는 문맥이므로, empathetic(공감하는)이 적절하다.

오답노트

① 슬픔 …… 시기하는　　　② 후회 …… 복수심에 불타는
④ 후회 …… 복수심에 불타는　⑤ 기쁨 …… 공감하는

29 ①

문제해설

연결어 However로 시작하여 교정에 자전거 보관대가 충분하지 않기 때문에 학생들이 자전거를 주차할 장소를 찾는 데 어려움을 겪고 있다는 내용으로, ①의 앞에서 점점 더 많은 수의 학생이 자전거를 타고 등교하고 있다고 했고, ①의 뒤에서 자전거를 둘 장소를 찾느라 많은 시간을 보내 수업에 늦는 결과가 초래된다고 했으므로, 주어진 문장이 들어가기에 가장 적절한 곳은 ①이다.

30 ④

문제해설

④ 진주어 to always love and care deeply about others에 대한 가주어 자리이므로 대명사 this를 가주어 it으로 고쳐야 한다.

오답노트

① '~이 되다'를 의미하는 불완전 자동사 go의 과거진행형 다음 주격 보어 자리이므로 형용사 right를 쓰는 것은 적절하다.
② '~하자마자 …했다'라는 의미는 〈주어+had+barely+p.p. ~ when+주어+과거형 동사〉와 같이 나타내므로 부사 barely는 적절하다.
③ 셀 수 없는 명사 money를 수식하는 자리이므로 수량형용사 much를 쓰는 것은 적절하다.
⑤ '계속 ~하다'라는 의미는 〈keep+동명사〉 구문이므로 동명사 crying을 쓰는 것은 적절하다.

31 ③

문제해설

건설적인 갈등이 의사 결정 과정에서 중요하므로 리더는 건전한 비판을 청하고 의견 차이를 건설적으로 활용해야 한다는 내용이다. 리더가 어려운 문제를 해결하려고 노력하기를 꺼리거나 아이디어에 대해서 의견 차이를 수용하기를 꺼린다면 효과적으로 전략을 세우거나 방향을 정할 수 없게 될 것이므로 ③ willing(기꺼이 하는)을 unwilling(꺼리는)과 같은 말로 바꿔야 한다.

32 ②

문제해설

역풍을 맞으며 달리면 속도가 느려져서 더 세게 밀고 나가야 하지만 이와 반대로 순풍을 맞으면 앞으로 나아가는 추진력을 얻게 될 것이므로, 빈칸에 들어갈 말로 가장 적절한 것은 ② '여러분을 앞으로 나아가게 하는 힘'이다.

오답노트

① 여러분의 방향을 안내하는 나침반
③ 여러분이 정면으로 맞서야 하는 도전
④ 여러분이 함께 경쟁해야 할 좋은 라이벌
⑤ 여러분이 자신의 최고가 되도록 영감을 주는 멘토

33 ⑤

문제해설

자동화의 시대가 미국 중산층에게 기회의 감소를 의미하며, 자동화로 인해

미국 중산층 남성의 일자리가 줄고 경제적 지위가 저하되어 그들의 상향 이동의 길이 막혔다는 내용이므로, 글의 제목으로 가장 적절한 것은 ⑤ '자동화 함정: 그것은 어떻게 미국 중산층에게 악영향을 미쳤나'이다.

오답노트

① 미국 산업 발전에 대한 간략한 역사
② 미국 중산층의 흥망성쇠
③ 1980년대 이후 기계화가 더 이상 작동하지 않는 이유
④ 미국 역사에서 중산층의 물질적 풍요

34 ④

문제해설

오늘날 우리가 직면하는 심각한 환경적 난제가 돈과 시장을 신성시하는 지배적인 이야기에서 비롯되었으므로 이러한 이야기를 생명과 지구를 중시하는 이야기로 대체하여 지구상의 생명 시스템의 복구와 회복을 시작해야 한다는 내용이다. 따라서 돈과 시장을 신성시하는 이야기가 우리의 개입 없이 아무런 방해도 받지 않고 현재의 궤도로 진행하도록 허락한다면 우리는 결국 파멸의 길에 이르게 될 것이므로, 밑줄 친 부분이 함축하고 있는 바로 가장 적절한 것은 ④ '우리는 우리 스스로 우리의 몰락과 죽음을 피할 수 없게 만든다'이다

오답노트

① 아무도 우리의 자연과의 동반자 관계에 대해 신경 쓰지 않을 것이다
② 환경 문제를 해결하려는 우리의 노력은 결실을 맺을 것이다
③ 생명 시스템의 복구와 회복은 저절로 일어날 것이다
⑤ 근본적인 사회 변혁은 우리가 통제할 수 없다

35 ③

문제해설

상상력은 흔히 무한하고 제약이 없는 것처럼 보이지만 사실이 아니며 지식을 제공하거나 새로운 지식을 생성해 내려면 제한된 범위 내에서 상상적 탐색을 해야 한다는 내용이므로, '지식의 생성은 학술 기관, 기업 및 공공 기관에서 직접 연구 및 실험 개발을 통해 공식적으로 일어날 수 있다.'는 ③은 글의 전체 흐름과 관계가 없다.

36 ①

문제해설

주어진 문장은 당시 중국에서 대부분의 교육받은 젊은이들이 관직을 얻기 위해 노력했지만, Zhang Heng은 대신 수학과 천문학을 배우며 여러 해를 보냈다는 내용으로, ① 앞에서 언급된 Han dynasty를 주어진 문장에서 at the time으로 받고 있고, 주어진 문장에서 언급된 mathematics and astronomy를 ① 뒤에서 these fields로 받고 있으므로, 주어진 문장이 들어가기에 가장 적절한 곳은 ①이다.

37 ①

문제해설

돈에 관한 부모의 가르침은 아이의 삶에 지속적인 영향을 미쳐 아이가 돈을 중심으로 설계된 평생의 삶을 살게 하거나 돈에 대한 박탈감을 피하기 위해 성인이 되어 과소비하는 경향을 초래할 수도 있다는 내용이므로, '돈에 대한 우리의 믿음과 행동은 우리 부모님에 의해 (A) 형성되기 때문에 돈에 관한 그들의(부모님의) 발언은 성인기에 우리의 금전적 결정이나 소비 습관에 대한 (B) 기초가 된다.'와 같이 요약할 수 있다.

오답노트

② 형성되다 …… 부담　　③ 반영되다 …… 기초

④ 꾸지람 받다 …… 부담   ⑤ 꾸지람 받다 …… 자산

38 ②

문제해설

얼룩말이 움직이는 동안 그것의 줄무늬가 포식자를 혼란스럽게 한다는 생각이 초기 이론이라는 내용의 주어진 글에 이어, 주어진 글의 내용을 This로 받아 시작하면서 얼룩말의 줄무늬가 포식자를 혼란스럽게 한다는 생각이 그럴듯한 가능성인 이유를 얼룩말이 현혹 효과와 혼란 효과의 상호작용으로부터 이익을 얻을 수 있기 때문이라고 설명하는 (B)가 오고, 움직임 현혹 가설이 얼룩말에서 연구되는데 이 분석은 얼룩말 줄무늬가 이동 정보 처리를 어렵게 만든다는 가설을 뒷받침한다는 내용의 (A)가 온 후, 최근의 연구는 얼룩말의 줄무늬가 곤충에 대한 보호 기능을 한다는 점에 초점을 맞추지만 이것이 현혹 가설과 서로 배타적이지 않은 관계라는 내용인 (C)로 마무리하는 것이 자연스럽다.

39 ③

문제해설

(A) 증가하는 개인주의와 늘어나는 정신 질환 사이에 있을 수도 있는 연관성을 고려할 때 세계에서 가장 개인주의적인 사회인 미국은 정신 질환의 범주에서도 최고일 것이므로 top(최고)이 적절하다. bottom은 '최하'라는 뜻이다.
(B) '부자병'을 '돈, 소유물, 외양과 평판에 높은 가치를 두는 것'으로 정의하며, 이것을 '이기적 자본주의'라고 부르는 것 때문으로 여긴다는 문맥이므로 attributes(~을 …의 결과로 여기다)가 적절하다. contribute는 '기여하다'라는 뜻이다.
(C) 자신의 돈, 소유물 등에 높은 가치를 부여하는 '부자병'이 '이기적 자본주의'에서 비롯되므로 '이기적 자본주의'가 강한 문화에서는 물질적 요소에 부여되는 상대적 중요성이 특히 중요할 것이다. 따라서 materialistic(물질적인)이 적절하다. spiritual은 '정신적인'이라는 뜻이다.

40 ③

문제해설

센서는 우주를 이해할 방대한 새로운 창을 열고 있으며 가까운 미래에 센서의 발전으로 과학의 대중화를 이루고 태양계 밖에 있는 행성의 대기를 분석하고 문명의 표시를 찾을 수 있을 것이라는 내용이므로, '과학을 대중화하는 것은 투표로 자연에 대한 질문을 해결하는 것을 의미하지 않는다. 그것은 접근성, 투명성 및 책임의 원칙을 완전히 통합하는 제도와 관행을 만드는 것을 의미한다.'라는 ③은 글의 전체 흐름과 관계가 없다.

41 ⑤

문제해설

큰 소리로 '감사합니다!'라고 말하는 것과 같은 겉보기에는 사소한 사회적 기본 예절이 다른 사람들에게 긍정적인 영향을 미쳐 그것이 사람들과 공동체 모두에게 많은 도움이 된다는 내용이므로, 글의 주제로 가장 적절한 것은 ⑤ '기본 예절이 다른 사람들과 공동체에 미치는 긍정적인 파급 효과'이다.

오답노트

① 사회적 배제의 위험성과 결과
② 일상생활에서 선을 배워야 할 필요성
③ 불친절과 무례함의 전염성
④ 다양한 사회적 상황에서 기본 예절의 중요성

42 ④

문제해설

상황이 어떠한지가 우리에게 중요한 만큼 상황이 어떠하지 않은지도 똑같

이 중요할 수 있다는 내용의 주어진 글에 이어, 원하는 것이 있지 않을 때, 음료나 음식에 특정한 성분이 없는 것, 기차가 서지 않는 것이 중요할 수 있으며 사별 또한 중요하다는 내용의 (C)가 오고, 사별의 중요성에 대해 부연 설명으로 사랑하는 사람이 존재하지 않을 때 그 사람의 부재에 대한 느낌은 엄청나다는 것과 상황이 특정한 방식이 아닌 것이 누군가에게 평범할 수도 있다는 내용과 관련된 (A)가 온 후, 역접의 연결어 But으로 시작하여 상황이 그렇지 않은 것의 몇몇 경우는 대단히 중요하다는 내용을 언급한 (B)로 마무리하는 것이 자연스럽다.

43 ①

문제해설

'마음 읽기'는 심리 상태가 다른 사람에게 있다고 생각하는 인지 능력이며, '사회 인지'는 심리 상태가 다른 사람에게 있다고 생각하지 않고 사회적 관습을 기반으로 그들과 성공적으로 상호 작용하는 것을 가능하게 해 준다는 내용이다. 사회적 관습은 서로 다른 역할을 하는 사람들이 어떻게 행동하리라고 우리가 기대하느냐에까지 확장되기 때문에 사회 인지를 바탕으로 우리는 다른 사람들의 심리적 상태에 대해 추론할 필요가 없이 그들과 상호 작용하는 것이 가능할 것이므로, 빈칸에 들어갈 말로 가장 적절한 것은 ① '다른 사람들의 심리적 상태에 대한 추론'이다.

오답노트

② 다른 사람들의 행동의 결과에 대한 기대
③ 우리의 인지적 사고 과정과 정신적 노력
④ 사회적 관습과 사회적 규범의 준수
⑤ 마음 읽기과 사회 인지에 대한 의도적인 생각

44 ④

문제해설

개인의 자유 의지를 상정하는 것은 일상적 태도와 판단을 정당화시켜 자유 의지의 문제가 우리의 자기 이해, 대인 관계뿐만 아니라 도덕적, 법적 관행에 현실적인 영향을 미친다는 내용이므로, 글의 제목으로 가장 적절한 것은 ④ '우리의 태도와 판단의 토대로서의 자유 의지'이다.

오답노트

① 자유 의지란 없다
② 자유 의지에는 그 한계와 문제점이 있다
③ 자유 의지에 비추어 본 형사 사법 제도
⑤ 자유 의지를 믿는 것은 여러분을 더 진정한 자신으로 느끼게 해 준다

45 ①

문제해설

비행기를 개발할 때는 먼저 이론을 분석한 다음, 모형을 만들고 실험을 하며 비행기가 땅에 안전하게 있으면서 조립되고, 조정되고, 테스트 되지만, 이와 달리 종의 진화는 항상 '비행 중에' 행해지기 때문에 충분히 기능적이고 경쟁력이 있어야만 순차적 변이가 가능한 어려운 과정이므로 비행기 개발에 비해 호화로움이 없는 과정이라고 볼 수 있다. 따라서 빈칸에 들어갈 말로 가장 적절한 것은 ① '호사'이다.

오답노트

② 반복   ③ 융통성   ④ 복잡함   ⑤ 적응

46 ③

문제해설

사람들이 자신들에 대한 다른 사람들의 인식에 영향을 주기 위해 소셜 미디어를 사용하지만, 소셜 미디어를 통해 제시된 이미지는 실제 자신의 모습과 크게 다르거나 동떨어져 있지 않다는 내용이므로, 글의 제목으로 가

장 적절한 것은 ③ 'SNS상에서 보이는 자아와 실제 사이의 편차는 거의 없다'이다.

오답노트

① SNS상에서 자기 표현의 한계
② SNS상에서 어떤 종류의 이미지가 나타나는가?
④ 관계 구축: SNS상에서 이미지 공유에 대한 동기
⑤ 소셜 미디어: 자기 표현과 자기 노출을 위한 훌륭한 무대

47 ③

문제해설

조직 집합 개념이 역할 군의 개념과 유사하다는 내용에서 '어머니'라는 가족 관계 내의 지위가 상대 지위의 정체성에 따라 다양한 역할 군과 연관되듯이 특정 조직도 특정 파트너와 경쟁자의 정체성에 따라 다양한 관계를 맺게 될 것이므로, 빈칸에 들어갈 말로 가장 적절한 것은 ③ '다양한 관계에 참여한다'이다.

오답노트

① 구체적인 작업 지침을 설정한다
② 구성원 간에 역할을 분담한다
④ 목표와 목적을 명확하게 명시한다
⑤ 제품과 서비스의 범위를 결정한다

48 ②

문제해설

Thiel과 같은 사람들은 고등 교육을 받는 것은 평균적으로 학생들이 더 많은 돈을 버는 데 도움이 될 수도 있지만, 대학 교육을 받지 않고 사업을 시작하기로 선택하는 사람들이 버는 것에 비해 반드시 비용 효율적이지는 않다고 지적한다는 내용이므로, 글의 주제로 가장 적절한 것은 ② '고등 교육의 비용 효율성에 대한 의혹과 의심'이다.

오답노트

① 교육 부문이 직면한 난제
③ 고등 교육의 비용 효율성을 측정하는 방법
④ 현재의 공교육 위기를 해결하기 위한 해결책
⑤ 학교 중도 탈락자들을 위한 체계적인 재교육 프로그램의 필요성

49 (1) ① → are (2) ③ → leads

문제해설

① a number of는 '많은'이라는 의미이므로 동사 is는 are로 고쳐 써야 한다.
③ 선행사가 앞 문장 전체인 계속적용법의 주격 관계대명사 which 다음의 동사는 단수 동사여야 하므로 lead를 leads로 고쳐 써야 한다.

오답노트

② 〈have trouble+v-ing〉는 '~하는 데 어려움이 있다'라는 의미이므로 finding은 적절하다.
④ 비교급 worse를 수식하며, '훨씬'이라는 의미를 갖는 부사 even은 적절하다.
⑤ 동사 take를 수식하는 부사 seriously는 적절하다.

50 facilities

문제해설

영영 뜻풀이는 '사람들이 사용할 수 있는 장소에 제공되는 방 또는 장비의 일부와 같은 것'이고, 내용상 자전거와 관련된 시설물이 부족하다는 내용이 되어야 한다. 따라서 '시설물'을 의미하는 facility가 와야 하며 총칭을 나타내므로 복수로 facilities를 쓰는 것이 적절하다.

51 어렵게 사는 분들로부터 생각지도 못한 과분한 친절을 받은 것에 감동받아서

문제해설

필자가 힘들었던 날 책을 팔기 위해 방문한 곳에서 어렵게 사는 노부부로부터 식사 대접을 받고, 삶에 관한 이야기를 들으며, 돈까지 받게 되면서 따뜻한 친절함에 감동을 받았다는 내용의 글이다.

52 Barely had I knocked on the door when an older woman opened it

문제해설

〈had+barely+p.p. ~ when/before+주어+과거동사〉 구문은 '~하자마자 …했다'의 의미이다. Barely가 문두에 있으면 〈조동사+주어〉로 도치가 이루어져 Barely had I knocked on the door로 쓴 후 when 절 뒤에서는 과거형 동사인 opened로 이어서 쓰면 된다.

53 ③ → disagreement

문제해설

기성의 사고에 도전하거나, 건설적인 갈등은 문제 해결과 효과적인 전략 수립에 매우 중요하다는 내용으로, 리더는 그러한 '의견 차이'를 즐기며 발전을 도모한다고 하는 것이 적절하므로, ③ agreement(동의)를 disagreement(의견 차이) 정도로 고쳐야 한다.

54 It is probably worth mentioning that Socrates was put to death for his beliefs

문제해설

'언급할 가치가 있는'은 〈worth+v-ing〉를 이용하여 is worth mentioning'으로 표현하며, 〈it ~ that〉 진주어-가주어 구문을 사용하여 It is probably worth mentioning that으로 시작하도록 한다. 〈put+사람+to death〉는 '~를 죽이다'는 뜻인데 Socrates가 주어이므로 수동태 was put으로 나타내도록 한다.

55 consequential

문제해설

제시된 영영 뜻풀이는 '중요한 결과와 영향을 가지는'라는 의미이고 문맥적으로 순풍이 '중요하지만' 간과되거나 잊혀진다는 내용으로 이어지는 것이 적절하므로 빈칸에는 consequential(중요한)이 적절하다.

56 as if it were your own athletic prowess

문제해설

〈as if+가정법〉을 사용한 문장으로 현재 사실에 대한 가정이므로 be동사는 were를 사용하고, '여러분 자신의 운동 기량'은 your own athletic prowess로 써 주면 된다.

57 (A) → have been left (B) → to attain

문제해설

(A) be left behind는 '~에 남겨지다'라는 의미로 주어 many와 수동의 관계여야 하므로 have left는 have been left로 고쳐야 한다.
(B) 〈allow+목적어+to-v〉이므로 목적격 보어로 to attain은 적절하다.

58 (A) opportunities (B) upward

문제해설

산업화 시대의 노동자의 상황과 비슷하게 자동화 시대의 노동자가 기회의

감소와 낮은 임금, 노동 시장에서의 탈락, 상향 이동의 기회 감소 등을 겪고 있다는 내용이므로, '자동화 시대의 노동자들은 (A) 기회가 줄어들고, 새로운 시대에 적응하면서 더 낮은 임금을 위해 일하거나 혹은 노동 시장에서 탈락하게 될 수밖에 없고, (B) 상향 이동의 기회를 잃기 시작한다는 점에서 산업화 시대의 노동자들과 비슷한 경험을 하고 있다.'와 같이 요약할 수 있다.

59 We do not have an environmental problem so much as we have a *story* problem

문제해설

⟨not A so much as B / not so much A as B⟩는 'A라기 보다 B이다'를 의미하는 구문이다. 보기에는 so much as가 있으므로 앞부분에는 We don't have an environmental problem이 오고 so much as 뒤에 we have a story problem으로 이어지면 된다.

60 ⑤ → uninterrupted

문제해설

⑤ 신성시되는 돈과 시장 이야기가 효과적인 개입 없이 또는 방해함 없이 진행된다면 파멸한다는 문맥이므로, interrupted(방해받는 상태로)는 uninterrupted(방해받지 않은 상태로)로 고쳐 써야 한다.

61 constraint

문제해설

상상력은 무한이고 제약이 없기에 거짓일 수 있으므로, 지식 제공을 위해선 상상력이 제한되어야 한다. 그러나 새로운 지식을 생성하는 것은 상상력을 어느 정도는 제약하면서도 그러한 제약 범위 내에서 탐색 활동을 허용해야 한다는 내용이 되어야 하므로, 빈칸에 들어갈 말은 전치사 without의 목적어이므로 동사 constrain(제약하다)의 명사형 constraint(제약)가 들어가야 적절하다.

62 (A) were (B) what (C) allowing

문제해설

(A) 주절에 would be가 등장하므로 가정법 과거의 동사 형태인 were로 고쳐 써야 한다.
(B) 전치사 beyond의 목적어이면서 '우리가 이미 알고 있는 것'이라는 의미로 선행사를 포함하는 관계대명사인 what으로 고쳐 써야 한다.
(C) 접속사 while에 주어와 동사를 생략한 분사구로서 의미상 주어 one과 능동의 관계이므로 allowing으로 고쳐 써야 한다.

63 (A) peak (B) fell (C) below

문제해설

(A) 2017-2018 회계 연도의 전체 물 소비는 15,386으로 가장 높은 수치이므로 peak(최대량)가 적절하다.
(B) 2014-2016 회계 연도 동안 전체 물 사용은 14,877에서 13,669로 떨어졌으므로 fell(떨어졌다)이 적절하다.
(C) 2018-2020 회계 연도 동안 평균 강수량은 347로 350보다는 아래이므로 below(~아래)가 적절하다.

64 with more than 15,000 gigaliters used

문제해설

⟨with+명사+분사⟩의 구문을 사용한다. '15,000 기가리터 이상의'를 나타내는 표현은 more than 15,000 gigaliters이며 이것과 동사 use와의 의미 관계는 수동이므로 과거분사 used로 쓴다.

65 an accurate chart of the stars, a flying machine, the first seismograph

문제해설

문학적 업적에 필적하는 다른 분야의 업적은 정확한 성도, 비행 장치, 최초의 지진계가 언급되고 있다.

66 Only later in his life did Zhang Heng hold a series of important government positions

문제해설

Only later in his life가 문두에 나와 의미가 강조되며 도치 구문을 형성하도록 한다. 시제가 과거이므로 did Zhang Heng hold로 도치하고 '일련의 중요한 관직'은 a series of important government positions로 쓴다.

67 Do you want to see your artwork displayed at an exhibition

문제해설

⟨want+to-v⟩와 ⟨see+목적어+분사⟩의 구문을 활용하여 영작하는데, see의 목적어 your artwork와 동사 display는 의미상 수동 관계이므로 과거분사를 사용하여 see your artwork displayed로 쓴다.

68 수여자는 총 18명이며, 모든 출품작이 전시된다.

문제해설

수상자 인원과 출품작 전시 개수에 대한 질문으로 연령 그룹은 7-12세와 13-18세로 두 그룹인데 각각 1등 1명, 2등 3명, 3등 5명이므로 총 18명이 수상을 받게 된다. 그리고 수상작만 전시되는 것이 아니라 모든 작품이 전시된다는 언급이 나온다.

69 Happy Mall

문제해설

질문은 행사 주최자에 대한 것으로 첫 문장에서의 '우리'는 최신 유행인 짧은 비디오 플랫폼인 ShortClip과 협력하여 이번 행사를 한다고 밝히고 있는데, 마지막에 상을 수여하는 곳이 Happy Mall임을 밝히고 있다.

70 validate

문제해설

제시된 영영 뜻풀이는 '무언가가 사실이거나 옳다는 것을 공식적으로 증명하다'라는 의미로 참가를 인증하기 위해 계정을 공개 설정하라는 내용이 되어야 하므로, 빈칸에는 validate(인증하다, 확인하다)가 적절하다.

71 (A) worse (B) obsession (C) deprivation

문제해설

(A) 아이들이 이해할 수 있도록 노력하는 대답도 돈에 대한 청사진에 각인되지만, 설상가상으로 식사 중에 지나가는 말로도 평생 가는 영향을 끼칠 수 있다고 하였으므로 (A)에는 Even worse(설상가상으로)가 되어야 하므로 worse가 적절하다.
(B) 돈이 부족하다는 개념은 일에 대한 집착을 통해 항상 충분한 돈이 있을 수 있도록 삶을 꾸려가고 일을 열심히 해야 하므로 (B)에는 obsession(집착)이 적절하다. negligence는 '태만, 부주의'라는 뜻이다.
(C) 박탈감을 느껴서 어른이 되어 이를 피하기 위해 과소비를 하게 될 수 있다는 내용이므로, deprivation(박탈)이 적절하다. satisfaction은 '만족'이라는 뜻이다.

72 (A) comprehend (B) blueprint

문제해설

돈에 대한 교훈에 대해서는 아이들이 이해하도록 하는 신중한 대답도 돈에 대한 개념에 영향을 끼치지만, 식사 중 지나가는 말로도 평생 지속되는 영향을 끼칠 수 있다고 하였으므로, '돈에 대한 교훈에 대해서는, 아이들이 (A) 이해할 수 있을 정도로 사려 깊은 대답뿐 아니라 돈에 대해 지나가는 말도 그들의 돈의 (B) 청사진에 평생 지속되는 영향을 끼칠 수 있다'와 같이 요약할 수 있다.

73 (1) ② → created (2) ④ → difficult

문제해설

② 의미상 주어 dazzle effects and confusion effects(현혹 효과와 혼란 효과)와 의미상 수동 관계이므로 created로 고쳐 써야 한다.
④ 〈make+목적어+목적격 보어〉의 구조에서 보어 자리에는 부사는 올 수 없으므로 difficultly를 형용사 difficult로 고쳐 써야 한다.

오답노트

① the high-contrast patterning을 수식하며 수동의 의미를 갖는 과거분사 thought는 적절하다.
③ 〈find+목적어+목적격 보어〉의 구문으로 목적어는 camouflaging via other mechanisms이고 목적격 보어에 형용사 difficult이므로 목적어 구를 이끌고 있는 동명사 camouflaging은 적절하다.
⑤ 비교급 smaller를 수식하며 '훨씬'이라는 의미를 갖는 much는 적절하다.

74 (A) protection (B) processing

문제해설

얼룩말의 줄무늬가 일으킬 수 있는 현혹 효과와 혼란 효과에 대한 연구가 이루어지고 있는데, 실제와 다른 방향으로의 움직임 신호를 생성하여 이에 대한 이동 정보를 처리하는 것을 어렵게 만든다고 한다. 따라서 '얼룩말 줄무늬는 사자와 하이에나 같은 포식자와 무는 곤충에 대해 (A) 보호의 역할을 할 수도 있는데, 이는 실제 움직임의 방향으로부터 다른 방향의 강한 움직임 신호를 만들어서 움직임에 대한 (B) 처리를 어렵게 만든다.'와 같이 요약하는 것이 적절하다.

75 (A) in which (B) figure (C) what

문제해설

(A) 선행사 Affluenza는 책이라는 공간적 개념으로 적용되며 관계사 뒤에는 완전한 문장이 이어지므로, in which로 고쳐 써야 한다.
(B) 주어는 Several other countries이므로 복수형 동사 figure로 고쳐 써야 한다.
(C) 전치사 to의 목적어 자리에 있으면서 선행사를 포함하고 있으므로 관계대명사 what으로 고쳐 써야 한다.

76 selfish capitalism

문제해설

James는 부자병을 돈, 소유물, 외모, 평판에 높은 가치를 두는 것으로 정의하면서 이것은 자신이 명명하길 '이기적 자본주의' 때문이라고 하였으므로, James가 생각한 부자병의 원인은 selfish capitalism(이기적 자본주의)이다.

77 commonplace

문제해설

센서의 발달로 태양계 밖에 있는 행성의 발견에 대해서도 흔히 있는 일로 되었다는 내용으로, 제시된 영영 뜻풀이는 '많은 곳에서 발생하거나 나타나고 특별한 일이 아닌 일'이므로 빈칸에는 commonplace(흔히 있는

일, 다반사)가 적절하다.

78 (A) enables (B) discovery

문제해설

센서의 발달로 태양계 밖 행성의 발견이 일상화되었고, 더 많은 분석이 가능해질 것이며, 아마추어 천문가들이 고성능의 기기를 사용할 수 있게 되면서 아마추어 과학이 대중화되고 새로운 행성의 발견에 큰 진척을 이루어낼 것이라는 내용이므로 '센서의 발달은 우주 탐색의 다양한 측면을 (A) 가능하게 할 뿐만 아니라, 아마추어 천문가들의 새로운 행성 (B) 발견에 기여한다는 면에서 과학의 대중화를 이끌 것이다.'와 같이 요약할 수 있다. analyze는 '분석하다', hinder는 '방해하다', creation은 '창조, 생성'이라는 뜻이다.

79 (A) exit → exiting (B) be → having been
     (C) blow → blowing

문제해설

(A) '주민들이 버스에서 내릴 때'라는 의미로 접속사를 생략하지 않은 분사구문이고 의미상 주어가 the natives로 능동 관계여야 하므로 현재분사 exiting으로 고쳐 써야 한다.
(B) '감사를 받았기 때문에'를 의미하는 분사구문이므로 배경의 시제보다 한 단계 이전의 일을 나타내고 있는 표현으로 having been으로 고쳐 써야 한다.
(C) wind는 분사의 의미상 주어로 wind와 의미상 능동의 관계이므로 현재분사 blowing으로 고쳐 써야 한다.

80 It initially struck me as a bit excessive

문제해설

'~에게는 …로 여겨진다'의 의미를 가진 〈strike ~ as …〉 구문을 활용하고, '조금 과한'은 a bit excessive로 표현한다. 시제가 과거이므로 It initially struck me로 쓴다.

81 (1) ② → negative (2) ③ → absence

문제해설

② 알려지나 과민증인 사람은 부정의 선호를 갖고 있다는 내용이 되어야 하므로 negative(부정의, 음성의)가 적절하다. positive는 '긍정의, 양성의'이라는 뜻이다.
③ 사별(bereavement)과 같이 소중한 사람이 없을 때, 그 부재의 느낌은 중요하다는 내용이므로, absence(부재)가 적절하다. presence는 '존재'라는 뜻이다.

82 there would be no human life on the planet if it were

문제해설

'만일 그렇다면(지구가 더 가까이에 있다면)'을 if 절로 표현할 경우, 'if it(the planet) were closer to the sun'인데 해당 구절이 앞 문장에 있으므로 were까지만 쓰고 나머지는 생략할 수 있다. 주절의 경우 〈there+be-v〉 표현을 사용하되, 가정법 구문이므로 'There would be'가 되도록 한다. '지구에는 어떤 인간 생명체도 없다'는 no human life on the planet로 쓴다.

83 (1) giving any thought to the psychological states that caused them
     (2) reasoning about their psychological states

문제해설

attribute psychological states to other people은 다른 사람이 어떠한 심리적 상태를 파악한다는 의미이므로 같은 의미를 표현한 본

문 중의 어구는 giving any thought to the psychological states that caused them(다른 사람의 행동을 일으킨 심리 상태를 생각하기)와 reasoning about their psychological states(다른 사람들의 심리적 상태 추론하기)이다.

84 (A) reason (B) anticipation

문제해설

마음 읽기와 사회 인지의 차이점에 대해서 설명하면서 마음 읽기는 타인의 심리 상태에 대해 생각하는 것이고, 사회 인지는 타인의 심리 상태에 대한 추론 없이 사회 관습에 의한 행동에 따라 타인과 상호 작용을 한다는 점에서 다르다는 내용이므로, '마음 읽기는 타인의 심리 상태에 대해 (A) 추론하는 인지 능력을 의미하지만, 반면에 사회 인지는 마음 읽기의 과정 없이 특정 상황이나 역할에 대한 사회 관습에 근거한 행동을 (B) 예상하면서 타인과 성공적으로 사회적 상호 작용이 존재한다는 측면에서 더 넓은 의미를 가지고 있다'와 같이 요약할 수 있다.

85 justification

문제해설

영영 풀이는 '무엇인가가 올바르며 도덕적으로 옳은 이유'라는 의미이고, 우리를 부당하게 취급하는 사람에 대한 분개와 도덕적 분노는 그 사람의 자유 의지를 상정하기 때문에 개인의 자유 의지를 상정하는 것은 일상적 태도와 판단을 정당화시킨다는 내용이 되어야 한다. 따라서 동사 justify(정당화하다)의 명사형인 justification(정당화)이 들어가야 적절하다.

86 (1) ① → that (2) ② → do we experience
(3) ⑤ → is

문제해설

① 뒤에 완전한 문장이 나오고 있고, assumption을 설명하는 동격절의 접속사가 필요하므로 that으로 고쳐야 한다.
② Not only가 문두에서 쓰여서, 구문이 도치되도록 해야 하므로 do we experience로 고쳐 써야 한다.
⑤ 주어는 A 'universal and persistent' foundation stone이므로 단수형 동사 is로 고쳐 써야 한다.

오답노트

③ 도덕적 분노를 느낄 때 대체로 우리는 정당화된다고 느끼게 되므로 주어 we와 수동 관계이므로 are justified는 적절하다.
④ 앞에 선행사가 없고 뒤에 불완전한 구조가 이어지므로 선행사를 포함하는 관계대명사 what은 적절하다.

87 accumulation

문제해설

제시된 영영 뜻풀이는 '시간이 지남에 따라 무언가가 양이 증가하거나 함께 수집되는 과정'이고, 종의 진화 과정은 새로운 비행기를 개발하는 것과 같이 절차와 순서가 있는 것이 아닌 그때그때 임시변통의 해결책이 점진적으로 축적된 것과 같다는 의미이므로 빈칸에 들어갈 말은 accumulation(축적)이 적절하다.

88 (A) modification (B) requirements

문제해설

비행 전에 일련의 여러 과정을 거치는 비행기 개발과 달리 진화는 진화적 변이가 지속적으로 축적되는 상시적 과정이기에 불필요한 중복과 낭비, 복잡성과 같은 문제가 있고, 새로운 필요에 대해 기존의 하드웨어를 사용하게 되는 문제가 있다는 내용이므로, '새로운 비행기를 개발하는 일은 비행 전에 지상에서 일련의 과정을 거치는 반면, 진화는 지속적인 진화적 수정

의 축적으로 인해 기능적이고 경쟁적인 (A) 변이를 요구하여 비효율과 현재의 하드웨어로 새로운 (B) 필요(요구 사항)를 통합하는 데 어려움을 초래한다.'와 같이 요약할 수 있다.

89 (1) ③ → untagging (2) ⑤ → corresponded

문제해설

(1) 타인이 게시한 이미지가 매력적이지 않거나 타인이 알게 하고 싶지 않은 것일 경우 태그를 해제한다는 내용이므로 ③은 untagging(태그 해제하기)이 적절하다.
(2) 이후 문장에서 관찰자들의 평가가 실제 사진과 다르지 않다고 하였으므로, 실제 개성과 더 밀접하게 부합한다는 내용이므로, corresponded(부합하는)가 적절하다.
obstacle은 '장애물', prejudice는 '편견', accorde는 '일치하다'라는 뜻이다.

90 (A) themselves (B) them (C) presented

문제해설

(A) express의 주어는 instagram users이고 자기 자신을 표현하다는 의미가 되므로 재귀대명사 themselves로 고쳐 써야 한다.
(B) portray의 주어는 those photos이므로 목적어인 그들은 Facebook users이므로 them으로 고쳐 써야 한다.
(C) '제시하다'라는 의미의 present는 뒤에 동사 are가 있으므로 분사 형태가 되어야 하고, the images와 수동 관계이므로 과거분사 presented가 적절하다.

91 analogy

문제해설

제시된 영영 뜻풀이는 '유사함을 보여 주려는 의도로 두 가지 상황, 프로세스 등을 비교하는 것'이라는 의미로 조직 집합이라는 개념이 역할 군이라는 개념에서 유추되어 개발되었다는 내용이 되어야 하므로 빈칸에는 analogy(유추)가 들어가야 적절하다.

92 (A) Similarly (B) For example (C) For example

문제해설

(A) 먼저 어머니라는 단일 지위가 상대방에 따라 다른 역할을 가진다고 하였고, 빈칸 이후에 조직체가 파트너와 경쟁자에 따라 다양한 관계에 참여한다고 하였으므로, 유사한 내용의 추가 언급에 쓰이는 Similarly(마찬가지로)가 적절하다.
(B) 조직체가 파트너에 따라 다양한 관계에 참여한다고 한 다음, 빈칸 이후에 식료품점과 공급자, 고객, 공무원과의 관계를 구체적 사례로 제시하고 있으므로, For example(예를 들어)이 적절하다.
(C) 근본적 개념은 간단하지만 그 영향은 상당히 다양하다고 한 후, 빈칸 이후에 다양한 요인에 대해 사례를 들어 설명하고 있으므로, For example(예를 들어)이 적절하다.

93 (A) misplaced (B) overpriced (C) choose

문제해설

(A) 이후 문맥을 통해 더 많은 교육에 대한 믿음이 부적절하다는 주장으로 이어지므로, misplaced(부적절한)가 적절하다.
(B) 고등 교육이 들인 돈의 가치를 얻지 못하고 있다고 주장하고 있으므로, overpriced(너무 비싼, 가치보다 비싸게 값이 매겨진)가 적절하다.
(C) Thiel이 학생들에게 돈을 주었고, 그들은 60개의 회사를 차렸다는 내용으로 이어지므로, 그들은 대학을 가지 않고 회사를 창업하기로 선택한 학생들이므로, choose(선택하다)가 적절하다. reject는 '거부하다', organize는 '조직하다', inexpensive는 '비싸지 않은'이라는 뜻이다.

94 how these students would have done without their education

문제해설

가정법 〈without+명사〉의 구문을 활용하여 먼저 without their education을 쓰고, 전체적 시제가 과거이므로 가정법 과거완료를 사용하고, 가정법 주절이 간접의문문 형태가 되어 〈의문사+주어+동사〉의 어순으로 how these students would have done로 쓰며 수설을 앞에 두라 하였으므로 앞쪽에 먼저 쓴다.

95 ③, ⑤ → thought

문제해설

생각과 느낌의 연관성을 설명하기 위해서 음료 자판기를 비유로 설명하였는데, 생각을 의미하는 것들은 the button(s), the interpretation이며, 느낌을 의미하는 것은 the desired beverage, our corresponding reactions, anger 등이다. 따라서 ③, ⑤번이 의미하는 바가 같으며, 이는 thought를 의미한다.

96 should I arrive at the interpretation / would ideally dispense

문제해설

〈보기〉에 if가 없으므로 if가 생략되어, 조동사 should를 사용하는 〈가정법 미래〉 문장으로 'should I ~'의 형태로 시작하도록 하고, 주절에는 조동사의 과거형 would를 사용한다. 따라서 should I arrive at the interpretation와 would ideally dispense로 차례대로 쓰도록 한다.

97 (1) ② → have elicited (2) ③ → noticing (3) ⑤ → comforted

문제해설

② 앞에 would와 함께 '만약 괜찮냐고 물었더라면'이란 의미로 가정법 과거완료 시제여야 하므로 have elicited로 고쳐 써야 한다.
③ '~를 할 수밖에 없다'라는 의미의 〈cannot help+v-ing〉 구문이므로 noticing으로 고쳐 써야 한다.
⑤ 그녀가 약간은 위안을 받은 채로 떠난 것이므로, 수동형 과거분사 comforted로 고쳐 써야 한다.

오답노트

① 의미상 주어 my flight와 수동의 관계이므로 be announced는 적절하다.
④ 선행사가 the point이고 이어지는 문장이 완전한 구조이므로 관계부사 where는 적절하다.

98 잡을 수 있는 따뜻한 손, 고통을 비추는 공감하는 눈, 기대어 올 수 있는 어깨

문제해설

the genuine empathy는 '진정한 공감'이라는 말로 글쓴이가 진실한 감정이 있는 곳에서 나올 수 있는 행위들을 마지막 문장 But it's not true — where there is real emotion, there can never be enough warm hands to hold, empathetic eyes to reflect the pain, and shoulders to cry on.에서 나열하고 있다.

Test 2

1번 —————————————————— p.229

• Word Test

1 추천, 복권　2 (강, 운하 등의) 물길, 수로　3 패들링
4 허가증, 허가　5 향상된, 개선된　6 분량
7 ~을 감행하다　8 활동　9 access　10 scenic
11 mobile　12 extraordinary　13 award
14 ensure　15 destination　16 come to a close

유형 1
❶ With　❷ behind　❸ scenic
❹ application

유형 2
❶ coming　❷ to be　❸ is used
❹ enhanced

유형 3
❶ water activities
❷ venture into extraordinary adventures
❸ the most scenic
❹ enhanced experience

2번 —————————————————— p.231

• Word Test

1 젖다　2 (텐트를) 치다, 설치하다　3 비탈, 경사
4 미세한　5 직물, 천　6 압도하다　7 참여[참가]하다
8 기어가다　9 second-guess　10 through
11 spray　12 range　13 dash　14 more or less
15 scramble　16 mist

유형 1
❶ far enough　❷ heavy　❸ have joined
❹ to

유형 2
❶ scrambled　❷ spraying　❸ to feel
❹ to throw　❺ to prepare

유형 3
❶ washing machine　❷ fine mist
❸ more or less　❹ at the last minute
❺ occurred to me

3번 —————————————————— p.233

• Word Test

1 소통가, 전달자　2 이해하다, 해석하다　3 소수
4 달리하다, 변화를 주다　5 안심되는, 신뢰할 수 있는
6 ~의 방식에 따라　7 ~을 특징짓다, ~의 특징이 되다
8 움직이다, 기능하다　9 방식　10 consciously
11 flexibility　12 educated　13 possibly
14 adapt　15 preference　16 dramatically
17 majority　18 arena

유형 1

❶ understand　　❷ flexibility　　❸ minority
❹ what　　❺ in

유형 2

❶ creating　　❷ to vary　　❸ adapting
❹ to communicate　❺ characterizes

유형 3

❶ rather than　　❷ are different from
❸ No matter what method you choose
❹ more educated guesses

4번 — p.235

• Word Test

1 영속성　　2 해당[상당]하다, 나타내다, 대표하다
3 계속 ~을 하다　　4 대부분, 큰 규모　　5 잠시 멈추다
6 드문　7 표면　8 중력　9 ~에 영향을 받지 않는
10 ~을 따라가다, ~에 대해 계속 파악하고 있다　　11 reflect on
12 remarkably　13 degradation　14 fool
15 habitable　16 immense　17 file
18 the vast majority of　19 contemporary
20 campaign

유형 1

❶ lies　　❷ habitable
❸ contemporary　❹ which　　❺ little
❻ that

유형 2

❶ keeping　　❷ contain　　❸ knows
❹ Going　　❺ believing

유형 3

❶ depend on　　❷ reflect on
❸ despite all that　❹ along with

5번 — p.237

• Word Test

1 전략　2 동일하게　3 거의, 사실상　4 본질, 본성
5 이론　6 긴급한　7 통제된 방식으로 행동하는
8 뒷받침하다　9 evidence　10 organized　11 fit
12 effective　13 approach　14 seize
15 matter　16 emerge

유형 1

❶ that　　❷ the more　　❸ than
❹ with　　❺ that

유형 2

❶ have　　❷ supports　　❸ studying
❹ disciplined　❺ needed

유형 3

❶ preferred learning style
❷ equally effective
❸ seize an opportunity
❹ in general

6번 — p.239

• Word Test

1 비인격적인, 인간미 없는　　2 분리하다　　3 영향을 미치다
4 대규모의, 대량의　　5 분명하게 보여 주다, 규정하다
6 능력　7 significance　8 consumption
9 capitalist　10 interconnected　11 ritual
12 monetary

유형 1

❶ obvious　　❷ whose　　❸ where
❹ that　　❺ separates

유형 2

❶ defining　　❷ lies
❸ are purchased　❹ is

유형 3

❶ in contrast to　　❷ in modern society
❸ case of monetary gifts　❹ massive activity
❺ be entirely separated

7번 — p.241

• Word Test

1 ~을 가져오다, ~이 생기게 하다　　2 전체　　3 번영하다
4 시도하다, 착수하다　　5 긍정적인　6 전환
7 (역경 등을) 헤쳐 나가다, 견디다　　8 unsustainability
9 planetary　10 planet　11 potential
12 sustainable　13 aspiration　14 nurture

유형 1

❶ transition　　❷ what　　❸ positive
❹ but also

유형 2

❶ realizing　　❷ to nurture　　❸ weathering
❹ is　　❺ to find

유형 3

❶ come from re-visioning
❷ are afraid of weathering
❸ more positive process　❹ bring about
❺ strong evidence

8번 — p.243

• Word Test

1 인용구　2 간결함　3 관련된　4 설문 조사
5 공유하기에 적절한　6 인용되는　7 exclusive
8 factor　9 spokesperson　10 contain
11 journalist　12 account for

유형 1

❶ what　　❷ that　　❸ cited
❹ relevant　❺ that

유형 2

❶ makes　　❷ was　　❸ Containing
❹ involving　❺ is

9번 ——————————————— p.245

• Word Test

1 인상적인 2 장애가 있는, 손상된 3 정식의
4 동향, 변화, 움직임 5 연주 6 재능 7 시들해지다
8 3인조, 트리오 9 창의성 10 존경하다
11 embrace 12 gain 13 format 14 praise
15 popularity 16 standard 17 self-taught
18 organize 19 advent 20 display

유형 1

❶ greatest ❷ which ❸ impaired
❹ formal ❺ impressive

유형 2

❶ is considered ❷ displayed ❸ starting
❹ performing ❺ was admired

유형 3

❶ of all time ❷ set a new standard
❸ early talent for music ❹ concentrated on
❺ the advent of

10번 ——————————————— p.247

• Word Test

1 팽팽하게 하다 2 기기 3 넣다, 끼우다 4 촉진, 가속
5 이점, 혜택 6 민감한 7 조립하다 8 초과한; 과도
9 품질 보증(서) 10 감소 11 operate
12 stimulation 13 fabric 14 purchase
15 manufacturer 16 pregnant 17 effect
18 wrinkle 19 instrument 20 circulation

유형 1

❶ device ❷ reduction ❸ sensitive
❹ wet ❺ anything

유형 2

❶ to become ❷ to avoid ❸ gets
❹ to remove ❺ Included

유형 3

❶ Effects and Benefits
❷ acceleration of blood circulation
❸ Usage Information ❹ sensitive skin
❺ attempt to

11번 ——————————————— p.250

• Word Test

1 발견하다, 탐지하다 2 이용 가능한 3 먹다
4 친환경의 5 동굴 6 extraordinary
7 on board 8 book 9 turtle
10 packed lunch

유형 1

❶ extraordinary ❷ where ❸ on
❹ which

유형 2

❶ to watch ❷ swimming ❸ depending
❹ included

유형 3

❶ the most extraordinary ❷ The tour includes
❸ snack bar on board
❹ Lunch is not included

12번 ——————————————— p.253

• Word Test

1 (부당하게) 이용하다 2 능력 3 계산하다
4 접근 권한, 접근 5 저하시키다 6 붕괴, 방해
7 물리적인 8 재래식의, 비핵의 9 유효한 10 유용성
11 acknowledge 12 perceive 13 intrusion
14 flaw 15 authorized 16 disclosure
17 derive 18 nuclear 19 overwhelm
20 roughly

유형 1

❶ where ❷ from ❸ degrade
❹ valid ❺ it

유형 2

❶ calculated ❷ obtaining ❸ make
❹ to determine ❺ has

유형 3

❶ By contrast
❷ previously undisclosed flaws
❸ seemingly valid information requests
❹ one of the most famous instances

13번 ——————————————— p.255

• Word Test

1 배치 2 평평한, 생기가 없는, 무미건조한 3 특성, 속성
4 무표정한 5 ~에 부합하다[들어맞다], ~을 따르다
6 선호하다, 편들다 7 고수, 충실 8 정밀(성), 정확(성)
9 허리 10 경직된, 엄격한 11 꺼림, (마음) 내키지 않음
12 배열하다, 정리하다 13 formula 14 depth
15 stereotypical 16 portray 17 conventional
18 persist 19 convey 20 glorify 21 hierarchy
22 faithfully 23 limb 24 adopt

유형 1

❶ to ❷ simplified ❸ that
❹ unique ❺ little

유형 2

❶ to adopt ❷ to depict ❸ drawn
❹ involving ❺ glorifying

39

유형 3

❶ rigid social hierarchy   ❷ attempt to
❸ in the most simplified manner
❹ conform to a strict formula
❺ unique viewpoint

14번 ——————————————— p.258

• Word Test

1 수용, 포옹   2 탐색, 탐구   3 불안한
4 (~에도 불구하고) 존속하다, 살아남다   5 분명히, 확실하게
6 친밀한   7 앙심에 찬, 복수심에 불타는   8 만족스러운
9 널리 알려짐   10 remotely   11 at heart
12 paradoxically   13 genuine   14 prospect
15 longing   16 fragility   17 ultimately
18 sphere

유형 1

❶ available   ❷ definitively   ❸ who
❹ they   ❺ prospect

유형 2

❶ won   ❷ to strive   ❸ building
❹ feel   ❺ Being

유형 3

❶ shortcut to friendship
❷ building up genuine bonds
❸ longing for   ❹ sign of failure

15번 ——————————————— p.260

• Word Test

1 나타내다   2 폐쇄   3 척도   4 오해를 일으키는
5 포착하다   6 분석   7 차이, 구별   8 오로지
9 적절한   10 오염   11 reflect   12 framework
13 conclude   14 substitute   15 perspective
16 analyst   17 contribute to   18 in isolation
19 indicator   20 limitation

유형 1

❶ distinction   ❷ Because of   ❸ that
❹ appropriate   ❺ comprehensive

유형 2

❶ to understand   ❷ viewed   ❸ realized
❹ to visit   ❺ Using

유형 3

❶ well-defined measures   ❷ related to
❸ negative changes   ❹ contribute to
❺ comprehensive economic analysis

16번 ——————————————— p.263

• Word Test

1 정확히   2 전문가   3 대성공   4 인물 사진
5 나타내다   6 더미, 무더기   7 사진작가
8 실물보다 못 나온   9 experimentation   10 junk

11 critically   12 in-between   13 viewer
14 discriminating   15 fraction   16 exposure

유형 1

❶ that   ❷ what   ❸ that
❹ quality   ❺ successful

유형 2

❶ to show   ❷ make
❸ discriminating   ❹ is   ❺ needed

유형 3

❶ with a poor exposure   ❷ discriminating eye
❸ end up in   ❹ creative energy
❺ part of the step-by-step development

17번 ——————————————— p.266

• Word Test

1 입력하다, 적어넣다   2 ~을 가능하게 하다
3 (생각나게 하는) 신호, 메모   4 예약, 약속   5 구체성
6 주다, 제공하다   7 유연성, 융통성   8 지연
9 illustration   10 put off   11 settle on
12 context   13 intention   14 overlook
15 interpret   16 automatic

유형 1

❶ flexibility   ❷ who   ❸ physician
❹ as   ❺ appointment

유형 2

❶ opening   ❷ to make   ❸ done
❹ to phone   ❺ to overlook

유형 3

❶ a degree of   ❷ make an appointment with
❸ take care of himself   ❹ lack of specificity
❺ attentional structure

18번 ——————————————— p.269

• Word Test

1 멸종한   2 제목   3 진가를 인정하다   4 관점
5 관여   6 동기를 부여하다   7 생물 다양성   8 보존하다
9 scarce   10 striving   11 vocabulary   12 awe
13 account   14 conservation   15 security
16 pursue

유형 1

❶ as   ❷ do we
❸ perspectives   ❹ automatically   ❺ extinct

유형 2

❶ to be   ❷ to appreciate   ❸ pressed
❹ goes   ❺ including

유형 3

❶ scarce resource   ❷ nature for its own sake
❸ goes extinct   ❹ diversity of nature

19번 ——————————— p.271

• Word Test

1 수행하다　2 사례　3 나타나다　4 건축물, 건축
5 공간의　6 도시 경관　7 방식　8 notable
9 footrace　10 dimension　11 notoriously
12 measurement　13 exterior　14 intersection

유형 1

❶ without　❷ Nevertheless　❸ and
❹ minimum　❺ where

유형 2

❶ fixed　❷ to design　❸ be played
❹ to undertake　❺ was

유형 3

❶ take place in　❷ exterior wall of a building
❸ a unit of measurement
❹ at the intersection

20번 ——————————— p.273

• Word Test

1 상관　2 동화　3 이겨 내다, 극복하다　4 포함하다
5 대모　6 성쇠, 부침　7 추상적인　8 마차
9 obstacle　10 weave　11 resign　12 helpless
13 suspense　14 heroine　15 bankrupt
16 rigid

유형 1

❶ antagonists　❷ greater　❸ because of
❹ abstract　❺ why

유형 2

❶ overcoming　❷ going　❸ resign
❹ be woven　❺ was disappointed

유형 3

❶ are full of
❷ faced an employer going bankrupt
❸ abstract discussion　❹ as usual
❺ felt helpless

21번 ——————————— p.277

• Word Test

1 ~에 기여하다　2 정도　3 추상적인　4 전문화, 분화
5 존재　6 제도, 기관　7 연대, 결속
8 ~에 견주어, ~에 비례하여, ~에 관련하여　9 공동 관리하다
10 공동의, 상호 간의　11 exact　12 benefit
13 universal　14 varying　15 common good
16 labour　17 owe　18 obligation　19 mediate
20 medical facility

유형 1

❶ that　❷ defence　❸ solidarity
❹ why　❺ those

유형 2

❶ living　❷ mediated　❸ paid
❹ to contribute　❺ varies

유형 3

❶ to varying degrees
❷ solidarity with fellow citizens
❸ are expected to
❹ existence of such expectations is universal

22번 ——————————— p.279

• Word Test

1 ~에 취약한, 영향받기 쉬운　2 노출　3 토양　4 독성의
5 위험한　6 다양하다, 각기 다르다　7 풍부한
8 요소, 원소　9 질병, 질환　10 기후, (특정 기후를 가진) 지역
11 unsanitary　12 derive　13 interaction
14 shell　15 geologic　16 contaminate
17 potentially　18 concentration　19 primitive
20 waters

유형 1

❶ which　❷ Primitive　❸ diseases
❹ where　❺ that

유형 2

❶ posed　❷ are　❸ harvested
❹ developed　❺ are

유형 3

❶ potentially hazardous　❷ live off the land
❸ In contrast　❹ complex interaction
❺ derived from soils

23번 ——————————— p.282

• Word Test

1 사회 기반 시설　2 전력망　3 지표
4 꼼짝 못 하는, 빠져나갈 수가 없는　5 뒤처지다
6 분산형의, 분권화된　7 원자재　8 이행, 실행
9 skip　10 suburb　11 aging　12 renewable
13 from scratch　14 land line　15 sustainability
16 harmful

유형 1

❶ than　❷ expensive　❸ inefficient
❹ much　❺ while　❻ where

유형 2

❶ to fix　❷ to rebuild　❸ to skip
❹ developing　❺ were
❻ to drive

유형 3

❶ from scratch
❷ stages of economic development
❸ decentralized renewable energy systems
❹ be stuck　❺ inefficient electrical grid
❻ are forced to

24-25번 ———————————— p.285

● Word Test

1 직관적인 **2** (역사적으로) 거슬러 올라가다
3 근본적인, 근원적인 **4** 반항 **5** 추론하다 **6** 이원론의
7 굴복하다, 양보하다 **8** 옹호자, 지지자 **9** 도덕
10 주관성 **11** 전념하다, 바치다 **12** 이해하다
13 objective **14** internal **15** adopt **16** soul
17 separation **18** genetics **19** unquantifiable
20 behaviorism **21** interpretive **22** humanities
23 approximation **24** evolutionary

유형 1

1 who **2** that **3** adopt
4 that **5** outside **6** and
7 that

유형 2

1 to understand **2** analyzed
3 be understood **4** devoted **5** to embrace
6 understand **7** yielding

유형 3

1 Echoes of this debate **2** religious methods
3 devoted to **4** dualistic separation
5 underlying claim

26-28번 ———————————— p.288

● Word Test

1 어리둥절한, 당혹스러운 **2** ~에게 놀랍게도 **3** 편안한
4 알아차리다 **5** 우아한, 품위 있는 **6** (~에) 적응하다
7 몹시, 대단히 **8** 처음에 **9** freshman **10** passion
11 interest **12** switch **13** let ~ down
14 care **15** drill **16** follow in one's footsteps

유형 1

1 the youngest **2** while **3** had seen
4 that **5** shook **6** when
7 to fit **8** find

유형 2

1 Following **2** love **3** plays
4 to be **5** to get **6** running
7 relaxed **8** to leave

유형 3

1 the youngest of three daughters
2 seemed to absolutely love
3 Somewhat puzzled **4** shook her head
5 let them down **6** fit in
7 In the process

---

p.292

01 ①	**02** ③	**03** ③	**04** ⑤	**05** ③	**06** ⑤
07 ③	**08** ⑤	**09** ⑤	**10** ④	**11** ⑤	**12** ③
13 ⑤	**14** ③	**15** ②	**16** ④	**17** ②	**18** ③
19 ②	**20** ⑤	**21** ⑤	**22** ⑤	**23** ⑤	**24** ④
25 ④	**26** ⑤	**27** ④	**28** ①	**29** ⑤	**30** ③
31 ③	**32** ④	**33** ④	**34** ⑤	**35** ③	**36** ⑤
37 ②	**38** ②	**39** ③	**40** ④	**41** ①	**42** ③
43 ④	**44** ③	**45** ⑤	**46** ⑤	**47** ①	**48** ②

49 With the year coming to a close **50** ensures
51 남부 캘리포니아 사막의 외딴 곳을 탐험함 **52** It never occurred to me to prepare for a storm!
53 (A) → when (B) → what (C) → how
54 No matter what kind, the majority of, function differently from **55** (1) ③ → contain
(2) ⑤ → to file **56** 정치가들이 해양 관련 사안에 관해 운동을 벌이는 일이 거의 없다 **57** ⑤ → emerged **58** (A) task
(B) serve **59** whose value lies entirely in the capacity to purchase things **60** consumption
61 nurture **62** to bring about personal well-being, joy, health and flourishing as well as planetary health
63 the factor that was most likely to help, was the subject **64** (A) → cited (B) → participated
(C) → is **65** ⑤ → faded **66** is considered one of the greatest jazz pianists of all time
67 wrinkles **68** Do not assemble or operate this device with wet hands. **69** (1) ② → swimming
(2) ④ → included **70** allows you to watch the sea turtles and to swim in the most extraordinary
71 disclosure **72** it difficult or impossible to determine, is attacking **73** revived the Egyptian reluctance to record the natural world
74 몸통은 정면을, 머리와 허리, 팔다리는 측면을 그렸다.
75 real kindness **76** (A) to be known
(B) who[that] (C) in which[where]
77 ② → ignore **78** closing local beach A due to pollution causes more people to visit
79 (A) → to show (B) → opened (C) → needed
80 hidden photos **81** interpreting delay as something other than that **82** overlook
83 do we attempt to appreciate and protect nature
84 nature **85** (a) sporting (b) architectural
86 (A) fixed (B) to be played (C) means
87 (1) ② → scared (2) ③ → have (3) ⑤ → disappointed
88 Audiences generally identify more with people and characters in the stories than with abstract discussion. **89** mediated **90** 생산적인 성인일 때 공익에 기여하고, 그 대가로 어릴 때는 교육을, 아프거나 실직하거나 늙었을 때는 부양을 받음 **91** (A) → the way(that / in which)[how] (B) → where[in which] (C) → because
92 are more likely to be affected by, such as
93 ④ → forced **94** 사회 기반 시설을 지속 가능하게 다시 짓는 것은 매우 많은 비용이 든다.
95 can be traced, as far back as **96** 인간의 내적 상태는 과학적으로는 결코 조사될 수 없으며 직관적, 해석적, 심지어 종교적 방법을 통해 비과학적으로 이해되어야 한다는 견해
97 seemed that Emily absolutely loved
98 (A) passion (B) runner

01 ①

문제해설

주어진 문장은 한 해가 마무리되어 가는데 일상의 것은 뒤로하고 특별한

모험을 감행해 보라고 권하는 내용으로, ① 이후에 하천 스포츠 활동을 위한 하천 허가증을 받을 수 있도록 추첨에 응모하라는 구체적인 권유가 시작되므로, 주어진 문장이 들어가기에 가장 적절한 곳은 ①이다.

02 ③

문제해설

갑작스러운 홍수를 벗어나기 위해 비탈을 기어올라 어둠 속 마구 쏟아지는 빗속에서 텐트를 쳤다는 내용의 주어진 글에 이어, 텐트 안으로 기어들어가는 것을 세탁기에 들어가는 것에 비유하며 침낭이 완전히 젖으면서 피로가 압도했다는 내용의 (B)가 오고, 피로로 눈꺼풀이 무거워지기 시작했을 때 자신이 마지막 학기 봄 방학 여행으로 낚시 여행에 합류하지 않은 것에 대해 스스로 비판하는 내용인 (C)가 이어진 후, Instead로 시작하여 낚시 여행 대신에 폭풍우에 전혀 대비되지 않은 채 사막 탐험에 나설 결심을 한 것을 후회하고 있는 내용인 (A)로 마무리하는 것이 자연스럽다.

03 ③

문제해설

상대방의 행동 양식과 의사소통 방법에 맞추어 우리의 의사소통 방식에 변화를 줄 때 유연한 의사소통이 가능해지고 의사소통 능력이 극적으로 증가될 수 있다는 내용이므로, 글의 제목으로 가장 적절한 것은 ③ '듣는 사람의 말투에 따라 당신의 의사소통 방식을 조정하라'이다.

오답노트

① 당신의 생각을 말하는 것의 어려움
② 일상생활에서 의사소통 능력의 중요성
④ 의사소통의 장벽은 무엇이고 그것을 극복하는 방법
⑤ 의사소통의 부재: 그것이 우리에게 미치는 영향과 개선하는 방법

04 ⑤

문제해설

해양의 중요성과 그것에 대한 우리의 큰 의존성에도 불구하고 해양은 현대 정치에 의해 홀대받고 있는데 그것의 어마어마한 크기와 영속성 때문에 우리는 해양이 악화의 영향을 받지 않을 것이라고 오해할 수 있다는 내용이 되어야 하므로 ⑤ susceptible(영향받기 쉬운)을 immune(영향받지 않는)과 같은 말로 바꿔야 한다.

05 ③

문제해설

업무의 본질이 사람의 본성보다 더 중요할 수 있어 업무 유형에 따라 서로 다른 성격적인 부분이 나타나며 우리 성격의 서로 다른 부분은 서로 다른 유형의 목적에 도움이 될 수 있다는 내용이므로, 빈칸에 들어갈 말로 가장 적절한 것은 ③ '흔히 사람보다는 과제에 더 달려 있다'이다.

오답노트

① 가변적이고 변동하기 쉽다
② 사람의 본성을 최대한 활용하다
④ 구성원 간의 화합을 강조한다
⑤ 항상 구성원들의 모든 성격 유형을 고려한다

06 ⑤

문제해설

선물은 비인격적인 자본주의 경제와는 다르고 그것과 대조되는 사랑과 의식의 사적 세계를 분명히 보여 주는 방법이지만, 선물의 가치는 자본주의의 영향을 받을 수 밖에 없어 그 둘은 서로 분리될 수 없다는 내용이므로, '선물을 주는 것의 의미는 자본주의 경제에 의해 강한 (A) 영향을 받는데

이는 선물을 주는 것에 의해 분명히 표현되는 사랑과 의식의 사적 세계가 그것으로부터 완전히 (B) 분리될 수 없기 때문이다.'와 같이 요약하는 것이 가장 적절하다.

오답노트

① 부정되는 …… 밀착될   ② 훼손되는 …… 분리될
③ 훼손되는 …… 독립적일   ④ 영향받는 …… 밀착될

07 ③

문제해설

더 지속 가능한 생활 양식으로의 전환은 우리가 자연의 일부임을 깨달으면서 자연 속에서 인간의 위치를 다시 그려 보는 데서 출발한다는 내용이므로, '구체적으로 지구의 건강 분야는 지구 자연계에 대한 인간의 파괴가 인간의 건강과 지구 상의 모든 생명체에 미치는 영향을 분석하고 해결하는 사회 운동에 초점을 맞추고 있다.'라는 ③은 글의 전체 흐름과 관계가 없다.

08 ⑤

문제해설

회사 대변인의 인용문을 포함하는 것이 기사를 공유하기에 적절하게 만든다고 응답한 언론인의 비율은 8퍼센트이고 간결함이 효과가 있을 거라고 말한 언론인의 비율은 20퍼센트인데 ⑤는 more than half(절반 이상)이라고 했으므로 도표의 내용과 일치하지 않는다.

09 ⑤

문제해설

⑤ 동사 embrace의 목적어가 빠진 불완전한 구조를 이끌면서 선행사 a movement를 수식하는 절을 이끄는 자리이므로 관계대명사 what을 that으로 고쳐야 한다.

오답노트

① 주어 Art Tatum이 역사상 가장 위대한 재즈 피아니스트 중 한 명으로 여겨진다는 수동의 의미이므로 수동형 동사 is considered를 쓰는 것은 적절하다.
② 관계대명사 which절 내에서 선행사 their technical skills and creativity에 대한 동사가 필요하므로 과거형 동사 set을 쓰는 것은 적절하다.
③ 전치사 after의 목적어 자리이므로 동명사 starting을 쓰는 것은 적절하다.
④ '주로, 대개'라는 의미로 뒤따르는 전치사구 in the trio format을 수식하는 자리이므로 부사 mostly를 쓰는 것은 적절하다.

10 ④

문제해설

If anything gets into the jack, contact the manufacturer. Do not attempt to remove it yourself.에서 잭 안으로 무언가가 들어갈 경우 그것을 꺼내려고 하지 말고 제조 업체로 연락하라고 했으므로, ④는 안내문의 내용과 일치한다.

11 ⑤

문제해설

Lunch is not included. You're welcome to bring your own packed lunch, which can be consumed on board.에서 점심 식사는 포함되어 있지 않으며 선상에서 먹을 수 있는 도시락을 직접 싸 와도 된다고 했으므로, ⑤는 안내문의 내용과 일치하지 않는다.

12 ③

문제해설

물리적 공간에 존재하는 재래식 무기나 핵무기와는 대조적으로 사이버 무기는 불투명성으로부터 유용성을 얻는데 사이버 무기의 침입은 사용자의 허락이나 인지 없이 시스템에 대한 접근 권한을 얻어 시스템이 원래 의도된 용도에 맞게 쓰일 수 없게 할 수 있으므로 ③ available(이용 가능한)을 unavailable(이용될 수 없는)과 같은 말로 바꿔야 한다

13 ⑤

문제해설

고대 이집트 예술은 입체감이나 거리감을 표현하려고 시도하지 않는 등 자연계를 정확히 표현하기를 꺼려했는데, 이러한 그림 방식을 그대로 계승하여 중세 예술가들도 가장 단순화된 방법으로 형태를 묘사했다는 내용이므로, 글의 제목으로 가장 적절한 것은 ⑤ '고대 이집트 미술의 충실한 계승자로서의 중세 미술'이다.

오답노트

① 무엇이 고대 이집트 예술을 위대하게 만들까?
② 한 사람의 독특한 관점의 형태로서의 예술
③ 중세 미술은 고대 이집트 미술과 어떻게 다른가?
④ 사실적 입체감: 중세 미술의 뚜렷한 특징

14 ③

문제해설

진정한 우정은 모르는 사람에게 널리 알려지는 것을 추구하는 것에서 오는 것이 아니라 소수의 친밀하고 호혜적인 관계의 결실이라는 내용이므로, '의사소통 능력과 스트레스 관리 기술은 갈등 관리뿐만 아니라 관계 속에서 신뢰, 유대감, 안전감을 형성하는 데에도 필수적이다.'라는 ③은 글의 전체 흐름과 관계가 없다.

15 ②

문제해설

경제적 현상을 분석할 때 분리해서 보는 단순한 지표는 오해를 일으키는 관점을 제공할 수 있기 때문에 잘못된 결론을 도출하지 않기 위해서는 좀 더 포괄적인 경제 분석이 적용되어야 한다는 내용이므로 글의 요지로 가장 적절한 것은 ②이다.

16 ④

문제해설

주어진 문장은 역접의 연결어 Yet을 포함하여 그러한 숨겨진 사진들은 이미지 제작 과정에 결정적으로 중요하다는 내용으로, ④ 앞 문장에서 사진작가들이 사진 제작을 위해 많은 에너지와 시간을 투자하지만 사진 대부분은 그들이 기대하는 품질을 나타내지 못한다는 내용이 언급되고 있고 ④ 뒷부분에서 관객들에게 공개되지 않는 사진들이 창조적 대성공에 도달하는 단계별 발전 과정의 일부라는 내용이 언급되고 있으므로, 주어진 문장이 들어가기에 가장 적절한 곳은 ④이다.

17 ②

문제해설

명확한 기한과 과제를 정하는 것이 지연을 그것이 아닌 어떤 것으로 해석하는 것을 피하는 데 도움이 된다는 내용의 주어진 글에 이어, 건강상 문제로 인해 진료 예약을 고려하고 있는 Gary의 사례를 들어 주어진 글에 대한 예시가 시작되는 부분인 (B)가 오고, Gary의 계획에서 구체성이 결여된 것이 그에게 진료 예약을 미루고 있는 것에 대한 합리화의 여지를 준다는 내용의 (A)가 이어진 후, 앞에서 언급한 상황을 In such contexts(그러한 상황에서)로 받아 캘린더에 전화를 걸기 위한 구체적인 시간과 자동 알림을 입력하면 정해진 시간에 전화를 걸지 않는 것이 지연이라는 것을 간과하기 어렵게 될 것이라는 내용의 (C)로 마무리하는 것이 자연스럽다.

18 ③

문제해설

우리는 자연을 미래 세대의 안전을 위해 보존되어야 할 희소한 자원으로 취급하여 목표 지향적인 노력을 하려고 할 뿐 그것의 진가를 인정하고 보호하려는 시도를 거의 하지 않는다는 내용이므로 글의 요지로 가장 적절한 것은 ③이다.

19 ②

문제해설

(A) 스포츠는 건축물이 필요하지 않으며 들판이 여러 운동을 위한 운동장 역할을 할 수 있어서 영국 초창기 축구 경기는 고정된 크기 없이 도시 경관 전체에 걸쳐 열렸을 것이므로, fixed(고정된)가 적절하다. unfixed는 '고정되지 않은'이라는 뜻이다.
(B) 스포츠 건축물을 설계하고 짓기 위해서는 열리게 될 경기의 규칙과 그 활동을 수행하는 데 필요한 최소한의 공간의 크기에 대한 체계화가 마련되어 있어야 한다는 문맥이 자연스러우므로, undertake(수행하다)가 적절하다. overtake는 '~을 따라잡다'라는 뜻이다.
(C) 스포츠 건축물은 다양한 경기 규칙의 체계화와 설계 및 건축의 수단과 양식이 교차하는 지점에서 생겨나는 것이므로, emerges(나타나다)가 적절하다. disappear는 '사라지다'라는 뜻이다.

20 ⑤

문제해설

빈칸 앞에서는 어려움을 겪는 주인공의 구체적 사례를 통해 신데렐라와 인터뷰 대상자라는 중심인물에 대해 언급하고 있고 빈칸 뒤에서는 비즈니스 스토리텔링에서 중심인물이 한 명도 없을 때 인물들이 이야기의 본문에 엮어질 수 있다고 했으므로, 빈칸에 들어갈 말로 가장 적절한 것은 ⑤ '추상적 논의보다 이야기 속 사람들과 인물들에 더 동질감을 갖는다.'이다.

오답노트

① 그들이 이야기를 듣는 동안 마음을 졸이고 싶어 하지 않다
② 자신의 환상과 상상력을 자극하기 위해 만들어진 인물들을 좋아한다
③ 이야기가 먼저 결론부터 시작할 때 그것의 논리를 이해하고 따라가다
④ 착한 사람이 보답을 받는 행복한 결말을 가진 동화에 관심을 기울이다

21 ⑤

문제해설

역사를 통틀어 사람들이 대규모 집단으로 사는 데에서 오는 이득을 누리고 거기서 오는 위험을 관리하기 위해 자신들의 자원을 공동 관리해 왔다는 내용의 주어진 글에 이어, These benefits로 주어진 글에서 언급한 이득을 구체적으로 명시한 후, 집단이 커지면서 상호 간의 의무가 동료 시민과의 연대나 국가에 대한 임무로 변한다는 내용의 (C)가 오고, 그 예로 오늘날 사회적 약자 대부분이 국가의 비용에 의존하기 때문에 사람들은 생산적인 성인일 때 공익에 기여하고 어릴 때 교육받고 병들거나 실직하거나 늙었을 때 부양받을 것으로 기대된다는 내용의 (B)가 이어진 후, 이러한 기대(these expectations)의 속성이 문화적 규범, 제도, 정책과 법에 따라 다르지만 그런 기대가 존재하는 것은 보편적이라는 내용인 (A)로 마무리하는 것이 자연스럽다.

22 ⑤

문제해설

토양에서의 자연적 과정이 잠재적으로 위험한 지질 물질을 한 곳에 집중시
킨다는 내용의 글에서 칼슘이 자연 수역에 풍부한 아프리카와 아시아 일부
지역은 주혈흡충증을 유발하는 달팽이가 많지만, 남아메리카의 수역은 칼
슘이 부족해서 그 질병이 희귀하다고 했으므로 질병의 유발 원인이 칼슘의
자연적인 집중에서 비롯되었음을 알 수 있다. 따라서 빈칸에 들어갈 말로
가장 적절한 것은 ⑤ '집중'이다.

오답노트

① 감소 　　② 멸종 　　③ 진화 　　④ 번식

23 ⑤

문제해설

개발 도상국은 환경적으로 해로운 기술의 사용을 건너뛰어 지속 가능한 방
법으로 발전할 가능성이 있는 반면에 미국은 낡고 비효율적인 기술과 노후
화된 사회 기반 시설에 의존할 수밖에 없어서 지속 가능하게 발전하는 것
이 어려운 상황이라는 내용이므로, 글의 주제로 가장 적절한 것은 ⑤ '미국
이 지속 가능한 개발에 있어 뒤처지고 있는 주된 이유'이다.

오답노트

① 지속 가능한 발전에 대한 전 세계적인 접근
② 환경적으로 지속 가능한 개발에 있어서 미국의 핵심적인 역할
③ 많은 국가들의 현재 사회 기반 시설의 상태 비교
④ 환경적으로 해로운 기술의 사용을 막는 방법

24 ④

문제해설

몇몇 사상가들은 인간의 내적 상태를 과학적으로 조사할 수 없다고 간주
했으며, 행동주의 옹호자 Skinner조차 내적 정신 상태는 관찰이 불가능
하고 수량화할 수 없는 주관성을 지녀 객관적인 과학적 면밀한 조사의 범
위 밖에 속한다고 추론했으므로, 글의 요지로 가장 적절한 것은 ④이다.

25 ④

문제해설

빈칸 뒤에서 우리가 과학을 이용해 영혼, 감정, 사고, 도덕, 미를 완전히 이
해할 수 없다는 근본적인 주장을 했다는 내용이 이어지고 있는 것으로 보
아 몇몇 철학자들과 신학자들은 물질세계와 정신세계 간의 아주 오래된 분
리를 받아들였을 것이므로, 빈칸에 들어갈 말로 가장 적절한 것은 ④ '이원
론적 분리'이다.

오답노트

① 잠재적인 갈등
② 지속적인 조화
③ 합리적인 통합
⑤ 부자연스러운 공존

26 ⑤

문제해설

(a), (b), (c), (d)는 모두 Emily를 가리키고 (e)는 Emily의 코치를 가리
킨다.

27 ④

문제해설

She wasn't surprised to learn that Emily had a passion for

running.에서 그녀는 Emily가 달리기에 열정이 있다는 것을 알고 놀라
지 않았다고 했으므로, ④는 글의 내용과 일치하지 않는다.

28 ①

문제해설

Emily가 축구 선수로서 뛰어난 기량을 보였지만 축구에 대한 열정을 보
여주지 않자, 그녀가 달리기에 열정이 있다는 것을 발견한 코치가 Emily
가 축구팀에서 떠나는 것을 허락했고 이후 Emily가 여자 크로스컨트리 팀
에서 최고 주자로 팀을 결승전까지 이끌었다는 내용이므로, 빈칸에 들어갈
말로 가장 적절한 것은 ① 'Emily가 자신의 진정한 열정을 찾도록 도와주
었다'이다.

오답노트

② 달리기 클럽에 가입하려고 축구팀을 떠났다
③ Emily의 가족을 설득하는 데 어려움을 겪었다
④ Emily의 부족한 열정에 실망했다
⑤ Emily와의 관계를 회복할 방법을 찾았다

29 ⑤

문제해설

(A) with 분사구문에서 with의 목적어가 the year이고 목적격 보어와
의 관계가 의미상 능동이므로 현재분사 coming이 적절하다.
(B) to 부정사의 의미상의 주어 the chance와 to부정사의 관계가 의미
상 수동이므로 be awarded가 적절하다.
(C) 타동사 helps의 목적어 자리로 to부정사나 동사원형이 와야 하므로
manage가 적절하다.

30 ③

문제해설

주어진 문장은 필자가 눈꺼풀이 무거워지기 시작했을 때 자신의 봄 방학
휴일을 위한 활동 선택을 비판하기 시작했다는 내용으로, ③ 앞 문장에서
침낭이 완전히 젖으면서 피로가 압도했다는 내용이 언급되고 있고 ③ 다음
문장에서 낚시 여행에 친구들과 함께할 수도 있었다고 후회하는 내용이 언
급되고 있으므로, 주어진 문장이 들어가기에 가장 적절한 곳은 ③이다.

31 ③

문제해설

상대방의 행동 양식과 의사소통 방법에 맞추어 우리의 의사소통 방식에 변
화를 줄 때 유연한 의사소통이 가능해지고 의사소통 방법의 근거를 단지
자신의 선호에만 둘 수 없다고 했으므로, 빈칸에 들어갈 말로 가장 적절한
것은 ③ '유연성과 다른 사람들의 요구를 이해하는 능력'이다.

오답노트

① 관객들의 마음을 사로잡는 것
② 적절한 몸짓 언어 및 얼굴 표정을 사용하는 것
④ 간단하고 간결한 방식으로 자신의 요점을 전달하는 기술
⑤ 진정성과 듣는 사람을 위한 편안한 분위기를 조성하는 것

32 ④

문제해설

해양의 중요성과 그것에 대한 우리의 큰 의존성에도 불구하고 현대의 정치
는 해양을 홀대하고 있고 해양 및 그것과 관련된 사안에 관해 우리는 많은
관심을 두지 않는다는 내용이므로 글의 요지로 가장 적절한 것은 ④이다.

33 ④

문제해설

가장 효과가 있는 전략은 흔히 사람보다는 과제에 더 달려 있어 업무 유형에 따라 서로 다른 성격적인 부분이 나타난다는 내용이므로, '즉, 외향적으로 행동할 때 사람들은 높은 수준의 행복을 보고하고, 이것은 내향적인 사람과 외향적인 사람 모두에게 똑같이 적용된다.'라는 ④는 글의 전체 흐름과 관계가 없다.

34 ⑤

문제해설

선물을 주는 것의 의미는 자본주의 경제에 의해 강한 영향을 받는데 이는 선물을 주는 것으로 분명히 표현되는 사랑과 의식의 사적 세계가 자본주의 경제와 서로 연결되어 있어서 둘을 완전히 분리할 수 없기 때문이라는 내용이므로 ⑤ independent(독립적인)을 interconnected(서로 연결된)와 같은 말로 바꿔야 한다.

35 ③

문제해설

(A) 현재분사 realizing의 의미상 주어가 문장의 주어 we이고 목적어 역시 같은 대상을 가리키고 있으므로 재귀대명사 ourselves가 적절하다.
(B) the potential for reconnection의 내용을 부연하기 위한 형용사 역할의 to 부정사 자리이므로 동사원형 bring이 적절하다.
(C) show의 목적어에 해당하는 that절 안에는 주어 well-being에 대한 동사가 필요하므로 is가 적절하다.

36 ⑤

문제해설

his popularity faded in the mid to late 1940s with the advent of bebop — a movement that Tatum did not embrace.에서 그의 인기가 비밥의 등장과 함께 1940년대 중후반에 시들해졌다고 했으므로, ⑤는 글의 내용과 일치하지 않는다.

37 ②

문제해설

재래식 무기와 핵무기는 물리적 공간에 존재해서 그것들의 배치와 능력의 인식이 가능하다는 내용의 주어진 글에 이어, By contrast라는 대조의 연결어로 시작하여 대조적으로 사이버 무기는 불투명성으로부터 유용성을 얻는다는 내용의 (B)가 오고, 사이버 무기의 침입은 사용자의 허락이나 인지 없이 시스템에 대한 접근 권한을 얻어 시스템이 원래 의도된 용도에 맞게 이용될 수 없게 할 수 있다는 것에 대한 예시로 DDoS 공격을 언급하고 있는 (A)가 이어진 후, DDoS 공격을 In such cases로 받아 그런 경우 공격의 진짜 근원이 감춰질 수 있어서 누가 공격하고 있는지 알아내는 것이 불가능할 수 있다는 내용의 (C)로 마무리하는 것이 자연스럽다.

38 ②

문제해설

고대 이집트 예술 방식을 그대로 계승한 중세 예술가들은 엄격한 규칙이 존재하는 문화 속에서 단순화되고 정형화된 형태의 묘사를 선호했다는 내용이므로, 빈칸에 들어갈 말로 가장 적절한 것은 ② '엄격한 방식에 부합하는'이다.

오답노트

① 종교적 이상을 거부한
③ 현실과 반대로 표현되는
④ 인간성을 직접적으로 드러내지 않는

⑤ 형식에 구애받지 않은

39 ③

문제해설

진정한 우정은 모르는 사람에게 널리 알려지는 것을 추구하는 것에서 오는 것이 아니라 소수의 친밀하고 호혜적인 관계의 결실이라는 내용이므로, 글의 제목으로 가장 적절한 것은 ③ '진정한 만족은 소수의 참된 친구들로부터 온다'이다.

오답노트

① 명성과 우정 중 더 나은 것은 무엇인가?
② 참된 친구는 사람들이 생각하는 것에 신경 쓰지 않는다
④ 널리 알려짐을 추구하는 것: 진정한 우정으로 가는 지름길
⑤ 우정에 관한 한 '많을수록 좋다'가 항상 옳다

40 ④

문제해설

주어진 문장은 B 해수욕장에 대한 방문자 수만을 바라보는 분석가는 A 해수욕장의 폐쇄에 대한 고려 없이 단순한 지표만을 고려함으로써 잘못된 결론을 도출할 수도 있다는 내용으로, ④ 앞의 문장에서 오염으로 인해 A 해수욕장이 폐쇄되면 더 많은 사람이 오염되지 않은 B 해수욕장을 방문하게 된다고 가정해 보라는 내용이 있고, ④ 뒤의 문장에서 적절한 경제 분석 틀을 사용하면 오해를 일으키는 그러한 결론을 방지할 수 있다는 내용이 언급되고 있으므로, 주어진 문장이 들어가기에 가장 적절한 곳은 ④이다.

41 ①

문제해설

(A) 눈을 감고 있거나, 노출이 좋지 않거나, 관람객에게 보이고 싶지 않은 수많은 사진들이 편집 중에 삭제된다는 내용으로 보아 관객들은 전문가의 작은 일부의 사진을 보는 것이므로, fraction(일부, 부분)이 적절하다. friction은 '마찰'이라는 뜻이다.
(B) Joel Meyerowitz와 같은 거리 사진작가들이 수천 장의 사진을 제작하여 뛰어난 안목으로 자신의 관람객이 보기를 원하는 것을 선택할 것이므로, discriminating(판단력이 뛰어난)이 적절하다. indiscriminate는 '지각없는, 무분별한'이라는 뜻이다.
(C) 숨겨진 사진들은 창조적 대성공에 도달하는 데 필요한 실패와 실험의 단계들을 보여 주는 단계별 발전 과정의 일부여서 이미지 제작 과정에 중요할 것이므로, important(중요한)가 적절하다. unimportant는 '중요하지 않은'이라는 뜻이다.

42 ③

문제해설

계획에 대한 명확한 기한과 과제를 정함으로써 지연을 지연이 아닌 다른 어떤 것으로 해석하는 것을 피하는데 도움이 된다는 내용이므로, '우리의 주의가 과제를 향하도록 하고 방해하는 것으로부터 벗어나도록 조정하는 구조를 (A) 설계함으로써, 우리는 (B) 지연을 제멋대로 해석하려는 유혹을 견딜 수 있다.'와 같이 요약하는 것이 가장 적절하다.

오답노트

① 피함 …… 게으름   ② 피함 …… 실패
④ 설계함 …… 실패   ⑤ 우선시함 …… 지연

43 ④

문제해설

우리는 자연을 보존해야 할 희소한 자원으로 간주하고 목표 지향적인 노력을 하려고 할 뿐이며 자연의 다양성을 본질적으로 의미가 있고, 우리가 관

여할 가치가 있는 것으로 이해하는 어휘가 없다고 했으므로, 빈칸에 들어
갈 말로 가장 적절한 것은 ④ '자연의 진가를 인정하고 보호하려는'이다.

오답노트

① 자연을 충분히 이용할
② 자연의 모든 측면을 즐길
③ 순수한 호기심에서 자연과 접촉할
⑤ 자연이 우리에게 가르쳐 준 것이 있을지도 모른다고 생각할

44 ③

문제해설

들판이 여러 운동을 위한 운동장 역할을 할 수 있고, 여러 스포츠가 자연의
설계되지 않은 장소에서 이루어질 수 있음에도 스포츠 건축물은 역사를 거
슬러 올라가 스포츠상의 그리고 건축상의 이유 양면에서 의미가 있다는 내
용의 글이다. 따라서 '스포츠와 스포츠 건축물의 세계화와 관련된 긴장감
은 거금의 돈이 팬들과 경기 사이의 오래된 관계에 어떻게 영향을 미치는
지를 중심으로 돈다.'라는 ③은 글의 전체 흐름과 관계가 없다.

45 ⑤

문제해설

청중은 일반적으로 추상적 논의보다 이야기 속 사람들 그리고 인물들과 더
동질감을 가지므로 비즈니스 스토리텔링에서 중심인물이 한 명도 없을 때
인물들이 이야기의 본문에 엮어질 수 있다는 내용의 글이다. 따라서 글의
제목으로 가장 적절한 것은 ⑤ '효과적인 비즈니스 스토리텔링을 위해 인
물을 포함시켜라'이다.

오답노트

① 위대한 동화들의 공통적인 특징
② 가벼운 이야기는 비즈니스 환경에 활력을 불어넣을 수 있다
③ 비즈니스에서의 사실적 스토리텔링의 장단점
④ 무언가를 협상할 때 자신만의 이야기로 시작하라

46 ⑤

문제해설

⑤ the rights and obligations를 받는 대명사 자리로 형용사구 of
the wider society의 후치 수식을 받고 있으므로 them을 those로 고
쳐야 한다.

오답노트

① the benefits와 the risks를 공통으로 수식하면서 뒤에 주어가 빠진
불완전한 구조가 이어지고 있으므로 주격 관계대명사 that을 쓰는 것은
적절하다.
② 불완전 자동사 become의 주격 보어 자리이므로 형용사 abstract를
쓰는 것은 적절하다.
③ 의미상의 주어인 schools ~ unemployment benefits를 수식하
는 자리로 '비용을 대는'이라는 의미상 수동의 관계이므로, 과거분사 paid
를 쓰는 것은 적절하다.
④ and를 중심으로 to contribute와 병렬을 이루는 자리에서 to부정사
의 to가 생략되어 있으므로 동사원형 get을 쓰는 것은 적절하다.

47 ①

문제해설

토양에서의 자연적 과정이 잠재적으로 위험한 지질 물질을 한 곳에 집중
시킨다는 내용의 주어진 글에 이어, 주어진 글에서 언급된 hazardous
geologic materials를 these elements로 받으면서 이러한 요소들
에 의해 제기되는 건강 위험은 인간이 환경과 상호 작용하는 방식에 따라
좌우되는데 토지에 의해 살아가는 낙후된 문화는 어떤 질병에 취약한지에

대해 구체화한 내용의 (A)가 오고, 대조의 연결어 In contrast로 시작하
여 더 선진화된 사회의 건강 위험을 언급한 후 어떤 질병들은 인간, 곤충,
기후, 그리고 환경에 있는 특정 요소의 자연 집중 사이의 복잡한 상호 작용
을 반영한다는 내용의 (C)가 이어진 후, 이에 대해 자연에 집중된 칼슘의
양에 따라 주혈흡충증이라는 질병이 지역에 따라 다르게 나타난다는 예시
를 들고 있는 (B)로 마무리하는 것이 자연스럽다.

48 ②

문제해설

(A) 립프로깅을 통해 개발 도상국이 선진국에서 사용되었던 낡고 비효율
적인 기술의 이행을 건너 뛴다면 환경에 해로운 경제 개발 단계를 거치지
않게 될 수 있으므로, avoiding(피하게 되는)이 적절하다.
(B) 개발 도상국들에서 사람들이 더 지속 가능하게 살 수 있는 도시
에 개발을 집중시킨다면 도시 주변의 녹지 공간은 보호될 것이므로,
preserve(보존하다)가 적절하다.

오답노트

① 피하게 되는 …… 줄이다   ③ 규제하는 …… 훼손하다
④ 규제하는 …… 보존하다   ⑤ 겪는 …… 훼손하다

49 With the year coming to a close

문제해설

〈with+(의미상) 주어+분사〉는 동시 상황을 나타내는 분사구문으로 자주
쓰이는데, '~가 …하는[인] 상황에서', 혹은 '~을 …하면서'라는 의미로 사
용된다. with 뒤의 주어 the year와 동사 come은 능동의 관계를 나타
내므로 come을 현재분사 coming으로 쓴다.

50 ensures

문제해설

'어떤 일이 일어나거나 이루어졌는지 확인하다'라는 의미의 단어는
ensure(틀림없이 하다, 보장하다)이며 주어가 It이므로 단수형 동사
ensures가 적절하다.

51 남부 캘리포니아 사막의 외딴 곳을 탐험함

문제해설

'나의 활동 선택'이라는 의미로 글 후반부 head out to explore ~
desert에서 친구들과 낚시 여행을 가는 대신 외딴 사막 지역을 탐험하기
로 했음을 알 수 있다.

52 It never occurred to me to prepare for a storm!

문제해설

to부정사 진주어를 '폭풍우에 대비하는 것'이라는 의미가 되게 to
prepare for a storm으로 쓴다. occur to me는 '나에게 (어떤 생각
이) 떠오르다'라는 의미이므로 가주어 it 뒤에 두는 데 빈도부사 never는
일반동사 앞에 오는 것이 자연스러우므로 occur 앞에 쓰며 시제는 과거
이므로 It never occurred로 쓴다.

53 (A) → when (B) → what (C) → how

문제해설

(A) 완전한 문장 구조가 이어지고 '우리와 다른 사람들과 대화할 때'라는
의미가 되어야 하므로 부사절의 접속사 when으로 고쳐야 한다.
(B) 앞에 선행사가 없고 불완전한 구조가 이어지므로 선행사를 포함하고
있으면서 '~하는 것'이라는 뜻을 담고 있는 관계대명사 what으로 고쳐 써
야 한다.
(C) '아마도 어떻게 반응할까에 대한'이라는 의미를 나타내므로 how로

고쳐 써야 한다.

54 No matter what kind, the majority of, function differently from

문제해설

'어떤 종류의 ~이[을] ...라고 해도'라는 의미는 no matter what kind of로 쓰고, '~의 다수'라는 의미의 the majority of를 이용하여 '대부분의 사람들'이라는 표현을 만든다. '움직일 것이다'라는 의미의 will function을 쓰고 부사구 differently from이 오도록 하면 된다.

55 (1) ③ → contain (2) ⑤ → to file

문제해설

③ 〈few of+복수명사〉가 주어로 쓰인 경우 복수 취급을 하므로 contains는 contain으로 고쳐야 한다.
⑤ '~하도록 유혹받다'는 〈be tempted to-v〉이므로 to file로 고쳐야 한다.

오답노트

① 〈분수 표현+of+명사〉는 of 뒤에 나오는 명사의 수에 일치시키는데 surface가 단수이므로 단수 동사 lies는 적절하다.
② 주어 anyone이 forgive의 대상이 되므로 수동형 be forgiven은 적절하다.
④ emerge를 강조하는 do동사로 2016년에 있었던 사건이므로 과거형 동사 did는 적절하다.

56 정치가들이 해양 관련 사안에 관해 운동을 벌이는 일이 거의 없다

문제해설

our politicians ~ ocean-related issues에서 해양이 도대체 거기에 있기나 한 것인지 의아해 할 정도로 정치가들이나 정치와 관련된 사람들이 무관심하여서 정치가들이 해양 관련 사안에 관해 운동을 벌이는 일이 거의 없게 되었다는 내용이 나와 있다.

57 ⑤ → emerged

문제해설

성실성은 처리해야 할 일이 어렵고 긴급할 때, 그리고 심지어 특별히 체계적이도 근면하지도 않은 사람에게도 나타났다고 하는 것이 문맥상 자연스러우므로 ⑤ vanished(사라졌다)를 emerged(나타났다)와 같은 말로 바꿔 써야 한다.

58 (A) task (B) serve

문제해설

업무의 본질이 사람의 본성보다 더 중요할 수 있어서 업무 유형에 따라 서로 다른 성격적인 부분이 나타날 수 있다는 글로서, '하나의 학습 스타일이 성공에 가장 효과적인 접근 방식은 아니며, 오히려 가장 효과적인 전략은 그 사람의 본질보다 (A) 업무의 본질에 더 의존할 수 있고, 우리 성격의 다른 부분들은 다른 유형의 목표에 (B) 기여할 수 있다.'와 같이 요약할 수 있다.

59 whose value lies entirely in the capacity to purchase things

문제해설

'그것의 가치'가 관계절의 주어가 되어야 하고, 10단어로 해야 하므로 of which 대신에 whose value로 표현한다. '전적으로 달려 있다'는 lies entirely in으로 쓰며, '구매할 능력'은 capacity to purchase로 표현

하고 뒤에 목적어 things를 쓴다.

60 consumption

문제해설

'연료나 에너지 같은 것을 사용하거나, 또는 사람들이 사용하는 양'라는 의미의 단어는 consumption(소비)이다.

61 nurture

문제해설

'어린 아이, 동물 또는 식물이 성장하고 발달하는 데 필요한 보살핌과 관심을 제공하다'라는 의미이고, 우리가 분리된 존재가 아니라 영원히 생물권을 보살펴야할 책임이 있는 전체의 일부라는 내용이므로 빈칸에는 nurture(보살피다, 육성하다)가 적절하다.

62 to bring about personal well-being, joy, health and flourishing as well as planetary health

문제해설

〈not just [only] A but also B〉는 'A뿐만 아니라 B도 또한'이라는 의미로 〈B as well as A〉로 바꿔 쓸 수 있다.

63 the factor that was most likely to help, was the subject

문제해설

선행사 the factor(요인)을 수식하는 관계절의 주격 관계대명사 that을 쓰고 이어 '가장 ~할 것 같다'라는 의미를 나타내는 〈be most likely +to-v〉 구문을 활용한다. 시제가 과거이므로 관계절의 be동사도 was로, 보어 역할을 하는 the subject앞에도 과거형 was를 사용한다.

64 (A) → cited (B) → participated (C) → is

문제해설

(A) '두 번째로 많이 인용되는'이라는 수동의 의미가 되어야 하므로 과거분사 cited로 고쳐야 한다.
(B) 주격 관계대명사 바로 뒤의 동사가 와야 하는 자리이므로 과거형 participated로 고쳐야 한다.
(C) the percentage가 주어로 단수 취급하므로 동사 is로 고쳐야 한다.

65 ⑤ → faded

문제해설

바로 앞에 'Tatum이 많은 재즈 음악인들에게 존경을 받고 있었음에도 불구하고'라는 표현이 나오고 있으므로 그의 인기가 '하락했다'라고 해야 자연스럽다. 따라서 ⑤ soared(올랐다)를 faded(시들었다)와 같은 단어로 고쳐야 한다.

66 is considered one of the greatest jazz pianists of all time

문제해설

'~로 여기다'라는 의미는 is considered로 쓰고, 보어로 '가장 ~한 …중 하나'라는 표현인 〈one of the+형용사의 최상급+복수명사〉를 활용한다. of all time은 문장 끝에 오게 한다.

67 wrinkles

문제해설

'나이가 들면서 피부에 생기는 선'이라는 의미의 단어는 wrinkle(주름살)이며 맥락상 복수형 wrinkles가 적절하다.

68 Do not assemble or operate this device with wet hands.

문제해설

부정명령문에 쓰이는 Don't ~ 대신 축약형이 아닌 Do not ~ 형식의 표현을 사용한다. '젖은 손으로'는 with wet hands로 쓴다.

69 (1) ② → swimming (2) ④ → included

문제해설

② '~하기를 즐기다'라는 의미는 〈enjoy+v-ing〉이므로 swimming으로 고쳐야 한다.
④ 점심은 포함되지 않는 것이라는 의미이므로 수동형 과거분사 included로 고쳐야 한다.

오답노트

① '가이드가 동행된다'는 의미의 과거분사형 형용사 guided는 적절하다.
③ 부대상황을 나타내는 분사구문으로 현재분사 depending은 적절하다.
⑤ 콤마 뒤에서 앞의 선행사 your own packed lunch를 부가적으로 설명하고 있는 계속적 용법의 관계대명사 which는 적절하다.

70 allows you to watch the sea turtles and to swim in the most extraordinary

문제해설

〈allow+목적어+to-v〉을 활용하되, to-v 부분이 접속사 and로 병렬되고 있다. 따라서 to watch the sea turtle와 to swim in the most extraordinary를 병렬시키면 된다.

71 disclosure

문제해설

빈칸 앞에는 재래식 무기는 파악이 되고 대략 계산이 가능하지만, 사이버 무기는 불투명성으로부터 유용성을 얻는다는 내용이다. 또한 빈칸 뒤에서 '그들의 사이버 무기의 침입이 undisclosed flaws(공개되지 않은 결함)를 이용해 발각되지 않고 네트워크나 시스템에 접근할 수 있다'고 했으므로 빈칸에는 disclosure(공개[폭로])임을 추론할 수 있다.

72 it difficult or impossible to determine, is attacking

문제해설

make 뒤에 가목적어 it을 넣어서 '~을 알아내기가 어렵거나 불가능하게 만들다'는 의미가 되도록 make it difficult or impossible to determine로 쓴다. 관계절의 be동사로 현재진행형에 사용되는 is가 나왔으므로 attack은 is attacking으로 표현한다.

73 revived the Egyptian reluctance to record the natural world

문제해설

'부활시켰다'에 해당하는 과거시제 동사 revived 뒤에 목적어에 해당하는 명사구를 만들어 주면 되는데 '이집트인들의 꺼림'을 the Egyptian reluctance로 쓰고 이를 수식하는 to부정사구를 써서 완성한다.

74 몸통은 정면을, 머리와 허리, 팔다리는 측면을 그렸다.

문제해설

고대 이집트인들이 사람을 묘사하는 특징은 글 중반부의 the torso was drawn from the front, but the head ~ were drawn in profile 에 잘 나타나 있다.

75 real kindness

문제해설

바로 앞 문장 '그러나 진정한 호의는 대중의 영역에서 결코 구할 수 없다'에서 주어인 real kindness(진정한 호의)를 가리킨다.

76 (A) to be known (B) who[that] (C) in which[where]

문제해설

(A) '사람들에게 알려지는 것을 애쓴다'라는 의미가 되어야 하므로 수동형 to be known으로 고쳐야 한다.
(B) It ~ that 강조구문으로 강조 대상이 the very anxious로 사람들을 나타내므로 that 대신에 who를 쓸 수도 있다. 따라서 what을 who 또는 that으로 고쳐야 한다.
(C) 완전한 문장 구조가 이어지고 있으므로 which를 in which 또는 where로 고쳐야 한다.

77 ② → ignore

문제해설

경제적 가치를 인간의 활동과 분리해서 보면 잘못된 관점을 제공할 수 있다고 전제한 뒤 이를 뒷받침하는 내용이 이어지고 있다. 단순 활동 지표는 비사용자에 의해 실현된 값 혹은 측정되지 않은 활동과 관련된 이익을 무시한다라고 해야 문맥상 자연스러우므로 ② reflect(반영하다)는 ignore(무시하다)와 같은 말로 바꿔 써야 한다.

78 closing local beach A due to pollution causes more people to visit

문제해설

주어부인 '오염으로 인한 지역의 A 해수욕장 폐쇄'는 동명사를 써서 closing local beach A due to pollution으로 표현한다. 그 뒤에 '~가 …하는 원인이 되다'라는 표현으로 〈cause+목적어+to-v〉를 이용하는데, 동명사구 주어가 단수이므로 causes more people to visit로 쓰면 된다.

79 (A) → to show (B) → opened (C) → needed

문제해설

(A) choose 뒤에는 목적어로 to부정사가 오므로 to show로 고쳐 써야 한다.
(B) '열리다'라는 의미를 나타내는 수동태 표현이 되어야 하므로 과거분사 opened로 고쳐 써야 한다.
(C) '창조적 대성공에 도달하기 위해 필요한'이라는 의미로 수동의 의미를 나타내므로 과거분사 needed로 고쳐 써야 한다.

80 hidden photos

문제해설

in-between photos('중간에 있는' 사진들)는 사진작가들에게서 공개되지 않고 어딘가에 저장되어 있는 숨겨진 사진들을 말한다. 따라서 hidden photos와 같은 의미이다.

81 interpreting delay as something other than that

문제해설

'~에 대한 길을 열어 주다'라는 의미를 나타내는 〈open the door to+명사(구)〉에서 to는 전치사이므로 동명사 interpreting을 이어 써 준다. something other than that은 '그것과 다른 어떤 것'이라는 의미를 갖는다.

82 overlook

문제해설

'어떤 것을 인지하지 못하거나 하지 못하다'라는 의미의 단어는 overlook(간과하다)이다.

83 do we attempt to appreciate and protect nature

문제해설

부정어 rarely가 주어 앞에 나오면 도치가 이루어지는데 동사가 일반동사(attempt)이고 주어가 we, 시제는 현재이므로 do, does, did 중에서 do를 주어 앞에 쓴다. '~하려고 시도하다'는 〈attempt+to-v〉로 표현한다.

84 nature

문제해설

자연을 바라보는 인간의 시각이 단순히 '보존'이라는 명목 하에 이루어지고 있고, 자연에 대한 본질적인 이해를 하지 않는다는 내용으로, '우리는 자연을 보존해야 할 희소한 자원으로 간주하고 이를 위해 노력하지만, 자연을 경이로움과 경외의 원천으로 이해하려는 시도는 거의 하지 않는다.'와 같이 요약할 수 있다.

85 (a) sporting (b) architectural

문제해설

빈칸 다음에 스포츠 건축물을 짓기 위해서는 경기 규칙과 이에 따른 경기장의 규모 등이 정해져야 한다고 말하고 있고 마지막 문장에서도 스포츠 건축물이 경기 규칙 체계화와 건축물로서의 속성을 다 내포하고 있다고 말하고 있는 것에서 빈칸에 들어갈 말은 reasons(이유)를 꾸며 주는 sport와 architecture의 형용사인 sporting(스포츠상의)과 architectural(건축상의)이 적절하다.

86 (A) fixed (B) to be played (C) means

문제해설

(A) 전치사 without 다음에는 명사(구)가 나와야 하며, 여기서는 dimensions가 without의 목적어이고 의미상 '고정된 크기'여야 하므로 과거분사 fixed로 고쳐야 한다.
(B) 앞의 명사 the game을 수식하는 to부정사로 의미상 수동 관계이므로 to be played로 고쳐야 한다.
(C) '설계와 건축의 수단과 양식'이라는 의미가 되어야 자연스러우므로 '수단'의 의미를 갖는 명사형 means로 고쳐야 한다.

87 (1) ② → scared (2) ③ → have
(3) ⑤ → disappointed

문제해설

② 시계 때문에 주어인 신데렐라가 무서워하는 것이므로 scaring(놀라운, 겁주는)은 scared(무서워하는, 겁먹은)로 고쳐야 한다.
③ Both of these examples는 '이들 두 가지 예 모두'라는 의미로 복수를 나타내고 있으므로 동사는 has 대신 have로 고쳐야 한다.
⑤ customer가 주어이므로 disappointing(실망감을 주는)은 disappointed (실망하는)로 고쳐야 한다.

오답노트

① 〈the+비교급, the+비교급〉 구문이 사용되었고 interesting의 비교급은 more interesting이므로 적절하다.
④ 선행사 five reasons 뒤에 이유의 관계부사 why는 적절하다.

88 Audiences generally identify more with people and characters in the stories than with abstract discussion.

문제해설

청중은 일반적으로 추상적 논의보다 이야기 속 사람들 그리고 인물들과 더 동질감을 가지므로 비즈니스 스토리텔링에서 중심인물이 한 명도 없을 때 인물들이 이야기의 본문에 엮이질 수 있다는 내용의 글이다. 글의 중반부에 있는 Audiences generally ~ abstract discussion.이 요지에 해당하는 문장이다.

89 mediated

문제해설

'두 사람이나 단체들 사이의 의견 차이를 끝내려고 노력하다'라는 의미의 단어는 mediate(중재하다)이며 앞의 are와 함께 수동형이 되어야 하므로 과거분사인 mediated로 써야 한다.

90 생산적인 성인일 때 공익에 기여하고, 그 대가로 어릴 때는 교육을, 아프거나 실직하거나 늙었을 때는 부양을 받음

문제해설

예전에는 가족 내에서 해결하던 일을 요즘에는 국가가 관여해서 지원하거나 관리하는 방식으로 바뀌었으며 이런 기대가 있는 것은 각 나라의 문화적 배경이나 규범, 제도, 정책 등의 영향을 받기는 하지만 보편적 현상이라는 것으로 '이러한 기대' 바로 앞 문장에 잘 나타나 있다.

91 (A) → the way(that / in which)[how]
(B) → where[in which]
(C) → because

문제해설

(A) 선행사 the way를 수식하는 관계절이 이어지는데 완전한 절이고 관계부사 how는 스스로 선행사 역할까지 하는 경우가 대부분이라 the way나 how 둘 중 하나만 쓴다. 혹은 the way that, the way in which도 가능하다.
(B) parts of Africa and Asia를 선행사로 하고 완전한 구조의 문장이 이어지므로 관계부사 where 또는 in which로 고쳐 써야 한다.
(C) 〈주어+동사〉가 있는 절의 형태가 이어지므로 because of는 because로 고쳐 써야 한다.

92 are more likely to be affected by, such as

문제해설

'~할 가능성이 더 크다'는 〈more likely+to-v〉로 표현하는데 '~에 의해 영향을 받다'라는 수동태가 되어야 하므로 to 다음에 be affected by가 이어 나오도록 한다. '~와 같은'이라는 의미의 표현은 such as이다.

93 ④ → forced

문제해설

④ 예전에 세워져 노후화하고 비효율적인 시설 때문에 불편을 감수해야 하는 고충을 언급하고 있는 내용이므로 일상적인 업무를 수행하기 위해 먼 거리를 운전하는 것은 free(자유롭게 ~하는)가 아닌 forced(억지로 ~해야 하는)로 고쳐야 한다.

94 사회 기반 시설을 지속 가능하게 다시 짓는 것은 매우 많은 비용이 든다.

문제해설

지속 가능성 지표는 개발 도상국과 같이 신흥국에서 높게 나타날 수 있는데, 그것은 이미 선진국에서 겪었던 낡고 비효율적인 기술의 이행을 건너뛰어서 해로운 환경을 피할 수 있고 미국과 같이 노후화 된 나라에서는 기반 시설을 다시 짓거나 교체하는 데 너무 큰 비용이 든다는 것이 It will be very expensive to rebuild our infrastructure to be more sustainable.에 잘 나타나 있다.

95 can be traced, as far back as

문제해설

trace는 '(기원을) 추적하다'라는 의미를 나타내며 can과 결합한 수동태 표현은 can be traced이다. as far as는 '~만큼 멀리'라는 의미이므로 as far back as로 쓰면 '~까지 거슬러 뒤로 멀리'라는 의미의 표현이 된다.

96 인간의 내적 상태는 과학적으로는 결코 조사될 수 없으며 직관적, 해석적, 심지어 종교적 방법을 통해 비과학적으로 이해되어야 한다는 견해

문제해설

바로 앞에 나오는 문장인 the internal ~ religious method를 가리키는데 이것은 인간의 내적 상태는 과학적으로 결코 조사될 수 없고 직관적, 해석적, 또는 종교적인 방법을 통해 비과학적으로 이해되어야 한다는 견해이다.

97 seemed that Emily absolutely loved

문제해설

〈주어+seemed to-v〉 표현은 '~는 …한 것 같았다'라는 의미이며 〈It seemed that+주어+과거형동사 …〉로 바꿔 쓸 수 있다

98 (A) passion (B) runner

문제해설

축구 선수였던 Emily가 하고 싶은 운동을 하도록 도와준 코치 덕분에 훌륭한 달리기 선수가 되었다는 내용의 글로서, '위대한 축구 선수를 포기했지만, 코치는 Emily가 (B) 달리기 선수로서 진정한 (A) 열정을 발견하는 것을 도울 수 있었다.'와 같이 요약할 수 있다.

Test 3

1번 p.330

• Word Test

1 전문가   2 제출하다   3 누수
4 수여[지급] 판정을 내리다   5 처리하다, 다루다   6 보험
7 구체적인, 특정한   8 천장   9 minimal
10 internal   11 estimate   12 adjuster
13 lift   14 extent   15 claim   16 assessment

유형 1

❶ that   ❷ where   ❸ what
❹ both   ❺ until

유형 2

❶ to address   ❷ had lifted   ❸ based
❹ arrived   ❺ holding

유형 3

❶ insurance adjuster   ❷ specific errors
❸ based on what he saw
❹ extent of the damage
❺ as soon as possible

2번 p.332

• Word Test

1 (어떤 나이가) 되다   2 다량, 소나기   3 알레르기가 있는
4 어린이집, 탁아소   5 매우 귀중한   6 콩
7 포럼, 공개 토론(의 장)   8 불안하게 하다   9 incident
10 dairy   11 supportive   12 emergency room
13 a host of   14 bite   15 recipe   16 seriously

유형 1

❶ seriously   ❷ anyone   ❸ figure
❹ safely   ❺ invaluable

유형 2

❶ had   ❷ to have   ❸ called
❹ to make   ❺ order

유형 3

❶ was seriously allergic to   ❷ emergency room
❸ In response to   ❹ figure out
❺ were emotionally supportive

3번 p.334

• Word Test

1 영역, 왕국   2 독자, 청중   3 실시하다, 행하다
4 ~에 기여하다   5 주로   6 치약   7 학회, 회의
8 대학의, 학문의   9 실험   10 innovation
11 publication   12 magnetic   13 target
14 capability   15 via   16 analyze   17 lab
18 purely

유형 1

❶ that   ❷ successful   ❸ hard
❹ primarily   ❺ that

유형 2

❶ have   ❷ to move   ❸ doing
❹ want   ❺ to disseminate

유형 3

❶ blood banking   ❷ contributed to
❸ realm of invention
❹ spend long hours
❺ other academic researchers

4번 ———————————————— p.336

• Word Test

1 유지(관리)   2 예언   3 소개하다   4 놀랄 만한, 현저한
5 소문을 내다   6 유인, 동기   7 시도, 노력   8 축제, 파티
9 고무하다   10 exhibition   11 do the trick
12 poetry   13 demanding   14 rally
15 in light of   16 humming   17 relevant
18 up for

유형 1

❶ that   ❷ while   ❸ more
❹ that   ❺ relevant

유형 2

❶ shooting   ❷ continued   ❸ to rally
❹ to showcase   ❺ to do

유형 3

❶ in light of   ❷ far beyond maintenance
❸ prepare to showcase their work
❹ raise the bar

5번 ———————————————— p.339

• Word Test

1 ~의 이익을 생각하다, ~을 보살피다   2 결론을 내리다
3 배려하는   4 알아내다   5 (행동으로) 보여 주다, 실증하다
6 considerate   7 falsely   8 distinguish
9 immediately   10 merely

유형 1

❶ that   ❷ from   ❸ considerate
❹ sometimes   ❺ whom

유형 2

❶ teaching   ❷ is   ❸ to show
❹ hearing   ❺ to benefit

유형 3

❶ distinguish good from not so good leaders
❷ care about others
❸ demonstrate overtly   ❹ figure out
❺ have themselves in mind first

6번 ———————————————— p.341

• Word Test

1 조립하다   2 보이지 않게 하다   3 의식상의, 의식을 위한
4 융합시키다, 결합시키다   5 해체하다, 분해하다   6 유형의
7 유지하다   8 ~에 의존하다   9 연속성

10 preservation   11 exact   12 cyclical
13 heritage   14 oral   15 physical   16 folk
17 local   18 vegetation

유형 1

❶ similar   ❷ continuity   ❸ who
❹ from   ❺ tangible

유형 2

❶ perpetuating   ❷ matters   ❸ being
❹ retaining   ❺ fused

유형 3

❶ every twenty years   ❷ rely on oral traditions
❸ cultural heritage   ❹ tangible objects

7번 ———————————————— p.343

• Word Test

1 지지하다   2 위협하다   3 관리   4 ~에 …을 제공하다
5 열정적인   6 무시하다, 간과하다   7 일반적으로
8 창의력   9 unique   10 activism
11 perspective   12 initiative   13 administrator
14 vehicle   15 lawsuit   16 detailed

유형 1

❶ to   ❷ although   ❸ effective
❹ successful   ❺ sensitive

유형 2

❶ solving   ❷ overlooked   ❸ promoting
❹ to begin   ❺ are

유형 3

❶ detailed information   ❷ unique perspective
❸ systems of governance   ❹ lasting programs
❺ threatened sensitive ecosystems

8번 ———————————————— p.345

• Word Test

1 백 만   2 참여   3 population   4 tourism

유형 1

❶ groups   ❷ who   ❸ higher
❹ that

유형 2

❶ shows   ❷ was   ❸ aged
❹ participated

유형 3

❶ participated in tourism   ❷ number of people
❸ higher than

9번 ———————————————— p.347

• Word Test

1 머리 위에   2 절약하다, 보존하다   3 희귀한   4 서식지
5 주된   6 짝짓기를 하다   7 심각하게   8 포식자
9 처벌을 받을 수 있는, 형에 처해질 수 있는   10 soar

11 wingspan 12 chick 13 diet 14 distract 15 flap 16 destruction 17 endangered 18 mammal

유형 1
❶ birds ❷ during ❸ the other ❹ habitat ❺ fewer

유형 2
❶ beginning ❷ to soar ❸ conserving ❹ to distract ❺ to recover

유형 3
❶ main diet ❷ at the top of a mountain ❸ habitat destruction ❹ every two years

10번 ——————————— p.349

• Word Test

1 전문적인 2 최대한 3 ~에 적합한 4 해안 5 야외의 6 exploration 7 activity 8 limited 9 participant 10 equipment

유형 1
❶ adventure ❷ participants ❸ years ❹ for

유형 2
❶ offer ❷ specialized ❸ following ❹ limited

유형 3
❶ outdoor activities ❷ rock climbing ❸ specialized equipment ❹ fill up fast

11번 ——————————— p.352

• Word Test

1 뒤쪽의 2 지지대 3 도움 4 적절한 5 이동; 이동시키다 6 보통의 7 고정하다 8 lean 9 distance 10 footrest 11 attendant 12 clearance 13 operate 14 upright

유형 1
❶ as ❷ less ❸ proper ❹ attendant

유형 2
❶ to transport ❷ To open ❸ to secure ❹ entering ❺ transferring

유형 3
❶ less than ❷ rear wheels ❸ move forward ❹ step on

12번 ——————————— p.355

• Word Test

1 혁신 2 가설 3 포유류의 4 인지의, 인식의 5 섭취하다, 소비하다 6 얻다, 획득하다 7 적응하다

8 (음식이 입안에서 느껴지는) 질감 9 잡식성의 10 dissonance 11 exploration 12 disgusting 13 diet 14 habitat 15 paradox 16 balanced 17 ingredient 18 evolve

유형 1
❶ sameness ❷ because of ❸ whether ❹ that ❺ than

유형 2
❶ to attain ❷ to adapt ❸ eating ❹ surrounding ❺ to eat

유형 3
❶ tire of the sameness ❷ lead to anxiety ❸ have an aversion to ❹ at the same time ❺ cognitive dissonance

13번 ——————————— p.357

• Word Test

1 전략적인 2 회계 3 동일하다 4 손금 보는 사람 5 중독 6 보상 7 ~에 전념하다 8 얻다, 획득하다 9 아마도, 추측건대 10 rush 11 investor 12 mythical 13 inherently 14 shop-front 15 sensation 16 unnoticeable 17 executive 18 acute

유형 1
❶ where ❷ which ❸ such as ❹ a little ❺ perception

유형 2
❶ is met ❷ equates ❸ to predict ❹ resolving ❺ (to) experience

유형 3
❶ pleasure of prediction ❷ such as ❸ are devoted to ❹ inherently uncertain ❺ pay lots of money

14번 ——————————— p.360

• Word Test

1 피험자, 연구 대상 2 왜곡 3 소유물 4 판단하다 5 분류하다 6 실험 7 꾸러미 8 categorization 9 perceive 10 artificially 11 actually 12 estimate 13 label 14 investigate

유형 1
❶ experiments ❷ in which ❸ into ❹ that ❺ differently

유형 2
❶ caused ❷ was ❸ to estimate ❹ asking ❺ being

유형 3
❶ a set of ❷ do the same ❸ grouped the lines into two sets ❹ one another

15번 — p.362

• Word Test

1 상호 의존성   2 완수하다   3 높이 평가하다
4 가장 가까운, 인접한   5 영향   6 열등한   7 범죄
8 분산시키다   9 공정성   10 collectivism
11 empathy   12 conflict   13 tolerate
14 expose   15 task   16 accountable
17 loyalty   18 complement

유형 1

❶ loyalty   ❷ where   ❸ less
❹ complements   ❺ it

유형 2

❶ completing   ❷ to write
❸ had received   ❹ to blow   ❺ leads

유형 3

❶ inferior performance
❷ sense of group belonging   ❸ instead of
❹ In short   ❺ conflict with justice

16번 — p.364

• Word Test

1 ~에 접근하다   2 위협   3 결론짓다, 끝나다   4 공학
5 활용하다, 이용하다   6 심리   7 보안   8 탁월한
9 immune to   10 scope   11 method
12 resistant to   13 hypothetical   14 contest
15 exploitation   16 obtain

유형 1

❶ foolish   ❷ that   ❸ prominent
❹ which   ❺ who

유형 2

❶ is   ❷ were asked   ❸ to give
❹ knowing   ❺ is

유형 3

❶ gaining access to
❷ As foolish as it may sound
❸ immune to   ❹ except for

17번 — p.366

• Word Test

1 적응, 순응   2 두드러지게 하다, 강조하다   3 경쟁적인
4 대개, 자주   5 고치다   6 ~과 함께, ~과 협력하여
7 강화하다   8 대체로, 일반적으로   9 version
10 personality   11 nurture   12 nature
13 predisposition   14 ambitious
15 interpersonal   16 amplify

유형 1

❶ during   ❷ enhancing   ❸ competitive
❹ extraversion   ❺ that

유형 2

❶ to act   ❷ including   ❸ are
❹ ends   ❺ exaggerated

유형 3

❶ More often than not   ❷ existing potential
❸ as a result   ❹ adaptation to those jobs

18번 — p.368

• Word Test

1 혼동하다   2 전문가   3 결단력 있는, 결정적인   4 반증
5 모든 것을 다 아는 듯한   6 후보자   7 ~을 생각해 내다
8 ~에 직면한   9 alternative   10 implication
11 unsure   12 without qualification   13 rigid
14 come to *do*   15 open-mindedness   16 tone

유형 1

❶ which   ❷ rigid   ❸ candidate
❹ implication   ❺ as

유형 2

❶ admire   ❷ faced   ❸ to have
❹ speaking   ❺ is

유형 3

❶ come to admire people   ❷ news commentator
❸ faced with   ❹ sign of expertise

19번 — p.370

• Word Test

1 새벽   2 흡수하다   3 우뚝 솟다, 최고 한도에 이르다
4 정확한, 틀림없는   5 온도   6 ~과 같다   7 희미한, 약한
8 표면   9 cool   10 ray   11 emit   12 exceed
13 incoming   14 atmosphere   15 horizon
16 outgoing

유형 1

❶ decrease   ❷ little   ❸ faint
❹ does the incoming radiation   ❺ than

유형 2

❶ shining   ❷ emitting   ❸ grows
❹ equal

유형 3

❶ all night long   ❷ In fact   ❸ at dawn
❹ solar radiation

20번 — p.372

• Word Test

1 부   2 접근, 이용   3 사망률   4 주장하다
5 출산율   6 적절한   7 빈곤, 가난   8 절대적인
9 위생 시설   10 영양   11 distribution
12 accompany   13 alter   14 shelter
15 birth control   16 desperate   17 lessen
18 official   19 professional   20 maintain

유형 1

❶ population   ❷ which   ❸ mortality
❹ adequate   ❺ too

55

❶ decided to ❷ enthusiastic over
❸ similar to ❹ As to the final outcome
❺ give depth to ❻ aside from
❼ preferable to

p.389

01 ③	02 ③	03 ④	04 ⑤	05 ③	06 ④
07 ①	08 ①	09 ③	10 ⑤	11 ②	12 ①
13 ⑤	14 ④	15 ④	16 ⑤	17 ⑤	18 ③
19 ③	20 ⑤	21 ②	22 ⑤	23 ④	24 ③
25 ⑤	26 ③	27 ③	28 ②	29 ⑤	30 ④
31 ②	32 ③	33 ②	34 ④	35 ③	36 ⑤
37 ④	38 ②	39 ③	40 ⑤	41 ④	42 ④
43 ④	44 ②	45 ⑤	46 ⑤	47 ②	48 ④

49 (A) that[which] (B) caused[had caused]
(C) what 50 a leak 51 recipe
52 ② → never 53 researchers 54 researchers
had taken active steps to move those discoveries into
the realm of invention 55 Jordan's remarkable
level of energy throughout the night following a
demanding game 56 (A) while (B) that[which]
(C) participate 57 ④ → benefit
58 the benefits 59 20년마다 해체되어 유사한 재료로
다시 만든 정확한 복제품이 같은 장소에 조립되는 것 60 who
scraped the chalk figure every seven years to keep it
from being obscured by growing vegetation
61 ⑤ → threatened 62 partnerships between
students and university staff and administrators
63 65 years or over 64 participation
65 ③ → distract 66 (A) birds (B) conserving
(C) the other 67 suitable 68 (A) experience
(B) specialized (C) fill 69 (A) to be used (B) to
permit (C) engage 70 attendant
71 taste dilemma 72 drives humans to eat
beyond our biological imperative as we eat more and
more variety 73 ④ → increasing
74 (A) predict (B) pay 75 the distortions caused
by categorization 76 ④ → differently
77 loyalty 78 충성도 자극을 받은 사람들은 열등한 수행
능력에 대해 동료 이용자를 기꺼이 고자질하려는 마음이 덜했다는
것 79 companies 80 (A) resistance
(B) divulge 81 nurture ends up amplifying
characteristics that were already there to begin
with 82 nurture 83 ③ → rigid
84 무조건적으로 또는 의심의 여지 없이 말하면서 모든 것을 다 아는
듯한 어조를 취하는 것 85 들어오는 태양 복사 에너지가 나가는
적외선보다 더 커질 때 86 ④ → larger
87 population control 88 (A) wealth (B) basic
89 (A) platform (B) (to) gain 90 ④ → raise
91 enzymes 92 unpromising 93 ③ → clear
94 the psychological contract
95 the law of small numbers 96 1000번의 공정한
동전의 던지기 후에 Soros 또는 Bozos가 가령 475번의 앞면에
비하여 525번의 앞면을 던져서 상대보다 훨씬 앞서 있을 확률이 훨씬

더 큰 것 97 ④ → different 98 (A) warmest
(B) believing

01 ③

문제해설

앞 문장에서 주택 파손에 대한 보험 회사 직원이 오직 남쪽 지붕창만 점검
한 후, 남쪽 지붕창에 대한 파손만 평가를 했지만, ③뒤 문장에서 진짜 큰
피해는 북쪽에 있었으며 직원이 제대로 피해 규모를 자세히 살피지 않았
다고 설명하는 글이므로 남쪽 지붕창의 피해는 북쪽에 비해 적다는 내용이
문맥상 자연스러우므로, ③의 maximal(아주 많은)을 minimal(아주 적
은)과 같은 단어로 고쳐야 한다.

02 ③

문제해설

필자는 알레르기가 심한 아들을 위해 유제품, 콩과 계란이 없는 케이크 조
리법에 대해 특정한 웹 사이트에 질문을 게시했고 그 사이트에서 활동하
는 다른 부모들로부터 안전한 케이크 조리법뿐만 아니라 다른 지원도 받
았다는 내용의 글이다. 주어진 문장에서의 They는 ③의 앞 문장에서의
parents on the site를 지칭하며, 그들이 필자에게 공유해 준 것은 안
전한 케이크 조리법이다. 그리고 ③뒤 문장에서는 도움을 받은 예시들을
언급하고 있으므로, 주어진 문장이 들어가기에 가장 적절한 곳은 ③이다.

03 ④

문제해설

④ 주절의 동사 present가 있으므로 분사가 와야 하는 자리로 의미상 주
어 Researchers와 능동 관계이므로 현재분사 targeting으로 고쳐야
한다.

오답노트

① if가 생략된 가정법 형태이므로 주어 researchers와 도치가 된 동사
had는 적절하다.
② 〈want+목적어+to-v〉의 구조이므로 to matter는 적절하다.
③ designing, conducting과 접속사 and로 병렬되고 있으므로
analyzing은 적절하다.
⑤ 복수 명사 audiences를 가리키므로 those는 적절 하다.

04 ⑤

문제해설

Michael Jordan이 스스로 여러 가지 활동을 지속적으로 함으로써 활
력을 유지할 수 있었던 것처럼, 학생들도 스스로 교실에서 할 수 있는 평범
한 활동을 통해 동기를 부여받을 수 있으며, 학생들에게 새로운 활기를 불
어넣어 줄 유인책의 예로 자신의 작품 전시, 체육 발표, 뮤지컬 공연, 시 축
제 등을 준비하고 참여하는 것들이 있다는 내용의 글이므로, 글의 제목으
로 가장 적절한 것은 ⑤ '학생들에게 활력을 불어넣는 탐구'이다.

오답노트

① 삶을 위한 학생의 재능 발굴
② 지속성: 성공으로 가는 길
③ 운동선수들의 자기 실현적 예언
④ 무패의 정복에 대한 도전

05 ③

문제해설

이 글은 좋은 지도지와 니쁜 지도자를 구별할 때, 나쁜 지도자는 항상 먼

저 생각하는 것은 자신의 이익이며, 심지어 다른 사람들의 불행에 관해 들을 때 슬퍼하고 있는 것처럼 보여도 늘 궁극적으로 자기 이익만을 생각하는 사람으로 공공연하게 자신이 사려 깊다는 것을 거짓으로 보여 준다는 내용의 글이므로, 빈칸에 들어갈 말로 가장 적절한 것은 ③ '그릇되게'이다.

오답노트

① 진심으로
② 단호히
④ 비밀스럽게
⑤ 사심 없이

06 ④

문제해설

일본의 Shinto Grand Shrine, 영국의 White House of Uffington, 구전 동화 등의 문화유산이 보존될 수 있었던 것은 문화마다 그들의 유산을 일상에서 정기적으로 재창조하며 보존한다는 내용의 글이므로 '비록 나라마다 가진 문화유산은 다르지만, 수 세기 동안 그들의 문화재를 그들의 삶에서 (B) 정기적으로 사용하고 상호 작용함으로써 그들의 유형과 무형의 문화재를 (A) 보존한다.'와 같이 요약하는 것이 가장 적절하다.

오답노트

① 유지하다 …… 일시적인
② 결합하다 …… 정기적인
③ 부활시키다 …… 일시적인
⑤ 설립하다 …… 영구적인

07 ①

문제해설

(A) 대학 내 환경 문제 해결을 위한 과정에서 자원을 찾고 정보 수집을 통해 창의적으로 기여할 수 있다는 내용이 문맥상 자연스러우므로, contribute(기여하다)가 적절하다. discourage는 '단념시키다'라는 의미이다.
(B) 학교에서의 재활용 프로그램을 시작하고 홍보한 학생들의 창의적인 사례를 들며, 학생들이 효과적으로 환경 변화를 촉진하는 그들만의 체계를 갖고 있다는 내용이 문맥상 자연스러우므로, effective(효율적인)가 적절하다. ineffective는 '비효율적인'이라는 의미이다.
(C) 다른 사례로 위협받고 있는 생태계를 보호하기 위해서 대학생들이 압력과 행동주의로 환경 문제를 해결했다는 내용이 문맥상 자연스러우므로, threatened(위협하다)가 적절하다. protected는 '보호하다'라는 뜻이다.

08 ①

문제해설

'In all of the age groups, the number of people who participated in tourism was over 30 million.'에서 관광 여행에 참여한 사람의 수는 모든 연령 집단에서 3천만 명이 넘었고, 여행 관련 설문에 참여한 수는 알 수 없으므로, ①은 글의 내용과 일치하지 않는다.

09 ③

문제해설

심각한 멸종 위기에 처한 희귀하고 강한 새인 필리핀 독수리의 유일한 포식자는 인간이지만, 1995년부터 필리핀의 정부로 보호 명령을 받고 있다는 내용의 글이므로, 글의 제목으로 가장 적절한 것은 ③ '인간: 미래의 친구인가 적인가?'이다.

오답노트

① 새들의 사냥 기술
② 원숭이 포식자의 숨겨진 정체
④ 맹금류의 특별한 점
⑤ 멸종위기에 처한 필리핀 독수리의 구조

10 ⑤

문제해설

For questions, call us at ~.에서 캠프 관련 문의를 유선상으로 받고 있으므로, ⑤는 글의 내용과 일치하지 않는다.

11 ②

문제해설

The lock to secure the back will engage automatically.에서 등받이를 고정하는 잠금장치가 자동으로 채워질 것이라고 했으므로, ②는 글의 내용과 일치하지 않는다.

12 ①

문제해설

미각 딜레마라는 것은 인간이 새로운 음식을 탐구하고 싶어 하는 반면 새로운 음식을 시도하는 것에 대한 불안과 두려움을 느낄 수 있다는 내용의 글로서, 새로운 음식에 대한 반감과 먹고자 하는 욕구가 동시에 있다는 역설적 측면을 언급하고 있기에 빈칸에 들어갈 말로 가장 적절한 것은 ① '역설'이다.

오답노트

② 목적
③ 규칙
④ 획일성
⑤ 의도성

13 ⑤

문제해설

확실성에 대한 욕구는 중독성이 있을 수 있고, 확실성에 대한 욕구가 충족되면 뇌에서 즐거운 반응을 일으킨다. 그래서 사람들은 확실성을 갈망하는데 그들을 찾고 큰 비용도 지불한다는 내용의 글이므로, 글의 제목으로 가장 적절한 것은 ⑤ '예측 가능성에 대한 우리의 중독 이해하기'이다.

오답노트

① 특이한 위협의 안락함
② 모두를 위한 미래 예측
③ 미지의 세계에 대처하는 전략
④ 불확실성의 기쁨과 고통

14 ④

문제해설

④ that절 속에서 once로 시작하는 부사절 다음에 주어가 the subjects가 오고 동사가 와야 하는 자리인데, 과거 시제여야 하므로 perceive를 perceived로 고쳐야 한다.

오답노트

① 〈One of+명사〉가 주어일 때, 주어 one에 수를 맞추므로 단수 동사 was는 적절하다.
② the next in the bunch를 선행사로 하며 불완전한 문장이 이어지므로 관계대명사 which는 적절하다.
③ '~하도록 요청하다'라는 의미로 〈ask+목적어+to-v〉의 형태가 되어야

하므로 to estimate는 적절하다.
⑤ 전치사 as 뒤에 전치사의 목적어로 동명사 being을 쓰는 것은 적절하다.

15 ④

문제해설

④주어 sense에 수 일치를 시켜야 하므로 lead를 단수 동사 leads로 고쳐야 한다.

오답노트

① where 뒤에 완전한 절이 이어지고 선행사가 marketplace이므로, 관계부사 where는 적절하다.
② 충성도 자극을 받은 시점이 열등한 수행 능력을 보인 동료를 고자질하는 시점보다 이전에 일어났으므로 과거완료 had received가 적절하다.
③ showing의 목적어로 완전한 절을 이끄는 명사절의 접속사 that을 쓰는 것은 적절하다.
⑤ 앞 문장의 The sense of group belonging and interdependence를 가리키는 It이 의미상 주어로 diffuse와는 능동의 관계이므로 분사 diffusing은 적절하다.

16 ⑤

문제해설

주어진 문장의 These employees는 ⑤의 바로 앞 문장의 주어인 90% of the employees를 지칭하는 것으로, 사회 공학에 영향을 받지 않는 조직이 없다는 것을 증명하기 위해 보안 학회에서 주최한 대회 참가자들이 보낸 링크를 클릭한 90%의 직원들은 발신인이 누군지 알려고 하지 않았다는 내용이다. 따라서 주어진 문장이 들어가기에 가장 적절한 곳은 ⑤이다.

17 ⑤

문제해설

선천성과 후천성 모두 사람의 성격을 형성하는데 영향을 미치지만, 후천성이 사람의 타고난 성향을 증폭시킨다는 내용으로, '후천성은 선천성과 함께 작용한다'라는 말이 의미하는 바로 가장 적절한 것은 ⑤ '유전적 특징은 사람을 형성하는 데 있어 환경적인 요인들과 작용한다.'이다.

오답노트

① 사람의 잠재력은 교육을 통해 개발될 수 있다.
② 배양된 특성은 유전적 요인보다 더 강력하다.
③ 유전적으로 미리 결정된 특성은 비유전적 특성에 영향을 미친다.
④ 적응력은 사람의 성격 형성에 지배적인 역할을 한다.

18 ③

문제해설

"훌륭한 사색가"와 "전문가"라는 두 가지 사고 기준을 혼동하는 경우가 있는데, 전문가들은 주로 모호한 태도를 보이지 않으며 확신에 찬 어조를 취하는데, 예시로 모든 것을 아는 어조를 말하는 정치인들을 전문가로 생각하는 사람들이 있다고 설명하는 글이므로, 제목으로 가장 적절한 것은 ③ '훌륭한 사색을 전문성과 혼동하다'이다.

오답노트

① 정치인의 신념 왜곡
② 우리는 어떻게 생각하고 말해야 할까?
④ 의사 결정자들을 존경하는 것에 대한 함정
⑤ 인지와 합리성의 엄격한 기준

19 ③

문제해설

③ 부정어 Not until이 문두에 위치하여 주어와 동사가 도치된 구문이기 때문에 주어가 the incoming radiation이므로 do를 단수 동사 does로 고쳐야 한다.

오답노트

① 불가산 명사 radiation을 수식하는 수량 형용사로 little은 적절하다.
② 주어가 the Earth로 의미상 능동이므로 현재분사 emitting은 적절하다.
④ 두 개의 미래 사건 중, 온도가 최솟값에 도달하게 되는 시점이 들어오는 태양 복사 에너지가 나가는 적외선보다 더 커지는 시점보다 먼저 발생하게 될 것이므로 미래완료 will have reached는 적절하다.
⑤ '~로서'라는 의미의 명사(구)를 이끄는 전치사 as는 적절하다.

20 ⑤

문제해설

⑤ 앞에 있는 grow or buy와 접속사 or로 병렬되고 있으므로 maintaining을 maintain으로 고쳐야 한다.

오답노트

① 동사 follows를 수식하므로 부사 closely는 적절하다.
② 뒤에 주어와 동사를 포함한 완전한 절이 나오므로 접속사 because는 적절하다.
③ '~하는 것을 돕다'는 〈help+to-v〉가 되므로 to reduce는 적절하다.
④ 주어가 people이므로 복수 동사 live는 적절하다.

21 ②

문제해설

디지털 기술의 도입으로 소비자들의 구매 결정 과정이 바뀌었으며, 소비자들의 구매 과정을 효과적으로 지원할 수 있는 강력한 플랫폼을 만들고 유지할 수 있는 기업은 시장에서 경쟁 우위를 갖게 될 것이기 때문에 네트워크 효과와 소비자들의 행동 및 욕구에 대한 지식이 수요 주도적 접근 방식과 함께 성공적인 기업을 뒷받침하는 원동력이 된다는 내용의 글이므로, 빈칸에 들어갈 말로 가장 적절한 것은 ② '원동력'이다.

오답노트

① 독점권
③ 제품 인지도
④ 경제적 통찰력
⑤ 눈에 보이지 않는 경쟁력

22 ⑤

문제해설

크릴과 같이 가망이 없는 동물로 여겨졌던 것에서 예상 밖의 과학적 발견이 이루어질 수 있으므로 크릴뿐만 아니라 지구의 모든 생물학적 재산을 소중하게 여겨야 한다는 것이 문맥상 자연스러우므로, ⑤ overlook(간과하다)을 ⑤ value(소중히 여기다)와 같은 단어로 고쳐야 한다.

23 ④

문제해설

직장 내의 심리적 계약은 공식적이지 않은데, 그것은 직원들이 문화적으로 얼마나 다양한지에 따라 조직의 구성원 간에 다르게 해석될 수 있다는 내용의 글이므로, '세계화와 인력이 인공지능으로 대체되는 등의 기술상 큰 발전으로 심리적 계약의 중요성을 규정하는 변화가 생겼다.'는 ④은 글의 전체 흐름과 관계가 없다.

24 ③

문제해설

작은 수의 시도로는 우리가 기대하는 확률적 결과를 얻기가 어렵다는 작은 수의 법칙을 설명하고, 그것의 예시로 동전을 천 번 던지면 앞면과 뒷면이 반반 나올 것이라고 기대하지만 실제로는 앞뒷면이 공평하게 반반 나오는 것을 보기에 충분하지 않은 시도라는 내용의 글이므로, 글의 제목으로 가장 적절한 것은 ③ '가능성에 대한 우리의 인식에 도전하다'이다.

오답노트

① 동전 뒤집기: 경기는 얼마나 공정할까요?
② 동전 뒤집기의 높은 위험과 수익
④ 게임 세계에서의 확률의 법칙
⑤ 도박꾼의 오류에 대한 수학적 해부학

25 ⑤

문제해설

작은 수의 시도로는 우리가 기대하는 확률적 결과를 얻기 어렵다는 내용의 글로서, 10,000명의 사람들이 동전을 1,000번 던지면 상당수의 사람이 꽤 좋은 기록으로 끝나거나 같은 수의 사람이 꽤 아쉬운 기록으로 끝날 경우가 일어날 것이라는 내용이 문맥상 자연스러우므로, (e) greater(더 많은)를 equal(같은)과 같은 단어로 고쳐야 한다.

26 ③

문제해설

필자는 특정한 정치 집단을 주제로 한 논문을 쓰는 소녀를 지도하게 되었다는 주어진 글 다음에 논문을 심사하는 Maples 선생님과 정치적 관점이 달라 걱정이 된다는 소녀를 안심시키려는 내용의 (C)가 이어지고, 소녀를 안심시키려는 필자의 시도는 실패했지만, 결과적으로 논문은 성공적이었다는 (D)가 이어진 후, 소녀를 돕기 위해 필자가 어떻게 했는지를 설명하는 (B)로 이어지는 것이 자연스럽다.

27 ③

문제해설

소녀의 논문을 채점하게 될 Maples 선생님의 정치적 관점이 소녀의 것과 달라서 선입견을 갖고 채점하는 것은 아닌지에 대한 걱정을 하고 있다는 것이 문맥상 자연스러우므로, (c)의 excited(신난)를 worried(걱정된) 등으로 고쳐야 한다.

28 ②

문제해설

"As far as politics go, ~ mine are probably similar to those of Ms. Maples"에서 필자의 정치적 관점은 Maples 선생님의 것과 더 비슷할 수 있다고 언급하고 있으므로, ②는 글의 내용과 일치하지 않는다.

29 ⑤

문제해설

⑤ 선행사가 없고 불완전한 구조가 이어지므로 based on의 목적어 역할을 하는 명사절을 이끄는 관계대명사 what으로 고쳐야 한다.

오답노트

① 동사 need의 목적어로 to-v가 올 수 있으므로 to address는 적절하다.
② 타일들이 들뜨게 된 것은 편지를 보내는 과거 시점 이전에 일어난 일이므로 과거완료 had lifted는 적절하다.

③ 앞 문장에서의 목적어 a leak을 가리키는 This는 적절하다.
④ 뒤에 완전한 절이 이어지고 선행사가 dormer's south side이므로, 관계부사 where은 적절하다.

30 ④

문제해설

foodallergickids.org라는 웹 사이트에서 다른 부모들로부터 케이크 조리법을 공유 받았다고 했으므로, ④는 글의 내용과 일치하지 않는다.

31 ②

문제해설

혁신적인 상품 개발이 대학 연구실에서 기원했다는 사실을 언급하는 주어진 글 다음에, 연구원들이 그 발견들을 발명의 영역으로 옮긴 덕분이라는 내용의 (B)가 이어져야 한다. 이어서 (A)의 By doing so와 those inventors는 (B)의 연구원들이 연구물을 학문적 흥미로 남기지 않고 발전시킨 것을 가리키며, 세상을 바꿀 수 있었다고 언급하고, 연구한 결과물을 어떻게 그리고 누구에게 알릴지 찾아볼 때, 학술지 등뿐만 아니라 상업적 역량이 있는 사람들과도 공유하라고 요구하는 내용의 (C)가 그 뒤를 잇는 것이 글의 순서로 가장 적절하다.

32 ③

문제해설

이 글은 여러 가지 일을 하며 지속적인 활력을 유지했던 뛰어난 운동선수 Michael Jordan과 같이, 학생들도 자신에게 중요한 유인책을 통해 새로운 활기로 동기를 부여받을 수 있다는 내용의 글이므로, 빈칸에 들어갈 말로 가장 적절한 것은 ③ '새로운 활기로 동기를 부여받다'이다.

오답노트

① 두려움을 성장으로 재구성하다
② 실패에 대한 두려움으로 방해를 받다
④ 기대에 부응하기 위해 압박을 받다
⑤ 그들의 안락 구역을 떠날 준비가 되다

33 ②

문제해설

② 앞에 동사가 이미 있으므로 when 뒤에 주어가 생략된 분사구 형태가 되어야 하므로 heard를 능동의 현재분사 hearing으로 고쳐야 한다.

오답노트

① that절에서 주어가 the main way이므로 단수 동사 is는 적절하다.
③ 주어 they가 목적어로 주어 자신이 온 것이므로 재귀대명사 themselves는 적절하다.
④ 명사 ways를 수식하며 '이득이 될'이라는 의미의 형용사적 용법 to benefit은 적절하다.
⑤ 뒤에 완전한 절이 이어지고 있고 say의 목적어가 되는 명사절의 접속사 that은 적절하다.

34 ④

문제해설

일본의 Shinto Grand Shrine, 영국의 White House of Uffington, 구전 동화 등의 다양한 문화유산이 정기적으로 재창조되어 보전되는 방법에 관한 내용의 글이므로, '구전은 젊은 세대들이 그들의 조상들의 지혜와 박식한 삶의 철학과 같은 문화의 중요한 측면들에 대해 가르쳐줌으로써 그들이 세상을 이해하도록 돕는다.'는 ④은 글의 전체 흐름과 관계가 없다.

35 ③

문제해설

전국의 학생들이 계획하고 지지해왔던 학교 재활용 프로그램이나 압력과 행동주의로 생태계를 보호한 사건 등의 사례를 통해 학생들이 대학교 내 환경 문제를 해결하는데 창의적으로 기여 할 수 있다는 내용의 글이므로, 빈칸에 들어갈 말로 가장 적절한 것은 ③ '캠퍼스 환경 문제를 해결하고'이다.

오답노트

① 학생 단체 정부를 소개하고
② 모범적인 학생 리더십을 보여 주고
④ 사회적 신념을 가진 사회 운동가들을 결속시키고
⑤ 환경 봉사 프로그램을 홍보하고

36 ⑤

문제해설

⑤ 과거 1995년부터 필리핀 독수리들이 보호되어 왔으므로 were를 현재완료 have been으로 고쳐야 한다.

오답노트

① fact를 선행사로 하며 주어가 필요한 불완전한 문장이 이어지므로 관계대명사 that은 적절하다.
② '하는 것을 허용하다'라는 의미의 〈allow+목적어+to-v〉의 형태이므로 to soar는 적절하다.
③ 뒤에 명사(구)가 나왔으므로 전치사구 Because of는 적절하다.
④ 주어 predators가 복수이므로 복수 동사 are가 적절하다.

37 ④

문제해설

인간의 음식 선택에 관해 쓴 Paul Rozin은 음식 선택 가설을 통해 인간이 새로운 음식을 탐구하고 싶어 하는 반면 그것을 시도하는 것에 대한 두려움을 동시에 느끼는 역설을 만들어내고, 이런 딜레마가 인간의 음식 선택 습관에 영향을 미친다는 내용의 글이므로, 글의 주제로 가장 적절한 것은 ④ '음식 선택 습관에 영향을 미치는 요소들'이다.

오답노트

① 인간 (혀의) 미뢰의 호기심
② 다양한 음식 섭취의 이점
③ 균형 잡힌 식단 유지의 필요성
⑤ 건강하게 먹기 위한 우리의 생물학적 체제의 역할

38 ②

문제해설

불확실성이 우리에게 위협으로 느껴질 수 있기 때문에 인간은 확실성에 대한 갈망을 충족하기 위해서 불확실성을 해소하려고 하며, 삶의 본질적인 불확실성에도 불구하고, 인간은 불확실성을 덜 느끼려고 상당한 금액을 지불한다는 내용의 글이므로, 빈칸에 들어갈 말로 가장 적절한 것은 ② '불확실성을 덜 느끼다'이다.

오답노트

① 특이점을 알아차리다
③ 혼란 속에서 질서를 발견하다
④ 그들의 감각을 만족시키다
⑤ 풀리지 않는 수수께끼를 풀다

39 ③

문제해설

'But before asking the other subjects to do the same, they

artificially grouped the lines into two sets~.'에서 다른 피실험자들에게 똑같은 요구를 하기 전에 인위적으로 선을 두 세트로 묶은 것은 연구원들이었다고 했으므로, ③은 글의 내용과 일치하지 않는다.

40 ⑤

문제해설

주어진 문장의 주어진 It은 ⑤의 바로 앞 문장의 '구성원들 사이의 집단 소속감과 상호 의존성'을 지칭하고 목적어 it은 ⑤의 바로 앞 문장의 to tolerate the offense(범죄를 용인하는 것)을 가리키는데, 집단 소속감과 상호 의존성이 흔히 사람들이 속한 집단 내의 범죄를 용인하고, 범죄를 용인한 행위에 대해 책임감을 덜 느끼게 하는 영향을 미친다는 내용이므로 주어진 문장이 들어가기에 가장 적절한 곳은 ⑤이다.

41 ④

문제해설

④ 앞 문장의 단수 명사 a URL을 가리키는 것이므로 them을 it으로 고쳐야 한다.

오답노트

① 완전한 절이 이어지므로 think의 목적절을 이끄는 명사절의 접속사 that은 적절하다.
② which는 information을 가리키므로 동사 utilize(활용하다)와는 수동이어야 하므로 과거분사 utilized는 적절하다.
③ '~하는 것을 거절하다'라는 의미는 〈refuse+to-v〉이므로 to give는 적절하다.
⑤ 〈how 의문사+형용사+주어+동사〉의 어순으로 전치사 on의 목적절 속의 how는 적절하다.

42 ④

문제해설

주어진 문장의 those jobs(그러한 직업)는 ④의 바로 앞부분에 나오는 '인적 네트워크 형성과 개인 간의 한담을 나누는 것을 필요로 하는 직업'을 가리키는 것으로, 외향적인 사람들이 많은 인맥 관리와 개인 간의 한담을 나누는 것을 요하는 직업을 선택함으로써 그들의 외향적 성향이 더 두드러지게 나타난다는 내용이 언급되어 있으므로, 주어진 문장이 들어가기에 가장 적절한 곳은 ④이다.

43 ④

문제해설

④ 주어가 a person 단수이므로 are를 단수 동사 is로 고쳐야 한다.

오답노트

① two different standards for thinking을 선행사로 하며 목적어가 필요한 불완전한 문장이므로 계속적용법의 관계대명사 which는 적절하다.
② 전치사 of의 목적어 자리에 동명사 being은 적절하다.
③ '~하기에 충분히 …하다'라는 의미는 〈형용사+enough+to-v〉이므로 to have는 적절하다.
⑤ their children을 선행사로 하며 불완전한 구조가 이어지므로 관계대명사 who는 적절하다.

44 ②

문제해설

복사 에너지에 의한 지구의 표면 온도 변화 과정을 묘사하는 내용의 글이므로, '지구뿐만 아니라 별을 포함한 다른 물체들도 온도에 상관없이 복사 에너지를 방출하고 흡수한다.'는 ②가 글의 전체 흐름과 관계가 없다.

45 ⑤

문제해설

Piel의 연구에 따르면 경제 발전으로 부의 분배를 바꾸면 인구 억제가 가능하다고 언급하지만, 그럼에도 불구하고 전세계적으로 빈곤율이 존재하며 증가하고 있으며 그것을 보여 주는 사례로 경제적 발전을 이룬 선진국에 해당되는 미국을 언급하는 내용의 글이므로, 글의 요지로 가장 적절한 것은 ⑤이다.

46 ⑤

문제해설

디지털 기술의 도입으로 기업들이 소비자들과 소통하기 위해 경쟁 우위를 갖추어야 하는데, 소비자들의 구매 과정을 효과적으로 지원할 수 있는 강력한 플랫폼은 기업으로 하여금 시장에서 경쟁 우위를 갖게끔 원동력을 제공해 준다는 것이 문맥상 자연스러우므로, ⑤ limit(제한하다)를 provide(제공하다) 등과 같은 단어로 고쳐야 한다.

47 ②

문제해설

글의 중반부에 다른 동물의 효소 작용은 온도가 떨어짐에 따라 급격하게 느려진다고 하였고, 반대로 크릴은 극한의 환경에서 더 강력해진다고 하였으므로 ②은 글의 내용과 일치하지 않는다.

48 ④

문제해설

직장 내에서의 심리적 계약은 보통 공식적으로 표현되지 않으며, 문화적으로 다양한 직원들이 속해있는 직장에서 사람마다 생각하고 있는 심리적 계약에 대한 기대가 다양하다는 내용의 글이므로, 빈칸에 들어갈 말로 가장 적절한 것은 ④ '심리적 계약에 대한 기대'이다.

오답노트

① 이익을 만드는 데 초점을 맞춘 의무
② 기업 문화를 배양하는 것에 대한 불만
③ 관계의 중요성에 대한 신념
⑤ 사회에 공헌하는 방법에 대한 인식

49 (A) that[which] (B) caused[had caused] (C) what

문제해설

(A) 선행사는 the claim이고, 목적어가 누락된 불완전한 구조가 이어지므로 관계대명사 that 또는 which로 고쳐야 한다.
(B) 과거분사 had lifted와 등위접속사 and로 병렬되고 있으므로 caused 또는 had caused로 고쳐야 한다.
(C) 선행사가 없으며 이어지는 문장이 완전한 구조가 아니므로 관계대명사 what으로 고쳐야 한다.

50 a leak

문제해설

앞 문장에서 강풍으로 인해 지붕에서 많은 타일들을 들뜨게 하여 생긴 '누수(a leak)'를 가리키는 말이다.

51 recipe

문제해설

'특정 음식을 요리하거나 준비하기 위한 일련의 지침'이라는 의미의 단어는 recipe(조리법)이다.

52 ② → never

문제해설

글쓴이에게는 심한 알레르기가 있는 아들 Noah가 있다. 글쓴이는 직접 생일 케이크를 만들어 본 적이 없었고, 그 아들이 생일 케이크 먹기를 원했다는 내용이므로, 문맥상 always(항상)를 never(한 번도 ~않다)와 같은 말로 바꿔 써야 한다.

53 researchers

문제해설

빈칸 (A)가 포함된 문장은 이 성공한 혁신들에 기여한 발견들은 '연구자들'이 그 발견들을 발명의 영역으로 옮겨 갈 적극적 조치를 취하지 않았다면 아마도 순전히 학문적으로 흥미로운 것으로 남았을 것이라는 내용이고, 빈칸 (B)가 포함된 문장은 '연구자'는 세미나, 학회 포스터와 발표, 저서의 장, 그리고 학술지 출판물을 통해 자기 연구를 공개한다는 내용이다. 따라서 빈칸 (A), (B)에 공통으로 들어갈 단어는 복수형으로 쓴 researchers[Researchers](연구자들)이다.

54 researchers had taken active steps to move those discoveries into the realm of invention

문제해설

By doing so에서 so는 앞 문장에서 언급된 researchers had taken active steps to move those discoveries into the realm of invention(연구자들은 그 발견들을 발명의 영역으로 옮겨 갈 적극적 조치를 취했다)을 가리킨다.

55 Jordan's remarkable level of energy throughout the night following a demanding game

문제해설

it은 문장의 앞부분에서 언급된 Jordan's remarkable level of energy throughout the night following a demanding game(힘든 경기 후 밤새도록 지속된 Jordan의 놀랄 만한 수준의 활력)을 가리킨다.

56 (A) while (B) that[which] (C) participate

문제해설

(A) 뒤에 〈주어+동사〉가 있는 절의 형태가 나오므로 during은 while로 고쳐야 한다.
(B) a self-fulfilling prophecy가 선행사이고 불완전한 구조가 이어지므로 주격 관계대명사 that 또는 which로 고쳐야 한다.
(C) The invitation to show에서 show, perform과 접속사 or로 병렬되고 있으므로 participating을 동사원형 participate로 고쳐야 한다.

57 ④ → benefit

문제해설

나쁜 지도자들은 다른 사람들에게 이득을 주는 방식으로 일할 때, 그들은 늘 자기 자신을 먼저 염두에 두고 있다는 흐름이므로, 문맥상 harm(피해를 끼치다)을 benefit(이득을 주다)과 같은 말로 바꿔 써야 한다.

58 the benefits

문제해설

범죄학자들이 범죄의 가해자를 알아내기 위해 돈을 주시하는 것처럼, 나쁜 지도자를 알아내기 위해 주시해야 할 것은 바로 the benefits(이득)이다.

59 20년마다 해체되어 유사한 재료로 다시 만든 정확한 복제품이 같은 장소에 조립되는 것

문제해설

밑줄 친 부분이 있는 앞 문장의 내용을 바탕으로 this form of preservation은 '일본의 Ise에 있는 Shinto Grand Shrine이 20년마다 해체되어 유사한 재료로 다시 만든 정확한 복제품이 같은 장소에 조립되는 것'임을 알 수 있다.

60 who scraped the chalk figure every seven years to keep it from being obscured by growing vegetation

문제해설

지역 주민들을 의미하는 locals를 부가 설명하는 주격 관계대명사 who 다음에 '백악 형상을 긁어냈다'라는 의미의 scraped the chalk figure를 쓴다. '7년마다'는 every seven years로 쓰고, '~이 …하지 못하게 하다'의 의미를 나타내는 〈keep+목적어+from v-ing〉와 '~에 (의해) 그것이 보이지 않게 되는 것을'은 동명사의 수동태인 being obscured by를 결합하여 쓴다.

61 ⑤ → threatened

문제해설

대학 캠퍼스의 환경 문제 해결을 위한 학생들의 참여에 대한 글로서, 한 전기 공급 회사가 투자를 회수하게 되었는데, 그 회사가 계획한 수력 발전소가 민감한 생태계와 토착민들을 위협했기 때문이라는 흐름이 적절하므로, 문맥상 ⑤ guarded(지켰다, 보호했다)를 threatened(위협했다)와 같은 말로 바꿔 써야 한다.

62 partnerships between students and university staff and administrators

문제해설

가장 성공적이고 지속적인 프로그램은 '학생과 대학 직원 및 관리자 간의 협력(partnerships between students and university staff and administrators)이다.

63 65 years or over

문제해설

'관광 여행에 참여하지 않는 사람들의 백분율 비율이 관광 여행에 참여한 사람들의 그것보다 더 높은 연령 집단'은 65 years or over(65세 이상)이다.

64 participation

문제해설

영영 풀이는 '무언가에 참여하는 과정'이라는 의미로 빈칸에는 participation(참여, 참가)이 적절하다.

65 ③ → distract

문제해설

독수리 두 마리가 함께 사냥할 때, 한 마리는 원숭이 무리의 주의를 분산시키기 위해 머리 위로 활공하고, 그동안에 다른 한 마리는 사냥감을 급습한다는 흐름이므로, 문맥상 ③ attract(주의를 끌다)를 distract(주의를 분산시키다)와 같은 말로 바꿔 써야 한다.

66 (A) birds (B) conserving (C) the other

문제해설

(A) '~ 중의 하나'는 〈one of the+복수명사〉이므로 복수형 birds로 고쳐야 한다.
(B) 앞에 동사 allows가 있으므로 분사가 와야 하는 자리이다. 앞문장 내용(낮 동안 산에서부터 나무에서 나무로 내려오며 사냥하는 것)을 가리키는 This가 의미상 주어로 conserve와 능동의 관계여야 하므로 현재분사 conserving으로 고쳐야 한다.
(C) 두 마리가 함께 사냥을 한다고 했으므로, 한 마리는 one으로, 남은 한 마리는 the other가 되어야 한다.

67 suitable

문제해설

'특정 목적, 사람, 또는 상황에 알맞은'이라는 의미의 단어는 suitable(적합한)이다.

68 (A) experience (B) specialized (C) fill

문제해설

(A) 앞에 '다양한'이라는 의미의 a range of가 있으므로 activity를 복수 명사 activities로 고쳐야 한다.
(B) 명사 equipment를 수식하는 '전문화 된, 전문적인'이라는 의미의 과거분사형 형용사 specialized로 고쳐야 한다.
(C) rooms 또는 spaces 같은 공간 개념이 주어로 올 때, '가득 차다'라는 의미를 갖도록 능동의 fill up이 쓰인다. 따라서 filled는 fill로 고쳐야 한다.

69 (A) to be used (B) to permit (C) engage

문제해설

(A) The Green Medical Transport Chair를 가리키는 주어 it이 to use의 행위의 대상이므로 to부정사의 수동태형 to be used로 고쳐야 한다.
(B) '적절한 여유 공간이 있도록 하기 위해서'의 의미가 되도록 목적을 나타내는 부사적 용법의 to permit으로 고쳐야 한다.
(C) 접속사 Before를 생략하지 않고 쓴 분사구문 뒤에, 주절은 주어가 생략된 명령문이므로 동사원형 engage로 고쳐야 한다.

70 attendant

문제해설

'다른 사람, 특히 중요한 위치에 있는 사람이나 아픈 사람을 돌보는 일을 하는 사람'이라는 의미의 단어는 attendant(간병인, 돌보는 사람)이다.

71 taste dilemma

문제해설

밑줄 친 내용은 '인지 부조화의 한 형태로, 우리의 음식 선택 습관을 둘러싼 역설'이라는 의미로 글 전반부에 '사람들은 균형 잡힌 식단을 얻기 위해 다양한 재료를 섭취하지만, 같은 것에 싫증을 느낄 수 있고 호기심으로 인해 새로운 맛과 질감을 경험하고 싶어 하는 것'에서 알 수 있듯이, 다양하게 섭취하지만 같은 것에 싫증을 느끼는 것이 부조화이고 역설의 내용이다. 이것을 가리켜 '미각 딜레마(taste dilemma)'라고 하였다.

72 drives humans to eat beyond our biological imperative as we eat more and more variety

문제해설

'인간을 먹도록 몰아간다'는 〈drive+목적어+to-v〉 구문을 이용하여

drives humans to eat으로 나타내고, '생명 유지의 필수 요소 이상'은 beyond our biological imperative로 쓴다. '~하면서'의 접속사 as 와 함께 '점점 더 다양한 음식을 먹다'는 eat more and more variety 로 쓴다.

73 ④ → increasing

문제해설

확실성에 대한 갈망이 충족될 때, 보상의 느낌(기쁨)이 있다는 내용의 글로서, 회계 및 컨설팅의 일부분은 전략적인 계획과 예측을 통해 경영 간부들이 증가하는 확실성에 대한 인식을 경험하도록 도움으로써 수익을 창출한다는 흐름이므로, ④ decreasing(감소하는)을 increasing(증가하는)과 같은 말로 바꿔 써야 한다.

74 (A) predict (B) pay

문제해설

확실성에 대한 갈망이 충족될 때 기쁨을 통해 보상을 받는다는 내용의 글이므로, '우리의 뇌는 사물에 대해 확신하는 것을 좋아하고 결과를 (A) 예측할 수 있을 때 기분이 좋지만, 우리가 불확실하다고 느낄 때 그것은 두렵게 느껴질 수 있으므로 사람들은 더 확실하게 느끼기 위해 기꺼이 돈을 (B) 지불한다.'와 같이 요약하는 것이 가장 적절하다.

75 the distortions caused by categorization

문제해설

끈의 길이를 그룹 A와 B로 나눈 피험자 집단이 그룹별 끈의 길이가 더 비슷하다고 느낀 이유는 첫 문장의 the distortions caused by categorization(범주화로 인한 왜곡)에 잘 나타나 있다.

76 ④ → differently

문제해설

실험자들은 그 끈이 어떤 그룹에 속한다고 생각되면 그 피험자들은 그 끈들을 다르게 인식한다는 것이 자연스러우므로, 문맥상 ④ similarly(같게)를 differently(다르게)와 같은 말로 바꿔 써야 한다.

77 loyalty

문제해설

빈칸 (A)가 포함된 문장은 우리는 이용자들이 과업을 완수한 것에 대해 돈을 버는 온라인 시장인 Amazon의 Mechanical Turk를 이용하는 사람들에게 '충성도'가 미치는 영향을 연구했다는 내용이고, 빈칸 (B)가 포함된 문장은 연구를 시작할 때, 우리는 몇몇 참가자들에게 '충성도'에 관한 에세이를 쓰도록 했다는 내용이다. 따라서 빈칸 (A), (B)에 공통으로 들어갈 단어는 loyalty(충성도)이다.

78 충성도 자극을 받은 사람들은 열등한 수행 능력에 대해 동료 이용자를 기꺼이 고자질하려는 마음이 덜했다는 것

문제해설

밑줄 친 부분이 있는 앞 문장의 내용을 바탕으로 This finding(이 연구 결과)은 '충성도 자극을 받은 사람들은 열등한 수행 능력에 대해 동료 이용자를 기꺼이 고자질하려는 마음이 덜했다는 것'임을 알 수 있다.

79 companies

문제해설

빈칸 (A)가 포함된 문장은 일부 '회사'와 조직은 그들이 사회 공학의 위협에 저항력이 있다고 생각한다는 내용이고, 빈칸 (B)가 포함된 문장은 표적 '회사'의 직원들에게 걸었던 140통의 전화 통화에서 아무것도 내놓지 않았던 다섯 명을 제외하고는 거의 모든 직원이 정보를 누설했다는 내용이다. 따라서 빈칸 (A), (B)에 공통으로 들어갈 단어는 복수형으로 쓴 companies(회사)이다.

80 (A) resistance (B) divulge

문제해설

사회 공학은 모든 조직에 영향을 미치며 많은 사람들이 그것에 당한다는 내용의 글이므로, '일부 회사와 조직들이 자신들은 사회 공학의 위협에 대한 (A) 저항력을 가졌다고 오해하는 것과는 달리, 가상 공격을 당한 표적 회사의 거의 모든 직원들은 회사 정보를 (B) 누설하게 되었다.'와 같이 요약하는 것이 가장 적절하다.

81 nurture ends up amplifying characteristics that were already there to begin with

문제해설

주어 '후천성'은 nurture로, '특성을 증폭시키는 것으로 결국 끝나다'는 〈end up+v-ing〉를 이용하며 주어가 단수이므로 ends up amplifying characteristics로 쓰면 된다. '이미 처음부터 존재했던'은 목적어 characteristics를 주격 관계대명사 that을 이용하여. that were already there to begin with로 쓴다.

82 nurture

문제해설

개인적인 자질 중 이미 처음부터 존재했던 특성을 결국 증폭시키는 것은 nurture(후천성)라고 하였다.

83 ③ → rigid

문제해설

만약 우리가 전문가들을 존경한다면, 우리는 완고하다는 의미에서 결단력이 있는 사람을 존경할지 모른다는 흐름이고, 앞에 나온 decisive(결단력 있는)라는 단어와 호응되어야 하므로, ③ flexible(유연한, 융통성이 있는)을 rigid(완고한)와 같은 말로 바꿔 써야 한다.

84 무조건적으로 또는 의심의 여지 없이 말하면서 모든 것을 다 아는 듯한 어조를 취하는 것

문제해설

밑줄 친 부분이 있는 앞 문장의 a person who adopts a know-it-all tone — speaking without qualification or doubt에 나타나 있다.

85 들어오는 태양 복사 에너지가 나가는 적외선보다 더 커질 때

문제해설

복사 에너지에 의한 지구의 표면 온도 변화에 대한 글로서, 온도가 상승하게 될 때에 대해서는 글의 후반부 the incoming solar radiation will be larger than the outgoing infra-red, and so absorption will exceed emission and the temperature will rise as a consequence에 나타나 있다.

86 ④ → larger

문제해설

일출 후 어느 정도 시간이 지나서, 들어오는 태양 복사 에너지가 '더 커지게' 되어서야 비로소 들어오는 복사 에너지가 나가는 적외선 복사 에너지와 결국 같아진다는 흐름이므로, 문맥상 smaller(더 작은)를 larger(더 큰)와 같은 말로 바꿔 써야 한다.

87 population control

문제해설

Piel의 제안에 따르면, 사람들이 빈곤의 순환에서 벗어날 수 있도록 해 주고, 경제 발전이 밀접하게 뒤따르게 하는 것은 population control(인구 억제, 인구 통제)이다.

88 (A) wealth (B) basic

문제해설

부의 분배가 바뀌어야 인구 억제가 가능하지만, 아직도 세계적으로 절대적 빈곤에서 살고 있는 사람이 10억 명이나 된다는 내용의 글이므로, '(A) 부의 분배를 개선하는 것이 인구 증가를 통제하는 데 필수적이지만 10억 명이 넘는 사람들이 (B) 기본적인 생필품이 부족하며 빈곤이 증가하고 있다.'와 같이 요약하는 것이 가장 적절하다.

89 (A) platform (B) (to) gain

문제해설

디지털 기술의 도입으로 인한 변화와 관련된 내용의 글이며, '디지털 기술과 온라인 리뷰는 소비자 행동을 변화시켰고, 기업은 고객과 연결하고 경쟁 우위를 (B) 확보하기 위해 강력한 네트워크 효과가 있는 보완 제품 (A) 플랫폼을 제공하도록 촉구했다.'와 같이 요약하는 것이 가장 적절하다.

90 ④ → raise

문제해설

강력한 네트워크 효과를 통해 소비자의 전환 비용을 '높이는' 연결된 상호 보완적인 제품의 체계를 제공하는 플랫으로 경쟁 우위가 확보되고 유지된다는 흐름이므로, 문맥상 lower(낮추다)를 raise(높이다)와 같은 말로 바꿔 써야 한다.

91 enzymes

문제해설

빈칸 (A)가 포함된 문장은 그들(크릴)은 자연에서 알려진 가장 강력하고 특이한 소화 '효소' 중 일부를 가지고 있다는 내용이고, 빈칸 (B)가 포함된 문장은 크릴 '효소'의 놀라운 특징을 설명하는 내용이다. 따라서 빈칸 (A), (B)에 공통으로 들어갈 단어는 복수형으로 쓴 enzymes(효소)이다.

92 unpromising

문제해설

'만족스럽거나 성공할 것 같지 않은'이라는 의미의 단어는 unpromising(가망이 없는)이다.

93 ③ → clear

문제해설

문화적으로 동질한 환경에서는 추정되는 것이 일반적으로 이해되고 공유되기 때문에, 작동 중인 심리적 계약이 비교적 '명확할' 수 있다는 흐름이므로, 문맥상 unclear(불분명한)를 clear(명확한)와 같은 말로 바꿔 써야 한다.

94 the psychological contract

문제해설

문화적으로 다양한 직원들이 그들 사이에서 서로 매우 다른 기대를 가지도록 만드는 것은 the psychological contract(심리적 계약)이다.

95 the law of small numbers

문제해설

작은 수의 시도로는 우리가 기대하는 확률적인 결과를 얻기 어렵다는 것을 나타낸 법칙의 이름은 the law of small numbers(작은 수의 법칙)이다.

96 1,000번의 공정한 동전의 던지기 후에 Soros 또는 Bozos가 가령 475번의 앞면에 비하여 525번의 앞면을 던져서 상대보다 훨씬 앞서 있을 확률이 훨씬 더 큰 것

문제해설

this는 앞 문장 내용을 가리킨다.

97 ④ → different

문제해설

나는 그녀가 '다른' 관점을 볼 수 있도록 도왔을 뿐만 아니라 그녀 자신의 관심에 깊이를 더해 주려고 노력했고 책도 몇 권 소개해 주었다는 흐름이므로, 문맥상 same(동일한)을 different(다른)와 같은 말로 바꿔 써야 한다.

98 (A) warmest (B) believing

문제해설

자신이 논문 지도를 했던 한 학생에 관해 기억나는 일에 관해 한 선생님이 쓴 글로서, '한 교사는 정치 집단에 대한 연구 논문에 대해 어떤 학생을 도우면서, (A) 가장 따뜻한 관계로 이끌며 성공 이상의 무언가를 (B) 믿는 학생의 신념을 강화하려고 시도한다.'와 같이 요약하는 것이 가장 적절하다.

학생 여러분,
쉼 없는 일상에 지치시죠?

이제 스트레스로 인한 긴장
쉼으로 잠시 내려놓으세요

스트레스케어
쉼으로
시작하자

제조/판매 : (주)에치와이, 건강기능식품

하루 한 병으로 관리하는 **스트레스케어 쉼**

스트레스로 인해 긴장되는 일상을 쉼 없이 이어 나가는 학생 여러분께
hy 스트레스케어 쉼이 달콤한 휴식을 선사합니다.

스트레스로 인한 긴장 완화에 도움을 줄 수 있는 L-테아닌과 (일일 최대 섭취량 250mg 함유)
특허 프로바이오틱스 100억을 한 병에! 캐모마일, 레몬, 베르가못 향으로 상큼 달콤하게 섭취하세요.

마시는 스트레스케어 **쉼**